STUDIES IN
MEDIEVAL THOUGHT AND LEARNING

STUDIES IN MEDIEVAL THOUGHT AND LEARNING

FROM ABELARD TO WYCLIF

BERYL SMALLEY

THE HAMBLEDON PRESS

Published by The Hambledon Press
35 Gloucester Avenue, London N.W.1
1981

ISBN 0 9506882 6 6

History Series Volume 6

British Library Cataloguing in Publication Data

Smalley, Beryl
 Studies in medieval thought and learning
 from Abelard to Wyclif. — (History series; 6)
 1. Europe — Intellectual life — Addresses,
 essays, lectures
 I. Title   II. Series
 189   AZ603

Printed by Unwin Brothers Limited
The Gresham Press, Old Woking, Surrey

CONTENTS

ACKNOWLEDGEMENTS

The articles reprinted here appeared in the following places and are used here with permission.

1   *Fritz Saxl, 1890–1948*, ed. D.J. Gordon (Nelson, London, 1957), 93–100.
2   *Mélanges Offerts à René Crozet*, (Société d'Études Médiévales, Poitiers, 1966), 655–661.
3   Cahiers de Civilisation Médiévale, IVe Année (1961), no. I, 15–22.
4   Recherches de Théologie ancienne et médiévale, (1969), xxxv 78–99.
5   RTAM, xxxv (1968), 35–82.
6   *Church, Society & Politics*, ed. D. Baker (Blackwell, Oxford, 1975), 113–131.
7   Medieval and Renaissance Studies, II (1950), 179–82.
8   *St. Thomas Aquinas 1274–1974*, (Pontifical Institute of Mediaeval Studies, Toronto, 1974), vol. I, 10–71.
9   *Medieval Learning and Literature. Essays Presented to Richard William Hunt*, ed. Alexander and Gibson (O.U.P., 1976), 307–27.
10 RTAM, xxiii (1956), 277–320.
11 Medieval and Renaissance Studies, III (1954), 200–38.
12 Medieval and Renaissance Studies, IV (1958), 91–145.
13 RTAM, xxviii (1961), 285–330.
14 RTAM, xxx (1963), 154–9.
15 Journal of the Warburg and Courtauld Institutes, xxvii (1964), 73–89.

TO THE MEMORY OF

R. W. HUNT

FOREWORD

These fifteen reprints have been chosen as satellites to my three books. Chapters 1, 3 to 6, 8, 10 to 13 and 15 can be read as supplements to *The Study of the Bible in the Middle Ages*, now sadly out of date. I have been able to correct myself in the meantime, as well as profiting from corrections and information supplied by others. Chapters 2, 7, 9, 13 and 14 will serve as prefaces and postscripts to *English Friars and Antiquity in the Early Fourteenth Century*. The political theories of John Baconthorpe and Jean de Hesdin (Chapters 12 to 14) reinforce the thesis of *The Becket Conflict and the Schools*: the schoolmen concerned themselves with politics.

I have not updated editions or added to bibliographies except where they are strictly relevant for reasons of space.

Oxford, 1981   Beryl Smalley

PRIMA CLAVIS SAPIENTIAE : AUGUSTINE
AND ABELARD

A BELARD'S prologue to his *Sic et non* was regarded at one
time as the most significant and daring of his writings.
Modern scholarship has softened the colours. He was not original
in pointing out the conflicting opinions among his authorities or
in wishing to harmonise them by means of dialectic. The *quaestio*,
by means of which a difficulty would be raised and solved, went
back to patristic literature and earlier [1] ; it had been used in
conjunction with dialectic of a simple kind by Abelard's master
in theology, Anselm of Laon.[2] Today attention is shifting to the
contents of the *Sic et non* as distinct from its prologue. Abelard
provided students in theology with a formidable *instrument de
travail*, a compilation of authorities where they could look up
the various opinions held by the Fathers on topics disputed in
the schools.[3] This was a solid and lasting contribution to research,
the prologue standing for the *hors-d'œuvre*.

But when all has been said, the prologue remains a forceful
defence of doubt as a method of enquiry. Abelard meant to carry
the use of dialectic further than his predecessors had done. He
strains every nerve to adduce reasons and authorities in support
of his method, the most august of the latter being Christ himself,
who willed that He should be found, at twelve years of age,
sitting and questioning in the midst of the doctors.[4] The reasons

[1] G. Bardy, "La littérature patristique des *Quaestiones et responsiones* sur l'Ecriture
sainte," in *Revue Biblique*, XLI (1932), pp. 210 ff., 341 ff., 515 ff. ; XLII (1933), pp. 14 ff.,
211 ff., 328 ff.
[2] O. Lottin, "Nouveaux fragments théologiques de l'école d'Anselme de Laon.
Conclusions et tables," in *Recherches de Théologie Ancienne et Médiévale*, XIV (1947),
pp. 157 ff. ; "Manegold de Lautenbach, source d'Anselme de Laon," *ibid.*, p. 222.
[3] See the discussion and bibliography in J. de Ghellinck, *Le Mouvement Théologique
du XIIe Siècle*, Bruges [etc.] 1948, pp. 149–80.
[4] Migne, *Patrologia Latina* (hereafter P.L.), VOL. CLXXVIII, col. 1349 : ". . . iuxta
quod et Veritas ipsa *Quaerite*, inquit, *et invenietis* ; *pulsate, et aperietur vobis*. (Mt. VII.7.)

1

end in a magnificent crescendo. The first key to wisdom, Abelard says, is continual questioning : by doubting we come to enquire and by enquiry we come to truth. The last argument alone is the subject of the present study. It is well known and has often been quoted, but hitherto it has been considered only in its general application or in its immediate context. The preceding sentence gives a clue to Abelard's meaning which seems to have been overlooked.

B. Geyer and J. G. Sikes pointed out that Abelard was quoting from his own *Logica ingredientibus*.[1] In this earlier work he had to explain a passage in Boethius' commentary on his translation of the *Categories* :

> Fortasse autem difficile est de huiusmodi rebus confidenter declarare, nisi pertractatae sint saepe. Dubitare enim de singulis non erit inutile.[2]

He glossed it as follows :

> *Difficile est* . . . Sed utile est dubitare potius, quippe per dubitationem venitur ad inquisitionem, per inquisitionem pertingitur ad veritatem.

The prologue to *Sic et non* has both the quotation and the gloss :

> Haec quippe prima sapientiae clavis definitur, assidua scilicet seu frequens interrogatio ; ad quam quidem toto desiderio arripiendam philosophus ille omnium perspicacissimus Aristoteles in praedicamento *ad aliquid* studiosos adhortatur, dicens *Fortasse autem difficile est de huiusmodi rebus confidenter declarare, nisi pertractatae sint saepe. Dubitare enim de singulis non erit inutile.* Dubitando enim ad inquisitionem venimus ; inquirendo veritatem percipimus.

This passage provides an excellent sample of Abelard's mind at work. He thinks in the medieval manner by means of a commentary on an authoritative text. The reverence for authority is apt to conceal the originality in treatment. Abelard has taken a remark of Boethius on Aristotle, that it is useful to doubt in

---

[1] ed. B. Geyer, in *Beiträge zur Geschichte der Philosophie des Mittelalters* (Münster), XXI, 2 (1921), p. 223. See J. G. Sikes, *Peter Abailard*, Cambridge 1932, p. 83.

[2] Migne, P.L., VOL. LXIV, col. 238. Abelard ascribes the passage to Aristotle without distinguishing Boethius' part in it.

Quae nos etiam proprio exemplo moraliter instruens, circa duodecimum aetatis suae annum sedens et interrogans in medio doctorum inveniri voluit, potius discipuli nobis formam per interrogationem exhibens, quam magistri per praedicationem . . ."

the case of individual propositions in logic, and has given it a vastly wider application. In his prologue to *Sic et non* he goes further, changing a statement about logic into a generalisation about the right method in theology. The example of Christ asking questions of the doctors in the temple follows immediately afterwards. Its purpose is to give added solemnity and universality to the statement. It also enables Abelard to sandwich his defence of doubt and questioning between the authority of the foremost pagan philosopher and that of the founder of Christianity.

The context shows that he was inserting his argument into a still wider framework. He had in mind the prologue to St Augustine's *Quaestiones in Heptateuchum*. A comparison of the two prologues will bring out the resemblance. Abelard begins with verbal reminiscences of his source. Then he goes on to develop the argument in his own way, while keeping the sequence of ideas. His defence of enquiry, supported by the quotation from "Aristotle," corresponds to a statement on the same lines by St Augustine. To make the parallel manageable I have omitted the quotation ascribed to Aristotle from the prologue to *Sic et non* and slightly abridged the prologue to the *Quaestiones*.

Augustine, Prol. to *Quaestiones in Hept.*, in Migne, P.L. VOL. XXXIV, col. 547.

Cum scripturas sanctas . . . legendo percurreremus, *placuit* eas *quaestiones, quae in mentem venirent* . . . stilo allegare *ne de memoria fugerent.*

Non ut eas satis explicaremus, sed ut cum opus esset, possemus inspicere ; sive ut admoneremur quid adhuc esset requirendum, sive ut ex eo quod iam videbatur inventum, ut poteramus, essemus et ad cogitandum instructi, et ad respondendum parati. Si quis igitur haec legere propter incultum in nostra festinatione sermonem non fastidierit, si quas quaestiones propositas invenerit nec solutas, non ideo sibi nihil collatum putat.

Abelard, Prol. to *Sic et non* in Migne P.L., VOL. CLXXVIII, col. 1349.

His autem praelibatis, *placet*, ut instituamus diversa sanctorum Patrum dicta colligere, *quando nostrae occurrerint memoriae*, aliqua ex dissonantia, quae habere videntur, *quaestionem* contrahentia, quae teneros lectores ad maximum inquirendae veritatis exercitium provocent et acutiores ex inquisitione reddant.

Nonnulla enim pars inventionis est, nosse quid quaeras . . . Non enim disputatio veritate sed veritas disputatione requiritur.

Haec quippe prima sapientiae clavis definitur, assidua scilicet seu frequens interrogatio . . . Dubitando enim ad inquisitionem venimus ; inquirendo veritatem percipimus.

It may be asked why Abelard does not mention Augustine by name in this passage, when he has just quoted a whole series of Augustinian works in support of his thesis.[1] The reason must surely be that he was making an allusion rather than an exact quotation. His readers would fill in the reference for themselves. The *Quaestiones in Heptateuchum*, so little studied today, was among the most popular of Augustine's works at a time when theology centred in lectures on the Bible. The *Glossa ordinaria* quotes it extensively, to give only one example. The glossator used nine out of the first ten questions,[2] and made a corresponding use of the rest, though I have not counted up the number exactly. We know that the *Glossa ordinaria* was compiled under the direction of Abelard's former master, Anselm of Laon. Another pupil of Anselm, Gilbert the Universal, prepared the section on the Pentateuch.[3] Abelard did not like these men [4] : they all read the same books, however. A classic work of Augustine on Scripture, in favour at Laon, the centre *par excellence* of theological studies during Abelard's youth, would be sure to be recognised even without a direct mention of its author. The implied parallel must have appeared plainly to his readers, whether they agreed with him or not. Moreover, we can set the prologue to *Sic et non* beside that to the commentary on the *Hexaëmeron*. Here Abelard makes a definite and pointed comparison between Augustine and Aristotle. Augustine writes :

[1] Migne, P.L., VOL. CLXXVIII, cols. 1346–7.

[2] This emerges from a comparison of *Quaestiones in Genesim*, Migne, P.L., VOL. XXXIV, cols. 548–50, with the corresponding part of the *Glossa ordinaria* on Genesis, ed. with the *Postills* of Nicholas of Lyre and the additions of Paul of Burgos, Lyons 1598, VOL. I. *Quaestio* III is the only one of the first ten to be omitted. The quotations in the *Glossa ordinaria* are not always verbally exact or correctly ascribed to their original. They may derive from some earlier compilation.

[3] B. Smalley, *The Study of the Bible in the Middle Ages*, Oxford 1952, pp. 60–1.

[4] *Historia calamitatum*, iii-iv, Migne, P.L., VOL. CLXXVIII, cols. 123–5 ; *Introductio in theologiam*, *ibid.*, col. 1056 ; see J. G. Sikes, *op. cit.*, pp. 265–6 ; B. Smalley, "Gilbertus Universalis and the problem of the *Glossa ordinaria*," in *Recherches de Théologie Ancienne et Médiévale*, VII (1935), p. 243.

quaerendo magis tanquam dubia, quam diffiniendo tanquam certa, quasi Aristotelicum illud attendens consilium. *Fortasse*, inquit, *difficile sit* . . .[1]

The quotation from Boethius on the *Categories* follows, just as in *Sic et non*. In his prologue to the *Hexaëmeron* commentary Abelard is making a specific parallel between Augustine's approach to the problems of creation as told in Genesis and the Aristotelian method of enquiry. Clearly, then, in the prologue to *Sic et non* he is pairing the Christian and the pagan philosopher in just the same way.

The reference must have seemed all the apter in that Augustine's questions on the Heptateuch arose in part from discrepancies between the various translations of Scripture.[2] Augustine says that he is comparing the Latin with the Septuagint :

> Cum scripturas sanctas, quae appellantur canonicae, legendo et cum aliis codicibus secundum Septuaginta interpretationem conferendo percurreremus, placuit eas quaestiones, quas in mentem venirent, sive breviter commemorando, vel etiam pertractando tantummodo proponerentur, sive etiam qualitercumque tanquam a festinantibus solverentur stilo allegare ne de memoria fugerent.

Similarly Abelard was collecting the sayings of the Fathers which contained discrepancies giving rise to questions. Of course the *De doctrina christiana* also gave encouragement to a Christian use of dialectic in a passage which Abelard knew and quoted elsewhere in his prologue.[3] But his thought here is closer to the prologue to the *Quaestiones*.

It seems therefore that his reasoning derived partly from Boethius on the *Categories*, partly from Augustine on the Heptateuch. There are two sets of parallels in the passage : Augustine and Aristotle, Augustine and Abelard. All three scholars are questioning. It was typical of Abelard to see himself in the pattern of the great thinkers of pagan and Christian antiquity.[4]

The comparison shows Abelard's debt. To appreciate his

---

[1] Migne, P.L., VOL. CLXXVIII, col. 732. J. G. Sikes points out the repetition of the quotation, *op. cit.*, p. 83, *n.* 1.

[2] For a discussion of Augustine's progress in learning Greek, see P. Courcelle, *Les Lettres Grecques en Occident de Macrobe à Cassiodore*, Paris 1948, pp. 137–53.

[3] Augustine, *De doctrina christiana*, II. 31 ; see G. Paré, A. Brunet and P. Tremblay, *La Renaissance du XIIᵉ Siècle. Les Écoles et l'Enseignement*, Paris [etc.] 1933, pp. 281, 292–3.

[4] E. Gilson, *Héloïse et Abélard*, Paris 1938, pp. 59–73, 179.

originality one must attempt a contrast. What did Augustine mean by his words and what did Abelard make of them ?

Augustine was writing as a former *rhetor* for men who had been trained in rhetoric ; this was the core of education in the schools of the late Empire.[1] At least three words in his prologue would ring a bell in the minds of educated readers : *memoria, inventio, eloquium* ; the sentence omitted in the last paragraph of the comparative texts reads :

> Quarum autem solutio placuerit, non ibi vile contemnat *eloquium* sed de aliqua participatione doctrinae potius gratuletur.

Rhetoric consisted in five things, of which Augustine has mentioned three : *inventio, dispositio, elocutio, memoria, pronuntiatio.*[2] The statement that no small part of *inventio* is to know what one is looking for sounds like some gloss on a rhetorical text. I have not been able to find any source for it in the Latin treatises on rhetoric. The closest that one comes is in the manual of Martianus Capella. He links *inventio* to the understanding of questions and arguments by means of wise scrutiny, and he gives it pride of place among the five parts of rhetoric in examining questions and adducing proofs :

> Inventio est quaestionum argumentorumque sagax investigatrixque comprehensio . . . Sed ex his inventionem certum esse potissimum, cuius opus est causae quaestiones excutere et argumenta idonea reperire.[3]

Martianus is thinking of the law court ; but what he says about *inventio* there could perfectly well be transferred to the investigation of difficulties in Scripture which occupies Augustine. At any rate, Martianus supplies the kind of context in which the expression "nonnulla pars inventionis est nosse quid quaeras" might well occur, although he does not actually say it. His manual was probably written too late for Augustine to have used it ; but

[1] H.-I. Marrou, *Saint Augustin et la Fin de la Culture Antique*, Paris 1949, VOL. I, pp. 47–83.

[2] Quintilian, *Institutio oratoriae*, III.3. There seems to be no proof that Augustine had actually read Quintilian, but his teaching was reproduced in later manuals, that of Julius Victor, for example (ed. C. Halm, *Rhetores latini minores*, Leipzig 1863, p. 373) ; see H.-I. Marrou, *op. cit.*, VOL. I, p. 48, *n.* 1 ; p. 49, *n.* 1.

[3] *Liber de arte rhetorica*, ed. C. Halm, *op. cit.*, p. 455.

it drew on a familiar school tradition. A study of late antique literature, including the Greek rhetoricians, might reveal a direct source. Greek rhetoric must have penetrated the Latin by many channels and have been familiar even when knowledge of Greek became uncommon in the schools of the Western Empire.

What interests us here is that rhetorical terms come naturally to Augustine ; he uses them when he wants to justify his scrutiny of the difficulties in Scripture. The next and final statement, that disputation is not sought by truth, but truth by disputation, is the kind of antithesis that he loved. It has less the air of being a school cliché than the remark about *inventio* ; it is no less obviously the fruit of his training in the art of persuasion.

Abelard has applied the same "processing" to Augustine's statements that he used for Boethius' commentary on the *Categories*. He converts a pair of rhetorical *formulae* into a plea for enquiry and dialectic. He leads up to this transformation of his source by giving a subtle twist to Augustine's argument in favour of setting questions. Augustine disclaims the intention of giving a sufficient explanation of his difficulties. He puts forward instead two different objects : we develop our own understanding and we prepare ourselves to answer ; to whom is not stated ; but he must have been thinking of Christian apologetics. Abelard stresses rather the virtue of questioning as a mental exercise, making young students more eager and quick-witted in the search for truth.

He introduces a note of greater seriousness by his use of the expression *clavis sapientiae*. "Keys of knowledge" was a biblical phrase (Lk. xi.52). It could be used in a narrow sense for initiation into some learned technique. Thus Guibert of Nogent had said that the writings of St Gregory supplied the keys to the art of moralising the text of the Bible.[1] Abelard substitutes *sapientia*, wisdom, for *scientia*, mere knowledge or skill.

The choice of a parallel in St Augustine's *Quaestiones in Heptateuchum* brings out more clearly what Abelard meant by advocating doubt and enquiry. No scholar today would describe him as a

---

[1] *De vita sua*, ed. G. Bourgin, Paris 1907, p. 66 : ". . . Gregoriana dicta, in quibus artis huius potissimum reperiuntur claves. . . ."

rationalist or sceptic. In this passage he is making plain the limits within which his doubts would be contained. Augustine, as appears from his prologue to the *Quaestiones*, did not doubt the truth of the Scriptures ; he only wanted to solve their difficulties. The first step in the process must be to define what they are. To pose your problem will bring you considerably nearer to its solution. Abelard implies that he is intending to do the same thing as St Augustine. But his task is even bigger. Whereas Augustine's authority had been simply the Bible in its different translations, Abelard had to reckon with the Bible plus the opinions of the Fathers, among them Augustine himself. *Sic et non* is presented as a modern version of the *Quaestiones*. The only difference is that Augustine had put forward tentative solutions to his questions ; Abelard contents himself with setting out the difficulties and postponing their solution to some future date. By doing so he was fitting his key into the lock, since the first key of wisdom is continual questioning.

Abelard has selected, combined and interpreted his authorities so that the result is something quite different from the original ingredients. In each case, what has been a commonplace statement, belonging to the teaching of the *Categories* on the one hand, probably of the *De inventione* on the other, gains new meaning. Ancient rhetoric and dialectic are pressed into the service of theology. The framework of early scholasticism conveys an earnestness which was lacking before.

The sources of a passage in *Sic et non* will have illustrated the central thesis of the Warburg Institute. These few remarks about them seem the right contribution to a volume dedicated to the memory of Saxl, the soul of the Warburg and the most brilliant and exciting exponent of the continuity of classical antiquity in later times.

2

A Pseudo-Sibylline Prophecy of the Early Twelfth Century in the *Life* of Altmann of Passau

The *Life* of St. Altmann includes a prophecy which experts on the medieval Sibyl have overlooked. Altmann, Bishop of Passau (1065-1091), was a strong gregorian ; he worked for reform as bishop, papal legate and writer, and suffered exile for his pains[1]. Historians of gregorian reform know and quote his *Life*, but they are interested in graver matters than pseudo prophecies. Another group of scholars use it as a source for legends about early german history. Somehow, the Sibyl has slipped through the net of the various specialisms.

The anonymous author was a monk of Göttweig in Lower Austria on the Danube, a house which Altmann founded and where he was buried. He intended it to be for canons regular, but they were replaced by a colony of benedictines from St. Blasien a few years after his death[2]. The editor, Wilhelm Wattenbach, dated the *Life* earlier than modern scholars do. The author says in his prologue that he writes at the command of Chadalhoh, Abbot of Göttweig (1125-1141). Wattenbach put it soon after 1125, because the author claims to have got his information from persons who had known and served Bishop Altmann[3]. This may have been a conventional phrase, however. The two references to informants hardly imply that they actually spoke to the author : a former butler of Altmann's, who became a monk at Göttweig, reported a miracle worked by his master, "to all"; Altmann's last days and death will be described briefly, *ut accepimus*[4]. In any case, old men about 1140 could have remembered the bishop from their youth or boyhood. The most serious difficulty in the way of an early date for the *Life* is that it also describes the death of Reginmar, Bishop of Passau (1121-1138). Wattenbach thought that this passage could have been added later. The author tells us how Altmann fostered religion in his diocese, contrasting its former squalor with its brilliance "now"[5]. Subsequently he complains that Reginmar has wrecked his predecessor's good work[6]. Wattenbach argued that the first passage was written before Reginmar had shown his hostility to monks, and that the second was added long afterwards. But the description of Altmann's reform in the *Life* (to be quoted below) is so rhetorical that it should not be used as evidence for dating. The author shows his

---

1. *M.G.H. SS.*, t. XII, p. 229-243. I shall refer to it as *Vita*. On Altmann, see R. BAUERREISS, *Kirchengeschichte Bayerns*, t. II, St. Ottilien, 1950, p. 51-52 and 233-236.
2. P. CLASSEN, *Gerhoch von Reichersberg*, Wiesbaden, 1960, p. 21.
3. *Vita*, p. 229 : "Ab his itaque qui eum praesentes viderunt, et eius obsequio familiarius adhaeserunt, quaelibet eius gesta studiose investigabo."
4. *Ibid.*, p. 235 and 239.
5. *Ibid.*, p. 234.
6. *Ibid.*, p. 240. Little is known of Reginmar ; see G. MEYER VON KNONAU, *Jahrbücher des deutschen Reiches unter Heinrich IV. und Heinrich V.*, t. VII, facs. 2, Leipzig, 1909, p. 179.

distance from the events he describes by his ignorance of them, as Wattenbach himself pointed out. Further, he neither mentions nor quotes from Altmann's polemical writing, although there was a copy at Göttweig, anonymous, it is true[7]. This *Streitschrift* was violent even of its kind, and would have helped the writer of his *Life* to present Altmann as a good gregorian. The manuscript tradition is late : the earliest surviving copy is late-twelfth-century, apart from a few leaves of the mid-century. A short account of the history of Göttweig up to 1156 comes at the end, and it is impossible to tell where the original finished[8].

It seems best to date it before Abbot Chadalhoh's death in 1141 and after Bishop Reginmar's, September 30, 1138. The story told of the latter's illness and death, foreseen in a vision, where he was condemned by a council at Rome for undoing Altmann's work for religion[9], would agree with a time when the monks were still smarting at his unfriendliness towards them. Hence the *Life* is a specimen of hagiography, written up from mainly second-hand material, some fifty years after the saint had died. This gives it an interest of its own: we see the author trying bravely to make bricks without straw.

His prologue, addressed to his abbot, explains that Altmann is not well enough known. The abbot has ordered that he should be "put on the map": the light hidden under a bushel must be displayed[10]. Perhaps the author felt that his light shone too dimly. The heroic phase of the investiture conflict had sunk into the past, as reformers tackled new problems. The miracles ascribed to Altmann were few and conventional. The monk of Göttweig may have hoped to catch the eye by fashioning a candlestick as elaborately as he could. Perhaps he belonged to that type of man, found in all ages, who likes to collect curious scraps of knowledge. His inclusion of papal letters addressed to Altmann suggests that he had a bent for research. For whatever reason, his *Life* resembles a museum. A sketch of its chief exhibits will serve as a background to the author's presentation of his Sibyl.

First of all he collects legends, supported by etymologies and even by archaeological evidence. Since Altmann came from Westphalia, his hagiographer thinks fit to give an account of the origin of the Saxons, of their threefold division and of the ecclesiastical geography of Saxony. He tells us that they descended from the army of Alexander the Great and that their name derives from the Saxon for "knife"[11]. Both items can be found in Widukind's *Saxon History* (I, 1 and 7), but our writer mentions no source other than tradition and goes into more detail. The situation of his monastery leads him to the early history of Eastern Germany. It is said to have been inhabited by the Goths, a warlike race, which traced its descent back to Mars; hence he tells of that wonderful sword, forged by Vulcan for Mars, lost for thousands of years and rediscovered by Attila, King of the Huns[12]. Jordanes has the same story about the Goths' claim to be descended from Mars and about the sword, in his *Gothic History* (35) ; again there is no evidence of direct quotation. Our monk then explains the etymology of Göttweig. It comes from the Goths and from Wich; the popular pronunciation "Kotewich" is wrong. Wich is gothic for Mars. A leader of the Goths called Godfrey is said to have lived on Mount Göttweig and to have worshipped Mars, as ditches and ramparts still testify, as do ancient buildings

7. M. SDRALEK, *Die Streitschriften Altmanns von Passau und Wezilos von Mainz*, Paderborn, 1890, p. 25. But see *Lib. de lit.*, t. I, p. 470.

8. See WATTENBACH's introduction, *Vita*, p. 226-228. I have not been able to see the ms.

9. *Vita*, p. 240.

10. *Ibid.*, p. 228-229 : "Laudabile admodum opus... a me praecipis depromi videlicet vitam praeclari antistitis Altmanni stilo illustrari, ac lucernam iam diu sub modio tectam, ad illuminationem futuris saeculis ostentare..., ut illustris vir diu latens in tenebris, producatur in lucem videndus ab omnibus."

11. *Ibid.*, p. 229.

12. *Ibid.*, p. 237.

or idols still found there. Göttweig seems to have been the site of a military camp in roman times. Earthworks, inscriptions and idols have indeed been found there[13]. A description of this pleasant hill, which reads almost like a modern holiday brochure, follows. It is situated in *Noricum Ripense*. Hence we pass to the provenance of the Bavarians, who came from Armenia and invaded the land under their leader Bavarus, driving out the natives. Norix, son of Hercules, conquered it "after many days" and called it after his name. Here he founded the city Tiburtina, which is now Ratisbon. Ripensis is now called Orientalis because hills have been raised and the bank of the Danube is fertile with ploughed fields and vineyards on all sides[14]. The legend that the Bavarians came from Armenia and that their land was conquered by Norix, son of Hercules, makes its first appearance in written form in the *Annolied*. This poem was written probably 1080-1085 by a monk of Siegburg in praise of Archbishop Anno of Cologne. It also has the story that the Saxons descended from Alexander the Great's army. The monk of Göttweig is the second writer known to have mythologised Bavarian history in this way[15]. He may have read the *Annolied*, since he venerated St. Anno and Siegburg abbey, as we shall see. But if that was his source, he treated it very freely, omitting some details and adding others.

His wish to connect his people with classical antiquity, as was fashionable, may help to explain why he introduces the Sibyl into his account of Altmann's reform. He does not make much display of classical learning elsewhere, apart from saying of a man who was punished by lameness that he still "limps like Jacob, or indeed Aeneas"[16]. Jacob's limp was authentic (Gen. XXXII, 31); Aeneas' seems to derive from Aeneid, XII, 476-7, where the hero is wounded:

> interdum genua inpediunt cursumque recusant,

— a forced parallel.

Secondly, he claims to quote from a rare book, the tenth letter, addressed to St. John the Evangelist in exile, which closes the Pseudo-Dionysian *corpus*. I say "claims" because his so-called quotation is wide of the mark. He finds it the only adequate comment on the wickedness of Altmann's clergy in resisting reform and in driving their bishop out of his see. The parallel between Altmann and St. John, two holy exiles, must have struck him. Sinners will have only themselves to blame when they get separated from the good at the Last Judgment, having already separated themselves in this life:

> Quid hic dicendum vel scribendum ? Hoc utique quod Dyonisius Ariopagita scribit ad Iohannem apostolum in Pathmos exilio relegatum dicens : 'Ut quid ab impiis Christus crudelis, quia in iudicio separabit malos a bonis ? Nonne multum

---

13. *Vita*, p. 237 : "Mars autem lingua eorum dicitur Wich ; ergo a Gothis et Wich mons vocatur Gotewich, non ut vulgus dicit Kotewich. In hoc monte fertur quidam dux eiusdem gentis, nomine Gotefrit, habitasse, et ibi Wich, id est Martem deum coluisse ; quod adhuc fossae et valli testantur, et antiqua aedificia vel idola ibi reperta." See G. PASCHER, *Römische Siedlungen und Strassen im Limesgebiet zwischen Enns und Leitha*, in *Der römische Limes in Österreich*, t. XIX, 1949, p. 40-41. This notice on Göttweig has a reference to our *Vita*.
14. *Vita*, p. 237 : "Et quia Noricum nominavimus, ethimologiam eius, si placet, exprimamus. Bawari traduntur ab Armenia oriundi. Qui cum magna multitudine de finibus suis egressi, hanc terram sunt ingressi, et expulsis aboriginibus, pro eis habitaverunt, et terram de nomine ducis sui Bawaro, Bawariam nominaverunt. Hanc post multos dies Norix filius Herculis expugnans, Noricum ex suo nomine vocavit ; in qua et civitatem Tiburtinam, quae nunc Ratispona dicitur, aedificavit. Ripensis autem, quae nunc Orientalis dicitur, ideo vocatur, quia subductis montibus ripa Danubii undique vineis et arvis foecundatur."
15. On all these legends, see A. BORST, *Der Turmbau von Babel*, t. II, 1, Stuttgart, 1958, p. 592-594; t. II, 2, Stuttgart, 1959, p. 669-671. Further work on sources of the *Life* might be rewarding, but lies outside my scope here.
16. *Vita*, p. 236.

dolent in eorum cohabitatione, et nimium exultant, in eorum separatione ? Graves sunt eis etiam ad videndum, quos timent eis pessimis viis fore impedimentum. Iuste ergo iustus iudex eos in iudicio ab invicem separabit, dum illos supplicio, istos aeterno gaudio mancipabit.'[17]

The relevant passage in John Scot's translation reads :

Quid mirum si Christus vere dicat, et discipulos iniusti civitatibus exagitent, ipsi quae sunt secundum dignitatem sibimet attribuentes et a sanctis polluti distincti et redeuntes ? Neque enim in saeculis venturis causalis erit ex se iustarum separationum Deus, sed ex Deo omnino se ipsos segregantes[18].

The anastasian gloss on *separationum* (about 875) stresses the point that sinners, not God, are responsible :

Notandum quod non Deus auctor sit separationis sive segregationis peccatoribus stationis sinistre, sed ipsi sibi auctores horum sunt peccatores penitus se ipsos segregantes a Deo[19].

Our author's "quotation" has no verbal resemblance to the original or to the gloss. It sounds like embroidery on dimly remembered reading. However, it was unusual for a monk writing in Austria before the mid-twelfth century even to know the contents of a Pseudo-Dionysian letter. Latin scholars were coming to know the *corpus* better than formerly in the first half of the twelfth century : Gerhoch of Reichersberg used it in his commentary on the Psalms from that on Ps. XIII onward ; his commentary on Ps. I-XX appeared early in 1146[20]. But the longer, more theological books of the *corpus* drew more attention and seem to have been quoted more often than the letters.

Thirdly, the monk of Göttweig makes a notable contribution to the literature of visions of the other world, by placing his monastery in Paradise. A certain man, secular in habit, but spiritual in faith and deed, "whether in the body, I know not, or out of the body" (II Cor. XII, 2), was carried to Hell, where he saw many unbearable torments and many persons of princely and middling rank, whom he knew, suffering there. He learnt from them "and told us afterwards" for what sins they were being punished. Then he was led to a flowery mead, bright and fragrant, and full of thousands of persons rejoicing. Here was a marble mount, delightful to look upon, where he held to it that he saw the monastery of Göttweig shining in great splendour. Inside it he saw Bishop Altmann with glittering dress and countenance among the brethren, whom he knew, and had a long talk with him. The visionary saw, too, the monastery of Siegburg in the same fair setting. Here was Bishop Anno with his brethren, from whom he received many orders, which he told on his return[21]. Anno, Archbishop of Cologne (1056-1075), paired with Altmann as a founder of monasteries. Like Altmann he was buried in one of his foundations, in this case Siegburg, also on a hill (Michelsberg near Cologne). Like Altmann he was driven out of his episcopal city by a revolt. His kinsmen the Archbishop of Magdeburg and the Bishop of Halberstadt played a leading part in the Saxons opposition to Henry IV; St. Anno died out of royal favour[22].

---

17. *Vita*, p. 234.
18. *Dionysiaca*, éd. Ph. CHEVALLIER, t. II, Bruges (undated), p. 1572-1573. I choose John the Scot's translation because the monk of Göttweig would have been most likely to see it. None of the variants given in this edition help to establish any verbal similarity.
19. On these glosses, see H.F. DONDAINE, *Le corpus dionysien de l'Université de Paris au XIIIe siècle*, Rome, 1953, p. 35-37. I quote from ms. Oxford, St. John's College 128, fol. 211 v° of the tenth to eleventh century. Ms. Oxford, Bodl. Laud. misc. 639, of the twelfth century, lacks this part of the *corpus*.
20. CLASSEN, *op. cit.*, p. 114-119.
21. *Vita*, p. 240.
22. W. SCHLESINGER, *Kirchengeschichte Sachsens im Mittelalter*, t. I, Cologne, 1962, p. 109.

The ingredients of this vision are familiar enough. The visionary sees persons known to him suffering for their sins and then others enjoying their reward in the bright light and sweet scents of Paradise[23]. Two marble mounts "of immense height and incredible beauty" appear in Hetto's account of the vision of Wettin, Abbot of Reichenau in the early ninth century. A river of fire, where many known to Wettin were in torment, flowed round the two mounts ; but no inhabitants are mentioned[24]. No vision known to me, apart from that in our *Life*, transports whole monasteries to the Elysian fields. The closest parallel comes from Adomnan's *Life of St. Columba*, probably written 688-692. An irish monk saw the whole island of Iona lit up by angels as they came to fetch St. Columba's soul when he lay dying ; but the monastery itself remains on earth[25]. The Irish had a special fondness for visions of the other world : Tundal for instance in a vision recorded by Helinand under the year 1149 saw four bishops, all named, in Paradise[26]. We hear in Altmann's *Life* that an irish monk called John visited Göttweig in the bishop's lifetime ; the bishop loved him for his religion and enclosed him (in a hermit's cell presumably) near the church there. John saw Altmann in a dream after his death and received instructions to purge the abbey, whose inmates had grown lax[27]. Perhaps the picture of two marble mounts, each crowned by a monastery with its holy patron, owed something to Irish influence : the recluse may have told stories of visions about Hell and Paradise in graphic detail.

The word "marble", signifying splendour and firmness, fascinated the monk of Göttweig. He opposes it to "wood", which is softer and rots easily. When Altmann entered his diocese he found that almost all the churches in it were built of wood and empty of furniture. Their priests were "wooden" too in the sense of being married, occupied with worldly business and ignorant of *divina officia*. Now, however, almost all the churches of the diocese are of stone and are adorned with books, pictures and other ornaments as a result of his care. Most important of all, they are well guarded by chaste and learned men. The writer adds a glowing account of Altmann's work for religion and his foundation of monasteries[28]. This leads him straight on to the pseudo-sibylline prophecy, which plays on the contrast between wood and marble :

> For he (Altmann) was the marble pillar in God's house about which the Sibyl is said to have prophesied, when she had divided the ages (of the world) according to the various metals. She wrote that a great house was to be raised up, supported by seven kinds of pillars ; the first were golden, the second silver, the third bronze, the fourth iron, the fifth marble, the sixth wooden ; the seventh and last were of reed. This she foresaw in the spirit would be, but we have already seen it happen. For the great house raised up is the church built of living stones, whose breadth stretches over the whole world. Its golden pillars were the apostles ; then came their successors, shining like silver in their chastity and eloquence ; the bronze pillars were the doctors, sounding sweetly as bronze with the roar of their teaching. The iron pillars were the martyrs, patient in tribulation and winning through all adversity like iron. The marble pillars were the bishops, upright in faith

23. See H.R. PATCH, *The Other World according to Descriptions in Medieval Literature*, Cambridge (Mass.), 1950, p. 104-107.

24. Referred to *ibid.*, p. 104-105. *M.G.H. Poet. lat. aevi carol.*, t. II, p. 268 : " His igitur dictis assumpsit eum idem angelus et duxit per viam amoenitatis immensae praeclaram. In qua dum pergerent, ostendit ei montes immensae altitudinis et incredibilis pulchritudinis, qui quasi essent marmorei videbantur. "

25. *Adomnan's Life of Columba*, éd. A.O. and M.O. ANDERSON, London, 1961, p. 530 ; on the date, see p. 96. I have to thank Dr C.J. HOLDSWORTH for this and the two following references. See his *Visions and Visionaries*, in " History, " t. XLVIII, 1963, p. 141.

26. *Chronicon*, lib. XLVIII, in *P.L.*, t. CCXII, col. 1038-1055.

27. *Vita*, p. 240-241. He came to Southern Germany with St. Marianus Scotus and many other irish monks : see *Vita s. Mariani Scoti*, in *AA. SS.*, feb., t. II, p. 368.

28. *Vita*, p. 234.

and firm in deeds.   Among them Bishop Altmann, like veined marble, underpinned God's house with his diverse virtues, and adorned the times by word and example up to the end of his life.   The wooden pillars are carnal prelates, wrapped up in earthly concerns alone ; they are easily rotted by vice, as is wood by worm, and break at a touch.   The pillars of reed are simoniacs, who enter, not through Christ, the gate, but climb over the wall, as it were, by means of money.   They slaughter and lose the sheep, feed not Christ's flock but themselves, take the milk and wool, buy all spiritual things as Simon did and sell them like Giezi ; and so they sink down like reed under the weight of the building of God's house[29].

Again familiar features combine with unfamiliar.   The theme of the church, God's house, as a building was as commonplace as the abuse of simoniacs as hirelings and false shepherds. The living stones were God's faithful people ; the pillars were apostles, doctors or bishops[30]. Gregory VII had complained in a letter to the princes and people of Germany that the lombard bishops, "who ought to be pillars in God's church", had no place in her structure[31], as schismatics and enemies.   The metal and fabric symbolism also drew on tradition[32]. St. Augustine taught in his *City of God* (XVIII, 23) that the Sibyl had prophesied the birth of Christ by means of verses ; the first letters of the lines spelled out the name of the Saviour in greek.   To make her prophesy the spread of Christianity throughout the world was a natural extension.   St. Augustine, however, divided world history into six ages, corresponding to the six ages of man ; the last, featuring decrepit old age, began after the Nativity[33]. Pseudo-Bede's Sibyl distinguished nine generations of men ; Christ was born in the fourth and chose his disciples in the fifth ; the ninth generation was marked by wars among kings, followed by the coming of "a salian king", Conrad II (1024-1039).   Sackur, who edited Pseudo-Bede, thought that the latin version originated in Lombardy in Conrad II's reign[34]. Neither of these two divisions of world history, whether sixfold or ninefold, begins with the apostles, as does the monk of Göttweig's.   Both cover all human history, whereas the monk of Göttweig limits himself to church history.   I know of no earlier scheme of division starting from the apostles, though variants on the theme appear later in the twelfth century. Anselm of Havelberg divides the ages of the Church on earth into six, of which his own age was the fourth[35].   His *Dialogues*, according to their prologue, were written for Pope Eugenius III, 1145.   Anselm had an optimistic view of the present age, seeing the foundation of new religious orders as a good sign.   Gerhoch of Reichersberg was gloomier : his *Fourth Watch of the Night*, written in 1167, gives a fourfold division ; the first age of the Church lasted from Christ to Constantine, the second from Constantine to Pope Gregory I, the third from Gregory I to Gregory VII, and the fourth from Gregory VII onwards.   Each age had its Antichrist in chief, the last of whom was still to come, and its lesser Antichrists.   Those of

29. *Vita*, p. 234 : " Erat namque in domo Domini columna marmorea, de qua fertur praedixisse Sibilla, cum distinxisset saecula per diversa metalla, scribens domum magnam erigendam, septem generibus columnarum fulciendam : quarum primae essent aureae... "   The passage is too long to quote in full.
30. See J. SAUER, *Symbolik des Kirchengebäudes und seiner Ausstatung in der Auffassung des Mittelalters*, Freiburg im Breisgau, 1902, p. 102, 134 and *passim*.
31. *Epistolae collectae*, nº 20, éd. P. JAFFÉ, in "Monumenta gregoriana. Bibliotheca rerum germanicarum," t. II, Berlin, 1865, p. 546.
32. J.B. PITRA, *Spicilegium Solesmense*, t. II, Paris, 1855, p. 275, 283, 292, 347, 420-421.
33. For the various periodisations of history current in the middle ages, see J. SPÖRL, *Grundformen hochmittelalterlicher Geschichtsanschauung*, Munich, 1935, *passim*, especially p. 120-121.
34. Pseudo-Bede also spread to Germany, E. SACKUR, *Sibyllinische Texte und Forschungen*, Halle, 1898, p. 125-137.   The Sibyl prophesies the coming of Boniface, Marquis of Tuscany, in Donizo's *Vita Mathildis*, written at Canossa (1111/12-1115), ed. L. SIMEONE, *R.I.S.*, t. V, 2, 1930, p. 32; on the date, see p. 111.   On later sibylline texts, see E. JAMISON, *Admiral Eugenius of Sicily, His Life and Work*, London, 1957, p. 22-32, 226-233, 295-303; she gives an up-to-date bibliography; see also B. SMALLEY, *Flaccianus " De visionibus Sibyllae,"* in " Mélanges offerts à Étienne GILSON," Toronto/Paris, 1959, p. 547-562.
35. *P.L.*, t. CLXXXVIII, col. 1149-1160.

the last age are money-grubbers and the roman people[36]. Neither Anselm of Havelberg nor Gerhoch of Reichersberg attaches his periodisation to a sibylline prophecy.

The monk of Göttweig's chronology is so confused that one wonders whether he thought of his prophecy as representing a time sequence at all. The martyrs, oddly, come after the apostles and doctors. The age of good bishops like Altmann is followed by an age of worldly prelates and then by that of simoniacs. This might look like an anticipation of Gerhoch if anything else in the *Life* suggested so pessimistic an outlook. But nothing in it would lead one to suppose that the writer believed himself to be living in an age of exclusively bad bishops. Nor does he show any interest in Antichrist. I would prefer another explanation. I suspect that having run through metals and started on fabrics, marble, wood and reed, he slid into a "morality" and began to moralise their properties, forgetting that they were intended to signify ages of the Church. What began as periodisation ends as a little sermon on good and bad prelates. The sequel bears me out. The writer goes on to praise Altmann in a mixed metaphor :

> But Bishop Altmann upheld the frame of God's house by the four cardinal virtues as though by posts. By them he raised up those committed to him from earthly, to heavenly things, as though in a four-wheeled chariot. He showed prudence in providing for his future by live works. Fortitude strengthened him when he flinched not from threats of the earthly empire. He put on justice when he led the errant back into the way of truth. He clove to temperance when he exceeded not the mean in any one of these. O man worthy of all praise and commendation, who converted water into the relish of wine, after Christ's example![37]

The account of the miracle by Altmann's butler follows on at once.

Our hagiographer, it seems, picked up some hitherto unknown version of a pseudo-sibylline prophecy, and wove it, not very skilfully, into his praise of Altmann and blame of bad prelates. The Sibyl served many good causes in the middle ages : she was quite obliging enough to prophesy in favour of a gregorian bishop.

---

36. CLASSEN, *op. cit.*, p. 295, 426-427.
37. *Vita*, p. 235 : "Episcopus autem Altmannus machinam domus Dei quatuor principalibus virtutibus quasi quatuor fulchris sustentavit, quibus sibi commissos quasi in quadriga de terrenis ad caelestia sublevavit. Prudentia quippe floruit, dum sibi in futurum vivis operibus providit ; fortitudo hunc roboravit, dum minas terreni imperii non formidavit..."

Note:

On pseudo-sybilline prophecies see now P.J. Alexander, 'The Diffusion of Byzantine Apocalypses in the Medieval West,' *Prophecy and Millenarism: Essays in Honour of Marjorie Reeves*, ed. Ann Williams (London, 1980) 56–71.

3

Les commentaires bibliques de l'époque romane : glose ordinaire et gloses périmées

Le problème des origines et de la première diffusion de la glose ordinaire ne semble pas avoir bénéficié du travail intense qui se fait actuellement autour de l'histoire des études bibliques de l'époque romane. Ce que nous en savons pourrait se résumer en peu de mots[1]. Déjà au temps de Cassiodore on lisait la Bible à la lumière des commentaires des saints Pères de l'Église. Le moyen le plus commode de le faire, pour des lecteurs ou débutants, ou pour des gens pressés, était d'étudier un texte glosé. On extrayait des morceaux choisis afin de les copier soit dans les marges, soit entre les lignes du texte sacré. La page sainte, *sacra pagina*, se présentait comme texte de base pour tout enseignement théologique au haut moyen âge. Le moine ou le clerc qui prononçait les mots *sacra pagina* ne voyait pas un texte tout cru ; il se figurait plutôt un texte entouré de sa glose. Pour lui, et le texte et les gloses représentaient des *auctoritates*. Il avait sûrement regardé une image, dans quelque manuscrit enluminé des Évangiles, qui lui montrait saint Matthieu, par exemple, en train de rédiger son évangile sous la dictée d'un ange, ou du Saint Esprit symbolisé par la colombe. L'iconographie de saint Grégoire le montrait, de même manière, écrivant les *Moralia in Iob* sous la dictée de la colombe perchée sur son épaule. Or saint Matthieu et saint Grégoire faisaient autorité dans les écoles.

Qui donc a confectionné ces recueils de gloses entourant le texte pour le préparer à l'usage des fidèles ? Nous ne le savons pas ; nous ne le saurons jamais, et pour cause : les compilateurs restent anonymes. Ils se contentaient, en général, de piller les saints Pères, n'ajoutant rien de leur propre, ou du moins très peu. La provenance même d'un texte glosé ne nous renseigne pas. Le recueil a pu être copié sur un texte provenant de n'importe où.

La nouvelle poussée de vie intellectuelle qui se manifestait dans les esprits vers le milieu du XIe siècle devait augmenter le nombre des recueils. Les chaires se multipliaient ; les élèves se groupaient autour des maîtres ; ils avaient besoin de livres de classe. Le professeur se croyait obligé de se faire transcrire un recueil ancien ou bien d'en compiler un nouveau. Il pouvait également (c'était normal, je crois) ajouter des gloses sur une page qui n'en était pas assez chargée à son goût. On commençait même à y insérer des explications personnelles du maître. Le recueil pouvait contenir de l'ancien et du nouveau à la fois. *Tot glosae quot magistri*, ou peu s'en faut. L'enseignement se dispensait dans des centres divers. Les écoles des abbayes commençaient à fermer leurs portes pour se borner à l'internat. Les écoles des cathédrales se multipliaient au contraire. Maîtres et étudiants déménageaient librement pour s'en aller ailleurs. Partout où il y avait école de théologie, le maître devait faire des

1. B. SMALLEY, *The Study of the Bible in the Middle Ages*, 2ᵉ éd., Oxford, 1952, p. 46-66, 224-230. Depuis lors, O. LOTTIN, *Psychologie et morale aux XIIᵉ et XIIIᵉ siècles*, t. V, Gembloux, 1959, p. 142-188 ; *A propos de la date de deux florilèges concernant Anselme de Laon*, dans « Recherches théol. anc. et médiév. », t. XXVI, 1959, p. 307-314 ; D. VAN DEN EYNDE, *Literary Note on the Earliest Scholastic « Commentarii in Psalmos »*, *Complementary Note*, dans « Francisc. Stud. », t. XIV, 1954, p. 121-154 ; XVII, 1957, p. 149-172.

cours sur la page sacrée, mais les bibliothèques n'étaient pas standardisées. Le maître pouvait apporter son matériel de classe dans ses bagages ; il pouvait se contenter de ce qu'il venait de trouver là où il s'installait de nouveau. On devine les inconvénients d'une telle façon de procéder. Le texte sacré, copié au milieu de la page, faisait l'élément constant de son enseignement, avec des variantes dues au copiste, bien entendu. Les gloses, au contraire, elles, variaient selon le manuscrit. Le compilateur les avait choisies à sa guise. Il avait abrégé, remanié, simplifié comme bon lui semblait. Une standardisation allait s'imposer du moment que les maîtres se concentraient à Paris d'une manière définitive. Une glose de la Bible entière, qui s'appellerait la « glose ordinaire », devint en effet un livre de classe obligatoire. Le maître faisait cours sur un texte entouré de la glose ordinaire. De Paris, cette glose, dite ordinaire, se répandit dans toute la Chrétienté médiévale, là où l'on parlait le latin comme langue commune. Les anciens appareils, que je vais appeler des « gloses périmées », sont entrés dans l'oubli ; ils étaient démodés ; on ne les copiait plus.

La glose dite ordinaire s'enracina dans le sol de Paris. Elle n'était pas une invention parisienne pourtant. Elle doit son origine à maître Anselme de Laon et à son équipe. Son école devança celles de Paris comme centre préféré de tout amateur des études sacrées. Maître Anselme est mort l'an 1117 ; nous lui devons la compilation de la glose ordinaire du psautier, de l'évangile de saint Jean et des épîtres de saint Paul. Son élève, maître Gilbert l'Universel, se chargea de gloser le Pentateuque et les quatre prophètes, le livre des Lamentations y compris. Pour ce qui concerne les autres livres de la Bible nous sommes encore dans le vague. Nous savons que maître Raoul, frère et collègue de maître Anselme, y est pour quelque chose, surtout pour le premier évangile. Nous savons que maître Gilbert de la Porrée s'en est mêlé ; un prologue de l'Apocalypse, attribué à ce maître célèbre, est entré dans la glose ordinaire. Il est assez probable, mais la preuve nous fait défaut, que Gilbert de la Porrée compila la glose du dernier livre de la Bible.

La glose ordinaire du psautier et de saint Paul fut élargie par Gilbert de la Porrée d'abord, et ensuite par Pierre Lombard. Les professeurs du XIIᵉ siècle finissant parlaient couramment de la *media glosatura* de Gilbert de la Porrée et de la *maior* ou *magna glosatura* de Pierre Lombard[2]. Pour l'enseignement du psautier et de saint Paul on se servait normalement de la moyenne ou de la grande glose. Pour tous les autres livres bibliques on se contentait de la glose ordinaire.

Voilà à peu près ce que nous savons. Voici maintenant ce que nous ne savons pas : comment la glose ordinaire, produit de l'école de Laon, se distinguait-elle des gloses périmées qu'elle remplaçait ? Concurrence d'abord, oubli ensuite. Pouvons-nous tracer des lignes d'affiliation entre la glose de Laon et les gloses périmées ? Il y a déjà longtemps que j'ai étudié les gloses de saint Paul à ce point de vue. On constate avec clarté que le maître de Laon prit un recueil plus ancien comme base du sien. Depuis plusieurs mois j'ai essayé de faire la même chose pour d'autres livres de la Bible. Deux manuscrits de l'an 1100 environ nous serviront comme échantillons de gloses périmées. Le ms. Oxford, Trinity College D. 20 (=T) est écrit de plusieurs mains, aux traits quelque peu archaïques, et qui pourraient être françaises (Pl. IX). Cela vaut pour les initiales enluminées aussi. Des griffonnages sur les feuilles de garde nous indiquent que ce codex se trouvait en Angleterre au XVᵉ siècle. C'est tout ce que l'on sait de sa provenance. Il contient deux livres glosés, l'évangile de Matthieu suivi par le livre de Job ; en troisième lieu nous avons un commencement de l'Apocalypse (le reste est perdu) également glosé. Une confrontation de pages choisies du Matthieu avec les endroits correspondants de la glose ordinaire a montré une ressemblance complète. Toutes les gloses de *T* se retrouvent dans la glose ordinaire, mais celle-ci contient plus de gloses que *T* ; elle se présente

2. Les deux œuvres de Pierre Lombard sont imprimées dans P. L., CXC-CXCI. Gilbert de la Porrée n'a pas encore trouvé son éditeur ; voir M. SIMON, *La glose de l'Épître aux Romains de Gilbert de la Porrée*, dans « Rev. d'hist. ecclés. », t. LII, 1957, p. 51-80.

comme une version amplifiée. Il est intéressant de noter que M. l'abbé Chatillon vient de trouver des livres glosés, dans le fonds de Saint-Victor à la Bibliothèque Nationale, qui ressemblent à la glose ordinaire, mais qui ont moins d'ampleur[3]. On peut en déduire que le compilateur de la glose ordinaire de Matthieu se servit de quelque fonds commun. Il copia des gloses qu'il venait de trouver quelque part ; ensuite il y ajouta d'autres gloses, copiées d'un second recueil et ainsi de suite. Tout autre est le cas pour la glose de Job. Ici le compilateur du haut moyen âge n'avait pas ce choix de commentaires patristiques qui devait embarrasser quand il s'agissait de gloser le premier évangile. Il avait sous les yeux les *Moralia in Iob* de saint Grégoire ou bien un abrégé : ce n'était pas difficile. Cela nous permet de souligner le fait que nos gloses n'ont plus rien de commun. Les deux glossateurs, de *T* et de la glose ordinaire, se réfèrent à saint Grégoire, mais ils semblent avoir travaillé indépendamment l'un de l'autre. Ils ne choisissent pas toujours les mêmes morceaux des *Moralia*. Lorsqu'il leur arrive de choisir le même, ils l'abrègent chacun à sa manière. Le glossateur de l'Ordinaire — ou bien son devancier — se montre le plus intelligent des deux. Il travaille plus librement. Il ne craint pas de simplifier son original afin d'en rendre la lecture plus facile. Il résulte de cette enquête que le glossateur du Job de *T* ne contribua pas au développement de la glose ordinaire. Un recueil circulait, au tournant du siècle, qui n'aura pas la chance de survivre. L'équipe de Laon l'ignorait ou, si par hasard elle le connaissait, elle le méprisait à tel point qu'elle n'admettait pas qu'il fasse partie de son grand appareil. On obtient un résultat semblable en confrontant les deux séries de gloses de l'Apocalypse. Elles représentent deux traditions distinctes. J'incline à penser que les deux glossateurs ont puisé à des sources diverses. Le manuscrit *T* nous a démontré que le chercheur qui s'évertue à éclairer la préhistoire de la glose ordinaire devra s'apprêter à étudier chaque livre de la Bible à part.

Notre deuxième échantillon de glose périmée se trouve dans un manuscrit de la Bodléienne, Rawl. G.17 (cote 14750 du *Summary Catalogue*), que je vais appeler *R* (Pl. X). Sa provenance est inconnue. Il fut écrit probablement peu après l'an 1100, peut-être au Nord de la France, mais sûrement pas en Angleterre. Il contient le livre de Job glosé. Le volume est de petit format, commode à manier, quoique l'écriture soit plus grande et plus lisible que celle de *T*. Quant à sa ressemblance avec la glose ordinaire, ce manuscrit nous rappelle les rapports qui existent entre la glose du Matthieu dans *T* et la glose ordinaire. Il y a ressemblance complète sauf pour deux détails. Les gloses *marginales* de *R* se retrouvent presque toutes dans la glose ordinaire ; les compilateurs de cette dernière se servirent d'un recueil qui correspondait à *R*, ou peu s'en faut. Ils ne se croyaient pas obligés de l'améliorer ni de l'amplifier, tandis que les gloses *interlinéaires* de *R* ne correspondent pas du tout avec la glose ordinaire. C'est une complication dont le chercheur devra tenir compte.

La deuxième différence est autrement intéressante. Je ne m'attendais pas à recueillir des gloses originelles dans un recueil du XIIᵉ siècle commençant. On croyait — ainsi raisonnais-je — que saint Grégoire avait tout dit. On se bornait sans doute à en faire des résumés et à simplifier ses phrases. Il fallait du courage pour ajouter quelque chose, si mince que ce soit. Mais nous avons affaire dans *R* à un esprit éveillé, qui avait le souci de comprendre le sens littéral de la Bible. J'ai remarqué huit gloses marginales dans le recueil *R* qui manquent dans la glose ordinaire de Job ; elles ne se retrouvent pas dans le recueil *T* non plus. Le glossateur de *R* ne les avait pas prises chez saint Grégoire. Le contraste entre ces huit gloses, propres à *R*, et les autres, extraites des *Moralia*, est si fort qu'il saute aux yeux du lecteur qui tourne les pages : c'est comme une fleur sauvage poussant dans une plate-bande de jardin soigné.

---

3. J. CHATILLON, *Richard de Saint-Victor*, « *Liber exceptionum* », Paris, 1958, p. 70-71.

Examinons de près ces gloses.

1. *Numquid virere potest scirpus absque humore? aut crescere carectum sine aqua?* (IOB, VIII, 11).
   « Carex est herba que secat manus, *carectum* locus in quo crescit, et dicitur carex, caricis. » (*R*, fol. 15 v°).

Saint Grégoire supposait que ses lecteurs comprendraient le mot *carectum ;* il n'avait pas envie de leur donner une leçon de botanique. Notre glossateur puisait dans un dictionnaire quelconque. Papias lui offrait une explication légèrement différente[4] ; ni saint Isidore ni Raban Maur n'auraient pu le renseigner là-dessus.

2. *... et quasi meridianus fulgor consurget tibi ad vesperam* (XI, 17).
   « Vespera corporis finis est appropinquatio » (fol. 22 v°).

Le glossateur a flairé une métaphore. Il nous explique que son auteur veut dire : « quand tu approches de la fin de ta vie ».

3. *Inquillini domus mee* (XIX, 15).
   « Ab incolo, quasi extranei domus » (fol. 62 v°)[5].

Encore une glose lexicographique.

4. *Quis mihi det ut exarentur in libro, stylo ferreo?* (XIX, 23-24).
   « *In libro*, id est in cordibus humanis ; *stilo ferreo*, id est firma auctoritate » (fol. 63 v°).

De nouveau le glossateur entreprend de nous expliquer la métaphore.

5. *... et gaudium hypocritae ad instar puncti* (XX, 5).
   « Manus dum pungitur cito se retrahit, sed punctio manet » (fol. 64).

Saint Grégoire lui-même, cette fois, se fait un devoir de nous expliquer la comparaison. Il regarde les choses d'une manière livresque. *Punctum* pour lui signifie le point que fait le scribe en maniant son *stylus*. Il nous propose le contraste entre le point et la ligne que trace le même scribe. La joie des hypocrites ressemble à la première et non pas à la seconde de ces deux espèces de notations : « In puncto enim stylus mox ut ponitur levatur, nec mora ulla agitur ut per exprimendam lineam trahatur » (P. L., CLXXV, 1083). Le glossateur de *R* nous révèle une mentalité plus concrète. *Punctum* pour lui veut dire piqûre ; elle est vite faite, mais le mal en reste. Il exprime sa pensée en se servant d'un dicton populaire.

6. *Interiora mea efferbuerunt* (XXX, 27).
   « *Interiora* Iob erant uxor et amici qui efferbent in eum » (fol. 53 v°).

Notre glossateur pense que Job voulait raconter les maux que lui faisaient sa femme et ses amis.

7. *... ossa mea aruerunt prae caumate* (XXX, 30).
   « Cauma frigus gelu vel estas secundum quosdam » (fol. 54 r°).

Les renseignements qu'il cherchait cette fois lui faisaient défaut. Est-ce que *cauma* veut dire le froid ou la chaleur ? Il n'en savait rien.

8. *... et ad Deum formidolosa laudatio* (XXXVII, 22).
   « *Formidolosa* est gentibus. Si enim Deus non pepercit naturalibus olivis, timeat sibi oleaster inserta (*sic*) » (fol. 78 r°).

Le glossateur fait un pas en avant : il croit que Job se référait aux *gentiles* et il se souvient d'un

---

4. PAPIAS, *Vocabularium*, Venise, 1485, fol. 26 : « Carex herba acuta vulgo lisca, caricis corripit penultimum ; carectum locus herbe. » Le glossateur de *R* ne se servait pas de Papias cependant ; ses gloses lexicographiques n°ˢ 3 et 7 en fournissent la preuve.
5. Plusieurs cahiers ont été déplacés par le relieur. Je suis l'ordre du texte biblique et non pas celui des feuillets du manuscrit.

texte de saint Paul, qui défend aux *gentiles*, olivier sauvage, de se glorifier en face des Juifs olivier cultivé par le Seigneur : *tu autem cum oleaster esses, insertus es in illis... Si enim Deus naturalibus ramis non pepercit, ne forte nec tibi parcet* (ROM., XI, 17-24).

Je n'ai pas la certitude que toutes ces gloses proviennent de la même main. Elles sont écrites par le même scribe qui copiait les autres ; elles n'ont pas l'air d'avoir été ajoutées après coup, ce qui donne à penser qu'elles remontent plus loin dans le passé. Une addition au prologue de Job dans le recueil *R* suggère qu'il ne faut pas remonter trop loin cependant. Il s'agit de *materia* et d'*intentio* : *Materia huius libri est ipse Iob, talis scilicet omnimoda temptatione temptatus. Intentio est instruere nobis exemplum victorie et patientie...* (fol. 1 v°). L'idée de transférer l'*introitus* des grammairiens aux procédés de l'exégèse des livres sacrés ne remonte pas plus haut que la fin du XIᵉ siècle, que je sache[6]. Si donc cette addition au prologue et les huit gloses originelles proviennent toutes de la même main, nous avons le droit de situer notre anonyme vers l'an 1100 ou peu après. En tout cas le recueil témoigne d'un intérêt pour le sens littéral qui poussa le glossateur à proposer des explications de la poésie orientale, si déroutante pour les occidentaux. Ses contemporains les auraient cherchées en vain chez saint Grégoire. Il est peu probable que notre anonyme ait pu survivre assez longtemps pour étudier les commentaires d'André de Saint-Victor, ce savant épris du sens littéral. Ils lui auraient plu. Cet anonyme fut un humble devancier de maître André.

Passons à la glose ordinaire elle-même. Je viens de feuilleter les pages de quelques exemplaires du XIIᵉ siècle, venant de la Bibliothèque Nationale ou de la Bodléienne. S'ils n'apportent pas de lumière sur les problèmes que je posais à l'instant, ils se signalent par des particularités intéressantes. Le manuscrit B.N. lat. 84 appartenait à l'abbaye cistercienne de Notre-Dame de Bonport[7]. C'est un beau manuscrit contenant les quatre livres des Rois, glosés, aux enluminures assez jolies. Une main contemporaine ou presque (deuxième moitié du XIIᵉ siècle) a ajouté de nombreuses notes dans les marges. Leur auteur anonyme ne se mêle pas de commenter le texte. Son seul but, semble-t-il, est d'en contrôler les mots. Il a entre les mains un autre exemplaire des livres des Rois glosés. Il confronte les manuscrits en démontrant et les ressemblances et les variantes de texte qui l'intéressent. Son travail inclut et le texte et la glose. On trouve maintes gloses de cette espèce dans les Bibles glosées des XIIᵉ-XIIIᵉ siècles ; rien de plus normal. Ce qui frappe ici ce sont les lettres « M.G. » qui précèdent toutes les notes. Comment faut-il les traduire ? *Media* ou *magna glosatura* sont exclues, pour la simple raison qu'il n'existait que la glose ordinaire pour les livres des Rois. Il s'agit plutôt d'un *Magister G*, qui se serait occupé en quelque sorte de la glose ordinaire de ces quatre livres de l'Ancien Testament. On peut supposer qu'il faisait cours sur le texte pourvu de la glose ordinaire, ou bien qu'il en possédait un exemplaire soigneusement corrigé. On pourrait même aller plus loin et postuler provisoirement le compilateur de la glose ordinaire des Rois : l'annotateur du manuscrit B.N. lat. 84 nous indiquerait un *liber magistri*. Et Étienne Langton et Hugues de Saint-Cher se réfèrent à une version de la glose ordinaire des Prophètes attribuée à Pierre Lombard[8]. Ce dernier n'avait pas compilé la glose ordinaire de cette partie de la Bible, mais il y a lieu de croire qu'il avait légué aux écoles un texte qui passait pour bon et pur. Gilbert l'Universel, Gilbert de la Porrée ? La lettre *G* nous laisse l'embarras du choix entre tous les Guillaume, les Godefroi, etc. Il vaut mieux laisser ici un point d'interrogation en attendant des recherches plus approfondies.

Le manuscrit B.N. lat. 105, psautier glosé de provenance inconnue, mais probablement française, nous offre un trait inattendu. Il date de peu après le milieu du XIIᵉ siècle, je crois. Le fait même que

---

6. R. W. HUNT, *The Introductions to the « Artes »...*, dans « Studia... R. J. MARTIN », Bruges, s. d., p. 85-112. Cette addition au prologue de l'ordinaire se retrouve dans Laud. lat. 93 (voir plus loin, p. 21). Les gloses de *R* nᵒˢ 1 et 5 sont passées dans Bodl. Auct. D. 14 (4114), glose ordinaire des XIIᵉ-XIIIᵉ siècles.

7. COTTINEAU, *Répertoire...*, col. 432-433.

8. SMALLEY, *The Study of the Bible*, p. 220.

la glose est « ordinaire » suffit pour nous suggérer une date assez reculée dans la diffusion de l'ordinaire ; on arrivait vite à préférer la *Media* ou la *Magna* pour la lecture du psautier ; il s'ensuivait que l'ordinaire était moins répandue. Le lat. 105 nous frappe tout de suite à cause de son écriture soignée et de la magnifique lettre *B* au commencement du premier psaume. Sur cette première page, insérées dans la glose ordinaire, mais distinguées par leur couleur rouge, nous lisons trois phrases, que je ne reconnais pas.

> *Beatus vir.* Ab honesto incipit.
> *in cathedra pestilentie non sedit.* Ab utili.
> *erit tanquam lignum.* A possibili.

Le clerc ou le moine qui se fit faire ce beau manuscrit devait attacher une grande importance à ces trois phrases ; autrement il n'aurait pas pensé à les faire écrire à l'encre rouge. Nous entendons là quelque souvenir d'une leçon de rhétorique, écho de tel procédé conseillé aux orateurs, idée d'un maître de la page sacrée qui était passé par les arts libéraux, *ancillae sacrae scripturae*. Il brûlait de les faire servir à l'étude des psaumes. Quoi qu'il en soit, nous assistons à une rencontre touchante entre David et Cicéron.

La bibliothèque de Trinity College, Cambridge, possède une belle série de livres glosés, écrits pour la plupart au tournant des XIIe-XIIIe siècles, et provenant de l'abbaye cistercienne de Buildwas (Shropshire)[9]. Conservés en bloc par quelque hasard, tandis que maintes collections de la même espèce ont été amoindries et dispersées par suite de la suppression des maisons religieuses, ils témoignent encore de la volonté des dirigeants de Buildwas cherchant à se procurer des copies convenables de la glose ordinaire de la Bible. On les corrigeait avec beaucoup de soin. On notait des variantes dans les marges. On s'occupait, de surcroît, à standardiser l'ordonnance des gloses :

> Quidam tamen libri habent istas duas glosas sic positas et sine modo (ms. 12 [B.1.13], fol. 2 r⁰, marge inférieure).
> *Manus in manu* (glose de PROV., XI, 23) : quidam hanc parvam glosam ponunt pro continuatione super. Alii dividunt (*ibid.*, fol. 20 v⁰, marge inférieure).

Nous retrouvons des notes semblables chez les maîtres d'école, qui se souciaient de l'ordonnance des gloses sur lesquelles ils faisaient leur cours[10].

Les manuscrits 49 (B.2.6, Exode glosé), 58 (B.2.15, Isaïe glosé) et 117 (B.4.3, petits prophètes glosés) nous montrent en outre le mot *Ser-*, parsemé dans les marges. Il faut lire *sermo*, car l'annotateur nous précise : « Ser(mo) ad prelatos » à propos de la glose d'EXODE, XXV, 24 (ms. 49, fol. 83 r⁰). On se servait de la Bible glosée non seulement pour les études et la *lectio divina* du cloître, mais aux fins de la prédication aussi. Le moine qui était invité à faire un sermon pouvait feuilleter les pages des livres glosés afin de trouver un thème convenable. Même procédé chez les maîtres de la page sacrée ; ils joignaient la *lectio* à la *praedicatio*, en suggérant aux élèves et des textes et des thèmes à utiliser dans la prédication[11].

Le problème le plus intrigant qui se pose au chercheur concerne le progrès marqué par les scribes de l'époque. Le scribe du XIe et du XIIe siècle commençant copiait le texte sacré sur une colonne tracée dans la page, en laissant plus ou moins de place libre aux marges et entre les lignes. Au glossateur de se débrouiller ensuite. L'espace mis à sa disposition ne variait pas en rapport avec le nombre des gloses à transcrire. Or la glose devenait forcément plus épaisse là où le texte avait plus d'importance

9. N. R. KER, *Medieval Libraries of Great Britain*, Londres, 1941, p. 9.
10. SMALLEY, *op. cit.*, p. 217-219.
11. *Ibid.*, p. 254.

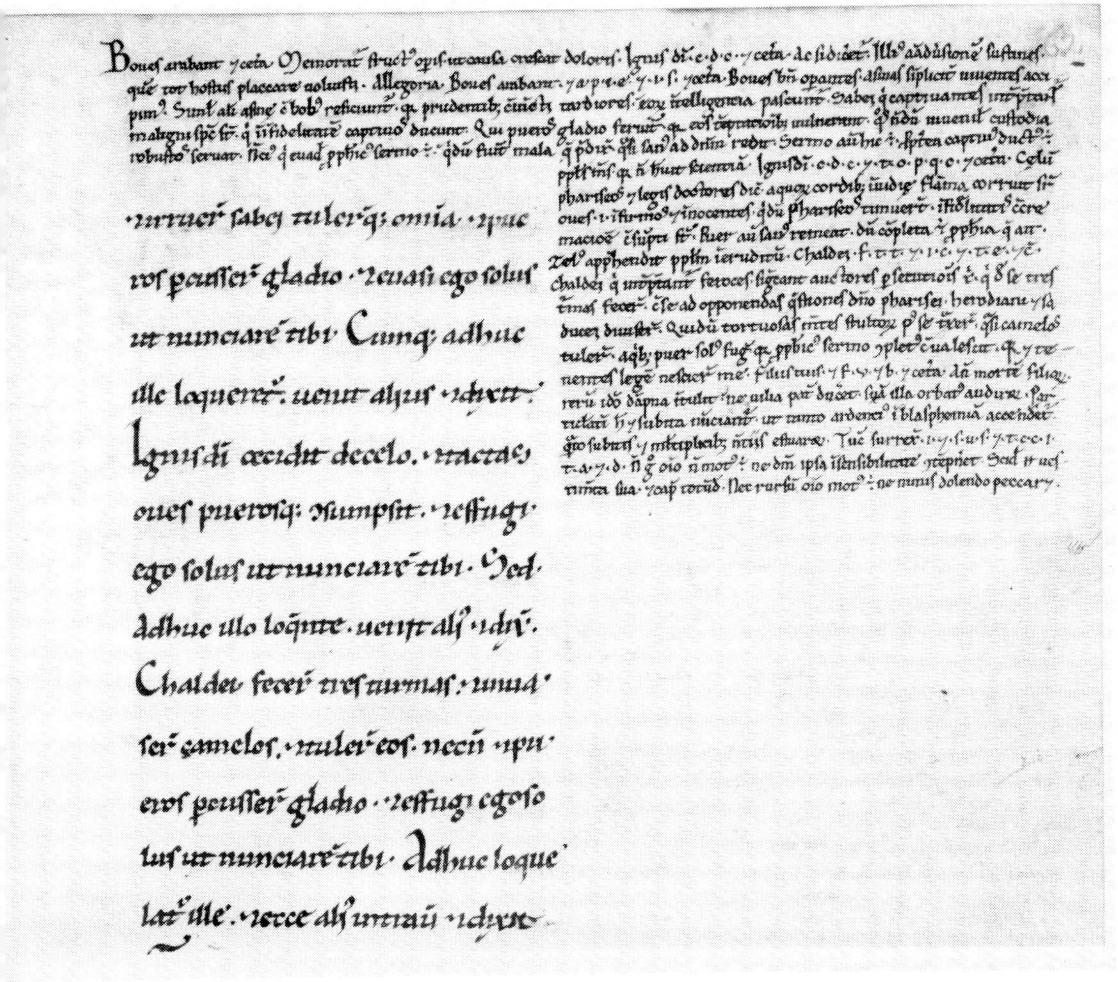

(Medieval Latin manuscript, glossed. Main text — Job 1:14–18 — in the lower left column:)

…nuncier sabei tulerq; omnia ·que
ros percusser gladio ·euasi ego solus
ut nunciare tibi Cumq; adhuc
ille loqueret· uenit alius ·dixit
Ignis di cecidit decelo· ·macta
oues puerosq; ·sumpsit· ·effugi
ego solus ut nunciare tibi· ·Sed·
adhuc illo loqute· uenit alius ·dixit
Chaldei fecer tres turmas· ·unua
se· camelos· ·tuler eos· necñ ·pu
eros percusser gladio ·effugi ego so
lus ut nunciare tibi· Adhuc loque
lat ille· ·ecce alius untau ·dixit

FIG. 1. — Bibliothèque Bodléienne. Manuscrit Oxford, Trinity College D. 20, fol. 62.

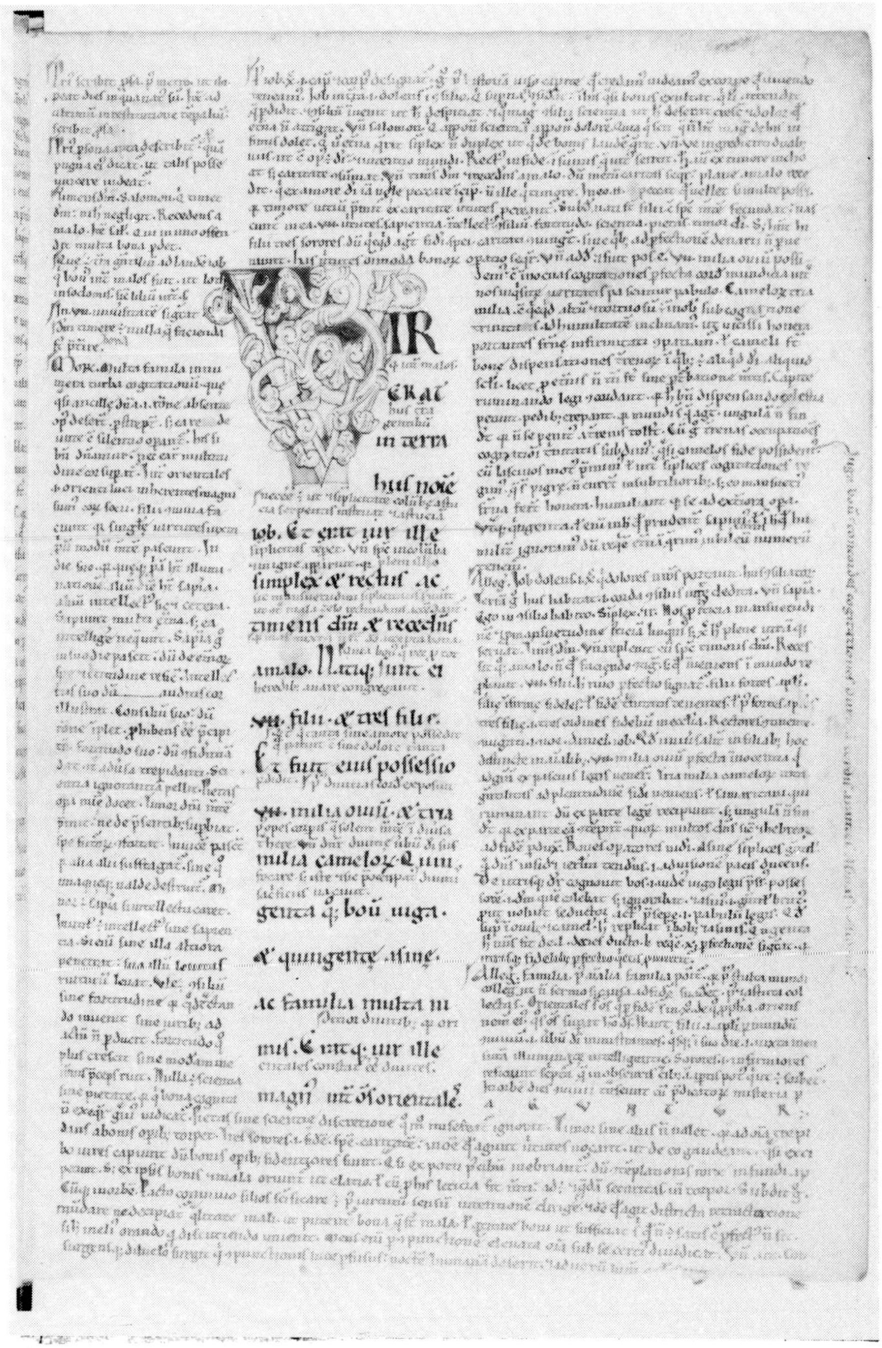

FIG. 2. — Bibliothèque Bodléienne. Manuscrit Rawl. G. 17 (cote 14750 du *Summary Catalogue*), fol. 2 r°.

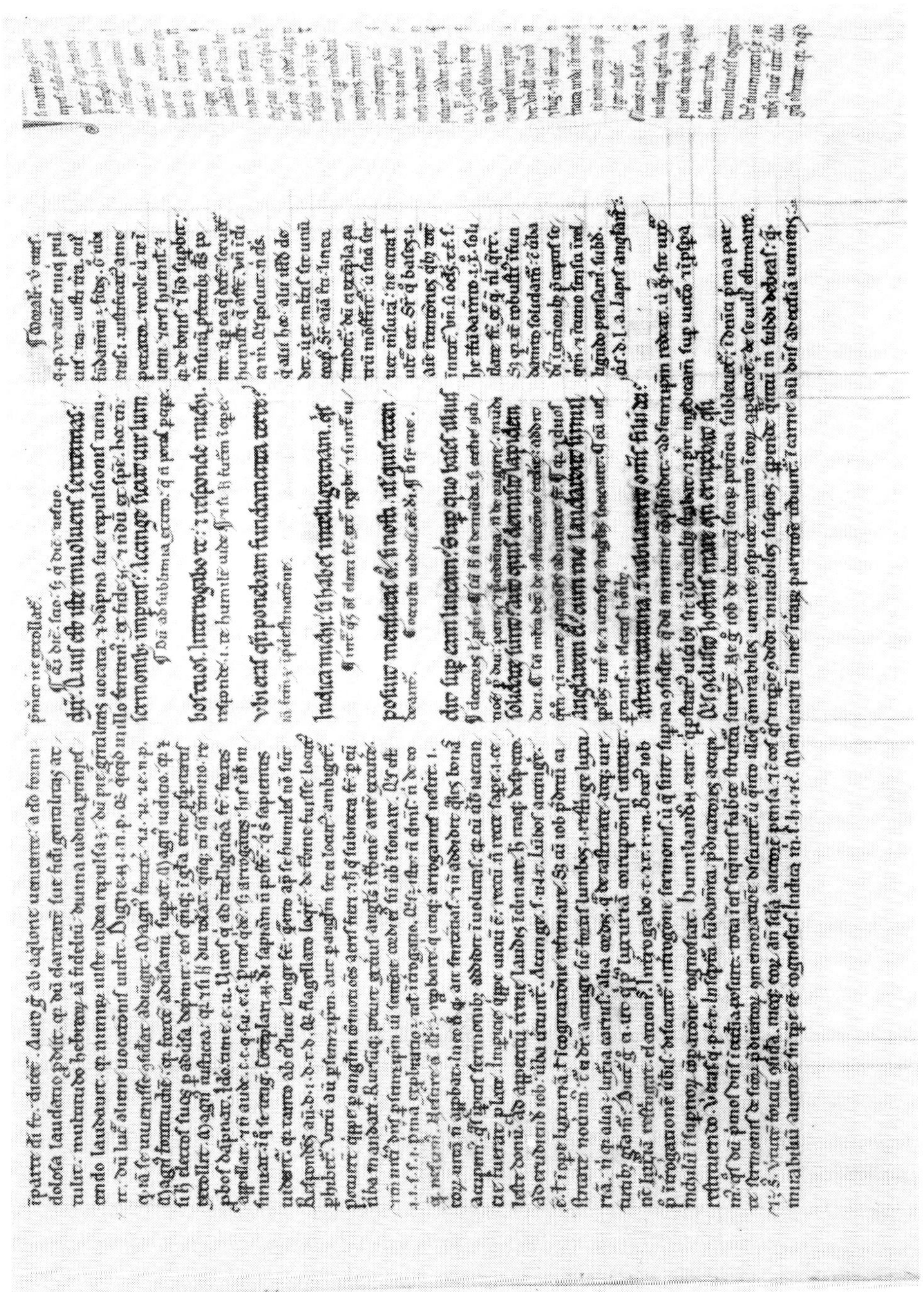

FIG. 3. — Bibliothèque Bodléienne. Manuscrit Laud. Lat. 93, fol. 11 v°.

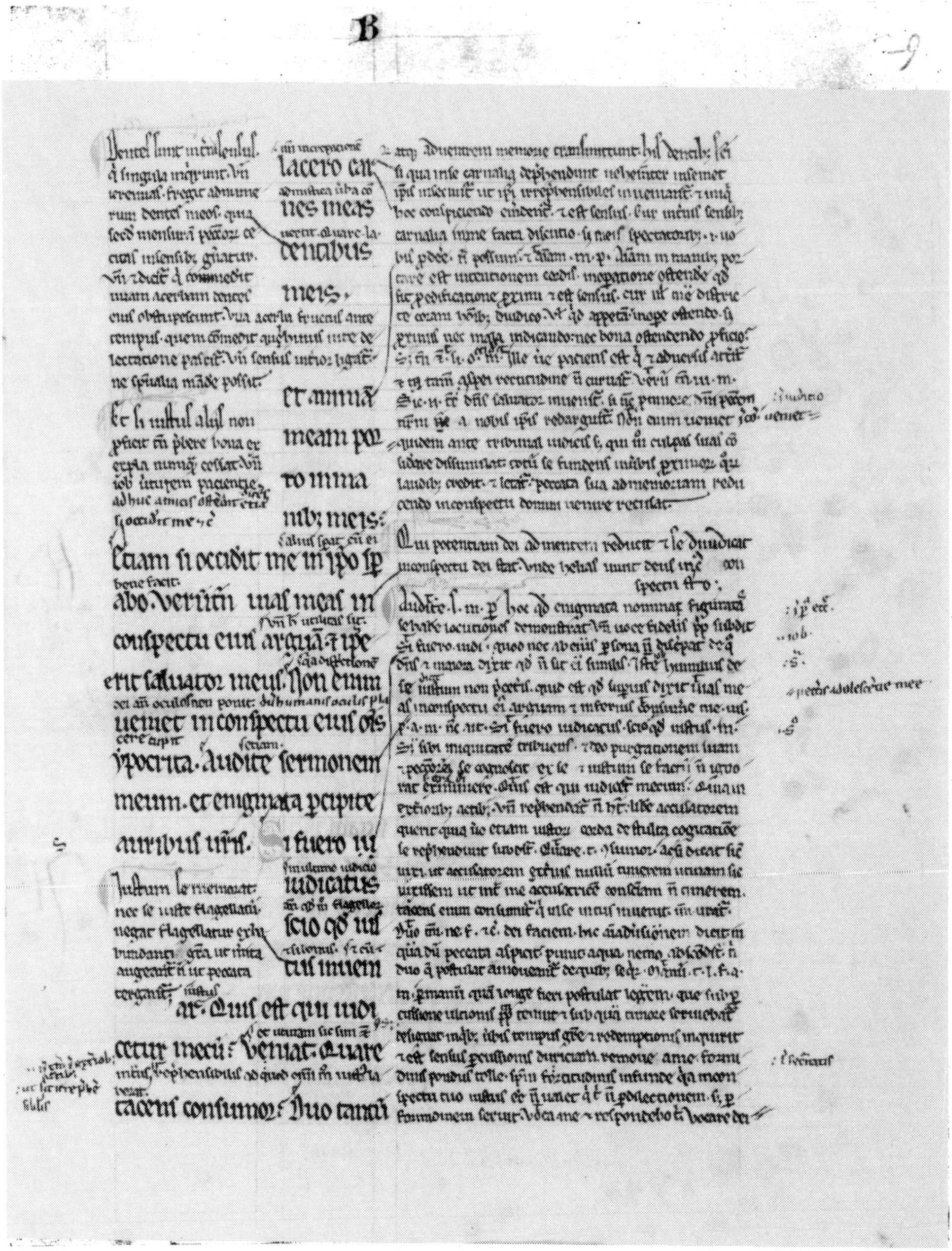

Fig. 4. — Bibliothèque Bodléienne. Manuscrit Laud. Misc. 441, fol. 29.

au point de vue de la doctrine. Les premiers chapitres de la Genèse attiraient beaucoup plus de commentaires que des textes de l'Ancien Testament de portée historique. Le glossateur ou copiste des gloses se voyait obligé de remplir les marges avec tant de textes que le résultat était à peine lisible : certaines fois, au contraire, il lui arrivait de laisser les marges presque vides. La beauté de la page sacrée et le gaspillage du précieux parchemin étaient également en jeu. Le manuscrit *T* nous offre un exemple de gaspillage propre à scandaliser les économes. Les gloses y sont comprimées dans le coin de la marge droite supérieure. Tout le reste est libre (Pl. IX). Les gloses, au surplus, erraient partout, à défaut de colonne. La difficulté restait insurmontable tant que les gloses n'étaient pas encore standardisées. La diffusion de l'ordinaire imposait une solution. Les copistes du milieu du siècle ne la trouvèrent pas : ils continuèrent à transcrire le texte d'une manière uniforme, sans rapport avec la glose. Que l'on considère par exemple le Laud. lat. 93 de la Bodléienne (Pl. XI), livre de Job, copié avec la glose ordinaire, provenant de l'abbaye royale de Saint-Denis. L'écriture est évidemment française ; je la daterais de la fin du XIIᵉ siècle environ. Une main du XIIIᵉ a écrit « Ioh'es Seyre » dans la marge inférieure du fol. 171 vᵒ. C'était un moine de la maison sans doute. Un certain Guillaume Sere, moine de Saint-Denis, est inscrit au nécrologe datant de l'an 1254 ou peu après [12]. Je le signale en passant comme exemple des renseignements à tirer des *marginalia* de ce genre de manuscrits. Celui qui commanda ce beau volume n'épargna pas les frais : il s'agit d'une édition de luxe de seconde classe pour ainsi dire. Les gloses sont déjà rangées en colonnes. Pourtant les copistes ne savaient pas éviter une mauvaise ordonnance. Les pages sont trop remplies ou trop vides ; s'il arrive au lecteur d'admirer le juste milieu, il s'aperçoit tout de suite que c'est là un effet du hasard. Il faut attendre la fin du siècle, à moins que ce ne soit le commencement du XIIIᵉ, pour assister aux noces définitives entre le texte et la glose. Un livre de Job glosé (actuellement manuscrit Bodl. Laud. misc. 441), nous réjouit par ce spectacle d'un couple uni. L'entente est parfaite. Le scribe qui devait copier le texte l'organisait en vue des gloses dépendant de chaque passage. Il prévoyait l'ensemble en se donnant beaucoup de peine pour inventer des effets décoratifs (Pl. XII). Je citerai également les manuscrits B.N. lat. 65 (Genèse glosée), et Trinity College, Cambridge, 90 (B.3.11, les petits prophètes glosés), provenant de Christ Church, Canterbury, comme types de gloses bien ordonnées par rapport au texte. En descendant dans le temps le lecteur est gâté ; il trouve normale la belle ordonnance qui précédemment lui faisait si forte impression. Il faut ajouter que cet effet heureux résultait d'une avance à tâtons. Il y avait un stade intermédiaire où le copiste du texte se rendait compte des besoins de son camarade, ou peut-être des siens, dans la tâche de copier les gloses. Il lui laissait plus ou moins de place selon que les gloses s'annonçaient ou nombreuses ou éparses. Le travail cependant était encore coupé en deux au lieu de se faire d'un seul jet. Je n'en veux pour preuve que les deux psautiers glosés manuscrits B.N. lat. 105-106. Le texte et la glose sont fiancés, pour ainsi dire ; ils ne se sont pas encore épousés.

Un autre raffinement inventé à la même époque concerne l'écriture de la glose. N.R. Ker vient de nous expliquer que les scribes anglo-normands commençaient vers 1170, semble-t-il, à se servir de deux types d'écritures, pour le texte et les gloses respectivement. Ils copiaient le texte d'une écriture aux traits anguleux, aux hastes élancées ; l'effet était imposant, mais il avait l'inconvénient de remplir beaucoup d'espace. Cet espace, ils l'économisaient en copiant les gloses d'une écriture plus ronde et plus courte [13]. Il serait intéressant de chercher un développement analogue dans les *scriptoria* continentaux. Il faudrait se demander en même temps si l'amélioration de l'ordonnance de la glose se répandit à partir d'un seul centre ou si le mérite en revint à des *scriptoria* divers, car il se peut que les mêmes besoins aient partout exigé une solution.

---

12. M. Félibien, *Histoire de l'abbaye royale de Saint-Denis en France*, Paris, 1706, p. 216. Le dernier abbé inscrit au nécrologe est mort le 4 mars 1254.
13. Ker, *English Manuscripts in the Century after the Norman Conquest*, Oxford, 1960, p. 2-3.

Je voudrais indiquer, pour terminer, un programme de recherches qui s'impose. Il implique un travail d'équipe, travail de longue haleine, travail coûteux aussi qui exigerait des subventions. On dresserait la liste des manuscrits des livres bibliques glosés (latins, il va sans dire), antérieurs au milieu du XIIᵉ siècle environ. On la ferait en se servant des catalogues de bibliothèques ; ensuite on les contrôlerait sur place. La paléographie n'est pas encore à l'état de science tout à fait exacte ; il n'est cependant pas trop difficile de distinguer les manuscrits du tournant XIᵉ-XIIᵉ siècles de ceux qui leur succédèrent. Les livres glosés de cette époque sont nombreux, mais non pas innombrables. On prendrait la glose ordinaire comme point de départ. On classerait les gloses périmées selon qu'elles s'approchent ou s'éloignent de la glose ordinaire. Que faudrait-il choisir comme témoin principal de cette dernière ? Je prendrais sans hésiter le texte imprimé avec les postilles de Nicolas de Lyre et les additions de Paul de Burgos, etc. Le choix fera froncer les sourcils : il paraîtra lâche au premier abord, mais à tort. Étant donné que nous n'avons pas d'édition moderne et critique, il faudra en préparer une tout en retraçant les origines. Les chercheurs, ayant achevé de classer les manuscrits, seraient à même d'éditer la glose ordinaire dans la forme qu'elle prit en sortant des mains de maître Anselme de Laon et de son équipe. Une telle édition est bien souhaitable. Elle aiderait aux recherches qui se font actuellement dans les domaines les plus variés. Les études littéraires en bénéficieraient aussi bien que les études théologiques. Feu dom Wilmart réclamait surtout une édition de la glose du psautier. Un savant qui s'occupe des commentaires bibliques du XIIᵉ siècle vient de se plaindre[14] de la corruption du texte de la glose du psautier en particulier. Mais il faudrait interroger les manuscrits au sujet des méthodes des glossateurs. Ceux du cercle de Laon choisissaient parmi les recueils qui précédaient les leurs. Le faisaient-ils entièrement au hasard, ou se souciaient-ils de chercher au loin pour trouver les plus propres à leurs besoins ?

Poursuivons notre enquête imaginaire et supposons que nous ayons la preuve que les maîtres de Laon agissaient librement, rejetant telle glose tout en lui préférant telle autre, qu'ils croyaient faire œuvre d'amélioration, voire de réforme, nous étudierions alors quel principe de choix ils adoptaient : choix aveugle ou conscient, stupide ou intelligent. Quel qu'il ait été, ce choix allait déterminer la forme que prendrait l'enseignement scripturaire de tout le moyen âge. A quel moment et dans quel milieu prit-on la glose de Laon comme base des cours ? Comment arriva-t-il que la glose de Laon eut la fortune de devenir « ordinaire » ? Voilà des questions supplémentaires que nos chercheurs devraient se poser. Puis ils nous raconteraient l'histoire de l'embellissement et de la diffusion de cette glose.

Mais comme il est à craindre, hélas, que les subventions fassent défaut, j'entrevois un projet de travail plus modeste. On pourrait se borner à une seule étude portant sur une seule ville. Qui classerait tous les psautiers glosés de Paris aurait déjà fait un travail utile. On pourrait tracer ensuite du point de vue paléographique l'histoire des fiançailles et du mariage du texte avec sa glose. J'espère avoir démontré, en exposant mes modestes fouilles, que le chercheur se constituera en passant un fichier riche de surprises. Il saisira sur le vif les idées que se faisaient les lecteurs de l'Écriture sainte au moyen âge, idées confiées aux marges des livres bibliques. Il n'y a pas meilleur moyen de leur arracher leur pensée.

14. D. VAN DEN EYNDE, *Autour des « Enarrationes in Evangelium sancti Matthaei » attribuées à Geoffroi Babion*, dans « Recherches théol. anc. et médiév. », t. XXVI, 1959, p. 51.

Note:
Dr. Christopher de Hamel has now made a thorough study of the development of gloss lay-out, *The Production and Circulation of Glossed Books of the Bible* (unpublished D.Phil. thesis, Bodleian Library, Oxford, 1978); 'The Manuscripts of Herbert of Bosham', *Manuscripts at Oxford: an exhibition in memory of Richard William Hunt (1908–1979)*, ed. A.C. de la Mare & B.C. Barker-Benfield (Oxford, Bodleian Library, 1908) 39–41.

On the earliest witnesses to the Gloss of Laon see now my 'Some Gospel Commentaries of the Early Twelfth Century', *Recherches de Théologie ancienne et médiévale*, xlv (1978) 147–180.

4

An Early Twelfth-Century Commentator on the Literal Sense of Leviticus

This anonymous author has escaped notice hitherto because his commentary takes the form of glosses, inserted into what at first sight looks like a standard copy of the *Gloss*. As we have no clue to his identity, I shall call him ' X '. His commentary survives in two copies only, as far as I know. There may be others ; but it cannot have been widespread in Belgium, France or England, where I have examined many glossed copies of Leviticus. X rewards study : he was a pioneer of biblical scholarship in a modest way ; he also reflected on theological problems connected with the observance of Old Testament *legalia*.

Our two known copies are in MSS *Bodl. Laud. lat. 14 (L)* and *Valenciennes 25 (V)*. The former came from the Cistercian abbey of Eberbach near Mainz [1], the latter, where text and glosses are incomplete, from the Benedictine abbey of St Amand [2].

> *L* : three MSS bound together in a 17th cent. binding, 8 3/4 × 6 1/2 in.
>
> > I, foll. 1[ra]-29[ra] : a commentary on Scripture by Albert of Siegburg, Genesis to Hebrews[3].
> > foll. 29[ra]-30[rb] : a short commentary on the New Testament (anonymous).
> > inc. : *Incipit Matheus. Ad seriem novi testamenti prius ponitur Matheus, de quo sicut de aliis pauca excipiam...*
> > expl. : *... quatuor milia, quatuor evangeliste.*
> > fol. 30[rb-va] : a moralisation of the properties of animals
> > inc. : *Dicitur in naturalibus...*
> > expl. : *... terra es et in terram ibis.*
> > *Finis adest operi, pocula ferte michi.*
> > foll. 30vb-31vb : four sermons for Advent [4].

---

1. See L. H. COTTINEAU, *Répertoire topo-bibliographique des abbayes et des prieurés*, Mâcon 1935, 1117-1118. Colonised from Clairvaux, 1135.

2. *Ibid.* 2581-2582.

3. F. STEGMÜLLER, *Repertorium biblicum* no. 1066.

4. None of the sermons found in *L*, I-II is listed by J. B. SCHNEYER, *Wegweiser zu lateinischen Predigtreihen des Mittelalters*, Munich 1965. They are all schematic and conventional.

II, foll. 32^v-34^r : three sermons.

fol. 34^v : beginning of a sermon.

fol. 35^r : the Benedictions of the Patriarchs (*Gen.* 49, 1-29) without commentary, followed by a mnemonic poem on the dating of Easter.

fol. 35^v : extract from a liturgical text for Easter.

Presumably both I and the slight scrapbok represented by II came from the Charterhouse of Mainz [5] : ' Codex carth. Mo(guntin)ensis ', partly cut off by the binder, is written in a 15th cent. hand in the bottom corner of fol. 1^r. I is written in 14th cent. German hands, red initials, II in German hands of the 14th or 15th cent. in single columns.

III, foll. 36va-114rb (fol. 36^r is blank) : text of Leviticus with prefatory, marginal and interlinear glosses.

Prefatory glosses, fol. 36^{va-b} : inc. : *Esicius : Querendum est quare iste liber...*

expl. : *... ut non optinet principium.*

Glosses, fol.. 37ra-114rb : inc. : *Ad litteram : Ideo appellabatur tabernaculum testimonii, quia in eo erat archa...*

expl. : *... designabat illud ad decimam pertinere.*

fol. 114^v : *Ex libris* inscription of St Mary of Eberbach in a 13th cent. hand ; fol. 115 is blank.

Written in the mid-12th cent., or perhaps earlier, in northern France or the Rhinelands. The glosses, written by a single hand, are contemporary with the text. The scribe uses the dipthong for *ae*, though not invariably. He makes careless mistakes, such as ' dubito ' for *debito* and ' fonsitan ' for *forsitan.* Blank spaces have been left for the initial V of the text and for capitals in the text. The lay-out of glosses in relation to the text is untidy and ill-planned, as is the case in early glossed books of the Bible [6]. Most glosses are headed *Ad litteram* or *Allegorice* or *Moraliter.* Most of those headed *Ad litteram* are not derived from the traditional sources and are the work of X. The incipit and explicit given above are from his marginal glosses.

V [7] : Text of Leviticus, breaking off at 14,14, ... *per extremum auricule dextere,* with marginal and interlinear, but no prefatory glosses, foll. 2ra-32vb. ' pars levitici glosata ' written in a 12th or 13th cent. hand, fol. 1^r ; fol. 1^v is blank. The glosses are identical with those in *L,* except for the absence of prefatory glosses, as far as the text goes. The scribe broke off before the bottom of his page. Text and glosses are written in north French hands of the mid-12th cent. A space is left blank for the initial *V* of the text. The first words of the glosses, *Ad litteram* etc., are rubricated.

Text of Job, up to 4,19, ... *fundamentum, consumentur,* with marginal and interlinear glosses, written by different, but roughly contemporary hands. This is a traditional compilation of glosses from St Gregory's *Moralia* with no glosses specially attached to the literal sense.

V belonged to the abbey of St Amand. It is not listed among the books added to the library 1150-1168 [8], and so may have been there earlier.

5. Cottineau, *op. cit.* 1798. Founded 1308.

6. B. Smalley, *Les commentaires bibliques de l'époque romane : glose ordinaire et gloses périmées,* see above, pp. 17-24.

7. See the description in *Catalogue général des manuscrits des bibliothèques publiques de France, Départements,* t. 25, Paris, 1894, 202.

8. L. Delisle, *Le Cabinet des manuscrits de la Bibliothèque impériale* I, Paris 1868, 307-319 ; II, 1874, 448-458.

L and *V* (up to *Lev.* 14, 14) contain glosses on the literal sense of Leviticus, supplementary to the predominantly spiritual exegesis found in the glosses derived from traditional sources. X, the anonymous glossator, nowhere explains to us the purpose or motive of his undertaking. The prefatory glosses, found in *L*, where he might have added a few words of explanation, had he wished, are all of the traditional type. The mixture of newly devised literal and traditional glosses in the same compilation has at least one precedent : a text of Job with glosses, of unknown provenance, now MS *Bodl. Rawl. G. 17*, written probably soon after 1100 in northern France, includes eight glosses on the literal sense. None of them derives from the *Moralia*, the source of the other glosses. This anonymous glossator tries to determine the meaning of some rare words in his text and to explain some biblical metaphors [9]. A thorough study of early compilations of glosses might produce more examples.

What relationship, if any, has the *L* and *V* collection of glosses to the standard *Gloss* on Leviticus ? Gilbert the Universal compiled the *Gloss* on the Pentateuch and the Prophets, and, as it now seems, on Kings also [10], at some time before he was appointed to the bishopric of London in his old age, late in 1127 [11]. Copies of individual books of the text and its *Gloss* came into circulation before the mid-twelfth century, but the *Gloss* on the whole Bible, a product of the school of Anselm of Laon, spread outward from Paris only after its adoption by Peter Lombard. Only then did it displace the many diverse collections of glosses which had done duty in schools and convents hitherto [12]. I shall ignore X's glosses for the moment and concentrate on the traditional type of glosses which go with them. I compared the traditional-type glosses in *L* with a copy of the *Gloss* in MS *Bodl. Auct. E. inf. 7 (S.C. 2130)*. The latter forms part of the *Gloss* on the Pentateuch copied under the direction of Herbert of Bosham for Archbishop Thomas Becket [13].

---

9. B. SMALLEY, *op. cit.* above 19–21

10. R. WASSELYNCK, *L'influence de l'exégèse de S. Grégoire le Grand sur les commentaires bibliques médiévaux*, in *Rech. Théol. anc. méd.* 32 (1965) 186-191. The argument for Gilbert's authorship of the *Gloss* on Kings might well be extended to cover Josue, Judges and Ruth.

11. B. SMALLEY, *Gilbertus Universalis Bishop of London (1128-1134) and the Problem of the " Glossa Ordinaria "*, *ibid.* 7 (1935) 237-240. Gilbert is first heard of among the clergy of Auxerre in 1110 and witnessed a charter there as *magister* in 1120. He was appointed to London late in 1127 and consecrated on Jan. 22 in the following year, being *grandaevus* at the time.

12. On some of these early collections see B. SMALLEY, *Les commentaires bibliques de l'époque romane, op. cit.* above.

13. C. R. DODWELL, *The Canterbury School of Illumination 1066-1200*, Cambridge 1954, 106-109. Experts on illumination differ on the question whether

Since Herbert was a pupil of Peter Lombard and edited the Lombard's *Magna glosatura* on St Paul and the Psalter, his glossed Leviticus inspires confidence, as a good witness to the text.

To begin with the prefatory glosses : the first in *L* correspond exactly to those in the *Gloss*. Four others from the *Gloss* are not found in *L* ; they include the gloss ascribed to the compiler, Gilbert the Universal, 'Rabanus ab Esicio... composuit'. Two other glosses found in the *Gloss* appear in *L* in shortened form and with some differences in wording [14]. When we turn from the prefatory glosses to those on the text, we find much greater divergence : the matter common to *L* and the *Gloss* is scattered and very rare. Different excerpts have been chosen from St Augustine's *Quaestiones* on Leviticus and from Raban Maur's commentary. The following comparison will show vividly how the same passage from Raban has been re-worded in the *Gloss* and in *L* on one of the few occasions where the same excerpt has been chosen :

RABAN on *Lev.* XXI (PL 108,488).

Sed ut Moyses dignitatem commendaret et ostenderet aperte, quia aliis quidem pauca, ipsi vero omnia Deus loqueretur, propter eius iustitiam et imaginem quam gerebat Christi, similiter et nos docens habere mentem ad quaecumque maiores et perfectione (*sic* perfectiores ?) dixerint, scientes quia continue ipsi superna operatione (*sic* contemplatione ?) fruuntur...

L, fol. 91[ra].	MS *Auct. E. inf. 7*, fol. 145[rb].
Per hoc quod Dominus Moysi loquebatur et Moyses populo, sanctorum prelatorum dignitas commendatur, et docemur mentem elevare ad audienda quecumque dixerint, cum ipsi superna contemplatione fruantur.	Moisi dignitatem commendat ; aliis enim pauca, ipsi vero loquitur Deus omnia, quia iustus est et imago Christi est. Nos quoque monet maioribus et perfectioribus attendere, qui continue fruuntur superna visione.

The lesson that God's speech with Moses should teach subjects to heed their spiritual superiors, as presented by Raban, has been slightly abridged in *L*, as compared with the *Gloss*, and has become more specific : *prelati* replace *maiores et perfectiores*. The *Gloss* keeps rather closer to the original, including the point, omitted in *L*, that Moses was righteous and a type of Christ.

---

the Bosham MSS were prepared by French or English artists. Early printed editions of the *Gloss* show comparatively few variations from twelfth-century MSS, but it seemed safer to use Herbert of Bosham's copy as being closer to the text used at Paris.

14. *L*, fol. 36[va-b] ; MS *Auct. E. inf. 7*, foll. 115[va]-116[rb].

The traditional-type glosses in *L*, therefore, represent one of those early compilations which gave way to the all-conquering *Gloss* in the third quarter of the twelfth century. The fact that a few glosses are the same in both can be explained easily. Gilbert the Universal probably took an existing compilation to serve as a basis for modification and expansion. Hence we should expect to find at least a minimum of common material underlying most of the early twelfth-century collections, with the *Gloss* among them.

X's glosses, on the contrary, have no counterpart elsewhere. The most likely and economical hypothesis to account for their presence would be that he took over or perhaps compiled for himself a set of traditional-type glosses, to which he added his own glosses on the literal sense of his text. Otherwise we must suppose that a third person added them from a commentary on Leviticus by X, which is now lost. It does not really matter which hypothesis we choose. The commentary does not survive, if it ever existed at all : we have only the glosses. They amount to a commentary, if we take them as a whole. Written out in continuous form, they would be longer than Hugh of St Victor's *Notulae* on Leviticus [15] and would be comparable with Andrew's [16]. Neither Hugh nor Andrew of St Victor expounded the whole text : they limited themselves, as X did, to passages which struck them as needing clarification.

It must be said at once that X made no use of either Hugh or Andrew on Leviticus. Their work would certainly have helped him, if he could have read it. Both Victorines transliterated Hebrew words, compared the Hebrew with the Latin text, and recorded information given them by contemporary Jews. X's ignorance of their writings puts him probably before the mid-twelfth century. Hugh's *Notulae* on the Octateuch belong to the earliest set of his works. Dr D. Van den Eynde dates them before 1125. He argues that Hugh must have begun his career as a writer before 1120, judging from the number of books he produced in this first stage of his activity [17]. We know that Hugh's books spread wide and fast, but they took

---

15. PL 175, 74-84.

16. I compared *L* with MS *Bodl. Laud. lat. 105*, foll. 111va-114va, for Andrew on Leviticus. Andrew began by transcribing Hugh's *Notulae* and then added comments of his own. Hence a reader of Andrew would also read Hugh on Leviticus. On Andrew see my *Study of the Bible in the Middle Ages*, Oxford 1952, 112-185 and *L'exégèse biblique du 12e siècle*, in *Entretiens sur la renaissance du 12e siècle*, ed. M. DE GANDILLAC and E. JEAUNEAU, Paris 1969, 273-283. My pupil Miss G. TEN KATE is completing a doctoral thesis on Andrew and his Hebrew sources.

17. *Essai sur la succession et la date des écrits de Hugues de Saint-Victor (Spicilegium Pontificii Athenaei Antoniani, 13)*, Rome 1960, 40-45, 207.

longer to reach some libraries than others : the bibliophile of St Amand added the *Notulae* to his collection 1150-1168 [18]. We may safely conclude that X was not in touch with St Victor and hence that he cannot have lived near Paris. It would be unsafe to put him before 1125 or thereabouts on the grounds that he did not know Hugh's work, and so make him a precursor of Hugh, since his teaching suggests a date well after the first decade of the century [19]. Hence there is no proof that he came first in the field, but he entered it independently, owing nothing to the Victorines.

Data on his status and dwelling place are scanty. That he was a qualified teacher appears from his use of the first person : he writes *arbitror* and *respondemus*, when discussing theological questions [20], in the manner of one who is licensed to instruct pupils. The phrase *sicut presens pagina videtur intimare* suggests that he may have been lecturing on the sacred page. His approach to his text differs sharply from that of monastic commentators ; therefore he can hardly have been a monk, dedicated to spiritual exegesis by the very fact of his profession. Membership of a house of canons regular need not be excluded. He consulted Jews, so he must have worked in an urban centre, where he could tap the learning of the synagogue. My guess would be that he taught in a cathedral school in northern France. To compensate for his reticence about himself he at least reveals his attitude and opinions : we learn what and how he thought.

His aim as a commentator was to analyse and describe the Old Testament *legalia*. To that end he would explain the grammatical construction where he found *inusitata locutio* (fol. 52va), and would adduce rhetorical techniques, to explain repetition for example :

> Breviter repetendo predicta magis reddit attentos auditores ad ea obser-vanda (fol. 63va).
> Repetitio eiusdem rei propter confirmationem (fol. 83vb).

He scrutinised his text in order to bring out precise details, taking an interest in such questions as which sacrifices were offered at public expense and which at private :

> On *Lev.* 8,2 : De hoc vitulo et de ceteris pertinentibus ad consecrationem sacerdotum videtur quod de publico sumptu sumerentur, sicut et vestes eorum (fol. 54ra).
> On 9,2 : Apparet quod hunc vitulum et arietem offerebat de proprio sumptu et pro peccato suo (fol. 56rb).
> On 16, 3-5 : Videtur quod superiora animalia, id est vitulum et arietem, emebat sacerdos de proprio, sed et ista populus de communi comparabat (fol. 75va).

---

18. DELISLE, *op. cit.* II, 458, n° 304.
19. See below, p. 42.
20. *L*, foll. 44rb, 81rb.

Sometimes he fell back on his own observation or ingenuity : the gridiron used for baking flour offerings (2,7) resembled that used for cooking fish and other foodstuffs ' in our time ' (fol. 39ra) ; the tabernacle was purified by annual sacrifice (16, 32) just as churches were reconciled after crimes had been committed there (fol. 76va). He did not understand the meaning of ' stroke ' (14, 54), but made several guesses :

> Lex omnis lepre et percussure : nescio quid hic appelletur percussura, nisi lepra que carnem ledit et quodammodo percutit, iuxta quod dicere solemus hominem percussum, quem infirmari videmus, vel nomine percussure hic sola lepra appellatur que loco percussure, id est vulneris, pullulat (fol. 72rb).

The rule against marriage with a kinswoman raises the question why God should have forbidden in Leviticus what he had allowed to Abraham and Sara. X answered that it was for some cause unknown to us, or else his purpose was to widen the circle of loving relationships :

> On 18,6 : Cum autem Abraham patriarcha non sit culpatus de hoc quod sibi copulavit Saram, ... queri potest quare Dominus modo prohibuit talibus personis copulari. Ad quod respondemus quod vel propter causam nobis incognitam hoc precepit Dominus, vel ut caritas inter plures dilataretur, quod fit cum a proximis mulieribus abstinent et cum remotioribus lege coniugali copulantur (fol. 81rb).

Two sources, and two only, could present themselves to X, if he wanted further information : Josephus and contemporary Jews. He exploited Josephus to the full. Many glosses are ascribed to Josephus and X refers to him in his own comments. Collation with the original showed that X copied verbally, apart from making minor changes and abridgements, from the Latin translation of *The Antiquities of the Jews*. ' The Latin Josephus ' was a medieval favourite and an obvious source [21]. Contemporary rabbis supplemented him quite naturally in the eyes of medieval exegetes. The biblical story left much to be clarified. St Jerome and Pseudo-Jerome [22] had set the example of consulting Jews on the literal sense of the Old Testament in order to fill up the gaps in their knowledge. God's revelation to Moses, as the Jews believed, included oral as well as written matter : the *Mishnah* enshrined both together. Christian scholars, for their part, expounded Scripture in the light of tradition, making no clear

---

21. See *The Latin Josephus* I (ed. F. BLATT, Copenhagen 1958).

22. The *Quaestiones in libros Regum* by an anonymous scholar writing about 800 were ascribed to St. Jerome ; see PL 23, 1329-1402. For an example of their use in the twelfth century see B. SMALLEY, *L'exégèse biblique du 12e siècle*, *op. cit.* 278-279.

distinction between the text and patristic, at least in the twelfth century. Hence they took it for granted that their Jewish teachers would recount Jewish traditions in answer to queries. The rabbis were living books, authorities on the literal sense of *legalia*, which they still observed. X shows no signs of supposing that his procedure in questioning contemporary Jews is anything out of the ordinary, although it is one of the earliest recorded.

His *Hebraei* are as anonymous as the Victorines', but some of their information can be traced. It was all *peshat*, exegesis of the literal sense of the Law. X recorded no legends of the kind picked up by later Christian scholars from their Jewish teachers. His account of the method of tithing flocks and herds (*Lev.* 27, 32) comes straight from the *Mishnah*. On many texts his *Hebraei* made general statements, which probably derived from the *Mishnah*, but omitted its precise details. They may have drawn on their standard commentary by Rabbi Salomon of Troyes (Rashi), who died in 1105. It is possible, however, that their comments coincide with Rashi's only because they were purveying common traditions. On *Lev.* 11, 34, they told him that they were allowed to eat meat which had been in contact with unclean things, in spite of the prohibition of the Law; this may have been a relaxation necessitated by medieval living conditions. Experts on *Judaica* may be able to fill in and specify X's sources more accurately. The following list of his quotations from Jewish informants will at least give some idea of the type of data which he elicited from them in his efforts to understand the nature of the Law and how it was put into practice.

> On 4,3 : *delinquere faciens populum*, scilicet de ceremoniis Domini male docendo, scilicet talia que fieri non deberent vel facienda et docenda pretermittendo. Si autem aliud grande peccatum per ignorantiam faceret simili oblatione mundaretur. Si autem ex deliberatione peccaret, dicunt hebrei quod a pontificatu deponeretur (fol. 41[va]).

> A distinction is made between deliberate and unwitting transgression, *Hor.* 2, 3-6 [23].

> On 4,7 : His omnibus liquet altare thimiamatis fuisse extra velum, quod etiam habet assertio hebreorum (fol. 42[rb]).

> Rashi ad *Exod.* 30,6 [24].

> On 4,27 : *Quod si peccaverit anima...* Si autem ex deliberatione peccaret, dicunt hebrei quod multum verberabatur vel et occide-

---

23. See H. DANBY, *The Mishnah*, Oxford 1933, a translation into English with notes and indexes.

24. *Pentateuch with Targum Onkelos etc. and Rashi's Commentary*, translated and annotated by M. ROSENBAUM and A. M. SILBERMANN, 2 vol., London 1940.

batur. Unde dicitur in libro Numeri : *anima que per superbiam...*
Verbum etiam Domini contempsit (fol. 43va).

Num. 15,30. This could derive from Rashi on *Num.* 15,30, and more generally from penalties prescribed in *Mishnah*.

On 6,14 : *Hec est lex sacrificii.* Iuxta hebreos hic iterum agitur de
simila, quam homines sponte offerebant sine animalibus ... (fol.
48rb).

Perhaps from Rashi *ad loc.*

On 6,17 : *erit sicut pro peccato.* Peccatum est quando committitur
illud quod est prohibitum velut furtum ; delictum est quando deseri-
tur illud quod preceptum est, velut Deum diligere et parentes honorare ; vel, ut hebrei dicunt, illud solum dicitur hic delictum quod
fiebat in ipsam personam Domini, precepta sacrificiorum eius et
aliarum ceremoniarum transgrediendo (fol. 48va).

On 7, 11-12 : Talium vero hostiarum due erant manerie, quarum
una appellabatur *thoha* [25], id est laus, et eam offerebant homines
gratias agentes Deo specialiter pro quibusdam causis, ut dicunt
hebrei, scilicet ideo quod eos liberasset a captivitate vel infirmi-
tate vel tempestate maris, vel ab errore deserti, per quod erraverant
(fol. 50va).

From Rashi *ad loc.*

On 7,13 : Illud quoque in Exodo legitur : *Non immolabis super*
fermentato sanguinem victime mee, referunt hebrei tantummodo ad
paschale sacrificium, quando nichil fermentatum poterat offerri vel
comedi (fol. 51ra).

From Rashi on *Exod.* 23,18 and 34,25.

On 7,14 : Dicunt hebrei quod reliqui panes edebantur ab aliis
sacerdotibus et non ab hominibus offerentibus, quamvis carnes
harum hostiarum edebantur partim a sacerdotibus, partim ab offerentibus (fol. 51^r, interlinear gloss).

Rashi *ad loc.* says that the bread remaining over was eaten by the owners ;
perhaps X got his information wrong.

On 7,16 : Hic agit de alia maneria pacificorum... Et quia in hac
oblatione non facit scriptura de panibus mentionem, ideo hebrei
dicunt quod fiebat sine panibus (*ibid*).

From Rashi *ad loc.*

On 7,19 : Hoc de sola carne hostiarum precipitur, nam de alia
carne non consecrata, licet aliquid immundum tangeret et immunda

---

25. See below, p. 37

fieret, tamen iuxta hebreos licebat immundis hominibus vesci (fol. 51ᵛᵇ).

Perhaps derived from Rashi *ad loc.*

On 11,34 : Cum dicat cibum et quodlibet aliud immundum fieri contactu morticinorum, videtur quod non liceret hebreis vesci cibis a morticinis vel ab alia re immunda contactis ; non enim licebat eis immundis uti. Et tamen hebrei dicunt sibi licitum esse vesci carnibus a morticino vel ab alia re immunda contactis (fol. 62ʳᵇ⁻ᵛᵃ).

On 17,3 : Dicunt hebrei Dominum hic vetasse ne populus toto tempore dum erat in castris prope tabernaculum nec etiam ad vescendum occideret aliquod animal quod offerri posset, nisi iuxta ritum pacificorum illud ante tabernaculum offerret ; postea vero a Domino permissum esse dicunt quod in terra promissionis causa vescendi licite occiderent animalia ubicumque manerent, quod confirmant per verba Moysi sic dicentis : *Locus quem elegerit Dominus, si procul fuerit, occides de armentis...* (fol. 79ʳᵃ).

Perhaps derives from Rashi on *Deut.* 12,22.

On 17,7 : Iuxta hebreos ante prohibuit animalia que offerri poterant occidere nisi coram tabernaculo, hoc autem prohibet in omni loco idolatriam (fol. 79ᵛᵃ).

On 19,27 : Videtur precipere ne rotunda fiat tonsio in circuitu, sed iuxta hebreos vetat ne in rotundum, id est ne penitus auferant capillos de capite quin aliqui remaneant (fol. 85ʳᵃ⁻ᵛᵇ).

Perhaps from Rashi *ad loc.*

On 20,18 : ... sicut hebrei dicunt, hic agitur de illo qui scienter hoc faceret, ibi de illo qui ignoranter hoc faceret... (fol. 88ʳᵃ).

Bek. 3,6 explains the difference between incurring uncleanness deliberately and by accident.

On 27,32 : Dicunt hebrei quod animalia decimanda in aliquo loco includebantur, de quo tam artus exitus erat quod inde non poterant nisi unumquodque per se egredi. Stabat autem pastor ante exitum tenens virgam tinctam recenter colore rubeo, et quodcumque decimum veniebat tangebat virga, et affectum macula coloris rubei designabat illud ad decimam pertinere (fol. 114ʳᵃ).

Bek. 9,7. Perhaps from Rashi *ad loc.*, but the detail seems closer to the *Mishnah.*

X went further : he struggled with the Hebrew tongue. I list below the passages where he refers to the Hebrew text and notes how it diverges from the Latin Vulgate. His transliterations of Hebrew words are generally incorrect, but this may have derived from the mistakes of his copyists, who would have lacked the knowledge to cope with them, and who perhaps had a badly written exemplar to decipher. It is interesting to see that X at first relies on what the Jews told him was in their text ; from *Lev.* 7, 14 onwards he writes : *in hebreo habetur* ; finally, on *Lev.* 27, 16, he writes : *in hebreis codicibus*. It sounds as though he graduated from taking down oral information to inspecting the written word. His Jewish teachers may have shown him their text and helped him to spell out the characters. Even that would have been an advance for a beginner. Miss G. Ten Kate kindly gives me notes on these pasages. I make no comment where X's Latin translation of the divergent reading in the Hebrew text is correct.

On *Lev.* 1,1 : Primo agit de quodam genere oblationum quod hebrei *minha* vocant. Nos autem illud vocare possumus munus placens vel sic aliquo modo (fol. 37rb).

Mishnah can mean grain-offering and would apply to *Lev.* 2 better than to the animal-offering prescribed in *Lev.* 1. X uses it in a general sense to mean a gift expressing reverence, which would be a possible sense of the word.

On 1,8 : Ubicumque nos habemus *iecur*, dicunt hebrei *epar* se habere (fol. 38ra).

This comment is obscure, since both words have the same meaning in Latin. *Epar*, however, may be a scribal mistake for the Hebrew *pader*, meaning kidney suet.

On 1,10 : Hic dicunt hebrei se habere *masculinum* non *anniculum* (fol. 37va).

On 3,1 : Post oblationem quam hebrei *haddi* vocant, agit de hostia pacificorum (fol. 40rb).

V also has *haddi* (fol. 4ra).

The transliteration *haddi* corresponds to no known Hebrew word which could apply to the offerings prescribed in *Lev.* 2. Probably the scribes misread the word in the exemplar.

On 5,5 : Hebrei habent *super holocaustum*. Precipitur igitur ut illud quod cremebatur de oblatione pacifica poneretur in eodem igne, ubi cremebatur holocaustum (fol. 40vb).

On 7, 11-12 : Talium vero hostiarum due erant manerie, quarum una appellabatur *thoha*, id est laus, et eam offerebant homines gratias agentes Deo specialiter, pro quibusdam causis, ut dicunt hebrei (fol. 50va).

The transliteration should read *thoda*, a thank-offering ; again we may have a scribal mistake.

On 7,12 : Ubi nos habemus *colliridas*, dicunt hebrei se habere tale nomen quod *turtellos spissos* significabat (fol. 51^r, interlin.).

This is a description of the offering, that is, ' cakes made of mixed flour, with oil ', rather than a translation of the Hebrew.

On 7,14 : *unus pro primitiis offeretur Domino*. In hebreo non habetur *primitiis* (*ibid.*).

On 9,20 : In hebreo habetur : *cremavit adipes in altari* (fol. 57va-b).

On 19,9 : In hebreo habetur : *non consummabis angulos metendo* (fol. 83va).

On 20,20 : In hebreo non habetur *absque liberis morientur*, sed *soli morientur* (fol. 88ra).

The Hebrew word means ' childless ' ; X is right in that it is an adjective, not a substantive and proposition.

On 22,29 : Hic agitur de quodam speciali hostia pacificorum, que iuxta hebreos *thoa*, id est laus appellatur (fol. 94ra).

Again the Hebrew *thoda* has been wrongly transliterated or transcribed, as on 7,11-12.

On 27,16 : Hec vero diversitas consecrationis aperte declaratur in hebreis codicibus, qui habent *cothex*, quod sanctum interpretatur, ubi de rebus agitur consecratis, que redimi possunt. Ubi autem agitur de illis que non possunt redimi, habent *herhun*, quod interpretatur anathema, id est ab usu communi separatum (fol. 112vb).

The correct transliterations are *codesh* and *cherem*, but their interpretations are correct.

We shall now look more closely at X's attitude to *legalia*. He held to the traditional pattern of literal and spiritual exegesis. When he could find no literal reason for a precept, he supposed that it had been given to signify a mystery :

On 22,27 : Determinat post quot dies a nativitate sua poterant offerre animalia. Ignoramus autem quare ante hunc terminum (ea) offerri prohibeat, nisi hoc factum sit pro significatione misterii. *Die autem octavo :* ignoramus etiam quare hoc sit prohibitum nisi pro significatione misterii (fol. 94ra).

On 25,31 : Miramur quare aliud preceperit de domibus urbium et aliud de domibus villarum. Forsitan (MS Fonsitan) hoc fecit propter solam significationem misterii (fol. 103vb).

On 27,6 : Mirum est quare in quadam etate iubeatur dare mulier pretium dimidium respectu viri et in aliis etatibus plus quam dimidium, nisi hoc factum sit pro significanda diversitate misteriorum (fol. 111ra).

Thus he accepted the spiritual sense of the precepts, but left its explanation to the Fathers.

He differs from most of his predecessors, however, in his concept of the Old Law as an historical institution. Earlier commentators on Leviticus had felt that Christian apologetics obliged them to pick holes in *legalia*. Many precepts struck them as irrational, inconsistent, trivial and impossible to observe ; their literal sense made nonsense. Such precepts 'cried out as with voices', to quote Ralph of Flaix, calling to Christians to interpret them according to their spiritual senses only. They had no true literal meaning ; they conveyed a spiritual message instead [26]. X, on the contrary, believed that all precepts had a true literal sense, even though he could find no reason for some of them. He handled the denial of a literal sense with a cautious firmness. The ban on certain foods as unclean seemed to clash with the text in Genesis, saying that God saw all his creation as good ; hence the unclean creatures had been interpreted as signifying vices. Raban Maur allowed that the lawgiver might have aimed at restraining the greed of the Jews, but held that his true intention was spiritual [27]. X, with an eye on Raban, pointed out that some foods were forbidden as a danger to health, and others, such as pork, on account of their (moral) significance. The latter, he implies, was not hidden from the Jews, but formed part of their education :

> On 11,1 : Hic docet que iuxta legem veterem sunt munda et ad esum licita, et que immunda et ad esum illicita. Et nota cum omnis creatura Dei sit bona iuxta illud : *Et vidit Deus quod erant omnia bona* [28], tamen Dominus prohibuit in lege quedam comedere tamquam immunda, sive propter infirmitatem hominum ut morticina et venenosa, sive propter significationem, ut porcum et quedam alia (fol. 60rb).

> On 11,43 : Prohibet ne se peccando contaminent, quod facerent aliquid de predictis contra precepta comedendo, et maxime vitia que in predictis significantur imitando (fol. 63rb).

The command not to enter the sanctuary except once a year was partly to test obedience, since entry would have been no sin in itself, and partly to signify its mystery :

> On 16,2 : Non esset peccatum assidue post velum intrare et ea videre que ibi erant, nisi Deus prohiberet. Prohibuit autem partim propter experimentum obedientie, propter significationem misterii partim (*sic*) (fol. 75vb).

---

26. B. SMALLEY, *Ralph of Flaix on Leviticus*, below, pp. 49–96.
    Ralph of Flaix may well have written after X, who shows no signs of having read him, but Ralph belonged to the old spiritualist tradition. X had certainly read Raban Maur, an earlier exponent of it.
27. PL 108, 351 : « ... et si ad modicum castigare Iudaeorum gastrimargiam volebat, tamen vera legis consideratio manifesta est et spiritualis praeceptorum expositio, qualesque oportet legi studium dantes docendi intentionem legislator habet ».
28. *Gen.* 1,31

Raban expounded the commemorative sounding of trumpets (23, 24) as a prediction of the Resurrection [29]. X added that it was meant to encourage the Jews to rejoice in memory of what they were celebrating as well :

> Id est feriabilis et solemnis dies, cuius celebritas et observatio omnibus debebat esse in memoria. Hoc autem quod die illo tubis clangebant fiebat ad maiorem exhortationem letitie et maxime propter misterii significationem (fol. 97[ra]).

He smoothed out those difficulties which his Christian sources pointed out to him. A good example is his comment on the precept against mating Diverse Kinds (19, 19). Raban called it ' ridiculous ' ; he cited the passage in Kings, where David ordered Sadoch and Nathan to set his son Salomon on *his* mule, thus proving that he rode a mule himself (*III Reg.* 1, 33), to argue that prophets and ' spiritual men ' did not keep this precept ; a mule, as the offspring of Diverse Kinds, should have been abominated [30]. X mentions David's mule to show that the Jews were allowed to buy offspring of Diverse Kinds from the gentiles, but not to breed them. His Jewish informants may have told him so from the *Mishnah* [31], though he does not cite their opinion here :

> David mulam habuit super quam iussit poni Salomon, quando fecit eum regem, unde apparet quod licebat eis animalia ex coitu diversorum animalium propagata ab alio populo comparare, sed non ad ea propaganda sua iumenta conmiscere (fol. 84[va]).

X also took pains to reconcile precepts which seemed to contradict each other. The command to cook and eat the ram sacrificed at a priest's consecration (8, 31) contradicted an earlier command to burn the whole of this sacrifice (6, 23), or so it seemed. He solved the riddle by distinguishing between various kinds of sacrifice :

> Cum hic iubeat comedere carnes arietis qui immolatus erat pro consecratione sacerdotis, queri potest qualiter illud sit verum quod superius

---

29. *Ibid.*, 509 : « Hoc et memoriale tubarum est : praedicat enim Salvatoris resurrectionem... »

30. *Ibid.*, 452-453 : « Haec quodammodo ad litteram videntur esse ridicula. Unde nec ita ea custodiri a prophetis et spiritualibus invenimus... Nam intende quid ad Sadoch sacerdotem et Nathan prophetam et ad Banayan David dicebat : *Ponite filium meum Salomonem in mulam meam* ; dicens enim *meam*, ostendit quia et ipse in mulam sedebat. Si autem iumenta commisceri alterius generis animantibus, id est asinum equo commisceri lex vetuit, et abhominabile hoc erat, oportebat et ea quae fiebant, et ea quae nascebantur ex eis procul dubio abominari ».

31. *Kilaim* 8,1 (*ed. cit.*) : " Diverse Kinds among cattle are permitted to be reared and maintained, and it is only forbidden to breed them. It is forbidden to mate Diverse Kinds of cattle one with another ".

dictum est : *Omne sacrificium sacerdotis igne consumetur nec quisquam comedet ex eo.* Sed illud superius de solo sacrificio simile intelligi potest ; vel sic exponatur quod omnis oblatio quam post consecrationem de sumptu suo et pro se offerebat sacerdos, igne penitus erat consumenda. Hic autem aries pro sua consecratione oblatus erat, et forsitan (MS fonsitan) de sumptu publico (fol. 55va).

He felt protective towards the Old Law. It had been a viable code in its time, although now the New Law had superseded it. He defended its viability against those who saw it as a mere tissue of contradictions and absurdities. The method of *concordantia discordantium* would serve to make a case for its coherence. Here he agreed with Hugh of St Victor, probably unknowingly. Hugh also taught that *legalia* had had a moral function : the ritual and prohibitions of the Old Law inculcated obedience, kindled devotion and signified that uncleanness was to be avoided, by forbidding pork, for example. Hugh also presented the Old Law as an historical institution as well as a book of mysteries [32].

What value did X attach to the observance of *legalia* in Old Testament times ? I shall transcribe the four glosses where he considers the problem. Then I shall try to deduce his opinions. These will lead on to the further question : how do they fit into the framework of early scholastic debates on the effects of circumcision and of the legal sacrifices on the Old Testament Jews ?

(1) On 2,10 : *Sanctum sanctorum,* id est valde sanctum comparatione aliarum rerum Deo sanctificatarum. Hec enim oblatio tante dignitatis erat quod non poterat comedi nisi in atrio et a solis maribus generis sacerdotalis, cum multa alia sanctificata aliis personis et in alio loco liceret comedere. Ideo autem sancta reputabantur quia rem sanctam significabant, vel ideo quia cum essent Deo consecrata augebant sanctitatem eorum qui illis digne utebantur, sicut faciunt ecclesiastica sacramenta, que illis antiquis multo sunt digniora (fol. 39rb).

(2) On 4,26 : *Et dimittetur ei.* Hinc apparet quod non solum post adventum et passionem Christi remissa esse peccata hominibus, cum tempore legis post penitentiam et sacrificium offerentibus peccata remitterentur, que tamen nullatenus arbitror remissa esse in efficatia illius legalis et figuralis sacrificii, sed in efficatia figurati et veri sacrificii, quod Christus in ara crucis obtulit. Si cui vero videtur quod ante passionem non remitterentur peccata, cum pro eis restaret pena et in sanctis, qui detinebantur in tenebris, simili modo videri potest quod parvulis in baptismo non remittatui

---

32. *De sacramentis* I, xii, 9 (PL 175, 360-361) : « *De mobilibus et superadditis praeceptis...* Pro exercitatione quidem ut plurima essent in quibus erudiendorum obedientia probaretur, et devotio excoleretur... Mandavit etiam eadem lex a carne porcina abstinendum ; opera scilicet immunditiae vitanda significans. Ad hunc modum aliorum quoque animalium tam volucrum quam piscium et eorum quae in terra versantur quaedam ab esu humano excipit ».

culpa, cum in eis restat pena, dissolutio scilicet corporis et anime. Quod autem ante passionem remitterentur peccata testatur Dominus in evangelio, sic dicens : *Confide fili, remittuntur peccata tua* [33]. Hoc idem propheta declarat, dicens : *Dixi : Confitebor adversum me iniustitiam meam Domino ; et tu remisisti impietatem peccati mei* [34] (fol. 44[rb]).

(3) On 6,3 : *Et quodlibet aliud ex pluribus fecerit.* Queri potest an ista satisfactio sufficeret ad hec peccata delenda que fiebant ex conscientia ; et dici potest quod pro eis inferebatur pena, et insuper addebatur illa satisfactio, sicut victus esset peccator (fol. 47[va]).

(4) On 12,6-7 : *Pro filio, sive pro filia, deferet agnum.* Queri potest utrum pro peccato pueri fieret hec oblatio, cui octavo die per circumcisionem dimissum erat peccatum originale, nec adhuc erat in ipso actuale. Itaque dicatur quod non pro preterito vel presenti peccato pueri fieret hoc sacrificium, sed pro futuris evitandis, sicut post baptismum, in quo fit plenaria remissio, eucharistia pro futuris malis cavendis assumitur. De filia vero, quia non circumcidebatur, dici potest quod per hoc sacrificium mundaretur de originali. De matre quoque, que forsitan in gignendo peccaverat, dici potest quod pro eius peccato fieret sacrificium, vel etiam, quamvis non peccasset, ab immunditia mundaretur, quam de effusione sanguinis contraxerat. Quod autem hoc sacrificium fieret pro infantulo, convincitur non solum ex hoc loco, sed etiam ex evangelio, ubi legitur : *Cum inducerent puerum Iesum parentes eius, ut facerent secundum consuetudinem legis pro eo* [35]. Quod autem pro matre etiam fieret oblatio (apparet) ex istis verbis presentibus : *Orabit pro ea sacerdos et sic mundabitur* (fol. 64[rb]).

To begin with the effects of circumcision : the view that it remitted original sin under the Old Law, as baptism did under the New, had become common opinion by the mid-twelfth century [36]. X takes it for granted (4). To the related question, how women were freed from the taint of original sin, he answers tentatively that the sacrifice offered for a daughter by her parents replaced circumcision :

De filia vero, quia non circumcidebatur, dici potest quod per hoc sacrificium mundaretur de originali (4).

Two sentence collections of the school of Anselm of Laon and William of Champeaux, *Augustinus. Semel immolatus est Christus* and *Dubitatur a quibusdam,* give the same answer :

Et tamen mulier, licet non sit circumcisa, sollempnibus tamen hostiis et oblationibus ab originali peccato purgata est [37].

---

33. *Mt.* 9,2.
34. *Ps.* 31,5.
35. *Lc.* 2,27.
36. A. LANDGRAF, *Dogmengeschichte der Früscholastik* III, 1, Regensburg 1954, 67.
37. H. WEISWEILER, *Das Schrifttum der Schule Anselms von Laon und Wilhelms von Champeaux (Beitr. zur Gesch. der Philos. und Theol. des Mittelalters* 33, 1/2), Münster 1936, 289, 333.

Peter Lombard ascribes this opinion to *quidam*. For himself he prefers to hold that women were freed from original sin by means of faith and good works, their own or their parents[38]. Hugh of St Victor had held this second opinion as to faith : women were saved by faith alone, though he adds that they were purified also by means of sacrifices, oblations and other rites [39]. Neither Hugh nor the Lombard admitted the efficacy of sacrifices in remitting original sin for women. X was consistent in his view of the effects of sacrifices, as we shall see.

He discusses also the question whether actual sins could be forgiven under the Old Law (2). His answer is ' yes ' : actual sins were forgiven to those who did penance and offered sacrifice. This was not in virtue of the legal and figurative sacrifices prescribed by the Old Law, but rather, he thinks, because they prefigured the true sacrifice which Christ offered up on the altar of the Cross. He goes on to attack the opinion that sins were not forgiven before the Passion. The argument used to support it was that even those holy men who died before the Redemption suffered the punishment due to sin, when they were imprisonned in the shades. Rupert of Deutz, for example, had insisted on this view [40]. X disallows the argument. It would follow, he objects, that infants are not freed from guilt in baptism because they remain subject to the punishment of dissolution by death :

> Si cui vero videtur quod ante passionem non remitterentur peccata, cum pro eis restaret pena et in sanctis, qui detinebantur in tenebris, simili modo videri potest quod parvulis in baptismo non remittatur culpa, cum in eis restat pena, dissolutio scilicet corporis et anime.

---

38. *Sent*. IV, 1, 8 (ed. Quaracchi 2, 1916, 749 : « Quaeritur autem de viris, qui fuerunt ante circumcisionem, et de feminis, quae fuerunt ante et post, quod remedium contra peccatum habuerint.

Quidam dicunt, sacrificia et oblationes eius valuisse ad remissionem peccati. Sed melius est dicere, illos qui de Abraham prodierunt, per circumcisionem iustificatos ; mulieres vero per fidem et operationem bonam, vel suam, si adultae erant, vel parentum, si parvulae ».

39. *De sacr*. I, XII, 2 (PL 175,350) : « Porro feminae in populo circumcisionis sola fide salvabantur, sacrificiis et oblationibus, aliisque legis caeremoniis purificatae ; ipsam quoque circumcisionem fide suscipientes, et in eis qui carnem illam susceperunt, venerando participantes ».

40. See his *Comment. in Evangelium S. Iohannis*, written in 1115 (ed. R. HAACKE, in *Corpus Christianorum, Contin. mediev.*, 9, Turnhout 1969, 36) : « Haec autem gratia uel reconciliatio in legis caeremoniis... praefigurabatur tantum, non etiam conferebatur. Quia uidelicet quamuis iusti uel sancti patres omnes, ubi dormierant, apud inferos... detinebantur ».

Ibid. 61 : « Unde patres antiqui quamlibet iusti ad inferos descendebant ueterem praevaricationis portantes ignominiam actualium quoque peccatorum non omnino coenum effugientes, quin aliquam contraherent sordem uel maculam, quam carnibus taurorum aut sanguine hircorum emundari impossibile erat ».

See also *ibid*. 144.

He ends by quoting from the gospel and the psalmist to prove that sins were forgiven before the Passion. The closest parallel to his opinion that I have found occurs in a sentence of William of Champeaux : the Jewish sacrifices, though they could not effect full salvation, conferred some remission of sins in virtue of what they prefigured, as believed by faith :

> Sacrificium Iudeorum de animalibus oblatum, dignum donum uidebatur et quotidie, uel per singulos annos iterabatur, nec poterat perfectam reddere salutem. In fide tamen figurati aliquam peccatorum faciebant remissionem. Christus uero oblatus totius mundi peccatis, et preteritis, et presentibus, et futuris sufficiens, digna hostia factus, perfectam salutem fecit... [41]

The late Dom Lottin found this sentence in a group ascribed to William of Champeaux in three sentence collections which belonged to St Amand (now MSS *Valenciennes 14, 73* and *180*), as well as elsewhere [42]. St Amand also possessed a copy of X on Leviticus. The coincidence is suggestive. Did X make use of *florilegia* at St Amand ? However that may be, his views on the effects of legal sacrifices in remitting original sin for women and actual sins for all connect him which the school of Anselm of Laon and William of Champeaux. He fits into the scholastic milieu of the second and third decades of the twelfth century, when their sentences were being circulated and studied.

In two other glosses he takes for granted what he proved to his own satisfaction here. Thus he asks whether the sin offering prescribed for faults (6, 3-6) sufficed to wipe out sins committed knowingly (*ex conscientia*) ; he answers that a punishment was inflicted in such cases and the sacrifice (*satisfactio*) was added to it (3). Later he asks why sacrifice had to be offered on behalf of a child whose original sin had been remitted by circumcision and who had not yet committed any actual sin (4) ; he answers that the sacrifice was offered not on account of past or present sins, but to avoid sins in future. He compares this sacrifice, made after the child's circumcision, to the practice (current in his time) of admitting newly baptised infants to communion, ' to ward off future evils ' [43] ; communion is given after baptism, even though the latter confers full remission of original sin :

> Itaque dicatur quod non pro preterito vel presenti peccato pueri fieret hoc sacrificium, sed pro futuris evitandis, sicut post baptismum, in quo fit plenaria remissio, eucharistia pro futuris malis cavendis assumitur.

41. O. LOTTIN, *Psychologie et morale aux XIIe et XIIIe siècles* 5 (Gembloux 1959) 212.

42. *Ibid.* 189, 211.

43. On the baptismal communion of infants see *Dict. d'archéol. chrét. et de liturgie* 3 (1914) 2444 ; it was general up to the thirteenth century.

Both glosses show X assuming that sacrifices remitted actual sins, just as circumcision remitted original sin. His parallel between the sacrifice offered on behalf of a circumcised child and the baptismal communion of infants suggests a tendency to evaluate the legal sacrifices in terms of those Christian sacraments which they prefigured.

Did X go so far as to hold that *legalia* conferred grace or increased merit ? It seems that he did, to judge from his comment on *sanctum sanctorum* (*Lev.* 2, 10). He explains that sacrifices were accounted holy because they signified a holy thing, or because, being consecrated to God, they increased the holiness of those who used them worthily, just as do the ecclesiastical sacraments, which are of much more worth than the old ones (1). It would follow that X allowed that *legalia* conferred grace on persons who used them worthily, though they had less value than the sacraments of the New Law. He was running ahead of current opinion, if so. The view that observance of *legalia* conferred grace gained acceptance more slowly than the view that circumcision remitted original sin. Hugh of St Victor taught that the sacraments of the Old Law were not sacraments in the proper sense of the word, since they were mere signs : they signified sanctity, but did not sanctify [44]. Peter Lombard made the same distinction : the sacraments of the Old Law were signs only ; those of the New Law conferred grace [45]. It was for this reason probably that neither writer would grant that sacrifices remitted original sin for women in lieu of circumcision. Neither wished to rate the legal sacrifices too highly. The problem received much attention in the schools. Many authorities and many considerations were brought forward, such as the contrast between servile fear and filial love as motives for obedience to the divine commands. X's opinion came to be accepted in some quarters, but it was put in terms more sophisticated than he could have conceived : the legal sacrifices were justificatory as *opus operans* ; the Christian conferred grace as *opus operatum* [46].

The only twelfth-century master who to my knowledge professed an opinion akin to X's was Peter the Chanter. Significantly, he

---

44. *De sacr.* I, xii, 10 (PL 175, 363-364) : « Sciendum vero quod haec omnia non talia sacramenta intelligere debemus, qualia superius sacramenta quae proprie sacramenta dicuntur, esse debere definivimus ; sed in his et huiusmodi quaedam ob hoc solummodo sacramenta vocata, quia sacrarum rerum signa fuerunt. Sic ergo aliud est sacramentum sanctificationem significans tantum, et sanctificatione sanctificans ; aliud non sanctificans, sed significans tantum ».

45. *Sent.* III, xl, 3 (*ed. cit.* 2, 734) : « Distat autem Evangelii littera a Legis littera : ... diversa etiam Sacramenta, quia illa tantum significant, haec conferunt gratiam ».

46. LANDGRAF, *op. cit.* 21-59.

hazards it in a commentary on Leviticus. The Chanter has been quoting Ralph of Flaix on the anointing of Aaron (*Lev.* 8, 12). Ralph wanted to impress on his readers the dignity of Christian priest-hood. How much does it confer on those who receive it in devout fear, when it meant something even to the Jews, estranged or soon to be estranged from God, and who had the form only ! The Chanter copies this passage from Ralph anonymously. Then he deduces from it that *legalia* conferred virtue and increase of virtue on those who approached them worthily. This he holds to be true :

> Hinc colligitur quantum timentibus Deum et pie accedentibus sacra conferat unctio, si nec apud illos vacare potuit, qui alieni a Deo, aut certe continuo alienandi, sacramenti solam formam gerebant [47].
>
> Argumentum quod digne accedentibus sacra legalia virtutes et augmen-tum virtutum conferebant, quod quidem verum est (MS *Eton College 14*, fol. 6rb) [48].

He shows more caution in his *Summa de sacramentis*. Here he debates at length the question whether the observance of *legalia* was meri-torious. The arguments *pro et contra* and the authorities brought forward on either side leave him hesitant ; he cannot make up his mind to declare for either [49].

The Chanter was teaching in the late twelfth century and had not read X on Leviticus. The ressemblance between the view he expresses in his gloss and X's view on *legalia* is more than mere coincidence, however. In the first place, they were both commenting on a text. A teacher of Scripture could allow himself more freedom to throw out ideas of his own than he could when he submitted to the more rigid discipline of the theological *quaestio*. The latter forced him to take all the consequences of his position into account. The Chanter may have changed his mind on the wholesome effects of observing *legalia* when he compiled his *Summa* towards the end of his life. It is more likely that he felt less inclined to commit him-self to a personal conclusion on so controversial a topic. In the second place, they were both commenting on Leviticus. This book cast a spell on its exegetes, if they interested themselves in the literal sense of the Old Law. A scholar who lived with the Jews in

---

47. *Com. in Lev.*, lib. VI, cap. 2, Marburg 1536, 80.

48. See F. STEGMÜLLER, *Repertorium biblicum*, no. 6457.

49. PIERRE LE CHANTRE, *Summa de sacramentis et animae consiliis*, ed. J. A. DUGAUQUIER (*Analecta mediaevalia namurcensia*, 4), Louvain 1954, I, 1, 13-17. The conclusion reads : « In ceremoniis triplex erat status pro variis tem-poribus. Primum tempus quando illa sola erant, scilicet ante tempus gratie ; tunc qui illis utebantur, obediendo ex caritate, merebantur secundum quosdam, secundum alios non ; et nisi uterentur illis peccarent mortaliter ».

imagination and tried to understand their cult would come to hope that *legalia* in Old Testament times benefited observers in some positive way ; surely they merited and grew in virtue by fulfilling worthily all the duties imposed on them ? Hence X and the Chanter had a common starting point, which would account for their sympathetic approach to *legalia*. His sessions with Jewish teachers had a similar effect on Andrew of St Victor, though he expressed it differently. Andrew ventured onto the more dangerous ground of Old Testament prophecy and was fascinated by its Jewish interpretation.

X can have had little influence compared with the Victorines. The prestige of their abbey ensured that it would be they who catered for the new interest in biblical scholarship, while X remained unknown or forgotten. His glosses must have gone to the scrapheap when the early compilations went out of use to make room for the standard *Gloss* of Paris. His out-of-date setting served him badly from the point of view of success in the schools. Yet X is a precious witness to the fact that biblical scholarship developed independently of St Victor and in centres other than Paris. X may even have anticipated Hugh of St Victor ; the lack of any precise date for him makes it impossible to be certain. The anonymous glosses on the literal sense of Job, already mentioned, point to the same independent revival of learning [50].

What motives drove scholars to study the literal sense of the Old Testament books ? That is one of the darkest problems connected with the twelfth-century revival. Hugh of St Victor explained at length why the 'literal foundation' ought not to be neglected [51]. But a rather shallow foundation for the superstructure of the spiritual senses had satisfied most exegetes in the early middle ages. Whence came the sudden urge to dig wider and deeper, to study Hebrew and to question rabbis ? We might have found an answer to the problem if X had written an explanatory preface to his glosses. He did not do so, or else it has vanished and our clue with it.

* * *

A second visit to the Municipal Library at Valenciennes enabled me to verify that the glosses on Job, following X on Leviticus, do not correspond to the standard *Gloss* either, but represent an earlier compilation. Some glosses have verbal parallels with those

---

50. Above, **p. 29.**
51. *De Scripturis sacris* V (PL 175, 13-14) ; *Erudit. Didasc.* VI, 1-10 (ed. C. H. BUTTIMER, Washington 1939, 113-128).

of the *Gloss* ; many are extra, but show no sign of original scholarship like X's. I also took a closer look at another early glossed Leviticus from St Amand, no. *24*. It is written in a hand of the twelfth-century, rather later than that of *25* (*V*). The glosses here derive from three sources : (1) many are exact parallels with those of the standard *Gloss* ; (2) Hugh of St Victor on Leviticus is quoted by name (fol. 1va) : " Hugo historice. Liber Leviticus... " (from PL 175, 74-77) ; other quotations from Hugh are anonymous, for example (fol. 5ra) : " Historice. Àd ostium tabernaculi. In uno eodemque loco... " (*ibid.* 77) ; (3) the glossator has made a selection of glosses from X, verbally identical, and therefore probably copied from *V* ; these, too, are anonymous and generally headed ' Historice '. He stopped drawing on Hugh and X before he reached chapter 8. His last historical gloss, drawn from X in this case, occurs on 7, 18 (fol. 29vb) : " Historice. Ita irrita fiebat oblatio... reus erat ". The combination of Hugh of St Victor and X on the literal sense of Leviticus witnesses to care for biblical scholarship at St Amand and shows that X had some influence there.

Note:
On Pseudo-Jerome see now Avrom Saltman, *Pseudo-Jerome Quaestiones on the Book of Samuel, edited with an introduction* (Studia Post-Biblica ed. J. C. H. Lebram xxvi, Brill, Leiden, 1975).

5

Ralph of Flaix on Leviticus

Alberic of Trois-Fontaines records under the year 1157 :

> Florebant hoc tempore quidam viri nominabiles, quorum unus Zacharias Crisopolitanus de ordine Premonstratensis apud S. Martinum Laudunensem fecit volumen illud egregium super quatuor evangelia, quod unum ex quatuor appellatur, et Radulfus ille niger monachus Flaicensis in territorio Belvacensis fecit opus super Leviticum per 20 libros dispositum, quod predicatur et probatur magnificum [1].

Ralph's twenty books on *Leviticus* became indeed the standard commentary up to the mid-thirteenth century at least. The manuscripts numbered by F. Stegmüller witness to its use in monastic libraries [2]. It appears on the Paris stationers' list of 1275-86. No other monastic work has this distinction apart from St. Anselm's and St. Bernard's [3]. A study of *marginalia* in copies which belonged to religious houses shows that it was read with careful appreciation. A study of early scholastic lectures on *Leviticus* shows that the history of this book of the Law boils down to a history of the masters' attitude to Ralph's commentary. What did *claustrales* and *scholares* alike find to admire in it ? An answer to this question has two kinds of interest : we learn something about the moral and intellectual ethos of a Benedictine abbey, St. Germer of Flaix, at a time when the Cistercians and other reformed Orders had put the black monks on the defensive ; we can watch the influence of monastic exegesis in the cloister and the schools at a time when the latter overshadowed the former, whichever version of the *Rule* was followed.

In this paper I shall study the commentary itself, leaving its after-life to a later occasion. My second paper will deal with the manuscripts and with quotations and notices by medieval writers and teachers. The printed edition of Ralph on *Leviticus* (Marburg/Cologne 1536) [4] was made from a good manuscript. Collation shows suprisingly

---

1. *Chronica* (MGH, *Script.* XXIII, 843-844).
2. *Repertorium biblicum*, no. 7093. I am not here concerned with the other commentaries listed by Stegmüller, which are of doubtful authenticity.
3. H. Denifle and E. Chatelain, *Chart. Univ. Paris.* I, 644, 649 n., no. 530.
4. Reprinted in *Maxima Bibliotheca veterum Patrum* XVII, Lyons 1677. I have used the 1536 edition and refer to its pages and columns throughout, slightly modifying the punctuation and spelling.

few and insignificant variants in all the copies that I have seen. Their original would have been a well-written, correct text, prepared with care in a monastic scriptorium. I shall therefore quote from the edition, which is quite adequate for my purpose now.

Alberic's chronicle gives the only date that we have. Zachary of Besançon, who pairs with Ralph under 1157, is recorded at Besançon 1134-1138 and wrote his *Unum ex quatuor* about 1140 [4]. Proceeding by analogy we might suppose that Ralph's activity fell into the years before 1157 too. The obituaries of the province of Rheims are being prepared for publication, but no notice of Ralph has come to light [5]. That is hardly surprising, since he never held the office of abbot or prior. The earliest datable copy of his commentary on *Leviticus*, from Corbie, now MS *Paris Nat. lat. 11564*, was produced 1174-1178 [6]. Monastic scribes and their supervisors of the late twelfth and early thirteenth centuries knew who he was. MS *Paris Nat. lat. 379*, fol. 220ra, has the rubric :

> Explicit liber XXus explanationis super leviticum edite a domno radulfo flaycensi monacho doctore precipuo et eximie conversationis viro.

The same explicit appears in the Corbie manuscript already mentioned. The praise of Ralph as a person may stem from living memory. MS *Paris Nat. lat. 378*, fol. 1ra, specifies ' sancti germani flaviacensis ', an easy mistake for St. Germer : this copy comes from Foucarmont, Rouen. The most common ascription is to ' Domnus Radulfus monachus Flaviacensis '. Then confusion set in. MS *Paris Nat. lat. 18201*, a fragment in a hand of the late twelfth century, has a rubric added in a thirteenth-century hand, fol. 65 :

> Incipit prologus magistri radulphi super librum leviticum [7].

Perhaps he was mistaken for Ralph of Laon or perhaps it was assumed that the author of a school text must have had the title of master. The bibliographers realised that Ralph was a monk. Ignorant of

---

4. D. Van den Eynde, *Les « Magistri » du Commentaire « Unum ex quatuor » de Zacharias Chrysopolitanus*, in *Antonianum* 23 (1948) p. 3 ; B. de Vregille, *Notes sur la vie et l'œuvre de Zacharie de Besançon*, in *Analecta Praemonstratensia* 41 (1965) 293-309.

5. I owe this information on the Rheims obituaries to the kind enquiries of Mlle M.-Th. d'Alverny. On St. Germer see L. H. Cottineau, *Répertoire topobibliogr. des abbayes et des prieurés*, Macon 1935, II, 2710 ; E. Lesne, *Histoire de la propriété ecclésiastique en France* II, Lille 1926, 148, 151 ; VI, Lille 1943, 34.

6. See L. W. Jones, *The Scriptorium at Corbie : the Library*, in *Speculum* 22 (1947) 196.

7. Mlle M. Dulong has kindly described this MS for me ; the fragmentary copy of Ralph on *Leviticus* in it is not listed by Stegmüller.

Alberic's notice, however, they made wild guesses as to his date, and located him at Flavigny[8] instead of Flaix (or Fly) or even at Fulda. The anonymous compiler of the history of St. Germer of Flaix, working in the seventeenth century, could only record the conflicting data which he found in earlier notices. He ventured a personal opinion, in default of evidence, that Ralph lived and wrote at Flaix 1090-1110, basing it on the fact that Guibert of Nogent flourished at the same time : the two writers struck him as having much in common[9].

St. Germer, a small abbey, owes its literary fame to Guibert. He was educated and made his profession there, and enjoyed reading in its well-stocked library. He used to stay there sometimes even after his election as abbot of Nogent-sous-Coucy[10]. If Ralph entered religion at an early age, as was customary, he would have known his senior. Guibert's writings will prove useful as a background to Ralph's. St. Bernard's letters 67 and 68 will be useful too[11]. Bernard wrote to the abbot of Flaix, Hildegard (d. April, 1123), excusing himself for having received a monk, whom the abbot reclaimed. The monk had begged to be admitted to Clairvaux because his abbot had forced him to practise medicine for the benefit of seculars, to the peril of his soul. Bernard reports his pleading :

> Cogebat servire, imo ipse serviebat per me, non Deo, sed saeculo, quando, ne saecularium malevolentiam incurreret principum, mederi me compellebat etiam tyrannis, raptoribus, excommunicatis. Quod animae meae periculum cum ei nunc privatim, hunc palam suggesissem nec profecissem... fugio meam damnationem...

Abbot Hildegard, according to the next letter, tried to shift the blame from himself to the fugitive : he did not deny that the latter had practised medicine outside the house, but claimed that he had neither known nor consented. The monk's version, as reported by Bernard, sounds the more plausible. The correspondence paints a picture of an abbey plagued by its neighbours, which is familiar from Guibert's *De vita sua*. ' Tyrant ' was the chroniclers ' term for a rebellious lord[12] ; he was often excommunicate for robbing churches.

---

8. On Flavigny see COTTINEAU, *op. cit.*, I, 1149. This abbey was not in the diocese of Beauvais and was not dedicated to St. Germer.

9. MS *Paris Nat. lat. 13890*, p. 376-379.

10. *De vita sua* (ed. G. BOURGIN, Paris 1907, II-XXXII, 66).

11. PL 182, 174-179 ; *Bernard de Clairvaux (Commission de l'histoire de l'Ordre de Cîteaux*, 3), Paris 1953, 234.

12. WILLIAM OF MALMESBURY, *Gesta regum*, lib. III, par. 249 (*Rolls Series* II, 308-309), describes the north of England before the Conqueror's harrying as ' nutricula tyrannorum '. SUGER, *Gesta Ludovici cognomento Grossi* (ed. A. MOLINIER, Paris 1887), 59, 60, 80, 83, calls the rebel vassals of the Isle de France ' tyrants '.

Hence Bernard writes of ' tyrants, robbers, excommunicates '. A harassed abbot would have thought medical services a small price to pay for mollifying such persons. We shall see, moreover, that the monks of Flaix interpreted their *Rule* as allowing service to laymen. Cure of their ruffian souls posed problems which Ralph discusses. Bernard's defence of his action turned on cap. LXI of the *Rule*. The abbot of Flaix had urged that a monk from a ' known monastery ' must not be received at another house. St Germer, he stated, was known as far off as Rome. Bernard answered that ' known ' meant ' known to the receiving abbot '. He knew nothing of Flaix and had never heard it mentioned before ; it was in a strange land and in a different ecclesiastical province.

Artistic fame did come to St. Germer within two decades of Hildegard's death. The monks rebuilt their church in the late ' thirties in an advanced gothic style, which was fine enough to be copied elsewhere [13].

We must turn from our thin material for Ralph's abbey to his long commentary, to see whether internal evidence may lead us to date it more closely. In the first place we know that its composition stretched over six years. Ralph either wrote or dictated it : there is no pretence that it represented sermons, though he had used the matter for teaching purposes. He tells us in his prologue to lib. V that he comes back to his task now that spring is here [14]. In his prologue to lib. VIII he writes that this is the fourth summer since he began : distracted by business and worn by cares, he let the third season go by without adding anything [15]. He showed the completed part to friends, who had time to read it before he replied to their

---

13. R. DE LASTEYRIE, *L'architecture religieuse en France à l'époque gothique* I, Paris 1926, 16-18. The date is uncertain, but the translation of a relic of St. Germer to Flaix from Beauvais in 1132 would have brought pilgrims and made it desirable to build a new church. It is worth noting that Eustace, abbot of Flaix, was sent to England on a preaching mission for the Crusade by Innocent III ; he won great renown as a revivalist and miracle worker ; see C. R. CHENEY, *Hubert Walter*, London 1967, 75-76. The abbey was therefore widely known in 1200.

14. 63a : « Iam hyems transiit,... flores visi sunt in terra. Revertetur ergo ad ceptum officium etiam lingua nostra... »
This probably refers to dictation. Ralph sometimes addresses his readers (see 106b), but never his hearers.

15. 108a : « Quarta iam volvitur estas, tertia consumpta, in qua variis occupationibus distracti, multisque anxietatibus fatigati, opusculo huic nostro nihil contulimus. Nunc, concessa nobis requie,... ad interiora maris, huius velificare, conamur ».

criticism in lib. XVI [16]. If conditions in winter always made work impossible, his progress must have been slow.

A passage on the coming of Antichrist suggests a rough *terminus ante quem* for his work up to lib. XVIII. Ralph's treatment of the theme is personal and has historical interest ; so the piece is worth studying in detail, quite apart from its date. He starts from the text : *Ecce autem egressus filius mulieris Israelitis, quem pepererat de viro Aegyptio inter filios Israel, iurgatus est in castro cum viro Israelita* (*Lev.* 24,10). Ralph interprets it as a prophecy of Antichrist, without any authority in his sources. The ' wrangler ' of mixed birth seems to frighten Moses, breaking into his silent converse with God so unexpectedly. Surely the Lawgiver must be foretelling the distant future by the inspiration of the Holy Spirit :

> Videtur legislator quasi conturbatus loqui, et ab illo silentio in quo Dominus loquebatur secum, ad rem subitam et inopinatam perterritus exclamasse. *Ecce* inquit, *egressus*... Quis est iurgator iste nec gentilis nec iudeus, nativitatis sue confundens originem. qui ... colloquium illud familiare... suis iurgiis interrumpit ? Dicat unusquisque quod senserit. Nobis videtur quod ad extrema sancte ecclesie tempora Spiritu sancto illuminatus oculos legislator direxerit et antichristi previdens adventum, tribulationis illius immanitate commotus, cum filius ille perditionis non tantum uni viro israeliti iurgium excitabit, sed adversus omnes Deum pie colentes apertas inimicitias exercebit, in hec verba prorupit... Quisque enim ille fuerit, cuius iuxta litteram iurgium hic introducitur, ea que dicuntur de eo ad antichristi personam congruissime referuntur [17].

Ralph assembles texts from the New Testament to prove that Antichrist will be born of Christian parents, the new Israelites, and that he will receive high office in the Church. The gentile father signifies the stronger, unregenerate side of his nature. Ralph gives it as his opinion that the time for Antichrist's coming draws near. Instead of pointing to visible signs, such as wars or divisions in Christendom, as one might expect, he dwells on his contemporaries' utter indifference to the question. Men who profess to be full believers draw the line at Antichrist ; or else, if they do believe in his coming, they put it off for centuries, as a mere dream. How different was the attitude of the early fathers, especially St. Gregory and St. Cyprian ! We, living later, and so having more reason to expect him, are lulled by a false security :

> Huius maligna arguitur cogitatio, quia post diuturnam ecclesie pacem quasi tempestas irruens, cum repentinum se ingerit, eo magis insidias suas

---

16. 244a. See below, p. 96
17. 267a.

valere suspicatur, quo securis et quiescentibus presentatur. Talis est hodie status ecclesie. Videas homines fidem quidem integram profitentes, cum quibus, si de ultima persecutione et antichristi adventu sermonem habeas, pene videntur hoc futurum non credere, aut si credunt, quasi per somnium inde cogitantes, post multa secula futurum conantur astruere. Nulla autem existimo manifestiora adventus eius indicia... [18] Ante nos sancti patres de huius adversarii immanitate sollicitabantur, iamiamque affuturum suspicabantur, sicut in dialogo pape Gregorii, sed et beati Cypriani aliorumque legimus martyrum scriptis [19]. Nos vero, qui post multas generationes hic nati sumus, et fini iam propinquavimus, incauta securitate torpemus [20].

The next step in the argument is to show that the peace enjoyed by the Church at the present time goes with a state of things forecast in Scripture as a prelude to the End. Ralph had too much caution to calculate dates or name names ; he condemns millenarians elsewhere [21] ; but he felt bound to risk an interpretation of the seven heads and ten horns of the beast (*Apoc.* 17,7) and of the four beasts and ten horns (*Dan.* 7,1-8). Following Jerome and Bede [22], he interprets them as signifying those powers which have ruled or shall rule over the world. The seven heads signify respectively the Assyrians, Medes, Persians, Greeks, Carthaginians, Romans and Antichrist. The four signify respectively the Assyrians, Persians, Greeks and Romans. Ten horns would arise from the head of the fourth beast, according to Daniel. Jerome interpreted these as a prophecy that ten kings would divide up the Roman empire between them. An eleventh horn would ' pluck up ' three of the ten kings ; the eleventh horn signified Antichrist. Ralph applied the prophecy to the contemporary world : the Roman empire, he says, is now divided up

---

18. Ralph here quotes *I Thess.* 5, 3-4.

19. This seems to be a general reference to *Dialog.* IV, and to *Ad Fortunatum*. On Cyprian in medieval libraries see J. DE GHELLINCK, *L'essor de la littérature latine au XII⁰ siècle*, II, Brussels 1946, 87 ; *Le mouvement théologique du XII⁰ siècle*, 2nd ed., Bruges 1948, 18, 243.

20. 268a-b.

21. 68a on *Lev.* 7, 17, *quidquid autem tertius invenerit dies, ignis absumet*, traditionally interpreted as referring to the Last Judgment (see RABAN MAUR, *Com. in Lev.* ; PL 108, 314) : « Quia vero non solum huiusmodi voluntas tunc inutilis est, sed etiam prava opinio nunc plurimum noxia, si quis eternitatis tempore hec nostre mortalitatis subsidia credat esse necessaria, quod a quibusdam millenariis, qui mille annos carnalis conversationis post resurrectionem inducere conati sunt, satis pueriliter disputatum est, apte subiungitur... »

22. JEROME, *Com. in Dan.* (*Corpus Christianorum, ser. lat.* 75a, 837-850). Jerome links Daniel's dream with the Apocalypse. BEDE, *In Apoc.* (PL 93, 183-184), refers to Daniel. RALPH seems to have worked out the names of the ten powers for himself and fills in some historical details ; the names of the four come from JEROME. See also A. LUNEAU, *L'histoire du salut chez les Pères de l'Église. La doctrine des âges du monde*, Paris 1964.

into many parts. He takes the number ten as denoting plurality rather than a specific figure, and does not say which kings have divided up the empire. They would have added up to more than ten, had he counted all the kingdoms of twelfth-century Christendom. Nor does he predict which of them is going to ally with Antichrist.

It followed from the fact of division that Antichrist might come at any moment. He would ' pluck up ' or associate with him three of the kings now reigning in place of the Romans and would proceed to his conquests. Ralph supports his forecast by quoting another text : *Five are fallen, one is, and the other is not yet come (Apoc.17,10)* St. John was writing under the rule of the sixth world power, the Roman : *one is* ; the seventh would be Antichrist's. The sixth has already come to an end by division ; therefore the seventh cannot long be delayed :

> Porro septimum huius bestie caput regnum erit antichristi, quod inter decem cornua quarte bestie parvulum orietur. Inter minutias quippe romani imperii, quod iam per multa divisum est, antichristus consurget, et primo, tribus regibus sibi consociatis et a Christi fide, quam prius tenebant, evulsis, incertum est autem qui illi futuri sint, deinde totum mundum occupabit et potentior ceteris regibus apparebit. Merito ergo Iohanni, qui sub romano scripsit imperio, de septem regnis istis ab angelo dictum est : *Quinque ceciderunt, unus est, et alius nondum venit.* Quinque enim ex hiis regnis, que supra memoravimus, iam transierunt. Romani tunc regnabant ; antichristus nondum venerat... Decem reges omnes hos in quos romanum imperium divisum videmus intellige. Quia enim necesse non erat ut certus eorum numerus exprimeretur, pluralitas tantum per denarium designata est [23].

The historical interest of Ralph's observation will leap to the eye. Where is the medieval empire, ' transferred ' from the Romans to the Franks and the Germans ? He ignores it. He does not say when the division ' now ' obtaining was made. A French tradition rejected the universality of the empire as revived by Otto I [24]. Hugh of Fleury held that the Frankish kingdom had been separated from the Roman empire ever since the battle of Fontenoy (841) [25]. Innocent

---

23. 269a-270a.

24. G. A. BEZZOLA, *Das Ottonischen Kaisertum in der französischen Geschichtesschreibung des 10. und beginnenden 11. Jahrhunderts*, Graz/Köln 1956.

25. *Modernorum regum Francorum actus* (MGH, *Script.* 9, 376-377) : « ... Prevaluit enim adversus eos Francorum exercitus. Ab illo tamen die usque nunc manet regnum Francorum ab imperio Romanorum seiunctum atque divisum ».

385 : « Karolus tamen, eorum frater iunior, quem ceteri fratres exheredare volebant, victoriam obtinuit ; et ab illo die usque in hodiernum diem regnum Francorum manet ab imperio Romanorum seiunctum ac separatum ».

See A. FUNKENSTEIN, *Heilsplan und natürliche Entwicklung. Formen der Gegenwartsbestimmung im Geschichtsdenken des hohen Mittelalters*, Munich

III in *Per venerabilem* (1202) legalised the tradition by declaring that the king of France had no temporal superior. Ralph had gone further, coolly assuming that all kings had the same status. His assumption throws light on the question whether the empire had any substance in the twelfth century outside Germany and the old ' middle kingdom '. Ralph at least gives a firm negative.

This also suggests a date for his commentary. He says that he spoke to a bored audience when he predicted the imminent coming of Antichrist. Writers of the mid-twelfth century certainly showed little sense of urgency [26]. But the papal schism of 1159 stirred up Gerhoh of Reichersberg to predict that the final conflict was at hand [27]. A major conflict in the Church would have presented itself to Ralph as matter for speculation, especially as Alexander III took refuge in northern France. Ralph's dismissal of the empire as non-existent would have been intelligible in the reign of Conrad, who never had an imperial coronation (1138-52). Its much advertised revival by Frederick Barbarossa from 1152 would have made it difficult to pass over the empire so calmly. Hence a date for the first eighteen books of the commentary may be fixed as probably before 1152 and almost certainly before the papal schism of 1159 [28]. Such a date would be consistent with Alberic's *floruit* 1157.

1965, 92-93. HUGH OF FLEURY dedicated his book to the Empress Matilda, daughter of Henry I of England. She married the emperor Henry V, in Jan., 1114. Hugh brought his book on the miracles of his abbey up to 1117, which suggests that he died soon afterwards ; see *Lib. de lite* II, 59.

26. HUGH OF ST. VICTOR held that the end would not come until the gospel had been preached to all nations, *De sacr.* II, XVII, 1 (PL 176, 597). I cannot agree that Rupert of Deutz and Anselm of Havelberg expected the imminent coming of Antichrist ; see PH. DELHAYE, *Le Microcosmus de Godefroy de Saint-Victor* II, Lille 1951, 68 n. They hold to tradition in believing themselves to be living in the sixth age of the world, but do not speculate on its end : see RUPERT on the Apocalypse (PL 169, 1139-1141) ; ANSELM, *Dial.* I, XIII (ed. G. SALET, in *Sources chrétiennes* 118, Paris 1966, 108-119). Andrew of St. Victor's interpretation of Daniel's dream contrasts with Ralph's. Andrew holds, even against Jerome, that the Roman empire will never be divided ; the ten kings will appear successively, not simultaneously ; hence Antichrist will conquer the empire as a whole. Andrew, however, does not suppose that Antichrist is at hand. See B. SMALLEY, *The Study of the Bible in the Middle Ages*, 2nd ed., Oxford 1952, 380-382.

27. P. CLASSEN, *Gerhoch von Reichersberg*, Wiesbaden 1960, 193-234.

28. John of Salisbury connects Barbarossa's attempt to revive the empire with the schism of 1159 ; see his letter 124 of June/July 1161, *The Letters of John of Salisbury (1153-1161)*, ed. W. J. MILLOR and H. E. BUTLER, revised by C. N. L. BROOKE, 207 : « Promittebat enim se totius orbis reformaturum imperium et urbi subiciendum orbem, eventusque facili omnia subacturum, si ei ad hoc solius Romani pontificis favor addesset... Non invenit adhuc qui tantae

Turning to the content, it will be well to note what readers will not find. Ralph avoids theological questions, nor does he show any interest in mysticism as distinct from piety. There is one reference to the contemplative mind, ' si vacare voluerit, ut Deum agnoscat, theoricis illuminationibus roborata '. An echo of Pseudo-Dionysius [29] ? If so, it stands alone.

His attitude to the pagan classics is more positive. Some of his friends found it shocking that he should have inserted *testimonia* from pagan books into a commentary on Scripture. He tried to satisfy them briefly, as they were dear friends, although he could have brushed their objections aside [30]. His apology for quoting pagan authors resorts to the standard arguments : the captive gentile woman may be married to an Israelite after mourning her parents in isolation [31] ; take what is true, while rejecting *superstitiosa figmenta*, quoted from *De doctrina Christiana* [32]. These commonplaces are touched by personal regret that such wise men had no hope of being saved. Ralph's lament for good pagans has its place in a tradition which goes from St. Augustine to Dante : he echoes St. Augustine's sentiments as expressed in *Ep.* 164, though he may not have read it [33] :

> Et quidem in eorum scriptis multa reperiuntur que placeant, que cum sacris paginis magnam consonantiam habeant, cum aut rerum investigant

---

consentiret iniquitati, ideoque... Balahamitam sibi ascivit pontificem, per quem malediceret populo Dei ».

Ralph could hardly have failed to notice these events, had he written at the time.

29. 121b. See HILDUIN's translation : « illuminantes vero replere divino lumine ad theoricum habitum et virtutem castissimos mentis oculos... » (*Coelest. Hierarch.* 111 (ed. PH. CHEVALLIER, *Dionysiaca*, II, Bruges, undated, 794-795). GUIBERT OF NOGENT knew the *corpus, Moral in Gen.* (PL 156, 50) : « Quis Areopagitae Dionysii mysteria digne intelligat ? » Ralph may therefore have known of its existence, at least.

30. Lib. XVI, cap. 2 (244a) : « Hec igitur, licet paulo longius digressi simus, inserere placuit, non solum quod propositum fuerat explanare intendimus... sed etiam quibusdam ex amicis occurrere, qui se moveri dixerunt, cum in scripture sacre tractatu nonnulla gentilium librorum testimonia a nobis invenissent assumpta. Qui licet in hac obiectione sua minus que (a) doctoribus conscripta sunt, frequentasse fuerint visi, quia tamen charissimi erant, non potuerunt contempni. His igitur suademus ut brevi hac satisfactione contenti sint, quia si lex operis suscepti nos permisisset latius evagari, multa suppeterent animo que possent adiungi ».

31. *Deut.* 21, 12-13 ; JEROME, *Ep.* XXI and *Ep.* LXX (PL 22, 385, 665-666) ; see J. DE GHELLINCK, *op. cit.* 94-95.

32. II, XVIII, 28.

33. *Ep.* 164, II, 4 (CSEL 44, 524-525) ; see P. BROWN, *Augustine of Hippo*, London 1967, 308.

58

naturam aut humanos mores examinant, recepti nonnunquam etiam in
ipsius divinitatis notitiam. Deus enim, teste apostolo, revelavit illis. Quia
tamen i lum nescierunt, sine quo nemo ad Patrem redit, non nos eorum
consolatur sapientia, ut salvari posse credamus, quos Mediatoris nec sanguis
abluit nec salutaris hostia reconciliavit. Inde est quod eorum nonnunquam
et dicta suscipimus et damnationem dolemus... Sic quoque et hæc mulier
plangit apud nos parentes suos, cum plangere nos compellit, et ea stimulante
quorum miramur ingenium dolemus exitum... Mense autem integro de-
flentur, qui cum nihil unquam egerint per quod iram evaderent sempiternam, tota vita sua steriles fuisse planguntur... [34]

Ralph accepted the older view, which condemned even good pagans.
It was being softened while he wrote ; but he was out of touch with
the schools [35].

The *testimonia* from pagan books are as follows :

1) CICERO, *De officiis* I, 43, 88, 101, 136. Ralph gives the title
in one place ; otherwise he refers to ' auctor romane eloquentie '.
The first quotation is preceded by praise :

> ... etiam illi qui perfectam Dei cognitionem minime habuerunt, Dei
> tamen munere illuminati, quod veritatis attingere potuerunt nobis utilius
> quam sibi scriptum reliquerunt.

He mentions *De amicitia* in his prologue together with *De civitate
Dei* and *De consolatione Philosophiae* as examples of books whose
titles derive from their subject matter. Cicero's praise of Caesar from
Pro Ligario XII, 35 is recalled to illustrate *Lev.* 19,18 : *Non quae-
res ultionem* [36]. These works of Cicero were all current at the time :
Ralph knew them at first hand, it seems.

2) HORACE, generally referred to as ' poeta ', *Ep.* I, 10, 32-33 ;
41 (the latter quoted twice), 16, 50-51, 67-68 ; *Carm.* II, 2, 9-12 ;
Ars poet. 25-26 [37]. The *Odes* were not often quoted and Ralph's
choice of verses from the *Epistles* are not mere tags either.

3) SENECA, *Ep. moral.* 2,1 ; 2,4 ; 3,2-3 ; 23,3 ; 42,3 [38]. Seneca's

---

34. 243a-244a. Ralph refers several times to *Rom.* 1, 19-22, and developes the
theme of the captive gentile woman, pagan wisdom, mourning her parents,
the pagan sages, from St. Jerome.

35. L. CAPÉRAN, *Le problème du salut des infidèles*, 2nd ed., Toulouse 1934,
124-126, 172-184.

36. 138b, 13a, 16b, prologue to lib. I (unpaginated), 199b. The reference to
mercy in connexion with Caesar was a topos. St. AUGUSTINE refers to *Pro
Ligario* XII, 37 in *De civ. Dei* IX, v ; JOHN OF SALISBURY quotes the same
passage, *Policraticus* VIII, VII (ed. C. C. WEBB, Oxford 1909, II, 264). Ralph
quotes a different passage, however.

37. 198b, 53a, 72b, 128a, 112a, 206b-207a, 278b.

38. 148a, 264a, 203b, 148a, 117a.

Letters 1-88 circulated in a separate volume and was the only one available in France in the mid-twelfth century [39].

4) PLINY, *Nat. hist.* VIII, 25 ; X, 8, 12, 47. Ralph borrowed descriptions of the unclean creatures listed in *Lev.* 11 [40].

5) The so-called *Disticha Catonis*, a boys' school book. Ralph quotes verses against paying heed to dreams [41].

6) Wise sayings ascribed to anonymous sages. They correspond to the following in Walther's list : 6036*a*, 11122*a*, 19619*a*, 25181, 31544*b*,1, 31960 [42]. Two are not in Walther's list :

a) on the distinction between mental and physical chastity :

> Quidam sapiens : Incesta, inquit, damnari nulla potest, nisi violatum est corpus [43].

b) on precepts :

> Quidam de mundi huius sapientibus : Precepta, inquit, quibusdam tradenda, quibusdam inculcanda sunt [44].

We have nothing out of the ordinary here, but it is the fruit of personal reading. Ralph reflects the increased interest in classical studies found even in monastic circles of his day ; he also appealed to the later masters of the sacred page, who larded their lectures with similar *testimonia* of ever-widening scope.

We turn now to his exegetical sources and the use he made of them. Ralph wrote too early to use the *Gloss*, which spread from the Paris schools in the second part of the twelfth century. Possibly he had some *antiqua glosa* of a type superseded by the triumphant *Gloss* [45].

---

39. See M. SPANNEUT, *Sénèque au moyen âge*, in *Rech. Théol. anc. méd.* 32 (1964) 32-42 ; L. D. REYNOLDS, *The Medieval Tradition of Seneca's Letters*, Oxford 1965, 17-34, 104-124.

40. 116b, 113b-114b.

41. 209b-210a, from *Disticha Catonis* (ed. M. BOAS, Amsterdam 1952), XVI, 140, also in H. WALTHER, *Lateinische Sprichwörter und Sentenzen des Mittelalters*, Munich, 1963-67, no. 30027 ; but Ralph's quotation is closer to the original.

42. 5a, 53a, 12b, 109b, 74b.

43. 136b.

44. 293a.

45. B. SMALLEY, *Les commentaires bibliques de l'époque romane : glose ordinaire et gloses périmées*, above, pp. 17-25. Copies of the *Gloss* circulated in separate books before it was adopted as a text at Paris and subsequently everywhere else where the Latin Vulgate was read. Hence Ralph might have had a copy of the *Gloss* on Leviticus, but I can find no evidence that he used one. There is some common material, but it derives from the use of common sources.

He used it discreetly, if so. He seems to have studied the *originalia*.
Where his predecessors did not satisfy him, he gave his own opinion.
One example will show how he worked. Aaron and his sons are forbidden to drink wine or any other intoxicant, *quando intratis in
tabernaculum testimonii* (*Lev.* 10,9). The question arose : was perpetual
abstinence enjoined on all Levites all the year round ? St. Augustine
had answered that the command to drink no wine ever applied to
the high priest only, since he had to enter the tabernacle daily, in
order to cense the altar, whereas the other priests did not. They
could drink wine on their off-duty days [46]. Ralph found no evidence
for this view, though it was taught by ' an outstanding doctor '.
He felt sure that the high priest would have appointed vicars to
replace him, when illness or necessary business prevented him from
carrying out his daily duties at the altar of the tabernacle ; hence
it seemed probable that the high priest and his sons organised some
sort of rota, which enabled them all to drink wine sometimes. He
was pondering the problem, when all clouds of doubt were dispelled
by the day's lesson from Chronicles (I, 6,49) : *Aaron vero, et filii
eius, adolebant incensum super altare holocausti et super altare thymi-
amatis, in omne opus Sancti sanctorum.* Here was proof that the high
priest and his sons shared the duty between them [47]. Ralph was

---

46. *Quaest. in Lev.* XXXIII (*Corpus Christianorum, ser. lat.* 33, 198) : « Quando
ergo eis bibere licebat, quandoquidem in tabernaculum eis cotidie necesse erat
introire et accedere ad altare propter continuam servitutem ? ... etiam necesse
erat intrare summum sacerdotem propter incensum continuationis. Non enim
semel in anno intrabat, ... propter incensum autem cotidie ».
See also *Quaest. in Lev.* LXXXII-III (*ibid.* 226-227). Ralph does not accept
St. Augustine's answers here either.

47. 102a-103a : « Queritur de Aaron et filiis eius, utrum perpetuo vino absti-
nuerint. Cum enim quotidie ad altare accesserent ad hostias offerendas, ... ergo
omni die tabernaculum intrabant... Si igitur sine cessatione omni die et ad altare
immolaturi accedebant, et in ipsum intrabant tabernaculum, ... perpetuo itaque
vino abstinebant, ... nisi forte filii Aaron, cum plures essent, in ministerio sibi
succedebant, unusquisque vicis sue hanc vini abstinentiam servaturus. De
Aaron vero, si verum est quod quidam inter doctores precipuus asseruit, sui
tantummodo iuris esse super altare thymiatis adolere incensum, certum est
quod quotidie tabernaculum intrabat, unde et vini usum nunquam admittebat.
Quod tamen nescio unde probari possit... Cum enim illa nulla die posset intermitti
mane et vespere, fieri non poterat ut summus pontifex aliquando non egrotaret,
vel in via esset... Quid enim, nonne et ad uxorem suam aliquando accedebat,
saltem ut susciperet filium, qui in eodem sibi pontificatu succederet ? ... Sed
necesse erat hanc [oblationem] vicariis illius nonnunquam committi. Sed quid
plura dicam ? Omnes dubitationis nebulas hodierna lectio depulit, que ex Para-
lipomenon volumine improvisa sane auribus nostris insonuit. Sic enim ibi scriptum est : Aaron et filii eius adolebant incensum ... Patet igitur, ut estimo, ... non
solum ad pontificem solum, sed ad sacerdotes quoque reliquos pertinere ».

drawing on his own experience. A medieval monk, accustomed to drinking wine at table, with water kept for penance, could hardly believe that the Jewish high priest was obliged to perpetual abstinence ; he supposed, too, that service at the altar would have been as well organised as it was in his abbey. The reading of Chronicles, one of the less familiar parts of Scripture (probably in refectory, where the Bible would be read out consecutively through the year), brought sudden enlightenment. We see here that he did not copy his sources mechanically.

Ralph made lavish use of St Augustine. The *Locutiones* and *Quaestiones* were the closest equivalent to a text book that he had, though they did not provide a running commentary. He turned to them constantly on Leviticus, and also on Genesis, Exodus, Deuteronomy and Judges [48] ; he quotes what Augustine says of them in his *Retractationes* [49], also Augustine's exegesis of *Deut.* 28,66 from *Contra Faustum* [50] and his comments on *Ps.* 18, and on *Ps.* 65, 15, *Holocausta medullata...*, apropos of sacrifices prescribed by the Law [51]. *Ep.* XLVII on swearing is brought to bear on *Lev.* 19, 12, *Non periurabitis* [52]. The definition of 'superstition' from *De doctrina Christiana* throws light on *Lev.* 19, 26 [53]. On *Lev.* 21, 9, a text prescribing the death penalty for the unchaste daughter of a priest, Ralph notes the ancient Romans' severity to a lapsed Vestal Virgin as recounted in *De civitate Dei* [54]. His quotation of sibylline verses probably comes from the same source [55]. He quotes from Augustine on the First Epistle of St John as *in libro de charitate*, a title sometimes found

---

48. 32b, *Loc. in Gen.* CXXXVI (*Corpus Christianorum, ser. lat.* 33, 394), repeated 247a ; 158b, *Loc. in Exod.* CXXVII (*ibid.* 418-419) ; 35b-36a, *Loc. in Deut.* LVI (*ibid.* 450-451) ; 38a, *Loc. in Iud.* XXIII, *ibid.* 461 ; 195b, *Quaest. in Exod.* CXXXIX, *ibid.* 134-135 ; CLX (*ibid.* 145-146).

49. 39a-b : « Unde beatus Augustinus in libro recapitulationum [*sic*] scripsisse se septem libros de septem libris divinarum scripturarum se commemorat...» From *Retract.* II, LIV (PL 32, 651).

50. 258a-b : « Hinc beatus Augustinus contra Faustum agens, cum illud legis capitulum in manibus haberet, *Videbitis vitam tuam pendentem* ... quod quidem varios intellectus parit, Filius, inquit, evangelii... » From *Contra Faustum* XVI, 22 (CSEL 25, 466).

« In hac igitur occultatione nihil aliud, ut dicit beatus Augustinus, nobis innotuit, nisi quod in eadem celebritate ipse figurabatur, sed non intelligebatur ». From *ibid.* 21, 463. This second quotation, following on the first, is not verbal.

51. 264b, *Enar. II in Ps.* 18, 1 (*Corpus Christianorum, ser. lat.* 38, 105) ; 170b-171a, *Enar. in Ps.* 65 (*ibid.* 39, 853).

52. 197b, *Ep.* XLVII, 2 (CSEL 34, 131).

53. 209a, *De doctr. Christ.* II, XX (30) (*Corpus Christ., ser. lat.* 32, 54).

54. 220b, *De civ. Dei* III, V (CSEL 40, 114).

55. 131a : « Hoc et sibyllinis versibus ante predictum fuerat : Cum iacet... gazam ». See *De civ. Dei* XVIII, XXIII (*ibid.*).

in medieval catalogues [56]. His mention of St Monica's conversation with a holy man, included in a list of examples to show the miraculous effects of tears, need not have come directly from the *Confessions* [57]. Finally he quotes Augustine *in quodam sermone de penitentibus*, *Sermo* 393, perhaps spurious [58]. Ralph availed himself of those works which would help him to expound his text ; he fought shy of the more metaphysical.

The *Rule* of St. Benedict served as a guide to exegesis. Ralph shared the contemporary view that the Fathers were inspired, just as the biblical writers were : his was an expanding Bible, not a closed one. So he draws a parallel, Gregorian in origin, between Moses, the lawgiver of the Jews, and ' our lawgiver ', St. Benedict, ' full of the spirit of righteousness ', as St. Gregory teaches [59]. ' I shall not keep silent on how well he agrees with this chapter ', Ralph writes when he moralises leprosy as the sin of pride on *Lev.* 13,6, *si obscurior fuerit lepra*. He then quotes the *Rule*, LVII, 1-3, on the humility required of monastic craftsmen [60]. His skill in adapting the *Rule* is worth illustrating. He moralises the offering of firstfruits of corn, *Lev.* 2, 14-16. Green ears must be burnt and broken small ; so a man must renounce his own will and bend to another's, when he offers himself to the Lord. He must pour out the oil of gladness and the incense of prayer to obtain God's help. Part of his gift was reserved for the priest ; so our sacrifice is divided between God and men. A text from Ecclesiasticus commends ' the wonderful agreement between these mouthpieces of the Holy Spirit ' [61].

> Legislatorem nostrum hic respiciam, qui quod Moyses depinxit in frugi-
> bus, in moribus expressit. Hic igitur, cum continentium et perfectam
> viam arripientium rudimenta imbueret, quasi ignem spicis virentibus
> adhibens, in primo gradu timorem Dei et carnalium desideriorum castiga-

---

56. 71a : « ... de quo beatus Augustinus in libro de charitate : Si nondum, inquit, idoneus es mori pro fratre... » From *In ep. Ioh. ad Parthos* (PL 35, 2018). For the title in medieval catalogues see G. NORTIER, *Les bibliothèques médiévales des abbayes bénédictines de Normandie*, in *Revue Mabillon* 50 (1960) 237.

57. 10b, *Confess.* III, XII.

58. 41b : « Beatus Augustinus in quodam sermone de penitentibus : Quisquis, inquit, positus in ultima necessitate... » From *Serm.* 393 (PL 39, 1714). See *Clavis Patrum Latinorum*, in *Sacris erudiri* 3, 1951, 57.

59. See E. MANNING, *Observations sur la présence de la « Regula Magistri » à Subiaco*, in *Rech. Théol. anc. méd.* 33 (1966) 339.

60. 142a : « Legislator noster, quem papa Gregorio attestante spiritu omnium iustorum plenum fuisse didicimus, qualiter huic capitulo concinat, non tacebo. Artifices, inquit, si sunt in monasterio... »

From *Benedicti Regula*, ed. R. HANSLIK (CSEL 75, 1960, 132).

61. 17a-b.

tionem proponit [62], secundo et tertio de earum confractione nos admonens : Secundus, inquit, humilitatis gradus est, si propriam quis non amans voluntatem, desideria sua non delectetur implere. Tertius vero, ut quis pro Dei amore omni obedientia se subdat maiori, imitans Dominum... [63]

Predictus ille pater noster, in primo humilitatis gradu oleum nos superfundere primitiis nostris monet, cum dicit : Bono animo a discipulis obedientiam preberi oportet, quia hilarem datorem diligit Deus... [64] De thuris quoque impositione nos instruit, cum in prefatione operis sui : Ad te, inquit, sermo meus dirigitur, quisque abrenuntians propriis voluntatibus, Domino Christo vero regi militaturus, obedientie fortissima atque preclara arma assumis : inprimis, ut quidquid agendum inchoas bonum, ab eo perfici instantissima oratione deposcas [65]. Libet hic etiam ex scriptura filii Sirach versiculum unum inserere et organorum Spiritus Sancti admirabilem consonantiam commendare. Bono animo, inquit, gloriam redde Deo... [66] Quod hic habes, bono animo gloriam redde Deo, hoc doctor noster dixit, bono animo a discipulis obedientiam preberi oportet... Item quod hic legis,... doctor noster exposuit cum ait : Nam cum malo animo si obediat discipulus, iam acceptum non erit Deo... [67]

Quod igitur et hec oblatio sacrificia cetera in duo partitur et pars illius Deo, pars hominibus ascribitur, evidenter ipse qui cetera in primo humilitatis gradu exponit. Hec ipsa, inquit, obedientia tunc acceptabilis erit Deo et dulcis hominibus, si quod iubetur non tepide, non tarde aut cum mumure vel cum responso nolentis efficiatur... [68]

Ralph also quotes the *Rule* on the abbot's duty to control his steward [69].

St. Gregory's name appears about sixty times, far more often than any other's. Dr. R. Wasselynck has taught us to look for Gregory *via* Paterius, who collected *Gregoriana* on books which Gregory had not expounded [70]. Sure enough, Ralph used Gregory-Paterius on Leviticus. Just as he used Augustine's *Locutiones* and *Quaestiones* on books other than Leviticus, so he used Gregory-Paterius on Exodus, Ecclesiasticus and Jeremias [71]. He also read Gregory in the original, quarrying in the *Moralia, Homiliae, Cura pastoralis* and *Dialogi*.

---

62. VII, 10-12 (*ibid.* 41-42).

63. VII, 31, 32, 34 (*ibid.* 45-46).

64. V, 16-18 (*ibid.* 37).

65. Prol. 3-4 (*ibid.* 1-2).

66. *Eccli.* 35, 10.

67. V, 16-18 (*loc. cit.* 37).

68. V, 14-15 (*ibid.* 37).

69. 12b : « Legislator noster, cum contra propositi superbiam abbatis zelum accenderet... Cogitet tamen abbas... » From LXV, 18, 22 (*ibid.* 155).

70. *L'influence de l'exégèse de S. Grégoire le Grand sur les commentaires bibliques médiévaux*, in Rech. Théol. anc. méd. 32 (1965) 165-192.

71. On *Exod.* 30, 34 (PL 79, 746), 174a ; on *Eccli.* 34, 7 (*ibid.* 936-937), 209a ; on *Ierem.* XLI, 5 (*ibid.* 975), 148b. Ralph quotes Paterius anonymously or as ‘ Gregory ’, as the custom was.

The range is impressive. Abridgments of the *Moralia* were available ;
compilations from other books were made in the twelfth century ;
but Ralph does not seem to have used them. The latter may have
appeared too late for him or else have been inaccessible [72]. He knew
St. Gregory at first hand. Like Guibert of Nogent before him, he
pondered the Gregorian sayings as the best key to exegesis [73]. Ralph
would differ from St. Augustine, as we have seen ; ' the most blessed
Gregory ' [74] is never criticised.

References to other *sancti* are few. Ralph quotes the famous saying
of St. Ignatius :

> Frumentum ego sum Dei ; bestiarum dentibus molar, ut panis mundus
> efficiar.

He could have found it in St. Jerome's *De viris illustribus* or in a
legendary [75], but he ascribes it to St. Irenaeus, reporting St. Ignatius [76].
He must have made a mistake. *Contra haereticos* was the only work
of St. Irenaeus known to the West at the time, and was extremely
rare [77] ; it does not contain the saying of St. Ignatius. St. Ambrose
is mentioned once only : he instituted psalmody in order to raise
the spirits of Christian people when they were suffering persecution
from heretics [78].

Ralph looked up Josephus on the Jewish sabbaths and jubilees [79],
and called him to witness that the threat *Ita ut comedatis carnem
filiorum vestrorum* (*Lev.* 26,29) was fulfilled during the Roman siege

---

72. H. FARMER, *William of Malmesbury's Commentary on Lamentations*, in
Studia monastica 4 (1962) 308-309. Malmesbury may have been the first, apart
from Paterius, to compile *Deflorationes* from books other than the *Moralia*.

73. *De vita sua* (*op. cit.* 66) : « Coepi igitur... Scripturarum commentis inten-
dere, Gregoriana dicta, in quibus artis huius potissimum reperiuntur claves,
crebrius terere... »

74. 56a.

75. PL 23, 635 ; *Acta SS*. Feb. 1, 28.

76. 11b : « Unde Irenaeus Lugdunensis, de inclito martyre loquens Ignatio :
Sicut dixit, inquit, quidam ex nostris pro martyrio Christi damnatus ad bestias :
Frumentum ego sum... »

77. A. SIEGMOND, *Die Überlieferung der griechischen christlichen Literatur
in der lateinischen Kirche bis zum zwölften Jahrhundert*, Munich 1959, 89-90.
The letters of St. Ignatius had been translated ; but Ralph is obviously quoting
at second hand.

78. 264b : « Sub hereticorum persecutione a patre nostro beatissimo Ambrosio
Mediolanis psalmodia legitur instituta ad relevandum tribulationis illius pondus,
ne scilicet populus christianus meroris tedio contabesceret ». PAULINUS in his
Vita juxtaposes the persecution by heretics and the institution of ' antiphons,
hymns and vigils ', but does not relate them, *Vita S. Ambrosii* (PL 14, 31).

79. 242a, from *Antiquit.* III, x, 7 ; 291b, from *ibid.* III, xii, 3.

of Jerusalem [80]. No other author is mentioned by name. Ralph certainly used Raban Maur on Leviticus ; he took the Latin translation of the LXX version from Raban on some of his texts [81]. There are other echoes, but no continuous reference. The account of the unclean creatures (*Lev.* 11) draws on Pliny, as we have seen, on St. Isidore's *Etymologies* (quoted anonymously) and on Raban. I have failed to find any other exegetical source, and not for want of trying.

Finally, Ralph illustrates his text from contemporary practice. *Ponetque manum super caput hostiae, et acceptabilis erit* (*Lev.* 1,4) recalls the assent by hand when parties to a suit ratify their agreement to a decision [82]. Moses ' repetitions remind him of painting : a painter will first draw his lines ; he seems to have finished, when in fact he has not ; secondly he adds his colours and puts in the missing touches. St. Gregory had used the simile of painting : a dark foundation makes the colours show up better. Such comparisons were not uncommon [83]. Ralph uses his very aptly and freshly.[84] He notes continuity, as he saw it, between the Law and the liturgy of the Church. On the anointing of Aaron and his sons (*Lev.* 8,10-13), he remarks that the same rite is still observed : priests receive holy oil on the hands only, whereas kings and bishops have their heads anointed [85]. This indeed was the practice in France. Study of Old Testament

---

80. 302b : « ... et Iosephus idem factum testatur in Ierusalem dum a principibus romanorum obsideretur ». From *De bellis* VI, III, 4.

81. 4a, 34b, 44a, 50b, from RABAN, *Com. in Lev.* (PL 108, 318, 277, 288, 318).

82. 2b : « Manus impositio devotionem offerentis insinuat. In omni enim placito, cum ad propositam sententiam diversorum consensus expetitur, per manus appositionem significatur. Tunc quippe hiis que dicta sunt se favere demonstrant, cum manus accomodent ».

Experts on legal procedure in the middle ages whom I consulted on this very unspecific reference kindly tell me that they can find no evidence for assent by hand. It might be local, unwritten custom, perhaps.

83. *Moral.* XXXII, 14 (PL 76, 691) : « Sicut enim niger color in pictura substernitur ut superiectus albus vel rubeus pulchrior ostendatur... » See also Y. LE-FÈVRE, *L'Elucidarium et les Lucidaires*, Paris 1954, 112-113, 142.

84. 47a : « ... a capite repetens, quod minus est singulis addit, morem pictoris imitans, qui aliquam depingens imaginem eius lineamenta prius ponit et quasi totam consummat, cum in ea nihil perfecerit. Mox denique membra singula recurrens, colores addit et singulis quod deesse videt, apponit. Pari forma legislator omnia retractans que dixerat, quibusdam repetitis, que iam tradiderat, quedam nova addit ».

85. 81a : « Qui ritus usque hodie servatur. Nam regum et pontificum capita oleo sacro perfunduntur, qui autem minoris ordinis sunt sacerdotes unctionem istam in manibus solis accipiunt ».

kingship had inspired it. Revival in the middle ages soon came to mean survival[86].

His method is unsystematic. Some books of the twenty begin with a prologue, where Ralph takes the opportunity to add thoughts which have occurred to him in the meantime. We have to wait until the prologue to lib. XIV to find his classification of the biblical books and their contents; the prologue to lib. XV classifies the four senses of Scripture. Instead of expounding his text first in the literal, then in the spiritual sense, he may reverse the order and begin with the spiritual, after which he writes: ' Quia igitur ad littere explanationem descendendum est... '[87] This rambling procedure may well result from his many interruptions; he picked up his work again after long intervals[88]. The background was *lectio divina*, meditative reading and exposition, with a preference for the spiritual senses[89].

A clear purpose runs through the twenty books, none the less. Ralph aimed first and foremost at refuting Jewish arguments for the benefit of his brethren at Flaix. The monks had been discussing among themselves the objections put forward by Jews. As the argument went to and fro, he saw that the simpler brothers did not know what to think of it. Their faces expressed bewilderment. Only the Church's teaching supported them, which they had sucked up with their mothers' milk, but as prejudice rather than reasoned assent. He reflected with sorrow how many men professed the Christian faith and yet how few of them had understanding. A man who believed

---

86. P. E. SCHRAMM, *Das Alte und das Neue Testament in der Staatslehre und Staatssymbolik des Mittelalters*, in *La Bibbia nell' alto Medioevo*, Spoleto 1963, 229-256; *Der König von Frankreich*, 2nd ed., Weimar 1960, 157-158.

87. 168b.

88. He wrote consecutively, though intermittently, making cross-references: 169b, in lib. XII, cap. I : « De hac autem eius oblatione in secundo huius volumine ... prolixius tractatum est. Qui voluerit, illic requirat... De qua eius hostia qui plene scire desiderat in sexto requirat volumine ». 246a, lib. XVI, cap. IV has a reference back to lib. XIII.

89. 1a, Ralph compares the study of Scripture to the paralytic of the Gospel, who was let down through the tiles to be healed (*Luc.* 5, 19) : « Christus namque sub opacitate sanctarum reconditus scripturarum, cum ab infirmis mentibus, repellente turba phantasmatum et variarum cogitationum tumultu impediente, adiri non possit, usu sancte lectionis, remoto velamine littere tanquam tegulis ipsum celantibus, investigandus est ».

3b : « Ut ergo quod rogamus etiam impetrare possimus, componamus in altari ligna, ut scilicet per studia et scripturarum meditationem assiduam igni Spiritus sancti materiam preparamus ».

On *lectio divina* see J. LECLERCQ, *L'amour des lettres et le désir de Dieu*, Paris 1957, 70-86; H. DE LUBAC, *Exégèse médiévale, les quatre sens de l'Écriture*, Paris 1959-1964, passim.

out of mere conformism, with little education in Scripture, did not yet understand what he believed. Mere conformism was Ralph's bugbear, as we shall see. His prologue gives a surprising account of a debate, not between Jews and Christians, be it noted, but among religious, some of whom put the Jewish arguments so forcefully as to sound convincing :

> Cum inter socios aliquando sermo de iudeorum contentionibus haberetur, quibus veritatem obruere et suam nobis conantur inducere cecitatem, dum nunc pro nobis, nunc pro illis ratio redderetur, visum est nobis inter verba quorundam auditorum animos fluctuare, et sicut minus eruditorum se status habet, tanquam flatibus contrariis, sic diversis persecutionibus actos, nunc hac, nunc illac assensum suum in partes alterutas declinare. Licet igitur hoc aperte pronuntiare confunderentur, vultu tamen ipso videbantur protestari se quid magis sequendum esset penitus ignorare, nisi quod ecclesiastice doctrine, quam cum lacte matris biberant, quasi quoddam preiudicium sustinebant. Ingemuimus re vera et cum dolcre cepimus retractare quod licet multis communis sit veritas nostre professionis, paucis tamen est concessa ipsius intelligentia veritatis. Difficile est autem ut immobilem fidei sue constantiam servet et non vacillet aliquantulum, cum coeperit contrariis obiectionibus inquietari. Quisquis ideo tantum credit quod alios credidisse cognoscit, sola scilicet multitudinis autoritate confisus, minus tamen scripturis imbutus, nondum intelligit quod credit [90].

Ralph undertook to clear up doubts by expounding Leviticus, one of the darker Mosaic books, which generally struck its readers as tiresome rather than edifying. Custom dictated that a monk should justify himself for writing at all. Were his confused brethren, then, a mere literary fiction [91] ? I think not. Informal disputations took place between Jews and Christians in northern France and elsewhere ; the ecclesiastical authorities forbad them as dangerous to faith, suggesting that the rabbis could defend themselves well [92]. Guibert of Nogent describes the judaising policies of John, count of Soissons (d. 1118) [93]. Kings and magnates would protect ' their '

---

90. The prologue is unpaginated.

91. There has been much debate on the real existence of the fool, whom St. Anselm set out to refute by proving God's existence ; see A. HAYEN, *Saint Anselme et saint Thomas*, in *Spicilegium Beccense* I, 1959, 69-85. There was a lively discussion of the subject at the Congress at Bec.

92. On Judeo-Christian debates and their prohibition see G. KISCH, *The Jews in Medieval Germany*, Chicago 1949, 520 ; S. W. BARON, *A Social and Religious History of the Jews*, 2nd ed., V, New York 1957, 108-137 ; H. DE LUBAC, *op. cit.*, II, 1, 148-181 ; for a detailed study of anti-Jewish treatises and references in the eleventh century see B. BLUMENKRANZ, *Les auteurs chrétiens latins du moyen âge sur les Juifs et le Judaïsme* (*Études juives*, 4), Paris 1963.

93. *De vita sua* (*ed. cit.*, 208-210).

Jews for financial reasons ; Jews were exploitable [94]. Their exploiters
were not secret converts to Judaism, as some churchmen suspected,
but the very suspicion may have bred doubt. Guibert also tells the
story that he heard a clerk disputing with a Jew in a house at Laon.
The clerk, overcome by the ' windiness ' of his opponent, gave it
up and resorted to a kind of ordeal instead [95]. Guibert wrote his *De
incarnatione contra Iudaeos* in order to reprove the ' judaising ' count
and to strengthen the faith of a Jewish boy, who had been saved
from a pogram and given to St. Germer ; he was baptised and received
into the community [96]. The monks of St. Germer, therefore, could
have heard Jewish arguments either at first or second hand, and
have discussed their truth. At the same time Christian scholars were
enlisting the help of rabbis in Old Testament exegesis. Andrew
of St. Victor, expounding in the literal sense, went so far as to be
accused of judaising on the messianic prophecies [97]. Ralph shows
no signs of familiarity with Victorine exegesis, but he may have
heard that consultations with Jewish scholars had come into fashion.
He seems to include Christians in his attacks on those exegetes who
busy themselves with ' the letter ' of Scripture : they, too, must
be refuted. It is interesting that the Jewish problem should have
struck him as so urgent, whereas heresies did not trouble him. ' There
are many questions on the part of men. While there is life there is
questioning ', wrote Hugh of St. Victor [98]. Twelfth-century scholars
propounded diverse methods for answering questions. Ralph had his.

The question that loomed largest for him was the Jewish claim
for the immutability of the Law. Presumably it was presented in
the debate among his colleagues. He could also have found it in anti-
Jewish polemic. Guibert put it in his *De incarnatione contra Iudaeos* :

> Et quomodo legem a Deo de coelis praebitam, imo ipsius digito exaratam,
> vocum terroribus, lampadum fulgoribus et montis exhalationibus promul-

---

94. H. G. RICHARDSON, *The English Jewry under the Angevin Kings*, London
1960 ; G. I. LANGMUIR, ' *Iudei nostri* ' *and the Beginning of Capetian Legislation*,
in *Traditio* 16 (1960) 207-209.

95. PL 156, 528.

96. *De vita sua* (118-120). STEGMÜLLER, no. 2887, ascribes a commentary on
Lamentations to ' Guilelmus Iudaeus ' of Flaix. I have read a copy in MS *Paris
Nat. lat. 575*, XII /XIII century. It seems to me from the content to be too late
to have been written by the Jewish convert at Flaix, a contemporary of Guibert ;
the Guilelmus Iudaeus who died in 1202 seems more likely ; see STEGMÜLLER,
no. 2899. In any case, the author of the commentary on Lamentations shows no
special knowledge of Jewish exegesis.

97. B. SMALLEY, *The Study of the Bible in the Middle Ages*, 2nd ed., Oxford
1952, 97-195.

98. *De sacramentis Christianae fidei* II, XIV, 9, translated by R. J. DEFARRARI,
Cambridge, Mass., 1951, 423 (PL 176, 570).

gatam, nulli genti a saeculo datam mutare poterimus ? Et si leges hominum constant, quis Dei praecepta destituit ? [99]

Ralph may have found it in another book, Gilbert Crispin's *Disputatio Iudaei et Christiani*. Written at an uncertain date towards the end of the eleventh century, it had a wide diffusion both in England and on the continent [100]. Gilbert Crispin, abbot of Westminter, belonged to St. Anselm's circle. St. Anselm had visited Flaix when he was prior of Bec and had talked to Guibert [101]. Gilbert Crispin's Jew makes the same claim for the Law of Moses :

> Si uero eam minime obseruandam discitis, culpandus est Moyses, cui nobis eam inani uanitate a deo tradidit obseruandam... Legislator nil excipit, sed universaliter ea omnia mandat obseruari, uos autem ad uestrum arbitrium legis et mandatorum obseruantiam determinatis [102].

He argues that the Law stands as a whole, whereas Christians pick and choose from it in an arbitrary manner.

Ralph fastened on one line of argument against the Jewish claim and ignored any others. Scripture, rightly understood, offerred the surest proof. He included the LXX translation, following St. Augustine, because the translators had been inspired : ' multa in verbis mysticis ad placitum suum mutaverunt ' [103]. Hence a LXX variant could be used in argument [104]. Ralph defended the validity of scriptu-

---

99. PL 156, 517.

100. For the most recent discussion of the date see R. W. SOUTHERN, *Saint Anselm and his Biographer*, Cambridge 1963, 90-91 ; he argues for 1092-3 as the date when the material was being prepared ; Dr. BLUMENKRANZ would put it later. On the diffusion of the *Disputatio* see his *La 'Disputatio Iudei cum Christiano' de Gilbert Crispin*, in *Revue du Moyen Age latin* 4 (1948) 243-245.

101. *De vita sua* (66-67).

102. Ed. B. BLUMENKRANZ, in *Stromata patristica et mediaevalia* 3, 1956, 28.

103. *De doctrina Christiana* II, xv, 22. P. BENOIT, *L'inspiration des Septante d'après les Pères*, in *L'homme devant Dieu. Mélanges offerts au Père Henri de Lubac* I, Lyons 1963, 186, writes : « Jérôme a porté un coup très dur à la Septante et à son inspiration. Augustin est un des derniers écrivains chrétiens à lui résister ouvertement ». He underestimates Augustine's influence on medieval exegetes.

104. 44a on *Lev.* 5, 15 : « Sciendum vero quod ubi hebraica veritas, quam nostra translatio sequitur, *duos siclos* ponit, LXX transtulerunt : qui emi possit quinquaginta siclis argenti siclo sanctuarii. Spiritu enim prophetico, ut credimus, interpretantes, multa in verbis mysticis ad placitum suum mutaverunt, ubi tamen spiritualis sensus idem esset, hinc maxime legis intentionem ostendentes, eamque figurative loqui insinuantes, quam legem interpretantes quasi alia a lege proferunt, eadem tamen que lex aliis figuris exprimunt ».

Ralph goes on to the legend of the LXX translators and explains that they meant to prophesy to the gentiles : « ... Dicant enim, qui errasse eos existimant, quo pacto credendum est LXX sapientes eatenus errasse ut per ignorantiam

ral proof from Scripture itself. Even St. Peter, an eyewitness of the
Transfiguration, recalls us to Scripture, knowing that evil spirits
can deceive : *Sed habemus certiorem propheticum sermonem*. Even
the martyrs' witness is indecisive. Heresy has its martyrs ; Scripture
has to judge between true and false martyrdom :

> Unde beatus Petrus, cum ad insinuandam Domini Iesu divinitatem
> vocis paterne mentionem fecisset, quam ipse audierat de celo allatam,
> cum esset cum eo in monte sancto, quia tamen etiam per malignos spiritus
> similia fieri possunt ad hominum deceptionem, ad scripturas continuo
> nos revocavit, dicens : *Sed habemus certiorem...* [105] Fidei vero nostre muni-
> mentum est in auctoritate sanctorum martyrum... Sed quia etiam in heresi-
> bus martyres inventi sunt,... inter ipsos quoque martyres scriptura diiudi-
> cat et sanctorum ab iniquis causam discernens eorum qui pro vera fide
> passi sunt pietatem commendat... Hoc igitur perpendentes, cum adversus
> iudeorum subsannationes armari vellemus, ad sacre legis considerationem
> apposuimus animum, cui subditi ipse videri volunt, sed eius intentionem
> nequaquam intelligunt [106].

The demonstration from Scripture turns on one idea : the Jews
'fail to perceive the brightness of Moses' countenance' [107], sharing
the blindness of all but a small minority of their forebears. Ralph
distinguishes between the Jewish multitude and an élite. The holy
patriarchs and prophets had a revelation of Christianity :

> All whom the spirit of prophecy touched foresaw the calling of the gen-
> tiles in the fullness of time, before it came to pass. They foresaw, they fore-
> told, they yearned [108].

Their own people would be stripped of grace and would lose the
glory of priesthood. The prospect grieved them, but they took com-
fort in the thought that no human wishes could alter divine Providence [109]. The revelation included Christian values : the dignity of

---

pro duobus siclis quinquaginta ponerent, et non potius scienter, rationabili
scilicet aliqua causa perspecta, siclorum numerum commutarent ».

They raised the price commonly paid for a goat to that of a horse in order
to point to a mystery : « Quid igitur ipsius numeri mutatio sibi velit et tanta
littere dissonantia quomodo in spiritu conveniat, advertendum est ».

See RABAN, PL 108, 288 for the LXX version. The Hebrew text has only
shekels in the plural.

105. From *II Petr*. 1, 19.
106. Unpaginated prologue.
107. Prologue, see *Exod*. 34, 35.
108. 251a : « Vocationem gentium in consummatione temporum futuram
omnes quod propheticus spiritus attigit previderunt antequam fieret. Previde-
bant, prenuntiabant et donec fieret suspirabant ».
109. 97a : « Sic sancti patriarche et prophete, qui paterno affectu populo
illi pre-erant, cum per spiritum prophetie spoliandum eum in consummatione
temporum sacerdotali gloria et divina privandum gratia presentirent, licet gentis

virginity was not hidden from Moses, nor the taint of even lawful
wedlock [110]. The élite had to speak to an ignorant, carnal people.
Some of their teaching had timeless value and would never be superseded. What of those ritual precepts, which the Gospel would super-
sede ? Ralph answers that these were prophecies, figures and sacraments of the Christian faith. Some things were told plainly, without
the veil of allegory, so that the rank and file could understand [111]. They
needed instruction in the lesser commandments ; otherwise they
would have known nothing of religion and would have observed the
signs only [112]. Divine wisdom condescended to lisp in teaching them
as though they were infants [113], and held out the promise of apples as
though they were children [114]. The ceremonies and ritual precepts of the
Law, however, had a mystical sense which escaped their understanding.

Ralph passes over two current interpretations of the Old Law.
He puts the Jewish people into a lower spiritual age group than
did Guibert of Nogent. The latter chose a traditional division : law
of nature for children, written law for adolescents, law of grace for
adults [115]. To Ralph the Jews were no better than children. According
to Honorius Augustodunensis, the ritual precepts had a plainer
function : they were given to the Jews to prevent them from sacrificing to idols, as they had done in Egypt [116]. Ralph preferred to dwell

---

sue calamitatem charitatis visceribus egre ferrent, inde tamen consolabantur
quod illius hec erat dispositio, cui nulla contraire potest humana conditio ».

110. 232b : « Non igitur latebat Moysen que esset dignitas virginitatis, cum
summo pontifici non viduam, non repudiatam, sed tantum virginem nubere
concedebat. Non latebat eum que esset in thoro etiam maritali contaminatio,
... cum post coitum, cum post partum mulier purificari iubebatur ».

111. 212a-b, on *Lev.* 19, 15 : « Ad coercitionem carnalis illius populi posita
sunt que sequuntur, qui, cum sensu parvulus esset, ad enodanda mysteria fuit
invalidus. Quod igitur propter illos dicebatur, sic utique dici oportebat, remota
scilicet allegoriarum nube, ut ab eis caperetur ».

112. 191a : « Quia igitur perfectam iustitiam adumbrare tantum suis ceremoniis poterant, non etiam adimplere, saltem preceptis minoribus fuerunt imbuendi,
ne sic in signis servirent religioni ut religionis ipsius prorsus fierent alieni ».

113. 231b on *Lev.* 22, 22 : « Miramur tamen, misericors Pater, ... quod sapientia tua, ut nostre insipientie conformetur, adeo se deponat ut cum infantibus
istis quodammodo balbutiat ».

114. 293a, on *Lev.* 26, 3-4 : « Quia vero etiam ipsi in scriptura habent quod
capiant et competentibus sibi promissis ut Deo serviant excitantur, apparet
quod divina providentia cum eis loquens quasi cum pueris agit, quibus poma
promittit ».

115. PL 156, 519 : « Sub Moysi vero quasi adolescentem a pristinis vilitatibus
aliquantulum sublevare et aliqua de viro sentire compelleret ».

116. See Y. LEFÈVRE, *op. cit.*, 433 : « Cur concessit Deus Judaeis legalia
sacrificia, cum non auferrent peccata ? Ne idolis immolarent. Quem ritum in
Aegypto positi didicerant ».

The allegorical significance of the legal sacrifices is added.

exclusively on the prophetic value of the Law. He anticipates the question : how could it educate the Jews to observe precepts whose significance they could not grasp ? He answers that it could not be other than useful for them to obey God's orders in some things at least, however blindly they did so [117]. He argues against contemporary Jews that their ritual precepts were given, not as good in themselves, but as bearing the image of goodness. Their own books prove it, since the prophets and the psalmist witness that God rejected blood sacrifices in favour of the interior sacrifice of the heart : *Dedi eis praecepta non bona*, said Ezechiel (20,25) [118]. That was a traditional line of argument : medieval exegetes took little, if any, account of changing attitudes to cultic observance in the Old Testament writings.

Ralph was more original in drawing a parallel between the teaching methods of the prophets and those of the lawgiver. The prophets taught and prophesied by means of actions as well as words, whereas now we rely on words for the most part. He cites examples from Ezechiel (12,7), Isaias (20,2-3) and Ieremias (13,3-7) [119]. Here he pointed to a feature of the prophets' technique, the importance of actions and gestures to convey their message, which is still stressed in modern studies [120]. Regarding Moses as a prophet, he went on to argue that Moses had the same purpose : he taught and prophesied by means of outward signs, that is, by prescribing actions, when he gave the Jews their laws [121]. The comparison is ingenious, but misleading : it ignores the contrast. The prophetic gestures were intended to make the words of the prophets clearer and more impressive

---

117. 190b : « Multa hactenus mystica populo illo antiquo servanda lex tradidit, in quibus fidei sive sanctorum morum umbra esset sola, non veritas, quorum etiam observantiam non intelligentibus quid protenderent ? In eo quidem utilis erat, quia Deo precipienti in quibuscumque obedientiam exhibere inutile esse non poterat ».

118. Prologue : « Non enim intuentur claritatem vultus Moysi, quod ex eorum libris facile probari potest. Nam cum per prophetam testetur ipse legislator quod dederit eis *precepta non bona*, quis non videret quod in preceptis illis non ipsam iustitie bonitatem, sed iustitie solam dicat esse imaginem... Sicut ergo supra dictum est, non sunt bona huiusmodi precepta, sed tamen boni ipsius ac religionis formam habentia ».

Four of Ralph's proof texts on the prophets' repudiation of the legal precepts on sacrifice had been quoted by Guibert (PL 156, 520-521), but not *Mich.* 6, 6-8 and *Ierem.* 7, 21.

119. Prologue : « Quod enim maxime nunc verbis agitur, hoc in illo populo prophetico etiam visibilibus signis tunc exhibeatur, ut non sola pronuntiatione vocis, sed etiam rerum sacramentis fieret significatio veritatis. Hoc in multis eorum operibus tam manifeste apparet ut contradictionis nullus locus sit ».

120. See for instance J. LINDBLOM, *Prophecy in Ancient Israel*, Oxford 1965, 51-53.

121. See below, n. 124.

to all. Ralph establishes this point ; but then he goes on to ascribe a different intention to Moses. The legal precepts, as Ralph understood them, were meant not to clarify, but to hide. They were couched in a secret sign language, whose sense escaped, and was designed to escape, all but a few initiates. The temple and the tabernacle served the same purpose. They had a hidden meaning for the élite. Both were to be built according to a divine exemplar (*I Paral.* 28, 19 ; *Exod.* 25,40). The concept went back to *Hebr.* 8,5 : *Qui exemplari et umbrae deserviunt coelestium, sicut responsum est Moysi, cum consummaret tabernaculum.* David and Moses saw figures or pictures by which they taught what to believe, what to hope for and how to live [122].

A traditional argument supports his interpretation. Abstract the secret meaning, and you have a mass of useless, irrational detail, unworthy to be recorded by such great men. Take the blood sacrifices prescribed by the Law. Was Moses just raving or playing some childish game with rumps and grease [123] ? No : he showed by referring to his exemplar that when he ordered certain things to be done he meant his orders to convey something different [124]. Ralph appealed to St. Paul : the precepts were figurative in two ways ; they were

---

122. Prologue : « Rex David, cum filio suo Salomoni tradit expensas templi et quid agendum sit instituit eum, quantum mysterium in hiis lateat, que visibiliter construuntur, docet dicens : *Omnia*, inquit, *venerunt scripta Domini ad me, ut intelligerem universa opera exemplaris*... Spiritu sancto docente, ... intellexerat quid homini credendum, quid sperandum qualiterque esset vivendum... congrua posset imago formari. Inde et Moyses ipse, cum de hiis que ad tabernaculum pertinent, Deo secum loquente, docetur : *Inspice*, ait Dominus, *et fac secundum exemplar.* Quid igitur succenset mihi iudeus, si dicam mosaicas traditiones umbraticas esse ? »

See BEDE (PL 91, 422) and RABAN MAUR (PL 109, 412) on the revelation to David and Moses, which they expressed allegorically in the structure of the temple and the furniture of the tabernacle.

123. 93b on *Lev.* 9, 19 : « Quid putamus cause esse ut adipes concremandi pectoribus superimponerentur ? Responde mihi iudee. Moyses iste tuus, quem ad celum laudibus effers, ut quid tot inutiliter agit ? ... Nonne verum tibi videtur quod apostolus noster asserit, hec omnia non solum figuraliter dici cum scribuntur, sed etiam in figura facta esse cum celebrarentur ? Alioquin delirare videbitur tanti viri sapientia ut puerorum more in extis et caudibus et adipibus pecorum ludum exercere ».

Ralph makes rather free use of *I Cor.* 10, 11 : *Haec autem omnia in figura contingebant illis ; scripta sunt autem ad correptionem nostram.*

124. Prologue : « ... et ipse testetur iuxta exemplaris sibi proposti formam hec omnia se constituisse et dum hec ordinaret aliud intendisse, et ceteros quoque sapientes illius temporis, qui per Spiritum sanctum agebantur, hunc tenuisse modum ut maxime per parabolas populo loquerentur et plerumque, verbis non contenti, locutionis formam visibilibus signis imitarentur ».

written down as figures ; they were also acted out as figures, when they were celebrated [125]. To sum up Ralph's thesis in his own words :

> Opera igitur que non solum videntur, sed etiam intelliguntur, preter speciem quam corporeis oculis offerebant, utique signa erant et aliud quod a prudentibus tantum caperetur, figuraliter continebant [126].

So far, Ralph has remained on the common ground of patristic tradition, as it had reached him [127], though he touches it up with some personal observations. The lure of a secret sign language carried him further. He presents the ritual precepts as a divine cryptgram. Even that did not satisfy him. He hoped to prove his case against the Jews by arguing that ' the letter ' made nonsense in some places : therefore we must understand it as a mystery. All precepts had a mystical significance of course ; but some had no literal sense at all. Ralph here chose one strand of tradition and pursued it remorselessly [128].

The search for apparent absurdities in the literal sense in order to pass straight to the mystery is the weakest side of Ralph's exegesis. He avoided the worst pitfalls. Thus he never denied a literal sense to a text because it expressed a metaphor or a figure of speech, nor did he reject the literal sense of a narrative or a law because it was morally shocking [129]. His classification of the biblical books according to their predominant mode of speech shows that he had pondered the problem. He begins with ' histories ', in which he includes the Pentateuch, the historical books of the Old Testament, the four gospels and the Acts of the Apostles. The psalms and the prophets are prophetic, although they contain plain as well as prophetic speech. The sapiential books are partly proverbial and partly prophe-

---

125. See above, n. 124.

126. Prologue.

127. Ralph may have read Origen's homilies on Leviticus in the Latin translation, though he does not quote them ; he was influenced by Augustine's teaching on the patriarchs' and prophets' ; see M. PONTET, *L'exégèse de S. Augustin prédicateur*, Paris 1944.

128. GILBERT CRISPIN made the same point in his *Disputatio* (*ed. cit.* 29) : « Diuino quidem sensu legis mandata intelligenda esse dicimus, quia si humano ea omnia sensu et ad litteram accipimus, multa sibi inuicem aduersantia et multum repugantia uidemus ».

129. 119b on *Lev.* 11, 37 : tales of crimes committed must be accepted as literally true, quoted by DE LUBAC, *op. cit.* II, 11 ,146.

194a-b on 18, 22 : « Multi, cum in scripturis talia reperiunt, abominantur, avertunt auditum et pene, si audiunt, legem divinam, quia in ea talia scripta sint, reprehendere nituntur, sed meminisse debemus quod superius legimus... Scriptura igitur sacra multa in suis immunda recipit, quorum tamen tactu non contaminatur ».

tic. The book of Job contains all three modes, historical, prophetical and proverbial. Ecclesiastes contains both proverb and *simplex doctrina*. The latter is found in the Pauline and Canonical epistles. Ralph then explains that his classification is not watertight : each book includes some or all of the diverse modes of speech : the historical books are called so, not because they are that only, but because history predominates in them [130]. Yet his thought on the subject did not save him. We shall watch him at work. In the passages which follow, the mystery is substituted for the literal sense, not based upon it.

Ralph puts his text through a sieve, as it were, to sift out the absurdities. Will it ' stand according to the letter ' or not ? If not, then the Christian exegete has scored a point against the Jews, proving that Moses had intended to teach a mystery. It amounts to a learned game and Ralph played it fairly by keeping to the rules ; he tried to ' save the letter ' wherever possible [131]. For example, he tried to work out the reckoning of the jubilee years, *Lev.* 25,53, which struck him as inconsistent and therefore absurd. Then he concluded that he had done his best ; perhaps further study might have enabled him to do even better, but the task was difficult and unprofitable if completed :

> ... hec de littere contrarietate dicta sint, que pluribus in locis adeo vel dubia vel quasi sibi repugnans apparet, ut vix et cum magno labore, diversis hinc et inde capitulis consideratis, que ad eundem sensum referenda videntur, aut eluceat quod dubium fuit aut consonet quod quasi contrarium prius apparet... Hec idcirco prolixius prosecuti sumus ut excusatos redderemus nos, sicubi forte iudaicam litteram non ad plenum investigare potuimus,

---

130. 204a-b : « Unde constat, libri historiales aut prophetici seu etiam proverbiales dicuntur, non quod hoc vel illud solum sine quantulacumque alterius admixtione habeant, sed quod hoc aut illud ex maxima parte contineant sic vocari... Cum in precedenti libro legislator multa simplice protulisset eloquio, ... item quedam subiungit que iudaice quidem ad litteram relata simpliciter prolata videantur, mysterio autem suo reddita proverbia esse sentiuntur ».

131. 99a-b on *Lev.* 10, 6, the Levites are forbidden to mourn for dead relatives : « In promptu est advertere quod illis interdicit quod aliis tamen conceditur. Viget igitur hic potissimum figura, ut in aliis libri huius locis. Littera tamen ita salvari potest ».

He explains the text as teaching that affliction must be patiently borne. Moreover, it would have been unfitting to rend newly consecrated garments in sign of grief, and put dust on newly anointed heads. AUGUSTINE raised the question, *Quaest. in Lev.* XXXII and LXXXI (*ed. cit.* 198, 225), but Ralph found his own answer.

205a-b : Ralph harmonises the apparently conflicting precepts *Lev.* 19, 20 and *Deut.* 22, 24 : « Videtur lex sibi sancire contraria... Potest itaque littere sensus hac satisfactione fulcire ».

que multis in locis et multum sudoris affert invenienda et parum utilitas inventa [132].

His reasons for rejecting the letter are various. First of all the legal precepts contradict one another. Leaven bread is forbidden as an offering, *Lev.* 2,11, and commanded 7,13. Here the conflicting mandates seem to cry out, as though with voices, that they need a spiritual interpretation, where the meaning of leaven will be consistent [133]. On the second text he accuses champions of the letter of passing over the contradiction in triumphant tones :

> Videant littere sectatores qualiter hunc locum transeant. Si enim littere hereamus, lex sibi contraria sancit... ; ipsius littere repugnantia nos ad spiritualem sensum compellit [134].

Secondly, the letter must be rejected when it goes against common sense and experience. One such rejection turns on a conjunctive. The ban on drinking wine before entering into the tabernacle is followed by the text : *Ut habeatis scientiam discernendi inter sanctum et profanum, inter pollutum et mundum* (10,10). Ralph finds the passage ridiculous because he takes *ut* as causal : wine taken in small quantities does not so impair the senses as to prevent one from distinguishing between a camel and an ox or a pig and a sheep. The wise writer would not have made himself a laughing stock ; we must seek out the mystery [135]. The site of the tabernacle, 16,16, gives rise to a similar problem : why was it specially mentioned, when it was part of the holy place ? Here the letter is absurd because unnecessary : it ' does not help itself ' [136]. The command to pay the hireling his wage by

---

132. 291a-b.

133. 14a : « Impugnat seipsam legis littera. In sequentibus quippe panes fermentati precipiuntur offerri. Sed nimirum verba littere, dum collata sibi convenire nequeant, aliud in se, aliquid quod queratur ostendunt, ac si quibusdam vocibus dicant : Dum nostra vos conspicitis in superficie destrui, hoc in nobis querite quod ordinatum sibique congruens apud nos valeat intus inveniri. Ad spiritualem igitur intelligentiam confugiamus. Ubi enim littera solvitur spiritus stat, quia hic aliud, ibi vero aliud fermentum significat ».

134. 64b. See also 245b on *Lev.* 23, 17-20 : « Si quis vero litteram pertinaciter sequatur, non video quis in hiis duobus capitulis evadende contrarietatis exitus inveniatur ». Also 308a on *Lev.* 27, 11 : « Angustias hic patiatur iudeus si interrogetur qualiter iuxta suam litteram recte possit Domino vovere quod Domino non licet offerre ».

135. 103a : « Quid igitur ? Totane ista est utilitas propter quam Aaron et filii ipsius etiam modici vini usum... intrantes tabernaculum debeant abicere, ut scilicet camelum a bove, suem ab ove discernere sufficiant ? ... Ridiculum est hoc et a sapientia tanti scriptoris prorsus alienum. Querendum est igitur huius loci mysterium ».

136. 176b : « De tabernaculo exteriori hoc dicitur... Nonne cum tabernaculo et sanctuarium inter eos fixum fuerat ? Ergo quia littera sibi non subvenit, ad mysterium recurrendum est ».

the day, 19,13, could hardly have been observed : workers willingly agree to be paid less often ; indeed they accept weekly wages in some cases. Here, however, Ralph granted that the command might have a literal sense, since it taught generosity [137]. Some texts are too irrational and trivial to have a literal sense : why should God have accepted the fruits of the fourth year particularly (19,24) [138] ? Why should a field which has been vowed to the Lord be priced as though it were to be sold forthwith (27,16) [139] ? The threat that in time of dearth ten women shall bake bread in one oven (26,26) is absurd: a siege does not reduce the number of ovens available [140]. Ralph might have ' saved the letter ' of this text by reflecting on conditions in a beleaguered city. He could not see why the priest who offered a victim as a holocaust should be allowed to keep the skin (7,8). The skin of birds would be useless. Those who follow the letter in all things might reply that the precept applied only to the skin of an ox or a sheep. Let them keep their straitjackets ! Ralph prefers the spiritual sense [141]. Sometimes he seems to depart from his own rules by choosing the spiritual sense just because it is easy and ob-

---

137. 197b-198a : « Quia tamen nescio si quisquam modo inveniatur qui hoc semper observet et frequentissime etiam cum gratia et favore operariorum contingit ut operis sui mercedem eadem die non recipiant, sed usque in tertiam aut quartam diem vel septimam libenter se differri sustineant, videtur mihi in tam festina recompensatione mercedis que populo illi indicitur formam apparere sacramenti... Cum igitur et hic eis precipitur... forma est divine liberalitatis que illis imponitur ut qui verum Deum colere docebantur ad eius similitudinem et morum sanctitate quodam vivendi genere traherentur ».

138. 206b : « Iudaico quippe animo agit qui occidentem sequens litteram a tanto auctore opus suum estimat improbari... Nulla est igitur ratio... »

139. 309b : « Movet me... quod ea que Domino voventur statim venundari precipiuntur... Perturbetur hic iudeus, nam materiam non habet perturbationis intelligentia veritatis ».

140. 301b-302a : « Hic satis apparet quod quecumque premissa sunt allegorice discutienda sunt. Hoc enim ad litteram, nisi desipere velit, nec iudeus accipiet. Quomodo namque in urbe obsessa clibanorum possit esse penuria ut non nisi in uno panes coquerentur ? ... Mysterium igitur discutiamus... Huiusmodi namque deliramentis plena est lex, si iudaico sensu nihil preter litteram ibi cogitetur ».

141. 61b : « Convenio autem eos qui in omnibus litteram solam sequuntur... Numquid avicula illa excorianda erit ut pellis eius, ad nihil utilis, tradatur sacerdotibus ? Ridiculum est ita sentire... Sed respondeant forsitan in bove tantum et ove hoc preceptum servandum, hec enim animalia pelles habere que aliquam utilitatem sacerdotibus conferre possint. Contenti ergo sint angustiis suis. Nos vero liberiori pede gressum moventes et libertatem spiritus sequentes libere astruimus ».

44b on 5, 15 : « Nam de hoc presens legislatio agere videtur, sed has angustias patiatur littera. In spiritu vero libere astruimus ».

vious as against the difficulty of the ' letter '. Thus he comments
on *Ad omnem mortuum non ingredietur omnino* (21,11) :

> What is easier if you refer it to Christ ? What more difficult than if you
> avert your eyes from him ?

The text refers to sin : who was sinless but Christ [142] ?

Precepts concerning hygiene presented obvious difficulties to a
westerner of the twelfth century. *Lev.* 11, 34 declares food to be unclean if water has been poured over it. A Jew might give as the
reason that a dry body is less liable to infection than a wet one ;
Ralph brushes it aside [143]. He ought to have considered St. Augustine's
suggestion that the text referred to water from an infected vessel [144].
Lev. 11,36 declares cisterns to be clean, like springs or running water ;
yet nothing is more likely to be polluted by a corpse [145]. Provisions
for leprosy in clothes and houses (13,47 and 14,36) struck him as the
clearest proof for his thesis by their absurdity. How could clothes
and walls be leprous ? He comments delightedly :

> Cum in plerisque locis, imo pene ubique satis appareat, legem spiritualiter
> intelligendam esse, dum ea sepius loquitur que nisi ad mysteria relata
> fuerint insipida prorsus et fatua sentiunt, nescio tamen si alicubi apertius
> quam in hoc lepre tractatu, ubi vestis leprosa et sicut sequentia continent
> domus leprosa introducitur [146].

Ralph would accept the literal sense, however, of a precept which
impressed him as edifying. Raban Maur had interpreted *Lev.* 19,33,
on protecting strangers in the land, as just a prophetic warning to
the Jews : they would try to expel gentiles who came to the faith
' at the end of time ' [147]. Ralph agrees that it may well be so, but the
prima littere superficies is so full of kindness as to attract the reader

---

142. 222a : « Quid manifestius, si ad Christum referas ? Quid difficilius, si
ab illo oculum avertas ? Quis enim sine peccato fuit in mundo nisi qui peccatum
tulit de mundo ? »

143. 118a : « Dicat iudeus, littere sue emulator, ut hanc legislationis istius
qualemcumque proferat rationem, quod scilicet corpus aridum non tam facile
polluti cadaveris sordes contrahit sicut aqua perfusum. Nos vero ridicula ista
parvipendentes, qui mystice omnia precipi et mystice ab eis fieri cognovimus,
facti huius mysterium perscrutemur ».

144. *Quaest. XXXVII in Lev.* (*ed. cit.* 203).

145. 119a : « Contraria videtur lex loqui. Si enim quidpiam per appositionem
morticiniorum contaminari potest, quid magis quam cisterna, in quam cadaver
delapsum, cum putrefactum fuerit, totam aquam illam corruptione sua abo-
minabilem reddit ? Sed littere imbecillitas ad spiritum nos mittit ».

Ralph probably took *cisterna* to mean a small tank of stagnant water.

146. 139b.

147. PL 108, 460.

and make him slow to seek further [148]. He adds a little homily on kindness to pilgrims and penitents. Touching as this may be, it brings out the selective and subjective character of his approach.

I have dwelt on his arguments against the Jews, but not to reprove him for misplaced ingenuity. It is rather to redress the balance. The Père de Lubac has considered the rejection of the literal sense as impossible or absurd in patristic and medieval exegesis; he finds it infrequent :

> Tout compte fait, de quelque genre d'« impossibilité » qu'il s'agisse pour la lettre, les cas de quelque importance jugés tels à tort sont peu nombreux. Si l'on désire quelquefois un peu trop vite échapper à quelque apparente « absurdité », plus souvent l'absurdité prétendue était le fait d'une interprétation littérale abusive, prônée par les ennemis de l'Écriture et de la foi chrétienne, dans une intention de dénigrement [149].

The book of Leviticus lent itself to the discovery of apparent absurdities. My illustrations from Ralph's commentary will have shown that the above estimate is too optimistic. Ralph has made a system out of the search for absurdities and consequent rejection of the letter when it does not pass his tests. I turned the pages of Rupert of Deutz on Leviticus in order to compare his comments with Ralph's. Rupert was less concerned to refute the Jews, but he will reject the letter on occasion, raising the same objection as Ralph on the text *Lev.* 10,10 [150]. On *Lev.* 7,19 he rejects the letter where Ralph accepts it [151].

Andrew of St. Victor belongs to a different world. Consider his brief comment on the precepts dealing with leprosy in clothes and

---

148. 211b : « O preceptum pietatis ! O digna sacris legibus institutio ! Forsitan aliquis dixerit iam hic prophetice iudeos argui quod in fine temporum gentes ad fidem accedentes repellere voluerunt et pristinos errores suos illis exprobare coeperunt. Et probabile satis est hoc iam intendisse scriptorem, sed prima littere superficies tanta benignitate plena est ut lectorem statim ad se trahat et ad aliud investigandum pigrum efficiat ».

149. *Op. cit.* II, II, 146.

150 PL 167, 795 : « Ergone idcirco non bibent vinum ut discernere queant inter bovem et camelum, inter hircum et choerogryllum ? Nam huiusmodi discretio, si simplicem sequaris litteram, postmodum subscripta est... id est, austeram prohibentur sequi legis litteram ».

151. *Ibid.* 782 : « Ergone postquam combusta fuerit igni, tunc demum *qui mundus fuerit vescetur ex ea* ? Hoc itaque, iuxta litterae corticem, stare non potest, sed iuxta interiorem spiritus medullam, certum est... »

RALPH, 68b : « Non ad illam quam tactu immundi immundam factam dixerat, hoc referendum est, sed quoniam de carne sanctificata preceperat, ut nihil tangeret immundum, addidit quoque ut non nisi a mundis comedi debuisset ». There are some similarities between Rupert and Ralph, but my comparison suggests that there was no dependence ; neither wording nor content woudl indicate that Ralph had read Rupert.

houses. They puzzled him, too ; but he did not dismiss ' the letter '
out of hand as nonsense :

> We have not seen leprosy in clothes or houses or suchlike in our regions
> or times, unless perhaps the law calls leprous certain stains, which certainly
> often appear on them. But what stain is leprous and what is not, it would
> be hard to find anyone to judge [152].

He leaves the question open, with a scholar's caution, suggesting
that distance of time and place may supply the answer. It is a more
scientific attitude. Andrew accepted the Law, in spite of its difficulties
and inconsistencies, as an historical institution, which could be studied,
though not always understood. To Ralph it was *illa umbratica traditio*
and hence mere words on his page. The Paris masters, faced with
the two approaches, Ralph's and Andrew's, would slowly move
towards Andrew's, using the spiritual senses, but supposing a literal
sense in the texts they expounded. The beauty of the spiritual interpretation in the middle ages has been praised to the skies ; its confu-
sions have been underrated ; Andrew has been accused of ' dryness '.
But which of the two approaches led to a clearer understanding of
the development of sacred history ? Ralph shows, moreover, that
the search for mysteries had an ugly side, when it was used for polemic
against the Jews : it led him to waste of effort, complacency and
insult.

The pity was that he had sound impulses as an exegete. He was
nothing if not consciencious. Where he allowed a literal sense, he
brought all the primitive erudition at his disposal to clarify it for
his readers. His sources on Leviticus were scanty ; he had to do
much for himself. He asked sensible questions. Why did the Lord
make special mention of Moloch, the god of the Ammonites, when
he forbad idolatry ? Other neighbouring tribes had their idols too.
Ralph gave as the reason that the Ammonites had the custom of
passing their children through fire as an offering to Moloch [153]. He
explained the rare word *spatulas* (*palmarum*) correctly as derived

---

152. MS *Oxford Bodl. Laud. lat. 105*, fol. 114[rb] : « Lepram in vestibus vel
domibus vel huiusmodi, de quibus lex agit, in nostris partibus vel nostris temporibus non vidimus, nisi forte lepram dicit maculas quasdam, quas in huiusmodi
frequenter inveniri constat. Sed que macula sit leprosa, que autem non, qui
diiudicare nosset non facile inveniri posset ».
Andrew wrote his commentary on the Pentateuch towards 1148.
Rupert of Deutz made the ingenious suggestion that ' house ' referred to a
tribe, whose members had contracted leprosy (*op. cit.* 814).

153. 213a on *Lev.* 20, 2-5 : « Movet tamen me cur Dominus, ab idolorum cultu
populum suum deterrens, idolum precipue ammonitarum elegit... Erant enim
et alia idola, que a proximis gentibus colebantur,... quibus omnibus pretermissis,
de solo Moloch mentionem facit ». He refers to *IV Reg.* 23, 10.

from *spata* in reference to their shape ; they are ' what we call *spicas* '. He probably meant young shoots, having looked it up in the *Etymologiae* [154]. The grammatical construction of the text interested him ; he would note an unusual word order [155] and a mode of speech. *Lev.* 7,8 is synedoche, 11,35 hyperbaton ; 8,30 and 26,36 are hyperbole [156]. *De doctrina Christiana* would have taught him to apply grammar to the study of Scripture : synedoche is listed among the rules of Tyconius [157], but he used the hints for himself. The accusative case in *Lev.* 8,9 puzzled him, since his Bible had *Cidarim quoque texit caput.* *Cidarim* was a common variant for *Cidari* [158]. The Hebrew has a preposition : *And he put the mitre upon his head* (English revised version). Ralph knew no Hebrew and never thought of checking his Latin text ; so he ventured a guess, which was wrong but excusable, that the translator tried to keep the original Hebrew idiom ; hence his Latin was ungrammatical [159]. Again Ralph was trying to apply what Augustine had taught him on the peculiarities of Hebrew. He had the will, if not the skill, to do so. His careful scrutiny of the literal sense gave the Paris masters data which they could not have found elsewhere.

The spiritual interpretation, or rather the homiletics it led to, show Ralph at his most sympathetic. He would probably have wished to be judged on his prowess in this field, since it reassured and edified his readers. In principle he distinguished three spiritual senses, allegorical, moral and anagogic [160]. In practice he did not schematise, preferring the comprehensive term ' mystery ' : ' Nota grande et utile mysterium ' [161]. Nor did he use *distinctiones* or lists of spiritual meanings. Their absence gives his commentary ease and freedom.

---

154. 261a on *Lev.* 23, 40 : « *Spatulas* vero *palmarum* illas existimo quas nos spicas dicimus. Spatule namque dicte sunt quia scilicet spatarum formam videntur pretendere ». See ISIDORE, *Etymol.* XVII, III, 15 : « Spicam de maturis frugibus abusive dicimus ; nam proprie spica est cum ... aristae adhuc tenues in modum spiculi eminent ». On *spata* XVIII, VI, 4 : « Alii spatam Latine autumant dictum, eo quod spatiosa sit, id est lata et ampla ; unde et spatula in pecoribus ».

155. 118a on *Lev.* 11, 34 : « Inusitata est ista constructio... Sic igitur ordinanda est tota huius capituli contextio... » See also 86a and 104a.

156. 62a, 118b, 86b-87a, 303b.

157. *De doctr. Christ.* III, XXXV, 50.

158. *Bibl. lat. vulg.* (ed. H. QUENTIN, II, Rome 1929, 369).

159. 76a : « Non est nostre locutionis ut sic dicatur : texit caput cidarim, ut dici solet : docuit me lectionem seu : induit me tunicam ; sed habet hebrea lingua locutiones suas, quam, puto, interpres in hoc loco ut sequeretur minus latine loqui elegit et lingue, quam transferebat, proprietatem expressit. *Cidarim* ergo, inquit, *texit caput* ».

160. 217a-218a.

161. 87b.

Guibert of Nogent had recommended the moral sense as more useful than the allegorical : men needed instruction in morals, whereas the faith (taught by allegory) was now known to all [162]. Ralph's experience had shown him that the faith still needed defenders, and the content of Leviticus drew him to allegory : the sacrifices prescribed by the Law prefigured the Cross and the sacraments, the Levites Christian priesthood. Sometimes he turns to anagoge. In his prologue to lib. XII he writes that the lawgiver has been describing the trials of the righteous ; now he comforts them with the hope of heavenly rewards. Ralph moves easily from Moses' intention to a prayer to Jesus, ' our hope in tribulation ' [163]. There remained plenty of scope for the moral interpretation of Leviticus. This was a more personal task : allegory was standardised ; moralities could be freely adapted to suit the teacher and his readers. The teacher could express himself, if he chose.

Ralph seized on the opportunity to set forth his *Weltanschauung*. We might expect to find that *contemptus mundi*, which Dr. Bultot has described for us. Far from it. In contrast to the ideal of withdrawal, our monk prefers ministry. Secular men have a place in the Church and may win merit, even though they cannot devote themselves wholly to God : Ralph wanted to help them. The first chapters of his commentary read like a manifesto, and the theme is sustained to the very end. He says at the beginning that the two types of offering prescribed by the Law signify two orders of men in the Church. Some men offer themselves as a holocaust by renouncing the world ; others make peace offerings. Unsuited to pursuit of the higher virtues, they aspire to medium goodness and avoid crime as far as they can. They do not strip themselves of all their possessions, but use them for God's service. Hence their offering is hallowed, even when not accompanied by spiritual fervour [164]. As weaker members, they

---

162. *Liber quo ordine sermo fieri debet* (PL 156, 26).

163. 167a on *Lev.* 16, 1 et seq. : « Hucusque ergo legislator iustorum agones descripserat... Sed quia in laboribus non durat perseverantia nisi remunerationis expectatio consoletur, iustum erat ut quibus celestem indixerat pugnam, aperiret etiam quanta eis in celestibus post victoriam gloria reservetur. De spe igitur nostra audituri sumus, de spe quam tu, domine Iesu, miseris mortalibus tribuisti. »

164. 1b : « Hostias vero pacificas offerunt, qui ad culmen perfectionis minus idonei, quamquam celsiora virtutum merita minime assequantur, per mediocrem tamen conversationem pacem cum Deo faciunt, pro viribus precaventes ne odium illius per criminalem offensam incurrant. Hii, licet omnia sua non deserant, de hiis tamen que possident fideliter Domino ministrant ; et idcirco carnes eorum... nondum quidem spirituali fervore absumuntur, sed sanctificate quidem sine criminis admixtione ex magna tamen parte offerentium voluptati deserviunt ».

do not aspire to the heights, but would save themselves by keeping out of the depths [165]. Riches need not be condemned ; their use may gain credit when their owners avoid pride and luxury [166]. Knights may conform to public custom by wearing splendid dress, while despising worldly glory and abasing themselves inwardly [167]. Religious sometimes receive temporal office without loss of humility or disloyalty to their habit [168]. Ralph has a humane passage on old men, of whom God asks nothing more than that they should wait patiently for death [169]. He repeats himself towards the end of his commentary to drive home his point ; his insistence comes out in the phrasing. The faithful fall into two groups, stronger and weaker. The latter must do their best in their different circumstances :

> Iam superius semel et iterum discrevimus, duo esse fidelium genera. Unum enim est robustius, quod perfectionis amore temporalia postponere et, ut Deum plenius possideat, eligit in hoc mundo nihil possidere. Aliud vero infirmius est, quod, licet divinas leges attendat et secundum illas agat, quantum tamen eisdem legibus docetur non esse contrarium, temporali iocunditate fruitur, coniugiis inherens, filios generans et possessiones terrenas non solum sibi, sed etiam sue successioni procurans. Qui autem huiusmodi sunt, necesse est (ut) in suo genere vitiis resistant et criminum incentores spiritus debellare contendant [170].

---

165. 18a : « Sunt quippe nonnulli, qui quamvis summa virtutum fastigia non ambiant, offensum tamen Deum habere refugiunt, indeque, licet bona summa non expleant, mala tamen summa devitant... quia salvari quidem volunt, sed sufficit eis si salventur, quamvis inter extrema sancte ecclesie membra computentur ».
The idea comes from RABAN on Leviticus (PL 108, 265), but has been elaborated.

166. 115a : « Istos ergo lex propter presentem non reprobat abundantiam quia, licet multa possideant, ad usum ea non ad superbiam retorquent erogandoque ac dispensando que possident ex abundantia transitorie facultatis meritum comparant eternitatis ».

167. Ibid. (a moralisation of the creatures allowed as food, Lev. 11, 22) : « Porro locusta... iure militaribus aptabitur, qui splendore habitus sui publice consuetudini satisfacientes omnem temporalem gloriam parvipendunt et se etiam dum foris elevant intus abiciunt ».

168. Ibid. : « Bruchus vero... eorum nobis pretendit speciem qui in religionis habitu constituti, si temporalibus subleventur honoribus, nec mentis deserunt humilitatem nec habitus sui mutant deformitatem ».

169. 307a-b on Lev. 27,7, Sexagenarius et ultra... : « Non est Deus immoderatus exactor ut hoc ab homine extorqueat quod vires eius novit excedere. Etate igitur fessos, et qui ad laborem minus idonei sunt, iam quidem non cogit laborare, sed transacti laboris remunerationem precipit expectare. Spes itaque sola ab eis exigitur, ut sicut fortes in opere fuerunt, dum viguit etas, sic nunc cum iam laborare non possunt, in expectatione sue mercedis inveniantur longanimes.

170. 295a.

He set standards for his *mediocres*. Doing their best meant restraining their passions, keeping peace and showing kindness [171]. Alas for the ignorance of men who think that almsgiving suffices to please God, when they may be adulterers, robbers and perjurors [172] ! Virtue involves doing good, not just refraining from sin. Some pass their days in eating, sleeping and chattering, yet think themselves very religious because they abstain from theft, robbery and murder. They strike at the sins of others without seeing their own. Many, both seculars and men vowed to continence, simply follow the herd and accept the way of life which they take from others, on the authority of the crowd, without thinking for themselves or looking for eternal reward ; they live innocently, not in order to please God, but rather to conform outwardly to men. Their innocence is useless, if they lack charity [173]. Innocence and simplicity, indeed, may serve as an excuse for idleness : those too feeble to labour should at least be humble [174]. Mere sheeplike respectability was not a common target for medieval moralists, nor does it fit into our picture of ' an age of violent contrasts '. But Ralph had observed it and felt strongly on the subject.

He also disliked the ' holier than thou ' attitude of the new religious Orders. St. Bernard's letters to the abbot of Flaix were remembered perhaps, and still rankled. Ralph moralises the pig, which

---

171. 19b on *Lev.* 3, 4-5 : « Necessario igitur in hostiis pacificis adipum concrematio commendatur, quoniam, licet in vita carnale, compescendi sunt tamen carnales affectus, ne per eorum intemperantiam subito ipsa conversationis mediocritas, qua servatur pax est homini, deseratur... Sed nec hoc sufficit ad pacem cum Deo custodiendam, nisi cum virtute continentie pax ad proximos et animi mansuetudo servetur ».

172. 231a : « O quam lugenda est humana ignorantia ! Videmus etiam nonnullos, qui cum in seculari conversatione se offerant Domino, si de facultatibus suis pauperibus tribuant, in hoc se placituros existimant, cum sint fortasse adulteriis fedi, crudeles in rapinis, in periuriis Dei ipsius contemptores ».

173. 21b : « Videmus namque quamplurimos, qui dormiendo, comedendo, vanis sermocinationibus intendendo vitam consumentes, quia tamen a furtis, rapinis (et) homicidiis manus continent, religiosissimos se arbitrantur ;... peccatis alienis insultant, sua non vident. Multi huiusmodi et in vita seculari et in continentium conversatione inveniuntur, qui tamen, bonis corporalibus admixti, quasi oves gregem sequentes, pene absque deliberationis proprie iudicio absque remunerationis eterne intuitu, formam vivendi, quam ab aliis sumunt, multitudinis auctoritate tracti, specietenus custodiunt,... innocenter vivendo, non ut Deo placeant, sed ut hominibus conformentur, invigilant. Horum innocentia inutilis est, quia quidquid fecerit homo, nisi ex charitate hoc fecerit, nihil ei prodest ». An Allusion to *I Cor.* 13, 3.

174. 20b : « Qui vero sola innocentia et simplicitate contenti sunt, (ut) timeant semper necesse est, ne tanquam inutiles et infructuosi beatitudinis illius participartione iudicentur indigni... Unde isti qui ad labores invalidi sunt, saltem per humilitatem placere debent ».

was forbidden as food. The pig, a dull, dirty animal, signifies those who set up their own superstitions as a Rule, deciding on what is to be done or not done from their own tradition rather than from the authority of divine law. It is great foolishness for each man to choose a religion for himself, as he pleases, without consulting God's will. Such observance does not clean him. The man who is superstitious about his habit does not regard the uncleanness of his soul. You may abstain from some things which divine law has not forbidden, deciding what is to be sought or shunned according to your own judgment; you will not achieve true righteousness thereby [175]. The passage reads as a veiled attack on new interpretations of the *Rule*, which Ralph regarded as arbitrary, and superstitious additions to it. Poverty alone does not confer virtue, he says elsewhere. Many poor men lack the means, but not the wish to do harm. Hence, although unknown to men on account of their lowliness, they are despicable in God's sight. We must not regard all poor men as saintly, but must distinguish between them, as the Law teaches [176].

Ralph's attitude to the laity recalls Guibert's. The latter had considered the problem of rich men, who used their power for evil and stood out for bestial cruelty, but who feared divine judgment and made at least some reparation for their wickedness. He dared not despair of their salvation, provided that they did not presume on their good works, even though they could not or feared to lay aside their role in the world [177]. Both Ralph and Guibert were devotees

---

175. 111a on *Lev.* 11, 7 : « ... quia superstitiose multa observantes, non ex auctoritate legis divine, sed ex sua traditione agenda aut non agenda constituunt... Isti quoque per suem designati sunt, quod fatuum animal est et immundum. Magna namque stultitia est, cum propositum sit nobis Deo placere, unumquemque super religionis censura vel divinam voluntatem consulere, sed pro libidine voluntatis proprie sibi religionem statuere ; sed nec mundare potest huiusmodi observatio. Dum enim homo quedam superstitiose super habitum suum decernit, anime sue immunditiam non attendit... quia licet a quibusdam abstinueris, quorum tibi usum sanctio divina non interdixerit, dum pro tuo arbitrio sequenda aut fugienda discernis, iustitie veritatem obtinere non poteris ».

176. 109b-110a : « Neque enim ad iustitiam satis est pauperem fuisse. Sunt namque multi qui malum quod in animo concipiunt, opibus destituti, explere non possunt. Sunt ergo quamplurimi qui etiam propter nimiam inopiam hominibus sunt ignoti, Deo autem propter morum ignobilitatem contemptibiles et immundi. Ne igitur pauperes omnes sanctos estimaremus, docet lex quam in pauperum numero distinctionem facere debeamus ».

177. *Moral. in Gen.* (PL 156, 52) : « Per *bestias terrae* quidam intra Ecclesiam figurantur, ferali animo et crudelitate insignes, qui licet per potentatum secularem quem gerunt multa mala perpetrent, tamen, ad cor redeuntes, saepius de Dei iudicio valde extimescunt et plurima beneficia proinde impendunt. Qui si

of St. Gregory. He, after all, had preached to the laity as well as to religious. The Gregorian tradition contrasted in some ways with the more exclusive teaching of ascetics, who wrote for a spiritual élite. Such writers took an unhopeful view of the chances of salvation except in a hermitage or monastery [178]. Ralph, by avoiding this austere outlook, came closer to the 'masters of the sacred page'. The Paris programme was to evangelise the whole world. The masters preached themselves and trained their pupils to preach to the widest possible audience [179].

Their chosen instruments for reforming the laity were the pulpit and the confessional. Guibert had written a treatise on preaching [180]. Ralph refers to the preacher's technique : he must discuss vices as well as virtues, praising the latter and rebuking the former. Hence he must meditate on what he will tell to the people [181]. This advice looks forward to manuals on the seven deadly sins and to the theme of the scholar meditating on the sacred page as a preparation for preaching, which would become commonplace. Ralph also satirises society : he points to legal corruption [182] and to the misbehaviour of clergy, who cheat the people and set a bad example [183]. Satire

---

humiliter agunt nec de bono opere securitatem peccandi accipiunt, etsi a mundiali cura prorsus expediri non possunt, aut metuunt, dicere non audeo quod huiusmodi desperandi sint ».

178. R. BULTOT, *La doctrine du mépris du monde* IV, *Le XIᵉ siècle*, Louvain / Paris 1964. Dr. Bultot has been accused of exaggeration and of an unhistorical approach ; see the review by J. BATANY, in *Annales : économies, sociétés, civilisations* 20 (2), 1965, 1006-1014. The texts on *contemptus mundi* which he cites are nonetheless telling.

179. M.-D. CHENU, *La théologie au douzième siècle*, Paris 1957, 257-265 ; M. PEUCHMAURD, *Le prêtre ministre de la parole dans la théologie du XIIᵉ siècle*, in *Rech. Théol. anc. méd.* 29 (1962) 52-76.

180. *Liber quo ordine sermo fieri debet* (PL 156, 21-32).

181. 119a : « Sed quoniam incumbit predicatoribus sanctis necessitas ut non solum de virtutibus, sed etiam de vitiis disputent, illas scilicet laudando, ista autem reprehendendo, coguntur in meditatione sua utraque suscipere, ut tam de vitiis quam de virtutibus, quod deinceps in populi auribus loqui debeant antea mente pertractent ».

182. 46a-b : « Multi sunt qui vim palam inferre non possunt, sed rem proximi calumniantes et causam suam ad commune iudicium referentes, corrupto iudice, ex eius sententia quasi iuste quod suum non est invadunt ».

On the difficulty of obtaining impartial justice at the time see Y. BONGERT, *Recherches sur les cours laïques du Xᵉ au XIIIᵉ siècles*, Paris 1949.

183. 69a : « Ego tamen hanc legalem sententiam magis arbitror ad ecclesiasticos viros pertinere,... quia oblationes quas pro peccatis suis populus Deo offert in usus proprios accipiunt,... morum suorum perversitate eum exacerbant... Qui talia agunt digni sunt morte nec solum qui faciunt ea, sed etiam qui consentiunt facientibus ».

of this kind would ring through the Paris classrooms. Above all, the masters would preach repentance.

Modern scholars have paid more attention to the development of the doctrine of penance in the schools than to its place in homiletics. The two were complementary. Masters of the sacred page cleared the way for the canon of the Lateran Council of 1215, enjoining annual confession to a priest on all the faithful. Lecturers on Scripture had urged the faithful to go to confession : picturesque *exempla* were used to persuade them. If we turn to Stephen Langton's lectures on the Twelve Prophets, given at Paris about 1200, in a manuscript from the Cluniac Priory of St. Andrew's, Northampton, now MS *Oriel College, Oxford 53*, we find that the rubricator has noted in the margin some twelve places in the lecture on Osee alone, where Langton has mentioned confession : ' Commendatio confessionis et detestatio celationis ' is the most pungent [184]. It will be interesting to see how Ralph fits into this pattern. He recommends confession to a priest, which must be full and not partial. The flour to be made as a sin offering (*Lev.* 5,11) signifies that we should offer up our hidden sins of thought and deed by revealing them :

> ... Quid in simila nisi latentium cogitationum et criminum, in quibus peccator sibi soli notus est, p∂r confessionem expositio intelligitur... Quod tamen in potestate habeat, faciat ; similam offerat, et mala que apud se celabat, per confessionem sacerdoti prodat... Dignum est enim, ut qui peccatorum suorum confessionem facit, consumet eam, omnia que ad memorial revocare potest Domino pandens, non alia prodens, alia abscondens [185].

105a : « Pastor quippe morti obnoxius est si ecclesie sibi commisse affectum non amore divino succendere, sed ad se potius referre contendat ».

184. Fol. 123rb. Other rubrics include : *De contritione, confessione et satisfactione* (97va) ; *De cogitatione punienda non solum per contritionem, sed per confessionem* (fol. 101ra) ; *De perfecta memoria peccatorum et circumstantiarum* (fol. 109va) ; *De confessione circumstantiarum peccati* (fol. 119rb). Twelve references in the rubrics (plus one in the text which the rubricator did not notice, fol. 105ra) is a good proportion for the 38 leaves of the lecture on Osee. Langton's lecture-commentaries on Scripture, where he insists on the inclusion of circumstances in confession, would have provided useful material to Dr. J. GRÜNDEL, *Die. Lehre von den Umständen der menschlichen Handlung im Mittelalter* (*Beitr. zur Gesch. der Philos. und. Theol. des Mittelalters*, 39), Münster 1963.

185. 41a-b. Again 308b : « ... per confessionem mala a nobis commissa sensibus exponuntur alienis et ad alterius notitiam perducuntur » ; 312a, on *Lev.* 27, 19 : « Quia vero in hoc loco idem est redemptor et emptor, hic enim non emit ut perdat, sed ut possideat, super estimatam precii quantitatem iubetur ut quintam partem super adiciat, ut scilicet devotioni presenti precedentium quoque delictorum et eorum que nec n unc vitare potest confessionem adiungat »

Earlier on in the commentary he has described confession as a prelude to absolution, quoting the crucial text *Mat.* 18,18. His language is imprecise ; *doctor* and *sacerdos* are used as almost interchangeable terms ; but the gist is there : the sinner needs a mediator, as well as instruction on the satisfaction he is to make. Ralph is commenting on *Lev.* 4, 25 : *Tinget sacerdos digitum in sanguine hostiae pro peccato...* :

> *Tinget sacerdos...* Sacerdos qui Christi aut prepositi cuiuspiam typum habet... Docemur quippe per hanc sanguinis participationem luctu et afflictione nostra primum doctoribus satisfaciendum, deinde per eorum absolutionem nimirum quibus claves regni commisse sunt ad divinam indulgentiam pertingere. Doctoribus quippe dictum est : Quecumque ligaveritis super terram ligata erunt et in celo. Sed et quicumque sunt electi, si sanctitatis gratia prediti sunt, Deo eos familiares esse non dubium est. Accedendum itaque ad illos, vulnera per confessionem pandenda, flendum coram eis... Sicque commissa nostra et meritis lavent et potestate relaxent. Decet enim peccatorem hec humilitas, ut sine mediatore aliquo iusto petere indulgentiam non presumat... Sed sufficere non debet humana gratia. Illa enim maxima, illa tota intentione poscenda est, sine qua salutis humane nulla spes esse potest. Cum ergo iam homines tibi ignoscunt, tunc ad Deum gemitum tuum converte... Si vero sacerdos quilibet doctor hic accipitur, ipse quoque in sanguine nostro digitum tingere debet, penitentie scilicet nostre co-operari per doctrinam suam,... ut admonitione eius instruamur, qua humilitate et homines iustos placere et Deum nobis repropitiare possimus. ... Non enim sufficit peccata deseruisse, nisi congrua satisfactione quod inique perpetratum est aboleatur [186].

It seems from this passage, the most explicit in the commentary, that Ralph shared the uncertainties of contemporary writers on penance [187]. He wavered between the medicinal and the sacramental aspects. Two questions concern him. The first is dismissed briefly. Suppose there is no bishop at hand or the pastor is unheeding ? Then you must do his work for him : study to offer a clean mind to God [188]. Ralph did not mention confession to a layman, though it was widely recommended at the time [189]. The second question

---

186. 33a-35a.

187. P. ANCIAUX, *La théologie du sacrement de pénitence au XII⁰ siècle*, Louvain 1949 ; L. HÖDL, *Die Geschichte der scholastischen Literatur und der Theologie der Schlüsselgewalt (Beitr. zur Gesch. der Philos. und Theol. des Mittelalters*, 38, Heft 4), Münster 1960.

188. 2b on *Lev.* 1, 5 : « Fundunt ergo filii Aaron sanguinem, quia doctores sancti assiduitate sua de discipulorum cordibus malitiam expellunt. Sed quoniam propter Dei timorem hoc agitur, hec ipsa effusio Dei oblatio est. Tu quoque, si desit episcopus, si pastor incuriosus sit, pastoris circa te vices exequere et mentem tuam, studio adhibito, mundam Deo prebe ».

See ANCIAUX, 16, HÖDL, 82 on the problem of confession to unworthy priests or in the case where no priest is available.

189. ANCIAUX, 34-35.

concerns sick-bed confessions. Ralph always found the problem of motive perplexing. A man may leave secular life to take up 'spiritual studies'; but his intention remains in doubt; pride in his new learning may have moved him [190]. What of confession without repentance ? Many confess for fear of death, only to return to their sins, which they have renounced in confession, if they get well again. Can a human eye look into their minds ? Are they just 'bidding farewell' to their sins, not hating them as yet, out of sheer fright ? To God all is open. Man cannot examine such a confession to see whether it be true or false, nor promise certain forgiveness to him who makes it. Ralph goes on to quote the dilemma as it was described in the *Sermo ad penitentes* (no. 393), ascribed to St. Augustine and cited in treatises on penance [191]. The preacher here warns his congregation that the priest cannot judge the sincerity of a death-bed repentance [192]. Ralph may also have read *De vera et falsa penitentia*; it circulated widely under the name of Augustine from about 1140 or earlier [193]. Ralph softens its teaching, giving gentle advice to the unwilling penitent and to his confessor on how to pray in a seemingly desperate emergency :

Confessio quippe quam nullus comitatur fructus boni operis, quamque interni gemitus non commendant, incertum est utrum a Deo accipiatur. Multos quippe videmus timore mortis confiteri. Si tamen contigerit eos convalescere, mala quibus per confessionem abrenuntiaverunt repetunt et canum more ad vomitum redeunt. Cum ergo confiterentur, numquid humanus oculus interiora eorum penetrare poterat ut adverteret eos crimina que prodebant nondum detestari, sed timore exterritos quasi eis valefacere ? Deo vero omnia manifesta sunt. Homo itaque, sicut confessionem huiusmodi utrum vera an falsa sit nequit examinare, ... sic nec certam venie spem confitenti promittere. Beatus Augustinus in quodam sermone ad penitentes : Quisquis, inquit, positus in ultima necessitate... tene certum...
    Qui enim peccata sua nec probabilius vivendo corrigere nec saltem ea digne deflere potest, puto verecundia exigit ut indignum se divina misericordia iudicet, nec impudenter et quasi libera fronte eam sibi conferri exoret. Petat tamen, sed quasi non petendo ; speret, sed quasi desperando, dum et se indignum venia confitetur, et tamen sola Dei misericordia fieri posse credat ut salvetur. Huius orationis forma est ubi Deum rogantes dicere solemus ut dimittat que conscientia metuit et adiciat quod oratio non presumit... [194]
Quod vero eandem similam sacerdoti tradere iubetur, manifestum est, quia confessionem suam sacerdoti debet offerre qui confitetur... Quapropter

---

190. 76a : « Item si quis seculares conventus fugiens spiritualibus se tradat studiis, adhuc in dubio est qua intentione hoc agat, ne forte adeptione scientie inflari magis appetat quam edificari ».
    191. ANCIAUX, 30 n.
    192. PL 39, 1714-1715.
    193. ANCIAUX, 15-16.
    194. From the Collect for the eleventh Sunday after Pentecost.

bonus pastor, qui subditi pene desperati recipiat confessionem, intercessionis sue misericorditer beneficium ei impendat, et apud Deum, si fieri possit, pro reo obtineat quod reus ipse meritis suis obtinere se posse desperat... Necesse est ut periclitanti compatiens pro diluendis, que sibi revelata sunt, eius criminibus saltem brevi tempore in precibus coram Domino compungatur,... quantum in se est, expiare contendens [195].

He also considers the case of a robber or usurer, who repents and seeks medicine for his guilt. Ralph addresses the confessor: tell him that if he cannot find his victims and return his illgotten gains, he should dispense them well; his alms are less deserving than if he were giving the fruits of honest labour; nevertheless, they suffice to make worthy satisfaction [196]. Here again, Ralph wanted to reassure the penitent.

The question whether monks had the right to exercise pastoral care was being hotly debated. Secular clergy contested and monks defended it. Ralph never mentions the controversy, but he assumes that religious will act as confessors and spiritual advisers to laymen. His commentary witnesses to the fact that objections and prohibitions failed to prevent twelfth-century monks from undertaking cure of souls, in their own churches at least [197]. He wrote for colleagues whose activities would not be confined to *opus Dei* and *lectio divina*.

I have left to the last a unique passage where Ralph makes an excursion into psychology. He defines *anima* on *Lev.* 4,2: *Anima*

---

195. 41b-42a. *De vera et falsa penitentia* has a warning passage on 'poenitentia sera' (PL 40, 1127-1128, cap. XVII: « ... Multos solet serotina poenitentia decipere. Sed quoniam Deus semper potens est, semper potest etiam in morte iuvare quibus placet... Si quis est igitur qui veram tunc quaerat poenitentiam, expectet Dei clementiam, maiorem sentiens Dei bonitatem sua nequitia ».
The author, however, does not consider what help may be given to a sick man who is frightened, but not truly repentant.
196. 15a: «Munera quoque de fermento offeruntur Domino, cum aliquis usuris sive rapinis et furtis assuetus, denuo compunctus, misericorditer erogat quod crudeliter aggregavit. Si enim conversus egerit penitentiam et reatus sui medicinam a te quesierit, quid tandem dabis ei consilium nisi ut amicos faciat sibi de mammona iniquitatis, et si non invenit quibus reddat quod rapuit, bene ipse distribuat quod male usurpavit? Que tamen munera non eius sunt meriti quomodo si de iustis laboribus daretur elemosina, sufficit eis ut preterite rapacitatis dignam satisfactionem obtineant ».
197. See now M. CHIBNALL, *Monks and Pastoral Work*, in *Journal of Ecclesiastical History* 18 (1967) 165-172. Mrs Chibnall distinguishes between ministry in monastic churches attended by laymen and ministry to lay patrons on the one hand, and service of parish churches on the other; the former was frequent, the latter rare. Ralph probably had the former in mind.

quae peccaverit ex ignorantia, in order to find what meaning it had in the context of the Law. A comparison with other scriptural texts, where *anima* signifies mere physical life, decided him that Moses used it to denote carnal man, preoccupied with bodily things, too ignorant or too feeble to know or to obey God's will. Before reaching this conclusion, Ralph defines *anima* in its higher sense as part of the human *compositum,* body and soul. Here it has a threefold *vis* ; the first is sensual life, the second reason, which he thinks must include memory, the third is in appetite, which may be directed either to bodily things or to wisdom. We are bidden to love God with all three forces of the soul. Ralph's sources for this passage baffle me. There are echoes of well-known definitions by Augustine and Isidore, but the content is not truly Augustinian [198]. The only verbal identity that I can find is with Pseudo-Augustine, *De spiritu et anima.* Ralph does not refer to it or give any warning that he is quoting at all. Moreover, his concealed quotations come from the middle of the book, cap. XXXVII. The authorship and date of *De spiritu et anima* are still unknown. Dr. G. Raciti rightly rejects the authorship of Alcher of Clairvaux, but does not carry conviction in arguing for Peter Comestor's [199]. Dr. C. H. Talbot points to a copy listed in a catalogue of 1158 at Prüfening [200]. If it was already in circulation at this date, then Ralph, writing before 1159, could have used it. Like most of his contemporaries, he would have supposed it to be by St. Augustine. An alternative explanation would be that he drew on its sources. While scholars agree that *De spiritu et anima* forms a pastiche of quotations, no one as yet has identified them in detail [201]. I have not discovered the source of the passage reproduced by Ralph, and can only hope that some reader may enlighten me. The following transcript will show the parallels between Ralph's commentary and *De spiritu et anima* and their context in his discussion of *anima.*

---

198. H. Ostler, *Die Psychologie des Hugos von St. Viktor (Beitr. zur Gesch. der Philos. des Mittelalters,* 6, Heft 1), Münster 1906, gives a useful list of sources currently quoted by twelfth-century writers on *anima.*

199. *L'autore del « De spiritu et anima »,* in *Rivista di Filosofia neo-scolastica* 53 (1961) 385-401.

200. *Ailred of Rievaulx : De anima (Mediaeval and Renaissance Studies,* Supplement 1), London 1952, 49, quoting G. Becker, *Catalogi Bibliothecarum antiqui,* p. 212, no. 66.

201. The author seems to have drawn on Isaac abbot of l'Étoile, *De anima,* but the passage in question does not come from here, nor is there any evidence that Ralph knew Isaac's work ; on Isaac see W. Meuser, *Die Erkenntnislehre des Isaac von Stella,* Freiburg i.Br. 1934.

92

RALPH, lib. II, cap. IV, on *Lev.* 4,2
(24a-b).

De spiritu et anima, cap.
XXXVII (PL ʇ0, 808).

Anima substantia est invisibilis, pars hominis, ex qua homo cum corpore compositus est [202].

Hec triplicem habet vim. Prima est qua in corpore et per corpus utitur, vita sensualis, qua corpus vegetat et per corporis sensus exteriora ista sentit et discernit. Secunda est quam apud se exerit, per quam non solum ea que corporis sensus attingunt multo apertius perscrutatur ac discutit, sed et multa a sensibus aliena perquirit et plerumque, cum *bene viget*, et ad ipsius Dei notitiam erumpit. Hec non tantum in natura quid lateat, verum et in moribus humanis deprehendit quid deceat. Hec ratio dicitur, cuius etiam exercitium, quo circa *secretorum* indagationem utitur, ratiocinatio vocatur. Huius quoque *finis*, *cum ad* eorum *que diu quesivit notitiam pervenerit, intellectus seu intelligentia nuncupatur*. In hac parte *memoriam* computandam existimo que, licet et in hiis reperiatur animantibus que ratione carent [203], in rationalibus tamen *rationis consors et co-operatrix est*. Nam *sine ea ratio nec ad incognita procedere nec cognitorum scientiam poterit retinere.*

Tunc *finis* eius, si *bene viget*, *cum ad notitiam secretorum, que diu* investigando *quesivit, pervenerit, intellectus seu intelligentia nuncupatur...*

Memoria etiam *consors et co-operatrix est rationis ; sine ea ratio nec ad incognita procedere nec cognitorum scientiam retinere potest...*

Nimirum quippe, cum latentia querimus, ex cognitis ad incognita ratiocinando transimus. Quod si nulla est cognitorum memoria, necesse est ut et incognitorum nobis inventio denegetur. Tertia autem anime vis in *appetitu* est que seu ad ea que per corpus sentit seu ad scientie lumen et sapientie pulchritudinem voluptate quadam animam rapit. Hec igitur in quibusdam corporis *voluptatibus delectatur*, in quibusdam vero, contemptis carnis illecebris, ad mores optimos et ad vite honestatem pertingere conatur.

Humanus *appetitus*, ... si carnis *voluptatibus* pascitur, carnalis sive animalis nominatur. Si spiritualibus desideriis *delectatur*, spiritualis nuncupatur.

---

202. ISIDORE, *Different.* II, 27 (PL 83, 83) : « Anima est substantia incorporalis... invisibilis... » For *compositum* see AUGUSTINE, *De Trin.* XV, VII, 11 (PL 42, 1065), *De quantitate animae* I, 1, 2, (PL 32, 1036).

203. On memory in irrational creatures see AUGUSTINE, *Confess.* X, XVII, CLAUDIUS MAMERTUS, *De statu animae* (PL 53, 723). I owe these references to TALBOT, *op. cit.* 73, 77.

De hac itaque triplici anime virtute scriptum est : Diliges Deum tuum ex toto corde tuo et ex tota anima tua et ex tota mente tua [204]. Ex corde scilicet, ut anime affectus in Deum tendant, ex anima, ut hoc etiam quod in corpore vivit et per corpus opera Dei sentit in laudem eius amoremque proficiat, ex mente quoque, ut humana cogitatio, memoria, ratiocinatio investigando Deo et cognoscendo deserviat. Omnis ergo anime virtus charitati divine militare debet, quod breviter quidam evangelista conclusit dicens : ex omni virtute tua [205].

Anima itaque cum substantialiter dicitur et vitam sensualem et rationis acumen motumque appetitus in se comprehendit.

Dicitur autem et aliter anima, non ut substantia illa incorporea, sed vita eius infima, que in corpore et per corpus subsistit, intelligatur. Inde scriptum habes : Factus est homo in animam viventem [206], et : qui perdiderit animam suam propter me, inveniet eam [207]. Sed et quod paulo ante commemoravimus ex toto corde et ex tota anima Deum diligendum. Hinc [208] igitur, cum homo totus incumbit, cum sensibus sue carnis deditus a spiritualium contemplatione excluditur, animalis sive carnalis appellatur. Inde habes in apostolo : Animalis homo non percipit ea que sunt spiritus Dei [209], quia, ut diximus, mediam illam partem appetituum infime immergens superioris, id est rationis, lumen amittit. Sed et carnales vocat quosdam apostolus : Non potui, inquit, vobis loqui quasi spiritualibus, sed quasi carnalibus. Lac vobis potum dedi, non escam [210]. Sensibus enim suis dediti spiritus mysteria capere idonei nondum erant.

Invenies quoque huiusmodi hominem non solum *animalem* aut *carnalem*, sed et carnem animamve vocari. Habes in Genesi : Non permanebit spiritus meus in hominibus istis, quia caro sunt [211]. *Appetitus* quippe *humanus inter ima et summa* medius, cum plerumque in utraque divisus, sibimetipsi contrarius sit, quod ille expertus fuerat qui dicebat : Video aliam legem in membris meis, repugnantem legi mentis mee [212].

Humanus appetitus inter summa et ima positus...

In quantumque partem totus transierit, eius merito et nomen sortitur, et cum solis *carnis voluptatibus pascitur*, caro *nominatur*. Econtra vero, si spiritualium trahitur pulchritudine, si in sapientie

... si *carnis voluptatibus pascitur*, carnalis sive animalis *nominatur*.

204. From *Deut.* 6, 5 and *Mat.* 22, 37.
205. *Marc.* 12, 30.
206. *Gen.* 2, 7.
207. *Mat.* 10, 39.
208. Ed. *Huic.*
209. *I Cor.* 2, 14.
210. *I Cor.* 3, 1-2.
211. *Gen.* 6, 3.
212. *Rom.* 7, 23.

amplexus estuans voces illas suas facit : Hanc amavi et exquisivi a iuventute mea, et quesivi mihi sponsam assumere eam, et amator factus sum forme illius [213], audiet ab apostolo : Vos in carne non estis, sed in spiritu [214]. Unde et *spiritualis* seu etiam spiritus, qui eiusmodi est, *nuncupatur.*

Si spiritualibus desideriis delectatur, *spiritualis nuncupatur.*

Apostolus ad Corinthios : Spiritualis, ait, iudicat omnia [215]. Et in psalmo : Qui facit angelos spiritus [216]. Animam vero nuncupari hominem, non ad substantie significationem, sed ad infirmitatis vitiique denotationem, lex tibi in hoc loco erit in testimonium : *Anima,* inquit, *cum peccaverit per ignorantiam.* Animam quippe hominem appellavit, qui animalem vitam agens et in hiis infimis que per corpus sentit occupatus, divinam voluntatem aut per ignorantiam nescit aut per infirmitatem implere non sufficit.

Several points of interest emerge from this passage. First, Ralph sought conscienciously to determine the meaning of *anima* in his text. He realised that the biblical writers used it in a different sense from the Fathers. Secondly, he made a personal choice from the various traditions which offered themselves when he defined *anima* taken *substantialiter.* He avoided any suggestion that the body was the prison of the soul. He did not raise the problem of how the soul became contaminated by the body. He omitted to mention divine illumination as a condition of perception and understanding. It would be strange if his omissions were not made deliberately, seeing how large these aspects of the subject loomed in earlier writings. Ralph gives the impression of thinking that body and soul could work harmoniously together provided that man directed his appetite aright. He also gives a personal slant to the object sought by *appetitus.* Its aim should be to seek and to know God and to love him. When Ralph broached this part of his subject, he showed clearly that morals interested him more than metaphysics or mysticism. Reason, he wrote, could discern things foreign to the senses and might even, if healthy, aspire to knowledge of God himself ; then he added immediately : ‘ This (reason) apprehends not only what is hidden in nature, but also what is fitting in human behaviour ’. Later he wrote that appetite, rightly directed, might snatch up the soul to ‘ the light of learning and the beauty of wisdom ’, and distinguished between two types of appetite, baser and higher : some men delight in bodily pleasures ;

---

213. *Sap.* 8, 2.
214. *Rom.* 8, 9.
215. *I Cor.* 2, 15.
216. *Ps.* 103, 4.

others, spurning the forbidden things of the flesh, aim at good conduct and a worthy life. He pitched his tone lower than many writers on the soul, from St. Augustine onwards. Applying his *triplex vis* to the precepts to ' love the Lord thy God ', he explained them for all men.

Historians of early scholasticism may despise him as backward and unenterprising. So he was, from the point of view of speculation. But consider what he avoided by comparison with a crude popular exposé of the body-soul relationship. It comes from twelfth-century additions to the manual on theology compiled by Honorius Augustodunensis :

> Cum vero anima carni juncta fuerit, concupiscentiam ab ea trahit. Duas autem vires animae inesse nullus dubitat, unam qua corpus vivificat, alteram qua invisibilia considerat. Et illa qua corpus vivificatur animalitas vel carnalitas vel sensualitas nominatur ; illa autem quae invisibiliter contemplatur spiritus vel mens vel intellectus nuncupatur. Inferior ergo pars animae, quae animalitas vocatur... tantum in terrenis delectatur et idcirco caro appellatur... Superior autem vis animae, quae spiritus vel interior homo nominatur, spiritualia et caelestia scrutatur, caduca respuens invisibilium contemplatione delectatur et ideo carni adversari perhibetur [217].

The contrast is all the more striking in that Honorius' annotator shows some verbal parallels with Ralph and *De spiritu et anima*, where these two agree. But the annotator knows only a *duplex vis animae* ; Ralph's *triplex vis* enabled him to paint a more subtle picture of the human *compositum*.

The Benedictine tradition of scholarship had a late flowering in Ralph on Leviticus. It was a fine flower. Surrounded by simple brethren, who could not answer Jewish objections and who criticised him for quoting pagan writers, he succeeded in producing a standard commentary. It had unusual freshness at a time when so many contented themselves with making a mere *catena* of *auctoritates*. He thought things out for himself and selected his sources to suit his ideas, whether he was discussing psychology or the coming of Antichrist. Where tradition was uniform, as on the spiritual interpretation of the Law, he carried it to absurd conclusions ; but that resulted from his probing mind. He had a rare tolerance for the laity, combining monastic *lectio divina* with the missionary concerns of *magistri sacrae paginae*. Ralph on Leviticus was a personal work,

---

217. Y. LEFÈVRE, *op. cit.*, 232-239, 419-420.

and a black monk's brain-child, just as surely as St. Bernard on the Canticle was Cistercian.

ADDENDUM : A passage in the prologue, omitted from the edition and from the majority of MSS, tells us that Ralph set his oral teaching into writing at the request of his colleagues, and that it took him six years to do so : *Paris Nat. lat. 14248* (12th cent. from St Victor), fol. 2va-b : « Deinde monuerunt nos ut quod familiari fuerat sermone tractatum stilo traderetur et paginis, ne de memoria laberetur. Quem laborem, licet occupatissimi, iuxta illorum voluntatem suscepimus, et per sex annos opus inceptum consummavimus ».

6

ECCLESIASTICAL ATTITUDES
TO NOVELTY *c.* 1100 – *c.* 1250

NOVELTY in this paper refers to a new idea or institution. I shall not distinguish between religious, social and political novelties, since medieval churchmen did not do so. The church concerned herself with every aspect of christian life: any change in men's way of living affected her either directly or indirectly and generally the former.

I shall begin by quoting four examples of attitudes to novelty. My first two come from the late eleventh and early twelfth centuries. One will illustrate an attitude to new ideas, the second to a new institution. The distinction is artificial, but convenient. Men normally think up ideas in order to justify or criticise institutions. First listen to an anonymous opponent of Manegold of Lautenbach. Manegold contributed an extremist theory to papal polemic in the gregorian reform movement in order to explain and justify Gregory's action in declaring the emperor Henry IV deposed and absolving subjects from their oath of allegiance (1085). His opponent cries:

O nova lex, O dogma novum, noviter fabricatum![1]

This anonymous imperialist uses 'new' as a smear word. Manegold's doctrine is *bad*, just because it is *new*. The phrase 'new and unheard of' rings through anti-gregorian polemic from the beginning of the investiture contest. My second example is hackneyed, but irresistible. The monk Guibert of Nogent describes how the townsmen of Laon rebelled against their bishop and attempted to set up a commune. Guibert calls 'commune'

> a new and detestable name for an arrangement whereby the people pay the customary head tax, which they owe their lords as a servile due, in a lump sum once a year; . . . and all other financial exactions which are customarily imposed on serfs are completely abolished.[2]

[1] *MGH Lib de lit*, 1, p 431. On Manegold see W. Hartmann, *Manegold von Lautenbach Liber contra Wolfhelmum, MGH Quellen zur Geistesgeschichte des Mittelalters* 8 (1972) pp 11–14; K. J. Leyser, 'The Polemics of the Papal Revolution', *Trends in Medieval Political Thought*, ed B. Smalley (Oxford 1965) pp 47–51.
[2] *De vita sua* iii, 7; trans by J. F. Benton, *Self and Society in Medieval France* (New York 1970) p 167. Guibert was born 1065 (?) and died *c* 1125.

Guibert sums up the conservative reaction to the communal movement in northern France in his own excited way. Here again, *new* means *bad*.

Passing to the mid-thirteenth century, I shall illustrate an attitude to new ideas from a sequence in honour of St Francis of Assisi, ascribed to friar Thomas of Celano, who died soon after 1260. The saint is praised for his novelty:

> Novus ordo, nova vita
> Mundo surgit inaudita.[3]

The words 'new and unheard of' here denote good instead of bad. Next comes Robert Grosseteste bishop of Lincoln, defending his mode of visiting his diocese at the curia at Lyons in 1250. His inquisitorial method of detecting abuses had raised a storm of protest. Such inquisition was 'new and unaccustomed', its victims complained. Grosseteste justified his reform programme to the pope and cardinals as follows:

> Every new measure which plants, fosters and perfects the new man, and which harms and destroys the old, is a blessed novelty, wholly pleasing to him who came in order to renew the old man by his own newness.[4]

The text of St. Paul, *to put off the old man . . . and put on the new* (Eph. iv, 22–24) underlies the argument. Grosseteste claims that any measure of ecclesiastical discipline which aims at correcting and improving fallen man will be pleasing to God, however novel it may be. He went on to the corollary: any measure which was not framed to achieve this end came from the devil. His strong language amounts to a provocative rephrasing of the canon law maxim that custom, however old and venerable, must give way to truth, as defined by the church.[5] The bishop assumed that Innocent IV and his cardinals would agree with his view that new institutions to promote reform came from God, while obstruction on grounds of custom was devilish.

[3] *Analecta Franciscana* 10, p 402.
[4] . . . Quibus ego respondi: Omne novum, quod novum hominem instituit, promovet et consummat, veterem hominem corrumpit et destruit, benedictum novum est et omnino acceptum ei qui veterem hominem venit sua novitate renovare. See S. Gieben, 'Robert Grosseteste at the Papal Curia, Lyons, 1250. Edition of the Documents', *Collectanea Franciscana* 41 (1971) p 376. On Grosseteste's visitations see J. H. Srawley, 'Grosseteste's Administration of the Diocese of Lincoln', *Robert Grosseteste Bishop and Scholar*, ed D. A. Callus (Oxford 1955) pp 151–5; on royal objections to his procedure see F. M. Powicke, *The Thirteenth Century* (Oxford 1953) pp 454–6.
[5] See especially G. B. Ladner, 'Two Gregorian Letters', *Studi Gregoriani* 5 (1956) pp 225–42.

An emotional change has come about in some hundred and fifty years. *New* has ceased to be a dirty word. It may carry the sense of 'improvement'; in that case it is praiseworthy. God has changed sides; he is no longer safely conservative. The picture obviously needs shading. I have made it look too black and white. In the first place, defence of novelty began in the first stages of gregorian polemic. Gregory VII had two lines of defence for his policies: he was making no new decrees, but was merely repeating what had been ordered by the holy canons and the holy fathers; alternatively, he could devise new measures to correct new abuses by virtue of his authority as vicar of St Peter. But shading does not hide the contrast. The innovator defends himself as best he can. The burden of proof lies on him. His best line of defence is an appeal to the good old days before abuses arose. 'Novelty' looks better if he presents it as having been 'heard of' in the past. It is not his fault that wicked men have forgotten it in the present.[6]

My shading pencil goes to work again on the thirteenth-century welcome to novelty. Conservatives still attacked changes which struck them as 'new and unaccustomed', especially if the changes hurt vested interests. The new orders of mendicant friars ran the gauntlet of such attack. They undertook duties prescribed for both canons and monks, instead of obeying the statutes of the fathers, who allocated these duties to separate religious orders. So a bolognese rhetor complained about 1226, echoing a common criticism.[7] The anti-mendicant polemic led by William of St Amour in the fifties turned largely on the question of novelties in religion introduced by the friars.[8] But shading sets off the contrast again. The champions of novelty have moved from defence to attack. They glory in novelty and have no idea of sneaking it in under cover of a mere return to the past. The very concept of return to the past was presented differently. St Francis and his sons imitated Christ; but their imitation was novel, because no christian, not even the greatest saint, had ever set about it in the franciscan way. If they misread the past, they did so to stress their novelty, not to excuse it. St Bonaventure, among many other arguments, chose to defend the friars along lines similar to Grosseteste's apology for his inquisitorial procedure on visitations. In *De septem donis Spiritus sancti* (1268) Bonaventure answered the objection that

[6] *Ibid* pp 221–4 and the same author's *The Idea of Reform* (Cambridge, Mass., 1959).
[7] Quoted by J. Koudelka, 'Notes pour servir à l'histoire de S. Dominique II', *Archivum Fratrum Praedicatorum* 43 (1973) p 27.
[8] [M.-M.] Dufeuil, [*Guillaume de Saint-Amour et la polémique universitaire Parisienne 1250–1259*] (Paris 1972).

mendicant religion was 'fictitious and of new institution'; we might translate the phrase as 'new-fangled'. He did not dispute the charge, not here at least, but held that however 'fictitious and new' it might be, the order was good, since it led men to follow Christ. That was found compatible with the view that the franciscan rule or way of life was not something new, but a renewal.[9]

A novelty could now be judged on its merits, instead of being 'presumed guilty'. How account for the change? The pace of events imposed it. Unprecedented phenomena sprang up like mushrooms. To observe is to evaluate, especially for men whose interests are affected and who have been trained to moralise. In some cases the novelty was accepted tacitly without any acknowledged *volte face*. No cleric to my knowledge stated that the communal movement was 'a good thing after all'. But towns gained privileges and became more or less self-governing corporations, with or without bloodshed, so extensively that communes and *bonnes villes* turned into a fact of life. A moralist like Stephen of Tournai complained that townsmen abused their privileges; he did not urge that the privileges should be withdrawn. Theologians and civil and canon lawyers settled down to analyse and classify the various kinds of corporations and 'universities' which they observed. Their studies were objective, penetrating and realistic, as the late Pierre Michaud-Quantin has shown in his book on thirteenth-century notions of *universitas*. The college, commune and *studium* ceased to be novelties to schoolmen; they were now data to be examined.[10]

Other new movements had such obvious usefulness for the regulation of christendom that their momentum could hardly be put into question. No member of society could escape the impact of canon law, least of all the lawyers who studied and helped to make it. The development had critics. St Bernard deplored the amount of legal business, which, as he thought, prevented the pope from attending to the more important duty of pastoral care. But even his reproach to Eugenius III in his *De consideratione* admits that the pope could do little

[9] *Opera* 5 (Quaracchi 1891) p 492: Dicit 'ordo fictitius est, de novo institutus . . .' . . . Carissimi! quantumcumque sit ordo fictitius et novus, est tamen bonus . . . *Ibid* 8 (1898) p 393, *Expositio super Regulam*: . . . Non est ergo haec Regula aut vita nova res, sed procul dubio renovata . . .
On the authorship of the *Expositio* see now S. Clasen, 'Bonaventuras Expositio super regulam Fratrum Minorum', *S. Bonaventura 1274–1974* (Grottaferrata, Rome, 1974) 1, pp 531–70, where the contested ascription to Bonaventure is rejected in Bonaventure's favour.
[10] *Universitas, expressions du mouvement communautaire dans le moyen âge latin* (Paris 1970).

more than try to control the flood of appeals to Rome; there was no stopping them from coming in.[11] Canon lawyers were not allergic to the charge of novelty. Their work immunised them. No amount of *concordantia discordantium canonum* could cover up their innovations. A recent study of the twelfth-century canonists' attitude to the early church as a standard of righteousness has shown that they were well aware of its distance from the contemporary church. They saw many divergencies in discipline and in permitted practices from the arrangements of the early christians as described in the new testament. Changing times required new measures to meet new needs. Canonists did not feel guilty on that account.[12] Untroubled by nostalgia for the past, they saw the church as an expanding concern. Canon law was a growth industry, beneficial to christendom in general and to themselves in particular.

Heresy posed a new problem to defenders of novelty, and forced them to apologise. They had to find reasons for what canonists took for granted. Heretics, the waldensians in the forefront, reproached catholics for having departed from the customs of the early church. The wealth of the medieval church had brought abuses, laxity, litigation and a host of rules and practices which had no authority in scripture. An obvious answer to the sectaries' charge was *Tu quoque*: they, too, made new regulations for their members. It was true, since every religious organisation has to make rules to guide its faithful and keep them up to scratch. But the pendant to *Tu quoque* is that two blacks do not make a white. Catholic apologists went further and defended innovation as wholesome and God-given. I shall quote from two anti-heretical treatises to illustrate the type of argument put forward and to show how defence of novelty gained in depth and assurance. Neither of my writers was original in his ecclesiology. The interesting point is the way they deployed their arguments.

Master Prepositinus of Cremona (or Pseudo-Prepositinus; the authorship is still disputed) wrote probably in the early years of the thirteenth century. He met the heretics' objection: 'Ecclesiastical institutions are superfluous; Christians are bound to obey the ten commandments and the faith of Christ only, and not the institutions of men.'[13] Prepositinus answered that Christ's guidance to his church

[11] *S. Bernardi Opera* 3 ed J. Lerclercq and H. M. Rochais (Rome 1963) pp 435–9.
[12] G. Olsen, 'The Idea of the *Ecclesia Primitiva* in the Writings of the Twelfth-Century Canonists', *Traditio* 25 (1969) pp 61–86.
[13] *The Summa contra Haereticos ascribed to Praepositinus of Cremona,* ed J. N. Garvin and J. A. Corbett (Notre Dame, Indiana, 1958) pp 158–63. The chapter heading *Contra*

was a continuous process. He left his commandments to us in the gospels; he commanded other things through the apostles, and he now commands other things through the church. Taking a leaf from the canonists' book, the writer points out that masters in the schools recognise changes when they say: 'This *decretum* has been abolished, or its force is altered by the sequel or by a custom contrary to it.' He then makes a distinction between the various types of commandment. Ecclesiastical institutions are not precisely additions to the gospels; they prepare us to understand God's commands and to follow them more easily. The church of today fills in details, as though a master should order a servant to cross the sea and leave it to a friend to tell him when and where, and what provision to make for his journey. Prepositinus makes a far-reaching claim when he quotes the text: *He who is not with me is against me* (Mk. 9, 39). Therefore, what is not against Christ must be for him. In this light he interprets the role of doctors and prelates, who supply what the apostles failed to make plain when the church orders christendom by the revelation of the Holy Spirit. He allowed them a wide scope indeed. To put his view in modern language, he contrasted the static church of the sectaries with the dynamic church of the catholics; ecclesiastical institutions grow out of their originals by a healthy drive for survival.

The dominican inquisitor, Moneta of Cremona, working in Milan, wrote his *Adversus Catharos et Valdensienses* in 1241 or perhaps some ten years later.[14] He offers us a bolder sweep of history. The church has had a continuous existence since the time of Abel. Moneta uses this traditional theme against the heretics skilfully. A church which exists throughout time must necessarily change with the times. She has passed from the law of nature, through the written law to the law of grace. Continuity must include innovation. The jews themselves made good additions to their institutions, as when the Rechabites were established and when David recruited singers for divine service. We read in their *Acts* that the apostles altered some arrangements of the early church. How much more then must the church of today add her quota to the long history of changes, divinely ordained? Current

---

Passaginos is mistaken, since the *Passagini* believed in the obligation to keep both the Old and the New Law. On anti-heretical tracts *c*1185–1200 see C. Thouzellier, *Catharisme et Valdéisme en Languedoc à la fin du XIIe et au début du XIIIe siècle* (2 ed Louvain/Paris 1969) pp 49–129.

[14] G. Schmitz-Valckenberg, *Grundlehren katharischer Sekten des 13 Jahrhunderts* (Munich 1971) p 4.

abuses do not justify the heretics' action in leaving the church. Abuses simply show the other side of the coin; they are part of the church's history from the beginning. Moneta has absorbed innovation into his *Heilsgeschichte*.[15]

The sharpest polemic on innovation in the twelfth century centred on the rise of new religious orders. These proliferated: there were white monks, black and white canons regular, military orders and hermits, living singly or in groups. Traditionalists, including black monks and secular clergy, attacked their novelties; the innovators defended themselves. A satirical poem by a secular canon of Chartres called Pain Bolotin provides a forceful example of attack; Pain wrote *c*1121–36 (?). He criticised hermits in particular, but all the new religious orders were *visés*. His poem strikes a sinister apocalyptic note, anticipating the anti-mendicant polemic of William of St Amour. 'We all know this novelty in religion,' he writes: 'We cannot doubt that false hermits presage the coming of Doomsday, when we see so many religious monstrosities arise.' The four horsemen of the apocalypse signify the four types of enemies of the church: pagans, persecutors, heretics and finally hypocrites. Pain interpreted the 'pale horse' as presaging hypocrites and identified them with hermits and other self-righteous innovators. Hence novelty is not only bad in itself; it prophesies something worse, that is the coming of Antichrist; the new orders make ready for him.[16]

Most of the combatants in the battle of words had to wage a war on two fronts. The black monks, traditionalist as they were, had to defend themselves against the secular clergy. The latter objected to the priesthood of monks plus their right to minister to the people outside the monastery and to take tithes.[17] The priesthood of monks was nothing new in the twelfth century; but it came under fiercer fire than formerly. It was certainly novel if one took the *Rule* of St Benedict as a standard. The early monks had not received holy orders, as opponents of monastic priesthood were quick to point out. The black monks therefore had to defend the change in their status. On the other hand, they attacked innovators such as the cistercians, since the stricter religious orders showed up the black monks' decline from their

[15] *Adversus Catharos et Valdensienses* (Rome 1743) pp 408, 443, 446.

[16] J. Leclercq, 'Le poème de Payen Bolotin contre les faux hermites', *Revue Bénédictine* 48 (1958) pp 52–68; see especially pp 74, 84, 81.

[17] On the whole subject see G. Constable, *Monastic Tithes and their Origins to the Twelfth Century* (Cambridge 1964) and M. Chibnall, 'Monks and Pastoral Work' *JEH* 18 (1967) pp 165–71.

early standards. The canons regular had to meet attacks from both
the secular clergy and black and white monks combined. Philip of
Harvengt, abbot of Bonne Espérance, a house of praemonstratensian
(white) canons, put it neatly when he wrote about 1158 that black and
white monks quarrelled with one another, only to join forces against
canons regular.[18]

The polemic gives us a birdseye view of changing attitudes to novelty. The first and commonest line of argument was to outbid
tradition by seeking to prove that what looked novel really went back
to antiquity. The combatants ransacked the old and new testaments
for precedents. Success in finding them obviated the charge of novelty;
failure would leave one's flank exposed. Both monks and canons
claimed Christ and the apostles as their predecessors. The monks held
that Christ and his apostles had lived as monks. Later on, they claimed,
as the number of christians multiplied and decay set in, those who
wished to maintain the early norm of life had separated themselves
from the main body of christians in order to live as religious.
Therefore monks had priority over other christians. The canons
denied that Christ and his apostles had lived as monks. Monasticism
was a later development in the church. Therefore canons had priority
over monks. The old testament provided its quota of precedents. The
levites prefigured christian priesthood; that was unquestionable in
catholic tradition. Therefore all priests had priority over all other
churchmen. Both secular priests and canons regular made capital
out of the levites. The monks cashed in on them by claiming that
all those who received holy orders, as monks now did, derived from
the levitical priesthood as much as any other priests. They fell back
on the old testament prophets as a second line of defence. The prophets
and holy men of the old testament had lived as monks or hermits, thus
forging a link between the monasticism of the old testament and the
gospels.

The ingenuity which went into this search for biblical origins can
be illustrated by two contrasting examples. The first is academic and
scholarly. Professor Constable has edited the *Libellus de diversis ordinibus
et professionibus qui sunt in Aecclesia*, composed by a canon who called
himself 'R'.[19] He probably came from the diocese of Liège and wrote
in the period 1121-61. His attitude to the diverse religious orders

---

[18] D. Roby, 'Philip of Harvengt's contribution on the question of passage from one
religious order to another', *Analecta Praemonstratensia* 49 (1973) pp 69-100.

[19] Ed with transl. and notes by G. Constable and B. Smith (Oxford Medieval Texts 1972).

suggests that he was a canon regular, not of the strictest observance. 'R' set up as a peacemaker. His eirenic purpose was to justify diversity. The church had room for religious orders of all kinds, from the cluniacs and other black monks of milder observance, through the various branches of canons regular to the white monks. All of them enriched the church; all served christendom in their different ways. 'R' makes his point by finding precedents in both testaments for each and all of the orders in turn. His interest for us as an example is that his purpose gave him wider scope for precedent hunting than any other contestant, since he was justifying all ways of life and not one only. This collector of religions shows scholarly expertise. The editor's helpful table of concordances or parallels between biblical originals and the various orders brings it out at a glance. Each of the old testament tribes, whether dwelling in town or country, or centred on the capital city of Jerusalem, serves as a prototype for some present-day order, whose members commonly found their houses in towns or choose rural solitude. New testament characters offer a second set of prototypes. Hence all orders were needed and none was novel, if examined closely with an eye to the bible. Each one derived from an original whose function in ministry, prayer, contemplation and alms-giving corresponded to its own special brand of religion.

My second precedent hunter was an amateur enthusiast for antiquity. He leads us from the sphere of biblical scholarship to fantasy. The knights hospitallers of St John of Jerusalem had a strong incentive to make themselves respectable by disclaiming the charge of innovation. The military orders of knights templars and hospitallers grew in response to the needs of the crusades and of the latin colonists of Palestine. They broke with religious precedent in that their members were laymen, apart from their chaplains. Moreover, instead of taking vows of stability and expecting to remain in one house of the order, a novice put himself at the disposal of superiors who could send him anywhere at any time, to fight or to collect revenue or to rule over dependancies. He belonged to a supra-national network and his duties were fluid. The hospitallers at first served hospitals for the care of sick and poor pilgrims. They took over military service under pressure to help in the defence of Outremer. The resulting type of organisation was so new that even papal approval did not quench the knights' thirst for ancestors. And they owed it to themselves that the Hospital should rival the Temple.

The story, which took shape perhaps as early as 1140–1150, told

106

that the Hospital had been founded by Judas Machabeus; a garbled version of an incident recounted 2 Machab. 12, 43 authenticated the claim. Then Zacharias, father of St John the Baptist, the order's patron, served the Hospital until divine command released him and he was followed by 'Julian the Roman'. Julian belongs to the realm of fiction. The emperor Augustus sent him, an honest Roman, to collect tribute from the jews. His companions on the journey all perished in a ship-wreck; but Julian was saved by the Son of God and sent to serve the Hospital in succession to Zacharias. One version of the story is ascribed to the historian Josephus. The author of *The Jewish War*, widely read in its latin translation, cast his cloak over 'Julian the Roman'. Who was more likely to tell of his mission to Judaea? After this *tour de force*, it was child's play to put new testament scenes into a Hospital setting: here Jesus healed the sick; here lived his disciples and his mother after the ascension; St Stephen was the first Master of the order.[20]

Both canon 'R' and the unnamed fakers of the Hospital legend counter the charge of novelty by linking themselves to the past, much as a *nouveau riche* will pay genealogists to supply him with ancestors. In other words, they and their like admitted the blame attached to novelty, but parried it by stretching history like a piece of elastic in order to settle safely inside.

The cistercians had a readier answer. They were observing the *Rule* of St Benedict 'to the letter', stripping it of all those customs and relaxations which it had accumulated through the years. 'Innovator yourself!' they replied to their black monk critics. Customs added to the *Rule* were innovations, and bad ones, since they detracted from the primitive simplicity desired by the founder. The black monks defended changes, which they could not deny, on the grounds that christian charity obliged them to temper the wind to weaker brethren or that modern monks could not bear the rigours of old times; to insist on the primitive *Rule* would have meant ex-cluding many potential religious from the path of salvation. Apolo-gists for black monk institutions tended to be rather shamefaced. They could hardly defend the changes made to the *Rule* as good in them-selves, much less evolve any theory in favour of change.[21] Tradition confronted tradition; so the earliest tradition would win.

[20] J. S. C. Riley-Smith, *The Knights of St John in Jerusalem and Cyprus 1050–1310* (London 1967) pp 32–59.
[21] M. D. Knowles, *The Historian and Character and Other Essays* (Cambridge 1963) pp 50–75; 'Peter the Venerable: Champion of Cluny', *JEH* 19 (1968) pp 213–17;

The cistercian order, however, attracted men of intelligence as well as piety. The first breakthrough on the question of religious novelties came from cistercian circles, when white monks came to the rescue of other new orders. Novelties could be holy and blessed, without being hallowed by precedent. St Bernard's letter in praise of the knights templars springs to mind (1128–36). In *De laude novae militiae* Bernard stressed the newness of this military order. The crusade itself was a new movement and Bernard never doubted the righteousness of killing obstinate infidels. The holy war sanctified participants. God's holy places belonged to christians and cried out to be defended. Hence the templars represented a new and holy type of warrior, fufilling a new need. It is true that the abbot of Clairvaux cited biblical prophecies predicting the christian conquest of Jerusalem, which the templars helped to keep in latin hands. He fits the New Militia into God's plan of salvation; but the plan had room for novelties and indeed required them for its fulfilment.[22] The man who pitched into Abelard for his theological novelties justified a novel type of fighter.

Bernard's friend William of St Thierry defended the carthusians for their innovation in his *Golden Letter to the Brothers of Mont Dieu* (1144–8). William, former abbot of St Thierry, joined the cistercian order as a convert and wrote as a monk of Signy, to encourage the carthusians to persevere in their solitary way of life in spite of difficulties and criticism. This scholar monk had a keen awareness of the changes in all spheres of human activity which he observed. He saw them as a natural consequence of God's provision for mankind. God endowed man, even fallen man, with the natural wit he needed, not only for mere life, but for civilised living too. A sparkling passage in *The Golden Letter* describes the opportunities open to contemporaries. There were new discoveries in architecture, in sciences and arts and new varieties of positions and posts (choice of careers in the world). Such novelties could be exploited by good men and bad men alike. Their value depended on the purpose to which they were put by their users.

G. Constable, *The Letters of Peter the Venerable* (Cambridge, Mass., 1967) 1, pp 52–8, 2, pp 270–4; A. Wilmart, 'Une riposte de l'ancien monachisme au manifeste de Saint Bernard', *Revue Bénédictine* 46 (1934) pp 296–344; J. Leclercq, 'Nouvelle réponse de l'ancien monachisme aux critiques des Cisterciens', *ibid* 67 (1957) pp 77–94; C. H. Talbot, 'The Date and Authorship of the "Riposte",' *Studia Anselmiana* 40 (1956) pp 72–80.

[22] Ed cit 3, pp 213–39; on the date see *ibid* p 207. On criticisms of the templars see J. Leclercq, 'Un document sur les débuts des Templiers', *RHE* 52 (1957) pp 81–91.

William welcomed religious as well as secular novelties with the same proviso. The carthusian type was 'no empty pursuit of newness'. Novelty inhered in religion, and had done since the earliest times, from the prophets to Jesus and afterwards. He poured scorn on men who carped at 'the mere name of novelty': 'with their minds set in the old ways they do not know how to think new thoughts.'[23] This is an impressive attitude towards changes in both secular and religious affairs. I have to admit that William did not co-ordinate his ideas, but threw out his remarks in passing; he made no bridge between the two passages which I have quoted, though both must have sprung from the same process of thought.

To find a co-ordinated theory of religious change, we must turn to a white canon, Anselm of Havelberg. He certainly experienced changes in his own career. First a scholar, then a praemonstratensian canon, then bishop of Havelberg, a border diocese, a leader of the wendish crusade of 1147 as papal legate, an envoy to Constantinople, where he disputed with greek churchmen, he died as archbishop of Ravenna in 1158. Book 1 of his *Dialogues* (c1149) presents a theory of *Heilsgeschichte* specially designed to accommodate novelties.[24] Modern scholars have spilled rivers of ink on Anselm's theory. Briefly, he divided the history of the church into seven ages, corresponding to the seven 'states' of the apocalyptic prophecies. Elaborating on a traditional theme, he identified his own time with the fourth age, when the church was persecuted by hypocrites and false brethren. The hypocrites persecuted the church by decrying religious reform and new orders. Here he neatly reversed Pain Bolotin's identification of hypocrites as false hermits and other 'enthusiasts'. The whole history of the church, as Anselm told it, called for novelties as useful, indeed essential, to her well-being. He had already defended his own order of white canons against attacks on it by a black monk abbot on the score that the canons' mixed life of action and contemplation served a pressing need.[25] Now, in the *Dialogues*, he found a wider framework in which he could present novelties as a constant factor in the history of salvation and could praise variety. The diversity of

[23] On William of St Thierry see *DSAM* 6, pp 1241–63. I quote the English translation of *The Golden Epistle* by T. Berkeley, Cistercian Fathers Series 12 (Spencer, Mass., 1971) pp 32, 11–12; for the latin text see *PL* 184 (1858) cols 317, 310–11.

[24] *Dialogues* 1, ed with french translation and notes by G. Salet, *SC* 118 (1966); J. W. Braun, 'Studien zum Uberlieferung der Werke Anselms von Havelberg', *Deutsches Archiv* 27 (1972) pp 133–209.

[25] *Epistola ad Egbertum, PL* 183 (1858) cols 1119–20.

religious orders, including military orders, were beneficial to christendom. Anselm approved of diversity, as did canon 'R'. Unlike 'R', he saw no reason to defend it by searching for precedents; the old need not be good, nor the new bad in his view.

Anselm may perhaps have been influenced by Hugh of St Victor (d. 1141). The victorine master, too, saw the church's history as a continuous process through time. History provided the clue to his theology and to his account of the arts and sciences.[26] He does not come into the controversy on religious innovation as I have outlined it, since he never set himself to defend any particular novelty. It is significant that in his letter to the knights templars he differs from St Bernard in making no mention of their newness as an order; he simply encourages them to continue in the active religious life which they have chosen on the plea that the church needs them to fight for christians in the holy land.[27] Hugh was not a polemicist. He took for granted what his contemporaries picked on as a battlefield.

The debate on religious novelties has taken up a disproportionate amount of space. The reason is that they provoked more discussion than other kinds, because they touched *esprit de corps*. Individual writers sharpened their pens for the service of their orders. Rivalry, jealousy and competition for recruits and patronage made the argument a matter of bread-and-butter, as well as prestige. Genuine concern and perplexity on the question of where to find the perfect way of life raised the debate to higher levels. The 'crossroads' of religious life stirred seekers after perfection to agonising reappraisals.[28]

The anti-mendicant polemic and the friars' defence of themselves in the thirteenth century offers an anticlimax from the point of view of attitudes to novelty, although this pamphlet warfare has many other interesting features. Conservatives now fought with their backs to the wall. After the defeat of William of St Amour the friars' enemies aimed at restricting their privileges rather than at abolishing their orders. Perhaps the existence of so many 'bad' novelties in the crisis of christendom around 1200 in the shape of heresies and growing anti-clericalism called for 'good' novelties as a remedy. The rise of

[26] R. W. Southern, 'Aspects of the European Tradition of Historical Writing: 2. Hugh of St Victor and the Idea of Historical Development'. *TRHS*, 5 series, 21 (1971) pp 159–79.

[27] C. Sclafert, 'Lettre inédite de Hugues de Saint-Victor aux Chevaliers du Temple', *RAM* 34 (1958) pp 275–99.

[28] M.-D. Chenu, 'Moines, Clercs, Laïques. Au carrefour de la vie évangélique', *La théologie au XIIe siècle* (Paris 1957) pp 225–51.

populous cities and university towns, breeding grounds of heresy and of ignorance, as the parish system broke down, ensured a future for the friars They melted into the landscape with surprising speed.

We shall now turn to the schools. *De faire du neuf, d'etre des hommes nouveaux, les intellectuels du XIIe siècle en ont le vif sentiment.* This is professor Le Goff's impression of the scholars.[29] It is validated by their pushing self-confidence and by the titles which teachers of the liberal arts gave to their books: *Poetria nova, Rhetorica novissima*. Gerald of Wales, admittedly an individualist, prided himself on the novelty of his books on Ireland. Some even gloried in their claims to have discovered things new and unheard of, according to Hugh of St Cher, teaching at Paris 1230–1235[29a]

Theologians walked more warily. No theologian called his book *The New Theology*. There was much blame of 'overstepping the bounds set by the fathers in pursuit of vain curiosity'. Such blame served as a smokescreen, behind which the masters of theology produced new questions, new answers, and new attempts at synthesis. The proceedings against Abelard and Gilbert of la Porrée acted as a catalyst. From 1148 onwards the parisian theologians were left to censure themselves, without much interference from the hierarchy. Their language was so obscure, in any case, that few outside the élite really knew what they were at. Walter of St Victor's diatribe against new doctors and new doctrines (c1180) fell on deaf ears, as far as we know. The popes understood the usefulness of the schools to themselves and to christendom and protected them, as they did the mendicant orders. The pragmatic, optimistic attitude of the canon lawyers to novelty came into play; many of the popes had trained as canonists and depended on canon lawyers for advice and for business affairs. The 'new Aristotle' revived old fears; but the papal ban on the teaching of the *libri naturales* in the arts course did not prevent them from becoming set texts there. The monastic response to the rise of the schools illustrates how yesterday's novelty took its place as part of today's establishment: monasteries hired friars, trained in universities or *studia*, as lecturers to keep the brothers up to date on theology; both black and white monks founded houses of study for their members in universities. The monk student joined the seculars and friars as fellow academics.

It may be asked whether secular government had the same history

[29] J. Le Goff *Les intellectuels au moyen âge* (Paris 1957) p 14.
[29a]*Postilla in Bibliam* (Paris 1530–45) *ad* Eccles. i, 10.

of reaction to novelty as bad and final acceptance of it as possibly good. The modern historian sees developments in bureaucracy, law-making, and judicial and financial administration in the twelfth and thirteenth centuries which impress him just as much as innovation in other fields. My impression, as far as it goes, is that secular government gives us an exception to prove the rule. There were reasons for it. If we begin with churchmen at the receiving end of governmental development, we notice at once that novelties affected their pockets in the form of new exactions and new restrictions on clerical privilege. Governments continually laid new and heavier burdens on their subjects. Taxpayers, whether clerks or laymen, could hardly be expected to welcome royal and papal taxation as 'a good thing'; in fact they denounced it bitterly. Nor did their acceptance of it become less grudging as methods of assessment and collection gained in sophistication and efficiency, rather the reverse.

If we look at churchmen as participants in secular government, we might expect to find a more positive response. As chancellors, justices and counsellors or as lower-grade bureaucrats, churchmen helped to create and invent means by which power could reach out to wider areas. Bureaucrats are not given to speculation. It would have called for a gigantic effort of reappraisal to overcome the old notion that temporal power was punitive. Tradition presented it as a sad consequence of original sin, and 'good' only in so far as it quelled snatch-and-grab by keeping each man in his place in the social hierarchy. Appearances were for such a view: government in the twelfth and early thirteenth centuries concerned itself mainly with the repression of crime and rebellion and with warfare. Expenditure on warfare stimulated governments to devise new means of increasing their revenues more than any other demand on their budgets.[30] No amount of propaganda could avail in the long run to persuade victims of the new regulations that the wars would benefit them, when their rulers so often suffered defeat after pouring their subjects' money down the drain and then asking for more. It need not surprise us that civil servants kept off the task of justifying novelties. Their propaganda for the ruler, if it was entrusted to them, followed other lines. We hear of 'reforming the peace' and 'renewal of empire'. The best that can be done is to present the ruler as going back to the good old days. Again

[30] See for instance J. O. Prestwich, 'War and Finance in the Anglo-Norman State', *TRHS*, 5 series, 4 (1954) pp 19–44; J. M. Powell, 'Medieval Monarchy and Trade', *Studi medievali*, 3 series, 3 (1962) pp 420–524.

appearances and fact, too, explain why the very term 'novelty' was inapt to describe government measures, even those which we might now rate as constructive. They took place against a background of custom; they were often *ad hoc* and unspectacular. The practice of summoning representatives of estates or local communities to attend 'parliaments', which developed throughout most kingdoms of Europe, including the papal states, strikes us as significant and exciting. Contemporaries hardly noticed it, because they had been conditioned to the view that rulers should consult their free subjects at all levels.[31] The reforms of Henry II Plantagenet provide a litmus test of the civil service attitude to novelty. Richard Fitzneal in his *Dialogue of the Exchequer* and the author of *On the Laws of England*, ascribed to Glanvill, both take pride in the efficient working of angevin government. 'Glanvill' even calls the grand assize 'a royal benefit granted to the people by the goodness of the king acting on the advice of his magnates.'[32] But both writers aim at setting out how institutions work in practice. The question of novelty versus tradition does not come into it.

With that understandable exception novelty lost its stigma. Innovation could be beneficial in some cases. Nothing vague and general, like Bury's 'Idea of Progress' gained currency. Tradition was not devalued. It was simply that churchmen came to accept or even welcome efforts to improve and adapt out-dated institutions or invent new ones. The benefits of innovation are self-evident to us. They were not so in the early twelfth century, witness the mental labour expended on finding arguments to justify change. Some writers defended changes on the grounds that they were really antiquities in disguise, 'mutton dressed as lamb'; and that was a compliment, not an insult. Others defended them as useful to the church. The second was the more promising line. It expressed a view of the church in society and politics as a growing institution. The history of salvation showed that novelties formed part of the divine plan. Religion especially was presented as a process of incessant renewal; a tree puts out new shoots from the parent stem as the sap rises. St Thomas Aquinas normally tested institutions according to whether they conduced to 'the common good'. The way had been prepared for his attitude in the debates of his forerunners. The novelties themselves came first in time. They

[31] T. N. Bisson, *Assemblies and representation in Languedoc in the thirteenth century* (Princeton 1964) gives a general bibliography.
[32] Ed with notes and translation by G. D. G. Hall, *Medieval Texts* (London 1965) p 28.

battered on men's consciousness and forced them to take stock of new situations.

Finally, I shall raise a question which cannot be answered for lack of evidence. History would be a duller subject than it is if historians limited themselves to questions which admit of answers on the evidence available. My question here is whether current cosmological theories of change affected churchmen's attitude to changes on earth. Did physics and metaphysics have anything to do with reactions to novelty? To argue for this as a possibility one could begin with St Augustine. In his platonist or neoplatonist thought-world change meant decay. God punished fallen man by subjecting him to change together with the lower part of creation. Everything on 'our middle earth' tended to crumble and deteriorate. Man's foremost task in this life was to raise his eyes above earthly things and fix them on the eternal and un-changing, in so far as a sinful mortal could.[33] The individual could be converted and change for the better, as St Augustine had done, and could try to help his fellows; that was all. Readers of St Augustine and those educated in his tradition would tend to assume that changes must be from bad to worse. Granted that terrestrial institutions, however imperfect, saved man from the chaos brought about by original sin, then they were better let alone or else preserved from attack by would-be reformers. The divine order, adapted to an evil world, looked static and capable only of preservation, not of improvement.

The reception and study of the corpus of writings ascribed to St Denis the Areopagite offered an alternative picture of the universe, although medieval scholars often amalgamated the two traditions or attempted a synthesis.[34] The celestial and ecclesiastical hierarchies described by Pseudo-Dionysius (the ranks of angels corresponding to the ranks of prelates and priests and lesser orders) is static in that each creature, visible or invisible, has its own degree and must stay there. On the other hand, the members of each degree in the hierarchies must help those in the next lower degree to realise their potential and to move as far upward as their divinely fixed nature allows. Hugh of St Victor, who had a historical vision of the church proceeding through time, wrote an influential commentary on Pseudo-Dionysius.

William of St Thierry drew on another greek patristic tradition in

---

[33] H. I. Marrou, *L'Ambivalence du Temps de l'Histoire chez S. Augustin* (Paris 1950).
[34] R. Roques, *L'Univers Dionysien: structure hiérarchique du monde selon le Pseudo-Denys* (Paris 1954).

114

latin translation. He based his religious and philosophical thinking
on the theme of 'withdrawal and return'.[35] The whole of creation is
in a state of flux, *egressus/regressus*. Creatures flowed from the Godhead
and are returning to their source, thanks to the saving work of Christ
and the Holy Spirit. It is not a pantheistic view, since the creatures
retain their individualities. Motion implies change. We have seen
that William observed both secular and religious changes in the world
around him and welcomed them if they were rightly used. Did the
influence of greek patristic writings impart a sense of movement into
the more static picture of the universe handed down by the latins?

The concept of God as immobile mover went back to Boethius. It
was known to medieval scholars through his *Consolation of Philosophy*
and could serve as an argument to prove God's existence.[36] The
reception of Aristotle's *libri naturales* in the late twelfth and early
thirteenth centuries gave it new force and a significance which it had
not had before. Aristotle directed his readers' attention to the phenomenon of motion and change, which was central to his philosophy.
Hence 'generation and corruption' became scientific terms. The
notion of agency, moving potency to act, entered into the scholars'
view of their universe.[37] Change was a fact of life, not to be deplored
as an evil, but to be registered and studied. If change became 'natural'
in the teleological sense of the word, it lost some of its horror. It would
be far-fetched to suppose that even Grosseteste, for all his interest in
natural science, had it in mind when he praised 'good' novelties. But
the *libri naturales* formed the climate in which educated men lived
and thought. We are not always conscious of the way in which our
schooling in one subject seeps into our ideas on something quite
different.

A more down-to-earth suggestion comes from Walter Freund's
study of the notion of *Modernus* in the middle ages. In an excursus on
the meaning of *Novus* he points to use of the term in ancient and
medieval literature. It often denoted 'surprising' or 'unexpected' and
therefore 'frightening'. 'New' in this context expresses man's helpless-

[35] See above n 23. The theme of 'withdrawal and return' informs the *De divisione naturae*
of John Scot Erigena; but this early ninth-century book was not widely read in the
twelfth century; see *Iohannis Scotti Erivgenae Periphyseon*, ed I. P. Sheldon-Williams, 1
(Dublin 1968) pp 1–25, 32–3.
[36] P. Courcelle, *La Consolation de Philosophie dans la tradition littéraire* (Paris 1967)
pp 179–89.
[37] On latin translations and their dates see *Aristoteles Latinus*, ed G. Lacombe and others, 1
(Rome 1939) pp 49–61; 2 (Cambridge 1955) pp 787–8.

ness in face of a strange situation, which he cannot control; he feels all at sea because he has no precedent to guide him.[38] It might be argued that in the period *c*1100–*c*1250 men gained more control of their environment. Production and trade reached a higher level, in spite of war and famines. Economic prosperity may have pushed back the zone of the terrifying unknown a little further. Although churchmen generally distrusted merchants and their new business techniques, thriving trade and industry with the opportunities to raise the standard of living which they brought may have induced a greater sense of security. Bonaventure suggested that famines were a thing of the past when disputing at Paris in 1255/6.[39]

My provisional dossier on churchmen's attitudes to novelty will have shown that they became more positive in the period *c*1100–*c*1250. Conservatives and reactionaries are a constant factor in history. Spokesmen in favour of novelties won a verbal victory at least in this century and a half. They won it after a long and painful battle of words, and more than words only. Builders of institutions went about their work and contributed novelties without making a fuss. Lawyers and scholars took novelties in their stride. After posing some unanswerable questions on the intellectual background to this change, I shall end with one more question, which could be answered by someone willing to sift the evidence available for the late thirteenth and fourteenth centuries. Did novelty shed its newly acquired respectability and slip backwards, to become a term of abuse? The crises of the later middle ages make it seem likely that this would happen. Perhaps so, or perhaps there is no simple answer.

---

[38] *Modernus und andere Zeitbegriffe des Mittelalters*, Neue münstersche Beiträge zur Geschichtsforchung, ed K. von Raumer, 4, (1957) pp 107–8.
[39] Dufeuil pp 176, 183.

Note:
p. 109, n. 27, read Revue d'ascétique et de mystique for RAM.
The ascription to Hugh of St. Victor remains uncertain. See R. Baron, *Etudes sur Hugues de Saint-Victor* (Paris, 1963) 45

7

GREGORY IX AND THE TWO FACES OF THE SOUL

Soon after his accession to the papacy in March, 1227, Gregory IX wrote to the emperor, Frederic II, urging him to fulfil his vow to lead a crusade. The letter was written at Anagni, July 22.[1] Its tone is of fatherly advice and encouragement. Frederic has outstanding gifts of intellect and great potentialities for good in his character. Let him use them in the service of God and of the Christian people. Gregory introduces a note of warning: the emperor must beware lest his lower instincts should frustrate his natural abilities. Heaven forbid that this should happen, since now the welfare of this temporal world depends on his carrying out his promise.

In describing the excellence of Frederic's understanding the letter refers to the two faces of his soul, corresponding to its two powers, the *virtus motiva* and the *virtus comprehensiva*. The reference is intertwined with a biblical comparison. God has placed him as a cherubim with *a flaming sword, turning every way, to keep the way of the tree of life* (Gen. iii. 24). 'The way of the tree of life', as the letter subsequently explains, is the crusade, which Frederic must lead in order to free the holy places. 'The flaming sword, turning every way' (*versatilis*), is Frederic's soul, with its two faces, turned each in a different direction, and its two powers. These in their turn suggest its capacity for either good or evil. The passage reads:

Ad ostendendam viam ligni vite errantibus in invio mundi huius, posuit te Dominus quasi cherubim et versatilem gladium. Cum enim diligenti meditatione pensatur ratio in te illuminata dono intelligentie naturalis et imaginatio discreta in rei comprehensione sensibilis, que quasi versatilis una facie respicit rationem, alia naturam sensibilium intuetur, in te virtus motiva manifeste conspicitur qua possis inconveniens a conveniente distinguere et comprehensiva qua facile valeas conveniens et licitum obtinere. Donum sane tibi scientie desuper attribute et virtus perfecte imaginationis in manu opicifis resultantis quasi

---

[1] L. Auvray, *Les registres de Grégoire IX*, Paris, 1896, vol. I, col. 79, no. 142. The letter is dated here but not re-edited.

118

duo luminaria magna, duo dona celestia, viam ligni in qua vita nostra pependit
et terram promissionis ostendunt; ista duo vexilla que Deus erexit in anime tue
corporeis instrumentis tota sequitur militia Christiana, quin potius sequitur totus
mundus a paradyso pure conscientie merito sue prevaricationis exclusus. Et
ideo est summopere precavendum ne vexillum quod habes commune cum angelis,
intellectus viz. et affectus, inclines ad id quod habet homo commune cum brutis
scilicet et arbustis, sensum et nutrimentum, quia et amor sensibilium minuit
intellectum et effectum deformat delicati corporis nutrimentum. . . .

Absit a te hoc, fili charissime, a quo videtur modo vita huius mundi sensibilis
dependere. . . .[1]

If we subtract the biblical metaphors from this passage, we are left
with Avicenna's *De anima*. This was the source of the theory of the *virtus
activa* and *contemplativa*, or *motiva* and *comprehensiva* as they are called here,
and of the two faces of the soul.[2] The theory became popular through the
De immortalitate animae of William of Auvergne, quoting Gundissalinus.[3]
The date of William's treatise is not quite certain. He was teaching
theology at Paris by 1223 and Gregory appointed him bishop of Paris in
1228. His *De anima*, which quotes the *De immortalitate animae*, appeared
in 1230.[4] Gregory's allusion, however, seems to be closer to the actual
text of Avicenna than to Gundissalinus.[5] The theory had a brilliant future,
since it combined with the Augustinian teaching on the higher and lower
reason in the human intellect. The Franciscans especially adopted it and
made it a characteristic doctrine of their Order. M. Gilson has summarized:

On peut donc dire qu'il y a deux faces de l'âme: l'une par laquelle elle

[1]) J. L. A. Huillard-Bréholles, *Historia diplomatica Frederici II*, Paris, 1852, III, 7-8.

[2]) Avicenna, *Opera*, Venice, 1508, I, fol. 5ᵛ: Hec autem virtus activa est illa virtus quam habet
anima propter debitum quod debet ei quod est infra eam, scilicet corpus ad regendum aliquid. Sed
virtus contemplativa est illa virtus quam habet anima propter debitum ei quod est supra ipsam ut patiatur
ab eo et perficietur per illud et recipiat ex illo; tanquam anima nostra habeat duas facies, faciem scilicet
deorsum ad corpus, quam oportet nullatenus recipere aliquam affectionem generis debiti nature corporis.
Et aliam faciem sursum versus principia altissima quam oportet semper recipere aliquid ab eo quod est
illic et affici ab illo. Ex eo autem quod est infra eam generantur mores; sed ex eo quod est supra eam
generantur sapientie, et hec est virtus activa.

[3]) See J. Rohmer, *Sur la doctrine franciscaine des deux faces de l'âme*, Archives d'histoire doctrinale
et littéraire du moyen age, 2 [1927], 73-7.

[4]) P. Glorieux, *Répertoire des maîtres en théologie à Paris au xiiiᵉ siècle*, Paris, 1933, I, 315-20.

[5]) The text of William of Auvergne-Gundissalinus is quoted by J. Rohmer, *loc. cit.*, pp. 74-5.

regarde le corps qui est au dessous d'elle afin de le régir, c'est la vertu active
. . . l'autre par laquelle elle regarde l'intelligible qui est au dessus d'elle, afin de
le recevoir et de s'y soumettre: c'est la vertu contemplative.[1]

It is interesting to find that the papal chancery had seized on the religious
and moral implications of the doctrine as early as 1227, before the Friars
Minor had officially organized their schools.

Gregory's allusion to the two faces throws light on his own tastes
and education and on his attitude to learning. We know that he had
been a student, since he describes himself in a privilege to the university
of Paris as 'aliquando disciplinis scholasticis insudantes'.[2] His biographer
says that he was instructed in the liberal arts[3] and a contemporary calls
him 'litteratus'.[4] He is never referred to as 'magister' in contemporary
sources. It is difficult to fit a long period of study into the dates of his
career; Innocent III raised him to the cardinalate from being papal
chaplain and sub-deacon in 1198. There seems to be no ground for the
legend that he studied at Paris;[5] probably it was in a smaller school in
Italy. Dr. Haller has pointed out that Gregory was intensely receptive
to the new religious movements of his day and steeped in contemporary
piety.[6] As Cardinal Hugolino he wrote that the holy Cistercian abbot,
Rainer, whom he believed to have possessed the gift of prophecy, had
begun to initiate him into the spiritual life, but had died before completing the task.[7] He protected the memory of Joachim of Flora as well
as supporting St. Francis and the friars. The letter to Frederic II suggests
that he also sympathized with the promoters of the new arabic philosophy.
Perhaps it explains his wish to find a key place in the hierarchy for William

[1]) *Les sources gréco-arabes de l'augustinisme avicennisant*, Archives d'hist. doctr. et lit. du m.â., 4
[1929], 57.

[2]) H. Denifle, *Chartularium Universitatis Parisiensis*, Paris, 1889, vol. I, p. 127.

[3]) Muratori, *Scriptores rerum Italicarum*, vol. III, i, col. 575.

[4]) *Ignoti monachi Cisterciensis Chronicon*, ed. A. Gaudenzi, Naples, 1888, p. 38.

[5]) It is worth noticing in this connexion that Gregory states explicitly in his letter of Nov. 23,
1229, that William of Auvergne was unknown to him personally when he promoted him to be bishop:
. . . et nos ipsi qui auditu aurium potius quam experientia excitati te notis pretulimus et expertis.
(*Chartularium*, vol. I, p. 125).

[6]) *Das Papsttum*, Stuttgart, 1945, III, 47-8.

[7]) The letter is edited by Winckelmann, *Varietà*, Archivio di storia Romana, 2, 1879, p. 363.

of Auvergne.   The fact that he picked out the theory of the two faces shows his natural affinity to the Franciscan way of thought.

Gregory's letter to the regent masters in theology at Paris, July 7, 1228,[1] is much better known than his letter of the previous year to the emperor: it has got into the text-books.   Gregory warns the masters not to turn aside to secular learning nor to mingle 'the fictions of philosophers' with the word of God.   They are to teach a theology pure from all taint of secular science.   'Pratiquement impossible à suivre dans un milieu scolaire où ces fictions étaient en fait enseignées,' is M. Gilson's comment.[2] Undoubtedly, seeing that the pope himself used arguments drawn from Avicenna to persuade the emperor to go on crusade.   The prohibitions of lectures, public or private, on the *libri naturales* and their commentators were not intended to preclude private study, and papal warnings against secular science, from St. Gregory the Great downwards, ought not to be taken too literally.

Lastly, the letter to Frederic can be read as an example of the rhetorical technique of the papal chancery.   The rhetors of Bologna and other Italian schools were perfecting the art of persuasion for political and diplomatic purposes.   The study of rhetoric involved, not only style and formulae, but also the invention of those arguments which would be most likely to impress a given audience in given circumstances.[3]   The application to Frederic II and his Sicilian court is obvious.   Avicenna might succeed when Scripture failed to persuade him.

---

[1]) *Chartularium*, I, 114-6.

[2]) *La philosophie au moyen âge*, 2nd ed., Paris, 1944, p. 414.

[3]) See N. Rubinstein, *Political rhetoric in the imperial chancery during the twelfth and thirteenth centuries*, Medium Aevum, 14 [1945], 21-43.

8

WILLIAM OF AUVERGNE, JOHN OF LA ROCHELLE AND ST. THOMAS AQUINAS ON THE OLD LAW

I

INTRODUCTION

"Then I saw the patriarchs and prophets exulting in wondrous joy at having reached that country which once they greeted from afar, at witnessing the fulfilment of what they had foreseen in the spirit, and at having passed from weary waiting to eternal glory."

THESE words are spoken by *Desiderium vitae aeternae*, describing the joys of heaven in a dialogue *De custodia interioris hominis* ascribed to St. Anselm of Canterbury.[1] *Desiderium* expresses the medieval Catholic view of the Old Testament in pictorial form. Moses, both patriarch and prophet, gave a divinely revealed law to God's chosen people as a preparation for the New Law of the Gospel, which would come in the fullness of time. Then the ceremonial and judicial precepts of the Mosaic Law would be superseded, though the moral precepts would remain as having timeless value. So much was common doctrine throughout the middle ages. Readers will expect me to add that the ceremonial and judicial precepts of the Old Law were held to "prefigure" the New Law in their allegorical sense, being interpreted of Christ and the sacraments of the Church, and to signify moral teaching in their tropological sense.[2] So indeed I should have said before reading the *De legibus* of William of Auvergne. Since reading it, I prefer to say that belief in the allegorical and tropological interpretation of the Old Law was general, but not quite universal. Even supposing that it *was* universal, however, the common doctrine raised many questions on the nature and effects of the Mosaic precepts, which admitted of diverse answers. My aim in this paper is to study St. Thomas's place in the chain of question and answer: "...ici comme souvent, il synthétise une

---

1 *Memorials of Saint Anselm*, ed. R. W. Southern and F. S. Schmitt (Auctores Britannici Medii Aevi i, London 1969) 358. The tract originated in St. Anselm's circle; see ibid. 354-5.
2 See H. de Lubac, *Exégèse médiévale. Les quatre sens de l'Ecriture* (Paris 1959-1964).

122

large tradition, qu'il perfectionne en la dotant d'une forte structure intellectuelle", as Dom Gribomont wrote of his theology on the bond between the two Testaments.[3] The evolution of this wide tradition and its
complexity need more detailed analysis than they have received
hitherto.

The Law, as transmitted in the Old Testament, posed problems as
difficult, though different, for those who read it "all of a piece" as it
does for modern scholars who see it as "composite". Its divergent
traditions, its traces of magic and primitive rites, and the miscellaneous
grouping of many precepts were baffling. How could one reconcile a
God-given code, strange and anomalous as it was, with that beauty,
reason and harmony which belonged to the divine plan for the universe
and for man's place within it? Lack of the tools of modern research
closed one approach to the problem; but others were tried. A striking
change of approach came about in the twelfth and thirteenth century
schools.

The patristic tradition as known to medieval scholars stemmed from
the Latin translation of Origen. He approached the Old Law as an
apologist for the faith against both pagan philosophers and Jews and as
a preacher to Christians. To the Jews, who continued to observe their
Law, he exposed and derided the irrationality and seeming futility of
many precepts: he sought and found biblical texts where precepts contradicted one another; other texts commanded practices which were
"absurd" and even impossible to act upon; they made sense only if interpreted as figures of the Christian revelation to come. To pagan
philosophers he argued that the Old Testament should be read in its
spiritual sense. He urged upon Jews and pagan philosophers alike that
irrational, absurd and impossible precepts had the function of pointing
us to the need for a spiritual interpretation. Some precepts had no
literal sense at all; most of them demanded a spiritual interpretation of
"the letter". Origen admitted the historical reality of much of his text,
but history as such did not interest him.[4] As a preacher he couched his
teaching to the faithful in his spiritual interpretation of the Old
Testament. These homilies won for themselves a unique place in
medieval spirituality.[5] St. Gregory the Great's exegesis reinforced the

3 "Le lien des deux Testaments, selon la théologie de Saint Thomas", *Ephemerides
Theologicae Lovanienses* xxii (1946) 71.
4 R. M. Grant, *The Letter and the Spirit* (London 1957) 95-6; M. Simon, *Verus Israel. Etude
sur les relations entre chrétiens et juifs dans l'empire romain (135-425)*, 2nd ed. (Paris 1964) 87-
121, 189-203, gives a general background.
5 See among numerous studies on the subject J. Leclercq, *Receuil d'études sur S. Bernard et ses
écrits* (Storia e letteratura xcii, Rome 1962) passim.

stress on spiritual interpretation. Both Origen and St. Gregory contributed largely to the compilation of the *Glossa ordinaria* on the Pentateuch.[6] St. Jerome's Hebrew scholarship and St. Augustine's more
practical discussion of difficulties arising from the literal sense of the
Law also influenced the glossators, but could do little to alter a settled
mode of thought.[7] A monastic commentary on *Leviticus* by Ralph of St.
Germer of Flaix, written towards the middle of the twelfth century,
achieved the distinction, rare for a monastic book, of becoming a standard school text:[8] it was priced in the Paris stationers' list of 1275-1286.
Ralph on *Leviticus* came too late to be quoted in the *Gloss*, but excerpts from it were often copied into the margins of manuscripts of the
Gloss and it served as a standard supplement to the *Gloss* in lectures on
Leviticus until the late thirteenth century. Ralph's commentary on the
central book of the Law passed on the patristic spiritualist interpretation in its most extreme form. Paradoxically, he shows what a
literally minded exegete could make of it. The schoolmen therefore had
to come to terms with him, accepting, rejecting or modifying what they
found in the *originalia*, in the *Gloss* excerpts and in their standard
medieval commentary.

Ralph set out to dissuade his brethren at St. Germer from overrrating
Jewish arguments in favour of the permanence of the whole Mosaic
Law. The Jewish case for it was known to them, and perplexed the
more simple minded. He counter-attacked along three lines. God himself witnessed through his prophet Ezechiel "quod dederat eis praecepta
non bona" (*Ezech.* xx, 25).[9] Other texts from the prophets denounced
sacrifices as inefficacious or insufficient. This proved that the
ceremonial precepts given by Moses were not good in themselves, but
were merely "the image of righteousness" or "foreshadowings". Moses

---

6 R. Wasselynck, "L'influence de l'exégèse de S. Grégoire le Grand sur les commentaires
bibliques médiévaux", RTAM xxxii (1965) 157-204. Gilbert the Universal compiled the *Gloss* on
the Pentateuch, in concert with the circle of Anselm of Laon, at some time between c. 1110 and
1128; see B. Smalley, *The study of the Bible in the Middle Ages*, 2nd ed. (Oxford 1952) 60-62; "Les
commentaires bibliques de l'époque romane: glose ordinaire et gloses périmées", *Cahiers de
civilisation médiévale* iv (1961) 15-22; R. Wasselynck, op. cit. 186-92.

7 A gloss in the standard *Gloss* on *Lev.* xix, 27-28, a ban on shaving the beard and making incisions in the skin, offers a rational explanation; these things were forbidden as pagan practices:
"Sicut barbari faciunt....nec in honore demonum cicinnos nutrire et vovere, sicut student pagani
puerorum capita demonibus offerre, quod maxime videtur hic prohibere." It represents a garbled
version of Raban Maur's commentary on the text (PL 108, 457-458). But this type of explanation is
rare enough in the *Gloss* to stand out as remarkable.

8 B. Smalley, "Ralph of Flaix on Leviticus", above, p. 49.   I shall refer to it as
"Ralph". I also draw on material to be published in a paper in RTAM on "The influence of Ralph
of Flaix".

9 This text has been variously interpreted throughout the history of exegesis; see for instance
J. Lindblom, *Prophecy in Ancient Israel* (Oxford 1965) 184.

and the wise men of the Old Testament understood them in this manner. The divine revelation to Moses included a prophetic vision of Christ's coming and even of Christian values, such as the pre-eminence of virginity. The rank and file of the Jewish people, on the other hand, took the precepts in their literal sense, since they could not understand the inner meaning. Moses veiled his face, so that they failed to perceive the brightness of his countenance (*Exod.* xxxiv, 33-35). In the same way he concealed the prophetic secrets of the Law under dark sayings. Ralph goes on to make his third point: many precepts, besides being inconsistent with others or childish, would not "stand according to the letter"; that is, they could not have been observed; they had no literal meaning and were put there in order to prove to the wise that their true meaning must be sought in the spiritual sense only. Ralph examined each precept in the course of his commentary to test whether it could "stand according to the letter". For instance, an example to the contrary, which struck him as the most telling of all, was provision for leprosy in clothes and houses (*Lev.* xiii, 47, xiv. 36). "How can clothes and houses be leprous?" he asked.[10] It must be added that Ralph did his best to establish the literal sense where he thought he could do so, and he appreciated literal *moralia*. Precepts enjoining kindness to travellers and strangers called forth warm admiration. He credited observance of the Law with positive value, in that it taught obedience to the one true God. But the gist of his commentary is to present the Law as a cryptogram.

His readers had to cope with another tradition, deriving from St. Jerome and from contemporary Jewish rabbis. Master Andrew of St. Victor, stimulated by the example of his master Hugh, wrote commentaries on the literal sense of Old Testament books, beginning with the Pentateuch (before about 1147). He learned some biblical Hebrew and consulted rabbis on their exegesis. His Jewish teachers drew mainly on rabbinic tradition and on the standard works of Rabbi Solomon of Troyes (d. 1105) in what they told him.[11] There is no evidence to suggest that Andrew doubted the validity of the interpretation according to the four senses. He probably thought of himself as "laying

10 Quoted in "Ralph" 78: "Cum in plerisque locis, immo pene ubique satis appareat, legem spiritualiter intelligendam esse, dum ea sepius loquitur que nisi ad mysteria relata fuerint insipida prorsus et fatua sentiunt; nescio tamen si alicubi apertius quam in hoc lepre tractatu, ubi vestis leprosa et sicut sequentia continent domus leprosa introducitur". See "Ralph" 66-81 for anti-Jewish polemic.

11 See my *Study of the Bible in the Middle Ages*, op. cit. 83-185 and "L'exégèse biblique du 12ᵉ siècle", *Entretiens sur la renaissance du 12ᵉ siècle*, ed. M. de Gandillac and E. Jeaneau (Paris 1969) 273-293. My pupil Mrs. G. A. C. Hadfield (née Ten Kate) is preparing a doctoral thesis on Andrew's exegesis, with special reference to his knowledge of Hebrew and to his Jewish sources.

the literal foundation" for the spiritual interpretation, which he left to others. He was accused of "judaising" in his exegesis of the prophet Isaias, but never of a "judaising" approach to the Old Law. What distinguished him from Ralph was that he took for granted the historical fact of *legalia*. All precepts had a literal meaning for Andrew, even when it escaped him. He had never seen leprosy in clothes and houses; if the texts referred to stains, then who should judge which were leprous and which were not?[12] He did not dismiss these precepts as verbal puzzles. His factual approach to the Old Law had more importance than his discussion of its details. His treatment of them was skimpy compared with his much fuller comments on Old Testament history and prophecy. Like Ralph, he wrote after the compilation of the *Gloss*, but he supplied "masters of the sacred page" with a guide to the literal sense of those books which he expounded, until Nicholas of Lyre replaced him in the fourteenth century.

Discovery of an anonymous commentary on *Leviticus*, probably written in the 1120s or '30s in a North French school, shows that St. Victor was not the only centre of biblical scholarship. The anonymous commentator must have been a contemporary of Hugh of St. Victor, but he worked independently. He, too, learned Hebrew and drew upon rabbinic sources. He, too, accepted all precepts as literally true.[13] His commentary deserves mention here, even though it remained almost unknown, because it helps to account for Andrew's success in the schools. The Anonymous proves that the literal sense of the Law was evoking a new curiosity.

Masters of the sacred page preferred the Victorine approach to Ralph's. They came round to it slowly. Hugh had stressed that the literal foundation must be properly laid; Andrew obeyed him. At first, however, masters would quote Andrew on the literal sense along with Ralph and earlier sources, without noting the contrast of method. That is hardly surprising, seeing that Andrew never discussed method; he merely set an example by studying the literal sense. We can see how Ralph's influence persisted in a marginal note to the *Histories* of Peter Comestor on the precepts concerning leprosy: "It is clear that not all which is said of the diverse kinds of leprosy can be taken according to

---

12   Quoted in "Ralph" 80: "Lepram in vestibus vel domibus vel huiusmodi, de quibus lex agit, in nostris partibus vel nostris temporibus non vidimus, nisi forte lepram dicit maculas quasdam, quas in huiusmodi frequenter inveniri constat. Sed que macula sit leprosa, que autem non, qui diiudicare nosset non facile inveniri posset".

13   B. Smalley, "An anonymous commentary on the literal sense of Leviticus of the early twelfth century", RTAM xxxvi (1969) 78-99.

the letter".[14] Peter the Canter, in his lecture-commentary on *Leviticus* (c. 1170-1196), quoted much from Ralph and did not criticise his position at all. His blind acceptance of Ralph's method had an untoward effect, since Hugh of St. Cher borrowed from the Chanter in his postill on *Leviticus* (1230-1235). His borrowings included many quotations from Ralph; Hugh also quoted from Ralph directly. The Dominican master's postills on Scripture became a standard school text. Hence he popularised certain passages where Ralph had queried the literal sense or else rejected it outright. Nevertheless, rethinking on the validity of the literal sense was already in process: Hugh's incautious use of the Chanter did not deflect the current trend. Stephen Langton, teaching at Paris c. 1180-1206, took pains to discriminate between the senses. Annotators of the *Gloss* and the *Histories* of the late twelfth and early thirteenth centuries show an increasing anxiety to distinguish the senses from one another, deciding which glosses expound the literal sense and which the spiritual. Finally William of Milton or Middleton O.F.M. achieved clarity in his lectures on *Leviticus* about 1248.[15] He handles Ralph in a masterful way, quoting him independently of his sources on both the literal and the spiritual senses, distinguishing between them, and avoiding all those passages where Ralph had rejected "the letter".

The masters had worked out a method for the practical purpose of lecturing on the books of the Law. They treated it as an historical fact instead of trying to decode a cypher. But a satisfactory theory of the relations between the senses had to wait for St. Thomas. The trouble was that lecturing on Scripture, as practiced in the schools, gave masters little opportunity to discuss the Law as a whole. The master began with an introductory lecture on his book or group of books setting out the facts on authorship, date and intention, in so far as these were known to him. Then he expounded his text phrase by phrase. The procedure did not lend itself to discussion of general problems. Further, he aimed at making his text *praedicabilis*. He was instructing his pupils on their religious and moral duties as future prelates and preachers and was training them to preach in their turn: lectures provided raw material for sermons. Exegesis according to the four senses offered a commodious hold-all for the combination of biblical scholarship and

14 PL 198, 1206. It is not known whether the glosses printed in the Migne edition of the *Histories* were written by the Comestor himself or by a pupil or reader.
15 P. Glorieux, *Répertoire des maîtres en théologie de Paris au XIIIᵉ siècle* (Paris 1933/4) no. 304; A. B. Emden, *A Bibliographical Register of the University of Cambridge* (Cambridge 1963) 407. It is not certain that the Paris and Cambridge friars of the same name were identical, though it seems probable from the dates. The lectures on *Leviticus* must have been given in Paris, judging from the diffusion of manuscript copies.

homiletics. The proportion varied from one master to another; the ingredients remained the same. The Bible supplied every need. A writer of the late twelfth century, "B", a priest or canon of Troyes, lists a series of metaphors in praise of Scripture. Most of them are conventional enough, but one is striking. "B" compares "the letter" of Scripture to "a harlot, open to any sense whatsoever". He specifies:

> Sicut enim meretrix multis, immo quam plurimis, sese exponit, ita in littera multiplex est sensus: est enim sensus historialis, allegoricus, tropologicus. [16]

He expresses crudely but truthfully the aptitude of the biblical text to convey any Catholic teaching which the lecturer found suitable to his audience. To give one example: the creatures allowed or forbidden as food in the Law were traditionally interpreted tropologically as virtues and vices. The theme could be developed and spiced with satire on contemporary manners at the lecturer's pleasure.

The allegorical interpretation linked the two Testaments together. William of Auxerre explains the meaning of *rota in medio rotae* in Ezechiel's vision when writing his *Summa aurea* (1222-1225). Tradition taught that it signified the two Testaments: how do they form "a wheel within a wheel"? William gives a traditional answer: "The masters say that the New Testament is in the Old according to prefiguration, and the Old in the New according to exposition". [17] It is easy to see why the rules of their faculty obliged masters of the sacred page to lecture on a book of the Old and a book of the New Testament concurrently. The theme of promise and fulfilment gave unity to their piecemeal exposition of texts.

The *Summa aurea* makes a convenient bridge between lectures on Scripture and theological *quaestiones*, sentences, sentence-commentaries and treatises. This type of discussion encouraged deeper

16   Quoted by E. Jeauneau, "'Nani gigantum humeris insidentes'. Essai d'interprétation de Bernard de Chartres", *Vivarium* v (1967) 94-95. The writer tells me that the comparison "littera-meretrix" occurs in the *Quaestiones naturales* of Adelard of Bath, ed. M. Müller, *Beitr. zur Gesch. der Philos. etc.* xxxi (2) 1934, 12: "Omnis quippe littera meretrix est, nunc ad hos, nunc ad illos affectus exposita."

Adelard was referring to philosophic texts, not to Scripture. The context of his remark is: "...prius ratio inquirenda sit, ea inventa auctoritas, si adiacet, demum subdenda."

It is not clear whether "B. of Troyes" took his comparison directly from Adelard and applied it to Scripture or whether it was current when he wrote.

17   Ed. Paris, 1500, foll. 243vb-244ra. William of Auxerre is discussing the contrast between the burdens imposed by the Old and the New Law respectively. It is objected by some that Ezechiel's vision would imply that they were of equal weight. William has to answer the objection. I use the *Summa aurea* for illustration because it was widely read. On William of Auxerre see C. Ottaviano, *Guglielmo d'Auxerre* (*Biblioteca di Filosofia e scienza* xii, Rome 1950).

thought on problems arising from *legalia*.[18] First of all, did writers in a theological context regard all precepts of the Old Law as literally true? The answer is that we do find traces of the same confusion as appears in lectures on Scripture, but they are early and few. Peter of Capua in his *Summa* (c. 1201-1202) raises the question: Did the Old Law include precepts impossible to observe? He gives an opinion ascribed to "quidam" without committing himself: all precepts were imposed upon all Jews, not as binding each Jew to observe them all *ad litteram*, but as binding each to observe *ad litteram* such as he could, and to observe all "mystically", at least.[19] "Mystically" may refer to a spirit of obedience here; it is used rather ambiguously. Roland of Cremona, the first Dominican master to teach at Paris, takes Ralph's interpretation uncritically into his *Summa* (1228-1230):

> Likewise there was something in the Law which could not be understood according to the letter in any way, such as: *You shall eat the oldest of the old store: and new coming on, you shall cast away the old* (*Lev.* xxvi, 10). That precept would force the Jews to resort to the spiritual understanding....[20]

It seems strange that an innocent promise of abundance should have struck commentators as meaningless according to the letter, until we turn to the ingenious objection made by Ralph on the words *Vetustissima veterum comedetis*: why eat the *oldest* before the *old*?

> Let the Jew, who accepts the fleshly sense only of abundance, tell the reason why the *old* should be cast out and the *oldest* eaten, when they should rather have cast out the *oldest* and eaten the *old*.[21]

Ralph had interpreted the *stores* as the sacraments of the Old and New Laws respectively.[22] Hugh of St. Cher telescoped the passage into:

---

18 See especially A. M. Landgraf, *Dogmengeschichte der Frühscholastik* iii, 1 (Regensburg 1954) 19-108.
19 Quoted ibid. 34: "Quidam etiam dicunt, quod cuilibet erant omnia precepta, non ut ad litteram omnia observaret, sed quedam ad litteram, que posset, et omnia saltem mistice".
20 Quoted ibid. 59: "Similiter aliquid erat in lege, quod nullo modo poterat intelligi ad litteram, ut istud: vetustissima veterum comedetis et novis supervenientibus vetera abicietis. Istud cogebat iudeos recurrere ad spiritualem intelligentiam". I use the Douai version as the most faithful translation of the medieval Latin Vulgate.
21 *The New English Bible. The Old Testament* (Oxford/Cambridge 1970) 167. "Your old harvest shall last you in store until you have to clear out the old to make room for the new."
22 Ed. Marburg/Cologne, 1536, lib. XIX, cap. viii, pp. 295-296: "Que igitur sunt vetera, quae praedicuntur proiicienda? Nos vetera intelligimus legis sacramenta....Haec igitur vetera, novis supervenientibus proiiciuntur, quia dum novi testamenti suscipimus instituta, legis caeremonias servare contemnimus.....vetustissima veterum comedimus, quia iam non iustitiae figuris sub tempore datis oneramur, sed ipsius iustitiae, que apud Deum aeterna est, pane reficimur. Aliaque dicat iudeus, qui carnalem tantum in his amplectitur abundantiam, quae sit ratio ut vetera proiiciantur et vetustissima comedantur, cum quod vetustissimum est magis proiici, vetera vero comedi deberent. Quod si haec non solum in scripturis, verumtamen in nostris affectibus velimus advertere, vetus est cupiditas, quae veterem facit hominem...."

Obiectio contra iudaeos: nam et si vetera proiiciuntur, multo fortius vetustissima. Mystice vero non est obiectio.[23]

Roland would sometimes deny that his text had a literal or historical sense in his commentary on Job;[24] he carries over the ambiguity of terms into his *Summa*.

However, such passages are exceptional. Masters generally assumed that the precepts could be taken as literally true. The framework for their discussions was a saying, sometimes ascribed to St. Augustine:

The Law was given as a sign to the perfect, as a burden and scourge to the froward, as tutor to the simple and sucklings.[25]

The first phrase safeguarded the mystical sense of the Old Law, as understood by the élite, the second its penal character, and all three enabled theologians to interpret it as "burdensome" rather than nonsensical or absurd. William of Auxerre takes it in this way. He answers objections raised by texts from the prophets declaring that sacrifices were unpleasing to God. Such texts had figured in Ralph's arguments against the Jews. William gives three reasons for God's displeasure: the sacrifices were offered in the wrong spirit, without right intention; they were offered at the wrong time, after truth had dispersed shade (i.e. the prophets were foretelling the New Law); God did not prescribe sacrifices *voluntate absoluta, sed quasi coacta*. He imposed them as preventive of evil, not as good in themselves, to restrain the Jews from idolatry, just as he permitted divorce, since otherwise they would have

---

23   *Post. in Bib.* (Paris 1530-1545) i, fol. 120rb: "Obiectio contra iudeos: Nam et si vetera proiiciuntur, multo fortius vetustissima. Mystice vero non est obiectio. Nam vetustissima sunt unitas essentie trinitatis personarum, que comedere debet omnis homo et masticare dentibus fidei".

24   Quoted by A. Dondaine, "Un commentaire scripturaire de Roland de Crémone 'Le livre de Iob'", *Archivum Fratrum Praedicatorum* xi (1941) 124: "Sensus ystorialis hic nequaquam invenitur. Non enim piscatores, ut opinor, sagenas implent pelle ceti, neque gurgustium piscium capite illius." The text is *Iob*, x1, 26.

Roland's commentary followed his *Summa*, to which he refers in it; ibid. 118-123. Hence he may have used Hugh of St. Cher's postill, compiled soon after 1230.

25   William of Auxerre, *Summa aurea*, ed. cit. fol. 243va: Solutio: "ut dicit beatus Augustinus, lex fuit data perfectis in signum, duris et superbis in onus et flagellum, rudibus et mamotrectis in pedagogum"; ibid., fol. 101ra: "Lex data est rudibus in pedagogum, duris in flagellum, perfectis in signum."

See *Gal.* iv, 24: *Itaque lex paedagogus noster fuit in Christo*, also *Mat.* xxiii, 4; *Luc.* xi, 46. The saying occurs in various forms, as in Peter the Chanter's *Summa*, ed. J.-A. Dugauquier, *Analecta mediaevalia Namurcensia* iv (1954) 13: "Queritur de sacramentis legalibus que data sunt in signum perfectorum et iugum superborum et pedagogum infirmorum." It is found earlier in *Sententie divine pagine, Sententie Anselmi, Ysagoge in theologiam*; see the references given by Dugauquier, ibid; also Hugh of St. Victor, ed. O. Lottin, "Questions inédites de Hugues de Saint-Victor", RTAM xxvi (1959) 202, no. 27: "Multis de causis data est lex... Quibusdam de se presumentibus data est in onus... Quibusdam, scilicet perfectis, ut Moysi et Aaron et aliis iustis, data est in signum...."

None of the editors has identified the saying as a quotation.

killed their unwanted wives. William goes on to consider the objection that certain precepts were absurd. He tackles it apropos of a classic puzzle: why did the priest who sacrificed the red heifer have to cleanse himself afterwards? Rabbinic tradition, though William may not have known it, also regarded the precept (*Num.* xix, 1-10) as obscure: King Solomon understood the causes of all the sacrifices except that of the red heifer.[26] William classifies the impurity incurred by the priest as "burdensome"; he compares it to the ban on eating pork. Neither precept had any other literal cause or reason: the true cause must be sought in allegory or morality. Pork was forbidden in order to signify that we should not imitate a dirty, greedy animal. The sacrifice of the red heifer signified the Eucharist: the celebrant must beware of sullying his conscience after performing the holy rites. William at least allowed historical reality to precepts for which he could find no literal cause or reason beyond the fact that they were intended to be burdensome.[27]

Some theologians made an effort to clarify the link between St. Augustine's first and third phrases: the Law was given as a sign to the perfect and as a tutor to the simple. They asked themselves what it was like for the simple people, who had to perform burdensome, and to them incomprehensible duties. Simon of Tournai in his *Summa* (towards 1165) compared them to the simple laymen of his own day, who would recite the Lord's prayer with devotion, but without understanding; they knew only that it profited them to salvation.[28] Roland of Cremona probed further. The very fact that some precepts of the Law put a strain on belief would lead simple Jews to enquire from spiritual men or prophets what the true meaning was. Roland instances the sending of the scapegoat into the wilderness, carrying the sins of Israel written on a scroll tied to its head, and the apparent nonsense in

26 Quoted by Maimonides, *Guide of the Perplexed* iii, 26, translated by S. Pines with introduction and notes by L. Strauss (Chicago 1963) 507-8. The source is given by the editors.

27 *Summa aurea*, op. cit. fol. 243va: "Erant igitur multa in lege que ad litteram non habebant aliquam causam sue institutionis nisi onus et flagellum; secundum vero allegoriam et moralitatem causam aliquam habebant, sicut quod iudei non comederent carnes porcinas ad litteram non habebat aliquam causam nisi onus, sed secundum moralitatem patet ratio; non enim debemus imitari gulosos et immundos. Similiter immunditia illa, quam contrahebat sacerdos ex immolatione vitule rufe, tantum instituta fuit in onus secundum litteram, sed secundum moralitatem sacerdos ille qui immolabat vitulam rufam significabat sacerdotem nostrum qui confixit eucharistiam, qui postquam celebravit timere debet ne indigne contrectaverit. Unde immundum se debet reputare usque ad vesperem, id est usque ad contritionem que est finis et consumptio peccati".

28 Quoted by Landgraf, op. cit. 32: "Litteralis doctrina non erat superflua rudibus, licet non caperent spiritualem intelligentiam, quia venerabantur litteram continentem spiritualem intelligentiam.....Quo modo nunc aliquis simplex profert dominicam orationem non intelligens eam, et devotione prolationis et veneratione littere citra eius intellectum, quod orat, imperat et salvatur...."

the promise on the oldest and the old stores.[29] The Dominican friar, belonging to a later generation than Simon of Tournai, thought more highly of the intelligence to be found among the "simple". Both men were feeling their way towards a question which would be raised still later: why did the spiritual leaders and prophets of the Old Testament keep simple Jews in the dark, instead of enlightening them on the mystical significance of the legal precepts? Why did they fail to imitate Christian preachers, who expounded the spiritual senses of Scripture from their pulpits?

These were fringe problems, raised *en passant*. Theologians naturally took more interest in the effects of observance on the Old Testament Jews. What merit did observance of *legalia* confer? How far was it meritorious and justificatory? They had to harmonise many conflicting texts from the Bible and the Fathers.[30] A more positive evaluation of observance came slowly to the fore. It had been generally accepted that faith in God's promises as a ground for obedience conferred merit: the righteous men of the Old Testament were justified, even though they had to wait for deliverance until Christ came to save them.[31] Theologians reached agreement on the effects of circumcision at an early stage: circumcision had the same effect as baptism in that it freed from original sin.[32] The parallel between baptism and circumcision was so current as to find expression in poetry:

> Circumcisa caro lavit sub lege reatus,
> illud agens quod agit fons sub cruce sanctificatus,

wrote Hildebert of Lavardin (d. 1133).[33] The efficacy of other sacraments and ceremonies of the Old Law offered more difficulty and provoked much discussion. Eventually it came to be held that they did not confer grace, as did Christian sacraments; nor was observance meritorious in itself; but faith and charity sufficed to make observance meritorious and justificatory. The simple did not need to have explicit faith in the inner meaning of *legalia*; general belief in the Law's divine

---

29 Quoted ibid. 58-59: "Non enim poterat aliquis homo, qui sensum haberet, credere, quod ideo, quod hircus portabat cedulam, in qua erant scripta peccata iudeorum, in desertum, quod ideo eis erant dimissa peccata. Et ideo cogebantur credere in aliquem venturum, qui dimitteret peccata, vel ad minus cogebantur querere a viris spiritualibus vel a prophetis, quid hoc esset, et ipsi eis exposuisse misterium et ita fidem acquisivissent, et ita iustificati fuissent.... Similiter aliquid erat in lege, quod nullo modo poterat intelligi ad litteram....Istud cogebat iudeos recurrere ad spiritualem intelligentiam, et ita quodam modo iustificabat eos...."
30 Landgraf, op. cit. 59-60.
31 Ibid.
32 Ibid. 61-108.
33 *Carmina minora* no. 39 II, ed. A. B. Scott (Teubner 1969) 29. There is no evidence for the date of no. 39.

character and charity they did need. William of Auxerre and others reached a clearer formulation by distinguishing between *opus operans* and *opus operatum*. William answers the question "whether *legalia* justified" as follows:

> The *opus operans* is the action itself, that is the sacrifice of a bull or a lamb, which justified when it was done in charity. The *opus operatum* is the actual flesh of the bull or lamb which was sacrificed, which certainly did not justify. In the New Law, on the other hand, both *opus operans* and *opus operatum* justify, because the flesh of Christ (the *opus operatum*) is justificatory. Thus, when it is asked whether the sacraments of the Old Law justified, we grant that they did as *opus operans*, as the foregoing reasons have proved; but they did not justify as *opus operatum*.[34]

The outcome of discussion had been to raise *legalia* to a higher level than the Lombard had allowed them in his *Sentences*. By the early 1220s a more indulgent view was being taken of observance, if not of the literal content of *legalia*.

Perhaps the Catharist heretics in Italy and the *terra Albigensium* prompted the change of attitude. Cathars rejected the Old Testament as devilish: it emanated from the god of this bad visible world, in their view. Hence they forced defenders of the Catholic Church to stress the divine origin and beneficient character of *legalia*. Preaching missions and debates with heretics before and during the Albigensian crusades brought a spate of tracts against the heretics.[35] The crisis must have made an impression on teachers in the northern schools: some joined in polemic. Although its effect is elusive, we can suppose that the crisis stimulated thought in two ways: the Cathars made an arbitrary use of the spiritual interpretation, dismissing the literal sense altogether in favour of a spiritual sense, where it suited them, They therefore brought out the need for careful definition of the relationship between the senses in Catholic exegesis.[36] By attacking the Old Law as wholly evil, they led

34 *Summa aurea*, op. cit. fol. 243va. On the origin of the distinction between *opus operans* and *opus operatum* see Landgraf, op. cit. 54-60.
35 See Christiane Thouzellier, *Catharisme et Valdéisme en Languedoc à la fin du XIIᶜ et au début du XIIIᶜ siècle*, 2nd ed. (Paris/Louvain 1969).
36 Durand of Huesca, a Valdesian who returned to Catholicism and wrote against the heretics, gives examples of how the Cathars interpreted Gospel texts according to the spiritual sense only; he replies to them that the mystical sense does not destroy, but derives from the literal or historical sense; ed. Christiane Thouzellier, *Une Somme anti-cathare. Le liber contra Manichaeos de Durand de Huesca* (Spicilegium sacrum Lovaniense. Etudes et documents xxxii, 1964) 94, 149, 150, 159, 207. But Durand uses the mystical sense in a confused and ambiguous way himself on *Job* xxviii, 6: *Locus sapphiri lapides eius* etc.: "Sed nos sensum eorum exuflando, quia istorice non potest apte intelligi, ad sensum misticum recurramus....Et sic intelligenda est predicta sentencia beatissimi Iob, ab hereticis depravata" (258). His mystical interpretation is that the earth signifies the Synagogue, the source of Scripture, and the holy Jews of the Old Testament. What he has done is to reject the "literal sense" because it contains a metaphor, and pass straight to the allegorical

Catholic theologians to think more deeply about its literal sense as a guide to God's chosen people. The dualist heresies may explain in part why Maimonides' *Guide of the Perplexed* found eager readers, when it reached the schools in its Latin translation.

Maimonides or Rabbi Moses (1135-1204) finished his *Guide* soon after 1190.[37] Its contents interest us here only in so far as it deals with the Law. Maimonides, as a Jewish philosopher and practicing Jew, had much the same aim as his predecessor Philo Judaeus (d. soon after 40 A. D.). He wanted to harmonise the Law with a philosophic account of the deity and the cosmos, without compromising its sacred and binding character for Jews. Philo solved his problem by presenting the Law as an allegory, though he regarded its literal sense as true and binding on his people. The content of philosophy had changed since then. Maimonides had to take another road. He read Plato's *Republic* and noted its philosopher kings, also Aristotle's *Politics* with its insistence on the common good as a criterion for good government. The Jews for whom he wrote were perplexed by the untidiness and irrationality of their Law. Maimonides guided them not by allegorising, but by rationalising. He defended the political and religious value of the Law as it stood. He presented Moses in the dual role of a prophet and of a philosopher ruler, transmitting wise laws for the constitution and running of the Jewish state. The Law as a whole united the tribes of Israel and joined them together as a community, whose cult brought social and religious cohesion. Maimonides dwelt on the justice and mercy of many precepts and on the ethical values inculcated by commands such as those concerning good treatment of neighbours and pity to birds and beasts. Such precepts had "clear utility". His main argument on those precepts whose utility was not so clear amounted to a wide application of the principle that sacrifices and ceremonies aimed at weaning the Jews from idolatry. Moses taught his people to avoid the superstitions and pagan rites of the Egyptians and other gentiles, with whom they had contacts, by prescribing a cult which bore no resemblance to any other. This dictated the choice of animals to be offered as sacrifices and the mode of slaughter, for example. Maimonides "traces an impressive, but quite unhistorical picture of paganism in biblical times" in order to contrast Mosaic to pagan worship. The Jews, emerging from slavery in

---

sense. M^llc Thouzellier dates his *Liber* 1222-1223, *Catharisme*, op. cit. 299. Although, as she shows, Durand had had a good education and was well-read, he was out of touch with the northern schools, where the confusion between the metaphorical and the mystical senses of Scripture was being cleared up at the time.

37 On Maimonides' life and writings see G. Vajda, "La pensée religieuse de Maïmonide", *Cahiers de civilisation médiévale* ix (1966) 29-49, where a full bibliography is given.

134

Egypt and tainted by gentile customs, needed settled rules and prescribed ritual; without such precepts, they would have lapsed into idol
worship like their neighbours. Blood sacrifices, prohibitions and
purifications all led them to honour God and to feel a holy awe in his
presence. Maimonides does not explain why a code adapted to the state
of Jewish society at a particular point in its history should retain its
value after paganism had disappeared.[38] This failure on his part could
only increase his appeal to Christian readers, since they could fill the
gap in his argument. They saw *legalia* as a passing phase in the history
of salvation.

His explanation had the further advantage that the general covered
the particular. He presented the ceremonial precepts as "God's gracious
ruse" to draw men to himself;[39] hence not every detail need have a
cause assigned to it. Worship called for rules and regulations. Numbers
and kinds of offerings had to be specified; but specification was not
always significant in detail. The whole Law commanded nothing absurd; its seemingly petty orders could be subsumed in its general plan,
to provide for the common good of Israel.

The perplexing reproaches made by the prophets against sacrifices,
and Ezechiel's saying that the precepts were not good (xx, 25) fell into
place quite easily. Maimonides could explain the text of Jeremias:
*When I brought your forefathers out of Egypt, I gave them no com-
mands about whole-offering and sacrifice* (vii, 22), a dictum, he says,
"which has been regarded as difficult by everyone whose words I have
seen or heard."[40] The first intention of the Law was worship of the one
true God. The sacrifices, prescribed at a later stage, were only means to
an end. The prophets blamed the Jews for neglecting the first intention;
God reproaches his people through his prophets:

> You, however, came and abolished this end, while holding fast to what
> has been done for its sake. For you have doubted my existence...And still
> you continue to repair to the temple of the Lord, offering sacrifices,
> which are things that have not been intended in the first intention.[41]

The *Guide* offered reasons to an age in love with reason. It had another
point of contact with scholastic exegesis: its author shared the
philosophers' low opinion of the capacities of the common people. The
Law gave to the vulgar all they needed to know in the perfect city.[42]

38 Ibid. 46.
39 *Guide* iii, 32 and 45, ed. cit. 526, 580.
40 Ibid. iii, 26, 27, 508-510.
41 Ibid. iii, 32, 530-531.
42 Vajda, op. cit. 48.

Moses and the élite understood the philosophy behind the words. Scripture included all science and metaphysics. Significantly, Maimonides writes that to forbid formal worship and sacrifices would have been equivalent to forbidding formal prayers in favour of pure meditation in his own day.[43] His belief in a hierarchy of wisdom corresponded to the Christian teaching that the élite of the Old Testament already belonged to the New, in that they perceived the prefiguration of the Gospel in *legalia*. Hence the *Guide* accorded with Christian tradition in presenting the Law as wholesome for all, sufficient for the people, and a mine of deeper wisdom for the élite.

There is still no study of the text of the Latin translation.[44] The *Guide* was written in Arabic, but was soon translated into Hebrew and thence into Latin. Michael Scot has been credited with the Latin version on plausible evidence. He would have made it in Italy after leaving Toledo "by 1220 at the latest".[45] It used to be thought that William of Auvergne was the first schoolman to quote from the Latin version about 1230. We now know that Alexander of Hales O.F.M. anticipated him. Alexander quotes Maimonides' classification of the Old Testament precepts under fourteen heads in his *Glossa* on the *Sentences*, given as lectures at Paris while he was still a secular, probably 1223-1227.[46] He ascribes the quotation, copied in full, to "quidam expositor, licet non sanctus". As it comes towards the end of his *Glossa*, we can deduce that the Latin *Guide* had reached Paris not long before 1227, and that it made a quick entry into the schools. Alexander of Hales and William of Auvergne were followed by John of La Rochelle in his contribution to the *Summa* which goes under the name of Alexander, by Vincent of Beauvais O.P., the encyclopaedist, and by St Thomas.[47] The *Guide*

43   *Guide* iii, 32, 526. The two central places in Scripture for philosophic and mystical teaching were the account of creation and Ezechiel's vision of the chariot.

44   F. van Steenberghen has noted this as one desideratum among many, *La philosophie au XIII* siècle* (Louvain/Paris 1966) 339. For a list and analysis of some Latin MSS and the early editions, see W. Kluxen, "Literargeschichtliches zum lateinischen Moses Maimonides", RTAM xxi (1954) 23-35.

45   L. Thorndike, *Michael Scot* (London 1965) 28-29. Michael was at Bologna by 1220. It is not known when he entered the service of the emperor Frederich II, perhaps in 1220, perhaps not until 1224; ibid. 32-33.

46   *Glossa in quatuor libros sententiarum Petri Lombardi* ii (Quaracchi 1954) 471 (*Bibl. Franc. schol. med. aevi* xiv). The quotation is from the *Guide* iii, 36. It occurs in the earliest recension of the *Glossa*, designated by the editors as 'A'; a later recension, 'E', of the 1230s, adds 'Moyses' after "licet non sanctus". On the dates of the various books of the *Glossa*, see xii, 110*-116*, xiii, 21*; xv, 18* of *Bibl.Franc.* etc.

47   The best account of the Latin translation and its influence on the schoolmen is still J. Guttmann's "Der Einflüss etc." in *Moses Ben Maimon*, ed. W. Bacher, M. Brann and M. Simonsen (Leipzig 1908) 135-230. Guttmann could not have known of the recent research on Michael Scot nor of the quotation of the *Guide* in Alexander's *Glossa*, which was not discovered until 1946.

reached Oxford in time to be quoted by Richard Fishacre O.P. in his commentary on the *Sentences* about 1243; he quotes Rabbi Moses at least three times on the literal reasons for *caeremonialia*.[48] It is an impressive picture: the *Guide*, probably translated into Latin by Michael Scot in Italy soon after 1220, was used by a secular teacher at Paris soon before 1227, then by another secular, William of Auvergne, and then by Franciscans and Dominicans alike. A book catches on if it broaches problems which concern its readers and if its answers forestall or put more clearly what readers had in mind beforehand. The *Guide* had just this relevance in the early thirteenth century.

Still, much depended on the first Christian writer who sponsored the *Guide* in a big way. William of Auvergne was the first to unlock and display its teaching. Any suspicion of unorthodoxy on his part would have compromised it. On the other hand, a timid use would have blurred its significance. William was a theologian of high repute and unimpeachable orthodoxy. He grasped its meaning and drew out the implications boldly. We shall see how he fitted it into the framework of his doctrine. His commitment to it was so personal and so daring as to pose problems to his successors. We shall not understand St. Thomas's approach to the Old Law unless we begin by looking at its presentation in William's *De fide et legibus*. Since his ideas and his temperament coloured his use of the *Guide,* we must start by making a general study of William.

---

48 MS Oxford, Oriel College 43, foll. 333ra, 336rb, 338va on *Sent.* IV, i, 4,5,7. Fishacre quotes the opinions that uncleanness was instituted in the Law in order to induce feelings of reverence and fear, that all ceremonies were intended to strengthen faith in God and to prevent idolatry, and that regulations on circumcision had reasonable causes. On Fishacre see A. B. Emden, *A Bibliographical Register of the University of Oxford to A. D. 1500* ii (Oxford 1958) 685, and especially D. A. Callus, "The Introduction of Aristotelian Learning to Oxford", *Proceedings of the British Academy* xxix (1944) 259.

II

WILLIAM OF AUVERGNE

William came from Aurillac in the Auvergne.[1] He studied at Paris and then taught as a doctor of theology from sometime before 1222 to 1228; he was a canon of Notre-Dame by 1223. A disputed election to the bishopric of Paris brought him to Rome in 1228 to forward an appeal lodged by his chapter. Gregory IX quashed the election as uncanonical and provided and consecrated William to the bishopric, which he held until his death in 1249. His career as scholar and bishop corresponds to the ideal picture painted by masters of the Sacred Page in their sermons and lectures: the scholar must prepare himself for pastoral care by his study of Scripture; as master he will lecture, dispute and preach; finally, when raised to prelacy, he will practice what he has learnt and taught to his pupils. William strongly resembles Robert Grosseteste, his contemporary, bishop of Lincoln 1235-1253, another living model of a scholar bishop, as the scholars saw him.[2] Both William and Robert threw themselves heart and soul into the duties of pastoral care, striving to reform abuses, making visitations, preaching and promoting study, giving spiritual guidance and befriending the mendicant friars as precious helpers in their task. Both were strict disciplinarians. Both had to negotiate difficult business with their respective governments and with the papal Curia, though William showed more diplomacy and less intransigeance than his English colleague. Their output as scholars also has features in common. Both had an exceptionally wide range of interests. Neither of them used the normal scholastic mode of presentation, partly because they lacked the necessary feeling for system and order, and partly for the more positive reason that it would have cramped their style. They preferred to preach and teach and discuss theological problems in the same treatise, instead of using separate compartments. Further, they shared a rare gift of originality. The resemblance ends at this point, since each was original in his own way.

We have no comprehensive study of William, but detailed work on early scholasticism has built him up as an innovator: "He was one of the great thirteenth-century thinkers and has received less than his due only

---

1   See the notice and bibliography by P. Viard in *Dictionnaire de la spiritualité* vi (1967) 1182-92.

2   M. Gibbs and J. Lang, *Bishops and Reform 1215-1272* (Oxford 1934), *Robert Grosseteste Scholar and Bishop*, ed. D. A. Callus (Oxford 1953, reprinted 1969); S. Gieben, "Bibliographia universa Roberti Grosseteste ab an. 1473 ad an. 1969", *Collectanea Franciscana* xxxix (1969) 362-418.

because even greater men followed him".[3] His early lectures on *Proverbs*, *Ecclesiastes* and the *Canticle* show him as one of the first to bring the *Libri naturales* to bear on exegesis and to argue against current doubts on the immortality of the soul. His praise of the new religious Orders shows his receptivity.[4] His lectures on the *Canticle* struck Dr. Riedlinger as a marked contrast to the average school treatment of this book. William dwelt on the corruption of the Church, the bride of Christ, in more personal, violent language than any other exegete of the time permitted himself. His satire bit so deep that Hugh of Saint-Cher, basing his postill on William's, felt obliged to muzzle him. Hence William on the *Canticle* circulated through a Dominican medium with the mordancy softened.[5] We shall see how a Franciscan applied the same process to *De legibus*. William's *De bono et malo*, another early work (1223-1228), has been edited recently. It brings out his interest in human nature and his fondness for Cicero's *De officiis*.[6] His *Magisterium divinale*, a collection of tracts put together to form a *Summa*, serves the historian as a quarry for discovery of new or budding ideas. William's extensive early use of Arabic philosophers and scientists has been noted.[7] He was a precursor of St. Thomas in seeking rational proof for God's existence, rejecting St. Anselm's ontological argument.[8] He was a precursor, too, in his teaching on the unity of the soul; he was original on the problem of synderesis; he was one of the first Paris masters to attach liberty to the will[9] and to arrive at the concept of *Limbus puerorum*.[10]

Nowhere does he strike a line of his own more forcibly than in *De legibus*, which concerns us here. It formed part V (together with its twin, *De fide*) of the *Magisterium divinale*. A reference in *De legibus* to his *De sacramentis*, written about 1228, and another in his *De universo*, 1231-1236, date *De legibus* between these years. It therefore belongs to the beginning of his episcopate, probably about 1230.[11]

3   R. Weberberger, "*Limbus puerorum*. Zur Entstehung eines theologischen Begriffes", RTAM xxxv (1968) 128.

4   B. Smalley, "Some Thirteenth-Century Commentaries on the Sapiential Books", *Dominican Studies* ii (1949) 326-337; for MS Arsenal 64 read 84.

5   *Die Makellosigkeit der Kirche in den lateinischen Hohenliedkommentaren des Mittelalters* (BGPTM xxxviii, 3, 1958) 241-256.

6   J. R. O'Donnell, "Tractatus Magistri Guillelmi Alvernensis *De bono et malo*", *Mediaeval Studies* viii (1946) 245-299.

7   R. de Vaux, *Notes et textes sur l'Avicennisme latin aux confins des XIIᵉ-XIIIᵉ siècles* (Paris 1934) 17-22, 37-38.

8   A. Masnovo, *Da Guglielmo d'Auvergne a S. Tommaso*, 2nd ed. (Milan 1945-1946) i, 41.

9   O. Lottin, *Psychologie et morale aux XIIᵉ et XIIIᵉ siècles* (Louvain 1942-1960) i, 463; ii, 134-137, 340.

10   R. Weberberger, op. cit. 128-133.

11   J. Kramp, "Des Wilhelm von Auvergne *Magisterium divinale*", *Gregorianum* i (1920) 538-

William distinguishes himself from contemporaries by his grasp of a situation. He listened to men who did not raise their objections in formal academic debate. Hence he uncovers areas of doubt which might have gone unrecorded. To take a striking example: he attacks those who hold that the adherent of any faith, law or sect may be saved, provided that he believes sincerely that it comes from God. His deeds are pleasing to God, they say, provided that he does them for God's sake. William gives their reasons. An exclusive view of religion would mean that the multitude of the damned and the tiny proportion of the saved would reflect on God's mercy. Further, Christians presume in claiming salvation for themselves alone; and as only good Christians will be saved it follows that hell will be overcrowded: God could not be so pitiless as that. The background to such doubts was probably disputations with Jews and conversions to Judaism on the one hand.[12] The Church reacted by tightening regulations against the Jews and by burning the Talmud at Paris; William took a leading part in this. On the other hand, Islam was victorious in the Holy Land and the Reconquest of Spain disclosed hordes of Muslims, who resisted conversion. It was natural that Christians should wonder whether their religion counted as the only true one.[13] But William exposes an elusive frame of mind when he selects it for frontal attack. He does not say who the doubters were, only that they were numerous. He answers them by pointing out first that the doubter should have recourse to prayer: God will surely enlighten one who seeks the truth earnestly. Secondly, he compares the natural and supernatural orders: nature produces many vile in contrast to very few precious things; hence we need not be surprised that few go to heaven. Thirdly, he argues from God's love of justice.[14] St. Thomas's *Contra gentiles* shows up as a more sophisticated

---

584; ii (1921) 42-78. I have used a photographic reproduction of the Paris/Orleans, 1674 edition of William's *Opera*. My references will be to pages of vol. i. I have slightly altered punctuation and spelling. Collation of this edition with an early manuscript for selected passages is reassuring; variants are few and do not materially alter the sense where they occur; see appendix, below, p. 179.

12 For some recent work on disputations between Jews and Christians and on judaising Christians, see B. Z. Wacholder, "Cases of Proselytizing in the Tosafist Responsa", *Jewish Quarterly Review* N.S. li (1960-1961) 288-315; S. Stein, *Jewish-Christian Disputations in Thirteenth-Century Narbonne. An Inaugural Lecture delivered at University College London* (London 1969).

13 Doubt found collective expression in the parable of the three rings. Three sons each inherit a ring given him by his father. The rings look alike, but one is genuine and the others counterfeit. They stand for the three faiths, Christian, Jewish and Muslim. God, the Father in heaven, alone knows which is the true one. For variants of the story and its significance see M. Penna, *La parabola dei tre anelli e la toleranza nel medio evo* (Turin 1953).

14 *De Legibus* xxi, p. 60. Lottin, op. cit., ii, 409-411, points out that William of Auxerre also taught that prayer would be efficacious for the solution of doubts. There is a great contrast, however, between the types of doubt envisaged: William of Auxerre thought in terms of casuistry

140

argument on the same theme. It aimed at providing a reasoned defence of the Christian faith for use against Jews and Muslims and against Christians led astray by Greco-Arabic philosophy.[15] William's arguments are unconvincing in comparison, just as the objections that he answers are less intellectual. But William at least gives the simpler doubters a right to be heard. His willingness to confront objections will help to explain his attitude to exegesis.

His use of the *Guide* is already well known. It has been asked why he never quoted the author by name, whereas he did not scruple to name Avicenna. The reason is surely that Avicenna died in 1037 and Maimonides in 1204; hence he came within the conventional span during which later writers would not quote him by name; near contemporaries were called *quidam* or *aliqui*.[16] In the same way, Alexander of Hales had quoted him as *quidam expositor, sed non sanctus*, to distinguish him from Christian scholars, as we have seen. William advertised instead of concealing his debt to Maimonides. Alexander quoted from the *Guide* once only; he did not mention the author's rationalisation of precepts which had no obvious reason, such as the ban on wearing clothes woven of wool and flax together (*Deut.* xxii, 11). Such precepts were figurative, though Alexander accepted that they had a literal meaning (if not a reason) for the Old Testament Jews.[17] William, on the contrary, took over the leading idea of Maimonides: *legalia* aimed at weaning the Jews from idolatry; hence they forbad all practices which recalled pagan rites. William echoed the *Guide* on other reasons: the offering of unblemished beasts in sacrifice taught the honour due to God; the burning of offerings and the sending out of the scapegoat signified repentance, in that sins were symbolically destroyed or cast out, in order to teach the sinner to set his sins behind him.[18] He mentions the marvellous cures reported in the *Guide* in discussing the precepts on leprosy.[19] The influence goes deeper than mere quotation.

and scruples of conscience; William of Auvergne was concerned with the more fundamental question of rival religions.

15 M.-D. Chenu, *Introduction à l'étude de Saint Thomas d'Aquin* (Paris 1950) 247-254.

16 The reasons previously suggested (see Masnovo, op. cit. i, 118-124) are that William would not quote Maimonides by name because he was a Jew, and alternatively that the *Guide* was presented as a compilation, rather than as an original work. Neither reason convinces me.

17 *Glossa*, op. cit. 460-461: "Nam alia sunt praecepta mystica, alia non. Mystica autem, alia sunt caerimonialia, alia sacramentalia...Caerimonalia sunt quorum non est evidens ratio, quale est hoc: *Non indues contextum ex lino et lana*. Haec autem et illa dicuntur figurativa. Sed figurativa sunt rei faciendae, aut rei futurae....Quae autem sunt figurativa rei faciendae manserunt in thurificio et aqua benedicta." Ibid. 543: "Erit ergo duplex adimpletio (Veteris Legis), scilicet cum sacramenta Novae Legis succedunt aliis, et cum succedunt litteralibus intellectibus caeremonialium intellectus spirituales."

18 *Guide* III, 46, 584, 589, 591; *De legibus* viii, 38, 40.

19 Ibid. xi, 43.

William made the *Guide* his own. He will elaborate on the arguments, finding further evidence for those pagan practices and superstitions, which according to Maimonides the Law combatted by prescribing their opposites.[20] Even more interesting, he criticises Maimonides openly or by implication, in the belief that he, as a Christian bishop, could give better reasons for the literal causes of precepts than a Jewish philosopher could do.

William is both a personal and digressive writer. Professor Gilson points to the influence of Avicenna on his dialogue with his reader, addressed as *tibi*, and in his constant use of phrases like *revertamur ad id in quo eramus*;[21] the former at least could have derived from Maimonides as well. It will clarify his thesis, therefore, if we begin with his conclusion and then work backward through his proofs. He claims to have made the following points:[22] 1) seemingly absurd precepts had just and reasonable causes and hence must be understood in their literal sense; they were imposed on a simple people, needing to be weaned from idolatry; the time demanded them; 2) many similar bans obtain "among us" even today; certain practices are forbidden as superstitious and recalling Judaism or "Saracenism". All the more reason why the Old Law should have warded off contamination.

Why did William feel a compulsion to defend the literal reasons for *legalia*? The *Guide* stimulated him to go one better in doing so; but other influences worked on him. They appear in his account of the nature and purpose of law in general at the beginning of *De legibus*: nothing but the best was worthy of the divine lawgiver. Hence the Old Law had to fit into his concept of what law ought to be.

He begins with a few remarks on the law of nature, stressing its intrinsic character: laws imposed from without are not laws at all, properly speaking; moral values reside in the soul, radiating from divine wisdom.[23] St. Isidore's list of the attributes of good human law supplies the framework for William's. Isidore wrote:

Erit autem lex honesta, iusta, possibilis, secundum naturam, secundum

---

20 Ibid. xiii, 44.

21 "Avicenne en Occident au moyen âge", AHDLMA xxxvi (1969) 91-93.

22 *De legibus* xv, 46: "Licet autem ex his clarum tibi sit, et merito, quod iuxta litteram intelligenda sunt ea quae absurda videntur esse in lege, et quia causas habent iustas et rationabiles suae praeceptionis et suae prohibitionis, et quod tempus illud et populi ruditas et ineruditio idolatriaeque proximitas et vicinitas praecepta et prohibitiones huiusmodi requirebant, ostendimus etiam tibi quod magna pars eorum etiam apud nos extant, sicut prohibitiones observationum superstitiosarum, quas proxime enumeravimus, et quia etiam tales praeceptiones et prohibitiones fiunt apud nos propter speciem Judaismi et Saracenismi aliarumque superstitionum suspiciones. Et propter hoc merito ex similibus causis similes praeceptiones et prohibitiones primitivo illo populo, et idolatriae innutrito et circumquaque obsesso, multo fortius faciendae fuerunt."

23 O. Lottin, *Le droit naturel chez Saint Thomas d'Aquin et ses prédécesseurs* (Bruges 1931) 40, n. 1.

142

> consuetudinem patriae, loco temporique conveniens, necessaria, utilis, manifesta quoque...[24]

William renders this in his own words, quoting a current dictum in addition:

> Dicamus igitur quia lex verissima ratione nihil aliud est quam honestas legibilis, id est descripta religionis praeceptis, iuxta quod dictum videtur: lex est scriptum assistens honestis, prohibens contrarium...[25] Lex est honestas integra seu completa, legibilis et descripta litteris et ad observantiam imperata.[26]

The definition of good law sets the tone for William's treatment of *legalia*. The outward observance imposed on the Jews must have echoed the precepts of the law of nature and have measured up to the standards set by Isidore for good human laws. Taking the Ciceronian *honestum* as a starting point, he presents the Law of Moses as an *alphabetum honestatis*. True, it formed part, not the whole, of the perfect, eternal Law of the Gospel. Its function was to prepare an uneducated people to receive the Gospel, by teaching them their *alphabetum honestatis*, according to their limited understanding, "quia naturalis honestatis regulas continet et mandata." William justifies his description of the Old Law, which he will then prove in detail:

> The whole Law contains nothing which lacks a rational cause for commanding, forbidding or narrating. There is nothing absurd or irrational in it, and this appears clearly in many items which have obvious worth and usefulness.[27]

His defence aims at showing that the Old Law reached Isidorian standards. It was worthy or decorous (*honesta*); it accorded with nature; it was suited to its time and place; it was necessary and useful, just and possible; it was manifest, having been published and set down in writing. William realised only too well that his predecessors had found

24 *Etym.* II, x; V, xxi, ed. W. Lindsay (Oxford 1911). This passage from St. Isidore forms the subject of an article of the *Summa* (Ia2ae, q. 95, a. 3). It was so well known previously that we find it in a gloss added to a copy of the *Gloss* on the Psalter, soon after the mid twelfth century, MS Paris, B.N. lat. 105: *Beatus vir. Ab honesto incipit. In cathedra pestilentie non sedit. Ab utili. Erit tanquam lignum. A possibili.*
See B. Smalley, "Les commentaires bibliques de l'époque romane", above p. 17

25 This dictum, "lex...contrarium", was current in the thirteenth century, with slight variations. St. Albert ascribed it to Cicero, but it is not in his works; see O. Lottin, *Psychologie et morale*, op. cit. ii, 16-17.
26 *De legibus* i, 18. I cannot find the actual verbal source of William's definition of law; it may be his own.
27 Ibid. ii, 29. See also xvi, 47: "Et quoniam iam defendimus et declaravimus litteralem intelligentiam legis, in his quibus absurda penitus et nullatenus possibilia videbatur..."

many precepts quite the opposite; they had been regarded as unworthy, unfitting, useless or impossible to observe.

He first defends the multiplicity of laws: why did the *alphabetum honestatis* have to include so many precepts? Maimonides explained it on the grounds that the Jews had to be warned against many diverse kinds of idolatry. William adds two other reasons: children cannot understand generalisations; they need instruction in detail, just as bread must be broken before they can chew it;[28] secondly, God provided what would occupy their minds; the Law offered ample matter for study.[29] Scarcity of books and fewness of precepts would have turned the Jews towards profane learning and would have led them astray. This danger appeared later in their history, especially when they were overrun by the Saracens. Then they studied pagan philosophy, which led them to apostatise, since many precepts began to look absurd and futile.[30] William had Maimonides' apologetic purpose in mind at this point in his argument. The *Guide* was written for perplexed Jews, who doubted in consequence of their philosophic studies.

We pass from content to enforcement. Maimonides justified the harsh penalties imposed by the Law in the interests of good order: "To the wicked the existence of a judge who renders tyranny impossible is harmful and grievous."[31] William heartily agrees. He discourses at length on the need for *disciplina*. Men still have to be forced as well as taught to act rightly. He sums up as follows:

> This is the surest and firmest ground (of the judicial penalties), that discipline must be applied, and not teaching only.[32]

He goes on to argue against those soft-brained persons who illogically disapprove of the death penalty, while accepting the need for lesser deterrents.[33] The Church, as he noted, still had to legislate against the survival of pagan practices in the form of superstition and magic: "We shall refute those errors concerning idols which have existed, and still do," he says in his preface.[34] Many Old Testament laws against idolatry had kept their relevance. Maimonides could have given even more

---

28 *De legibus* i, 24. A common analogy for God's condescension to human understanding; see R. W. Southern and F. S. Schmitt, *Memorials of St. Anselm*, op. cit. 274: apples have to be cut up for children on account of their soft teeth and small mouths.

29 This idea derives from Augustine's *De vera religione* xvii, PL 34, 136.

30 *De legibus* i, 24.

31 *Guide* II, 39, 380-1; III, 35, 536.

32 *De legibus* i, 27.

33 Ibid. William's experience as a bishop on the need for *disciplina* corresponded to St. Augustine's, though William does not quote him; see Peter Brown, *Augustine of Hippo* (London 1967) 236-241.

34 *De legibus*, 2.

144

weight to the argument in their favour. William's sharpest criticism of
the *Guide* turns on the interpretation of *Deut.* xxii, 6: the wayfarer who
finds a nest with a sitting bird in it may take the young, but must let her
go, that he may prosper and have a long life. Maimonides grouped this
text among precepts which inculcated pity: if God requires mercy
towards birds and beasts, then how much more to men?[35] William
dismisses the explanation as laughable and childish. Had pity been the
object of the precept, then it would have been less cruel to take the hen
bird and leave the young; the blessing attached to the precept,
moreover, seems too great for so trivial an action. He explains it instead
as directed against magicians, who used birds and their eggs or chicks
for fertility rites and auguries: "Many fools still think it lucky to find
certain objects and keep them as pledges of good fortune: old women
cannot be weaned of the idea." Similarly, Christians still make incisions
in the skin and carry figures, drawn or engraved, just as the Jews were
forbidden to do (*Lev.* xix, 28); this is yet another detestable relic of
idolatry. The Church today would sternly correct persons who observed
Jewish or Saracen customs, even if these were harmless in themselves,
such as refraining from servile work on Saturdays.[36] William draws on
his experience as bishop and director of conscience here: he tells us in
De virtutibus that he used to be consulted on temptations by demons.[37]

He also brings his personal scientific interests to bear on the
diagnosis of leprosy by the priests of the Law. Earlier commentators
had stumbled over the references to "leprosy in walls" (*Lev.* xiv, 36).
Ralph of Flaix regarded it as the clearest proof of the absurdity of the
Law *ad litteram*; others had followed him or had done their best to
"save" its literal meaning.[38] William had no difficulty with the text. He
had himself been questioned about a stone in a certain abbey, which
was said to be "cancerous" because it was rotting away; and he had observed dry rot in wood.[39]

We see a gentler side of him when he christianises Old Testament
worship. The sacrifices were not prescribed with the sole intention of
weaning the Jews from idolatry, "as certain persons have held". *Quidam*
refers to Maimonides, who wrote:

> The first intention of the Law consists only in your apprehending Me
> and not worshipping someone other than Me....Those laws concerning

35   *Guide* III, 48, 600.
36   *De legibus*, xiv, 45-46.
37   Ibid. xi, ed. cit. 131.
38   See above, p. 123 n. 8.
39   *De legibus*, xi, 42-43.

sacrifices and repairing to the Temple were given only for the sake of this fundamental principle.[40]

William was hardly fair to his author, reading "*first* intention" as "one and only";[41] he could pick up hints on other purposes in the ritual precepts. However, he puts forward seven other reasons in addition to prevention of idolatry. The sacrifices were instituted to honour God and to teach the Jews to observe the rites which he alone had prescribed for them. The slaughter of animals signified God's justice and mercy; the Jews learnt the lesson that God in his justice could have visited them with death for their sins, instead of sparing them in his mercy. The act of sacrifice impressed on their minds what they read in their books. William invented a pious thought (*cogitatio*) which would have been used by those making sacrifice:

> Mors nobis imminebat quemadmodum istis animalibus, cui utique de iustitia tua tradere nos poteras, sed per misericordiam tuam vel liberati sumus vel liberari nos petimus, O Deus.

A cross-reference sends us to a later passage, where he invents prayers for use at sin offerings:

> He who slaughtered or burned the animals would state in deed, and also in word, as we believe: "The sins for which I offer these animals perish and vanish, just as they do".[42]

William wrote a treatise on Christian prayer, *De rhetorica divina*, the most popular of his books. It includes a choice of prayers for use by the faithful.[43] He could easily surmise what devotions would have suited the Israelites. The sacrifices were a memorial to divine goodness. The offerers gave part of them to God and kept part for themselves, to signify that they owed all to God's blessing. The sacrifices sanctified those who offered, cleansing them from the stains of their sins, by God's virtue and mercy. Here William commits himself to the much-discussed view that *legalia* sanctified.[44] They also brought men into closer relationship to God. The offering of gifts and sharing at the holy table made them seem in some way to be table-mates with him, just as the family table

---

40 *Guide* III, 32, 530; see also ibid. 527 and III, 29, 517-518 and III, 46, 582.

41 I checked the Latin translation of the *Guide* from MS Oxford, Bodl. 437, to see whether the translation had led William astray, but it has "prima intentio legis est", and "prima intentio...", foll. 91, 92, 93v, 94.

42 *De legibus*, ii, 29; xxiv, 72.

43 P. Viard, *Dict. de spiritualité* op. cit. 1190. He lists a "prayer to Moses" among them, which would be interesting, but it must be a mistake; I cannot find any prayer to Moses in *De rhetorica divina*.

44 He explains later that this was not *propria virtute*, in contrast to Christian sacraments. See below, p. 152.

146

brings men into closer relationship with their human parents. God indicated his presence from time to time by sending fire from heaven to consume his share of the sacrifices, as though in his stead. Sacrifices unified God's people, drawing many individuals together to make up one household and family. Sharing bodily food is the distinctive mark of the latter. Similarly sharing of spiritual food and drink makes one spiritual family and household. William defines "spiritual food and drink" as that which is hallowed, and where spiritual rather than bodily nourishment is sought. This definition enabled him to classify the Old Testament sacrificial meals as "spiritual". Finally, the sacrifices had a social-religious function in bringing men to worship together;[45] here again he draws on his experience:

> Food and drink cause men to assemble in the same place on the same occasion as nothing else does. That is why the Church has founded infirmaries, where physical refreshment is prepared; otherwise few or none would assemble there. Hence God in his great wisdom and mercy willed that food and drink should be shared in his house and at his altar, in order that the community of his people should be brought there and should be bound to them more closely. He willed that sacrifices should be sacred to him, in order that the people should partake of them as God's gifts and not as their own property, and as sacred, not common. The people would therefore acknowledge him as father of the family, who gave them life and food, and would refrain from evil, when they saw themselves admitted to communion or participation in holy things.[46]

William postulated that all his seven reasons for the sacrificial precepts would have been explained to the Jews in sermons. It could not have been otherwise. The wise and holy fathers of old would not have offered sacrifice without praises, blessings and discourses; they would not have left their people in total ignorance of divine matters. Who will believe that God's worship has ever lacked prayer and praise, seeing that these things are foremost and most pleasing to him in our services? The argument was hypothetical, as William knew. Evidence for prayers at sacrifice in the Old Testament is conspicuous by its absence. William got round it by suggesting that evidence had been lost, just as Maimonides had pointed to lost evidence on the nature of pagan

45   The *Guide* gave William a lead by implication on the subject of pilgrimage, III, 46, p. 592. The reason for the utility of pilgrimage is well known. For such a gathering results in a renewal of the Law, this being a consequence of people being affected by it and of the fraternity that comes about among them because of it. See also III, 39, 551 on the social function of the second tithe, which was to be spent on food in Jerusalem, and hence brought men together.
46   *De legibus*, ii, 29-30. The same point is made later: people would not frequent confraternity meetings unless cooked meals were provided; xxviii, 97.

practices.[47] "If these prayers and praises had come down to us", writes William, "they would have taught us clearly the causes and uses of this kind of rite".[48] A further reason for the sacrifices was to provide for the needs of the priests and leave them free to attend to divine service and to teach their people.[49]

William made a real effort to think himself back into Old Testament times. He tried to recreate the value and ethos of the Old Law, as administered by his predecessors, the levites, He could sympathise with them in their struggle to educate their flock. The Old Law, according to him, had a positive content, as well as a negative purpose against idolatry. Earlier Christian commentators had dwelt lovingly on the Tabernacle and its physical appearance. It took William to set up a pulpit beside the Jewish shrine. His historical method was anachronistic, in that he made the past look much like the present, as was usual in the middle ages. The interesting point is that he brought it to bear on the educative value of *legalia*, taken *ad litteram*.

Having expounded his own view, he turns to earlier exegesis. Commentators had interpreted the precepts all too often in a spiritual sense only. They had seen *legalia* as a veil or foreshadowing of the New Law and had neglected their literal value for the ancient Jews. William names no one, but he may well have directed his reproaches against Ralph of Flaix, since the latter's commentary on *Leviticus* was standard. The whole tradition, deriving from Origen and exemplified by Ralph comes in for criticism. Certain precepts had been classified as "absurd according to the letter". William turns the objection upside down. Absurd indeed they would have been, if they had lacked a literal meaning. The law-giver and his law would have been "barbarous", had they been incomprehensible. What could be sillier than to suppose that a wise prophet and lawgiver would have ordered his people to observe what they could not comprehend? It would have amounted to deception and mockery on his part. How could a leader and teacher fulfil his office unless he explained the law he gave? If he failed to do so, he would lead his people astray. To propound commandments which had no literal meaning, without announcing the fact, would have led the recipients to suppose a literal sense, where none was, or else left them, an ignorant people, to work out the secret, hidden meaning for themselves. Would a wise, loyal man refuse to speak openly to the people whom he had undertaken to teach? That would have involved him in

---

47   *Guide*, III, 29, 521.
48   *De legibus*, ii, 30.
49   Ibid.

148

fraud and dissimulation. William quotes a tag from rhetoric: "Sermo interpres animi est".[50] A lawgiver who refused to speak plainly would
have concealed his mind instead of revealing it. Moses had followers,
too. Would all later doctors of the law have left the people in ignorance
of its hidden meaning? The prophets at least would have mentioned it,
since God sent them to correct errors. According to the traditional
view, the precepts and bans of the Old Law were addressed to the "new
people", the Christians. They alone could understand the hidden
meaning, which was reserved for them and not for the ancient Jews.
William counters this objection. He begins by quoting St. Paul: *Now we
know that what things soever the Law speaketh, it speaketh to them
that are within the law* (*Rom.* iii, 19). He goes on to argue that the Law
had no need to carry an inner, spiritual meaning for the benefit "of us,
who were not yet there". There was no need for the Law to speak to us
in figures after the Church had been established, for then the Gospel
truth reached us, bare and plain. He thought it most unlikely that the
whole Jewish people, dedicated for so long to the study of their Law,
would not have discerned the error of taking it in its literal sense only,
if there had been another. William ends by anticipating a query which
might be raised. It occurred to him that he was claiming to understand
the moral value and rational character of *legalia* better than "the
modern Jews" did themselves: they ignored the literal reasons for their
laws. Was he not making the literal sense as difficult to grasp as the
spiritual? He answers that the learned men among the ancient Jews
would have understood well enough. The uneducated could have been
brought to understand quite easily, given the prevalence of idolatry
around them, which supplied the most obvious reason. That their former knowledge has perished is due to the passage of time, to their af-
flictions and dispersal and to their neglect of study. The reasons for
their negligence in studying their Law are avarice, to which the Jews
are prone, and love of gentile philosophy.

To sum up: William has anticipated St. Thomas in accounting the
whole intention of the sacred writer as included in the literal sense. Further, he was the first commentator, to my knowledge, to break away
from a narrow verbal concept of "the letter". Medieval exegetes had
been dogged by it. Even scholars who took the literal interpretation
seriously had still thought in terms of the *superficies litterae*. When
commenting on the literal sense of *legalia* they restricted themselves to
the exact form of the rites prescribed and took small pains to bring out
their meaning for the ancient Jews. True, William had the advantage of
writing in the framework of a treatise, instead of lecturing on his text,

50 Ibid. xv, 46, from Cicero, *De Legibus* i, 10: "Interpresque mentis oratio..."

clause by clause, as was done in the schools; but he also benefited from his careful reading of the *Guide*. Now he must leave the *Guide* and pass to the spiritual sense of *legalia*. So far, he has never denied that the Law has a spiritual sense for Christians. He has merely insisted that it had a literal sense for the Jews, who could understand it and profit from its lessons. *De legibus* presents it as an *alphabetum honestatis* and not as a veil or cryptogram.

What will he make of the spiritual meaning? The answer is rather elusive: perhaps it was intended to be. Conventional passages alternate with eccentric ones. William first states the proposition that Law of necessity has not only a literal, but a manifold spiritual meaning "from God", deducible from the literal, which enlightens the mind and edifies the soul. He proves it from the Law and the prophets themselves.[51] Many texts show us that the Law had an inner meaning. David the psalmist, to quote only one illustration, prayed that his eyes might be opened to consider the wondrous things of the Law (*Ps.* cxviii, 18). He had wit enough to understand the literal meaning of the Law (which William has already described as comprehensible even to simple men); therefore, he must have prayed for understanding of its higher meaning. The proof texts are buttressed by an argument from analogy. A human master teaches the pupils in his school according to their individual needs; some are dull and others clever. How much more does God, the supreme teacher, adapt his lessons to his pupils' various grades of intelligence? The Scriptures offer infinite variety, like a table groaning with good fare, where each guest will find nourishment suited to his appetite. William then launches into praise of Scripture of a traditional kind.[52] It sounds like part of a *principium*, the lecture in praise of Scripture given by a doctor at his inception. William may have used his own or borrowed from someone else.[53] So far, so good. Disconcertingly, however, he does not specify the content of the inner meaning which David prayed to have revealed to him. Did it refer to an understanding of the Old Testament prophecies of Christ? William may have presupposed that such was the case; but how odd that he fails to mention it!

51 Ibid., xvi, 47: "Patefaciemus post haec quia non solum litteralem intelligentiam habet lex. sed etiam spiritualem multiplicem a Deo, ut omnino intellectus illuminativus et aedificativus animarum, qui ex ea elici potest in ea necessario sit; et primum ostendemus hoc ex ipsius legis et prophetarum testimoniis."
William has already mentioned the existence of an élite among the Jews, though without elaborating on it; see cap. i, 23: "Quemadmodum nec omnes Hebraei temporis illius ad vetus testamentum pertinebant, ut dicit Augustinus: immo erant in populo illo qui ad novum pertinent" (*sic*).
52 Ibid., 47-8. Scripture is likened to a mine, having veins of precious metals and jewels, to a garden of delights, to a wine cellar and to a medicine chest.
53 None of the many sermons listed by J. B. Schneyer, *Wegweiser zu lateinischen Predigtreihen des Mittelalters* (Munich 1965) looks like a *principium* or inaugural lecture, but William must have given one.

There is still a chance for him to bring it in, since he passes to the spiritual senses of Scripture, after proving their existence. And here comes the novelty.[54] The spiritual interpretation, he tells us, proves a stumbling block to many; it strikes them as "imposition" rather than "exposition". He will try to satisfy them. His apology for the spiritual senses against their critics falls into four parts. Nobody can take offence at two modes of interpretation. Prophetic signs, expressed by means of deeds or speech were intended to be understood figuratively; he gives examples of what today we should call symbolic gestures or metaphors. On his own showing, these should really have been covered by the literal interpretation, since they belonged to teaching designed for instruction of Old Testament Jews. The third mode of interpretation is inoffensive also: we find a spiritual sense by drawing out the consequences of the literal. Thus bans on bodily idol worship had a moral significance: the command not to worship golden idols signified that plain gold must not be worshipped either, and forbad the sin of avarice. Paris masters of the sacred page classified William's third mode of interpretation as *moralitas secundum litteram*; they distinguished it from moralisation of texts, since it represented a deduction from the literal sense; it was not a "morality" in the strict sense of the term.[55] Logically, William should have included it in his account of the literal interpretation, since he argued that the precepts conveyed moral teaching according to their literal sense and reasons.

The fourth mode of interpretation gives offence to many. William sees the force of their objections and goes at least half way to meet them. This fourth mode is by comparison. There is no harm in it, if only exegetes would stick to comparisons instead of using signification. But they make things signify what they were never meant to, which is abusive. God did not teach in that way, when he spoke through his prophets. He used comparisons. William illustrates comparison in carefully chosen words:

> As a woman that despiseth her lover, so hath the house of Israel despised me (*Ierem.* iii, 20). God did not say that the woman's contempt signified the children of Israel's contempt nor that her lover signified himself.... Rather he expressed a mode or obvious likeness between the woman's contempt of her lover and the conduct of the children of Israel.

The prophet should serve as a model to exegetes. William continues:

> If exegetes and doctors would only speak in this way in their allegories and tropologies and anagogical interpretations, they would do justice to

54   See appendix, pp. 179-81 for the full text, which I summarise here in translation, giving references to the quotations in it.
55   B. Smalley, *The Study of the Bible in the Middle Ages*, op. cit. 234.

Scripture and would not insult the intelligence of their readers and hearers.

Instead, they make one thing signify another as a figure or prophecy, when it was neither said nor done in order to signify any other thing, which gravely offends their hearers. William gives a sample of this kind of distortion. He chooses the story of David's adultery with Bethsabee and the slaying of her husband Uria (II *Reg.* xi-xii). David acted as an adulterer, traitor and murderer. Yet he is said to signify Christ, while the good Uria is said to signify the devil. David's adultery with Bethsabee is said to signify Christ's pure, stainless union with the Church of the gentiles. This sort of teaching angers many. It destroys or at least weakens their faith in holy exposition of Scripture. William has picked on a current allegorical interpretation, deriving from St. Gregory's *Moralia*, as he must have known.

The objectors see two flaws in the use of signification. First, David's action was not intended to signify something else. Secondly, they think it most unlikely that the action was recorded in order to signify something else either. William (more or less identifying himself with them) explains how the David story may be used as a comparison: *just as* David loved Bethsabee and procured the death of her husband, *so* Christ loved the Synagogue and freed her from those who had held her in subjection, in order to honour her in spiritual marriage and make her his queen in heaven. If exegetes would make and explain such comparisons in a fitting way, they would run no risk of offending their hearers and would be listened to gratefully. Use of comparisons is a natural mode of teaching, found in Scripture, too. Commentators raise further scandal by their unskilled, fanciful inventions, which do violence to their text; they neglect St. Jerome's warning against excessive use of tropology. Instead of keeping to the point, they go off at a tangent, as when they interpret the branches and baskets in the dreams told to Joseph (*Gen.* xli) as signifying something different from what Joseph said they meant.

William closes this surprising chapter with a second conventional passage in praise of Scripture; but a trenchant summary of his views comes immediately after:

> We have explained that the Law has all the meaning proper to wholesome teaching, which can be deduced from it, in addition to its literal sense; but this is not whatever can be imposed abusively and violently upon it, repugnant to the letter. Such twisting of the Scriptures is not exposition, but rather abusive imposition. God in his goodness intended that all the meaning proper to wholesome teaching, which can be deduced from it *fittingly*, should be understood in Holy Scripture.

152

He has thrown overboard the current technique of lecturing on Scripture according to the four senses. Those *distinctiones*, which listed the properties of things for use in the spiritual exposition, rank by implication as idle fancies. Comparisons are admissable, significations are not:

> Verbum ergo significandi est quod in parte ista graviter offendit auditores atque lectores.[56]

Finally, William explains why *legalia* have been banned by the Church as superfluous under the new dispensation. Now, if ever, was the time for him to describe them as *umbra futurorum*. He does not. He explains instead that the sacrifices had no power to cleanse of themselves: they pleased God only because they demonstrated devotion and obedience and had useful purposes, such as maintaining the priesthood. The Church has found better ways of providing for divine worship and maintaining her priests.[57] Hence *legalia* no longer serve the needs of the new spiritual people, which has spiritual knowledge in the Gospel. William passes to two questions. First, why were *legalia* imposed on the righteous, as well as on the weak and ignorant, seeing that the righteous did not need symbolic actions to teach them to avoid sin and idolatry? Secondly, why did God withhold the true means of sanctification from his chosen people? The answer to the first question is that the righteous observed the ceremonial precepts in order to avoid scandal and schism. The second question receives the familiar answer that the people as a whole would not have understood them.[58] William now makes a new point: the prophets marked a further stage in education. They invited the people to spiritual worship and inner holiness, blaming mere outward observance.[59] The teaching of the prophets succeeded to that of the Law and came closer to perfection. Then at last, came the perfect excellence of the Gospels.[60] *De legibus* closes with an account of the

56 See appendix, below p. 180
57 *De legibus*, xxviii, p. 97: "Manifestum est quod postquam ista offeruntur, necesse habent illa cessare tanquam superflua quantum ad emundationem et sanctificationem, quare quamcito ista imposita et exposita sunt, cessare oportet illa, et ideo spirituali populo interdicta sunt merito, evangelio coruscante. Spirituali enim populo, hoc est spiritualia cognoscenti, nec necessaria sunt ad eruditionem neque ad emundationem vel sanctificationem neque ad eas quas diximus, scilicet ad conservationem et retinentiam in Dei honorificantia et cultu, neque ad alimoniam sacerdotum, cum alias et melius et honestius provideatur sacerdotibus spiritualibus. Quare manifestum est nullo modo ea esse necessaria. Deo autem accepta vel placita impossibile est esse, nisi propter utilitatem populi sui. Ergo manifestum est quia, facto spirituali populo, nec Deo placita sunt...."
58 Ibid., 98.
59 He quotes *Ierem*. iv, 3; vi, 10; ix, 26. The crucial text *Ezech*. xx, 25: *Dedi eis praecepta non bona* is not mentioned, however.
60 *De legibus*, xxviii, 99: "Unde postmodum per prophetas paulatim ad spiritualem cultum et interiorem sanctificationem invitati sunt, sicut apparet Hierem. 4, ubi dicitur... Iam igitur manifestum est, quia nec veritas nec virtus nec salubritas huiusmodi sacrificiorum causa fuit ut imponeretur populo Hebraeorum, sed sicut generaliter verum est quia pro rudibus et novitiis perfecta

seven sacraments of the Church, which have superseded the legal sacrifices. William's last opportunity to present the latter as figurative of the former has passed.[61] It follows that he could not allow the righteous of the Old Testament any presage of Christian sacraments.

The omission must have been intentional. We can see the influence of Maimonides in William's view of the superior type of wisdom possessed by the Old Testament élite. Like Maimonides, he restricts it to a higher concept of holiness and understanding of true religion or philosophy. It contrasted with external religion, though the latter had its uses, as wise men realised. This view in its turn sends us back to the beginning of *De legibus*, where William presents law in general as depending on the dictates of mind and heart. But this wisdom, it seems, excluded an understanding of *legalia* as *umbra futurorum*.

Full of curiosity, I turned next to William's lectures on Scripture, to his aids to preaching and to his sermons, to discover whether he put his theories into practice. Did he avoid allegories and tropologies, substituting comparison for signification? His lectures belong to an early stage of his career as a teacher. Here he used allegories and tropologies, as did everyone else.[62] He had not yet begun to criticise them. A study of his many unprinted sermons would have taken too long; but one has been edited, a university sermon, preached 1230-1231,[63] and therefore roughly contemporary with *De legibus*. Here he avoids allegories and tropologies altogether. His colleagues, Philip the Chancellor and others, preaching in the same year, use them freely.[64] William produced two aids to preachers, both undated. One has been edited by de Poorter. It does not mention the four senses. William dwells on the usefulness of fitting comparisons:

ab initio non traduntur vel imponuntur... Et doctrinae legis successit doctrina prophetarum tanquam perfectioni vicinior; tandem autem advenit evangelicae perfectionis excellentia, ultra quam non est quo se extendat in vita ista perfectio sanctitatis, et ideo praenominata rudimenta et initialia in adventu eius penitus cessaverunt et interdicta sunt toto orbe..."

61 Ibid. Several pages are dovoted to the sacraments of the Christian Church to conclude *De legibus*, but nowhere here are they described as having been prefigured or foreshadowed by *legalia*.

62 See B. Smalley, "Some Thirteenth-Century Commentaries etc" op. cit. 330. I looked again at the copy of William on *Proverbs* in MS Oxford, Bodl. 292. Here is a specimen of his exegesis: "*Dominus sapientia fundavit terram* (iii, 19): Ad litteram planum est...Mistice autem terram ecclesie fundavit Christus...*Stabilivit celos prudentia*. Celos vero enim contemplativos stabilivit...*Pes tuus non impinget* (23)... Pes autem iste caritas intelligitur..." (foll. 371vb, 372rb).

63 Edited by M. M. Davy, *Les sermons universitaires Parisiens de 1230-1231* (Etudes de philosophie médiévale xv, 1931) 149-53. William takes as his theme *Numquid ordinem caeli nosti* (Iob xxxviii, 33). He distinguishes the literal from the spiritual order of the heavens, but he includes in the literal interpretation of the text: "hujus caeli litteralis ordinem non videntur nosse. Ordo caeli litteralis possunt vocari stellae et hujusmodi... Secundus ordo caeli spiritualis et sublimis est, ubi sedet auctor universitatis, deinde seraphim..." (150).

64 Ibid. 161, 193, 244-5, 365.

154

> Convenienter rerum similitudo multum valet ad loquendum, sicut videri potest quando aliter rei natura sive proprietas explicatur.

Thus the Holy Spirit may be likened to fire or Christ to the sun, provided that the preacher explains the likeness. He stresses the need for logical order of ideas and he admits the use of *distinctiones, divisiones, interpretationes et definitiones*. The *distinctio*, which he cites as an example, lists only the literal senses of the word: "est pax peccatoris, praedicatoris etc".[65] The unprinted *De faciebus mundi* again recommends comparisons, drawn "from the book of nature and of art", with many examples.[66] Again it does not mention the four senses. So William satisfied me that he was consistent. He avoided allegories and tropologies, as soon as he had begun to reflect on their arbitrary character and had heard them attacked in the schools. Then he resorted to comparisons as a better mode of teaching.

One difficulty remained. William praised the Cistercian abbot, Joachim of Fiore, as having displayed *donum intellectus* in his commentary on the Apocalypse and in his *Liber concordie novi et veteris testamenti*. This passage, which has been discussed by students of Joachism, occurs in William's *De virtutibus*,[67] following next but one to *De legibus* in his *Magisterium divinale*. Joachim's type of spiritual exposition should not have pleased William on the evidence of *De legibus*. However, the praise of Joachim must be taken in its context. William is explaining how the "gift of understanding" differs from the spirit of prophecy and from faith. The prophet sees by divine illumination. The gift of understanding, on the other hand, enables us to discover the inner meaning of hidden things and signs:[68]

> Huic dono loquentur caerimoniae legis omnes et figurae,[69] similiter parabolae, aenigmata et visiones prophetarum, ut dicit Iob, quia intelligentia est opus in visione.[70]

In other words, prophets have the vision; those gifted with understanding expound their utterances. Men have the gift of understanding in varying degrees; it calls for effort and exercise. It may

65 A. de Poorter, "Un manuel de prédication médiéval", *Revue néo-scolastique* xxv (1923) 198, 203.
66 MS Oxford, Bodl. Digby 30, fol. 50-50v. On this treatise see H. Caplan, "Mediaeval *Artes Praedicandi*. A Hand-List", *Cornell Studies in Philology* xxiv (1934) 30; "A Supplementary Hand-List", ibid. xxv (1936) 20, 23.
67 M. Reeves, *The Influence of Prophecy in the Later Middle Ages* (Oxford 1969) 41-42.
68 *De virtutibus* xi, 152-3.
69 *Iob* xx, 3: *Spiritus intelligentiae meae respondebit mihi.*
70 *Dan.* x, 1.

attain to such clarity and sharpness as to resemble the spirit of prophecy. He cites Joachim as an example:

> Debes etiam scire quia istud donum, scilicet donum intellectus, tantae claritatis est et acuminis in quibusdam, ut valde assimiletur spiritui prophetiae, qualem crediderunt nonnulli fuisse in Abbate Joachim et ipsemet de seipso dixisse dicitur, quia non erat ei datus spiritus prophetiae, sed spiritus intelligentiae. Si quis autem inspexerit libros eius, quos scripsit super Apocalypsim et super concordiam duorum testamentorum, mirabitur donum intellectus in eo.

He goes straight on to explain that the gift of understanding differs from faith in that its object is deep, hidden matters, which are veiled in mystery or suggested by means of signification, whereas faith concerns basic principles. *Donum intellectus* carries neither the certainty of vision nor the certainty of truth which is arrived at by demonstration; exegetes of the Law and the Prophets do not use proofs, but "declarative narrations" only. The point of the definition comes at the end. William stresses that everything which is understood by *donum intellectus* can be acquired by teaching (*doctrina*). Every prophecy and mystery of which the gift confers understanding can be explained by teaching and set down clearly in writing by its possessor. Each virtue described in *De virtutibus* has its corresponding vice. The vice opposing *donum intellectus* is brutish idleness, which leads to neglect of study and reading.

De virtutibus raises the same problem as *De legibus*, in that William refers to exposition of the inner meaning of the Law and other mysteries without specifying its content. What manner of understanding them did *donum intellectus* confer? He does not tell us. His main aim in describing it comes out clearly, nonetheless. He was pleading for diligent application to study and teaching of the mysteries of Scripture. Joachim served as an example of a man who disclaimed the gift of prophecy (so it was said), but who applied himself to study and who published his studies for the benefit of others. Whether William accepted Joachim's findings, or whether he reserved judgment, cannot be decided from what he wrote. Joachim's exegesis, daring as it was, had no place for the mechanical allegories and moralities that William disliked. He wanted to keep abreast of current trends, as we know from his defence of the new Orders. Joachim's authentic writings were being discussed; the scandal which would break out on *spuria*, circulated by his disciples, had yet to come. William may therefore have been noting new ideas, perhaps without examining them.[71]

---

71 He certainly did not entertain any idea that a third and more spiritual age was still to come, since the gospel had brought full spiritual perfection within men's reach.

I have defended his consistency in applying his theories. Their internal coherence cannot be defended. William's account of the spiritual interpretation and its relationship to the literal is incomplete and muddled. As I understand it, he saw the spiritual interpretation as an extension of the literal; it was not to be "imposed" at the whim of the exegete. The story of David's adultery was not enacted or even recorded as an allegory: why impose allegory upon it? The thesis raised basic problems, which he did not formulate, on the relationship between the Old and New Testaments. The Old Law educated and prepared the chosen people to receive the New. He was sure of that. But was it a prefiguration, perceived by the wise, in addition to serving as an *alphabetum honestatis*? Had the Old Testament élite an implicit or explicit faith in the doctrines of the Trinity, the Incarnation and the Redemption? *De legibus* gives no answer. It raises questions instead; and these are crucial. We hear that many persons canvassed the exclusive truth of Christianity. Even more surprisingly, we hear that many persons took offence at the exposition according to the four senses. We cannot identify the former; the latter must have been students in the faculty of theology at Paris, since William writes that they read and heard expositions of Scripture. William deplores the first type of doubting, but shares the second. The vogue for allegorical interpretation of sacred texts has gone in waves. Each crest has been followed by reaction and "debunking". Yet it has always survived criticism.[72] We depend on *De legibus* for the surprising information that one period of reaction against allegory occurred at Paris in the second quarter of the thirteenth century.

William wrote under its impact. He threw out suggestions which would have altered the technique of medieval exegesis, had they been followed. They were not followed; allegory survived. William's theory suffered from a fatal combination of flaws. It was both original and inchoate, too original to appeal and too inchoate to be adopted. We shall see that it failed to win acceptance in the schools.

---

72 J. Pépin, *Mythe et allégorie. Les origines grecques et les contestations judéo-chrétiennes* (Paris 1958).

III

JOHN OF LA ROCHELLE

De legibus was quoted, though not swallowed whole. Much of it is woven into the texture of the *Tractatus de praeceptis et legibus* which forms part of the *Summa* ascribed to Alexander of Hales O.F.M. Modern research has established that John of la Rochelle O.F.M. compiled the *Tractatus*. It is older than the *Summa*. John collaborated with Alexander in preparing some parts of the latter, 1236-1245, but his teaching on natural law differs from Alexander's, as we have it in Alexander's *Sentences*, to such an extent that we must credit John with authorship of the *Tractatus*; it represented an original contribution to the *Summa*.[1] John was master of theology at Paris in 1238 and died in February, 1245. The exact date of his *Tractatus* is not known, but he must have been writing it during William's lifetime, while William was bishop of Paris, 1228-1249.[2] This would explain why he always quoted or referred to *De legibus* anonymously.

John quotes it verbally and sometimes slavishly. He copies out the passage on leprosy, where William wrote that he himself had seen dry rot in wood.[3] But slavish transcription of what appealed to him in *De legibus* went together with a critical and selective treatment of William's doctrine on the Old Law. This is important for two reasons: it shows how a contemporary reacted to the novelties in *De legibus*; it decided the form in which *De legibus* was passed on to the many readers of "Alexander's" *Summa*. Direct knowledge of William's treatise must have been rarer than knowledge of it *via* John's *Tractatus* as contained in the famous *Summa* of the Franciscan school.

John's reaction to *De legibus* can be put quite simply. He held to the traditional doctrine that *legalia* had not only a literal, but also a spiritual sense as signs, foreshadowings or figures of the New Law. William never said so: John keeps recurring to it in no uncertain terms. He classifies the precepts of the Old Law according to their three pur-

---

1 O. Lottin, op. cit. i, 128, 135; ii, 19, 52; W. H. Steinmüller, "Die Naturrechtslehre des Joannes von Rupella und des Alexander von Hales", *Franziskanische Studien* xli (1959) 310-422.

2 I shall quote the *Tractatus* from the edition in *Summa theologiae Alexandri Halensis*, part iii, vol. IV (Quaracchi 1948), using the editors' numbers and page references. They give exact references to both quotations from and allusions to the *De legibus*.

3 No. 518, p. 774. John copies "sicut vidimus".

poses: *moralia* clarified the law of nature; *iudicialia* repressed evil desires and served as a scourge for the wicked; *caeremonialia* signified the law of grace:

> ...figurae erant futurorum. et quantum ad hoc erat (lex) iustis in signum.[4]

William had described "signification" as a stumbling block.[5] John defends it explicitly. The ceremonial precepts were given

> ad manifestationem et testimonium futurae gratiae.[6]
> Sed lex Moysi, quantum ad figuralia, facit cognitionem
> credendorum et ad ipsam pertinet.[7]
> ...lex Moysi includit legem naturalem per explicationem in moralibus,
> legem vero gratiae per figurationem in caeremonialibus.[8]
> Lex quantum ad figuralia erat ducens in Christum.[9]

The figurative nature of the Old Law raises the question: did the ancient Jews who offered sacrifice according to its precepts understand their significance as prefigurations of the coming Redemption? The command of the psalmist, *sing ye wisely* (xlvi, 8), argues that they should have, since wisdom involves understanding. John answers that doctors and priests were bound to understand the true significance of their sacrifices explicitly. Simple men, on the other hand, were bound to realise only that they were pleasing to God, which carried with it an implicit understanding of their value as signs. He draws a parallel: scholars and prelates are bound to understand the articles of the faith explicitly, but simple men only implicitly.[10] It has already been stated that these figures were a sign of future grace *quoad perfectos*.[11] John adopts the traditional doctrine that *caeremonialia* carried signs of future grace for the Old Testament élite, who could understand their spiritual meaning, whereas the rank and file could not. Again he departs from *De legibus*. William never identified the inner meaning of the Old Law, as studied by the wise among the Jews, with prophecies or figures of Christ. He had asked why signs should have been written into the Old Law for the benefit of Christians, who were still unborn. John answers his query without raising it explicitly: The *figuralia* of the Old

---

4 No. 259, p. 367-8.
5 "Verbum ergo significandi est quod in parte ista graviter offendit auditores atque lectores". See below, p. 180
6 No. 259, p. 369.
7 No. 260, p. 370.
8 Ibid.
9 No. 262, p. 373.
10 No. 531, p. 807.
11 No. 267, p. 392.

Law still remain for us to read as past signs of the future, even after their fulfilment and abrogation.[12]

John's very arrangement of chapters shows how wedded to tradition he was. Before considering the literal sense of *caeremonialia*, he establishes that they had a spiritual sense in two chapters on *De intellectu praeceptorum caeremonialium*. This was to reverse the order of their treatment in *De legibus*. John begins by asking: "Utrum in caeremonialibus universaliter sit intelligentia litteralis", as some (William) have held.[13] He puts forward William's arguments in favour of the proposition: the legislator would have failed in his duty had he veiled his meaning instead of teaching his people plainly, and so on. His reply is that the alleged inconveniences are just the opposite: it is fitting that divine wisdom and divine law should be conveyed darkly. John's reasons betray some confusion, since he adduces both parables and metaphors to prove his point; these should have been included in the literal sense, strictly speaking. He adds that the spiritual sense was put there for the benefit of an élite. His conclusion is to deny the proposition, with the proviso that although it is not true *universaliter*, *most* of the precepts did have a literal sense and reason as well as a spiritual; *a few* of them, however, had a spiritual reason only.[14] Then he argues that they *all* had a spiritual meaning in a section headed "Qualiter in praeceptis caeremonialibus sit intelligentia spiritualis".[15]

Here he adapts William's account of the spiritual sense ingeniously to fit his thesis. First, he records objections to the spiritual interpretation. According to St. Augustine in *De doctrina christiana* all teaching is conveyed either by things or by signs. Some (William) ascribe a literal sense to all the ceremonial precepts. In that case, teaching is conveyed by things; these things cannot also be signs; consequently they convey no spiritual meaning. Secondly, it is abusive to deduce signs from things which were not intended to signify, and hence to seek a spiritual meaning in them (William again). Thirdly, the prophets taught by comparisons and not by significations; therefore it is unfitting to seek a spiritual interpretation where none was intended (William again).

---

12 No. 269, p. 398: "... immo adhuc habent eam (auctoritatem signandi) ut possit adhuc homo legere in ipsis; sed quod prius significabant ut futurum, modo significant ut praeteritum, et sic remanet significantia non mutata".

13 No. 516, p. 759.

14 Ibid., p. 760: "Ex iis igitur manifeste relinquitur non esse necesse in praeceptis caeremonialibus Legis universaliter esse sensum sive intelligentiam litteralem. Propterea breviter dicendum est, quod clarius erit in sequentibus, quod in aliquibus et pluribus praeceptorum caeremonialium praeter spiritualem intelligentiam sensus fuit et ratio litteralis, in aliquibus vero et paucis tantum ratio spiritualis, propter rationes praedictas quod infra manifestabitur".

15 No. 517, p. 760.

Fourthly, one thing designates another more fittingly and surely uni-
vocally than equivocally: a thing should have one meaning only. The
spiritual interpretation must be fitting. Therefore each word or deed
recorded in Scripture should have one spiritual meaning only. All the
holy expositors who find multiple meanings err in doing so. It is fitting,
too, that good should signify good, and bad, bad. John adduces William's objection to the allegorical interpretation of David's adultery
with Bethsabee as referring to Christ and the Church. He names St.
Gregory (as William had not done), so as to leave no doubt as to the
authentic source of the allegory. This last objection also derives from
William. All in all, John has made a fair and logical survey of William's
arguments against "abusive" allegories and moralities.

He answers them by making William argue against himself. The first
objection is disposed of by a distinction: the ceremonies were "things",
and as such they were ordered to the worship of the Creator; they were
also "signs", and as such they prefigured the Saviour's grace. He then
quotes William's defence of what William regarded as legitimate
spiritual interpretation, that is, the elucidation of metaphor or symbol,
deduction *per consequentiam* and teaching by the method of comparison. William's conventional praise of Scripture is quoted, with his
statement that all wholesome teaching may be drawn from it. John adds
a gloss of his own:

> Most fittingly are many meanings signified by one, in order that the
> Law's intention may correspond to God's goodness.

The gloss falsifies William's thought. John's sleight of hand is
remarkable. He has answered William's objections to the traditional
spiritual interpretation by manipulating William's own words and adding to them. The spearhead of William's attack has been blunted.

A more straightforward use of *De legibus* appears in the next chapter,
De ratione caeremonialium praeceptorum.[16] Having given priority to
the spiritual sense of the ceremonies, and denied a literal reason for
them *en bloc*, John felt free to approve the notion that many or most
had a rational cause *ad litteram*. He supplemented *De legibus* by a
direct study of the *Guide*, which is sometimes quoted by name independently of *De legibus*.[17] John copies at length from William's
defence of the precepts as rational and from his rebuttal of charges that
some of them were irrational, futile or absurd in the literal sense.

16 No. 518, p. 763. The full extent of John's use of *De legibus* is shown by the Quaracchi
editors in their admirable footnotes.
17 This also appears in the footnotes; John refers to Rabbi Moses, no. 263, p. 377 and to "Expositor legis Iudaeorum", no. 518, p. 763; there are other examples.

William's rather jumbled presentation of his defence is even improved upon. John classifies its heads in a more logical order. There were four reasons for the precepts in their literal sense. Some were necessary for the institution of religion, as were circumcision and the Passover, some to warn against error, some to promote worship of the Creator, and some for a compound of the last two reasons. John says apropos the third reason that three things are required to attract the rational mind to divine worship: decorum, dignity and cheerfulness (*decorum, honestum, iucundum*). These things appear in the precepts. Here we have an echo of William's account of Old Testament rites. John made further use of *De legibus* in a detailed study of the sacrifices,[18] "Utrum sacrificia legalia fuerint vera sacrificia". Oddly enough, he did not single out any precept as having no literal reason but only a spiritual, although he had refused to allow them a literal reason *universaliter*. His reservation protected him against the charge of too close adherence to *De legibus*, but did not need to be applied in particular, it seems. He dots the "i"s and crosses the "t"s in a later section headed "De differentiis sacrificiorum in Lege",[19] where he sets out the spiritual (allegorical and moral) interpretation of the sacrifices, in addition to the literal reason that they were instituted for the honour of God.

Hence the gist of William's rationalisation of *legalia* passed into school tradition via the *Tractatus*. John took just as much from *De legibus* as would fit into his conservative framework, and no more. But his quotations are full and verbal enough to convey some of the original warmth and power. William's defence of the literal reasons for the precepts became acceptable when once it had been isolated from its dangerous context. He was alive, and a highly respected prelate, when John wrote his *Tractatus*. John processed *De legibus* discreetly so as to avoid open criticism. One would like to know what William thought of the alterations.

18 No. 525, p. 797.
19 No. 537, p. 814.

IV

St. Thomas Aquinas

St. Thomas needed his clear mind when he turned to the literal and spiritual senses of Scripture: he had to fight a war on two fronts. On one front, he had to engage in a mopping up operation. Masters of the sacred page had widened the literal sense of Scripture so as to include verbal simile, metaphor, parable and symbolic action or gesture. Words and actions recorded in Scripture had to be explained according to their first intention; their spiritual interpretation was an addition, not a substitute. But the masters had worked their way to this method without accounting for it by any systematic reasoning, as far as we know. Consequently their terminology remained confused. Neither William of Auvergne nor John of la Rochelle achieved consistency in his handling of biblical metaphor and symbolism. Maimonides either raised or brought to a head a further problem on the literal interpretation of the Old Law. Had all its precepts, excluding *moralia*, some literal reason, as well as a literal sense (as a code actually given to the Jews)? Or were some precepts to be taken as irrational in their literal sense, apart from their divine purpose to prefigure the New Law? The question had wide implications, since it made scholars think about the legislator's aims in their historical context. On this front St. Thomas put forward a theoretical justification for the wider meaning now currently accorded to the literal sense, and distinguished it from the spiritual senses more clearly than had been done before.

On his second front, the traditional three spiritual senses had come under fire from William of Auvergne, voicing the objections of unnamed masters or students. St. Thomas was conservative enough to defend the spiritual senses. It would be interesting to know whether he read William's *De legibus*; if so, he met the attack in its full force. He certainly read and used John's *Tractatus*, where he could find a bowdlerised version of *De legibus* and perhaps guess at the original. Lottin, whose opinion must be respected, thought it probable that St. Thomas read *De legibus* directly and not only *via* the *Tractatus*.[1] I have

---

1   O. Lottin, *Psychologie et morale*, op. cit. iii, 592, 709. On St. Thomas's use of John's *Tractatus* see also G. Lafont, *Structures et méthodes dans la Somme théologique de Saint Thomas d'Aquin* (Paris 1961) 213.

found no textual proof that he did. More important, is the evidence of his *quaestiones disputatae*, given during his first regency at Paris, 1256-1259.[2] The regent master would announce the subject for disputation beforehand; then he presided over the exercise and "determined" at its close. Naturally he would choose a subject connected with some live issue, which would stir up interest and controversy.[3] Among the questions chosen by St. Thomas are: Whether Holy Scripture has senses other than the literal hidden in its words? How many spiritual senses are there? Are they to be found in writings other than Scripture? The choice of these three questions indicates that William's attack on allegories, tropologies and anagogies still had echoes in the schools. Some of St. Thomas's colleagues and pupils in the theological faculty must have doubted the validity of the fourfold interpretation, at least as currently practised, or wanted to be assured that it rested on a valid theory. He posted the problem for disputation in order to satisfy doubters.

The first question was crucial. Once the existence of a spiritual sense "Hidden in the Letter" had been established, it would be plain sailing to make the traditional threefold division of the spiritual into allegorical, moral or tropological and anagogical. The first two objections come from *De legibus*, retailed in John's *Tractatus*:

> Quia dictionibus semel sumptis non est utendum aequivoce vel multipliciter. Sed pluralitas sensuum facit multiplicem locutionem. Ergo in eadem locutione sacrae Scripturae non possunt plures sensus latere. Praeterea, sacra Scriptura ordinata est ad intellectum...Sed multiplicitas sensuum obnubilat intellectum. Ergo non debet in sacra Scriptura multi sensus esse.[4]

In substance it is objected that the purpose of Scripture is to instruct us clearly on one thing at a time. The third objection must have occurred to many masters of the sacred page in the course of their lectures: if there are several senses in Scripture, it will give rise to error, since interpretation will be arbitrary; the exegete will have no check on his arguments. The fourth follows on: the literal sense alone has authority in argument; therefore we cannot posit a spiritual sense as well. The fifth and last objection brings us back to William and John:

> Praeterea, quicumque sensus ex verbis alicuius trahitur quem auctor non intendit, non est sensus proprius; quia auctor per unam scripturam non

---

2 M. D. Chenu, *Introduction à l'étude de Saint Thomas d'Aquin* (Paris 1950) 241-242.
3 Ibid., 242-245; P. Glorieux, "L'enseignement au moyen âge. Techniques et méthodes en usage à la Faculté de Théologie de Paris au XIIIe siècle", *AHDLMA* xxxv (1969) 123-128.
4 *Quodl.* VII, q. vi, a. 1, ed. R. Spiazzi, i (Rome/Turin 1928) 145.

> potest intelligere nisi unum, quia non contingit plura simul intelligere, secundum Philosophum. Ergo non possunt esse plures sensus proprii sacrae Scripturae.

This gives the gist of William's argument which he illustrated by the story of David's adultery: we should keep to the sense intended by the sacred writer, instead of making him mean something else and turning his factual record into an allegory of Christ and the Church.

St. Thomas's solution of these problems is too well known to need more than a bare summary here.[5] He focussed attention on the twofold authorship of Scripture, human and divine, and hence on the diverse methods employed first by the human authors and then by the Holy Spirit who inspired them. The human authors would sometimes convey their teaching by means of metaphor, symbolism, analogy and parable. We find the same genres in pagan literature, especially in poetry. The literal sense includes all that the writer meant to express, a rule which applies to both sacred and profane literature. Prophecy and moral instruction, for instance, may be expressed in Scripture through figures of speech or action. We must include both the author's teaching and his way of putting it over to his audience in our reading of the literal sense. This definition of the literal sense as "all that the writer intended" cleared up a persistent muddle in terminology. The spiritual sense, in contrast to the literal, depended exclusively on the intention of God, the first cause and author of Scripture. God, as cause and author of all history, could give a significance to the events recorded and to the things described by the human authors of Scripture, which they, inspired though they were, could not possibly grasp, but which later revelation made plain. The Holy Spirit could express the divine meaning in figures over and above those employed by his human instruments:

> Sicut enim homo potest adhibere ad significandum aliquas voces vel aliquas similitudines fictas, ita Deus adhibet ad significationem aliquorum ipsum cursum rerum suae providentiae subiectarum.[6]

Hence the spiritual interpretation in its threefold division is "founded on the literal"; St. Thomas gave new content to the stock phrase. According to him, interpretation in the spiritual sense meant beginning from where the literal interpretation ended and only after it had been exhausted. His distinction between the senses made firmer ground for the rule (already partly accepted) that argument must proceed from

5 *Quodl.* VII, q. vi, p. 145-148. St. Thomas returns to the senses of Scripture in the *Summa* 1a, q. 1, a. 8-10. His treatment of it here is both more comprehensive and more succinct than in the *Quodlibet.* I have taken both the *Quodlibet* and this part of the *Summa* into account in summarising his solutions.
6 *Quodl.* VII, q. vi, a. 3, p. 148.

the literal sense only. God saw to it that everything needed for salvation should be found somewhere in Scripture according to the letter. The distinction between literal and spiritual senses enabled St. Thomas to mark off the Bible from other literature. In the Bible the actual course of the history recorded had a spiritual significance unknown to its actors and writers. That could not apply to any other kind of writing, but only to Scripture, of which the Holy Spirit was author and man merely the instrument.[7]

The solution neatly disposed of William's objections to the allegorisation of King David's misdeeds: they were not committed, nor probably were they recorded, in order to signify Christ's marriage to his Church; so William argued.[8] According to Thomist theory there could be no question of intention to signify either on the part of King David or of the historian. The Holy Spirit intended that the misdeeds and their record should have an allegorical significance, which was unrecognisable at the time. All carping at allegories, moralities and anagogies would cease when this touchstone was applied to them. Their justification in Thomist theory would make it otiose to resort to comparisons instead of significations, as William had urged upon exegetes. The spiritual interpretation could be used without doing violence to the sacred writers' intentions. It must have relieved the scrupulous: allegories, moralities and anagogies had divine authority, whereas comparisons represented mere human inventiveness.

Thomist doctrine on the four senses has been much discussed. Personally I see it differently after reading William's *De legibus*. Before that surprising experience I put too much emphasis on St. Thomas's care for a better definition and better understanding of the literal sense.[9] Now I would classify this as a mopping up operation, designed to remedy confusion and to justify deeper study of the literal sense. His more powerful guns, as I picture it in the light of *De legibus*, were trained in defence of the traditional fourfold interpretation against William's attack. Further study of the section *De veteri lege* in his *Summa* has confirmed my change of mind. St. Thomas was more middle-of-the-road than he seemed to me on first acquaintance with his teaching.

In any case, his doctrine on the senses is incomplete and leaves a gap to be filled in. He allows for Old Testament prophecies of Christ within the context of the literal sense. He justifies the allegorical interpretation, according to which historical events signify Christ and his

7 Ibid.
8 See above, p.151, and appendix, below, p. 180.
9 See my *Study of the Bible*, op. cit. 300-306.

members as shadows of truth; then he explains that when Christ is referred to (directly) by means of a simile or metaphor, this does not go beyond the literal sense; the image of *the stone cut out of a mountain without hands* in Daniel's interpretation of King Nabuchodonosor's dream (*Dan.* ii, 34) is given as an example of a prophecy of Christ according to the literal sense.[10] The problem how to distinguish passages which had a Christological meaning in the literal sense, as intended by the lawgiver or prophet, from those which were allegories, had already presented itself to exegetes. They were left to fumble. By what rules should the exegete judge whether a text which had been traditionally interpreted as a prophecy of Christ belonged to the literal sense or the allegorical? What limits should he set to the prophet's foresight? St. Thomas gave no guidance here. Did he offer guidance in the application of his own principles to exegesis? His literal exposition of the book of Job is a brilliant example: he treated the content as a discussion of the ways of divine Providence.[11] But the choice of this book suited his genius as a philosopher theologian perfectly. The precepts and institutions of the Old Law demanded a different approach. *De veteri lege* shows him applying the principles set forth in *De veritate* and at the beginning of the *Summa*.

A study of *De veteri lege* must begin with its sources. It fits into the framework of the whole section *De legibus*, a treatise on divine, eternal, natural and human law. St. Thomas had a strong feeling for the rational character of law in general. He has been claimed as a true jurist, in spite of his lack of legal training: "Saint Thomas se situe admirablement dans la ligne spirituelle des grands romanistes médiévaux."[12] We know that he read and pondered the *Guide*: he quoted Rabbi Moses independently and directly.[13] The going gets harder when we confront *De veteri lege* with its main secondary source, John's *Tractatus*.[14] The Dominican doctor took up the problems of the Old Law where the Franciscan had left off. He rearranged and rethought the *Tractatus*, though he neither copied it verbally nor mentioned it by name. No one as yet has collated the two. All I can undertake to do in this paper is to

10 *Quodl.* VII, q. VI, a. 2, op. cit. p. 147.
11 *Expositio super Iob ad litteram, Opera* xxvi, ed. Leon., 1965.
12 J. M. Aubert, *Le droit romain dans l'œuvre de Saint Thomas* (Paris 1955) 76, 79, 139.
13 See the thorough survey by J. Guttman, *Das Verhältniss des Thomas von Aquino zum Judentum und zur jüdischen Literatur* (Göttingen 1891) 33-92; on his criticism of Maimonides see H. Liebeschütz, "Eine Polemik des Thomas von Aquino gegen Maimonides", *Monatschrift für Geschichte und Wissenschaft des Judenthums* lxxx (1936) 93-96.
14 I have used the edition and translation with occasional minor changes in the new publication of the *Summa* on the Old Law by the English Dominicans, xxix (London 1969) by D. Bourke and A. Littledale. Unfortunately the editors confine themselves to cross-references and to authors quoted by name in the *Summa*. They ignore the relationship between the *Summa* on the Old Law and John's *Tractatus*. Otherwise the volume is very useful.

offer an impressionistic sketch of the order of questions and articles in
the *Tractatus* and the *Summa* respectively. The samples that I have
chosen relate to the nature and content of the Old Law and to the
ceremonies in particular. Sections on *moralia* and *iudicialia* will be
omitted. The comparisons will show that St. Thomas posed much the
same questions as John. Differences between the two scholars occur
mainly in the ordering of their material. St. Thomas sometimes altered
the sequence of articles given by the *Tractatus* inside one question;
sometimes he made more drastic changes.

Tractatus I	*Summa* 1a 2ae
Q.I: De latione Legis mosaicae	Q. 98
259 a.1) De utilitate lationis Legis	a.1) Utrum lex vetus fuerit bona
260 a.2) An lex Moysi sit necessaria ad salutem	(included in a.1)
261 a.3) De tempore lationis Legis	a.6) Utrum lex vetus convenienter data fuerit tempore Moysi
262 a.4) Quibus debuit dari Lex	a.4) Utrum lex vetus dari debuit populo Judaeorum
263 a.5) De Legis latore. An lex Moysi sit lata a bono et a solo Deo	a.2) Utrum lex vetus fuerit a Deo
264 a.6) Utrum lex Moysi sit lata a Deo per ministerium angelorum	a.3) Utrum lex vetus data fuerit per angelos

The *Summa* follows a more logical order than the *Tractatus*. St.
Thomas proceeds from the top downward. The Old Law was good; it
was given by God as necessary to salvation by the ministry of angels to
the Jews at a fitting time. His a.5 explains why the Old Law, given to
the Jewish people, as stated in a.4, was not binding upon all. St.
Thomas's a.5 corresponds to a much later article in the *Tractatus*,
where John considers a miscellany of questions, under the heading *De
personis* (no. 530).

Q.II of the *Tractatus* deals with points which St. Thomas had condensed into q. 98, a.1, *Utrum lex vetus fuerit bona*. A glance will show
how he abridged his source; one article sufficed for all the following:

Tractatus (265-268)

a.1) De continentia Legis quantum ad genera contentorum; a.2) De continentia Legis quantum ad qualitatem contentorum; (i) Utrum omne
quod continetur in Lege sit sanctum (ii) bonum (iii) iustum.

Tractatus	*Summa*
269 Q.III: De impletione legis Moysi per Christum	Q.106: De lege evangelica etc
271 Q.IV: De onere observantiae legis mosaicae	Q.107, a.4) Utrum lex nova sit gravior quam vetus
274 Q.V: De iustificatione per Legem[15]	Q.100, a.12; Q. 103, a.2.

St. Thomas preferred to tackle problems arising from comparison between the Old and New Laws after, not before, he had finished discussing the content of the Old Law. Again, his arrangement looks tidier than John's. The question whether observance of the legal precepts in Old Testament times justified the observers made a bridge between the two and fitted into discussion of the legal precepts. Hence it came earlier in the *Summa* than in the *Tractatus*.

Tractatus II, sect. iii: De caeremonialibus	*Summa*
516 Q.I, cap. i: Utrum in caeremonialibus universaliter sit intellectus litteralis	Q.102, a.2) Utrum habeant causam litteralem, vel solum figuralem
517 cap.ii: Qualiter in praeceptis caeremonialibus sit intellectus spiritualis	(included in a.2)
518 Q.II: De ratione caeremonialium praeceptorum. An habeant causam observantiae litteralem, an solum mysticam et figuralem	a.1) Utrum praecepta caeremonialia habeant causam (also included in a.2)
A. in generali	(also included in a.2)
B. in speciali	
1) in circumcisione	a.5) De causis sacrorum
2) in Phase	
3) in victu	a.6) De causis observantiarum
4) in vestitu	(included in a.6)
5) circa actum indifferentem	
6) circa immunditiarum cavendarum	
7) purificationis immunditiarum	
8) sacrificiorum, in genere, in speciali	a.3) De causis sacrificiorum
9) altaris	a.4) De causis sacramentorum
10) tabernaculi	(included in a.4)
11) circa ordinationem ministrorum	
12) circa ornatum sacerdotum seu ministrorum	
13) solemnitatum	

15 The numbers 270, 272-3 of the *Tractatus* deal with subordinate points. I have omitted them in order to make the scheme of my comparison clearer.

St. Thomas has succeeded in reducing thirteen articles to six by dividing ceremonies into categories: sacrifices, sacraments, sacred things and observances. He considers most of the points raised by John within the scope of fewer articles.

Tractatus	*Summa*
Q. III	
519 De numerositate caeremonialium	Q.101, a.3) Utrum debuerint esse multa caeremonialium praecepta
520 De differentia caeremonialium in genere	a.4) Utrum caeremonia veteris legis convenienter dividantur in sacrificia, sacra, sacramenta et observantias

Again, it was tidier to clear up the problem of why there were so many ceremonial precepts before descending to particular items and to group them under separate headings. St. Thomas therefore inverted John's order. As we have seen, he divided them into categories; and he saved himself from redundancy in considering their causes: John's thirteen articles are more than halved in the *Summa*.

My comparison will have shown that St. Thomas had the *Tractatus* on his desk or at least in his mind, when he compiled *De veteri lege*. The sketch will have given some idea of how he set its questions in his own order. He makes one major change of structure in that he treated the ceremonial precepts before instead of after the judicial.[16] A comparison of the internal matter of separate articles, where the questions coincide, gives the same impression: St. Thomas borrowed arguments *pro* and *contra* from John, sometimes conflating them. Thus in q. 101, a. 2, on whether the ceremonial precepts are figurative, he abridges six objections, taken by John (no. 516, p. 759) from William of Auvergne, into one:

> It is the duty of every teacher to make himself easily understood, as Augustine says. This seems necessary most of all in propounding a law, since its commands are conveyed to the people. Hence a law ought to be clear, as Isidore says. If then the ceremonial precepts were given as figurative of something, it would seem that Moses, in failing to explain what they figured, did not transmit them in a proper manner.

But he adds other objections of his own. His replies and conclusions often agree with John's in substance.

---

16 St. Thomas probably did so out of respect for the biblical text: *Haec sunt praecepta et caeremoniae atque iudicia* (*Deut.* vi, 1). He quotes it in q. 99, a. 4. A further difference between his treatment of *iudicia* and John's is that St. Thomas limits himself here to the judicial precepts of the Old Law, whereas John spreads his net wider; he discusses contemporary judicial problems.

There is no time for a more detailed collation here. St. Thomas restructured his source into a clearer, more logical pattern. He sorted out the pieces and fitted them together as it pleased him. What did he make of its doctrine? The short answer is that he rethought it in terms of his theory of causality.

This appears in his very first questions on the Old Law in general, "whether it is good", (q. 98, a. 1). St. Thomas replies to objections by defending the Old Law on the grounds that it conformed to reason by restraining the appetite and by forbidding all sins which are contrary to reason. Then he considers "the ordering of things to a given end". Human law is directed towards the temporal peace of the State, divine law towards bringing man to the attainment of his goal of eternal happiness. Hence the latter has to do more than regulate external actions: "it is required to make man totally equipped to share in eternal happiness, something which can be achieved only by the grace of the Holy Spirit". It follows from consideration of ends that the Old Law is good, but imperfect in comparison with the New Law; the conferring of grace was reserved to Christ. The crucial text: *I gave them statutes which were not good* (*Ezech.* xx, 25) has taken its place as the first authority *contra*. St. Thomas refers it to the ceremonial precepts, as had normally been done. Ralph of Flaix, representing the older tradition, had used it to discredit the educative value of *caeremonialia*, whereas William of Auvergne, following Maimonides, had taken *not good* as referring to the disposition of those who performed ceremonies unworthily. John of la Rochelle did not consider the Ezechiel text. St. Thomas steers a middle course. The ceremonial precepts were said by the prophet to be *not good* because they showed up man's need for cleansing (being instituted as sin-offerings etc.), but they did not (in contrast to the sacraments of the New Law) confer the grace by which men could be cleansed of their sins. Thus he relates the Ezechiel text to the nature and purpose of the Old Law; it was good, but imperfect.

He begins his discussion of the ceremonial precepts *secundum se* (q. 101, a.1) by framing a question of his own: "Does the reason of the ceremonial precepts reside in the fact that they concern the worship of God?" This question gives him scope to explain his principle. The ceremonial precepts, even those which at first sight do not seem to belong to divine worship, are particular applications of the moral precepts which order man to God, just as the judicial precepts are applications of those which order man to his neighbour. "Whatever is preparatory to a particular end comes under the science dealing with that end". The ceremonial precepts are rules of salvation, which order man to God. "Accordingly those which concern the worship of God are

called ceremonial". St. Thomas has stated his own formula just before
he begins to draw on John's *De legibus*, which cannot have been accidental. The theme of "ends" will recur even when he is borrowing.
Thus he answers the question (a. 2), whether the ceremonial precepts
had a literal cause or only a figurative, by relating them to their purpose: "The reason for whatever is done in view of an end must be
looked for in that end. Now the end of the ceremonial precepts was
twofold; they were ordained for the worship of God at that time, and for
prefiguring Christ". Their purpose was *ordinatio mentis in Deum*, as he
states repeatedly (q. 101, a. 2-4, q. 102, a. 1-5). He also fits *ordinatio*
into his doctrine on the body-soul relationship (q. 101, a. 2): "Worship
is twofold: internal and external. For since man is made up of soul and
body, both must be used for the worship of God, the soul by interior
worship, the body by exterior....As the body is ordered to God by the
soul, so exterior worship is ordered to interior".

We may now turn to his teaching on the significance of
caeremonialia. St. Thomas subscribed to and underlined John's
argument that they had both a figurative and a literal cause. Like John
he begins by establishing that they had a figurative cause: divine
teaching had to be adapted to a crude people; divine mysteries must be
expressed in figures (q. 101, a. 1). Like John he argues that they had a
literal cause as well (q. 102, a. 2). His arguments have a more cutting
edge than his predecessor's. The objections are (1) circumcision and the
sacrifice of the paschal lamb were signs only: how much more so the
other ceremonies? (2) the effect is proportionate to the cause. All the
ceremonial precepts are figurative. Therefore they have a figurative
cause only; (3) many precepts, such as the number of animals prescribed
for sacrifice, are indifferent in themselves; therefore they cannot have
any literal cause. He replies by arguing for a literal cause on the ground
that ceremonies provided for divine worship "at that time". They warded off idolatry, recalled God's goodness and disposed the mind to his
worship. St. Thomas draws a parallel between legal precepts and
prophetic words. The prophet spoke words which applied to his own
time and which also figured what was to come. Similarly, circumcision
and the passover signified God's covenant with Israel and her delivery
from Egypt according to their literal sense, but they also prefigured the
sacraments of the New Law. The other ceremonies likewise were instituted not only as figures of the future, but also to regulate divine worship there and then. The answer to objection (2) is that it would be conclusive only if the ceremonial precepts were given *solely* to prefigure the
future. The answer to the objection on indifferent precepts (3) disposes
of the whole difficulty once and for all, though particular cases come

up for discussion later. St. Thomas refers back to his treatment of particulars in human laws (q. 96, a. 1 and 6). Human laws should be ordered to the common good of the body politic in principle. Their particulars vary according to the will of their framers. In the same way "many particulars in the ceremonies of the Old Law have no literal cause, but only a figurative, though *taken in the abstract, they have also literal causes*". His parallel between human and divine laws enabled St. Thomas to steer a middle course. He avoided making a categorical statement that some precepts had no literal cause, as John had done; he avoided making the equally categorical statement that *all* precepts had a literal cause, as William had done. Divine and human laws alike, in Thomist theory, were directed to an end in principle, which covered particular applications.

The literal reasons for *caeremonialia* interested him. He studied their particulars, supplementing John by direct recourse to the *Guide*. He did not always agree with John. The Franciscan had argued, copying William, that the precept against boiling a kid in the milk of its dam (*Exod.* xxiii, 19) was directed against idolatry, and gave no other reason for it. The same applied to John's explanation for the precept not to take the hen with her young from a nest (*Deut.* xxii, 6). Here again, he followed William, who had scouted Maimonides' suggestion that such precepts inculcated pity. St. Thomas preferred to hold that they did inculcate pity, as well as warning against idolatry and superstition. He expands on the argument:

> As to the affection arising from sentiment, it is operative also with regard to animals; for since pity is roused by the sufferings of others, and animals can feel pain, man can feel pity for them. And if he is often moved in this way, he is more likely to have compassion for his fellowmen... Therefore the Lord, in order to stir to compassion the Jewish people, naturally inclined to cruelty, wished to exercise them in pity even to animals, by forbidding certain practices savouring of cruelty to them (q. 102, a. 6).

His thoughtful interest in literal reasons for particular precepts did not prevent him from tipping the balance in favour of John's defence of their figurative reasons. *Caeremonialia* as figures have a privileged place in the Thomist scheme. This comes out in the contrast made between ceremonial and judicial precepts (q. 104, a. 4). The judicial precepts were figurative in a different way from the ceremonial (q. 104, a. 2): "It seems to be characteristic of the ceremonial precepts that they were instituted as figures of something." They regulate divine worship; things pertaining to God must be conveyed in figures, as being beyond our reason, whereas what concerns our neighbour is not beyond our reason. St. Thomas explains that a precept may be figurative in two ways: "First, primarily and in itself, in that it was enacted primarily to be a figure of something. The ceremonial precepts were figurative in this way; for they were instituted in order to be figurative of something connected with the worship of God *and the mystery of Christ*". Here, then, he classifies under the heading "figurative" the purpose of the ceremonies, both as regulating divine worship at that time and as prefiguring Christ. He sees their primary meaning as figurative in both senses. The judicial precepts, on the contrary, were figurative only in the way that the whole history of God's chosen people was figurative: the judicial precepts of this people, like their deeds and wars, are interpreted allegorically and morally as well as literally. Those of gentile peoples differ from the Jewish in that they are not interpreted allegorically and morally; they have a literal meaning only. St. Thomas is applying his doctrine on the senses of Scripture: God, as the first author of sacred history, has given it a mystical content peculiar to Revelation. But *caeremonialia* have a special place within it. Their special character is brought out again on the question: "Do the judicial precepts bind in perpetuity?" (a. 3). St. Thomas answers that neither the ceremonial nor the judicial precepts bind in perpetuity: both have been voided by the New Law. But they were voided in different ways. The ceremonies "became not only dead, but deadly to those who should keep them after Christ had come, and particularly after the promulgation of the Gospel. The judicial precepts, on the other hand, are dead, since they have no binding force, but not deadly". The reason given is that "the ceremonial precepts were figurative primarily and in themselves, being instituted principally as figuring the mysteries of Christ yet to come. Consequently their observance would militate against the truth of faith, in which we profess that these mysteries are now fulfilled". A legislator today might re-enact Old Testament *iudicialia* without committing mortal sin, provided that he did not order them to be observed "as binding through enactment in the Old Law". "The judicial precepts were not instituted as figuring, but as ordering the state of that people, which was directed to Christ".

St. Thomas has made a clear statement: the ceremonial precepts were instituted *principally as figuring the mysteries of Christ yet to come*. Hence they fall into a different class; St. Thomas has set them apart from the rest of Old Testament history, including *iudicialia*. Their literal meaning for the Jews slips into the background, as soon as he contrasts them with the judicial precepts. He repeats the traditional allegories and moralities concerning ceremonies in what strikes a modern reader (and his modern editors) as tedious detail. Much of it is

borrowed from John, but the borrowing stems from St. Thomas's determination to apply his principle at whatever cost in tedium. A principle
was at stake indeed. Since the primary significance of ceremonies included their figurative meaning, that is, allegories and moralities, then
the latter must be set forth at length. It seems that William of Auvergne's neglect or rejection of the figurative sense of the ceremonies
had spurred on St. Thomas to emphasise it, whether he knew of
William's attack at first hand or indirectly. He defended the figurative
sense of the ceremonies at unusual length; such prolixity is too rare in
the *Summa* to be accidental. The theme recurs in other sections too:
Christ's passion was a true sacrifice, prefigured by the blood offerings of
the Old Testament, though truth surpassed its figure (3a, q. 48, a. 3).

Modern experts on Thomism put forward divergent views on the
structure and organisation of the *Summa*, seen as reflecting its author's
mind. Some would interpret the sequence as outlining the process of
withdrawal and return to God; others see it as Christ-centred;[17] others
find the key in the author's concept of *Heilsgeschichte*.[18] All agree on
one point: St. Thomas was constrained by his reasoning to interpret the
Old Testament ceremonies and sacraments as prefigurations of the
New; the structure and doctrine of the *Summa* demanded that he
should.

St. Thomas's re-shaping and re-thinking of John's *De legibus* thus
tied it into his *ensemble*. He produced a more convincing justification
of the figurative meaning of *caeremonialia* than had been offered
previously. It was more telling in two ways: St. Thomas gave a general
theory on the relations between the senses as a background; he understood and allowed for the new enthusiasm for discovering a literal
reason in the precepts. He both satisfied critics and upheld the
traditional view of ceremonies as figurative. A moderate position,
clearly argued, will often win acceptance. So it did here: we hear
nothing further of William's attack on "significations".

Finally we must ask the question: how much, in St. Thomas's view,
did Moses and other wise men of the Old Testament perceive of the
figurative meaning of ceremonies? The distinction between élite and
common herd belonged to tradition and could be taken for granted.
Ralph of Flaix ascribed understanding of the figurative meaning to
Moses and the élite, but denied it to the people, from whom, indeed,

17 G. Lafont, *Structures et méthodes dans la Somme théologique de Saint Thomas d'Aquin*
(Paris 1961), gives a summary of earlier views and his own.
18 M. Seckler, *Le salut et l'histoire. La pensée de saint Thomas d'Aquin sur la théologie de
l'histoire*, transl. from the German (Paris 1967).

their teachers took pains to hide it behind the veil of the literal meaning. William of Auvergne challenged this traditional view on the grounds that all precepts of the Old Law had a literal reason, which teachers were bound to explain to the people. He admitted that wise men could gain a deeper understanding by dint of study than could be conveyed to the people, but its content he never specified. William avoided stating that the deeper meaning acquired by study included understanding of the prefigurative value of *caeremonialia*. John of la Rochelle re-stated the traditional view in a modified form. His distinction between explicit and implicit belief enabled him to put it more precisely and to allow the Jewish people a better understanding of their rites: "modern" scholars and prelates are bound to understand and believe in the articles of the *credo* explicitly, but simple men only implicitly. Just so, ancient doctors and priests were bound to understand the true figurative meaning of their sacrifices explicitly, whereas the people were bound to implicit belief only. The people had only to believe that their sacrifices would please God for reasons which passed their understanding.

St. Thomas agreed with John and he explored the subject further. He decided in *De veritate* that the ancients knew the whole faith, *quasi in universali implicite credentes.*[19] But the elders and leaders of the people were bound to believe some truths of the faith explicitly. They were bound to explicit belief in the Trinity, even before the Fall. After the Fall, they were bound also to explicit belief in redemption to come.[20] Explicit belief in a future redemption carried implicit faith in the incarnation and passion with it (2a 2ae, q. 1, a. 1). All those who resisted the devil before Christ's passion were able to do so through faith in his passion, although it had not yet come to pass (3a, q. 49, a. 2). The faith of the ancients was the same as ours, apart from the difference in period. They believed, explicitly in some matters, implicitly in others, truths which would come about in the future, whereas we believe truths which have been manifested to us in the past. The ancient fathers, as teachers of this faith, received from God such knowledge as they needed to convey to their people at the time, whether openly or in figures. Full knowledge would come with Christ. Understanding was given by stages, as God adapted his teaching to men in the various periods of their history: boys have to learn the lesser things first, and a crowd must be brought to understanding of things unheard of previously by degrees.[21]

19 *De Veritate*, q. 14, a. 12; ed. R. Spiazzi i (Rome/Turin, 1948) p. 304.
20 Ibid. a. 11, p. 302-3.
21 *Summa contra gentiles* 4, 23; ed. Leon. (Rome 1934) 517.

St. Thomas accepted the traditional three stages: before the Law, under the Law, the time of grace.

Did revelation by stages mean that implicit belief in the figurative value of ceremonies became more explicit as time went on? We might expect the answer to be "yes", since St. Thomas says that those who lived closer in time to Christ had more explicit knowledge, giving St. John the Baptist and the apostles as examples (2a 2ae, q. 2, a. 1-2). But the answer is really "no". The negative comes out clearly in his questions on prophecy (2a 2ae, q. 174, a. 1-2). Moses was the greatest of the Old Testament prophets *simpliciter*. The quality of prophecy did not improve within each of the three stages of salvation (before the Law, under the Law, time of grace). On the contrary, the first revelation within each of the three stages excelled those following in its own stage. Hence the revelation granted to Moses excelled those granted to later prophets under the Law, just as the Gospel excelled anything which followed it in the time of grace. The Baptist and the apostles, therefore, shared in the first and best revelation of the third period. St. Thomas refused to admit a progressive revelation within each of the stages of the history of man's salvation. His refusal formed the crux of his case against the Joachites. He rejected their hope of a new gospel of the Holy Spirit. [22] It is more important here that he differed from William of Auvergne also. William had stated his belief in a progressive revelation "under the Law". The prophets of Israel, according to William, called their people to a more interior worship than the legal precepts enjoined. He presented the Law as wholesome and rational, but argued that it could be supplemented and improved upon, though not voided, before it ceded to the New Law of Christ. [23]

In the Thomist view of revelation the best comes first in each successive stage. That is why the figurative value of ceremonies and sacrifices claims a central place in his synthesis. They give coherence to his picture of the history of salvation. The ceremonial and sacrificial precepts conveyed implicit faith to the whole Jewish people, who practised them for the honour of God (1a 2ae, q. 101, a. 2). They all observed rites which signified the future expiation of sin by Christ. They shared in this expiation "by professing faith in the Redeemer in figurative sacrifices" (ibid. q. 102, a. 5). But the Jewish people were divided into two groups. The priests had more explicit knowledge than the rest, just as they played a more direct part in divine worship:

> Hence the high priest alone, once a year, entered into the inner tabernacle, the Holy of Holies, signifying that the final perfection of man is his

22 See M. Reeves, op. cit. 67-69, 161.
23 See above, p. 152.

entrance into that world. Into the outer tabernacle, the Holy Place, the priests entered daily, but not the people, who only had access to the court, because the people could conceive what was corporeal, but the inner meaning could only be seen by the wise through reflection (q. 102, a. 4, ad 4).

To the state of the Old Law the people and the priests were related in different ways. The people looked on at the bodily sacrifices offered in the court. The priests, however, were intent on the meaning of the sacrifices, since they had more explicit faith in the mysteries of Christ, and so they entered into the outer tabernacle, for some things were veiled from the people concerning the mystery of Christ, while they were known to the priests, though even to them they were not fully revealed, as subsequently in the New Testament (ibid.).

St. Thomas, like John of la Rochelle, transposed the distinction between priests and people, clergy and laity, as he knew it, back into the Old Testament. The priests of the Old Law shared with Moses and the élite a more explicit understanding of the ceremonial mysteries than was vouchsafed to the people. As he explained in *De veritate, minores* in Christian times were bound to have explicit faith in the creed in general and in the Church's teaching; explicit faith in each article of the creed could not be demanded of *minores* as it was of *maiores*. [24] The same sort of difference obtained under the Old Law.

To sum up the results of this long enquiry: St. Thomas on the Old Law stands out from his background as an intelligent conservative. He thought out the traditional doctrine and put his learning at its disposal. It corresponded to his most cherished convictions on the divine scheme of salvation. The patriarchs and prophets still "greet their country from afar". St. Thomas yielded to none of his predecessors in the foresight which he accorded to the Old Testament élite. Priests and elders understood the figurative meaning of ceremonies and sacrifices explicitly, though they could not foresee the Gospel story in detail. The whole Jewish people was bound to believe implicitly what their elders believed explicitly. *Caeremonialia* had a central place in revelation. Their significance broke through the limits which St. Thomas himself had set to the definition of the literal sense of Scripture. The spiritual sense of Scripture, as he taught elsewhere, eluded the sacred writers' understanding, having been put there by God: The New Testament alone revealed the spiritual senses to Christians. But Moses and the élite had a partial understanding of the mystical sense of ceremonies. "Partial" is perhaps too weak an adjective for the explicit faith and clear pre-view which enabled them to pierce the veil of their legal code, as St. Thomas imagined things.

24 *De Verit.* p. 303-4. See also *Summa* 2a 2ae, q. 2, a. 6.

Dom Gribomont has made the pertinent comment that St. Thomas in speaking of implicit (I would add "partially explicit") knowledge, always stresses knowledge of reality implied in the object, as clearly known. Today, as Dom Gribomont says, we think more of the consciousness of the knowing subject. We feel more curiosity about the sacred writers' psychology.[25] The insight applies to medieval scholarship in all fields. The medieval clerk read both profane and sacred books for the sake of their content, as sources of wisdom. His authors interested him less than their teaching; he did not envisage them clearly as persons. So we need not wonder that St. Thomas focussed his attention on the content, literal and mystical, of the Mosaic Law, without enquiring what Moses had in mind. Paradoxically, this neglect of the question has the result of making the Thomist treatment of the Old Law look less dated and anachronistic today than William of Auvergne's. St. Thomas avoided rash speculation on its historical setting. William floundered in a quagmire because he ventured on to the terrain of biblical and ancient history. The schoolmen as a class had little use for history as such and were ill equipped to deal with it. St. Thomas dammed up William's line of enquiry and turned speculation into more profitable channels. He clarified and fortified tradition, partly in reaction to William's attack on allegories and moralities. John had bowdlerised *De legibus*; St. Thomas supplied a powerful counter argument, sustained throughout his *Summa* wherever he touched on ceremonies. *De legibus* therefore had a negative rather than a positive effect: it provoked refutation. St. Thomas's genius took its toll, as genius will, in making men forget his predecessors.

And yet was it all gain that he put William's opinions on the shelf, to moulder there permanently? William's answer to the question "What do we know about Moses?" would amuse a modern biblical scholar.[26] But the questions he asked matter more than his naïve answers. What did Old Testament history convey to readers or hearers when it was first recorded? What was the lawgiver's purpose? What did the Law mean when it was first received? Few of the questions raised in the schools have kept such relevance today. William was no match for the Angelic Doctor in the middle ages. For that very reason he seems closer to us when he discusses the Old Law. St. Thomas had the better mind; William showed more curiosity and imagination.

25 Op. cit. (above, p. 12, n. 3), 80. The difference between medieval and modern approaches to authors makes it hard to adapt Thomist doctrine on the interpretation of Scripture to problems of modern exegesis and theories on inspiration and revelation; see the account of various attempts to do so by J. T. Burtchaell, *Catholic Theories of Biblical Inspiration since 1810* (Cambridge 1969) 131 and passim.

26 See. G. Widengren, "What do we know about Moses?", *Proclamation and Presence. Old Testament Essays in Honour of Gwynne Henton Davies*, ed. J. I. Durham and J. R. Porter (London 1970) 21-47.

APPENDIX

William's account of the spiritual senses in *De legibus* is so novel that it seemed advisable to check the edition from an early manuscript. The editors do not state what manuscripts they used. I chose MS Paris, Bibl. nat. lat. 15755 as the earliest available; it belonged to the Sorbonne. M^llc Marthe Dulong kindly described it and collated it with the edition for me. She puts it probably in the mid-thirteenth century. It is written in black ink in a rather tremulous hand, "more like a hand used for documents than a real book hand". The chapters are marked by red and blue initials. There are no chapter headings or numbers and no marginalia, at least on these pages. The manuscript has some variations from the edition, which do not alter the sense in any material way. Some of the manuscript readings are inferior to the edition; others suggest slight improvements. I transcribe the text of the edition (pp. 48-49), noting the MS variants in brackets (fol. 49vb).

Quarta significatio est per similitudinem rerum, quae non ad hoc factae sunt ut significent; et haec est quae multos offendit, et propter hoc quia abusivum eis videtur res ad (in) signa trahere, quae non ad significandum factae sunt, quale est id (illud) Hieremiae 8 (xiii):[1] Nunquid sicut facit figulus iste non potero vobis (*add.* facere) domus Israel, ait Dominus. Dissipatio enim vasis quae prius fiebat, et formatio vasis alterius (*add.* non ad hoc)[2] factae sunt ut significarent; et cum eis ad significandum usus est Deus (Dominus), neque offenderetur quis audiens huiusmodi expositiones seu interpretationes, si diceretur ei hoc modo: Quemadmodum dicit (ibi dixit) Dominus: Nunquid non sic facere vobis potero? ubi de significatione nihil locutus est, sed de similitudine tantum. Quemadmodum et Hieremiae tertio, non dixit quicquam de significatione, sed similitudinem et modum tantum expressit dicens: Quomodo si mulier contemnat amatorem suum, sic contempsit me domus Israel (*add.* etc).[3] Non dixit, quia contemptus huius mulieris significaret conteriptum filiorum Israel, nec dixit quod amator huius significaret ipsum, neque dixit quod dissipatio aut reformatio vasis prophetia esset vel parabola eius quod ipse operatus (operaturus) esset in populo Israel (*add.* hoc modo), vel quod figulus esset figura ipsius, sed expressit modum seu similitudinem notam inter opus figuli et opus suum, et inter factum mulieris contemnentis amatorem suum et factum populi Israel, quo modo si loquerentur sacri expositores et doctores in allegoriis et tropologiis suis (*add.* et) etiam anagogicis

---

1   xviii, 6.
2   The MS reading is better here: the breaking of one vase and the making of another were not meant to signify, but to resemble what God could do to Israel.
3   iii, 20.

interpretationibus, et scripturae satisfacerent et audientium sive legentium intellectus non offenderent. Sed quia dicetur (dicunt): "Tale quid significat tale quid, et est figura seu prophetia aut parabola talis rei", cum alterum propter alterum significandum nec factum nec dictum videatur, offendunt graviter audientes. Quemadmodum se habet in facto David et Uriae, quod legitur in 11 (*add.* secundi) et 12 Regum, ubi dicitur quod David, qui utique proditor erat in facto illo, et adulter atque homicida, significat Christum, Urias autem, vir sanctus et fidelis, diabolum (Dyabolus). Et iterum (*add* de) adulterina illa copula Davidis de (David et) Bersabee, proditione et homicidio execrabili[4] significat sanctissimum matrimonium et immaculatissimam copulam Christi et Ecclesiae de gentibus, quae (*om.*) auribus multorum multam indignationem ingerunt, fidemque sacrarum expositionum aut penitus in eis abrogant aut multum laedunt. Primum, quia istud non est factum ad significandum, nec verisimile est multis quod propter hoc sit scriptum. Si autem ita dicerent: "Quo modo rex David Bersabee adamavit et pro (MS pre) amore ipsius mortem viri procuravit, quo modo illam regali connubio honoravit et regali solio exaltavit, sic rex coelorum Christus Dominus synagogam adamavit et, procurata morte magistratus seu principatus eius, cui velut marito suberat, eam connubio suo spirituali honoravit et coelestis regni solio sublimavit", si, inquam, de modo tantum aut similitudine mentionem facerent, et ipsam similitudinem decenter et diligenter prosequentes exponerent, absque offensione ulla audientium hoc fieret. Eodem modo de Ecclesia de (et) gentibus, quod procurata morte diaboli, morte (*om.*) scilicet spirituali, cui velut marito suberat, unde et vocabat ipsum Bahalim, quod interpretatur vir meus,[5] quod sic et sic ei fecit, non solum pacifice, sed gratanter (graviter) etiam audiretur. Verbum ergo significandi est quod in parte ista graviter offendit auditores atque lectores, quamquam verum sit quod omnium duorum similium, quorum alterum est intellectui nostro propinquius, nobisque notius, signum naturale est id (*om.*)[6] minus noti atque ab intellectu nostro remotioris. Signum, inquam, est naturale illius et velut liber in quo legitur; unde et quasi natura docente altero ad alterum declarandum utimur. Hoc ergo modo sacri doctores et expositores sane et absque offendiculo ullo dicere possunt quia (quod) factum illud de Bersabee factum significavit ecclesiae de gentibus; significavit (*add.* inquam) propria similitudine, tanquam naturali designatione. Licet autem Spiritui sancto et scriptoribus eius notioribus similibus (similitudinibus)[7] uti ad minus nota significanda et declaranda. Secundo, propter rerum dissimilitudinem et nimiam (nimiamque distantiam), ubi magis violenta est significatio (significationis impositio)[8] in ipsis quam rerum significatarum expositio. Et in hoc errant imperiti multi, qui nesciunt qualiter tractandum sit verbum veritatis, sed ingenium suum, ut ait Hieronymus, facere nolunt ec-

---

4 Both MS and edition seem to omit several words: "dicunt quod" would make sense.
5 Jerome gives "vir eius" as the meaning of *Bala* (*Ios.* xix, 3), *Liber de interp. nom Hebr.*, PL 23, 802, but it does not relate to the context. William's allusion is obscure. Perhaps another passage has dropped out of the text.
6 A better reading.
7 A better reading.
8 A better reading.

clesiae sacrificium (sacramentum),[9] et propter hoc dixit super Abacuc: Tropologia libera est et tantum legibus circumscripta, ut pietatem sequatur in intelligentiae sermonisque contextu (intelligentia sermonisque contextum), nec in rebus multum inter se contrariis violenta sit copulandis.[10] Tertium, est ignorantia explicandi prosequendique similitudines, ex quo defectu accidit et illud quod diximus, ut non credatur expositionibus, maxime ubi ex similitudine potissimum significant. Cessante namque in his rerum similitudine, cessat et significatio apud audientes. Quartum, est ignorantia eius videlicet quod solum in negotio significat, sicut accidit in somniis quae exposuit Ioseph in 40 et 41 Genesis. Tres enim propagines et tria canistra panum propter numerum tantum significaverunt tres dies, de quibus agitur, et solus ternarius quantum ad dies (*om.*) illos significat. Erraret enim intolerabiliter qui canistra vel propagines in significationem dierum detorquere vellet. Propter hoc dictum est (*add.* quod) sacra scriptura est velut cithara, in qua non omnia sonant (sanant).[11]

9 Wrong reading.
10 On Abac. i, 6-11, PL 26, 1281-2: "Historia stricta est et evagandi non habet facultatem. Tropologia libera, et his tantum legibus circumscripta, ut pietatem sequatur intelligentiae sermonisque contextu, nec in rebus multum inter se contrariis violenta sit copulandis."
11 Wrong reading. See Augustine, *Contra Faustum*, PL 42, 463.

Note:
p. 126, line 1, read Chanter for Canter
p. 126, add to end of n. 15: See MS Paris, Bibl. nat. lat. 526. foll. 117va–166rb.

9

Oxford University Sermons
1290–1293

THE data collected by Little and Pelster in *Oxford Theology and Theologians c. 1282–1302*[1] have been used mainly in two ways hitherto. Their discoveries have thrown light on the careers and writings of individual masters and on university customs. The content of the *quaestiones* and sermons which they listed and ana-lysed so carefully still remains largely unexplored. Here I shall attack the sermons. Pelster listed 128 university sermons given at Oxford during the academic years 1290–3.[2] The preachers include Dominican and Franciscan friars, seculars, and an occasional guest speaker, such as Raymond Gaufredi, Minister General of the Franciscan Order. Some names are given; other preachers are anonymous; but when a friar preached, the church, whether of the Preachers or Minors, is noted, so that we know which Order the friar belonged to. Pelster described the two manuscripts which contain records of the sermons: Worcester Cathedral Q. 46 (= W) and New College, Oxford, 92 (= N). The two collections overlap: we have two texts in some cases, but not in all. Mr. G. Mifsud has given a fuller account of N in his thesis 'John Sheppey, Bishop of Rochester, as Preacher and Collector of Sermons'.[3]

I shall take the rich information provided by Pelster for granted and also the notices in Dr. Emden's *Biographical Register of the University of Oxford to A.D. 1500*.[4] Readers can look up all the Oxford men referred to in this paper for themselves. Nor is it necessary to offer a full bibliography of recent studies on medieval preaching.[5] These Oxford texts fit into the pattern of university

---

[1] O.H.S. xcvi (1934), abbreviated here as LP.
[2] LP, pp. 149–215.
[3] MS. Bodleian Library, Oxford, B.Litt. d. 177 (deposited 1953).
[4] Cited in this volume as *B.R.U.O.*
[5] See J. B. Schneyer, *Wegweiser zu lateinischen Predigtreihen des Mittelalters*

184   *Oxford University Sermons, 1290–1293*

sermons of the period. The preachers use the structure and techniques recommended in *Artes praedicandi*. This is clear from the specimen sermons of Hugh of Hartlepool O.M. and Simon of Ghent, edited by Little and Pelster from the collection.[1] My aim is to study the Oxford theologians' interests, concerns, and attitudes as expressed in their sermons. There is room for further inquiry. Given the number of sermons, the difficulty of the hands, and the carelessness of the scribes, I had to limit myself to a sketchy survey. A student who asked different questions, or even the same, would find much that I have missed out.

The preachers spoke as academics to students and colleagues. When preaching on saints' days, they appropriated saints who were reputed to have taught in the schools. Saint Clement, Pope and Martyr, studied philosophy before his conversion, according to the *Golden Legend*.[2] 'He was a schoolman, just as we are; afterwards he became a churchman', says Thomas Sutton O.P.[3] Saint Edmund of Abingdon, archbishop of Canterbury 1233–40, canonized in 1246, evoked possessive pride. An anonymous Dominican proclaims on Saint Edmund's feast day: 'He taught Arts and theology too in this town, to the great honour of the whole university, which nurtured and brought forth such a man. He was also a pastor of the Church and primate of this province.'[4] The chancellor, John Monmouth, quotes the words of 'our blessed archbishop Saint Edmund' on receiving the viaticum.[5]

An anonymous Franciscan gives a fuller version of the saint's exclamation on receiving Communion and relates his vision of the Christ Child, his vision of his dead mother while he was regent in Arts 'in this university', and his combat with the devil, whom he mastered by making the sign of the Cross.[6] His assiduity as arch-

(Bayerische Akademie der Wissenschaften, i, 1965), especially pp. 547–55, on sermons by scholastic preachers. On *exempla* see now C. Delcorno, 'L'exemplum nella predicazione volgare di Giordano da Pisa', *Istituto Veneto, Memorie*, cl. di scienze morali, lettere ed arti, xxxvi (1972), 3–121.

[1] LP, pp. 192–215.
[2] James of Varazze, *Legenda aurea*, ed. Th. Graesse (Leipzig, 1850), p. 779.
[3] W fol. 26ᵛ.   [4] N fol. 55ᵛ.
[5] W fol. 195ᵛ, in a sermon preached on Septuagesima Sunday, 1292. See C. H. Lawrence, *St. Edmund of Abingdon* (Oxford, 1960), p. 104, for the versions of this story. John Monmouth's comes close to that in the *Life* by Eustace of Faversham; see ibid., p. 218.
[6] W fols. 309ᵛ–310ᵛ, preached on 16 November 1290. See Lawrence, op. cit.,

bishop in daily preaching and hearing confessions is mentioned.[1] This friar refers to a 'holy book', by which he seems to mean Saint Edmund's life and example. On clerical learning the saint says and defines in what order, by what means, and to what end one should study. First one should learn what is more efficacious for one's salvation. The pupil should study more eagerly and carefully what most enables him to acquire love and worth, since that is divine science. The purpose should be to obtain one's eternal reward. That is how Saint Edmund studied. The friar contrasts the sordid motives of 'legists and sophists' with Saint Edmund's purity.[2]

His cult was not popular in the later Middle Ages outside Salisbury and Abingdon;[3] so it is interesting to find Oxford theologians appealing to him as a paradigm of the scholar and pastor, and telling of his life and miracles some fifty years after his death. He belonged to Oxford.

We find few specific references to Oxford customs. The preachers blame masters and scholars for the standard sins. The system by which bishops granted licences to beneficed clerks to absent themselves from their cures in order to study at universities comes in for criticism. Friar Nottingham O.P. does not question the purpose of the system, the promotion of study; but he finds fault with the clerks' neglect to appoint suitable priests to take

pp. 101–4. The preacher tells the stories in his own words; it is difficult to know which *Life* he used.

[1] W fol. 310ʳᵛ. This item could have been taken from several of the *Lives*.

[2] W fol. 310. The preacher compares the Cross to a book, in which the cries of the wicked and the songs of the just are read, apropos the story of how Saint Edmund overthrew the devil by the sign of the Cross. This text follows immediately; but something may have dropped out: 'In sancto etiam libro est specialiter legendum quemadmodum fecit beatus Eadmundus. Bene distinxit de doctrina clericorum et dicit (et) diffinit quo ordine, quo studio, quo fine quis addiscat. Quo ordine, quoniam illud est prius addiscendum quod saluti est efficacius. Quo studio, illud ardentius et attentius est addiscendum per quod maxime amorem et honorem [*sic*, honestatem or bonitatem?] adquirit addiscens. Talis est scientia divina. *Primum* enim *querite regnum Dei* . . . Quo fine, illud principaliter est addiscendum quo adquiritur premium sine fine mansurum . . . Ideo tertio modo addiscebat beatus Eadmundus, et eo modo non addiscunt omnes sophiste nec legiste . . .'

The 'holy' book cannot refer to Saint Edmund's *Speculum Religiosorum* and *Speculum Ecclesie*, ed. H. P. Forshaw (Auctores Brit. Med. Aevi, iii, 1973). Neither version of the *Speculum* has anything resembling this passage of the sermon.

[3] Lawrence, op. cit., pp. 4–5.

charge during their absence. They bargain as to payment; the character and competence of their substitutes do not weigh with them. The incumbent hardly ever resides in his parish, spending his time elsewhere, 'now at Paris, now at Oxford, now with a king or an earl'.[1]

The most valuable item of information concerns the study and practice of medicine at Oxford. Our knowledge of these is scanty for the thirteenth century, perhaps because 'the medical school remained the smallest of the higher faculties'.[2] John Westerfeld O.P. mentions it when outlining the conduct suitable to various groups of scholars in a sermon preached 14 June 1293. Artists should avoid arts which have been banned (as magic, presumably); lawyers should avoid numerous pleas and crooked counsels; medicos should avoid rash treatment in a critical case, where carelessness involves risk. Otherwise they may kill a patient unwittingly by their extravagantly concocted doses. It is one thing to practise and another to receive authorization to do so. Medicos 'in this university' are quite well controlled; but they follow the course for a year or two, or hardly that, and immediately buy a practice on their return home. Westerfeld suggests that the Oxford faculty of medicine, however small, had a tight organization and a significant number of students, though many went down without taking a degree. His complaint against unqualified doctors agrees with evidence already available on the impossibility of restraining quackery outside universities in northern Europe until the fourteenth century. Even then, royal regulations on the expertise required of physicians and surgeons were tentative and ineffective.[3]

Do the sermons tell us anything of Oxford attitudes to politics?

[1] N fol. 105ᵛ, W fol. 288. See L. E. Boyle, 'The Constitution "Cum ex eo" of Boniface VIII', *Mediaeval Studies*, xxiv (1962), 263–302.

[2] V. L. Bullough, 'Medical Study at Mediaeval Oxford', *Speculum*, xxxvi (1961), 600–12.

[3] W fol. 47: 'Etiam isti medici vitent medicationes presumptuosas in casu periculoso, ubi possint de levitate incurrere periculum. Quid enim si (per) potiones suas immodeste confectas interficiant vivum hominem contra conscientiam? Possunt vel ministrare vel potestatem ministrandi accipere. Verumtamen in ista universitate satis cohibentur; sed vix audie(n)t per unum vel per duos (annos?) istam scientiam et cum venerint in partibus suis statim baliam pactizarent.'

See V. L. Bullough, 'Training of the Nonuniversity-Educated Medical Practitioners in the Later Middle Ages', *Journal of the History of Medicine and Allied Sciences*, xiv (1959), 446–58. Mrs. Susan Hall kindly helped me on this point.

The years 1290–3 marked the calm before the storms roused by the Bull *Clericis laicos* of 1296 and the baronial opposition to Edward I of 1297. Edward's war taxation fell heavily on clergy and laity alike. There was grumbling in the early 1290s, but no united stand to resist him as yet.[1] Some of our preachers, notably William Hothum O.P., worked in government service as advisers and diplomats. They would hardly have attacked the Crown on grounds of oppression of the Church or extortion from the laity.

Henry Sutton O.M. struck a belligerent note in a sermon on Saint Thomas Becket, preached on 29 December 1292. Saint Thomas exposed himself to martyrdom in defence of righteousness and of 'the liberties of the commonwealth', while his fellow bishops took cover or even opposed him. Afterwards the king, who had proscribed Saint Thomas for no lawful cause, did humble penance at his tomb.[2] Sutton substituted 'the liberties of the commonwealth' for the more usual expression 'liberties of the Church' as the reason for Becket's martyrdom. His fellow bishops, it is assumed, ought to have backed him against Henry II on the wider grounds of 'public good'. If Sutton had a modern parallel in mind, however, he left his hearers to draw it for themselves. An anonymous preacher on the text Matthew 9: 8 states that a ruler is 'good' if he does not depart from justice, and that he is 'bound' to uphold the liberties of the Church. Again the preacher stops short here.[3] Otherwise we find banalities on the difference between the good king and the tyrant with no discussion of the problem of resistance to tyranny.

It is striking from the point of view of politics that preachers on Saint Edmund's day never mention his objections to royal misrule, although he had been a noted mentor of Henry III. I have found no reference to Robert Grosseteste at all. The bishop of Lincoln had no saint's day, since attempts to procure his canonization had failed; but it seems surprising that an Oxford scholar of his status

[1] Michael Prestwich, *War, Politics and Finance under Edward I* (London, 1972).
[2] N fol. 77, W fol. 104ʳᵛ: '. . . solus in torculari militans (pro) libertatibus reipublice, ceteris coepiscopis non solum latitantibus, sed etiam ex adverso astantibus . . . ferro compressus est.
[3] W fols. 311ᵛ–312ᵛ. LP overlooked this sermon, which comes between numbers 6 and 7 of the list. The text is from the Gospel for the 24th Sunday after Trinity; see J. Wickham Legg, *The Sarum Missal* (Oxford, 1916), p. 195. No. 7 is for the last Sunday before Advent. Sunday sermons were normally preached by a Dominican.

should have dropped out of mind. His memory could have supplied ammunition to attack tyranny of all sorts.[1] It was not used.

These preachers show their conformity in another way. They like to draw upon the etiquette of the royal court as a source of comparisons or *exempla*. Suppose that the king has given someone the rank of shield-bearer or groom; if he associates with knights and barons instead of keeping to his rank, does he not seem to be criticizing the king, who will certainly put him down? Similarly, we must avoid the sin of pride in God's sight. A man who pushed his way into the royal presence when dirty and badly dressed, and wanted to touch the king's cup, would deserve to be put to shame. Similarly, we must lead a clean life in God's sight. These two comparisons come from sermons by Thomas Sutton O.P.[2] An anonymous secular preacher insists on the respect due to noble rank in a sermon on the feast of Saint Edmund, King and Martyr (20 November 1292). He starts from the text: *Blessed is the land whose king is noble* (Eccles. 10: 17). Men of servile origin make worse rulers than others, he says. It is right to honour nobility. Paris practice offers an example. The chancellor there made no bones about conferring the licence on nobles, whereas he subjected others, however worthy, to long examination. Nobles are an adornment to learning; others are honoured for being learned.[3] This may be an echo of the conflict between the masters and chancellor of Paris university in the years *c.* 1280–90. The masters accused the chancellor of dispensing with the conditions required by the university in favour of a princely candidate, and of withholding the licence from duly qualified men.[4] The anonymous preacher seems to approve of the chancellor's snobbery. It is interesting that he turned to Paris when he needed an example of the honour paid to noblemen. There was less noble pressure on Oxford in this period.

All in all, the preachers are 'establishment-minded'. They

[1] S. Gieben, 'Robert Grosseteste at the Papal Curia, Lyons 1250. Edition of the Documents', *Collectanea Franciscana*, xli (1971), 340–99.

[2] N fol. 100, W fol. 281ᵛ.

[3] N fol. 46, W fol. 150: 'Sicut exemplo Parisius, (ubi) cancellarius, qui ibidem, nobiles faciliter licentians, alios, quantumque valentes, diu in examine tenuit, quia illi scientiam honorant, isti per scientiam honorantur.'

[4] H. Rashdall, *The Universities of Europe in the Middle Ages*, ed. Powicke and Emden (Oxford, 1936), i. 398–400. According to Master Robert of Sorbon (d. 1274) in *De conscientia*, ed. F. Chambon (Paris, 1902), p. 2: 'Multis enim magnatibus fit aliquando gratia ut licentientur sine examinatione.'

compensate for their conformity by harping on the virtue of humility in all walks of life. Saint Thomas Becket set an example of humility to modern doctors by preferring the office of teaching to the honour of the *magisterium*, according to Friar Bothale O.M.[1] Preachers on the feasts of Saint Simon and Saint Jude, of Saint Gregory the Great, and of King Edmund all stress the humility of the saints, and contrast it with the pride shown by modern prelates and rulers.[2] But this is religious, not social, teaching.

The sermons show concern for financial obligations. It was traditional to remind prelates that they should act as stewards, not owners, of the goods of their sees, as did Friar Nottingham O.P.[3] John Westerfeld O.P. takes a more modern line when he compares bishops to salaried employees. He gives an example: 'If you agreed with someone to perform a service, for which he should receive his food and clothing, and he scorned the office he was hired to fulfil immediately on his first day, he would be despised as proud and held in contempt.' 'You prelates', says Westerfeld, 'are certainly hired to do the work of pastoral care.'[4] The chancellor Simon of Ghent applies the same principle to scholars in an Ash Wednesday sermon. He accuses clerks of being laxer than laymen in their Lenten observance and less afraid of excommunication. Clerks who have fallen under the ban do not bother to get absolution until they come to take holy orders. Only then do they remember, and may have to go to the papal Curia to straighten out their 'irregularity'. University clerks should bear in mind that their friends may be making a great effort to support them in the schools, in order that they should profit themselves and others. Now these clerks are doing neither. Indeed, they are putting their parents' help and money to bad uses. Those who have hoped for their protégés' promotion now despair of it.[5] We have moved into a society where men get paid and are held to account if they break

[1] W fol. 246, from a sermon preached on 29 December 1290. Bothale may have got the idea that Becket declined to take a degree from the *Lives*, which state that he did not stay long in the schools; see L. B. Radford, *Thomas of London before his Consecration* (Cambridge, 1894).

[2] See the sermons by Raymond Gaufredi O.M., minister general of the Order, W fols. 294–298ᵛ, Richard of Winchester, W fols. 169–171ᵛ, and an anonymous Franciscan, W fols. 310ᵛ–311.

[3] W fol. 309. The classic piece on this subject was Saint Bernard, *De consideratione*, III, i. 2, *Opera*, ed. J. Leclercq and H. M. Rochais, iii (Rome, 1963), 432.

[4] W fol. 83ᵛ.   [5] LP, p. 212.

their side of the bargain. The preachers appeal to a cash nexus to reinforce their moral argument.

Turning to strictly academic matters, we may look for traces of two current quarrels. First, do the sermons reflect the controversy between mendicants and seculars, which raged at Paris from 1256 onwards? Here, too, we encounter a lull in the storm. No important contribution to the pamphlet warfare at Paris appeared between 1289 and 1301.[1] The quarrel did not boil up at Oxford until 1303, though it had been simmering for some years. The parties patched up a compromise, without, as far as we know, engaging in pamphlet warfare of the Paris type.[2] To find an English equivalent we have to wait for Fitz Ralph's attack on the mendicants, launched at Avignon in 1350.[3]

These sermons show that the friars made use of their opportunities to put out propaganda for their way of living. Friar Bothale O.M. preached a recruiting sermon on the feast of the Conversion of Saint Paul, telling an *exemplum* to illustrate the danger to one's soul of neglecting a religious vocation in favour of service to a wealthy patron.[4] Thomas Sutton O.P. presented 'voluntary poverty' as the only safe way to heaven. It is hardly possible for a wealthy man not to love his wealth, however much he tries: a rider on horseback cannot trample on the earth, since he is mounted, even though his feet turn downwards, as though he meant to.[5] The fiercest cry of all comes from William Leominster, regent master at Blackfriars, preaching a Lenten sermon in 1293. Certain hissers, 'not theologians, but diabologians' (because the devil speaks through them) persuade men to scorn 'our' call to despise the world. They gloss Christ's counsels of perfection to make them mean that earthly things should be put away in affection, but not in deed. Leominster compares Christ to a master,

---

[1] See Y. M.-J. Congar, 'Aspects ecclésiologiques de la querelle entre mendiants et séculiers dans la seconde moitié du xiiie siècle et le début du xive', *Archives*, xxviii (1961), 50. On the earlier stage of the conflict see M.-M. Dufeil, *Guillaume de Saint-Amour et la polémique universitaire parisienne 1250–1259.* (Paris, 1972).

[2] Rashdall, op. cit. iii. 70–4. For the Cambridge conflict, 1303–6, see M. B. Hackett, *The Original Statutes of Cambridge University. The Text and its History* (Cambridge, 1970), pp. 241–4.

[3] For a summary of the arguments put forward in this last stage of the controversy see K. Walsh, *The 'De Vita Evangelica' of Geoffrey Hardeby, O.E.S.A.* (c. 1320–c. 1385). *A Study in the Mendicant Controversies of the Fourteenth Century* (Rome, 1972), pp. 84–111.

[4] W fol. 256.   [5] N fol. 100^v, W fol. 282^v.

who teaches an Art, the Art of perfect living in this case. He hands down the Art to his pupils; they expound it, as he has taught them, by word and by deed, and pass it on to their followers. Then *you* (the diabologian) come along and find another way of expounding the Art. Who believes you? Some infidels![1]

Who were 'the hissers', who denied that voluntary poverty was a condition of perfection? Leominster seems to grant them academic status, since he calls them 'theologians or diabologians'. Either he refers to the secular masters at Paris or he points us to some underground current of opinion at Oxford. The seculars who preached at Oxford 1290–3 neither objected nor retaliated to the friars' arguments, and never attacked them. The sermons indicate that the friars of both Orders were mettlesome and touchy, but that the seculars minded their manners in the pulpit, whatever they may have taught in the schools.

The second quarrel concerned Thomism. Two successive archbishops, Kilwardby and Pecham, had followed the Paris precedent in condemning certain propositions as heretical. These included some which had been taught by Saint Thomas. In 1286 Pecham excommunicated Richard Knapwell O.P. for defying the ban of 1284. The ban was not lifted during Pecham's lifetime; he died on 8 December 1292. He had put the Oxford Dominicans between the hammer and the anvil, since chapters general of their Order enjoined the teaching of Thomist theology. Some of them disobeyed the ban. It failed to prevent discussion and development of Thomist doctrine at Oxford even before Pecham died. The

---

[1] N fol. 102, W fol. 284 (*bis*): 'Nescio quid est. Nos predicamus contemptum mundi et tanto magis se tenent homines ad oppositam partem, sicut quanto magis ventus flat, tanto fortius pastor pallium suum sibi retinuit (*sic*). Credo quod diabolus inmisit novam theologiam, immo diabologiam. Nos persuademus ad contemptum mundi tanquam consilium Dei. Ipsi glosant, (dicentes) quod illud consilium debet (ita) intelligi quod terrena sunt dimittenda affectu, sed non effectu, et dicunt breviter quod omnia consilia debent intelligi secundum affectum suum. Ecce argumentum contra. Ecce unus magister facit unam artem; non dico scientiam. Ipsemet exponit artem, et quia ars est, ideo exponit opere, et discipuli sui post ipsum opere eandem artem exponunt. Tu de novo venis et aliam expositionem invenis. Quis credit tibi? Immo aliqui infideles. Dominus noster Iesus Christus artem perfecte vivendi composuit et dedit totam regulam: *Si vis perfectus esse* . . . Ipse et discipuli sui artem exposuerunt opere et effectu et illud derivaverunt ad alios . . . Si ergo sint aliqui sibilatores, non theologi, sed diabologi, qui contrariam sententiam nobis proponunt, scitote non illos esse qui loquuntur, sed diabolus loquitur per eos.'

Leominster distinguishes an Art from a science because an Art can be practised, whereas a science cannot.

preachers of 1290–3 included two keen Thomists, Thomas Sutton and Robert Orford; another preacher, William Hothum O.P., had done his best to avert Pecham's action against Knapwell.[1]

We might therefore expect to hear sniping, if not gunfire, on the banned propositions in these sermons. No Dominican preacher refers to Saint Thomas or to his theology, nor do the Franciscan preachers mention him by name or criticize him. Only a secular preacher, Simon of Ghent, makes a controversial statement in the Thomist sense; the soul is the 'form and act of the body'. Simon uses it when urging scholars and clerks to behave as 'the form and act' of Christ's mystical body, the Church.[2] He was preaching on Ash Wednesday, 11 February 1293, several months after Pecham's death. Perhaps he felt that it was safe at last to pronounce on the unity versus plurality of forms question in public. Did it cause a stir in his audience, or had most Oxford scholars lost interest in the unity or plurality of forms, which had roused such passions less than ten years earlier?[3]

Feeling curious, I took soundings to see whether the Dominican preachers showed any signs of having studied Saint Thomas. Sutton and Orford obviously had, though they maintained a discreet silence when preaching. But had their confrères? Surely some hint would transpire if the works of Saint Thomas were being read at Blackfriars. It was difficult to find a test case, seeing that the preachers touch on theology mainly to reinforce their moral lessons. However, an anonymous Dominican, preaching on Saint Martin's day, 11 November 1291, raises a question discussed by Saint Thomas in *De magistro*: 'Can a man teach and be called master or is that for God only?' Our preacher does not put his subject into *quaestio* form; but he expounds it in such a way as to offer grounds for comparison with *De magistro*.

The question posed itself in the schools because Saint Augustine taught that God alone can be said to teach by his illumination of man's mind. Robert Bacon O.P., who lectured on the Psalter

[1] See now *Thomas von Sutton Quodlibeta*, ed. M. Schmaus (Bayerische Akademie der Wissenschaften, ii, Munich, 1969), pp. vii–xxiii.

[2] LP, p. 211: 'Ideo bene angeli scolares et clerici dici possunt; anima enim est forma et actus corporis. Sic et clerici forma et actus esse debent corporis Christi mistici.'

[3] D. A. Callus, 'The Origins of the Problem of the Unity of Form', *The Thomist*, xxiv (1961), 257–85; 'The Problem of the Unity of Form and Richard Knapwell O.P.', *Mélanges offerts à Étienne Gilson* (Paris/Toronto, 1959), pp. 123–60.

at Oxford in the 1230s, stated clearly on his text *Thou hast taught
me, O God, from my youth* (Ps. 70: 17) that God alone teaches us
interiorly by illumination of our intellect; human masters teach
us exteriorly. Hence a man is called master only by 'indulgence'.
Bacon alludes to *De anima* ii. 5 (417^b21–5), where the Philosopher
says that our knowledge comes via the senses; but he falls back
upon Saint Augustine, quoting the Gospel: *Be not you called
masters; one is your master, who is in heaven* (from Matt. 23: 8–9).
Bacon compares divine illumination of the intellect to the sun,
which illumines our sight, so that the sun itself and material things
become visible; similarly 'the sun of righteousness' illumines the
intellect, so that spiritual things may be seen. Hence, Bacon concludes, the name of master must be ascribed to God first and
foremost.[1] The discussion took a more sophisticated form after
Bacon's day. It came to involve theories of cognition and the part
played by the *intellectus agens* in the process of acquiring knowledge. Saint Thomas gave the question his full attention for that
very reason. The master's role in imparting knowledge also im-
pinged on the controversy on the mendicants' function in universities. To minimize the value of human endeavour in teaching
would have seemed to lessen the need for friar doctors and the
dignity of the *magisterium*.

To focus on passages which lend themselves to comparison:
the opinion that 'God alone teaches and can be called a master' is
supported by three authorities which reappear in our sermon.
They are Matthew 23: 8, Saint Augustine's *De magistro*, and the
Gloss on Romans 10: 17, *Faith cometh by hearing*: 'Although God
teaches inwardly, yet his herald proclaims outwardly.' They have
one authority for the contrary opinion in common: Saint Paul
says: *Wherein I am appointed a preacher and an apostle and teacher*
(2 Tim. 1: 11). Both compare what Aristotle says in his *Ethics* on
the inculcation of virtuous habits to the acquisition of knowledge.
There must be a natural inclination to the virtues as a beginning;
but they must be brought to full development by exercise.
Similarly, certain seeds of the sciences are already present within
us, which make it possible for us to learn them. Another point of
contact is their reference to Saint Augustine's *rationes seminales*.
Saint Thomas, arguing for the opinion that 'a man can teach and

---

[1] B. Smalley, 'Robert Bacon and the Early Dominican School at Oxford',
T.R.H.S. 4th ser. xxx (1948), 17.

be called a teacher', replies to an objection that the pupil's knowledge pre-existed according to the *rationes seminales* implanted in man's nature by God. He explains that they serve as a starting-point for the teacher to work upon. Finally, both Saint Thomas and our preacher deal with the certainty which arises from principles. It is objected, to the opinion that 'a man can teach', that one man cannot induce inner certainty in another, since he teaches by outward signs, which cannot bring certainty. Saint Thomas admits that certainty in a science derives from its principles. Therefore, the fact that something is known with certainty is due to the light of reason, by which God speaks to us inwardly, not to a man, who teaches outwardly, except in so far as the man resolves conclusions into principles (which alone bring certainty). He could not do so unless the certitude of principles were already in us. It follows from Saint Thomas's answer that, as he has explained previously, the human master works on given material; but he brings into act what was already present potentially in his pupil.[1]

There the resemblance ends. The anonymous preacher also wishes to stress the role of the human master; but he sets about it differently. His text, *I made that in the heavens there should arise the light that never faileth* (Ecclus. 24: 6), leads him to explain that God is the first principle, who produces and creates the others. He then quotes the *Ethics* and applies his proposition to the acquisition of knowledge, as Saint Thomas did. He then argues from Saint Augustine and Matthew 23: 8 that we need a human master to help us to make use of our knowledge, which we have derived from our senses. Next he adduces the missions of Saint Peter and Saint Paul, with supporting texts. Hence, he concludes, 'we are God's ministers' to our fellow men. He does not appeal to the Thomist concept of act and potency, and he chooses a different illustration to clarify his meaning. Saint Thomas compared the teacher to a physician, who helps nature to function properly. The physician is said to be the cause of health in a patient, because he co-operates with nature to effect a cure. Similarly, a man is said to be the cause of science in another, because he co-operates with natural reason. The Oxford Dominican prefers to present the

[1] *Quaestiones disputatae. De veritate*, q. xi, a. 1, ed. R. Spiazzi, i (Turin, 1949), pp. 223–8. For the text of the Oxford sermon and references see below, p. 325. I am most grateful to Dr. L. Minio-Paluello and to Fr. C. Ernst O.P. for their help on this text.

human master as God's 'instrument' in teaching. Therefore, being instrumental, we need divine grace as well as our natural capacity to perform our task.

Both doctors had the same intention: they wanted to uphold the dignity of the human *magisterium*, without denying that God was the primary source of knowledge. Saint Thomas was disputing; the Oxford doctor was preaching. That would account for the difference in tone. Nevertheless, Saint Thomas's *De magistro* would have been helpful and relevant to the Oxford friar's argument. He ignored it. The likeness comes down to a few obvious *auctoritates*, some of them already known to Robert Bacon, and a comment on a passage of the *Ethics*, which derives from a Thomist milieu. This does not prove that the Oxford friar had read Saint Thomas's *De magistro* or even his commentary on the *Ethics* directly. Indeed, it seems more probable that he had not. The comparison, for what it is worth, suggests that Thomist writings were little studied at Blackfriars. Sutton and Orford may have represented a small élite. It would be misleading to take them as typical.

Sutton himself makes an un-Thomist opposition between faith and reason, when he warns scholars that their faith is likely to waver because they put everything to the test of natural reason. The intellect, by its very nature, wavers if it cannot depend upon reason. This often happens in matters of faith, for which it is impossible for us to find a certain reason in this world. Thus a man who relies on his reason begins to waver. He must resist by faith.[1]

Nor did Thomist 'naturalism' appeal to the Oxford preachers. Saint Thomas modified the traditional teaching on *contemptus mundi* by allowing more value to secular pursuits and human effort, provided that they subserved a supernatural end, than had been customary.[2] At Oxford seculars and mendicants alike kept

---

[1] N fol. 58ᵛ, W fol. 27: 'Et ista fluctuatio temptat maxime viros scholasticos, eo quod assuescunt omnia inquirere per rationem naturalem. Natura intellectus est quod hesitet, si non habet rationem. Ita contingit sepe de fide. Qui est assuetus discutere per rationem omnia, ipse hesitans movetur a vento, eo quod non habet rationem certam de fide, de qua, cum in hoc mundo impossibile est certam rationem invenire, ideo innitens se penitus sue rationi incipit hesitare.'

Sutton goes on to quote St. Gregory on reliance on faith; *Moral.* X. x, *P.L.* lxxv. 931.

[2] On the opposing attitudes see R. Bultot, 'La Chartula et l'enseignement du mépris du monde dans les écoles et les universités médiévales', *Studi medievali,*

to the conventional ethics: 'Despise the world and its vanities' they cry in chorus.[1] It was uphill work. Leominster complained in a passage already quoted: 'The more we teach men to despise the world, the more they cling to the opposite side, just as the shepherd wraps his cloak more tightly round him, the harder the wind blows.'[2]

Since their message was not original, some preachers looked for new ways to put it across. Sunshine might succeed better than storm in getting the sinner to loosen his grip on his worldly affections. Leominster tried gentle encouragement instead of denunciation. Pursuit of virtue is like copying the alphabet; the master scribe will not blame a beginner who cannot do it exactly. Or take scaling a mountain: you show willing if you put your baggage down and climb as high as you can. A gardener just tries to make his plants grow as tall as possible.[3]

Other preachers resort to pagan learning as a bait for their audience. It was an old trick to make comparisons from the *Libri naturales*, helped out by bestiary and lapidary lore. The *Ethics* presented a more exciting challenge by raising the question of values. An anonymous Franciscan, preaching on Maundy Thursday, 1291, transposes the Gospel into Aristotelian terms.[4] Aristotle defines man as a rational animal, as a social animal, and as a civilized animal. To be rational means subordinating the passions to reason.[5] To be social is to love all one's fellow men and not one's kin only, as beasts do. Here the preacher quotes 'the Commentator' (Saint Thomas) on the *Ethics*.[6] To be civilized (*mansuetus*) is to 'observe a certain mean with respect to anger' and to keep one's temper, also to be humble, obedient, and tractable.[7] Our friar

ser. III, viii (1967), 784–834; R. A. Gautier, *Magnanimité l'idéal de la grandeur dans la philosophie païenne et la théologie chrétienne* (Paris, 1951), 443–66.

[1] See for instance a sermon by the secular master John Monmouth, W fols. 194–195^v.

[2] See above, p. 315 n. 1.

[3] W fol. 204, an Ash Wednesday sermon, 1292.

[4] W fol. 158^{rv}.   [5] *Pol.* vii. 13, 1332^{b}3–5.

[6] '. . . est homo animal sociale, ut dicit commentator super i Ethic.: Politicum animal est homo, politicum, id est sociale et communicativum.'

From Saint Thomas, *Com. in Ethic. Nicom.* i. 7, 1097^{b}11, ed. R. M. Spiazzi (Turin, 1964), p. 31: 'Homo naturaliter est animal civile.' See also *De regimine principum*, i. 1, ed. J. Mathis (1948), p. 1.

[7] He quotes *Topica*, v. 1, 128^{b}17–18, and alludes to *Ethic. Nicom.* iv. 5, 1125^b 25–6, and perhaps to Saint Thomas's commentary, op. cit., p. 222: 'Mansuetudo autem est quaedam medietas circa iras . . . vult mansuetus imperturbatus esse.'

explains that Jesus showed all these qualities both in life and in death. For instance, Christ's gift of his body to his disciples at the Last Supper resembled the 'social gift', which a friend makes to his friends on his departure as a memorial. Further, Christ's love for the commonwealth was great indeed, since he, so noble, exposed himself to a terrible death for its sake. Quotations from Cicero and Ecclesiasticus on friendship clinch this part of the argument.[1] The preacher has put much ingenuity into co-ordinating Aristotle and the Gospel, without sacrificing Christian doctrine and feeling. It is interesting that a Franciscan, not a Dominican, should have quoted Saint Thomas on the *Ethics*.

Another way to use pagan learning was to tell stories of 'the philosophers'. John of Wales O.M., who died probably in 1285, had promoted this method by drawing up collections of tales about the philosophers' lives and sayings. He intended them for retail in social converse and in sermons. The pagan sages set an example to Christians by their austere detachment from the world; Anaxagoras struck him as a *magnificus contemptor mundi*.[2] There were Dominican precedents too. Saint Albert told stories of pagan philosophers and expressed admiration for the Roman emperors, who were better than modern rulers, except for the one drawback of not being Christians.[3] However, John of Wales was more influential at Oxford.

John's sober tales must have whetted the appetite for more exotic fare. Pseudo-classical *exempla* came into fashion; stories are fitted into an imaginary setting with 'classical features'. An anonymous Franciscan gives us an early specimen in an Easter Week sermon of 1293 to illustrate his lesson that a wise man will accept his share of troubles, without complaining at the human lot: 'Note how the philosophers posited two jars on the threshold of the house of Jove. All who entered had to drink from both jars. According to the philosophers, Jove's house is the world; the two jars signify prosperity and adversity, which comers into the world

[1] *De amicitia*, iv. 15: 'ab omnibus seculis vix tres aut quatuor nominantur (paria) amicorum'; Ecclus. 6: 15, 10.
[2] *Compendiloquium* (Venice, 1496), pars iii. 1. fol. 181H. On John of Wales see now Balduinus ab Amsterdam, 'The Commentary on St. John's Gospel, etc', *Collectanea Franciscana*, xl (1970), 71–96.
[3] J. B. Schneyer, 'Alberts des Grossen Augsburger Prediktzyklus über den hl. Augustinus', *Recherches de Théologie ancienne et médiévale*, xxxvi (1969), 114. The sermons were preached in 1257 or 1263.

must taste.'¹ This pseudo-antique type of *exemplum* had a brilliant
future. The tale of the two jars reappears in a more developed
form in a collection probably made by an Italian Austin friar,
Michele da Massa Marittima (d. 1337), who seems to have drawn
on English material.² The Oxford Franciscan gives an early instance of its use. Two other Franciscan preachers tell the story of
the philosopher who fell into a ditch while star-gazing; but that
was an old favourite.³

John Westerfeld O.P., a lively preacher, made the most daring
use of the new technique. He may have belonged to the younger
age group, since he visited Bordeaux as proctor for the Cambridge
Blackfriars over twenty years later in 1316.⁴ His sermon for the
second Sunday after Easter shows him exploiting and distorting
the data on pagan religion assembled by Saint Augustine in his
City of God. John of Wales may have suggested the idea to Westerfeld; but he carried it further. Preaching on the Resurrection, he
tries to move his hearers to gratitude and pity for the death of the
Saviour by stressing the point that pagans regarded life as the most
precious of all good things. The Athenians believed that the sun
was 'the living god'. They judged Anaxagoras guilty and stoned
him for holding that the sun was merely a burning lantern.⁵
Westerfeld refers to the *City of God*: but he or his secondary
source (if he had one) embroidered on Saint Augustine, who told
the story in order to attack pagan beliefs as self-contradictory. He
did not say that Anaxagoras was 'stoned' by the Athenians either.⁶
Westerfeld presents the Athenians as having an inkling of the

¹ W fol. 270.
² B. Smalley, *English Friars and Antiquity in the Early Fourteenth Century*
(Oxford, 1960), pp. 265–71, 347, 377.
³ In one sermon it is referred directly and correctly to *Ethic. Nicom.* (vi. 7,
1141ᵇ), W fol. 268ᵛ; in another it is told in the more developed form which became
popular with preachers, W fol. 254ᵛ; see Delcorno, op. cit., p. 73. St. Peter
Damian was already using it as an *exemplum c.* 1067; see *Lettre sur la toute-
puissance divine*, ed. and transl. A. Cantin (Paris, 1972), pp. 460–2 and *P.L.*
clxv. 615.
⁴ A. B. Emden, *A Biographical Register of the University of Cambridge to
1500* (Cambridge, 1963), p. 630.
⁵ W fols. 213ᵛ–214, N fol. 112: 'Karissimi, si respiciamus bene ad gesta et
dicta antiquorum, videre poterimus quod etiam ipsi pagani vitam precipue pre
aliis eligibilem poneba(n)t, in tantum ut etiam deos vivos dicerent, ut manifeste
dicit Augustinus, de civitate Dei, 18, quod Anaxagoras apud Athenienses factus
est reus et lapidatus est, eo quod solem posuit ardentem lampadem, quem ipsi
deum vivum esse dicebant.'
⁶ *De civ. Dei* xviii. 41.

truth: they ascribed life to their gods; that was not Saint Augustine's intention.

We go on to Pythagoras: he first posited the soul's immortality and taught that it would receive rewards and punishments after death.[1] Westerfeld brings out the philosophers' expectation and hope of a future life. Saint Augustine attacked the pagan attitude to suicide by citing the death of Cleombrotus, who threw himself off a wall after reading Plato's book on the immortality of the soul, in order to pass from this life to a better one.[2] John of Wales had already told the story in a corrupt form; the name of the reader of Plato's book becomes its title, *Theobrotus*! John tells it to exemplify, not pagan error, but the philosophers' yearning for blessedness hereafter. Westerfeld puts it to the same purpose, and quotes it in the same form as John of Wales, who was probably his source. His praise of the philosophers leads up to the superiority of Christian doctrine: 'But they all lacked knowledge of the true life.' Christ alone promises true blessedness.[3]

Later in the sermon Westerfeld tells another story to illustrate Aristotle's saying that life is more precious to a virtuous man than to a bad one.[4] This tale had a long pedigree. Westerfeld probably got it from John of Wales; but he tells it vividly in his own words:

Agellius tells of a Stoic philosopher called Puplius that he had to cross the sea. When they ran into danger, he turned pale and was very upset. Someone said to him: 'You're a great man indeed, and yet you show fear at so small a thing. *I'm* not afraid!' He answered and said: 'You worthless fellow! It's no wonder that I worry about a philosopher's soul, whereas you've only to worry about a rascal's.' He made a very good answer, since life is more desirable to the virtuous man, as Aristotle says, than it is to another.

[1] W fols. 213ᵛ–214: 'Pictagoras etiam primo (im)mortalitatem anime posuit (et) etiam ei fore premia et penas post hanc vitam.' Knowledge of the Pythagorean doctrine of the soul was common. Westerfeld could have derived it from John of Salisbury's *Policraticus* vii. 4, ed. C. C. Webb (Oxford, 1909), ii. 104.

[2] *De civ. Dei* i. 22.

[3] W fols. 213ᵛ–214: 'Omnes aliam vitam commendebant et aliam huic vite preferebant. Ideo quidam paganus, ut dicitur in libro Platonis, qui liber vocatur Teobrodus, ubi disputatur de immortalitate anime, se precipitem muro dedit, ut transierit ab hac vita ad aliam, quam credidit multo meliorem . . . Omnes isti tamen veram vitam ignoraverunt.' See *Compendiloquium* pars i, cap. 8, ed. cit., fol. 177D–E.

[4] *Ethic. Nicom.* ix. 9, 1170ᵃ25–8; 1170ᵇ1–5.

Westerfeld proceeds to apply the tale and Aristotle's dictum to Christ.[1]

Lastly, he treats us to a risky joke in a sermon preached on 14 June 1293. Exhorting prelates to fulfil their function, he quotes Christ's command to Saint Peter, thrice repeated: *Feed my sheep* (John 21: 15–17): 'Know that Christ does not say *Feed* three times to authorize you to take three meals a day or to drink between meals, but tells you to *feed* your subjects by word, example, and temporal aid.'[2] Robert Holcot makes the same crack in his Wisdom commentary, though here it is a novice who claims three meals a day on the strength of the command to Saint Peter.[3] The fourteenth-century Dominican was a master of wit and humour. The joke accords with his character. But Westerfeld stands out as exceptional for his light touch among his fellow preachers.

To sum up: these sermons give a negative impression at first sight. The preachers keep quiet on both English and local politics. We hear only faint echoes of the quarrel between mendicants and seculars, and nothing of the ban on Thomism. The silence on Saint Thomas is not surprising, given that Saint Edmund of Abingdon is the only thirteenth-century scholar to be mentioned by name. But none of the preachers, except Simon of Ghent, makes any reference to Thomist doctrine, as far as I can see. The university sermon must have been the most taxing and thankless of academic exercises. The doctors may well have found it a chore. A clerical audience did not need that basic instruction on the creed and the sacraments which was suitable for laymen. The preachers in fact say little on the sacraments, though penance may be commended

---

[1] W fol. 214ᵛ: 'Ideo narratur de philosopho stoico, qui vocabatur Puplius. Agellius de eo narrat quod debuit transire quoddam mare, qui, cum ceperunt periclitari, pallere cepit et tristari valde, cui dixit unus: tu es tantus ac talis, et pro tam modico times, et ego non timeo. Cui respondens dixit; pessime ribalde, non est mirum (quod) ego sollicitus sum circa animam unius philosophi. Tu non es sollicitus nisi circa tuam animam nebulonis. Et optime respondit, quoniam vita est eligibilior ipsi virtuoso, ut dicit Aristoteles, quam alii, quoniam plurima consequitur delectatio ipsum virtuosum. Ex quo igitur Dominus noster fuit supra virtutes omnes, eius mors et privatio (vite) maius malum fuit.'
The tale came down through Aulus Gellius, Saint Augustine, John of Salisbury, and John of Wales. Westerfeld is the first to call the philosopher 'Publius'. The next chapter in *Compendiloquium* is headed 'De Publio et eius egregiis sententiis' (pars iv, cap. 11, ed. cit., fol. 209Q.). Westerfeld may have taken the name from there. See *Noct. Attic.* xix. 1; *De civ. Dei* ix. 4; *Policr.* vii. 3.

[2] W fol. 47ᵛ.
[3] Smalley, op. cit., pp. 192, 332.

in a Lenten sermon.[1] On the other hand, the stimulus of disputation was absent. How could one hold the attention, much less move the hearts or prick the consciences of blasé clerks?

Some preachers sought new answers to the problem. Here we come to the positive side of the sermons. Previously a gap opened out in the history of classical studies at Oxford. The didactic collections of tales about ancient philosophers made by John of Wales before 1285 seemed a poor preparation for the creative scholarship which began with Nicholas Trevet at the turn of the century and continued in the works of Thomas Waleys, John Ridevall, and Robert Holcot.[2] The preachers of 1290–3 do something to close the gap. None of them were classical scholars in the strict sense or book-hunters; but some had a spark of curiosity. His admiring interest in pagan antiquities sent John Westerfeld to the *City of God* as a source of information. He both recalls John of Wales and looks forward to Trevet and Waleys. An anonymous Franciscan tells the Gospel story in terms of the *Ethics*, as Thomas Waleys would do more daringly.[3] Another Franciscan tells a pseudo-antique *exemplum* of the type which appealed to Holcot and the compilers of *Gesta Romanorum*. Further research on Oxford in the later thirteenth century may uncover more evidence on Trevet's background. Already the first medieval commentator on *De civitate Dei* and *Ab Urbe condita* rises in a less meteoric fashion than he seemed to before. The 'classicizing friars' of the early fourteenth century had their humble forerunners.

APPENDIX
W fols. 302ᵛ–303

Ego feci in celis ut oriretur lumen indeficiens, in Ecclesiastico.[4] Karissimi, bene videtis quod quamvis lumen ad solatium hominum omnibus communicetur per illuminationem medii, est tamen a quodam principio, puta a corpore solari, et quia non solummodo ab illo producitur principio, sed etiam a Domino, ideo non solum est illud principium quod suo radio (MS. sui radii) medium illuminat, immo ipse Deus principium est, qui aliud principium producit et creat, de quo in Matheo: *Qui solem oriri facit super bonos et malos.*[5] Non igitur (solum)

---

[1] W fols. 276ᵛ–278.　　[2] Smalley, op. cit., pp. 45–202.
[3] Ibid., pp. 106–7.　　[4] 24: 6.　　[5] 5: 45.

tales res sunt principia a quibus exeunt alie, sed etiam Deus, qui talia principia voluit rebus imprimere, de quibus principiis dicit Sapiens, 6 Moralium, quod mores (? MS. ipse res) ante complementum preexistunt in quibusdam principiis.[1] Hoc etiam apparet in adnascentibus, quorum principia consistunt in semine, et quia tales a Deo producuntur, non solum dicitur homo principium, qui tales res seminat et plantat, immo Deus ipse.

Hec autem pro tanto diceremus, quia sicut est ita in moralibus, sic erit in speculativis. Deus enim quedam principia nobis impressit, que sunt per se cognita, in quibus que ad ipsa consecuntur necessario virtualiter preexistunt. Ex quo dico quod lumen illorum principiorum in cognitionem aliorum inducit. Ipse autem superior doctor noster est, qui ista nobis inmisit, unde Matheus: *Unus est magister vester.*[2] Etiam Augustinus: Docet ipse solus in terris, qui cathedram habet in celis.[3] Sed quia nostra cognitio intellectiva ortum habet a sensu, ideo sub istis exemplaribus proponuntur nobis quedam particularia exempla.[4] [fol. 303] Hinc est quod potest dici alius noster magister, quoniam *fides est ex auditu.*[5] Ideo oportet esse alium qui exterius annuntiet; ad Romanos: Quamquam Christus veritatem interius doceat, preco tamen exterius annuntiat.[6] 2° ad Tim.: *In quo positus sum ego doctor et magister.*[7] Christus ergo doctor et magister (est).[8]

Christus ergo doctor noster est interius illuminando, homo autem exterius annuntiando. Unde Augustinus, de doctrina christiana, cap. 3°: Cognoscimus Paulum apostolum, licet a Deo consecratum, ad hominem tamen missum, ut ecclesiam Dei confortaret, (et) etiam Petrum Cornelio missum. In Petro igitur ad Cornelium misso et Paulo ad centurionem significatur quod non solum ut ecclesie Dei copulentur a Deo consecrentur, immo istos ad hominem mittuntur. Cuius rationem

---

[1] Cf. Aquinas, *De magistro*, ed. cit., p. 225: 'Similiter etiam secundum ipsius sententiam in VI Ethicorum, virtutum habitus ante earum consummationem praeexistunt in nobis in quibusdam naturalibus inclinationibus, quae sunt quaedam virtutum inchoationes, sed postea per exercitium operum adducuntur in debitam consummationem.'
  The reference is to *Ethic. Nicom.* vi. 13, 1144^{b}1–17. Aquinas uses the same terminology in commenting on the passage; cf. his commentary on the *Ethics* vi, lect. xi, ed. R. M. Spiazzi (Turin, 1964), p. 346. See also St. Albert on the same passage, ed. Borgnet, *Opera*, vii (Paris, 1891), 459a–460a.
[2] 23: 8. Gloss. Ord. ad loc.: 'Qui illuminat hominem, quod non (facit) alius homo, sed tantum exerceat docendo; non intellectum prestat.'
[3] Cf. *De magistro*, cap. xlvi.
[4] Cf. Aristotle, *De anima* ii. 5, 417^{b}20–8.
[5] Rom. 10: 17.
[6] Cf. Peter Lombard, comm. ad loc (*P.L.* cxcii. 1479).
[7] Cf. 2 Tim. 1: 11.
[8] Peter Lombard, op. cit.: '*auditus autem per verbum Christi,* id est per gratiam Christi doctores evangelici.'

subdit: Abiecta esset humana conditio, si per homines hominibus nichil ministrari videretur, nec verificaretur quod templum sanctum Dei estis vos.[1] Quoniam sanctificamur per fidem, fides autem instituitur per auditum, auditus autem informatur per divini verbi annuntiationem, igitur a principio per annuntiationem verbi divini sancti efficimur. Igitur ad hoc quod hoc sit verum, *templum sanctum Dei quod estis vos,*[2] quia homines hominibus verba Dei annuntiant, illis hominibus delectando et difficilia exponendo, ideo, ut dicitur ad Corinthios: *Dei coadiutores sumus*[3] in dispensatione verbi Domini. Ideo sumus ministri Dei.[4]

Ministeria rationem instrumenti habent respectu principalis agentis. Instrumentum autem, ad hoc quod effectum intentum ab agente attingat, necesse (est) ut agens aliquid sibi imprimit ultra virtutem sibi ex natura propria impressam. Ideo, cum nos sumus quasi instrumenta Dei, indigemus aliqua spirituali impressione a Deo, que quidem impressio est divine gratie communicatio.

[1] *De doctr. Christ.* prol. 6.
[3] Cf. 1 Cor. 3: 19.

[2] 1 Cor. 3: 17.
[4] Cf. 2 Cor. 6: 4.

Note:

p. 197: The *exemplum* of the two jars derives from Homer, *Iliad* xxiv, 527, *via* Boethius, *De consolatione Philosophiae* II, pros. ii, 13.

10

John Russel O. F. M.

I

John Russel, 22nd lector to the Cambridge Franciscans, has left one letter, preserved in a formulary, two fragments of sermons, and two biblical commentaries, on the Canticle and Apocalypse. The main purpose of my paper is to study the commentaries. They are *catenae*, but in this lies their interest. Russel reveals himself by his choice and treatment of his sources, more especially of Abbot Joachim, thus helping us to gain a better understanding of certain trends in English academic circles around the year 1300. A survey of his sources will also tell us something of the books available in English Franciscan libraries of his time.

The letter and sermons fit naturally into an account of his career, which will include an attempt to date his commentaries. A description of the commentaries and of their sources will follow. Then I shall try to place him in the development of biblical studies at Oxford and Cambridge in the late thirteenth and early fourteenth centuries.

Our information about his career is concentrated on a very few years[1]. He was twenty-second regent master to the Franciscans of Cambridge, probably in the academic year 1292-93. He would have taken his degree at Cambridge, since there is no evidence for inception or regency at Oxford. Then he appears twice in a letterbook, contained in MS *Oxford, Bodl. Digby 154 (1755)*[2]. Miss Rosalind Hill, in her study of monastic letter-books, describes it as follows : 'From internal evidence it is possible that the letters were collected at the Augustinian priory of Bicester in Oxfordshire, although a Roger de Marlow, who wrote a number of them, was not at that time an Augustinian canon. The MS is written in two hands of the early fourteenth century' (except for two entries, which do not concern us). 'The MS

---

1. On Russel's career and writings see A. G. LITTLE, *The Grey Friars in Oxford*, Oxford 1891, 218 ; J. C. RUSSEL, *Dictionary of Writers of Thirteenth-Century England*, in *Bulletin of the Institute of Historical Research*, Spec. suppl. 3, 1936, 72-73 ; J. R. H. MOORMAN, *The Grey Friars in Cambridge*, Cambridge 1952, 205-206.

2. Numbers in brackets refer to the *Summary Catalogue* numbers.

206

belonged to the Premonstratensian abbey of Titchfield in the fifteenth century' [3]. One of the letters was sent from Edmund, earl of Cornwall, brother of King Edward I, to Brother Raymond, Minister General of the Franciscan Order (1289-1295), thanking him for some presents, 'que in octavis assumptionis Virginis gloriose per manus dilecti et domestici nostri, fratris Iohannis Russel... recepimus'. Edmund ends by recommending Russel to the Minister : 'Recommendamus vobis nominatum dilectum ac domesticum fratrem Iohannem familiarius quo valemus' (fol. 38). The letter is dated Aug. 29, 1293, at Edmund's manor of Beckley, a few miles from Oxford. The earl patronised the Franciscans : he and Blanche, his wife, founded the house for Minoresses in London, the first in England of its kind, in June of the same year [4]. This may have been the occasion of the Minister's gifts to him. He was also one of the chief builders of Greyfriars, Preston, Lancs [5]. It seems, therefore, that Russel was attached to his household as chaplain in the long vacation of 1293.

Edmund went to France towards the end of the year or early in 1294 and died on June 5, 1296 [6]. Russel had ceased to be in his service at least by the autumn of 1294. Another letter is by Russel himself and is addressed to his friend, Roger de Marlow. Here he explains that he meant to visit Roger when he attended the chapter of his Order at Oxford, which dates his letter in 1294 [7]. Unfortunately we know too little about the constitution of the English Franciscans to say in what capacity Russel might have attended his provincial chapter [8]. He had been prevented from making the visit to Roger by illness. He goes on to ask Roger for alms to provide himself with clothes for the coming winter. The item must have been included in the formulary as a model for a begging letter to a friend :

> Intime dilectionis amico domino suo, R. de M., suus frater, I. Rossel, amoris iugis terminum, qui terminari non novit. Veni ad capitulum fratrum nostrorum Oxonie, proponens vos personaliter visitasse, sed iam istud iter impedivit debilitas corporalis ; et quia recursus sit in necessariis ad dilectionem, ad vos confugio, ut securus supplici postulans exoratu, quatenus me

---

3. R. HILL, *Ecclesiastical Letter-Books of the Thirteenth Century*, privately printed, s. a., 183-184. I am most grateful to Miss Hill for lending me a copy of her privately printed thesis and for putting me on the track of Roger de Marlow.

4. W. E. RHODES, *Edmund, Earl of Lancaster*, in *English Historical Review* 10 (1895) 226.

5. *Ibid.*, 235 ; *Victoria County History of Lancashire* 2, 1908, 162.

6. RHODES, *op. cit.*, 227, 234.

7. *Victoria County History of Oxfordshire* 2, 1907, 129.

8. A. G. LITTLE, *The Constitution of Provincial Chapters in the Minorite Order*, in *Essays in Medieval History presented to Thomas Frederick Tout*, ed. A. G. LITTLE and F. M. POWICKE, Manchester 1925, 266-267.

vestrum, plus solito indigentem, in aliqua elemosina ad habendum vestitum pro ieme iam futura dignemini providere vice ista, quia non intendo talibus precibus de cetero vos gravare. Unde amore animarum dominorum vestrorum, qui vos dilexerunt et nutrierunt, ad presens hanc mihi gratiam faciatis, quem per latorem presentium transmittere secure valetis. Valeatis in valore antique amicitie et nove (fol. 37ᵛ).

At this period of their history the Minorites were still living from hand to mouth [9]. Russel had left the household of the richest prince in England 'poorer than usual', and depended on private charity for his winter garments. His friend, Roger de Marlow, was rector of the church of Harwell, Berks, in 1294 [10], an easy journey from Oxford. He entered the living after 1286 and had vacated it by June, 1310 [11]. On Jan. 8, 1302 he got leave of absence for study up to the following Michaelmas from his diocesan, the bishop of Salisbury [12]. The place is not stated, but was probably Oxford. He appears in the Patent Rolls as dean of the royal chapel of St Nicholas at Wallingford, Berks, in 1303 [13]. It seems that he had some connexion with Earl Edmund, who had endowed the chapel [14]; he is mentioned in an *Inspeximus* of 1301 as having witnessed a charter of the earl, dated Dec. 3, 1289 [15]. So when Russel begs from him 'amore animarum dominorum vestrorum', he may be referring to the family of their common patron, the earl of Cornwall. Roger de Marlow was thus an important person, with academic ambitions, though we do not know the extent of his studies [16]. The Oxford Dominican, Thomas Waleys, had just such a friend and helper, a beneficed clerk who had leave of absence to study at Oxford and probably met him there [17]. It is interesting to find cases of parish priests befriending mendicants.

By 1300 Russel had been sent to Leicester: 'He was licensed to hear confessions in the diocese of Lincoln in August 1300, being then a friar of Leicester, and as penitentiary for the archdeaconry of Lei-

9. W. A. HINNEBUSCH has shown how the English Dominicans depended on daily alms at this time, *The Early English Friars Preachers*, Rome 1951, 242-260.

10. *Calendar of Patent Rolls of Edward I, 1292-1301*, 119.

11. *Calendar of Papal Letters*, ed. W. H. BLISS, 1, 485, 2, 86; *Registrum Simonis de Gandavo 1297-1315*, ed. C. T. FLOWER and M. C. B. DAWES, Canterbury and York Society 2, 1934, 728.

12. *Ibid.*, 851.

13. *Calendar of Patent Rolls of Edward I, 1301-1307*, 197.

14. *Victoria County History of Berkshire* 2, 1907, 103-106.

15. *Calendar of Patent Rolls of Edward I, 1292-1301*, 608.

16. The correspondence in the letter-book relates mainly to ecclesiastical patronage and does not mention study.

17. B. SMALLEY, *Thomas Waleys O. P.*, in *Archivum Fratrum Praedic.* 24 (1954) 53-55.

208

cester in September 1305, being then at Lincoln'[18]. That is the last we hear of him. A. G. Little included him among the friars at one time resident in Oxford, though never a lector. We shall see that he worked in the Oxford library, since he used a book which must have been bequeathed by Grosseteste[19]. How long, or exactly when he was there, apart from his attendance at the chapter of 1294, there is no knowing.

The fragments of his sermons which survive suggest that he helped to preach the crusade of 1291. A. G. Little bought a small volume containing a collection of sermons in 1939, and was working on it at the time of his death. He left it to Bodley, where it has the shelf-mark *MS Lat. th. e. 24*[20]. The Keeper kindly allows me to quote the description from an unpublished part of the *Summary Catalogue* :

> In Latin, on parchment : written in the late 13th cent. in England : 180 × 120 mm., iv + 51 leaves : collation 13-27. 36-56. 68-88. A collection of sermons, incomplete at the beginning and end. The first two sermons are apparently by John Russel, a Franciscan, preaching the crusade of 1291... Bookplate of Devereux Viscount Hereford ; Joannes Dillon 7 (fol. 1ᵛ) ; bought by A. G. Little from E. van Dam, bookseller, and bequeathed to the Library, Mar. 17, 1946.

As the first two sermons only are ascribed to Russel, the rest being anonymous, we shall consider only the first two. The first goes on to one leaf, the beginning having been lost. It starts in the middle of a quotation, probably from a papal bull :

> 1... peregrini et promotores expeditionis terre sancte divina gratia consequentur. Hec ibi. Si ergo non vales accipere crucem, ut terram sanctam adeas, accipe crucem et da crucem, id est pecuniam cruce signatam, secundum tuam facultatem, ut meritum crucis obtineas. Hic autem debent articuli bulle de euntibus, de alios mittentibus, de subsidia conferentibus declarari pariter et exponi, ne decipiantur piis erroribus cruce signandi.

> Ut igitur de signo crucis concludam ex hiis dictis, quia crux Christi est et esse probatur...[21], ut signet suos fideles finaliter isto signo, signo videlicet crucis, et inter alios fratrem Iohannem Russel memorialis huius signi scriptorem, et hoc meritis sui patroni, beati Francisci, qui stigmata domini Iesu portavit in suo corpore signis quinis. Amen (fol. 2ʳ-2ᵛ).

> 2. A rubric introduces the second sermon :

> Memorialia de sacra cruce, que viris litteratis poterunt predicari.

---

18. Moorman, *op. cit.*
19. See below, p. 238
20. See *Bodleian Library Record* 2 (1947) 169.
21. Here comes a schematised *distinctio* on the expression 'signum crucis' with short comments by the preacher.

This sermon is complete apart from a leaf which has fallen out between the present foll. 2-3 :

Incipit : *Michi autem absit gloriari, nisi in cruce...* Ad Gal., cap. 6. Antequam loquitur de cruce crucifixi, assumo verbum eiusdem apostoli loquentis in epistola sua prima ad Cor. : *Non iudico me scire aliquid inter vos, nisi Christum, et hunc crucifixum.* Videtur quod apostolus in hoc verbo loquens de sua scientia... (fol. 2ᵛ).

Explicit : ...Ibi ergo gloriemur donec illa gloria venerit de qua dicit Psalmus : *Satiabor cum apparuerit gloria tua.* Ad quam nos perducat etc. Ave Maria pro fratre I. Russel (fol. 10).

The first item represents the end of a draft sermon, with instructions for preaching the crusade to the laity. The conditions of gaining indulgences as stated in the bull are to be read out and expounded to prevent misconceptions. The merits of the crusaders' cross are to be explained. The date must fall between the summer of 1290 and the spring of 1292. Nicholas IV issued a general call to a crusade in a bull dated Jan. 5, 1290 [22]. Archbishop Pecham began to preach it in person in July, but 'the loss of the latter part of his registers makes it impossible to know what arrangements were made for the general preaching of the crusade in his province' [23] : they might have thrown light on Russel's share in the preaching. Preparations went forward the following year and early in 1292. Then the project petered out with the death of Nicholas IV on Apr. 6, 1292. Affairs in France and Scotland deflected Edward I from fulfilling his promise to lead an expedition [24].

The second item is a sermon on the Cross of Christ, which is in no way concerned with a crusade ; Russel does not even mention the Holy Land. A contemporary crusading effort would have made his subject more moving, but the sermon itself, intended for a learned clerical audience, could have served for any occasion when the clergy forgathered. It was probably written at about the same time as the crusading sermon or earlier, since the two items were copied together. There would have been no point in transcribing a crusading sermon after the final collapse of the whole program. The fall of Acre in 1291 and the failure of Christendom to strike any counter blow at the Moslems put the crusading movement 'out of the sphere of practical politics' [25].

---

22. O. RAYNALDI, *Annales ecclesiastici ab anno 1198*, ed. J. D. MANSI, 4, Lucca 1749, 75-77. This is not the bull quoted by Russel, however.

23. D. L. DOUIE, *Archbishop Pecham*, Oxford 1952, 331.

24. F. M. POWICKE, *The Thirteenth Century, 1216-1307*, Oxford 1953, 266-268.

25. S. RUNCIMAN, *A History of the Crusades*, 3, Cambridge 1954, 427.

The crusading sermon is too scrappy to tell us anything about Russel's technique as a preacher. The sermon 'ad litteratos', lacking only one leaf, is much more informative. It follows the rules of the *artes praedicandi*. We have already seen from its incipit that it begins with theme and pro-theme. Next comes a quotation from Averroes on the *De anima*, which serves as a *captatio benevolentiae*. A preacher addressing a learned audience had to prove that he spoke the idiom of the schools, even when, as here, he was contrasting pagan philosophy with the true wisdom of the Apostle [26] :

> Videtur quod apostolus in hoc verbo loquens de sua scientia [27] alludat verbo philosophi, qui de scientia loquens ait in principio libri de anima : Bonorum, inquid, et honorabilium est scientia. Et causam quare hoc premittit philosophus explicat commentator, dicens ibidem in commento : Sic, inquid, incipit Aristoteles sermonicari de scientia, quod videlicet versatur circa bona et honorabilia, ut per hoc attrahat aliorum animos ad amorem scientie. Hec commentator [28]. Apostolus alio modo consilii volens attrahere alios ad habendam scientiam de misterio crucis, Christum Iesum gloria et honore coronatum iuxta prophete verbum proponit hic crucifixum, utpote quem nosse summa scientia est... (fol. 2ᵛ).

Russel then explains the significance of the four horns of the Cross *moraliter* as they refer to the four orders of Christians, the blessed in heaven [29], contemplatives and religious, prelates, and men leading the active life. We need not follow him through all the windings of his sermon, but we must note his quotations. Stephen Langton, he says, compares the Cross to a musical instrument :

> Qualiter autem cantus armonicus fuit formatus per crucem ostendit Stephanus Cantuariensis. Sicut, inquid, instrumentum musicum fit de corio exsiccato et super lignum extenso et sic redditur gaudiosa armonia, ut videmus timpano, sic quando pellis divina extendebatur super lignum crucis, proportiones armonice ibi sonabant (fol. 4ᵛ).

It would be difficult to identify the reference in Langton's vast and discursive commentaries, since Russel does not give the *locus*. The ingenious comparison is typically Langtonian, though not necessarily original. Russel may have found it in some collection of excerpts. The interesting point is that Langton should have been remembered so long after his death in 1228 ; his popularity as a commentator seems to have been on the wane in the late thirteenth century.

---

26. Th. M. Charland, *Les « Artes Praedicandi »*, Paris-Ottawa 1938, 39, 195, 262, 358.
27. An allusion to his pro-theme, *I Cor.* ii, 2.
28. Aristotle, *De anima cum commentariis Averrois*, Venice 1574, fol. 1ᵛ.
29. The loss of a leaf has left only a few phrases on this first order.

Russel quotes two commentators who will appear frequently in his biblical *catenae* :

> Nam sicut docet Hugo super Apocalipsim, super illud, *cantabant canticum novum* [30] : in cruce Christi fuit talis cantus, quod ibi erat proportio dupli ad simplum, quia ibi nostra mors destructa est per simplam mortem Christi. Erat insuper ibi proportio simpli ad triplum, quia de simplo sepulchro inferni mors eduxit suo sepulchro triduano. Erat insuper ibi proportio dupli ad triplum, quia nostra natura liberatur per eius trinam naturam. Erat etiam ibi proportio tripli ad quadruplum, cum mens attendit quod a peccato actuali, a peccato originali, a miseria penali destruendis quatuor ligna sunt compacta in cruce Christi (fol. 4ᵛ).

> Docet enim Alexander super Canticum quod in speculo vitreo non resultat imago, nisi plumbum subiciatur. Unde si vis quod imago crucis in te resultet, minores te, ut plumbum, et vilens te humiliter recognoscas (fol. 9).

The same quotation from 'Hugo' on the same text of the Apocalypse occurs in Russel's Apocalypse-commentary [31]. He makes much use of Alexander Nequam on the Canticle in his own Canticle-commentary [32]. The actual quotation from Nequam would be hard to trace in the absence of the *locus*. Another biblical commentator quoted in the sermon is 'Gilbertus expositor' ; Russel means Gilbert the Universal in a passage ascribed to him in the *Gloss* on *Exod.* vi, 16 [33]. The medieval preacher's fondness for rhyme comes out in a verse on the Cross, which I cannot trace :

> Metrice dicitur : in cruce rex alma passus fuit, hostia viva. Arbor erat palma, cedrus, cypressus, oliva (fol. 5).

The quotations from 'Hugo' and Nequam in the sermon help to date the biblical commentaries. The preacher is drawing on material collected by the biblical commentator and not *vice versa*. This is proved by the fact that the preacher quotes only once each two authors who contributed extensively to the biblical *catenae*. It follows that Russel composed his sermon at a time when he had already finished his *catenae* or when he had at least begun to collect material for them. We know that the sermon was written in 1290-91 or earlier. Hence Russel would have started work on his commentaries before about 1290-91. His sermon makes it plain that he was already specia-

---

30. *Apoc.* v, 9.

31. See below,   234.

32. See below, 220

33. *Glossa ordinaria cum postillis Nicolas de Lyra* etc. 1, Lyons 1589. Gilbert compiled the *Gloss* on the Pentateuch, making a few additions of his own ; see B. SMALLEY, *Gilbertus Universalis*, in *Rech. Théol. anc. méd.* 7 (1935) 253-255. Russel says : 'Et eadem verba dicit Gilbertus expositor : hoc etiam fuit propter misterium numeri ternarii...' (fol. 7).

lising on the Bible ; the predominance of biblical commentators in his quotations will speak for itself [34].

We can date the commentaries a little more closely. In both he refers to Pecham as 'Cantuariensis', which puts them after Pecham's consecration as archbishop on Feb. 19, 1279, and probably before his death on Dec. 8, 1292 [35], since Russel does not add 'bone memorie'. It looks as though both commentaries might belong to the regency at Cambridge, 1292-93. Russel would have been following the custom of lecturing on a book of the Old and a book of the New Testament concurrently. In both commentaries the quotations from 'Cantuariensis' come near the beginning, on the first two or three chapters. He could have been lecturing in the Michaelmas Term before Pecham's death early in December, 1292. The Apocalypse-commentary was certainly given as a lecture course ; Russel himself says so. The Canticle-commentary does not suggest lectures in its present form, but it may represent excerpts from or at least material for lectures. Russel most likely began to collect material before his regency ; so he could have used it when preparing his sermon. We may therefore put the commentaries into the academic year 1292-93, while not excluding the possibility that Russel put them into their final shape much later, when Pecham had been dead ten years or more, long enough to be referred to without an allusion to his memory.

II

We have four copies of Russel on the Canticle. The incipits and explicits are as follows :

> Prologue : '*Osculetur* etc. Cogitanti michi canticum promere laudis cuiusque ad honorem Virginis amorose, ipsa pia Virgo, rivos amoris scaturiens, ut prophetico alludam eloquio, inmisit in os meum canticum novum...'
> Text : 'Unde et hoc canticum sic incipit : *Osculetur* etc., videlicet rivus (amoris) os tam dignum, ut iam edoctum...'
> Explicit : '...te ducente, te iuvante, que illuc post filium tuum ascendisti, sicut virgula fumi ex aromatibus mirre et thuris'.

---

34. JOHN BALE credits Russel with a treatise *De potestate imperiali et papali*, giving no incipit ; see his *Index*, ed. R. L. POOLE and M. BATESON, Oxford 1902, 244. His editors refer to MS *London, Brit. Mus. Royal 18. A. LXXVI*. The subsequent publication of J. P. WARNER and G. F. GILSON. *Catalogue of Western MSS in the Old Royal and King's Collections* 2, 1921, 278, proves that this was written long after Bale's death ! It is dedicated to King James I (1603-25). Given Russel's overwhelming interest in biblical studies, one doubts whether he would ever have launched out into political theory. Bale may have confused him with some other writer.

35. F. M. POWICKE, *Handbook of British Chronology*, London 1939, 135.

London, MS Lambeth Palace Library 180, fol. 1ra-42vb ; 14th cent., from Christ Church, Canterbury ; list of contents headed 'fratris Thomas Stoyl' on the flyleaf. Thomas Stoyl entered the monastery in 1299 and died in 1333. A 15th cent. hand has written across the top of fol. 1 : 'Istam postillam composuit frater Iohannes Russel de ordine minorum'. The text has many corrections written in 14th cent. hands [36].

Munich, State Library, MS lat. 8827, fol. 15^{v}-65^{v} ; 15th cent., from the Munich Franciscans. Anonymous [37].

Oxford, MS Bodl. Can. pat. lat. 52, fol. 101ra-124vb ; 14th cent. Italian hand. Anonymous. A 15th cent. hand has written at the end of the volume : 'Statio huius libri est in quarta sede a latere canalis. Iste liber est monasterii Caritatis'. This must [38] refer to the Cistercian monastery in the diocese of Taranto, Lecce. Below in another hand, erased but still legible, is the inscription : 'Est monasterii sancti Bartholomei extra burgum Pusterle'. This refers to the house of Canons Regular of St. Bartholomew at Vicenza [39]. Russel on the Canticle is item no. 14 in a miscellany of devotional pieces, which includes one other complete commentary, Pseudo-Aegidius on the Canticle, fol. 173ra-185vb [40]. All the contents are written in 14th cent. Italian hands, but there are some notes in German in the same hand as the text to item no. 11, a mystical exposition of Nabuchodonosor's vision of the tree, *Dan. IV*, 7-9, fol. 59ra-75vb.

Rome, Apostolic Library, MS Vat. lat. 672, fol. 53^{r}-85^{v} ; early 14th cent., unknown provenance. Anonymous [41].

All four copies are anonymous, except for the ascription in a later hand in MS *Lambeth 180*. It is surely authentic. The choice of sources would label the commentator as 'circa 1300, English'. He has a number of traits in common with the author of our Apocalypse-commentary, ascribed to Russel by Russel himself, and with the author of the *Memorialia de sacra cruce*. He introduces his quotations in the same way : '... secundum (author's name)..., inquid,...' He uses the *catena*

---

36. M. R. JAMES and C. JENKINS, *Catalogue of MSS in the Library of Lambeth Palace* 2, Cambridge 1931, 283. Russel on the Canticle is the only item in the first of a number of fascicules making up the volume.

37. C. HALM and G. MEYER, *Catalogus codicum latinorum in Bibl. Reg. Monac.* 4, i, Munich 1874, 55. I owe this reference to the kindness of Dr R. W. Hunt, and have not seen the MS. Russel's commentary is not mentioned in the catalogue.

38. L. H. COTTINEAU, *Répertoire topo-bibliographique des abbayes et des prieurés* 1, Mâcon 1935, 603.

39. H. O. COXE, *Catalogus Codicum MSS Bibl. Bodl.* 3, 1854, 318-322 with notes by a former Keeper in the copy kept in Arts End in Bodley on MSS *Can. pat. lat. 52* and *60*.

40. F. STEGMÜLLER, *Repertorium Biblicum Medii Aevi*, Madrid, 1940-1955, no. 911. The copy in MS *Can. pat. lat. 52* lacks the prologue.

41. M. VATASSO and P. FRANCHI DE'CAVALIERI, *Codices Vaticani Latini* 1, Rome 1902, 527-529. Russel's commentary is the only item in the second of the fascicules making up the volume. F. STEGMÜLLER, *op. cit.*, no. 4919, has listed only MS *Lambeth 180*.

technique, as does Russel in the Apocalypse-commentary. He dedicates his commentary to the Blessed Virgin. Both the Apocalypse-commentary and the *Memorialia* end with a prayer to the Blessed Virgin, and Russel makes a point of praising her in the course of his exposition.

The Canticle-commentary belongs to a type which became current in the twelfth century [42]. Russel collects his excerpts from commentators who interpreted the Bride as the Virgin, the Bridegroom as Christ, or who could be understood in this sense. There is no reason to dwell on his borrowings from patristic or early medieval writers, down to the inevitable St Bernard [43]. I shall list the post-Bernardine commentators quoted by Russel in rough chronological order, and then note a few writers other than commentators whom he quotes occasionally. My transcripts come from MS *Can. pat. lat. 52*. The text is no worse than that in MSS *Lambeth 180* and *Vat. lat. 672*. All three MSS have many mistakes and the Bodleian was the most convenient to use.

Russel, as will soon appear, seldom quotes his authors with verbal exactness. Occasional differences in wording might derive from variations in the MSS, but they are so frequent as to preclude any idea that he meant to make accurate transcripts. He summarises, adds explanatory phrases, changes the interpretation and generally treats his authors as it suits him.

WILLIAM OF NEWBURGH (d. 1201).

'Willelmus Parvus' of Newburgh needs more introduction and comment than any other of Russel's sources. He owes his fame to his *Historia rerum anglicarum*, not to his Canticle-commentary. William was born at or near Bridlington in Yorkshire in 1136; he went to school and spent most or a good part of his life as a canon at the Augustinian priory of Newburgh, founded from Bridlington [44]. His commentary survives in three copies [45]. Hitherto no quotations from it have been discovered. The earliest of the three MSS gives a good picture of William's historical setting.

---

42. B. SMALLEY, *The Study of the Bible in the Middle Ages*, 2nd ed., Oxford 1952, 245 ; J. LECLERCQ, *Écrits monastiques sur la Bible aux XIe -XIIIe siècles*, in *Mediaeval Studies* 15 (1953) 100.

43. It may be of interest to note that he always quotes Pseudo-Haimo (PL 117, 295-398) as 'Remigius' ; see STEGMÜLLER, *op. cit.*, no. 3079, and no. 7218.

44. *Chronicles of the Reigns of Stephen, Henry II, and Richard I*, ed. R. HOWLETT, Rolls Series, 1, 1884, x-xxv ; *Dictionary of National Biography* 11, 360-363 ; J. C. DICKINSON, *The Origin of the Austin Canons*, London 1950, 295.

45. STEGMÜLLER, *op. cit.*, no. 3009.

Cambridge, MS University Library Gg. IV. 16 [46]. In Latin, on parchment : written probably in the late 12th cent. in England [47] : 26 × 21 cm. Illuminated initials. Miscellany of devotional works. The provenance is unknown, but the restrained and yet decorative capitals have a Cistercian look.

1. — 'Incipit prologus magistri Willelmi Parvi, canonici de Neuburc super Canticum Canticorum. In primis igitur considerandum videtur quomodo carmen istud nuptiale iuxta id quod intendimus dicatur Canticum Canticorum. Ut enim cantica distinguamus...' (fol. 1ra).

'Explicit prologus. Incipit tractatus magistri Willelmi super Canticum Canticorum. *Osculetur etc.* Vox annuntianti angelo credentis et in fetum gestientis Virginis est...' (fol. 1rb).

'...*Fuge, dilecte mi*, ad gloriam et laudem eiusdem sponsi, Dei et Domini nostri, Iesu Christi, qui cum Patre et Spiritu sancto etc. Amen ' (fol. 75rb). (dedicatory letter to Roger, without title in MS).

'Parui iussioni tue, venerabilis pater Rogere... filio commendare.

Laus tibi Virgo pia, celi regina Maria,

Auxiliare pia michi servo, sancta Maria' (fol. 75va).

The commentary is not divided into chapters. A later hand has added the chapter numbers of the Vulgate text in the margin.

2. — (Anonymous preface to the Canticle. No title in MS). 'Omnis anime motiones et universitatis conditor creavit ad bonum, sed usu nostro sepe fit ut res que bone sunt per naturam... (*ibid.*) '...plerumque prepostera' (fol. 77ra).

This may well represent a collection of prefaces joined together. The incipit of a preface found in some medieval Bibles, 'Si vis ascendere...' occurs near the beginning [48].

3. — (Robert of Tomberlaine on the Canticle. (a) incomplete) 'Beda (title in green letters), *Osculetur etc.* Os sponsi, inspiratio Christi, osculum oris, dulcis amor illius...' (*ibid.*) [49].

'...sol ergo eam decoloravit' (fol. 78ra) Rest of leaf blank ; fol. 76^{v}, 77^{r}, 77^{v} crossed through in red.

(b) The complete commentary of Robert of Tomberlaine is then copied out as a marginal and interlinear gloss round the text of the Canticle (fol 78^{r}-93^{v}). A note in the same hand as the commentary follows the explicit of the text : '*Explicit Canticum Canticorum Salomonis.* In emendatis exemplaribus non est sic, sed : *Incipit* sive *explicit Canticum Canticorum Salomon.* Cur non impressi hunc titulum ? Ne me lacerantes seipsos lederent cordis sui iudicio, quo parum sapiunt quid vituperio, quid laude sit dignum, qui si quid viderunt immutatum, supercilia dimittunt, corrugant nasum, ignorantes' (rest cut off by a binder).

---

46. *Catalogue of MSS preserved in the Library of the University of Cambridge* 3, Cambridge 1858, 161-162. This needs supplementing and correcting in some respects.

47. Dr O. Pächt tells me that he sees nothing in the MS to date it after about 1200.

48. STEGMÜLLER, *op. cit.*, no. 466.

49. *Ibid.*, no. 7488. Both the incomplete and the complete copy of the commentary omit Robert of Tomberlaine's prefaces.

The scribe evidently began to copy the commentary of Robert of Tomberlaine, wrongly ascribing it to Bede, and then decided or was told to begin again, leaving it anonymous and using a different lay-out.

4. — 'Sermo cuiusdam canonici Premonstratensis de Canone. In virtute sancte crucis et sacramento altaris magna est convenientia...' (fol. 94ra).

'...in tertio vera differentia' (fol. 98vb). This is the treatise on the Mass by Richard the Premonstratensian of Wedinghausen, printed with an ascription to John of Cornwall, PL 177, 455-470. One of the arguments put forward by Hauréau for Richard's authorship was the title in MS *Troyes 302*, from Clairvaux : 'Sermo de Canone, factus in capitulo Clarevallensi a quodam canonico de ordine Premonstratensi' [50]. The title in our MS is still very close to this.

5. — 'Epistola Ysaac abbatis Stellensis ad Iohannem Pictavensem episcopum de eodem. Domino et patri in Christo semper venerabili...' (*ibid.*)

'... ad quem conversi sumus, Iesum Christum, qui cum Patre et sancto Spiritu etc. Amen' (fol. 101ra). Rest of leaf cut off. Isaac de Stella on the Mass, printed by L. D'ACHERY, *Spicilegium*, Paris 1719, 449-451 [51].

6. — 'Epistola Petri abbatis sancti Remigii ad comitem Henricum Trecensem de opere sequenti. Domino et amico suo Henrico illustri...' (fol. 102ra).

'Continentia autem in hoc opere nostro de disciplina claustralium capitula ista' (fol. 102vb). A list of chapter headings follows : 'Incipiunt capitula huius libri...'

'Item prologus eiusdem abbatis ad Ricardum de Salisbire [52] canonicum Meritonie de eodem. Aut periti est aut experti iudicare de re cognita... (*ibid.*).

'Item prologus eiusdem ad eundem. Prolixum me fecit in hoc tractatu...' (fol. 103ra).

'Item prologus eiusdem ad eundem. Reddo cum usuris debitum...' (*ibid.*).

'Item epylogus ad eundem. Amicum discipline, Ricarde karissime...' (fol. 103rb).

'Incipit liber de disciplina claustralium et de auctoribus disciplinarum. Igitur (MS Ibitur) auctores huius discipline...' (fol. 103va).

'...super numerum. Explicit liber de disciplina claustralium' (fol. 120vb).

PL 202, 1101-1146. The prologue in the MS is much more subdivided than in Migne's edition, which does not give Richard's full name and title, as the MS does.

The flyleaf, fol. 121v, has notes in a 13th cent. hand, partly cut off by the binder, including some verses and interpretation of the names Willelmus, Thomas, Ricardus.

The miscellany in this volume comprises a wide range of writers

---

50. *Notices et extraits de quelques manuscrits de la Bibliothèque nationale* 24, 2, 1876, 145-146.

51. This is closer to our MS than PL 194, 1889-1899.

52. On John of Salisbury's brother, Richard, who entered the Augustinian priory of Merton in Surrey, see C. C. J. WEBB, *John of Salisbury*, London 1932, 2, 105, 111, 152. He witnessed deeds of the priory 1177-86 and about 1180 ; see A. HEALES, *The Records of Merton Priory*, London 1898, 32, 36.

on religious subjects. They stretch from the late eleventh to the late twelfth century. We find two Benedictines, Robert of Tomberlaine and Peter of la Celle, abbot of St Rémi of Rheims, a Cistercian, Abbot Isaac, a Premonstratensian and an Augustinian canon. Interest in textual emendation appears in the note at the end of the Canticle, preferring 'Salomon' to 'Salomonis'; it was an interest shared by Canons Regular and Cistercians, as well as by some secular masters of the twelfth century [53]. William of Newburgh takes his place in a circle of monastic authors, some contemporary with him, others older, who wrote on religious discipline and devotion.

The other two MSS are *Brussels, Bibl. royale 243 (1869)*, fol. 1-170, 13th cent., and *Cambridge, Gonville and Caius College 461 (734)*, fol. 81-151, 15th cent. They show that William of Newburgh's commentary continued to circulate in the later middle ages.

The 'Roger' to whom William dedicated his commentary was abbot of the Cistercian monastery of Byland [54], near Newburgh. He ruled Byland from about 1146 until his resignation in 1196, and died in 1199 [55]. William refers to Roger's long abbacy in his *Historia* [56]. The dedicatory letter is sufficiently interesting to be transcribed in full:

> Parui iussioni tue, venerabilis pater Rogere, atque opus laboriosissimum quod iniunxeras, cum multa tandem difficultate complevi. Factus sum insipiens, ne dicam impudens, audendo tam magna et que ultra modum excederent modulum meum, sed una michi apud Deum et homines tanti ausus excusatio est, quod tu me coegisti. Quis enim ego et quam idoneus, tot opacis scrutandis, tot secretis rimandis? Quid, inquam, est W., vero cognomine Parvus, ut post magnos patres novam et ab omnibus intentatam in Canticum Canticorum molitus explanationem dicatur? Sed, ut dixi, una michi tanti ausus excusatio est, tue sanctitatis imperium, quod utique spernere non potest, qui te novi ut ego. Denique post multam et diutinam fluctuationem meam, sicut nosti, cum tua me caritas vehementer urgeret, tandem orationibus tuis confortatus stilum arripui et que michi meditanti sive oranti in gloriam proprie genetricis Dominus revelare dignatus est ceris impressi. Suscepte siquidem materie novitas non me permisit via maiorum vestigiis trita incedere, sed novos cum summo labore moliri colles coegit.
>
> Opus autem in capite quadragesimalis ieiunii incoavi et vix ante sequentis

53. See R. WEBER, *Deux préfaces au Psautier dues à Nicolas Maniacoria*, in *Revue bénédictine* 65 (1953) 3-17.

54. According to a note seen by J.Leland in a copy in MS Queen's College, Cambridge, which has now disppeared; see *Dict. Nat. Biogr.*, *op. cit.*

55. F. M. POWICKE, *Walter Daniel's Life of Ailred Abbot of Rievaulx*, London 1950, 59. Roger administered the last sacraments to Ailred and attended his deathbed, *ibid.*, 59-61.

56. *Chronicles of the Reigns of Stephen* etc., *op. cit.*, 52.

anni quadragesimam absolvere potui, tum propter difficultatem materie, tum propter frequentes infirmitates meas atque alia negotia plurima, que me suscepto operi modico tempore vacare permiserunt. Huc accedit quod a me dictata in ceris nemo michi scribebat in membranis atque ideo dum duplex labor michi incumberet, opus vix cum anno finitum est ; et forte non improbe dixerim quia non in vacuum laboravi. Nam et ipse fructu laboris mei iam ex parte fruitus sum et multos, Deo volente, habundantius fruituros spero, sane ab omnibus, qui hunc laborem meum duxerunt non spernendum. Hanc michi vicissitudinem expeto, uti pro reverentia gloriose Virginis et Matris, cuius laudes ad excitandam sive exhilarandam piorum devotionem tam operose explicui, piis orationibus eius me studeant Filio commendare (MS *Cambridge, University Library Gg. IV. 16*, fol. 75rb-va).

The commentary must have been written before Roger's death in 1199 and probably before his resignation in 1196. It must have come before the *Historia*, which has been dated between early in 1199 and the spring of 1201. William makes an indirect allusion to his Canticle-commentary in the prefatory letter to the *Historia*, addressed to another Cistercian abbot, Arnold of Rievaulx. He says that he writes his history at Arnold's request and that he is undertaking an easier task than formerly ; it is a recreation to write history after scrutinising deep mysteries. The words echo his letter to Roger of Byland :

> Nunc autem cum cauta discretio vestra, non altis *scrutandis*, mysticisque *rimandis* insistere, sed in narrationibus historicis precipiat spatiari ad tempus, tanquam pro quadam ex facilitate operis recreatione ingenii, multo magis excusandi michi occasio tollitur [57].

The account of how the commentary was written throws light on the habits of monastic authors. William 'dictated' it on to wax tablets, but had to copy it on to parchment for himself, in default of a secretary ; hence it took him a disproportionate time to finish, from one Lent to the next. It is a sign of the remoteness of Newburgh that William should think he was doing something novel in composing a 'Mary-commentary'. He says that he could get no help from his predecessors. In fact, he does not quote earlier commentators by name, though a more thorough study might show that he relied on a library.

Russel frequently quotes a 'Willelmus'. Two examples will show that he meant William of Newburgh :

On 1, 9 : *collum tuum sicut monilia.*

Quasi diceret secundum expositionem Willelmi : Rigidum non est collum tuum per superbiam,	Quasi diceret : Non riget collum tuum per superbiam, sicut [85] collum eius de quo scriptum est :

---

57. *Ibid.*, 4.
58. From *Iob* xv, 26.

sicut collum eius est sicut (sic) versus Dominum erecto collo, sed est pia obedientia flexosum. Proinde non ornatur monilibus, sed in se ipso sicut monilia decoratur. Solet enim collum superbia rigidum monilibus ad ostentationem ornari ; eis quippe indiget, cum sine eis ipsum (MS ipso) turpe conspicitur. Porro obedientia humilis extrinsecum non querit ornatum, nam ut monilia ipsa pulchra cognoscitur (MS *Can. pat. lat. 52*, fol. 104vb-105ra).

cucurrit adversus Deum extento collo, sed est pia humilitate flectuosum.

Proinde non ornatur monilibus, sed in se ipso pulchrum est sicut monilia.

Solet enim collum superbia rigidum monilibus ad ostentationem ornari. Porro humilitas extrinsecum et peregrinum non querit ornatum, sed ad omnem ornatum sufficit sibi. Querat sibi superbia monilia quibus ornetur ; quippe indiget eis, cum in se ipsa turpis et feda sit. Humilitas vero non indiget monilibus, nec querit sibi monilia, quia pro monilibus ipsa sibi est, que nimirum pulchra est sicut monilia (MS *C. U. L.*, *Gg. IV, 16*, fol. 7ra).

On II, 7 : *Adiuro vos, filiae Ierusalem... ne suscitetis, neque evigilare faciatis dilectam...*

Willelmus : Piam matrem ob insigne filialis dilectionis vice proprii nominis dilectam vocat, que sane inter medios cleros dormiebat, hoc est, in medio duorum clerorum, cuius penne erant veluti penne columbe deargentate, cuius potest esse vox illud propheticum : Quis dabit michi pennas sicut columbe, et volabo et requiescam ?

Inter medios cleros, id est sortes. Clerus enim grece est sors latine. Una ergo sors fuit filii leva sive sinistra, sustentans per omne suffragium. Alia sors fuit ipsius dextera amplectantis per glorie patrocinium... [60] (fol. 108ra).

Vox est pie Iesu prohibentis importunitatem quarundam filiarum Ierusalem ab inquietatione dormientis matris. Hanc enim ob insigne filialis dilectionis vice proprii nominis dilectam vocat. Dormiebat sane pia mater inter medios cleros, hoc est, in medio duorum clerorum, et erant penne eius sicut penne columbe deargentate : Quis dabit michi pennas sicut columbe, hinc et volabo et requiescam ?... [59]

...cum dormiret in medio duorum clerorum, id est duarum sortium ; sors una dextera, alia sinistra... Sors dextera, incarnatio redemptoris,... sors vero sinistra, eiusdem redemptoris passio... (fol. 12rb).

Russel's quotations fill a gap in the history of William's Canticle-commentary. It was less neglected than we might have supposed. We can understand why it should have been copied in the fifteenth

---

59. *Ps.* LXVII, 14 ; LIV, 7.

60. Russel takes some liberties with his original here, interpreting the right and left hand rather differently from William of Newburgh.

century. All the same, it did remain isolated and never entered into the
school tradition : William of Newburgh breathes the spirit of eleventh
or early twelfth-century monastic piety. He is pre-scholastic in his
approach ; yet he avoids the personal mysticism of St Bernard and
his disciples. He seems an odd choice for a late thirteenth-century
Franciscan. There is an equally surprising parallel in the quotations
from Guibert of Nogent in a commentary on the Twelve Minor Prophets by another English Franciscan, William of Middleton, about
1250 [61]. What moved Russel and Middleton to dip into this monastic
past, a past lacking the authority of the Fathers and yet far removed
from contemporary modes of feeling ? Eclecticism ? certainly : perhaps
also the fun of quoting an author unknown to one's pupil's. But the
friars must have felt some affinity with these half-forgotten *claustrales*.

ALEXANDER NEQUAM (d. 1217).

Nequam supplies more material for Russel's commentary than
any other of his authors. Two examples will illustrate his manner
of quotation ; he quotes loosely and shortens his long original but
gives a correct reference to book and chapter :

On I, I :

Et sic introducitur illud canticum secundum Alexandrum, lib. 2
super Cant., cap. 2 : Ecce, inquid,
illustris rex Salomon, vir auctoritatis maxime profundeque intelligentie, carmen Virginis amatorium
ab osculo iocundo exordiens, ait :
Osculetur me... (fol. 101ra).

Ecce rex Salomon, vir auctoritatis maxime, profundissime canticum cantat canticorum [62]. Et ab
osculo iocundo exordiens... (MS
Oxford, Bodl. 356 (2716), fol. 55rb,
from lib. II, cap. 2).

On same text :

Unde Alexander, lib. 2, cap. 8,
litteraliter exponit illud de osculis
corporalibus, quibus sepius oscu-
latus est matrem suam Iesus parvulus, fons amoris, quem ipsa mater
appetit (fol. 101va).

Rubric :
Expositio dumtaxat historialis
eius quod scriptum est : *Osculetur...*
de beata virgine et Christo.
Text :
Iuxta quandam igitur litteralem
intelligentiam et simplicem, nonnunquam reperitur informatio sua-
vis... Patet autem quia pluries
iteravit (beata virgo), sepius dedit
filio suo oscula suavitatis (*ibid.*,
fol. 58vb-59ra, from lib. II, cap. 8).

61. B. SMALLEY, *William of Middleton and Guibert of Nogent*, in *Rech. Théol.
anc. méd.* 16 (1949) 281-291.
62. Eleven words, omitted by Russel, have been added in the margin here.

This commentary belongs to Nequam's monastic period, when he had retired from the schools to the important abbey of Augustinian canons at Cirencester. He was abbot 1213-1217 [63]. It is an enormously long treatise, dedicated to the Virgin :

> Non est autem intentionis nostre propositum epithalamium amoris exponere de Christo et ecclesia, quia multi nobilia opera tam eleganter quam diligenter super hoc edita sunt... Beata igitur Virgo ratione carnis assumpte a verbo sponsa est, quia humana natura sponsa est et anima Christi, sed sponsus est Christus (MS *Bodl. 356*, fol. 56[rb-va]).

It suited Russel : he liked the tender scenes in the life of the Virgin described by Nequam in profusion. Nequam did not use William of Newburgh's Canticle-commentary, writing in a more sentimental and pictorial vein than his predecessor. His greater popularity proves that he had more appeal for thirteenth and fourteenth-century readers [64].

THOMAS OF VERCELLI (d. 1246).

Russel quotes Thomas as 'Abbas Vercellensis' (fol. 102[va]) and 'secundum Vercellensem expositorem' [65]. He was using Thomas's third commentary on the Canticle [66]. This does in fact seem to have had more diffusion than the first or second.

On VII, 4 :

Oculi tui sicut piscine, ubi Vercellensis : oculus, inquid, pre ceteris sensibus ampliorem habet incomparabiliter cognitionem, adeo ut nomine visus sensus ceteri designentur, ut cum dicitur : vide quid oleat ; vide quid sapiat (fol. 120[vb]).

...quia sicut oculus pre ceteris sensibus ampliorem incomparabiliter habet cognitionem, adeo ut visus nomine ceteri designentur, ut cum dicitur : vide quid oleat et sapiat (MS *Oxford, Bodl. Laud. misc. 313*, fol. 33[v]).

The mystical tone of the Victorine canon, commentator on Pseudo-Dionysius and friend of Grosseteste [67], must have endeared him to

---

63. J. C. DICKINSON, *The Origins of the Austin Canons*, London 1950, 119, 188 ; STEGMÜLLER, *op. cit.*, no. 1168. Dr. R. W. HUNT has kindly allowed me to read his unpublished doctoral thesis on the life and work of Alexander Nequam.

64. For other quotations from Nequam on the Canticle, see below, **224**; also B. SMALLEY, *Robert Holcot O. P.*, in *Archivum Fratrum Praedic.* 26 (1956) 48.

65. MS *Lambeth180*, fol. 20[v], has 'expositorem' and currently refers to 'expositor Vercellensis'. So does MS *Vat. lat. 672*. MS. *Can. pat. lat. 52* always omits the 'expositor'.

66. STEGMÜLLER, *op. cit.*, no. 8201 ; and see the bibliography, *ibid.*

67. D. A. CALLUS, in *Robert Grosseteste, Bishop and Scholar*, Oxford 1955, 57-60.

Russel. True, Thomas was not writing a 'Mary commentary', but Russel could adjust the argument. Thus Thomas's comment on the verse just quoted really referred to the Seraphim. The adjustment is sometimes explicitly mentioned, as when Russel says on iv, 6 :

> Vercellensis exponit totum illud textum, et bene expositio sua alludit Virgini illi beate (fol. 114va).

He means rather that he can make the allusion out of it.

John Pecham (d. 1292).

Pecham composed a commentary on the Canticle when he was lecturing at the papal university, 1277-79 [68]. It probably represents his teaching there. The only surviving copies are in Italian libraries [69]. It would have been natural, however, for Pecham to bring his work with him to England, when he was appointed archbishop of Canterbury in 1279, and to give his autograph or a copy to the Minorites, his own Order. Russel quotes him as 'Cantuariensis'. There are a number of quotations, but not as many as those from William of Newburgh, Alexander Nequam or Thomas of Vercelli. Here are two examples :

On ii, 2 : *Sicut lilium inter spinas.*

Tamen Cantuariensis alio modo exponit istud de beata Virgine, quia sicut spina pungit, lilium non, sic fuit de beata Virgine et aliis mulieribus, quia sicut alie mulieres illecebrose excitant in hominibus motus corporales et in modis spinarum provocant concupiscentiarum punctiones, sic beata Virgo extinxit e contrario intuentibus excitatam concupiscentiam, quod satis videtur probabile, quia certum est secundum Ieronimum radios oculorum Christi tante fuisse virtutis potentie, quod homines rudes attraherent ad ipsum imitandum et ad comprehendendum eum prosternerent venientes, sicut ipse ait super illud Psalmi : Tanquam sponsus etc. (fol. 106va).

Plenissimum est illud verbum de Virgine gloriosa... Imo dicitur de ipsa quod, sicut illecebrose mulieres excitant in hominibus motus carnis, et in modum spinarum excitant concupiscentie punctiones, sic ipsa e contra extinxit intuentibus eam concupiscentiam excitatam, quod satis est probabile, quia certum est secundum Ieronimum radios oculorum Christi tante fuisse potentie ut homines rudes attraxerunt ad Christum imitandum et ad comprehendendum eum prostraverunt venientes, ut ipse dicit super illud verbum : Speciosus forma pre filiis... (MS *Laurent. Conv. sopp. 516*, fol. 172^v).

---

68. D. L. Douie, *Archbishop Pecham*, Oxford 1952, 43 ; A. Teetaert, *Bulletin franciscain*, in *Études franciscaines* 40 (1928) 304-305.

69. Stegmüller, *op. cit.*, no. 4845. I have used MS *Florence, Laurent. Conv. sopp. 516*, fol. 149-220. Mlle d'Alverny kindly verified Russel's quotations from this MS in a microfilm, lent by Fr. Delorme. The MS belonged to Santa Maria Novella.

On II, 3 : *fructus eius dulcis gutturi meo.*

...nec tantum est dulcis gutturi, imo dulcis est et visui, dulcis et auditui, sicut hic exponit Cantuariensis ; nam dulcis est gustui per masticationem sapidam, dulcis est visui per contemplationem limpidam, dulcis et auditui per inspirationem celicam. De dulcedine gustus dicitur : Quam dulce est domus. De dulcedine visus dicitur Eccles. II : Dulce lumen et delectabile est oculis videre solem... De dulcedine auditus per inspirationem celicam potest adduci illud Prov. 57 (sic) : Boni amici consiliis anima dulcoratur (fol. 107ra).

Circa quod sciendum quod fructus, qui in spirituali exercitio colligitur, dulcis est auditui, dulcis est visui, dulcis est gustui. Auditui per inspirationem, unde Prov. 27 : Bonis amici consiliis anima dulcoratur. Item, dulcis est visui per contemplationem, Eccles. 11 : Dulce lumen oculis, et delectabile videre solem. Item, dulcis est gustui per devotionem... (fol. 174vb-175ra).

Russel quotes once from a writer whom I cannot identify, Gerard, bishop of Mat(isconensis ?). The work quoted is a collection of homelies, whether on the Canticle or not is unclear. St Gerard, bishop of Mâcon 886-926, is not known to have left any homelies :

On I, 3 : *Introduxit me rex in cellaria sua.*

...et hoc est quod dicit Gerardus, episcopus Mat. [70] in omeliis suis : Solve, inquid, non vanam, non vagam, sed sacram et sanctam, tam [71] sacre ordinatam ad illud quod est supra, intra, iuxta, infra ; ad illud quod est supra per desiderii suspendium, ad illud quod est infra per continentie cinctorium, ad illud quod est iuxta, scilicet proximum, per vinculum virtutis concordie, ad illud quod est infra, scilicet mundum, per repudium labentis substantie (fol. 103ra).

Quotations from Peter de Riga's verse paraphrase of the Canticle in his *Aurora* stress the poetic character of Russel's *catena*. Here is one example :

Petrus in Aurora loquens in persona Virginis sic ait exponendo hunc textum : « In speciem nolite meam defigere lumen, » quia « me denigravit divini solis acumen » (fol. 103vb) [72].

It will be interesting to compare Russel's choice of authors with that of another English compiler of the later thirteenth century. He has

---

70. MS *Vat. lat. 672*, fol. 55, also has *Mat.-* ; MS *Lambeth 180*, fol. 4ra, has a blank space after 'Gerardus episcopus'.

71. MSS *Vat. lat. 672* and *Lambeth 180* both have 'tanquam'.

72. STEGMÜLLER, *op. cit.*, no. 6823-5. I checked the quotation from MS *Oxford, Bodl. 822 (2702)*, fol. 114^{v}.

left an anonymous set of extracts on the Canticle found in MS *Paris, Bibl. nat. 10726*, fol. 84-97 [73]. There is another copy in MS *Munich lat. 8827*, according to the catalogue [74].

It is the middle piece in a collection of items in different hands of unknown provenance. The Canticle-commentary is written in a hand of the late thirteenth century. The compiler has drawn on St Bernard, Alexander Nequam, Thomas of Vercelli (third commentary). So much he has in common with Russel, but he chooses different passages. He quotes extensively from Pseudo-Dionysius, twice with a mention of Grosseteste's commentary on him (fol. 89[ra], 91[va]), and from religious writings of the Victorines, Hugh and Richard. He differs from Russel in that he casts his net wider ; for instance he quotes St Basil on the Hexaemeron. 'The philosophers' play a greater part : Aristotle, Macrobius, Cicero and 'Plato in Thimeo' all appear. The difference arises partly from the fact that this is not a 'Mary commentary' like Russel's ; hence the compiler is less restricted in his choice. The most striking point of contrast is that he does not use either William of Newburgh or John Pecham. There is one quotation from 'Honorius monachus', a commentator not quoted by Russel [75].

III

Russel's Apocalypse-commentary exists in one copy in MS *Oxford, Merton College 172*. This volume is the last of a series, MSS *169-172*, containing a set of commentaries which originally covered the whole Bible. William of Nottingham II O. F. M., lector to the Oxford Franciscans about 1312, had them copied while he was 'actu regens' at the expense of Sir Hugh of Nottingham, a royal clerk and perhaps a kinsman of William. The commentaries are mostly by Nicholas Gorran, with a few other authors thrown in [76]. William himself while regent

---

73. STEGMÜLLER, *op. cit.*, no. 8201, 1.

74. See above, n. 37.

75. Fol. 84vb. I have not been able to find his quotation in the printed commentaries of Honorius Augustodunensis, however, PL 172, 347-518.

76. F. M. POWICKE, *The Medieval Books of Merton College*, Oxford 1931, 28-32, 162, 174-175 ; B. SMALLEY, *Some Latin Commentaries on the Sapiential Books*, in *Archives Hist. doctr. littér. Moyen Age* 18 (1951) 107-108 ; *Which William of Nottingham?* below, 249-87.

On William Reed, bishop of Chichester, who gave these MSS to Merton College, see also J. R. L. HIGHFIELD, *The English Hierarchy in the Reign of Edward III*, in *Transactions of the Royal Historical Society*, 5th series, 6 (1956) 124. It has been assumed until recently that William of Nottingham II copied these commentaries with his own hand, but Dr. R. W. Hunt and Mr N. R. Ker point out that there are in fact a number of different hands. It seems, therefore, that Nottingham merely supervised the scribes and of course chose the commentaries to be copied.

lectured on the Gospels in the harmony of Clement of Lanthony, producing a work of vast proportions. No wonder that he did not supervise the scribe of Russel's commentary closely enough to prevent the omission of words and lines here and there ; he must have had much else to occupy him.

MS *Merton 172* contains four items : 1 and 2 are Nicholas Gorran on the Canonical Epistles and on Acts, fol. 1ra-105vb [77] ; 4 is Hugh of St Cher on Acts, called 'postille communes', fol. 144ra-167vb [78]. The scribe has made many marginal notes and headings. He invokes 'Maria. Iesus. Iohannes.' on the top margins of fol. 144-145. The third item, which concerns us here, is Russel on the Apocalypse, fol. 106ra-143ra. The explicit gives Russel's name and Christian name and expresses the same devotion to Mary as does his Canticle-commentary.

Prologue. Incipit : '*Statuit septem piramides unam contra unam*, Mac. 13 [79]. Accedens ad expositionem Apocalipsis, beatissimo Iohanni luculentius approbate, inprimis assumo verbum Ioachim abbatis...' (fol. 106ra).

Text. Incipit : '*Apocalipsis Iesu Christi*. Nota bene quod ad hunc librum legendum premiationibus allicimur. Unde Apoc. cap. 1 : beatus qui legit verba prophetie huius. Glosa : vere beatus...' (fol. 106rb).

Explicit : '...et septem visiones. Septem insuper sunt littere in nomine auctoris ; nam Iohannes habet septem litteras, excepta h, que secundum Papiam non est littera, sed aspirationis nota. Septem enim sunt littere in nomine presentis compilatoris ; nam vocatur Iohannes, dictus Russel, de ordine minorum ; cui largiatur finaliter septenarius gratiarum, et hoc meritis et precibus illius Iohannis, insigniti septiformi spiritu gratie, cuius custodie deputata fuit illa mitis puella, quam angelus sic salutavit, dicens : Ave gratia plena' (fol. 143ra).

A partially erased, but still legible inscription follows :

'Explicit lectura fratris Iohannis Russel de ordine fratrum minorum super Apocalipsim'.

Then a note on the contents and scribe of the volume :

'In hoc volumine continentur postille fratris Nicolai de Gorham super omnes epistolas canonicas et super Apocalipsim, lectura etiam fratris Iohannis Russel super eundem librum, postille etiam communes super actus apostolorum ; quo qui usi fuerint, rogent pro anima domini Hugonis de Notingham, qui omnes expensas exhibuit habundanter, et etiam pro anima fratris Willelmi de eadem, per cuius laboriosam diligentiam taliter erat scriptum, etiam dum erat Oxon. actu regens'.

The rest of fol. 143 is blank.

The Apocalypse gave less opportunity for Russel to honour the

---

77. STEGMÜLLER, *op. cit.*, no. 5803-5810.
78. *Ibid.*, no. 3725.
79. *I Machab.* XIII, 28.

Virgin than did the Canticle ; but he refers the exposition to her wherever he finds it possible. Thus at the end of chapter xii he writes :

> Notandum est quod hec omnia de muliere in hoc capitulo exponuntur
> secundum quosdam de matre ecclesia, sed michi placuit melius expositio
> de Maria, presertim cum etiam ab expositoribus auctenticis sit assumptum
> (fol. 124va).

He invokes her in his final prayer, just before he gives his name and
commends himself to her and to St John. The prayer also states
that he is ending a lecture course and resumes its purpose :

> Et sicut hoc exemplo minister ecclesie petit dari plebibus gratiam bene-
> dictionis in ultimo misse, sic ego, recitator huius scripture, peto tribui
> vobis auditoribus gratiam benedictionis in conclusione et terminatione
> lectionum huius doctrine, quam in nobis confirmet tota Trinitas, gratie
> collatrix, Mater Dei, gratie imperatrix, persona Iohannis, gratie receptatrix,
> utpote qui fuit repletus septiformi spiritu gratie (fol. 142va).

Russel calls himself 'recitator huius scripture', claiming no originality for his commentary. We need not infer that he was merely a bachelor, 'reading the Bible with glosses'. His voice has a magisterial tone
whenever it rises above a recital. It seems unlikely, too, that a bachelor
would have dared to quote so dangerous an author as Joachim. Russel
was just a modest master, who felt that other expositors would have
more value for students than his own ventures in exposition.

The prologue is probably the least derivative part of the work.
It explains the 'four causes' of the Apocalypse and indulges in
the usual type of comparisons, which may have been freshly invented.
What follows is a string of quotations, divided into chapters corresponding to the Apocalypse text, with a short division at the head of
each chapter as a preface to the commentary. Russel gives a convenient list of his chief authorities near the end, when he discusses the
curse on anyone adding to the revelations (xxii, 18). It seems that
the curse might fall upon all expositors, he says. He answers by
distinguishing between the various meanings of 'appositio'. His expositors have made lawful additions, 'ut melius pateant gravia et
obscura'. Here is his list :

> ...videtur quod omnes hii doctores, quorum expositiones per vicem accepi,
> scilicet Ieronimus, Augustinus, Beda, Haimo, Ioachim, Berengarius, Rober-
> tus, Ricardus, Hugo, videtur, inquam, quod omnes hii sunt excommuni-
> cati (fol. 142^{rb-va}).

The expositors have been put in chronological order with the exception of Joachim. Russel inserts him between Haimo and Berengaudus,
instead of after Richard of St Victor. We need not consider the names

before 'Robertus'. Russel's use of the Fathers, of 'Haimo' and Berengaudus (whom he calls 'Berengarius') is quite normal and typical [80]. His choice of twelfth and thirteenth-century commentators is more interesting. It must be added that his list is not complete. Russel has mentioned only the names that he has been quoting most frequently.

ROBERT OF BRIDLINGTON (d. about 1160).

'Robertus' appears more often than any other name in the commentary. Russel calls him 'Robertus abbas' (fol. 106[va]) and says : 'per Robertum abbatem, insignem huius libri expositorem...' (fol. 106[vb]). He praises him : 'Robertus pulchre sic exponit :...' (fol. 109[vb]) ; 'sicut docet hic pulcherrime Robertus...' (fol. 142[vb]). The quotations come from the Apocalypse-commentary ascribed by Bale to the Augustinian canon, Robert, prior of Bridlington in Yorkshire [81]. It survives in two copies, MSS *Troyes 563*, fol. 1[ra]-105[vb],late 12 th cent., from Clairvaux [82], and *Oxford, Bodl. 864 (2735)*, fol. 69-146, written in the 15th cent. in England [83]. Russel is mistaken in giving Robert the title of abbot, since Bridlington was a priory ; perhaps he did not know the details of his expositor's life. Robert gives his own name in the capital letters at the beginning of his expositions of the seven visions, 'Roberti', but does not particularise further. He was an industrious compiler, who left commentaries on Exodus, the Twelve Minor Prophets and Pauline Epistles as well as on the Apocalypse [84]. He expounds the Apocalypse 'ex dictis patrum' according to the four senses in a 'safe' and traditional way, indulging neither in speculation nor in topical allusions [85].

---

80. Russel quotes occasionally from 'Ieronimus in originali', more often from Bede, 'Haimo' and Berengaudus (Pseudo-Ambrose) ; see STEGMÜLLER, *op. cit.*, n° 1640, 1711, 3122. St. Augustine left no Apocalypse-commentary and Russel does not quote Pseudo-Augustine ; see *ibid.*, no. 1495. He does, however, quote authentic works of St Augustine, and doubtless felt that his list of expositors would have been incomplete without this great name.

81. *Index*, ed. POOLE and BATESON, Oxford 1902, 388.

82. Described by J. LECLERCQ. *Le commentaire ue Gilbert de Stanford sur le Cantique*, in *Analecta monastica*, 1st series (*Studia Anselmiana*, 20), Rome 1948, 210.

83. Both MSS are listed by STEGMÜLLER, *op. cit.*, no. 7383. I have studied MS *Troyes 563* in a microfilm. Comparison of selected passages shows that the text is very similar in both MSS. Russel quotes loosely, *more suo*, but always recognisably. There is no need to pile up illustrations of his method.

84. On his life and writings see my papers, *Rech. Théol. anc. méd.* 7 (1935) 248-261 ; 8 (1936) 32-34 ; J. C. DICKINSON, *op. cit.*, 66-67 and *passim*.

85. The Apocalypse-commentary differs slightly from the others in that Robert does not give the names of his sources ; nor is he so obviously dependent

RICHARD OF ST VICTOR (d. 1173) [86].

We have seen that Russel lists Richard among his standard expositors. He quotes him by name throughout the commentary, though not nearly as often as Robert. His quotations can be verified from the text printed in Migne, PL 196, 683-888.

JOACHIM OF FIORE (d.1202).

Joachim also appears in Russel's list of authors. His Apocalypse-commentary is quoted throughout, much more often than is Richard's; Joachim comes second only to Robert as a favourite. The quotations can be found in the printed edition, Venice, 1527. Russel sometimes quotes verbally and sometimes, as he puts it himself, 'summatim'. His attitude to the Calabrian abbot can be expressed as 'cautious admiration'. To illustrate the admiration : — Joachim has pride of place, being chosen as the first commentator to be quoted in Russel's prologue ; immediately after his opening text Russel writes :

> Accedens ad expositionem Apocalipsis, beatissimo Iohanni luculentius approbate, in primis assumo verbum Ioachim abbatis in quodam libro introductorio in expositione istius libri. Magna, inquid, et singularis est prerogativa huius voluminis... Totum enim hunc librum numerus septenarius possidet, nec mirum (si) a Iohanne, celi camerario, scribitur, cui re cumbenti supra pectus Domini, habere septenarium donorum Spiritus sancti specialiter est concessum. Hec ille (fol. 106ra) [87].

On xviii, 14, *Et negotiatores terrae flebunt*, he quotes Joachim as being reported to have had the spirit of prophecy :

> ...Hec est litteralis expositio huius passus, secundum quam *negotiatores*

---

on the *Gloss*. There is no reason to doubt the ascription to Robert of Bridlington, however. The presence of his Apocalypse-commentary at Clairvaux is significant. He wrote on the Twelve Minor Prophets at the request of a Cistercian abbot, Gervase of Louth Park, and the monks of Clairvaux possessed a copy, MS *Troyes 224.*

86. On Richard of St. Victor see G. DUMEIGE, *Richard de Saint-Victor et l'idée chrétienne de l'amour*, Paris 1952 ; *Ives. Épître à Séverin. Richard de Saint-Victor. Les quatre degrés* etc., Paris 1955.

87. The passage in Joachim reads : 'Magna est et singularis prerogativa huius voluminis, quia magnus est Dei spiritus, quia in eo aperte loquitur voces suas (sic) ; per hoc enim quod librum istum septenarius totum possidet numerus... Nec mirum si a celi camerario scribitur, cui recumbenti supra pectus Domini archana speculari misteria et de torrente Spiritus sancti abundantius bibere datum est' (*Liber introductorius in expositionem Apocalypsis*, ed. Venice 1527, fol. 3rb). Russel has slightly abridged.

accipiuntur pro mercatoribus ad litteram. Ioachim tamen, qui, ut fertur, habuit spiritum prophetie, exponit istud de modernis sacerdotibus ecclesie, sic : Isti, inquid, *negotiatores terre* sunt sacerdotes bruti, qui nesciunt ea que sunt Dei... non licet [88]. Hec Ioachim (fol. 133ra).

He shows his caution by referring to the condemnation of Joachim's Trinitarian doctrine by the Lateran Council of 1215. He has just been quoting Joachim's explanation of the significance of *alpha et omega* (I, 8) ; Joachim expounds it of the Trinity 'diffuse et pulcherrime'. St Augustine, says Russel, teaches that flowers may be culled from thorns etc. ; so we may cull true and healthful doctrine (from Joachim) and reject what is erroneous. After this proviso he cites the condemnation :

> Ratio autem quare se exprimit per tales litteras, scilicet *alpha et omega* est ut insinuet misteria Trinitatis et unitatis et processionis personarum in divinis, sicut exponit Ioachim... In prima ergo littera greca signatur Trinitas personalis, cum dicitur *alpha*. Ioachim : alpha, quod est primum elementum apud grecos, idem est quod 'a', quod est primum elementum apud latinos ; 'a' autem est triangulatum elementum, in quo notatur personalis Trinitatis sacramentum. In sequenti elemento, scilicet 'o' reperitur rotunditas, et in hoc signatur essentialis unitatis individuitas. Hec Ioachim summatim. Diffuse enim tractat istam materiam et pulcherrime docet qualiter istud misterium Trinitatis et unitatis potest similiter colligi e litteris hebraicis [89].
>
> Notandum est autem quod ipse Ioachim aliter hoc exponit, dicens qualiter per illas duas litteras simul potest describi emanatio personarum in divinis. Nam in hoc elemento 'a' procedunt duo ab uno, in quo signari potest processus duarum personarum, scilicet Filii et Spiritus sancti ab uno originali principio, scil. Patre... Hec Ioachim [90]. Docetur lib. 16 *Contra Faustum*, in principio, quod de spinis florem debemus eligere, de herbis frugem, de muscis mella, de silvis poma, gemmas de abyssis, pisces de fluviis (MS fluvidis), sic inter erronea que vera sunt et salubria, hiis eiectis [91] ; *extra*. 1°, *Dampnamus* : Dampnamus et reprobamus libellum sive tractatum quem abbas Ioachim edidit contra magistrum Petrum Lumbardum... [92] (fol. 107va).

Russel keeps a sharp watch on his commentator throughout. Joachim expounds *Apoc.* xii, 15 of the sorrows of the Virgin when her Son was hanging on the Cross. He says that her torment, being men-

---

88. A verbal quotation, *ibid.*, fol. 200vb.

89. From Joachim on the Apocalypse, *op. cit.*, fol. 33vb-35va.

90. *Ibid.*, fol. 37^{ra-va}.

91. From *Contra Faustum* XVI, 1 (PL 42, 315). It is not a verbally exact quotation.

92. *Decret.*, lib. I, tit. 1, cap. II. Russel quotes at length from the condemnation of Joachim's anti-Lombard treatise, which is now lost.

tal, might be supposed to be the more grievous. Russel thought that Joachim exaggerated here :

> Qui hec et hiis similia pensaret, maiorem illius quam Christi putaret preponderare cruciatum, quia nimirum Christus in carne, illa, quod est gravius, cruciabatur in mente. Hec Ioàchim, cuius verbum est excessivum [93] (fol. 124rb).

Russel does not adopt the Abbot's prophecies of a third age of the Holy Spirit. He ignores Joachim's more controversial predictions and *a fortiori* the extravagant interpretations which were put upon them later. The Joachites had already run into trouble owing to their wildness and fanaticism. Russel never mentions their condemnation, but he must have had it in mind. He set aside what displeased him. The remainder, a slightly censored Joachim, he took for a first-class Apocalypse-commentary. The Abbot appealed him, strongly but exclusively, as an 'expositor'.

Instances of a similar use of Joachim occur in other Apocalypse-commentaries of the period. A review of them will show that Russel was in no way peculiar in his attitude. First comes an anonymous postill, *Vidit Iacob in somniis...*, often ascribed to Hugh of St Cher and printed among the works of St Thomas [94]. I have used the copy in MS *Oxford, Bodl. 444 (2385)*, fol. 28ra-177va. It was written in England or northern France in the second half of the thirteenth century. We would guess that the anonymous was a friar, since the Mendicants produced most of the biblical works of the last three-quarters of the thirteenth century. He shows a sympathy with poverty which makes it certain [95]. He wrote in the schools, as appears from his methods and procedure. We shall see later on that Russel used him, without giving him a name. I have not found any details in the postill itself which would carry us any further. For our present purpose it is enough to notice that the anonymous was cautious and orthodox. He refuses to speculate on the identity of *Gog et Magog* (*Apoc.* xx, 7) :

> Nos autem magis volumus glosis sanctorum adherere quam aliquid temere diffinire (fol. 164rb).

Yet this careful postillator quotes from Joachim once at least. He remarks the agreement between St Jerome and Joachim on the text *Apoc.* xi, 3-4, *due olive etc.* :

> Ioachim dicit, cui Ieronimus concordare videtur hic, quod hic dicitur

---

93. JOACHIM, *op. cit.*, fol. 156ra.
94. STEGMÜLLER, *op. cit.*, no. 3771.
95. See below, 236.

de duobus hiis in spiritu esse consummandum, non in littera, et quod hii
duo testes sunt duo ordines, qui ante finem mundi sunt venturi, qui et
due olive et duo candelabra dicuntur, quia et oleo caritatis ardebunt (fol.
97va) [96].

John Ridewall O. F. M., regent at Oxford about 1330, quotes Joachim twice in the surviving extracts from his *Lectura in Apocalyp-
sim* [97]:

> On II, 7 : 'Ioachim dicit duo tempora, unum tempus Filii, aliud tempus
> Spiritus sancti, quod tempus erit in fine seculi, et tunc utile erit advertere
> que hic inferuntur' (MS *Venice, Bibl. Marc. lat. 494 (1790)*, fol. 114ra) [98].

> On III, 7 : 'Ioachim dicit : si cupis habere caritatem Dei, ante omnia et
> super omnia deberes diligere psalmodiam, ita tamen ut non videaris ab
> hominibus nec aliud dicas quam ad laudem Dei et gloriam et gratiarum
> actionem' (*ibid.*, fol. 118rb) [99].

The original *Lectura*, which is now lost, may have contained many
more quotations of the same type. There is nothing to connect Ridewall with Joachism. His main interest seems to have been in mytho-
logy and in other classical studies.

The Friars Minor had a special liking for Joachim [100]. This may
account for his use by Russel and Ridewall, perhaps also by the
anonymous author of *Vidit Iacob in somniis...*, who may well have
been a Minorite. It does not account for his appearance in the Apocalypse-commentary of the Austin Friar, Agostino Trionfo (d. 1328).
This defender of the papal *plenitudo potestatis* must surely have set
the seal of orthodoxy on everything that he touched. His Apocalypse-
commentary survives in many copies [101]. The method he employs
there is to make a *catena* of extracts from earlier commentators for
each chapter or section of a chapter, and then to discuss the *dubita-
bilia*. The names of the authors quoted are generally written in red,
so that they stand out from the text. Joachim leaps to the eye as one
of the names occurring most frequently. Agostino Trionfo clearly

---

96. Joachim, *op. cit.*, fol. 148^{va-b}. Joachim himself refers to St Jerome.

97. Robert Holcot quotes Ridewall's *Lectura* about 1333-34 ; see B. Smalley,
Robert Holcot O. P., *loc. cit.*, 54-56 ; A. G. Little, *The Grey Friars in Oxford*,
Oxford 1892, 170-171.

98. A loose reference to Joachim, *op. cit.*, fol. 82va-84va, on *Apoc.* II, 7. Miss
M. E. Reeves kindly helped me to find these quotations.

99. Joachim, *op. cit.*, fol. 86ra.

100. See D. L. Douie, *The Nature and Effect of the Heresy of the Fraticelli*,
Manchester 1932, 22-48.

101. Stegmüller, *op. cit.*, no. 1546. I have seen the commentary in MSS
Rome, Bibl. apost. Vat. lat. 936, Urb. lat. 528, Oxford, Bodl. 138 (1908).

regarded him as a valuable guide, to set beside Jerome, Bede and Haimo. All four of our commentators, the anonymous, Russel, Ridewall and Trionfo, were quoting Joachim independently of one another. Each made his own choice of extracts. Each one, presumably, had a copy of Joachim's commentary before him.

Medieval scholars could distinguish between the merely heretical and the heretic. They quoted Origen and Berengar of Tours, both of whose names, as it happens, appear in the standard aid to Scripture, the *Glossa ordinaria*. Students would abstract the condemned doctrines and gratefully take what was left. Joachim lent himself to this selective process. The condemnation of 1215 had in no way impugned his character or spotted his reputation for sanctity. Recent research, moreover, has brought out the underlying orthodoxy of his ideas. He saw history as unrolling itself according to two patterns. The better known pattern is that of threes, culminating in a third age, which would be the age of the Holy Spirit. But he also used a pattern of twos, corresponding to the Old and New Testaments, a safer and more familiar arrangement. Both mattered to him [102]. His disciples experimented with speculations based on the pattern of threes. They proved its inherent dangers and incurred censure. When Joachism became suspect, the Abbot's admirers could fall back on the pattern of twos, and remain orthodox. Hence he did not only give rise to Joachism, though this was the more spectacular result of his writings. The less exotic part of them passed into the main stream of teaching on the Apocalypse. Joachim's influence on orthodox medieval exegesis deserves further study. It seems safe to say that even shorn of his prophecies his commentary on the Apocalypse must have strengthened the mystical tendency in exegesis, of the Apocalypse in particular. Nicholas of Lyre must have counteracted it to some extent ; he argues against Joachim, though without mentioning his name. But the diffusion of Agostino Trionfo's Apocalypse-commentary shows that Lyre had a strong competitor, who kept Joachim's name in the foreground.

---

102. M. E. REEVES, *The « Liber Figurarum » of Joachim of Fiore*, in *Mediaeval and Renaissance Studies* 2 (1950) 57-81 ; M. E. REEVES and B. HIRSCH-REICH, *The « Figurae » of Joachim of Fiore, ibid.* 3 (1954) 171-199. On Joachim's influence in northern Europe see W. BLOOMFIELD and M. E. REEVES, *The Penetration of Joachism into Northern Europe*, in *Speculum* 29 (1954) 772-793 ; R. FREYHAN, *Joachism and the English Apocalypse*, in *Journal of the Warburg and Courtauld Institutes* 18 (1955) 211-244. Unfortunately Freyhan was not able to use the former study, wich gives further proofs of Joachim's influence in England in the thirteenth century.

HUGH OF ST CHER ? (d. 1263).

Here is a puzzle. Russel ends his list of expositors with 'Hugo' and refers to 'Magister Hugo' and 'Hugo expositor'. Since he listed his expositors chronologically and put Hugh last, it seems certain that he meant Hugh of St Cher [103], whose postills on Scripture had become standard reference books by the late thirteenth century. Yet his quotations do not come from the printed text of Hugh of St Cher on the Apocalypse. They bear no relationship to it at all. Nor do they come from Pseudo-Hugo, *Vidit Iacob in somniis*. The postill printed under the name of Hugh of St Cher seems to be of doubtful authenticity [104]. Hence it may be useful to those interested in his postills to see some of Russel's quotations. The following are all that occur in Russel's commentary on *Apoc.* i-x. Russel's 'Hugo' was the author of a full, elaborate exposition and had a more than ordinary weakness for number-symbolism.

I, 5 : *et lavit nos.* 'Et secundum Hugonem expositorem : Ut perfecta foret ablutio, sanguinem fudit sub numero senario. In circumcisione enim fudit sanguinem germinalem, in sudatione sanguinem inter(ven)alem, in flagellatione sanguinem intercutaneum seu superficialem, in coronatione capitis, ubi sensus vigent, sanguinem animalem, in terebratione manuum et pedum sanguinem naturalem, in lanceatione [105] sanguinem vitalem' (fol. 107ra).

IV,2 : *sedes posita erat in coelo.* 'Magister Hugo sic exponit : Per celum, inquid, intelligitur divinitatis natura, cui proprietates celi competunt superintellectualiter. In hoc celo est sedes, quia sublimitas potestatis divine supra sedem sedens, Deus supra celum sedet [106], quia in se modo quiescit. Ipse enim solus se circumscribit per integritatem et se solo fruitur et sic se solo quiescit' (fol. 112rb) [107].

IV, 4 : *in capitibus eorum coronae aureae.* 'Dicit autem hic magister Hugo quod hoc premium corone iam est in eorum mentali capite, in quo iam vigent quinque sensus spirituales, quia in mentali capite eorum est contemplatio quasi (MS q.) infusa (MS infusus), gaudium quasi [108]... desiderium

---

103. Russel cannot have meant Hugh of St Victor. No Apocalypse-commentary has been ascribed to the latter, and Russel would have known that he was older than Richard of St Victor. He does, however, quote Hugh of St Victor on the *De arca Noe morali* simply as 'Hugo' : 'Hic de hoc libro pulcherrime loquitur Hugo, de arca Noe, lib. 2, cap. 14... Hec Hugo' (fol. 113ra). The quotation comes from *De arca Noe morali*, II, 11 (not 14) in PL 176, 643.

104. STEGMÜLLER, *op. cit.*, no. 3769-3770.

105. MS 'lasceationem'.

106. A word, phrase or line may have dropped out here.

107. Russel gives no indication as to where his quotation ends.

108. A line explaining the parallels to the first two senses must have dropped out here.

quasi olfactus, affectus quasi gustus, amplexus quasi tactus. Horum sensuum obiecta sunt clarifica pulchritudo, armonica aptitudo, odoris spira-
mentum, saporis delectamentum, lenitatis fulcimentum' [109] (fol. 112va).

IV, 9 : *et benedictionem.* 'Distinguit magister Hugo sic : quod benedictio
dicitur dupliciter, uno modo pro bona dictione, alio modo pro bona datione
et benedictionem bone dationis communicari debet benedicto bone dictio-
nis' (fol. 113ra).

V, 6 : '*In medio troni,* id est in intimo paterne substantie, secundum
magistrum Hugonem ; *et quatuor animalium, et in medio seniorum* ; per
quatuor animalia secundum magistrum Hugonem signantur patres evangelici, per seniores patres testamenti mosaici' (fol. 113^{va-b}).

V, 9 : *et cantabant canticum novum.* 'In qua quidem redemptione conso-
nantissimum erat canticum, sicut docet hic pulcherrime magister Hugo :
Ibi, inquid [110], fuit proportio dupli ad simplum, proportio simpli ad triplum,
proportio duorum ad tria, hoc est dyapente sive sesquitertia ; erat enim ibi
proportio dupli ad simplum, hoc est dyapason, quia Christus morte simpla
nostram (mortem) duplam destruxit...' [111] (fol. 114ra).

V, 14 : '*Et quatuor animalia,* id est patres novi testamenti, *dicebant : amen,*
id est confirmabant, secundum Hugonem' (fol. 114rb).

VI, 6 : '*Ne leseris,* hoc est : *non ledes,* scilicet in iudicio, secundum magistrum Hugonem' (fol. 114vb).

VI, 10 : '*Et clamabant voce magna* ; voce, inquam, intellectibili, non audi-
bili, secundum magistrum Hugonem' (fol. 115rb).

VI, 11 : *Et datae sunt illis singulae stolae albae.* 'Secundum magistrum
Hugonem, hec datio nichil aliud signat nisi anime supra se reflexionem et
beatificationis attentionem. Stola ista est gloria anime, que singula est
usque ad resurrectionem, quia usque ad illud tempus in sola anima percipiunt
glorificationem ; sed tunc gaudebunt stola bina, corpore iam resumpto.
Hec ille' (fol. 115rb).

VII, 2 : '*Ascendentem ab ortu solis,* id est a Patre, a quo naturaliter oriri
est eternaliter nasci, et sic orti ascendere est seipsum manifestare, secundum
magistrum Hugonem' (fol. 115vb).

VII, 3 : ...*quoadusque signemus servos Dei nostri in frontibus eorum.* 'Hic
emergit duplex questio, videlicet, que est ista vox cum exclamatione ?
Secundo, que est ista prohibitio cum ista exceptione [112], *quoadusque etc. ?*
Ad primum respondit Hugo : Dominum [113], inquid, voce magna clamare
hic in hoc libro nichil aliud est quam reproborum spirituum potestate(m)
impiosam (MS impiose) limitare, ne quantum velint possint nocere' (fol.
115vb-116ra).

---

109. Again no indication as to the end of the quotation.
110. MS adds 'ait' after 'inquid'.
111. I have omitted a long passage on number symbolism. Russel summarises
the same passage in his sermon ; see above, 283.
112. MS adds 'exclusione'.
113. MS 'Domini'.

VII, 11 : '*Et seniorum et quatuor animalium*, id est patrum novi et veteris testamenti, in quo circuitu stabant angeli parati semper ad iuvandum hebreos recipientes fidei signaculum, prompti etiam ad muniendum electam turbam gentium. *Stabant* etiam *in circuitu troni*, non intrinsecus, quia infinitum est quod in ipsa deitate latet interius, et creature capacitas est finita. Hec est expositio Hugonis (fol. 117ʳᵃ).

IX, 16 : *Et numerus equestris exercitus vicies millies dena millia.* 'Querit hic Hugo de isto numero appropriato istis equitibus, id est reprobis spiritibus, scilicet *vigies* vel *vities millies dena milia*, utrum debet intelligi litteraliter vel spiritualiter ; et respondit quod iste numerus non habet attendi penes litteralem sensum, quia plures sunt, sed penes prelature officium, hoc est penes respectum ad vitia quorum sunt principium ; et ideo dicuntur equites, nam presunt vitiis. Unde et dicitur spiritus superbie, spiritus fornicationis et huiusmodi. Sunt autem decem prevaricationes fundamentales, quia prevaricationes decalogi, que sunt negationes contra celsitudinem altissimi, abusio contra veritatem unigeniti, adversatio contra tranquilitatem paracleti, inhonoratio dignitatis, concussio fraternitatis, dehonestatio castitatis [114] facultatis, testificatio falsitatis, affectatio pollutionis, captatio possessionis : et hec habent triplex esse, scilicet in mentis consensu, in oris affatu, in opere seu actu, quorum primum, si in secundum reducitur, fuerit centum, que si in tertium reducitur (sic), fuerit mille. Insuper sunt decem peccata ad hec consequentia, que per has inducuntur prevaricationes, scilicet extollentia, invidentia, iracundia, tristitia, avaritia, luxuria, gule immoderantia, diffidentia, discredentia, contemptus, pertinacia ; et hec, si in illum millenarium reducuntur, faciunt decem milia. Item decem sunt quibus homo peccator per ista vitia iniuriatur, scilicet creator unus Dominus et angelici ordinis numerus novenarius [115]. Hec autem habent triplex esse, unum in mente divina, aliud in mente angelica, tertium in mente humana, quod si primum in secundum ducatur, et illud, sic ductum, ducatur in tertium, fiunt mille. Hec autem mille, si in predicta decem milia reducantur, fiunt milies decem milia. Per dicta autem vitia non solum peccator iniuriatur uni Deo, auctori nature, nec etiam novenario angelice creature ; iniuriatur etiam universe inferiorori(s) facture ; et hoc in numero consistit vicenario. Undecim enim orbes et sui ornatus faciunt duodecim, quatuorque sunt elementaria principia et quatuor mixta corpora, inanimatorum, vegetabilium, sensibilium, rationabilium, que simul sumpta constituunt viginti, in quorum singulum per omnia predicta mala peccatores offendunt. Hec igitur viginti, deducta in illa predicta, constituunt vigies milies dena milia. Unde ergo demones scelerati equites numerari convenit penes vitia seu peccata, quibus presunt. Hec Hugo' (fol. 120ʳᵇ).

X, 1 : '*angelum alium fortem*, scilicet in creando, in gubernando, in reparando, in propugnando, ait Hugo' (fol. 120ᵛᵃ).

---

114. Some words or a line must have dropped out here, since of the ten prevarications only eight are listed.

115. The text seems to be corrupt here.

Anonymous, *Vidit Iacob in somniis* [116].

Russel quotes this postill as 'expositor' and 'expositor moralis';
it does, in fact, concentrate on *moralitates*. Either he did not know the
author or he did not care to mention a contemporary by name. Two
examples will show his manner of quoting it.

On IV, 8.

*Et requiem non habebant die et
nocte*. Et dicit hic expositor quod
multi sunt similes philomene, que
nunquam cantat, nisi in estate,
sic multi nunquam Deum laudant
nisi (in) prosperitate (fol. 113ra).

Sed multi sunt similes philomene, que non cantat, nisi in
estate; sic multi non laudant
nisi in prosperitate (MS *Bodl. 444*,
fol. 54ra).

On VII, 16.

Sed hic movet expositor moralis
dubitationem de hoc quod hic
dicitur : *Non esurient, neque sitient
amplius*, quia contrarium habetur
in Ecclesiastico cap. 24, ubi dicitur
in persona Domini : Qui edent me
adhuc esurient... [117] Respondet
quod in esurie duo sunt, defectus
et affectus... (fol. 117rb).

...*amplius*.
Contra : Ecclesiasticus 24 : Qui
edent me adhuc esurient...

Solutio : duo sunt in esurie,
scilicet defectus et desiderium...
(fol. 74va).

A third passage will be quoted because it draws from Russel a
strong expression of his own opinion and this is unusual. He generally
contents himself with a 'recital' of what others have said. It also illustrates how a traditional interpretation could be made topical by
the alteration of a few words. According to Bede, the seven angels
with seven trumpets (viii, 2) signify the seven orders of preachers
who strengthen the Church against her seven orders of persecutors :
apostles v. Jews, martyrs v. Romans or gentiles, doctors v. heretics,
good Christians v. hypocrites or false brethren, the faithful few v.
Antichrist, God's messengers and then God himself v. the devil and
his allies at the end of the world [118]. The author of *Vidit Iacob in
somniis* calls the fourth order 'ordo *pauperum* predicatorum', thus
quietly identifying it with the mendicants. The problem then posed
itself : would the fifth order, which would resist Antichrist, be the
same as the fourth or would it be some new order ? If the latter, the

---

116. On this postill, see above, 230
117. *Eccli.* XXIV, 29.
118. Bede, *op. cit.* (PL 93, 154) and *Gloss., ad loc,*

mendicants must expect to be superseded. The author of *Vidit Iacob in somniis* can only hope that the fourth and fifth orders will be the same, on the analogy of the apostles ; many of these belonged to both the first and the second orders, resisting both the Jews and the Romans. He dare not determine. Russel believes much more definitely in the identity of the fourth and fifth orders. He seems to have felt more confident about the mendicants' lasting role in the Church. It is an interesting *nuance* of outlook. The only point he leaves uncertain is whether the faithful few who resist Antichrist will be exclusively recruited from the friars or not :

RUSSEL

Ita in ecclesia Dei secundum ordinem eam impugnantium erit semper ordo pro ea propugnantium. Firmiter autem estimo quod idem erit ordo predicatorum in quinto statu, qui et in quarto, hoc est ordo Christi pauperum, verbum Dei per mundum seminantium. Tamen si sit talium sive aliorum paucorum fidelium, non determino (fol. 118vb).

Vidit Iacob in somniis.

Nam bene potest fieri quod iidem sint predicatores in quinto statu, qui fuerunt in quarto, et sunt de quarto et de quinto ordine. Nam magis attenditur diversitas et ordo statuum ecclesie quam diversitas personarum sibi ad invicem succedentium. Apostoli enim multi et sub primo et sub secundo fuerunt. Sic etiam multi sub quarto et sub quinto potuerunt simul esse. Non tamen determino quod ita sit (MS *Bodl. 444*, fol. 81ra).

Lastly we have quotations from two Apocalypse-commentaries which are otherwise unknown. Since they are few and brief in each case it will be better to transcribe the quotations before commenting on them.

ROBERT GROSSETESTE (d.1253).

II, 6 : *facta Nicolaitarum.* '...Lincolniensis tamen : In 3º libro ecclesiastice historie, cap. 28, quiddam aliud de hoc Nicolao reperitur[119]. Tacta de factorum istorum nicolaitarum detestatione, statim subiungit de a(u)scultanda persuasione[120]. Unde dicit : *Qui habet aures.* Aliqui libri habent *audiendi*, sed non est textus apud aliquos doctores. *Audiant quid spiritus dicat ecclesiis* : regula generalis est, quando in scriptura *spiritus* sine additamento ponitur, tunc tota Trinitas hoc nomine frequentius nitetur (sic), ut hic et ibi : Spiritus est Deus, Ioh. 4º[121]. Verba sunt Lincolniensis' (fol. 109va).

119. EUSEBIUS, *Historia ecclesiastica* III, 29 (not 28), ed. T. MOMMSEN, Leipzig 1903, I, 261.
120. The corrector has added 'ad', but forgotten to alter 'auscultanda' to 'auscultandum'.
121. *Ioan.* IV, 24.

v, 8 : *phiales aureas.* 'Dicit autem Lincolniensis hic quod fiala est inferius coartata et superius dilatata ad modum galee enee, in quo notatur quod sancti habent non solum mortificationis strictitudinem, immo et devotionis latitudinem' (fol. 113vb).

v, 11 : *millia millium.* 'Lincolniensis habet *milies milia.* Quilibet (sic) adequabitur numeris electorum' (fol. 114ra).

v, 14 : *et adoraverunt viventem in secula seculorum.* 'Littera Haimonis et Lincolniensis est *et adoraverunt viventes in secula seculorum*' (fol. 114rb).

Russel is a good witness to the existence of an otherwise unrecorded work on the Apocalypse by Robert Grosseteste. The bishop of Lincoln bequeathed his books and papers to the Oxford Greyfriars. Gascoigne, a fifteenth-century student and admirer of his, saw copies of various biblical books, though not of the Apocalypse, with his notes in the margins, written beside the *Gloss* [122]. Russel must have found a glossed Apocalypse with wide margins annotated by Grosseteste in this way. It is quite likely that Russel piously copied all the annotations in Grosseteste's hand that he could find, which were few and scanty; or perhaps they amounted to more than he had time for. The few lines quoted show a mixture of devotion and of intellectual curiosity which was typical of Grosseteste as a biblical scholar. It was certainly his custom to correct his text [123].

We might suppose that a devotee of Grosseteste would quote Pseudo-Dionysius in his translation and use his commentary on it. Russel does not do so. He quotes twice from Hugh of St Victor's commentary on the *Angelic Hierarchy* [124]. His text is John Saracen's [125].

---

122. R. W. Hunt, in *Robert Grosseteste, op. cit.*, 121-145.

123. B. Smalley, *ibid.*, 70-97.

124. On xix, 5 : « Cuiusmodi debet hec laus esse docet Hugo super principium quarti capituli angelice ierarchie : Laudabimus, inquid, Deum non demonstratione et comprehensione, sed divina religione et perfecta gratiarum actione ; neque enim laudatur demonstratione quod est incogitabile, neque laudatur comprehensione quod est incomprehensibile... et hoc est perfectis gratiarum actionibus eum collaudare. Hec Hugo' (fol. 134ra). Russel is making a rough quotation from Hugh's commentary on *Laudabimus, inquam, principium omnis hierarchie* (PL 175, 1006).

On xix, 9 : 'Hugo super angelicam ierarchiam, lib. 8 : In illa, inquid, cena nonnisi unum ferculum ponetur, scilicet Deus et illud certe reficit et illud certe sufficit' (fol. 134va). From *ibid.*, on *Divino alimento repleti* (PL 175, 1066).

125. In the prologue : 'Dionysius, angelice ierarchie cap. primo : Neque, inquid, possibile est aliter nobis supersplendere thearchicum radium, nisi varietate sacrorum velaminum sursum active circumvelatum. Hec ille' (fol. 106ra). This corresponds to John Saracen's text, except that Russel adds 'est' and has 'sacrorum' for 'sanctorum'. Both could be mistakes on Russel's part or on the part of his copyists. See Dom Ph. Chevallier, *Dionysiaca* 2, Bruges, s. a., 733.

This is further evidence for the slow passage of Grosseteste's work on Pseudo-Dionysius into current use even in the schools of Oxford [126].

JOHN PECHAM (d. 1292).

I, 9 : *Ego Iohannes, frater vester.* 'Cantuariensis : Patrem se vocare poterat illorum quos per evangelium genuerat, sed maluit se dicere fratrem, quod sibi erat tutius et illis dulcius, et tale est quod est [127] humilius' (fol. 107vb).

I, 15 : *vox illius tanquam vox aquarum multarum.* 'Cantuariensis : *vox aquarum multarum* dicitur laus concurrentium populorum, infra 17 [128], aque multe, populi multi, hoc est gentes, que (MS qui) dum more labilium aquarum ad fidem concurrerunt, quasi vocem christiane laudis Domino persolverunt ; sed iam aqua habet vocem, hoc est sonum, sed non habet sensum. Multitudo iam conversa gaudet quodam sono, scilicet laude nominis christianitatis, sed non interius viget sensum christiane veritatis' (fol. 108va) [129].

I, 20 : *septem stelle, angeli sunt septem ecclesiarum.* 'Cantuariensis : Quoniam omnes transferentes secundum aliam similitudinem transferunt recte septem stellis, id est planetis [130], angeli, id est rectores ecclesie, potuerunt adequari, et hoc propter septenarium virtutum, que in eis debent reperiri. Possunt enim comparari Saturno propter maturitatis gravitatem, Iovi propter consolationis benignitatem, Marti propter correptionis severitatem, Soli propter sapientie resplendentiam, Veneri, que est stella matutina et vespertina, propter sollicitudinis vigilantiam, Mercurio propter doctrinam eloquentiam, unde quidam vocabant Paulum Mercurium, quia erat dux verbi [131]. Iterum (possunt comparari) Lune propter condescensionem variam secundum videlicet subiectorum exigentiam, exemplo doctoris gentium, qui dicit : omnibus omnia factus sum [132]. Hec ille' (fol. 108vb).

II, 2 : *tentasti eos.* 'Sed secundum Cantuariensem ex hoc verbo *temptasti eos* etc. elicitur quoddam dubitabile, presertim cum aliquem temptare multum sit inhumanum, et respondit : est temptatio curiositatis versute explorantis, et est temptatio auctoritatis seu attentive caritatis proinde probantis et investigantis. Prima est curiosorum et multotiens callidorum, de qua temptatione Ecclesiastici 13 : ex multa enim loquela temptabit te de absconditis tuis [133]. Secunda est prelatorum, quibus incumbit ex officio probare et investigare fidem et mores subditorum ; et hoc est similiter doctrina Haimonis' [134] (fol. 109rb).

---

126. D. A. CALLUS, in *Robert Grosseteste, op. cit.,* 60-61 ; H.-F. DONDAINE, *Le corpus dionysien de l'Université de Paris au XIIIe siècle,* Rome 1953, 20-21.

127. 'quod est' repeated in MS.

128. From *Apoc.* XVII, 15.

129. Russel does not indicate where this quotation from Pecham ends.

130. Something had dropped out of the text here ; 'transferunt' lacks its object.

131. *Act.* XIV, 11.

132. *I Cor.* IX, 22. The fable of the moon-goddess condescending to mortals may derive from FULGENTIUS, *Mithologia* II, 16 (ed. R. HELM, Leipzig 1898, 57-58).

133. *Eccli.* XIII, 14.

134. PL 118, 964-965.

None of Pecham's bibliographers has ascribed an Apocalypse-commentary to him. Yet Russel deserves to be trusted. He quotes Pecham on the Canticle correctly as 'Cantuariensis'. Pecham perhaps left an unfinished commentary on the Apocalypse, the fruit of some interrupted teaching period before he became archbishop. Where was a more likely place for it than the Oxford Greyfriars ? Pecham may well have given autographs or copies of his works to his own Order [135].

Reference books other than commentaries used by Russel include the *Corrogationes Promethei* of Alexander Nequam [136] and a much rarer work by Thomas Docking O. F. M. This Oxford friar, a prolific commentator on Scripture, left a book of corrections to the text, which is entered in the catalogue of Syon Abbey ; it may be the same as his biblical grammar-book, quoted by William of Nottingham on Clement of Lanthony [137]. Russel's quotation confirms one's impression that the two books are identical. After quoting the dictionaries of Huguccio and Brito on the word *Bilibris* (vi, 6), Russel compares the view of 'the venerable Docking':

135. The only other archbishop of Canterbury who could have been meant would be Stephen Langton. Russel, however, quotes Langton in his sermon as '*Stephanus* Cantuariensis' ; Pecham is quoted in his Canticle-commentary as 'Cantuariensis' without the Christian name. No commentary on the Apocalypse can be ascribed to Langton with any certainty. G. Lacombe suggested a very short commentary, occupying a few leaves only, as being possibly Langton's, because it was copied with other works of his in MSS *Chartres 288, Paris Maz. 177, Arsenal 64* ; *Studies in the Commentaries of Cardinal Stephen Langton*, reprinted from *Archives Hist. doct. littér. Moyen Age* 5 (1930) 150. This is not Russel's source for his quotations of 'Cantuariensis'.

136. On v, 1 : 'Nota qualiter depingitur sanctus Iohannes habens librum in manu sinistra. Respondet Nequam quod per sinistrum designatur presens vita, per librum doctrina, que hic est intra, non in futuro, quia tunc aperietur liber, in quo omnia relucebunt. Sed quid est quod Paulus cum libro in sinistra manu depingitur et cum gladio in dextera ? Respondet metrice : Mucro, furor Sauli, liber est conversio Pauli' (fol. 113[rb]).

Nequam comments on the opening of St Paul's Epistle to Romans : 'Solet autem a nonnullis queri : quid sit quod Paulus depingitur gladium tenens in dextera manu, librum vero in sinistra ? Ad quod dicendum est quia per gladium potestas designatur, per dexteram autem vita eterna, per librum doctrina, per sinistram vita presens... Ait tamen quidam, super hoc quod quesitum est rationem reddere volens : Mucro, furor Sauli, liber est conversio Pauli' (MS *Bodl. 550 (2300)*, fol. 75[va]). Dr. R. W. Hunt kindly helped me to trace this reference.

137. M. Bateson, *Catalogue of the Library of Syon Monastery*, Cambridge 1898, 221 ; B. Smalley, *Which William of Nottingham?*, below, 283-4. On Docking's life and writings see A. G. Little, *Franciscan Papers, Lists and Documents*, Manchester 1943, 98-121.

> Secundum venerabilem Dokkynge debet corripi, et quod in metris producitur, hoc est propter mutam et liquidam secundum eum (fol. 114vb).

The book quoted must have been concerned with the correct spelling, accentuation and declension of biblical words. Docking was regent at Oxford between 1260 and 1265 and was still at Greyfriars, although no longer regent, in 1269. The date of his death is not known. He may have been living when Russel referred to him.

I have not been able to identify Russel's 'auctor de mysteriis ecclesie'. His quotation suggests some treatise on the Mass, since it explains the significance of the position of the fingers when the priest raises his hand in blessing. Neither the *De mysteriis ecclesiae* of Pierre de Roissy [138] nor the poem of the same name by John of Garland [139] contains this passage nor anything like it, nor does it occur in the standard works on the liturgy.

> ...In cuius rei signum benedictio sacerdotalis in solempnibus misse omnibus parochianis missam audientibus in fine misse solempniter debet dari [140] ...Benedictio autem humana datur tribus digitis propter mysterium Trinitatis, secundum auctorem de mysteriis ecclesie [141]. Primus digitus, scilicet pollex, qui dicitur eo quod pre ceteris pollet, designat Patrem ingenitum, qui est principium totius divinitatis, secundum Augustinum. Secundus, scilicet index, qui ab indicando (dicitur), designat Filium unigenitum... Tertius digitus, scilicet medius, designat Spiritum Paracletum, qui est nexus et amor duorum. Hii autem tres digiti elevati, ut dictum est, quibus datur benedictio, designant tres personas Trinitatis. Duo alii digiti, qui deprimuntur cum datur benedictio, designare possunt simplicem ecclesiam inferiorem, scilicet triumphantem et militantem, que quidem ecclesie humili et inclinato capite, ut ita loquatur, optant ut illa benedictio invocata infundatur a tota Trinitate, datrice gratie (fol. 142vb).

Russel takes some slight interest in current discussions on the emendation of the biblical text, on the standardisation of chapter-divisions and on the relationship between classical and biblical gram-

---

138. H. KENNEDY, *Pierre de Roissy, Manuale de mysteriis ecclesiae*, in *Mediaeval Studies* 5 (1943) 1-38. Mlle d'Alverny kindly looked up the passage for me in MS *Paris, Bibl. nat. nouv. acq. lat. 232*, fol. 15 and 50^{v}.

139. L. J. PAETOW, *The Morale scolarium of John of Garland*, Berkeley 1927, 111-112. I looked for the quotation in the printed edition and in MS *Oxford, Bodl. Auct. F. 5. 6*, fol. 150-158.

140. The omitted passage explains the difference between divine and human blessing.

141. It is not clear whether the phrase 'secundum auctorem de mysteriis ecclesie' refers backwards or forwards and whether Russel found the whole passage in this unknown book. The words from 'Primus digitus' to the end may perhaps represent his own elaboration of what he found there.

242

mar. He likes to be on the safe side, with tradition and authority ;
a glance at a *correctorium* probably represents the extent of his studies
in this field ; thus he says on viii, 13 :

> Notandum est hic quod *canituri* est littera omnium doctorum ; tamen
> quidam volunt dicere quod non [142] est latinum ; unde dicendum est *can-
> turus...* [143]. Ergo vera littera est *canituri* non *canituri* secundum ipsos.
> Quicquid sit de hoc, communi littere et a doctoribus exposite est securius
> initendum (fol. 118vb).

He shows a strange ignorance in supposing that his authors had
used Bibles containing the system of chapters familiar to him, when
this had in fact been imposed on the text in the thirteenth century and
was still incompletely standardised [144]. Doubtless his late copies of
patristic and early medieval commentaries had been divided according to the thirteenth-century system. Hence his comment on viii, 1 :

> *Et cum aperuisset etc.* Hic incipit capitulum secundum Bedam, Hai-
> monem, Berengarium.. *Et vidi* etc. [145] Hic secundum aliquos incipit capi-
> tulum, sed expositores famosos sequamur (fol. 117va).

Almost his only excursion into profane learning occurs in his prologue. He explains the nature of St John's vision by a reference to
optics, a favourite study at Oxford :

> Dicit enim auctor perspective quod radii qui linealiter veniunt a re visa
> faciunt unam piramidem, cuius cona est in pupilla et basis in re visa, et
> illi radii inangulantur in centro pupilli, et per angulum illum piramidem
> (sic) formatur visus seu apprehensio visualis. Consimiliter secundum exposi-
> tores formabiles rerum visibilium imagines quadam piramidali presenta-
> tione oculo mentali beati Iohannis erant exhibite... (fol. 106ra).

This is a reference rather than a quotation [146] and may be at second-hand. It was in the Oxford tradition to use optics to elucidate
problems of vision in Scripture. Docking quoted long passages from
a *Perspectiva* in discussing the climate of the promised land and
Moses' view of it from Mount Nebo [147].

---

142. 'non' added by the corrector.
143. The objectors to *canituri* relied on PRISCIAN, conjugating 'cano', *Gram-
matici latini* 3 (Leipzig 1860, 466-467).
144. Bibliography in B. SMALLEY, *The Study of the Bible, op. cit.*, 333-334.
145. *Apoc.* VIII, 2.
146. This is not a textual quotation from AL HASAN in MS *London, British
Museum Royal 12. G. VII,* fol. 1ra-102vb, or from Pecham, ed. Venice 1504 ; but
there were variant versions of PECHAM's *Perspectiva communis* ; see L. THORN-
DIKE, *A John Pecham MS,* in *Archivum francisc. histor.* 45 (1952) 451-461. Nor
does it come from PTOLEMY's *Optica,* ed. G. GOVI, Turin 1885.
147. A. G. LITTLE, *op. cit.*

IV

John Russel was yet another English friar who specialised on biblical studies. Where does he stand in the succession ? An attempt
to classify will be impressionistic at present, but it may be useful as a
beginning. Russel had more in common with his younger contemporary in the Franciscan Order, William of Nottingham II, than with any
other Oxford or Cambridge exegete of the late thirteenth or early fourteenth century. Nottingham was regent at Oxford about 1312 and
subsequently Provincial. He could not borrow from Russel, since
they commented on different books, Russel on the Canticle and Apocalypse, Nottingham on the Gospels (in Clement of Lanthony's harmony) [148]. He showed his approval of Russel by choosing the latter's
Apocalypse-commentary to have copied with 'laborious diligence'
during his regency. The two friars resemble each other both in method
and in spirit. Both were mainly compilers, but we can distinguish them
from their colleagues best by using the *via negativa*. What interests
did they *not* share with other groups of commentators ? These interests
cut across the various Orders of friars, the two English universities and
any rigid chronological divisions.

First, our two Minorites do not bring natural science or observation
of the contemporary scene to bear on biblical history. Russel's allusion to optics in his prologue is an isolated flourish. Neither seems to
be interested in parallels from medieval custom. Here they differ from
Simon of Hinton O. P. and Thomas Docking O. F. M., whose works
must have been available to them [149]. Second, they have nothing in
common with the classicising group, comprising Thomas Waleys
O. P., Robert Holcot O. P. and John Ridewall O. F. M. of Oxford,
and the Cambridge Dominicans, William Dencourt, Thomas Ringstede
and Thomas Hopeman [150]. Members of this group treated their lec-

---

148. B. SMALLEY, *Which William of Nottingham ?*, *op. cit.* On medieval
Gospel-'harmonies', see H. SILVESTRE, *Le « De concordia et expositione quatuor
Evangeliorum » inédit de Wazelin II etc.*, in *Revue bénédictine* 65 (1953) 310-325.

149. A. G. LITTLE, *op. cit.* ; B. SMALLEY, *The Study of the Bible*, *op. cit.*, 316-
323.

150. B. SMALLEY, *Thomas Waleys O. P.*, in *Archivum Fratrum Praedic.* 24
(1954) 50-107 ; *Robert Holcot O. P.*, *ibid.* 26 (1956) 5-97 ; *John Ridewall's Commentary on « De civitate Dei »*, in *Medium Aevum* 25 (1956) ; S. L. FORTE,
Thomas Hopeman O. P. An Unknown Biblical Commentator, in *Archivum Fratrum
Praedic.* 25 (1955) 311-344. Hopeman seems to have been more concerned with
theological exposition than were other members of the group. This may have
been because he was commenting on St Paul. Surviving commentaries by the
others are all on books of the old Testament or on the Apocalypse.

tures on Scripture as a framework for *exempla*. They all had a strong bent for tales and comparisons drawn from the Latin classics. Their purpose obliged them to concentrate on *moralitates*. Hence the literal exposition of the text suffered. The activities of this group fall between the years about 1317-1350, that is after the regencies of Russel and Nottingham ; but John of Wales O. F. M. must count as a forerunner. He was regent at Oxford in 1260 and at Paris 1281-83 ; he died about 1303 [151]. John's compilations from the saying and deeds of ancient sages in his *Compendiloquium* and *Breviloquium* must have stimulated the classicising group [152]. His commentary on St Matthew, which survives in excerpts, and which probably represents his teaching at Oxford, contains much classical lore, though less in proportion than would become fashionable among his followers [153].

Russel and Nottingham stand outside this movement. The former is sparing with his classical allusions. A few well-worn phrases from Seneca make up the total. Nottingham is even more austere than Russel ; he seems to exclude the philosophers and poets entirely. He does not quote from John of Wales' commentary on St Matthew, although, if John had given it as a lecture course at Oxford, his successor in the chair at Greyfriars must surely have known of its existence. It looks as though Nottingham ignored it in order to show his disapproval of its display of classical learning.

Third, both friars eschew controversy, whether theological or political. Russel does not engage in it at all ; he handles Joachim with his gloves on. Nottingham achieves the even greater feat of commenting on the Gospels without raising the question of apostolic poverty,

---

151. GLORIEUX, *op. cit.*, no. 322.

152. W. A. PANTIN, *The English Church in the Fourteenth Century*, Cambridge 1955, 147-148.

153. MS *Oxford, Magdalen College lat. 27*, fol. 1-91 (STEGMÜLLER, *op. cit.*, no. 4514). This part of the MS is written in an English hand, fairly early in the 14th cent. A later hand has written on the flyleaf : 'In isto volumine continentur sermones diversi, numero 113'. The commentary has been divided into 103 sermons ; the last portion of it is undivided ; this would account for the remainting ten sermons. They are not genuine sermons, but excerpts from a commentary on St Matthew. There is no literal exposition, only *moralitates* and allegories. The Oxford origin of the commentary appears in the quotations from Clement of Lanthony. Clement was a twelfth-century commmentator on the Gospels, popular in England, especially among the Oxford Franciscans, but little known on the Continent (fol. 11, 33ᵛ, on *Mt.* IV, 2 and IX, 6). The loss of the first part of Clement's enormous commentary makes it impossible to verify the references, but John of Wales quotes from 'parts' and 'chapters', corresponding to Clement's division of his book. It is significant of the classicising tone of the commentary that John of Wales quotes John of Salisbury's *Policraticus* as a source for tales from Apuleius (fol. 72ᵛ ; see *Policraticus*, ed. C. C. WEBB, Oxford 1909, 2, 23).

although it inflamed his Order at the time. Their refusal to take sides differentiates them from Robert Holcot, who criticised the 'Donation of Constantine' in his lectures, and even more from John Baconthorpe O. Carm. Baconthorpe turned his postill on St Matthew into an impassioned plea for the claims and policy of Pope John XXII [154]. Fourth, neither Russel nor Nottingham shows any skill in biblical languages or any capacity for first-hand textual criticism. They content themselves with the standard books on their shelves. They share the defect with their predecessors, Hinton and Docking [155], and with all their successors who have been named so far. But they had the memories of Grosseteste and Roger Bacon to inspire them. Nicholas Trevet O. P. would prove that a return to the tradition of biblical scholarship was possible [156]. They just did not care for it.

Russel and Nottingham, both, ignore natural science and allusions to current events, classical *exempla*, controversies and the techniques of biblical scholarship : a long list of negatives. We should not, however, dismiss the two friars as being merely timid, narrow and ignorant. Their restraint is so marked as to seem conscious and self-imposed. It amounts to a silent protest against the squandering of energy. They concentrate on *lectio divina* with single-minded piety, instead of going off in other directions. The religious atmosphere of their classrooms must have comforted troubled spirits, and there were many. The future mystic, Richard Rolle, broke off his studies at Oxford to become a hermit [157]. Contemporaries voiced a growing conviction that learning and goodness agreed ill together. Pupils of Russel and Nottingham might have felt able to reconcile what others found contradictory. Their lectures would induce peace and recollection or boredom according to the temperament of the hearer : oasis to some, dull backwater to others, no doubt.

At this point the two begin to differ and to show contrasting traits of character. Both friars offer piety ; each has his own brand. Notting-

---

154. B. SMALLEY, *John Baconthorpe's Postill on St Matthew*, below, 289 - 343

155. Docking's lost grammar of biblical terms might show signs of linguistic skill if it were found. But he can only quote the Hebrew text *via* Andrew of St Victor in his commentary on Isaias (MS *Oxford, Balliol College* 29, fol. 76[ra] ; other acknowledged or unacknowledged borrowings from Andrew on Isaias are on fol. 18[va], 37[ra], 75[rb-va]).

156. B. SMALLEY, *The Study of the Bible, op. cit.*, 346-347, 351-352.

157. H. E. ALLEN, *Writings ascribed to Richard Rolle Hermit of Hampole and Materials for his Biography*, New York-London 1927, 55-56, 448-449. Rolle seems to have been a student of arts at Oxford and to have left his family to become a hermit during a long vacation.

ham's vast commentary on Clement of Lanthony deceives at first sight by reason of its cumbrous apparatus. A closer study reveals it as something more than a school product, a set of lectures on a Gospel-harmony. Nottingham is in the line of writers who aimed at a popular presentation of the Gospel. He anticipates the *Vita Christi* of Ludolf the Carthusian, written sometime in the third quarter of the four-teenth century. Ludolf developed earlier efforts to set forth the Gos-pels as a consecutive story, which should nourish devotion and medi-tation of an affective kind. His *Vita Christi* has been described as follows : 'It is... a meditation on the history of the life of our Lord Jesus Christ harmonised from the four Gospels. It is built up with commentaries of the Fathers and the scholastics, as well as with dogmatic and moral reflections of the author. Each chapter is reca-pitulated by means of a prayer which gives the quintessence of its thought' [158]. Nottingham in fact was working in the Oxford Francis-can tradition. His predecessor, William of Nottingham I, had had the harmony of Clement with Clement's commentary on it copied for the use of the friars in his province. He did so from devotion to the Name of Jesus and his aim was clearly to give his friars a conse-cutive story of Christ's life and Passion accompanied by an edifying commentary. William of Nottingham II replaced the old-fashioned exposition of Clement, drawn mainly from the Fathers, by another of his own composition, also mainly derivative, but more in keeping with the sentiment of his time. His commentary on Clement's har-mony resembles the *Vita Christi*, making allowance for the fact that he gave it as a lecture course. Ludolf could organise his more literary work as a book of devotion with more attention to the needs of de-vout readers. All the same, some of the sections in Nottingham's commentary end with prayers [159]. One late-fourteenth-century copy, MS *Oxford, Bodl. Laud. misc. 165*, has lively little pictures illustrating, the text [160]. They render the simplicity of the original admirably and strengthen its likeness to the *Vita Christi*. Ludolf's book was

---

158. M. I. BODENSTEDT, *The Vita Christi of Ludolf the Carthusian*, Washington 1944, 16 ; see also M. G. MCNEIL, *Simone Fidati and his De gestis Domini salva-toris*, Washington 1950, 65-70. Ludolf does not seem to have borrowed from Nottingham. He wrote his *Vita Christi* in the Rhineland, probably at Mainz ; see BODENSTEDT, 17. Nottingham's commentary on Clement was read mainly in England ; the common material is probably due to their use of common sources.

159. For instance, the flight into Egypt signifies penance and the return reconciliation : 'et tunc de Egipto penitentie vocaberis ad terram Israel, id est ad gloriam visionis eterne, ad quam nos perducat qui sine fine vivit et regnat. Amen' (MS *Laud. misc. 165*, fol. 68[vb]).

160. See M. RICKERT, *The Reconstructed Carmelite Missal*, London 1952.

often illuminated to help his readers to re-live the Gospel story, as he meant them to do. Nottingham stands out among late medieval popularisers of the Gospel only for his soberness. He shuns those apocryphal tales that Ludolf would find a stimulus to devotion [161], nor does he fill out the story with imaginery details ; compare, for instance, the vernacular *Cursor mundi*, where Mary and Joseph entertain the Three Kings for the night [162]. Nottingham even distinguishes between the plain text and the much more explicit iconographical tradition on the flight into Egypt (*Mt.* ii, 14) [163] :

> *Et secessit in Egiptum.* Quis autem puerum portavit vel quomodo Maria recessit, certum non habemus ex scriptura, sed tantummodo ex pictura, que liber est laicorum, in qua describitur Virgo sedisse super asinum et puerum in ulnis eius, quia si non, sed potius peditanto, tunc verisimile est quod Ioseph puerum portavit (MS *Laud. misc. 165*, fol. 68[va-b]).

But he shares with Ludolf and other fourteenth-century evangelisers the wish to see and to sympathise with his characters. He wants, just as they do, to incite his students to prayer and imitation of Christ. He is pointing forward to a new literary genre.

Russel equals the younger master in unction. His Canticle-commentary is a song in honour of Our Lady, his Apocalypse-commentary a devout meditation on the visions of Patmos. Here the resemblance between the two Minorites ends. Nottingham looks forward to popular devotions ; Russel looks backward. He feels most at home with monastic writers of the twelfth and early thirteenth centuries. Robert of Bridlington, William of Newburgh, Richard of St Victor, Joachim of Fiore (minus the Joachimites), Alexander Nequam and Thomas of Vercelli, these are his preferred authors. His interpretation of *lectio divina* owes less to St Francis and to St Bonaventure than to the patristic tradition and to the reformed monasticism of the twelfth century. Cistercians and Canons Regular had kept their appeal as spiritual guides for at least one English friar about the year 1290. They suggested to him his own personal answer to the increasingly secular outlook of contemporary homilists.

Russel chose, and what a splendid choice of books he had ! Either he found what he needed in Greyfriars or he visited and borrowed from other libraries. He had a wide range of commentaries from all periods, including the commentaries of Stephen Langton or at least some of

---

161. BODENSTEDT, *op. cit.*, 47-49.

162. Ed. R. MORRIS, for the Early English Text Society, 2, London 1875-76. 660-661.

163. A reason for his restraint may be that university masters did not customarily introduce apocrypha into their lectures on Scripture.

them ; he quotes Langton in his sermon. He had Docking's biblical grammar, which is now lost. He had Grosseteste and Pecham on the Apocalypse, which would be unknown but for his quotations. He sets us a number of bibliographical puzzles. We notice, too, the pride of place taken by Englishmen in his selection. His post-patristic commentators are either English or very familiar in medieval England. This probably reflects the bias of his libraries. Russel used the Greyfriars collection in its palmy days. The contents of the Franciscan library at Oxford began to be neglected and scattered even before the Dissolution [164]. He discloses some of its riches in making his *catenae*.

---

164. R. W. HUNT, *op. cit.*, 131.

Note:
p. 233: On Hugh of St. Cher and the *Vidit Iacob in somniis* on the Apocalypse see D. M. Solomon, 'The Sentence Commentary of Richard Fishacre and the Apocalypse Commentary of Hugh of St. Cher', *Archivum Fratrum Praedicatorum*, xlvi (1976) 367-377.
p. 240: On Thomas Docking see J. I. Catto, 'New Light on Thomas Docking', *Medieval and Renaissance Studies*, vi (1968) 135–149.
p. 248: On Robert of Bridlington see M. L. Colker, 'Richard of St. Victor and the anonymous of Bridlington', *Traditio* xviii (1962) 181–228.

11

WHICH WILLIAM OF NOTTINGHAM?

I

THE TWO WILLIAMS

'NOTYNGHAM super unum ex quatuor secundum Clementem Lantoniensem' was one of the ponderous aids to study that weighted the shelves of the theological section in an English library of the later middle ages: a commentary on a gospel harmony. Two Friars Minor called William of Nottingham have claims to its authorship. The aim of this note is to decide between them. The sources, method and doctrine of the work will be treated only incidentally.

The first William of Nottingham[1] was fourth Provincial of the English Franciscans, 1240-54. He died in 1254. Perhaps, at an earlier stage in his career, he studied under Grosseteste when the latter was lector to the Franciscans at Oxford.[2] He certainly promoted learning as an administrator by organizing the schools in his province.[3] A. G. Little ascribed the commentary to him on the strength of a passage in the *De adventu Fratrum Minorum*: "That the well-known *Commentary on the Gospels* called also *Unum ex quatuor*, or *De concordia evangelistarum*, by Friar William of Nottingham, was by this William, and not by his namesake, the seventeenth provincial of the English Minorites, is proved by Eccleston's words." Since Eccleston knew William very well, his testimony would be convincing. Modern scholars who have had occasion to mention the commentary have followed

---

[1]) See the notices on him in A. G. Little, *The Grey Friars in Oxford*, Oxford, 1892, pp. 182-5, and *Franciscan Papers, Lists, and Documents*, Manchester, 1943, p. 190. These books will be referred to as *Grey Friars* and *Papers* respectively.

[2]) Little says that he 'seems to have attended Grosseteste's lectures at Oxford'; *Grey Friars*, p. 183. The passage in Eccleston quoted in support of the statement only mentions his presence at a sermon, preached by Grosseteste in chapter when he was lector at Oxford; *De adventu Fratrum Minorum in Angliam*, ed. A. G. Little (Collections d'Etudes, etc., vol. vii, Paris, 1909), p. 123.

[3]) *Papers*, pp. 62, 131-2, 227.

Little. Only Fr. Perrier favours William II, without stating his reasons.[1]
One must ask, however, just what sort of work it was that Eccleston
attributed to William I. Eccleston writes:

> Ipse in scripturis sanctis studiosissimus erat et studentes studiose promovebat.
> In mensis extra refectorium lectionem semper habere volebat, et affectu specialis-
> simo nomen Jesu venerabatur, et verba sancti Evangelii devotissime recolebat;
> unde et super *Unum ex quatuor* Clementis canones perutiles compilavit, et ex-
> positionem, quam idem Clemens fecit, complete scribi in ordine procuravit.[2]

The first point to emerge from Eccleston's story is that William did
not read his work as a lecture in the schools. William never, in fact, held
the office of lector or was regent in theology. One would gather from
Eccleston that he composed it when he was Provincial. The sequence of
ideas in the passage would rather suggest that he had it read to him when
business obliged him to take his meals in private, 'extra refectorium': that
is, if we take *unde* as referring to his love for reading at table, as well as
to his devotion to the gospels and the name of Jesus. Eccleston says that
he compiled very useful canons. The last word here has the sense which
is given to it in the *Etymologies*. St. Isidore defines it as follows:

> De canonibus Evangeliorum: Canones Evangeliorum Ammonius Alex-
> andriae primus excogitavit. . . . Qui ideo facti sunt, ut per eos invenire et scire
> possimus qui reliquorum Evangelistarum similia aut propria dixerunt. Sunt
> autem numero decem. . . . Quorum expositio haec est. . . .[3]

Gospel canons, then, meant an apparatus for comparing and harmonizing
the four gospels. Clement, Prior of the Augustinian house at Lanthony,
who died about 1190,[4] had published an improved version of previous
canons; at least, its popularity shows that mediaeval students found it an
improvement. After composing his Harmony, *Unum ex quatuor*, he made
an 'enormous commentary on it that seems to be nearly all taken from

---

[1] In his list of fourteenth-century commentators on Scripture in C. Spicq, *Esquisse d'une histoire
de l'exégèse latine au Moyen Age*, Paris, 1944, p. 345.

[2] *De adventu, op. cit.*, p. 125.

[3] Lib. vi, cap. 15, ed. W. M. Lindsay, Oxford, 1911.

[4] See *Dictionary of National Biography*, suppl. 22, pp. 458-9.

older writers'.[1] William of Nottingham, according to Eccleston, had this commentary written out in full and in order. Eccleston probably means that the Harmony and its commentary were copied consecutively. They had sometimes been separated, circulating in different volumes. William I, by keeping them together, would be providing his friars with a book very suitable for reading and meditation of the Franciscan type. Readers or hearers would be able to follow the story of Jesus in its fullest possible detail, conflated from all four evangelists. He was also, in accordance with his policy of fostering learning, supplying an explanation of the differences between the gospels, as given by Clement, and relevant excerpts from the Fathers, as given by Clement in his commentary.

The second conclusion to be drawn from Eccleston is that William added nothing to Clement's exposition; his addition was to the Harmony. He compiled 'very useful canons' on the basis of Clement's *Unum ex quatuor*. William must have elaborated the Harmony in some way, leaving the commentary unaltered.

Apart from the activity described by Eccleston he left one sermon, copied in MS. Pembroke College, Cambridge, 265 fol. 192-6, in a hand of about the third quarter of the thirteenth century. It has no contemporary title; but the table of contents of the volume, written on the first flyleaf in a fifteenth-century hand, describes it as "Sermo bonus de obedientia fratris Willelmi de Notyngham". Other items in the miscellany that makes up the volume suggest a Franciscan provenance; there are works by Bonaventure, John of Wales, John of La Rochelle.[2] The sermon is simple

---

[1] R. W. Hunt, *English Learning in the Late Twelfth Century*, Transactions of the Royal Historical Society, 4th series, 19 [1936], 27. Clement's commentary was still being used in the fifteenth century. Thomas Gascoigne quotes it with approval, *Liber de veritate*, MS. Lincoln College, Oxford, lat. 117, pp. 455-6.

[2] M. R. James, *Catalogue of the MSS. in the Library of Pembroke College, Cambridge*, Cambridge, 1905, p. 243. Prof. J. C. Russell suggests that this may be the same as the "Epistola fratris Gulielmi Notingham de obedientia" noted by Leland, *Collectanea*, ed. Hearne, vol. IV, p. 16; *A Dictionary of Writers of Thirteenth-Century England*, Bulletin of the Institute of Historical Research, Special Suppl. vol. 3, p. 197. A note to the catalogue in the library of Pembroke College, Cambridge, records that the piece was partially copied by A. G. Little in 1921. I do not know that Little published it and he does not mention it in his notice of William in *Grey Friars*. The incipit is: "*Quia peregrini et advene ...* Secundum apostolum vigilanter providendum ...*", the explicit: "*... feliciter pervenimus. Quod nobis prestare etc. Amen*".

in form, having only a 'theme', i.e. an introductory text, and no 'protheme'.[1] It was certainly addressed to religious and probably to friars in a *studium*; the author mentions, among examples of obedience, the case where a person is ordered by his superior to get himself a Bible or to undergo a course of study, which he welcomes, feeling that he has it in him to be a good student.[2] The authorities quoted are in no way out of the ordinary. The most interesting is Anselm's *Liber de similitudinibus*, which appears three times.[3] This little piece, as far as it goes, agrees with what we know of William's zeal for education, but tells us nothing of his intellectual attainments.

William of Nottingham II was lector to the Oxford Franciscans about 1312 and seventeenth Provincial, 1316-30 (?). He attended the General Chapter of his Order in 1322,[4] had a royal licence to go overseas in 1324 and again to attend the General Chapter as Provincial in 1325.[5] Bale puts his death at Leicester in 1336.[6] While he was lector he copied manuscripts, now MSS. Merton College, Oxford, 166, 168-71, at the expense of Sir Hugh of Nottingham.[7] They are big volumes, comprising postills by Gorran and others on almost the whole Bible, copied by William with 'tedious solicitude' and 'laborious diligence'.[8] They must have cost his benefactor a good sum in parchment. Sir Hugh of Nottingham suggests some sort of family background for William II, since he may well have

---

[1] For the elaborate structure recommended in contemporary aids to preaching, see Th.-M. Charland, *Artes Praedicandi*, Paris, Ottawa, 1936. The protheme seems to have been introduced into actual sermons preached in England in the second half of the thirteenth century and to have been at least less common in the first half; see J. Sweet, *Some Thirteenth-Century Sermons*, Journal of Ecclesiastical History, [1953], 30.

[2] Fol. 192ᵛ: "Alicui iniungitur per obedientiam ut querat sibi bibliam . . . quod faciat cum labore et difficultate. . . . Alicui iniungitur obedientia ad studendum; libenter obedit, quia videtur ei competens obedientia, eo quod sentit se ad hoc faciendum bene dispositum, quoad bona naturalia et adquisita . . ."

[3] This work derived from St. Anselm's teaching, though it was not written by him, and became very popular in England; R. W. Southern, *St. Anselm and his English Pupils*, M.A.R.S. 1 [1941], 7-12.

[4] *Grey Friars*, pp. 165-6; *Papers*, p. 195; *Calendar of Patent Rolls 1321-24*, p. 75.

[5] *Ibid.*, p. 367, *ibid. 1324-27*, p. 119.

[6] J. Bale, *Index*, ed. Poole and Bateson, Oxford, 1902, p. 140.

[7] F. M. Powicke, *The Medieval Books of Merton College*, Oxford, 1931, pp. 174-5.

[8] B. Smalley, *Some Commentaries on the Sapiential Books of the Late Thirteenth and Early Fourteenth Centuries*, Archives d'histoire doctrinale et littéraire du Moyen Age, 18 [1950], 107-8.

been a kinsman. He was a civil servant earning a comfortable living at the Exchequer. He was employed there from 1291, as remembrancer 1305-7, then as keeper and engrosser of the Pipe Roll.[1] In 1313 he was still 'continuously engaged in the king's service at the Exchequer'.[2] He was presented to a number of churches and refused one benefice in the diocese of Lincoln.[3] The archbishop of York in 1300 licensed him to build an aisle to the church of St. Nicholas at Nottingham, to have an altar to St. Anne placed there and to have divine service celebrated in an oratory in his house in the same parish.[4] In 1302 he got leave for Master John of Nottingham to absent himself from his church of Clifton for a year of study.[5] We hear of him last in 1318 when two livings were declared void by the cession of Hugh of Nottingham who held them as a pluralist without papal dispensation.[6]

A note in two hands of about 1500 after the explicit of Nottingham on the gospels in MS. Balliol College 33 says that William of Nottingham was secular canon and precentor of York and afterwards joined the Order of St. Francis. The statement is too late to be trusted.[7] There is no trace of a canon or precentor called William of Nottingham in the registers of the archbishops of York in the late thirteenth and early fourteenth

[1]) *Calendar of Close Rolls 1288-96*, p. 246; *ibid., 1296-1302*, pp. 461-2; *ibid., 1302-1307*, pp. 68, 194, 235; *ibid., 1307-1313*, p. 2; *Calendar of Patent Rolls 1301-1307*, pp. 28, 309, 463, 519; T. F. Tout, *The Place of Edward II in English History*, Manchester, 1914, p. 348; *Chapters in the Administrative History of Mediaeval England*, Manchester, 1920, ii, 220 n.

[2]) *Calendar of Close Rolls 1313-1318*, p. 281.

[3]) He was presented by the king to Ivychurch, Kent, in 1293, to Doddington, Cambs., in 1298, *Calendar of Patent Rolls 1292-1301*, pp. 58, 95, 336. In 1307 the king granted the right of free warren to Hugh de Notingham, king's clerk, parson of the church of Bishop Hatfield, *Calendar of Charter Rolls 1300-1326*, p. 100. He declined the church of Barnack about 1297; the parson was instituted in that year, Mar. 6, *The Rolls and Register of Bishop Oliver Sutton*, ed. R. M. T. Hill (Publications of the Lincoln Record Society, vol. 43, 1950), ii, 138. He was commended to the church of Bunney for six months in 1294, *Register of Archbishop John le Romeyn*, ed. W. Brown (Surtees Society, vol. 123, 1913), i 322.

[4]) *Register of Archbishop Thomas Corbridge*, ed. W. Brown and A. Hamilton Thompson (Surtees Society, vol. 138), i 208. He is called "illustris Anglie regis clericus" and is given the title of *dominus*. Nothing remains of his church building at Nottingham, since St. Nicholas' church was pulled down in 1647, see *Thoroton's History of Nottinghamshire*, ed. J. Throsby, ii [1790], 100.

[5]) *Register of Archbishop Thomas Corbridge, op. cit.*, p. 243.

[6]) The rectory of Hatfield, Herts, and the parish church and chapel of Tatterigge in the diocese of Lincoln, *Calendar of Papal Registers, Papal Letters*, ii 172, 177.

[7]) See below, p. 265. Little was sceptical of the notice, *Grey Friars*, pp. 165-6.

centuries, though John le Romeyn had a clerk of that name with the title of *magiſter* 1286-91.[1]

William II left a commentary on the *Sentences*, now MS. Gonville and Caius College 300.[2] Leland noted among the books of the London Carmelites 'Notingham super omnes epiſtolas Pauli' with the incipit *Bonum visitationem*, and Bale a *determinatio pro lege Chriſtianorum* at the Franciscan convent at Reading.[3] These loſt works are more likely to belong to the second than the firſt William, since they would fit into his duties as lector. A note in an early sixteenth-century hand on the flyleaf of MS. Corpus Chriſti College, Cambridge, 305 may represent an independent tradition; it calls William 'Richard' and ascribes various works to him:

> Ricardus Notingham Anglus, sacrae theologiae doctor, scripsit lecturam sententiarum lib. 4, conclusiones ordinarias, commentaria in Mathaeum, Lucam et Pauli epiſtolam ad Romanos et Corinthios. Claruit anno 1320.

A tradition in the Order credited this William with the commentary on *Unum ex quatuor*. The liſt of Provincials in the fifteenth-century regiſter, printed by Brewer and re-edited by Little, has an entry on the seventeenth holder of the office:

> Frater Willelmus Notyngham doctor Oxoniae, qui fecit solempnem postillam super unum ex quatuor. iacet Leycestre.[4]

The work ascribed to him in this notice does not really correspond to that which Eccleſton ascribed to William I. A 'poſtill' suggeſts a continuous commentary on the sacred text and it usually implies an origin in the classroom.[5] 'Solempnis' might be translated 'of recognized academic

---

[1]) *Regiſter, op. cit.*; see the indexes to vols. i and ii under 'Maſter William of Nottingham'. It is unlikely that this is our William. If he had his M.A. by 1286, he might just have had time to join the Order and qualify in theology between 1291 and 1312; but he would have been over forty as lector, probably nearer fifty.

[2]) He was influenced by Duns Scot. See the bibliography in Rashdall's *Medieval Universities*, ed. Powicke & Emden, Oxford, 1936, iii 259, n. 3. The moſt recent paper is by C. Balič, "La valeur critique des citations des oeuvres de Jean Duns Scot", *Mélanges Auguſte Pelzer*, Louvain, 1947, pp. 531-56.

[3]) *Collectanea*, ed. Hearne, iv 52; *Index, op. cit.*, p. 141.

[4]) Appendix to *De adventu*, ed. Little, *op. cit.*, p. 147.

[5]) See P. Lehmann, *Mittelalterliche Büchertitel*, I Heft, Sitzungsberichte der Bayerischen Akad. der Wissensch., Philos.-hiſt. Kl. 1948, Heft 4, 1949, pp. 42-47.

importance'. Thus William II in his commentary on the *Sentences* quotes 'opiniones solempnium magistrorum' and says: 'audivi solempnem magistrum valde. . . .'[1] The postill on *Unum ex quatuor*, therefore, would probably represent a lecture course delivered by William while he held the chair at Oxford, though it might have been worked over afterwards. Anyway, it could not be the same as the 'canons' that William I attached to his transcript of Clement of Lanthony. Which of the two, the postill or the canons, has survived in the manuscripts?

II

THE EVIDENCE OF THE MANUSCRIPTS

(a) The complete work

The surviving copies are rich in information about their owners and even tell us what these owners thought of the book and its author. They were mainly English. Fr. Stegmüller has noted only one copy on the Continent and this is at Prague,[2] which had close relations with England in the late fourteenth and early fifteenth centuries. Many copies are imperfect, since the book was so large and cumbrous that it tended to lose its outside leaves. The illuminations also tempted thieves to cut out leaves or pieces of them. The commentary ascribed to William of Nottingham accumulated an apparatus consisting of tables and explanatory notes, and the Harmony of Clement of Lanthony (without his commentary) was sometimes copied before or after. The commentary is always divided into twelve parts, corresponding to the divisions of Clement's Harmony. Hence it is easy to identify, even in a fragmentary state. The following list could perhaps be supplemented by a thorough search in English and continental libraries. My description is meant to supplement, not to replace the catalogues, which are generally adequate. I have noted only the date, provenance, arrangement, ascription and any notices concerning the authorship and contents. More information could probably be collected

---

[1] Quoted by C. Balič, *A propos de quelques ouvrages faussement attribués à Duns Scot*, Recherches de théologie ancienne et médiévale, 2 [1930], 173, 176..

[2] *Repertorium Biblicum Medii Aevi*, Madrid, 1950, ii 430.

about the owners, and a liturgiologist could make better use than I have
of the tables of gospels and saints' days contained in many manuscripts.

The incipits and explicits of the complete work are:

Prologue

Da michi intelleĉtum et scrutabor legem tuam. . . . In psalmo. Dionisius de divinis
nominibus capitulo tertio dicit quod ante omne et maxime theologiam ab oratione
incipere eŝt utile, vel debitum secundum translationem Lincolniensis. Hec eŝt
etiam doĉtrina beati Augustini. . . .

Prologue of St. Jerome

Hic eŝt Iohannes. . . . Dividitur iŝte prologus in vi partes. . . .

Commentary

In principio erat verbum. . . . In primis eŝt sciendum quod totus processus
evangelicus principaliter dividitur in ii partes. . . .

Explicit of part xii

. . . ut possimus ad dona sempiterna pervenire que dominus ipse promisit,
ipso iuvante igitur qui vivit et regnat in secula seculorum. 'Amen.

CAMBRIDGE

PEMBROKE COLLEGE 192 [1]

Written in a fifteenth-century English hand, with illuminated borders and
initials. The initial on fol. 27 has been cut out. The order is as follows:
1. Prologue and Harmony of Clement of Lanthony, fol. 1-19ᵛ. It is
defective, lacking some of part iv and all of parts v and vi. The text
corresponds to that in MS. Bodl. Hatton 61 (4083), fol. 1-133, a twelfth-
century copy of the Harmony. A rubric, fol. 19ᵛ, in the same hand as the
text, explains the connexion between Clement's Harmony and Nottingham's commentary on it:

Explicit concordia quatuor evangeliorum Clementis. Notandum quod
sequens evangelice hiŝtorie continuatio, quam (MS. qui) primo cum intentione
redeundi, corrigendi et completius exponendi ŝtudiose colligit Frater W. de
Notingham, observat in pluribus ut in processu Clementis ipsum auĉtoritatibus
confirmando. In aliquibus tamen paucis rationabiliter discrepat ab eodem. In

¹) M. R. James, *Catalogue of MSS. in the Library of Pembroke College, Cambridge*, Cambridge,
1905, p. 179.

prima autem parte litteram illam *Fuit homo missus a Deo etc.* usque illuc inclusive *sed ex Deo nati sunt* ponit Clemens in primo capitulo partis secunde, in sequenti vero continuatione ponitur et exponitur continue, sicut ponitur in Iohanne. Item genealogiam salvatoris secundum Matheum ponit Clemens ſtatim in principio, capitulo secundo. Hic autem rationabilius eam ponit poſt septimum vel potius sextum capitulum, quod ideo dico quia hic preponit septimum capitulum sexto. Item genealogiam salvatoris secundum Matheum ponit Clemens parte secunda, capitulo quarto. Hic autem eam immediate convenienter coniungit cum genealogia secundum Lucam. Item illud Luce quarto, *Et ait illis: Utique dicetis michi hanc similitudinem: Medice cura teipsum etc*, ponit Clemens capitulo quarto partis tertie. Sequens continue interserit illud infra, capitulo oᴄtodecimo eiusdem partis. Et sic de aliquibus aliis, paucis tamen.

2. The ten Eusebian canons and an explanation, comparing them with Clement's Harmony, fol. 20-21. The heading is:

Expositio ex prediᴄtis quid sit canon et quot sint canones, quia decem.[1]

The table of ten canons follows, with an explanation:

Si vis ergo scire tabulam canonum evangeliarum, disponet cuiuslibet evangelice capitula per numeros. . . . In Clemente vero loco illius scribitur illud Iohannis, *Veſpere autem faᴄto*, et sic de multis aliis. Deo gratias.

This piece has not been taken from Clement's Harmony and differs from the prologues concerning canons to be found in mediaeval Bibles.[2]
3. A table relating the four gospels in order, according to their chapters, with the corresponding part of the Harmony and its commentary by William of Nottingham, according to its twelve parts, fol. 21-24. A rubric at the end explains the use of the table and points to further slight differences between Clement and 'the truth':

Ex prediᴄta tabula, si diligenter consideratur, patere poteſt satis clare ubi quidlibet contentum in quocumque evangelio, cognito eiusdem situ et loco, inveniri poterit in Clemente et hoc vel in se vel in suo simili seu equivalente. Ex eadem patere poteſt que et quot mirabiles anticipationes et prepoſterationes

---

[1] MS. Laud misc. 165, fol. 584ᵛᵇ has a slightly different and probably more correᴄt wording: "Supposito ex prediᴄtis quid sit canon et quot canones, dic quod decem, ut notatur inferius."
[2] F. Stegmüller, *op. cit.*, i 307-8.

processus hystoriales evangelice in tribus evangeliis, scilicet Mathei, Marci et Luce ponuntur, inter quos Lucas precedentis plures ponit. Patet etiam ex eadem quod in evangelio Iohannis nichil anticipatur, nichil preposteratur nisi in duobus locis tantum, scilicet in primo capitulo ibi, *Fuit homo missus a Deo*, et infra, *Et de plenitudine eius*, et hoc secundum processum et opinionem Clementis. Secundum tamen rei veritatem nulla videtur esse ibi anticipatio vel preposteratio, sed recta hystorie continuatio. Sequitur nunc tabula canonum evangeliorum.

4. A table partly erased, relating the gospel canons to the commentary, fol. 24-5.

5. The prologue and commentary, fol. 27-287ᵛ. It is incomplete; the top of the first leaf with its initial has been cut out, and some of part xi, with the whole of part xii has been lost. The leaves are numbered, beginning afresh with each part. The parts are distinguished by rubrics, 'incipit pars prima' etc.

DURHAM

CATHEDRAL A.1.

I have not seen this manuscript. Rud gives a detailed and even vivid account of it: "Codex hic grandis est et etiam elephantinus, totius Bibliothecae maximus; neque enim in eodem cum reliquis pluteo stare potest. Habet folia 380."[1] He identified it by the incipits and compared it with MS. Pembroke College 192. The arrangement seems to be almost identical with that in British Museum MS. Royal 4 E. II, to be described later. The script reminded him of MS. Durham A. 3, dated 1386. Thomas Langley, Chancellor of England 1405-7 and 1417-24, bishop of Durham 1406-37,[2] may have left it to the Chapter. His will, dated Dec. 21, 1436, and proved Dec. 17, 1437, has an entry:

Item lego eidem ecclesiae meae Librum vocatum Notyngham super Ewangelia.[3]

The arrangement, according to Rud, is:
1. Prologue of William of Nottingham's commentary.

---

[1]) T. Rud, *Codd. MSS. eccles. cathedr. Dunelm. cat. class.*, Durham, 1825, pp. 1-3.

[2]) *Dict. Nat. Biogr.*, xi 553-5.

[3]) *Catt. Vett. Lib. Eccles. Cath. Dunelm.*, ed. Raine (Surtees Soc., 1838), pp. 119-20.

2. List of chapters.
3. Commentary.
4. Table.
5. Table of canons.
6. Reasons for the order followed in each of the twelve parts. This must represent a transcript of the concluding section of Clement's Harmony, where he explains the 'ratio ordinis' of his Harmony in twelve parts, MS. Hatton 61, fol. 124-131ᵛ. Rud specifies the length as three pages, which would be about right.

LONDON

BRITISH MUSEUM, Royal 4 E. II.
The catalogue gives a full and excellent description;[1] I am noting only arrangement and provenance. The hand is late fourteenth-century English.
1-3. Prologue, list of chapters, and commentary, fol. 2-462ᵛ. This corresponds to items 1-3 in the Durham manuscript. The leaves have no mediaeval foliation, but the number and chapter of the part are marked at the top of each leaf.
4. Eusebian canons with explanation, fol. 463ᵛ-469ᵛ. This corresponds to item 5 in the Durham, item 2 in the Pembroke College manuscript.
5-6. Tables with explanation, fol. 463ᵛ-469ᵛ. They correspond to items 3 and 4 in the Pembroke College manuscript and presumably to item 4 in the Durham manuscript.
7. The reasons for the order followed in the twelve parts, fol. 470-1 corresponding to item 6 in the Durham manuscript.

The only difference between the Royal and Durham copies is that in the Royal the tables to the commentary come after, instead of before, the table of Eusebian canons. They both differ from MS. Pembroke College 192 in that the Harmony of Clement has been omitted, except for the 'ratio ordinis' at the end. And they both put what is left of Clement's Harmony at the end instead of at the beginning.

A colophon on fol. 471 reads:

In hoc volumine continetur expositio xii partium totius processus evangelici

---

1) Warner and Gilson, *Catalogue of Royal and King's MSS. in the British Museum*, London, 1921, i 92.

secundum ordinem et diſtinctionem Clementis. Quo qui usi sunt rogent pro anima domini Iohannis Leyre Rectoris ecclesie de Dodington, qui dictum volumen ad suum proficuum et honorem Dei quoad omnia fecit parari, pro anima etiam fratris Wyllelmi de Notingham, qui ſtudio laborioso predictam expositionem ex variis compilavit.

A verse follows, ending with the date 1381. John Leyre, parson of Great Doddington, Northants, was credited with a loan of ten marks to the Crown in 1379[1] and exchanged his living for that of Olney in 1390.[2] The monks of Evesham received the book as a present from their abbot, John Wykwon (abbot 1439-c. 1460),[3] on the feaſt day of St. Auguſtine (Aug. 28), 1458, according to an inscription on the flyleaf.

OXFORD

BODLEIAN LIBRARY, Laud misc. 165.
This is the moſt expensively produced and in many ways the moſt intereſting copy. It was written in the later fourteenth century by James le Palmere, who gives his name in the explicit, fol. 585:

> Explicit liber qui vocatur unum ex quatuor vel unus ex quatuor et differt a Clemente in multis. Evangelia concordat et plene super quatuor evangelia tractat et plures bonas queſtiones movet et solvit. Et qui iſtum librum diligenter inspexerit et secundum ea que scripta sunt in eodem vixerit vitam eternam habebit. Iſte liber eſt liber Iacobi le Palmere quem scripsit manu sua propria. Deo gratias.

> Libro finito lassatum me fore scito,
> Premia pro merito des michi te rogito.
> Hic liber eſt scriptus, qui scripsit sit benedictus.

An Exchequer clerk called James le Palmere was granted an annual pension in 1375 on account of his good service.[4] This is the only person of the name who seems a likely candidate for identification in the public records in print. In fact, the text does not seem to have been written all by the same hand; but the explicit is in the hand of the rubricator.

---

[1] *Calendar of Patent Rolls, Richard II, 1377-81*, p. 636. He also appears on the Close Roll of the same year, *Calendar of Close Rolls, Richard II, 1377-81*, p. 240.

[2] *Calendar of Patent Rolls, Richard II, 1388-92*, p. 180.

[3] *Chronicon Abbatiae de Evesham*, ed. W. D. Macray (Rolls Series, 1863), p. 338.

[4] *Calendar of Patent Rolls, 1374-7*, p. 82.

There are many illuminations of biblical scenes by at least three artists, in an English style of the late fourteenth century. They are vigorous and rather crude. Fol. 5-12 have been added to the original and contain an illumination of a more refined type.[1] The manuscript came into the possession of Thomas Arundel, who gave it to the monks of Christ Church while he was archbishop, 1396-1414. A picture on fol. 5 commemorates the event. It shows him sitting in his pastoral chair, which bears his arms on the back, pointing to a book open at a page saying: "quod factum est in ipso vita erat" (Ioh. i 3-4). Four Benedictine monks are grouped round him, one of them holding a book, presumably the gift to the Priory.

The top margin has a prayer: "Assit principio sancta Maria meo." Below the picture, in the same hand as the prayer, is an explanation of the table which follows. The archbishop's clerk and chaplain has compiled a table of contents of the volume, out of pity for students whose overwork leads to sickness and death or to diseases even worse than death. He dedicates his table to the archbishop. The passage demands transcription as an unusually personal introduction to an index:

Reverendissimo in Christo patri ac domino, domino Thome Arundell, divina gratia et brachio patris altissimi cooperante Cantuariensi archiepiscopo, capellanus et clericus suus simplex et humilis obedientiam et reverentiam tanto patri debitas et honorem. Motus etenim studii nimietate per quam multi incurabiles egritudines et morbos diversemode incurrerunt, de quibus aliqui moriuntur et aliqui, substantiali humiditate consumpta, de die in diem vergunt ad interitum quod est deterius quam privatio ipsa vitalis, igitur, pater reverende, ne per presentem librum vestrum, Notyngham videlicet super evangelia, multum diffusum atque prolixum et claustro vestro et huius ecclesie per litterature doctrinam in agro dominico fulgure mirifico deaurantem, — ne mens studentium rapiatur nimium extra modum, sed tanquam formosum germen fructificet et pullilet (sic) in addiscendis materiam seu scripta in eodem contenta, in hoc opusculo per modum tabule

---

1) Prof. Margaret Rickert writes (Sept. 28, 1951) in answer to my inquiry: "MS. Laud misc. 165 is interesting for its illumination because its style (at least in part, as in the first miniature) is so typically late fourteenth-century English; and, I presume, London. I am using it, among other similar MSS. for comparison with the English artists' miniatures in the Carmelite Missal which I have reconstructed (MSS. Add. 29704-5 in the British Museum). My monograph on the Missal is now in the press and should appear this autumn but may be delayed till spring." See now M. Rickert, *The Reconstructed Carmelite Missal*, London, 1952, p. 76, pl. XLIII.

elaborato in unum succinĉtius quo potui et brevius redegi. Sed cum idem liber
sit divisus in partes duodecim, eĉt notandum quod primus numerus partibus
deservit, secundus numerus foliis, et hee quatuor littere, videliĉt *a*, *b*, *c*, *d*, foliorum
columnis, ita quod per *a* notatur prima columpna folii, per *b* secunda, per *c* tertia,
et per litteram *d* quarta.

The table, fol. 5rb-12va, corresponds to the description; it begins:
"Abraham et eius multiplex commendatio, parte septima, folio xvii, a, b."
Since the leaves are numbered (in roman numerals) so as to begin afresh
for each of the twelve parts, the table of contents supplies a convenient
and clear guide to the volume. A later hand has made additions to the
table in the margins. Along the top of fol. 12^v a different hand has written:
"Frater Willelmus Notyngham de ordine minorum erat auĉtor huius libri,
ut infra, parte iiia, fol. viiio, col. iia." This refers to a passage in the text,
fol. 116rb, marked by a marginal note, "Nomen auĉtoris iĉtius libri." The
passage, where William of Nottingham refers to himself as author, will
be transcribed later. An erased inscription at the end of the table on
fol. 12^v can be partially read by ultra-violet light:

"Q . . . .
Da michi pignum."

The order is as follows:
1. Table relating the contents of the commentary, according to the order
of parts, to the chapters of the four gospels, fol. 1-4. It begins:

Hic incipit kalendarium super quatuor evangelia, videlicet super illo libro
qui vocatur unum ex quatuor.
Prima pars. Verbum, id eĉt filius Dei, fit ab eterno . . . Ioh. i.

It ends with a rubric:

Circa prediĉta ad eorum evidentiam eĉt notandum quod non omnia contenta in
unoquoque capitulo a singulis evangeliĉtis ponuntur, qui in fine uniuscuiusque
tituli supradiĉti exprimuntur, quamvis ut in pluribus hoc contingat, sed aliquando
in aliqua in omnibus, aliqua in aliquibus, aliqua in uno solo, quod infra in serie
manifeĉtius apparebit. Hoc etiam patere poteĉt per cotationes marginales superius
annotatas.

The 'cotationes' presumably mean the chapter numbers of the gospels, marked in the top margins throughout the commentary, to indicate the *loci* which are being expounded.

2. The table of contents compiled by the archbishop's clerk and chaplain, with the prologue, as already described, fol. 5-12ᵛ.

3. Prologue and commentary, fol. 13-484ᵛ. The inscription of ownership is written above the text, fol. 13:

> Doctor qui dicitur Notyngham super Evangelia de dono domni Thome Arundell', archiepiscopi Cant. in claustro Cant.

The rubric is:

> Hic incipit quedam nobilis expositio super quatuor evangelia et est, ut dicitur, ultima et melior omnibus aliis et vocatur unum ex quatuor et multum plenius et diffusius tractat quam Clemens et plura dubia solvit.

An unusual feature is that each part has its separate incipit and explicit. They have been carefully varied so that the wording is never the same. The aim is generally to bring out the relationship between Clement and Nottingham. For instance:

> Explicit quarta pars operis secundum processum Clementis, quem auctor huius libri prosequitur et in multis cum eo concordat, tamen eum in multis excedit et plenius et planius exponit et etiam tractat, ut patere potest intuenti, si bene inspiciatur (fol. 210ᵛᵃ); Hic incipit quinta pars huius operis secundum ordinem Clementis, quem ordinem auctor huius libri prosequitur in multis (fol. 211ʳᵃ); Explicit septima pars huius voluminis secundum distinctionem Clementis per Notingham compilata. Deo gratias (fol. 355ᵛᵃ).

That the commentary was at least looked at in the sixteenth century appears from a proverb written in a sixteenth-century hand at the bottom of a column, fol. 508ᵛᵃ: "The neer the cherch the fardest from god."

4. Table of Eusebian canons with explanation, fol. 584ᵛ-585, followed by note of ownership by James Palmer as transcribed above.

5. Table of gospels and holy days for the year, according to the Use of Sarum, with references to the number of the part and of the folio where the gospels are treated in the commentary, fol. 585ᵛ-588. The table is incomplete, breaking off in the middle of an entry, 'Sancti Dionisii

sociorumque eius'. This table is in a different hand from the rest of the volume.

It will be noted that the tables here are different from those in the copies described above, and that Clement's Harmony has been omitted.

BALLIOL COLLEGE 33.

This copy is dated by the donor. An inscription on the flyleaf (fol. 1) in a hand of about 1400 reads: "Liber domus de Balliolo ex legato magistri Iohannis Waltham subdecani ecclesie Ebor. quondam socii predicte domus, cuius anime propitietur Deus. Amen. Contentum: Notyngham super evangelia." Mr. Emden has been kind enough to identify Master John Waltham for me, which involved disentangling him from his namesake, the bishop of Salisbury. Mr. Emden further allows me to quote his notes on John Waltham's career. The relevant facts are as follows: Waltham was a nephew of John Thoresby, archbishop of York.[1] He must have been a fellow of Balliol before 1349 and got leave to study at Oxford for four years on June 29, 1358.[2] He had incepted in arts by 1352, had his B.C.L. by 1358[3] and was licentiate of Canon Law by 1368.[4] He was ordained deacon on May 22, 1361.[5] His large number of preferments culminated in his becoming subdean of York, Oct. 24, 1381.[6] He died in 1384 and his will, dated Aug. 20, 1375, was proved on Nov. 26, 1384.[7] He left to Balliol "bibliam meam, librum accordanciarum, Nothyngam super evangelia, liram super psalterium et liram super epistolas Pauli."[8]

The hand is late fourteenth century. There are illuminated borders and initials, of which the first, fol. 4, has been cut out.

---

[1]) *Calendar of Papal Petitions*, i 245.

[2]) Register of Gynewell, Linc. viii, fol. 56ᵛ.

[3]) *Calendar of Papal Petitions*, i 245; *Calendar of Papal Letters*, iii 608.

[4]) Register of Thoresby, York xi, fol. 67.

[5]) Register of Zouch, York x.

[6]) Register of Alexander Neville, York xii, fol. 81. He had been canon and prebendary since 1368, Reg. Thoresby, fol. 67, J. Le Neve *Fasti Eccles. Angl.*, ed. Hardy, Oxford, 1854, iii 205.

[7]) *Wills, Dean and Chapter of York*, Yorks Archæol. Soc., Record Series, p. 66. The notice by A. H. Thompson in Yorks Archæol. Journal, 25 [1919], 257-60, confuses the two John Walthams in some respects.

[8]) York, Dean and Chapter Library, Register of Wills for the Peculiar of the Dean and Chapter, 1321-1493. Mr. Emden very kindly sent me this extract.

1. Prologue and commentary, fol. 4-354. There is a verse at the end of part vi, fol. 189:

> Scribitur hic medium libri, sit laus data Christo,
> Qui michi subsidium scribendi prebuit isto [confiso].

Another verse after the explicit of part xii reads:

> Hic postillatus evangelicus liber iste
> Est consummatus, sit laus et honor tibi Christe,
> Scriptoremque tibi fac huius vivere gratum,
> Ac William N. cui scribitur, esse beatum.

An early sixteenth-century hand has written after the explicit:

> Iste Notyngham fuit canonicus secularis et precentor eboracensis ecclesie.

A hand of about the same date has added:

> et postea factus est frater de ordine sancti Francisci.

The leaves are numbered afresh for each part. The formula for the incipit for each part is either: "Hic incipit prima pars" or: "Incipit sexta pars secundum Clementem." There are many marginal notes in a hand of the late fourteenth or early fifteenth century, indicating an attentive reader, for instance, "Hic incipit notabilis collatio de sancto Iohanne baptista," (fol. 8ᵛ).

2. A table relating the chapters of the gospels according to their division by letters, *a-h*, to the parts and chapters of the commentary. It is written on both sides of a leaf which has been sewn to fol. 354 and folded over inside the cover.

The leaves at the beginning of the volume, fol. 1-3ᵛ are mainly blank or filled with notes referring to the commentary which amount to a fragmentary table of contents. A sermon of St. Augustine in praise of *lectio divina* is written on fol. 2ᵛ.[1] The title of another, *De periurio*, is written at the top of fol. 3; but the space for the sermon has been left blank.

---

[1] PL. 40, col. 1339.

MAGDALEN COLLEGE, lat. 160.

Fifteenth-century English hand with illuminated borders and initials, many of them cut out. Incomplete at the beginning. The mediaeval foliation begins at fol. 26; part i up to chapter 9 has been lost. William of Nottingham is mentioned as author in the incipit of part vi. The provenance is unknown. The exemplar was either the Laudian manuscript or some copy deriving from it.

1. Commentary from end of chapter 9, part i to end, fol. 1-297.

2. Eusebian canons with their explanation, fol. 297ᵛ, followed by the same concluding rubric as in the Laudian manuscript: "Explicit liber qui vocatur . . . vitam eternam habebit." The note of ownership by John Palmer and the verse have been omitted.

3. Table of gospels for the year with references to the commentary, fol. 297ᵛ-299ᵛ. It is similar to the corresponding table in the Laudian manuscript, but complete; the gospels of Masses for special occasions have been added.

4. A second table of the same kind, partly identical and partly differing from the first, fol. 300ᵛ-302.

5. Table of contents prefaced by the prologue of Archbishop Arundel's clerk and chaplain, fol. 302-308ᵛ. The heading is "Tabula in expositionem Willelmi Notyngham super quatuor evangelia." The text of the prologue is identical. There is some confusion in the order of items 4 and 5. The scribe broke off the table of contents, fol. 302, in order to copy the end' of his liturgical table, which had been left unfinished; there is a cross reference, fol. 301ᵛ: "Quere aliam partem huius tabule in proximo quaterno ad tale signum." Then he chose to begin the table of contents all over again, so that the prologue and beginning of the table, *Abraham* to *angeli*, have been copied twice. The leaves are numbered, beginning afresh for each part. Whoever prepared the table, however, lacked the courage to adapt it to the foliation of this particular copy. Sometimes the number of the leaf and the letter of the column, as found in the original, have been omitted, leaving only the part and chapter; sometimes number and letter have been added; but they do not correspond to those of the manuscript. Consequently the table is likely to mislead and would irritate rather than relieve the student for whom the archbishop's clerk and chaplain had intended it.

MERTON COLLEGE 156.

English hands of the second half of the fourteenth century. Illuminated border and initial on fol. 1. No other decoration apart from large blue and red initials. Given by John of Bloxham, Warden of Merton, 1375-87.[1] The last leaf has been cut out, so that the end of part xii of the commentary is missing. Some blank spaces indicate a defective exemplar. "Notyngham super evangelia" is written in a hand roughly contemporary with the text on the flyleaf.

1. Prologue and commentary, fol. 1-399ᵛ.
The part of the commentary and the biblical chapters expounded in the text are marked in the upper margins, but there is no mediaeval foliation. The incipits of the separate parts are short: "Incipit pars prima", with an occasional variant: "Hic incipit sexta pars Clementis". The book was rebound by Master John Burbach, 'sacre theologie professor' and chained in the library for the use of students. Burbach was fellow of Merton and 'theologus senior' of the University 1433-9.[2]

MERTON COLLEGE 157.

English hands of the later fourteenth century. Red and blue initials. Given by John Wood, bachelor in theology, fellow of Merton, and afterwards archdeacon of Middlesex, who died in 1475.[3] A strip of parchment bearing the title "Notyngham super Evangelia" with the note on the donor is pasted on the flyleaf.

1. Prologue and commentary, fol. 1-357ʸ. The part and number of the leaf, beginning afresh for each part, are marked in the upper margin.
2. A table of gospels for the year and for special occasions, with references to the part of the commentary and the number of the leaf. The numbers of the leaves have been added in a different hand and correspond with the actual foliation of this manuscript.

The incipits of the separate parts correspond roughly to those of MS. 156. A hand of about 1500 has written "Robert Inkyn ys a good son" and *probationes pennae* on the margin of fol. 3ᵛ of part vi.

---

[1] F. M. Powicke, *The Medieval Books of Merton College*, Oxford, 1931, p. 187.
[2] *Ibid.*, p. 199.
[3] *Ibid.*, p. 209.

The Balliol and these two Merton manuscripts show us the commentary in its simplest, least decorated form. All accessories have disappeared except for one table each in MS. Balliol 33 and MS. Merton 157.

ST. JOHN'S COLLEGE 2.

A notice pasted inside the cover reads: "Ex dono magistri Ioannis Stonor Generosi de Northstoke in Comitatu Oxon. 1609." Of the ten manuscripts given by Sir John Stonor in 1609, seven undoubtedly came from Reading Abbey.[1] The inscription of ownership in Reading books was on a flyleaf.[2] As this manuscript has lost a few leaves at the beginning, there is no way of confirming its Reading provenance. Late fifteenth-century English hand with illuminated borders, grotesques and stripes across the leaves. It has a table, dated Oxford, 1489, which may have been copied.
1. Prologue and commentary, fol. 1-339ᵛ. The prologue is incomplete, beginning towards the end. The table of Eusebian canons and their explanation have been inserted between part vi and part vii, instead of being put at the beginning or end of the commentary.
2. Table of gospels for the year with references to the parts of the commentary, as in the Laudian manuscript, fol. 339ᵛ. The next leaf has been cut out, so that the table is incomplete, only reaching Septuagesima Sunday.
3. Table of contents in alphabetical order, *Abba pater - Zorobabel*, with references to the commentary, fol. 340-70. It ends:

Explicit tabula sententiarum secundum ordinem alphabeti super doctorem Notyngham de concordia quatuor evangeliorum, edita Oxon. 1489 et completa tertia decima die mensis Iulii anni supradicti.

This table is fuller than that in any of the other manuscripts.
4. Table of *quaestiones* contained in the commentary, also in alphabetical order, fol. 370-76ᵛ. It ends:

---

[1]) See J. R. Liddell, *Some notes on the library of Reading Abbey*, Bodleian Quarterly Record, 8 [1935], 47-54; R. J. Stonor, *Stonor*, Newport, 1951, pp. 240, 261, mentions the Stonors of North Stoke.
[2]) N. R. Ker, *Medieval Libraries of Great Britain*, London, 1941, p. 86.

explicit tabula queſtionum quas movet Notyngham in opere suo de concordia evangeliorum.

This is fuller than the tables to the excerpted *quaeſtiones* which will be described when we come to the abridgments.

In this manuscript the columns are numbered, beginning afresh with each chapter. The columns are divided into ſections of varying length, each marked by a letter from *a* to *g*. This division of the columns, however, begins only at chapter 8 of part vii, fol. 185. The table of *quaeſtiones* refers to the column only, not the ſection. The table of contents sometimes gives the letter as well as the number of the column. Since it gives letters in some cases for parts of the commentary coming before part vii, chapter 8, where the letters begin, one imagines that the table has been copied from an exemplar with columns divided by letters all the way through. The letters in this manuscript muſt have been put in so as to correspond with the exemplar, though it was not done syſtematically. This would explain the unevenness of the divisions, which otherwise would have no reason.

PRAGUE

UNIVERSITY LIBRARY 1870 (X.C.17), fol. 94ᵃ-260ᵇ.[1]
Fifteenth-century. It has the usual incipit of the prologue, "*Da mihi intelleĉtum* . . . Dionysius de divinis nominibus . . ." and ends incomplete. No tables are mentioned in the catalogue. It is part of a miscellany, containing St. Albert's *Biblia mariana* and anonymous treatises on the Canticle "Benedicite omnia opera" and on the Gospel parables.

We can now answer our question, "do the manuscripts contain the canons of William I or the poſtill of William II?" The majority have both canons and a poſtill. A comparison between the contents of the manuscripts suggeſts a hypothesis. MS. Pembroke College 192 comes cloſeſt to the original apparatus prepared by William I for the use of his friars. It begins with the Harmony of Clement, which is followed by a table of Eusebian canons with an explanatory note. Here we have some-

¹) J. Truhlář, *Cat. cod. MSS. lat. qui in C. R. Bibliotheca publica atque Univ. Pragensis asservantur*, Prague, 1906, ii 59.

thing like the apparatus as described by Eccleston: William I had the Harmony of Clement, to which he added 'very useful canons', copied together with Clement's exposition. Then William II replaced Clement's exposition by a postill of his own. Here, with the addition of a few tables, we have the collection contained in MS. Pembroke College 192. Henceforward the natural tendency would be for the original apparatus to melt away, making room for the postill and an increasing number of tables to facilitate its use. In MSS. Durham A.1. and Royal 4 E. II Clement's Harmony has been drastically abbreviated. Prologue and treatise have been cut away, leaving only the 'ratio ordinis' at the end. This, moreover, has been pushed from the front to the back of the volume in both manuscripts. It has dropped out of the others altogether. The table of canons and their explanation survived and were joined to the postill, except in MSS. Balliol 33 and Merton College 156-7, where they, too, have disappeared. It remains to prove this hypothesis, in so far as it can be proved, by making a closer study of the postill. Could it have been written by William I or only by William II?

The dates of the manuscripts favour William II: not one is earlier than about 1350. Yet readers formed a high opinion of the postill. Its author had taken infinite pains to prepare an improved apparatus for the study of the gospels. It was the latest and best. It surpassed Clement's. It set one on the road to everlasting life. The book appeared in sumptuous copies. Tables were devised for the benefit of overworked students and of preachers: indeed, the manuscripts provide material for the history of early indexing. Readers also show an interest in the author's identity. Rubricators distinguish between Clement and Nottingham. MS. Laud misc. 165 has a note directing us to a passage where the author calls himself "Brother William of Nottingham O.F.M." MS. Balliol 33 has a note claiming him as canon and precentor of York. Prayers are asked for his soul. Even the very ownership of the manuscripts suggests popularity. It is surprising that so many private persons, as distinct from institutions, should have owned so expensive a book. A bishop of Durham and a sub-dean of York could afford it, while a Warden and a fellow of Merton might need it for their academic work; but it also belonged to a country parson and to James Palmer, who cannot have been a celebrity. A book so valued in the later Middle Ages is unlikely to have remained unknown for a century after it was written. Had William I been author of the postill one would have expected to find at least one copy dating from the thirteenth or early fourteenth century.

Other evidence confirms the conclusions to be drawn from existing manuscripts. The book makes a late appearance in library catalogues. Syon Monastery, founded 1415, had two copies. One of them contained tables resembling the set in MS. Laud misc. 165. The catalogue description is interesting both for its account of the tables and for its clear statement that the liturgical table was used for preaching:

Notyngham super unum ex quatuor secundum Clementem Lanthoniensem. Bona tabula super idem opus in principio libri. Capitula singulorum (sic) partium eiusdem operis in fine libri. Breviarium quoddam eiusdem operis secundum Clementem. Decem Canones de concordantiis Evangelistarum iuxta formam antiquam. Quotationes evangeliorum totius anni tam de sanctis quam de temporali in hoc Monasterio predicandorum secundum idem opus in principio libri.[1]

This gives us still another arrangement if the cataloguer has set the items in order. Clement's Harmony comes after the commentary, as in MS. Royal 4 E. II; it is followed by the Eusebian canons, as in the Pembroke College and Durham manuscripts.

A monk called John of Canterbury gave "Clemens super Euangelia" and "Exposicio Notyngham post Clementem super Euangelia" to St. Augustine's, Canterbury. As he also gave Fitz Ralph's *De quaestionibus Armenorum* and Walter Burley's commentaries on the *Ethics* and *Politics*,[2] he must have been living in the second half of the fourteenth century at earliest. There is no trace of the book in the catalogue drawn up in the priorate of Henry Eastry, Prior of Christ Church, Canterbury, 1284-1331, nor in the list of books which he gave to Christ Church.[3] We have seen that Christ Church obtained its copy through the gift of Archbishop Arundel. Exeter seems to have got one as part of a legacy on Jan. 22, 1411,

---

[1] M. Bateson, *Catalogue of the Library of Syon Monastery*, Cambridge, 1898, p. 67. The second copy, catalogued on the same page, either had no tables or was described less fully.

[2] M. R. James, *Ancient Libraries of Canterbury and Dover*, Cambridge, 1903, pp. 217, 263, 314.

[3] *Ibid.*, pp. 113-63. The item "Glose super unum ex quatuor", p. 105, now at Lambeth, MS. 142, is Peter the Chanter's gloss on a gospel harmony, according to the incipit; see F. Gutjahr, *Petrus Cantor Parisiensis*, Graz, 1899, p. 54.

when an executor of Master Robert Rygghe, formerly chancellor of the cathedral, delivered two books for the library, "quorum duorum librorum unus vocatus Notyngham qui incipit secundo folio lya".[1] There is no trace of it, however, in the inventory of Exeter books drawn up in 1506.[2] Three copies cannot be dated even by guesswork. Leland saw "Notingham super unum ex quatuor"[3] in the library of the London Franciscans and Bale two more, in the house of William Hanley and at Oriel College.[4]

We get the same evidence of lateness if we turn from the complete commentary to extracts.

(b) Abbreviations and excerpts

The abbreviators gathered round Nottingham like flies round a honey pot. The most popular abridgment was a collection of *quaestiones* extracted from his commentary and arranged in alphabetical order. We find what was probably the original form with the excerptor's name attached to it in MS. Merton College 68, fol. 121ra-201v. The volume is a miscellany containing some interesting pieces, including a *determinatio* by Robert Alyngton, Chancellor of Oxford University in 1393.[5] The compilation has a strongly anti-Lollard bias. Our excerpts, written in a fifteenth-century English hand, have the title in the same hand as the text:

Iste sunt questiones quas movet Notyngham in scripto suo super evangelia extracte secundum ordinem alphabeti per magistrum Iohannem Wykham (fol. 121ra)

The incipit is: "Abel. Queritur super illo dicto Mat. 23 . . .", the explicit, on the word *zizania*: ". . . per naturam, parte 9, cap. 9" (fol. 195ra). There follows a table of gospels for the year, beginning with the first Sunday in Advent according to the Use of Sarum, "Cum appropinquasset Iesus etc." and ending with a Mass for the dead (fol. 195ra-201ra). Each has a reference to the *quaestio* dealing with this particular passage, e.g.: "Quere questiones

---

[1] *Historical MSS. Commission. Various Collections*, vol. IV, p. 40. From the chapter acts book of Exeter, no. 3550, fol. 109b. Mr. J. Crompton kindly pointed this out to me.

[2] G. Oliver, *Lives of the Bishops of Exeter*, Exeter, 1861, pp. 366-378.

[3] *Coll.*, iv 50.

[4] *Index*, pp. 140-1.

[5] Powicke, *op. cit.*, pp. 206-7.

pertinentes ad hoc evangelium in verbo *honorare*. . . ." Finally comes a list
of those words which are the subject of *quaestiones*, from *Abel* to *zizania*
(fol. 201ra-201v), with the explicit just above it: "Expliciunt questiones
Notyngham super evangelia." The list is independent of that given at the
end of some manuscripts of the full commentary, which is much longer.
A collation of *quaestiones* and commentary shows that the extracts are
generally verbally identical with the original, though they may have been
shortened, but that the excerptor worked selectively; he copied only some,
not all of the *quaestiones* contained in the commentary.

Mr. Emden has kindly identified Master John Wykeham, too, and
allows me to quote his notes on Wykeham's career. Master John was one
of the many kinsmen of Bishop William of Wykeham who had an Oxford
degree. He was charged for the rent of a room in the Queen's College,
1398-9, and was still being charged in Michaelmas Term, 1408.[1] He was
ordained acolyte in 1396 and, after passing through the minor grades,
priest in 1398.[2] He had already been admitted rector of Stockton, Wilts, in
1395.[3] From then onwards he had a number of preferments; the last which
can be traced was in 1404, the year of his patron's death. William of
Wykeham made him a bequest of £50 for his inception in theology at
Oxford.[4] It is known that John Wykeham had taken his M.A.; whether
he actually did incept in theology is uncertain. The bequest, together with
his continued renting of a room at Queen's, suggests that he was studying
for a degree. The copying and rearrangement of extracts from a standard
work on the gospels must have been a useful way of getting up one's
subject for examination purposes. The table of gospels accompanying his

---

[1]) Queen's College, Long Rolls.

[2]) *Register of William of Wykeham, Bishop of Winchester* (Hants Record Society), i 339 bis, 343, 347.

[3]) *Register of John of Waltham*, Sarum, part i, fol. 95, Phillipps 81, 83.

[4]) Collated to be canon of the king's free chapel, Bosham, Sussex, Jan. 25, 1397; exchanged
May, 1397, *Register of Edmund Stafford, Bishop of Exeter*, ed. F. C. Hingeston-Randolph (1886), p. 147,
373; collated to be canon of Howden, Yorks, and prebendary of Thorpe, May 25, 1397, *Sede vacante
register of York*, part iii, fol. 206v; to be rector of Mapledurham, Buriton, Hants, Aug. 1, 1397, and still
rector in 1403, *Register of Wykeham, op. cit.,* i, 210, *Calendar of Patent Rolls 1401-1405*, p. 227; admitted
vicar of Steeple Aston, Wilts, Apr. 15, 1400, had vacated by June, 1400, *Register of Bishop Medford, Sarum*,
part iii, fol. 62v, 63v; collated to be rector of Colbourne, Isle of Wight, Nov. 2, 1403, vacated by May,
1404, *Register of Wykeham, op. cit.,* i 243, 245; to be rector of Brightstone, Isle of Wight, May 15, 1404,
vacated by June, 1404, *ibid.*, i 246; to be rector of Bishops Waltham, Hants, June 19, 1404, *ibid.*

quaestio collection, however, shows that its primary purpose was to provide material for preaching: you looked up the *quaestio* on the gospel for the day. They are not the type of long, elaborately worked out *quaestiones* familiar to the student of scholasticism in disputations, but give information in a simple 'question and answer' form. They deal with the literal sense of the text, it is true; but then the preacher was supposed to base his teaching on an explanation of the literal sense, before proceeding to allegories and moralities. The popularity of these alphabetically arranged *quaestiones* shows that they answered a need. There are six other copies and a seventh, which I have not seen, is reported to have been at the Franciscan convent at Ravenna.[1] A difference in incipit arises from the fact that the first lines of the text have dropped out, so that in all copies except the Merton College one the first *quaestio* is on Abraham instead of on Abel; the Ravenna copy also began at Abel. The text may be disposed a little differently, beginning: "*Abraham pater meus* . . . Ioh. viii, super quo queritur," or: "Queritur super illo dicto Christi, Ioh. viii," with the word *Abraham* in the margin. The explicits vary from copy to copy, since only two (or three counting that from Ravenna) reach the word *zizania*. The others break off short at various stages. The hands are all fifteenth-century English.

1. MS. Cambridge, Pembroke College 239,[2] fol. 112-237v, ending on *veritas*. Table in columns, fol. 237v-239v, headed: "Hic incipiunt questiones Notyngham secundum capitula quatuor evangeliorum." The table attaches the *quaestiones* to their chapters in the four gospels. Bale may have seen this copy; he mentions Nottingham's *Quaestiones in evangelia* among the Pembroke College manuscripts.[3] The volume also has 'distinctiones theologice' ascribed to 'Ianuensis' (Jacobus de Voragine), fol. 1-107v, and the *De venenis* ascribed to Grosseteste, fol. 240-254.[4] A former owner was John Sparhawk, D.D., Fellow of the College about 1420, who died in 1474.[5]

2. MS. Oxford, Bodl. 583 (2214), fol. 133-246, ending on *vendi in templo*,

---

[1] Spicq, *op. cit.*, p. 345, Stegmüller, *op. cit.*, ii 341. Bale saw a copy at Norwich, *Index*, p. 264.

[2] M. R. James, *Catalogue of Pembroke College MSS.*, *op. cit.*, p. 215.

[3] *Index*, p. 141.

[4] The attribution to Grosseteste is doubtful, S. H. Thomson, *The Writings of Robert Grosseteste* (Cambridge, 1940), pp. 268-70.

[5] He also owned MS. Cambridge, Gonville and Caius College 328.

followed by a table similar to that in the Pembroke College manuscript, fol. 246-7ᵛ, with a table of gospels for the year with their corresponding *quaestiones*, similar to that in the Merton College manuscript, fol. 247ᵛ. The explicit is: "Expliciunt questiones Notyngham super evangelia per annum, quaterni xxi, precium xxix s." A marginal note on fol. 147 against the word *credere* says: "Hic deficiunt septem questiones quas require in fine libri." There are in fact seven *quaestiones* missing between *credere* and *conficere*; but they have not been added at the end of the book. The only other item in the volume is the *Distinctiones theologice* of Jacobus de Voragine, as in MS. Pembroke College 239, fol. 1-132ᵛ. It was given to Bodley by the dean and canons of Windsor in 1612.

3. MS. Oxford, Bodl. Rawl. C. 572, fol. 1-260ᵛ, ending on *zizania*, as MS. Merton College 68, followed by table of gospels, fol. 260-269ᵛ, ending: "Explicit libellus questionum Notyngham quas movet idem doctor in opere suo de concordia quatuor evangelistarum." The flyleaves have *probationes pennae*, scribbles, a list of names beginning "Adam, Benett, Clement, Davyth", and several rhymes, in sixteenth-century hands, of which one on fol. ivᵛ reads: "Ihus marcy Lady helpe for [?] my dogge ys a parillus welp"; the dog's name is illegible.

4. MS. Oxford, Balliol College 75, pp. 2-208, ending on *Virgo Maria*. The work is not ascribed. Gerard Langbaine wrote "Questiones super difficultates Evangeliorum" over the incipit and "Desunt (ut videtur) nonnulla. Questionum finis imperfectus G.L." at the end. There are two Oxford university sermons, of which Coxe gives incipits and extracts, pp. 213-227; they are unconnected with either the *Quaestiones* or the full commentary of Nottingham; then comes a table to the *Quaestiones*, attaching them to the chapters of the gospels, pp. 228-234. It is a table of the usual type, but here it is obviously home-made. The owner of the book had the columns ruled and the names of the Evangelists written at the top and the chapters at the side; then he filled in the references to the *Quaestiones* himself, in an untidy, irregular way. On pp. 245-249 are short pieces and sermons ascribed to St. Augustine. There are a number of different hands but the general impression is of a miscellany made by a scholar for his own use.

5. MS. Oxford, Lincoln College lat. 78, fol. 12ᵛ-161ᵛ, ending on *Christus*; the words go as far as *Zacheus*, several *quaestiones* on *Christus* having been added

at the end; they consist mainly in cross references. The title is: "Questiones quas movet Notyngham in scripto suo super evangelia secundum ordinem alphabeti." Here the tables come at the beginning, first a table of words only, as in MS. Merton College 68, fol. 2-3ᵛ (Abraham to Zacheus), then the usual table of Gospels headed "Evangelia de temporalibus", fol. 3ᵛ-12. The scribe has written "Me tibi virgo pia genetrix commendo Maria", fol. 161ᵛ. The book was given by a great benefactor of Lincoln College, John Forest, canon of Lincoln and dean of Wells, who died in 1446.[1] He seems to have been interested in biblical commentaries, since he also gave Ringstead on Proverbs and Holcot on Wisdom (MSS. Lincoln College lat. 86 and 110).

6. MS. Paris, Bibl. nat.lat. 13,207, fol. 1-147, ending on *zizania*, "Explicit libellus questionum Notyngham super evangelia." A collection of *quaestiones* without heading, written in a different hand, fol. 148-62, seems to deal largely with matters concerning the parish clergy. A table to these *quaestiones* on the flyleaf, fol. iiᵛ, calls them "Questiones alique conscientiam serenantes". The first is: "Utrum presbiter parochialis debeat credere parochiano suo dicenti se esse confessum alteri." There is a table of words for the Nottingham *Quaestiones* (Abel-zizania), fol. i-iᵛ, and the usual Gospel table, fol. iii-xᵛ. This copy resembles MS. Rawl. C. 572 more closely than any of the others, ending on *zizania*, and having the same title, "libellus questionum". It still has its mediaeval wooden binding. It belonged to the collection made by Chancellor Séguier in the first half of the seventeenth century, then passed to de Coislin, bishop of Metz, who left it to the Abbey of St. Germain des Près in his will. The Abbey received his bequest in 1735.[2]

Another collection of extracts is found in MSS. Cambridge University Library Kk III. 27 and Gg III. 31. The excerptor is anonymous. He took a table of gospels for the year and arranged his extracts from the full commentary under each, giving the effect of a series of homilies for the Christian year. This has naturally led bibliographers to ascribe homilies as well as a commentary to William of Nottingham. A collation shows

[1]) See A. Clark, *A History of Lincoln College*, London, 1898, pp. 8, 12, 19; J. Le Neve, *Fasti Eccles. Angl.*, ed. Hardy, Oxford, 1854, ii 105; *Vict. Count. Hist. Somerset*, London, 1911, ii 168.
[2]) L. Delisle, *Cabinet des MSS. de la Bibliothèque nationale*, Paris, 1874, ii 46, 78-99, 360.

that the supposed homilies are mere extracts from the commentary. They have not even been organized as formal sermons, with theme and conclusion, but simply provide material for the preacher on the gospel for the day to use as he pleases. Here we have the connexion with preaching in its most direct form. The preacher had no need of a table; he just opened the book at the appropriate season of the year.

1. MS. Kk III. 27,[1] fol. 1-186v. Incipit: *"Cum appropinquasset Iesus. In hoc evangelio in littera circa honoris exhibitione tanguntur tria. . . ."* Explicit: ". . . Require in quarta dominica quadragesima. Explicit Gorhan super textum omnium evangeliorum totius anni que leguntur in ecclesia Sarum in dominicis diebus."[2] A fifteenth-century hand has corrected Gorhan to Notyngham.[3] The scribe has written "Assit principio sancta Maria meo" along the top margin of fol. 1.[4] There are many marginal notes giving cross references and directions to preachers, such as "melius in dominica palmarum" and "notate episcopi et prelati". They are additions, not found in the full commentary. The hand is fifteenth-century English and there is an illuminated border.

2. MS. Gg III. 21, fol. 1-246v.[5] This is closely connected with the former manuscript. Many of the marginal notes are the same and there is the same invocation to St. Mary on fol. 87v. The incipit and text correspond up to fol. 85v, ending with a passage corresponding to the explicit of the text in MS. Kk III. 27. The remaining leaves contain more extracts from William of Nottingham, designed to fill up gaps in the material for sermons for the year, so that weekdays are added to the Sundays provided for in the first part. It ends: ". . . in tristitia erit super mensam suam." A table of contents follows. The hand is fifteenth-century English. There is no contemporary title or ascription.

---

[1] *Catalogue of MSS. in the Library of the University of Cambridge*, Cambridge, 1858, iii 636.

[2] The gospels do in fact correspond with *The Sarum Missal*, ed. J. Wickham Legg, Oxford, 1916.

[3] The mistaken ascription to Gorran was not due to any verbal identity in the two commentaries. A comparison between Gorran (Antwerp, 1617) and William of Nottingham in MS. Laud misc. 165 shows a certain amount of common material, as one would expect to find in two commentaries on the same books, but no evidence that one was using the other as a source.

[4] The same invocation to St. Mary is found in MS. Laud misc. 165, see above, p. 212; this may point to the use of the Laudian manuscript or a derivative as the exemplar from which the excerpts were made.

[5] *Cat. of MSS. in the Library of the University of Cambridge*, iii 82.

MS. Corpus Christi College, Cambridge, 305 has extracts following the order of the original, written in a hand of the late fourteenth century, fol. 1-352v.[1] A preface explains that the abbreviator has picked out what he thought would be most profitable to the less educated. He goes on to give full instructions on the use of his tables. These enable the reader to find the explanation of the gospel for the day of the year and they also index the contents. He has used arabic numerals but has added the more usual roman ones, because some are ignorant of the arabic:

Incipit quedam extractio extracta ab illa magna compilatione que appellatur Notyngham super evangelia. In hac extractione non exponuntur omnia evangelia, sed aliqua que videbantur extractori fore magis proficua minus litteratis. Plura etiam evangelia hic solum exponuntur ubi sensus litteralis vel misticus posset videri deficilis (sic) minus litteratis. Et quia in hoc libello raro ponuntur evangelia secundum ordinem dierum in quibus communiter solent dici in ecclesia, sed frequenter secundum ordinem historie et aliqua etiam evangelia inter⟨ser⟩untur neque secundum ordinem dierum, neque cum respectu ad historiam immediate precedentem, neque ad historiam immediate subsequentem, sed quasi absolute considerata propter quandam specialem effectum in eis conceptum, ideo folio 214b incipit tabula huius libelli in cuius prima parte notatur quibus diebus et quibus festis evangelia in hoc posita solent dici in ecclesia, quoto folio per numerum algorismi signato et qua parte folii secundum ordinem harum litterarum a, b, c, d, e, f, g eorum expositio incipit. In secunda parte folii secundum ordinem harum litterarum a, b, c, d, e, f, g diverse materie et diversa notabilia in hac extractione contenta invenientur. Et quia aliqui ignorant numeros algorismi, ideo in fine tabule exponuntur per numeros communiores supra positos. . . .

He goes on explaining his system of references (fol. iiv). The bibliographical note on William of Nottingham in a late hand, transcribed above,[2] has been written underneath this preface.

The text, written in the same hand as the preface, has the usual incipit, *Da mihi intellectum* (fol. 1). It seems to be unfinished, breaking off after the comment on Mt v 12, ". . . paupere quam in quocumque divite" (fol. 339v). The original was so long and unmanageable that the excerpts fill a fat volume without reaching the middle. The leaves have arabic numbers, as

---

[1] See M. R. James, *Catalogue of the MSS. in the Library of Corpus Christi College, Cambridge,* Cambridge, 1911, ii 102-3.

[2] p. 254.

stated, and letters down the side of the page, which is written in a single column. The tables are on fol. 214-22ᵛ, as stated in the preface, breaking into the text in a rather peculiar way. They must have been copied from an exemplar, since they tabulate the second pàrt of the commentary, which has not been included in this incomplete copy. Moreover, the exemplar itself had an incomplete table of gospels. The scribe writes "vacat" in the margin and goes straight on to the table of contents.

Lastly there are three pages of excerpts in a commonplace book, written in a hand of about 1500, MS. Oxford, Bodl. 487 (2067), fol. 22-3 (not 22-38 as the catalogue states). The excerpts are headed "Ex prologo Notyngham de Concordia". The title is quite correct: they are shortened extracts from Nottingham's prologue dealing mainly with the four senses of Scripture. The book seems to have belonged to a John Curteys, Fellow of Winchester and New College, who died in 1509.

A survey of the extracts has cleared up the bibliographical confusion about the biblical works ascribed to William of Nottingham. We have reduced them to one commentary on the *Unum ex quatuor* of Clement. The *quaestiones* and homilies ascribed to him are merely rearranged excerpts from this one commentary. The purpose of all, with the exception of the few scholar's notes in MS. Bodl. 487, was to put an enormous book at the disposal of preachers or of less educated readers. The dates again point to William II. The simplest of the abridgments survives in one copy of the late fourteenth century. John Wykeham excerpted the *quaestiones* about 1400. The homilies are found in two fifteenth-century copies. Another, short set of extracts from the prologue was made about 1500.

III

THE POSTILL AND ITS SOURCES

We shall now turn to the postill itself. The form suggests that it originated in lectures on the text of the gospels. After a prologue of the normal scholastic type, setting out the four causes of the composition of the gospels, and a commentary on their prologues, the commentator discusses the connexion between his texts. He comments on each passage, in places where the gospels are synoptic, bringing out the different shades of meaning. He speaks of himself as "reading and expounding":

Quoniam, ut dictum est supra, maxime intendo seriem evangelii secundum Iohannem et ordinem observare, ideo inprimis prologum beati Ieronimi in evangelium eiusdem legam et exponam.

He quite commonly says "in littera iam lecta" when he wants to refer back to an earlier section. The lecturer on Scripture used to read out the text to his class and this is what Nottingham seems to be doing.[1] Moreover, he is teaching as a master of theology, certainly not as a bachelor. He speaks with authority. He has chosen to base himself on Clement after mature deliberation. The passage marked out by the annotator of MS. Laud misc. 165 as giving the name of the author comes at a point where the sequence of events in the gospel story can be variously interpreted. The commentator has to decide which of the existing harmonies to follow; he opts for Clement, reserving the right to differ should he find a better authority:

Et ideo Clemens suum unum ex quatuor post omnes alios ordinando composuit, sicut patere potest ex dictis suis in principio sui operis, et aliorum ordinem diligentius inspexerat. Quia etiam processum evangelicum diffusius, studiosius et efficacius quam aliquis predictorum exposuit, innitens quasi totaliter auctoritatibus plurimorum sanctorum, ideo ego, frater Willelmus de Notingham de ordine minorum, intendo ex nunc ordinem suum tenere, nisi fortasse inveniendo aliquem doctorum vel auctorem sollempniorem eo sibi contradicentem (fol. 116rb).

John Bale correctly noted that Nottingham "scripsit super Evangelia expositive et disputative". He raises and solves *quaestiones* and he is ready to give his own opinion on disputed points: "quod magis credo."[2] Much of his material has been borrowed, it is true. The rubricator of MS. Royal 4 E. II was also right when he stated that Nottingham "studio laborioso predictam expositionem ex variis compilavit". But this could be applied to most mediaeval commentators. One expressed oneself in one's

---

[1] B. Smalley, *The Study of the Bible in the Middle Ages*, 2nd ed., Oxford, 1952, 217-8.

[2] My quotations are from MS. Laud misc. 165 unless otherwise stated.

choice of authorities and in one's discussion of their differences. Clement's commentary, moreover, is by no means his chief authority. He had it on his desk, as he had the Harmony; we find him referring to it;[1] but a comparison has not brought out unacknowledged quotations or any noticeable similarity of treatment.[2]

Since William I was never regent in theology, the chances that he could have written a magisterial work of this kind are negligible. The argument can be clinched by internal evidence of date.

Both the sources and the general tone of a commentary can usually be relied on to date it. We may start with a number of pointers, which are significant though not conclusive. The prologue begins with the text *Da mihi intellectum, et scrutabor legem tuam* (Ps. cxviii, 34), followed by a quotation from Pseudo-Dionysius' *De divinis nominibus* "secundum translationem Lincolniensis". Grosseteste's translation probably dates from 1239-1243;[3] William I could easily have quoted him. On the other hand, the commentary on the *Sentences*, now definitely restored to William II, begins with a very similar text, *Da mihi intellectum, ut sciam testimonia tua* (Ps. cxviii, 125); he repeats it at the opening of each book.[4] He also quotes Grosseteste's commentary on *De divinis nominibus*.[5] Here would be a coincidence. Even stranger would be the appearance of a quotation from Pseudo-Dionysius at all at the opening of a biblical prologue of the mid-thirteenth century. Only towards the end of the century did commentators begin to double their introductory text from Scripture by a second text chosen from one of the Fathers.[6] By that time all the appropriate texts from Scripture must have been used for incipits, some of them many times over. Lecturers wanted to draw the attention of their audience at the outset by something new and striking. A second text, drawn from a wider, less familiar field, would give them their opportunity.

---

[1]) MS. Laud misc. 165, fol. 33vb: "Clemens autem in expositione sua accipit sic: quo autem modo fieri potest? et iterum ita quo ergo fieri potest modo etc.?" For the context see below, p. 234.

[2]) I compared the postill with the copy of Clement's commentary in MS. Bodl. 334 (2333).

[3]) D. A. Callus, *The Date of Grosseteste's Translations and Commentaries on Pseudo-Dionysius and the Nichomachean Ethics*, Recherches de théologie ancienne et médiévale, 14 [1947], 186-210.

[4]) Quoted by C. Balič, *op. cit.* (above, p. 206, n. 1), p. 171, 4, 7.

[5]) *The Writings of Robert Grosseteste*, Cambridge, 1940, pp. 57, 79.

[6]) See B. Smalley, *Some Commentaries on the Sapiential Books*, etc., *op. cit.*, p. 119.

Then we find William quoting 'correctores' when discussing the variant readings in his text.[1] The use of lists of variants and emendations to the Paris text of the Vulgate began towards the middle of the thirteenth century, if not earlier.[2] But the actual name, 'correctores', does not occur, in my experience, in any commentator working before the time of Nicholas Gorran, towards the end of the century.[3] Then a number of the *quaestiones* on the fourth gospel contained in the commentary, though not all, can be traced to St. Bonaventure's commentary on St. John.[4] Bonaventure lectured on St. John's gospel during his teaching period at Paris, 1253-7.[5] His commentary on Ecclesiastes, which belongs to the same years, had a great success in the schools; later masters reproduced *quaestiones* from it in their own postills anonymously,[6] just as William of Nottingham copied *quaestiones* from the gospel commentary. Given this parallel, it is improbable that Bonaventure and Nottingham were drawing on a common source for their *quaestiones*. The use of Bonaventure very nearly excludes William I. Even if the commentary on St. John came at the beginning of Bonaventure's teaching period, 1253, a quick book service would have been required for it to be quoted by a man who died in 1254.

Two quotations from Thomas Docking bring certainty. William quotes, in the same passage, Docking on St. Luke and Docking in 'his grammar'. William is discussing the meaning of *quomodo* in the question

---

[1] On John i 18: "Sed ut dicunt correctores nec grecum nec antiqui nec libri glosati nec Augustinus habent hic *nisi* vel *sed,* sed(ab)solute sine utroque *unigenitus Dei filius.*" (MS. Laud misc. 165, fol. 80rb.)

On John i 31: "Correctores dicunt hic quod grecum et antiqui et Augustinus habent *manifestetur Israel,* sine *in,* ita quod *ly* Israel sit dativi casus." (fol. 94ra.)

On John i 42: "Sic etiam ut dicunt correctores habent communiter moderni, sed, ut addunt, grecum et antique glose habent *filius Iohanna,* sed Augustinus *filius Iohannis.*" (fol. 95va.)

[2] It should be possible to identify the *correctorium* that William of Nottingham used; but only a selection on Proverbs has been printed; H. Denifle, *Die Handschriften der Bibelcorrectorien des 13 Jahrhundert,* Archiv für Lit. und Kirchengesch., 4 [1888], 263-311, 471-601. The identification, therefore, even with the help of Denifle's list of manuscript *correctoria,* would need a long piece of research.

[3] B. Smalley, *Some Commentaries on the Sapiential Books, op. cit.,* p. 110.

[4] Here are some examples taken from three different chapters: *S. Bonaventurae Opera* t. VI, Quaracchi, 1893, pp. 466-7, Q. ii on Ioan. xvi 25; p. 518, Q. vi on Ioan. xx 29; pp. 528-9, Q. iv, v, vi on Ioan. xxi 20-23, are found in MS. Laud misc. 165, fol. 302ra, 475va, 475vb, 481va. Not all of the *quaestiones* in William of Nottingham can be found in Bonaventure, however, and *vice versa.*

[5] P. Glorieux, *Répertoire des maîtres en théologie à Paris,* Paris, 1934, ii 37, 39.

[6] B. Smalley, *Some Thirteenth-Century Commentaries on the Sapiential Books,* Dominican Studies, 3 [1950], 41, 51, 72-3, 243-4.

put by Our Lady to the angel in the annunciation (Luke i 34). The references to Docking come just before a reference to the exposition of Clement of Lanthony (quoted above, p. 232, note 1).

Ex hac auctoritate accipiunt aliqui, ut Dokkingus, quod hec vox *quomodo* due dictiones sunt, velut si diceret: quis modus est quo fieret istud? Addunt etiam ad hoc glosam xxvii causa ii, capitulo *sufficit*, ubi dicitur sic: Licet hec interrogaret, non tamen dubitavit de verbis angeli, sed dubitavit quo modo istud posset fieri, ut sint due dictiones, 'quo' et 'modo'. De modo dubitavit, non de facto.[1] Ad hoc etiam addunt unam rationem talem: si enim esset una dictio, dubium esset utrum questio esset de facto an de facti modo, sed hoc dubium evacuatur si sint due dictiones. Certum est quod non de facto sed de modo facti est questio ista. Unde iste idem doctor in grammatica sua, capitulo de accentu, dicit sic opinando: de hac autem voce *quomodo* dicitur quod cum querit de re simul et de modo rei, tunc est dictio et acuit penultimam, unde vero supponit rem et querit tantum de modo, sicut fuit cum sacra virgo quesivit ab angelo *quo modo fiet istud?*, tunc est oratio. (MS. Laud misc. 165, fol. 33va-vb).

Neither quotation can be checked, but the first, at least, refers to a work which Docking is known to have written. His commentary on St. Luke survives only in a few pages of extracts in the compilation from English masters now at Paris, Bibliothèque nationale, MS. lat. 3183, fol. 190-3.[2] Docking's comment on this particular text was not included in the extracts. I compared them with Nottingham on the same passages in St. Luke, but could not find any resemblance. It would follow that William of Nottingham was using Docking on St. Luke for occasional consultation only; we must not expect to recover the lost work of Docking through William as a medium. The second work, the grammar, does not seem to have survived at all. A. G. Little, however, noted that Syon Abbey possessed a book listed in the index to the catalogue as "Dokkyng ordinis minorum in suis correctionibus super sacram scripturam abbreviatus".[3] The context of William's quotation suggests that Docking's

---

[1] Gratian, *Decretum*, secunda pars, Causa xxvii, Q. II, c. 2, Palea, *sufficit*, Gloss to *Cum ergo*, on "Voluntas non coitus facit matrimonium". See the *Decretum* with its *glossa ordinaria* ed. Strasbourg, 1472, vol. II, unfoliated, *ad loc.* It is a verbally exact quotation from the *Gloss* to the *Decretum*.

[2] A. G. Little, *Thomas Docking* in Franciscan Papers, Lists and Documents (Manchester, 1943), gives a notice of this manuscript, pp. 101-2. His 'fol. 170r-3v' should be corrected to '190r-3v'.

[3] *Ibid.*, 103. See M. Bateson, *op. cit.*, p. 221.

'grammar' dealt with biblical terms; so the grammar may be the same as the 'correctiones'.

Docking, to quote the notice of him by A. G. Little, "was seventh lector to the Friars Minor at Oxford, . . . and must have been regent master in theology for two or three years between 1260 and 1265. He had ceased to be regent master in 1269, but was still at Oxford . . . in that year."[1] It was natural that one of Docking's successors as lector should quote him, although his works, as far as is known, were not very popular in the fourteenth century. The quotation puts William I out of court. An allusion to Thomas Aquinas gives us an even closer date for William II. William is commenting on the story of the Visitation. He finds that all his sources make Our Lady stay with Elizabeth until after the birth of John the Baptist. He wonders, therefore, by what authority the commentator Theophilus, frequently quoted by Friar Thomas Aquinas, makes her withdraw before the birth:

> Et in hoc omnes postillatores concordant. Nescio ergo qua auctoritate unus Theophilus expositor, quem frequenter, immo communiter, allegat frater Thomas de Alquino, dicit sic: quando vero Elizabeth paritura erat, virgo recessit. . . . (MS. Laud misc. 165, fol. 39ᵛᵃ.)

The quotation comes from St. Thomas's *Catena aurea* on St. Luke under the name Theophilus.[2] "Frater Thomas" occurs in MS. Merton 157, fol. 17ʳᵇ, as well as in the Laudian MS. Merton MS. 156, fol. 19ʳᵃ, has "sanctus Thomas". It also has a reference to the *Summa Theologica* (2a 2ae, a. 1, q. 124) with the words "et hoc tenet Thomas" following on a question about the slaughter of the Innocents, fol. 35ʳᵇ, where the other two copies have no such reference. MS. Merton 156 must represent a later tradition.

---

[1]) *Ibid.*, 99.

[2]) I used the edition of the *Catena aurea* in the *Opera* of St. Thomas, vol. XV, Venice, 1593. For this quotation, see fol. 39ʳ. The Greek sources of the *Catena aurea* have not been studied. No fragments from Theophilus have been found in the Greek *catenae* on the gospels; see R. Devresse, art. 'Chaînes, exégétiques grecques', *Dictionnaire de la Bible*, Suppl. I, ed. L. Pirot, Paris, 1928, col. 1084-1233. Nor do the quotations in the *Catena aurea* occur in the Latin compilation on the gospels, wrongly ascribed to Theophilus, ed. T. Zahn, *Der Evangeliencommentar des Theophilus von Antiochen*, Forschungen zur Geschichte des neutestamentliche Kanons, 2 [1883], 29-85; see O. Bardenhewer, *Patrology*, translated from 2nd ed. by T. J. Shahan, Freiburg i. Br. and St. Louis, Mo., 1908, p. 67. St. Thomas's 'Theophilus', therefore, remains to be identified.

The 'frater' in the early tradition of the text puts the commentary before Thomas's canonization, July 18, 1323. It would fit the lectorship of William II, about 1312, very well indeed, and the rather grudging tone of his allusion agrees with the attitude of his Order at the turn of the century. This has been characterized as "thoroughly anti-Thomist, but the opposition was not given a clearly defined official expression".[1]

In spite of his scruple William has made extensive use of the *Catena aurea*. He quotes Theophilus many times, evidently by way of the *Catena*, since the quotations correspond,[2] and some of his other authorities, St. Basil, for instance, may have come from the same collection.[3] There is a parallel in his prologue, where he discusses the four senses of Scripture. He approaches the Thomist formulation, but does not adopt it whole-heartedly. The passage gives an interesting example of the way in which Thomas could influence, without radically altering, a deeply-rooted tradition. William quotes the current verse about the four senses:

> Littera gesta docet, quid credas allegoria,
> moralis quid agas, quid speres anagogia.

He proceeds to criticize it as too condensed and unclear. The literal or historical sense expresses the 'first intention' of the sacred writer. Hence it includes figures of speech and so it cannot correctly be described as simply narrative: "littera gesta docet." William gives a painstaking account of the difference between the literal sense, which includes both narrative and metaphor, and the mystical sense. Thomas, however, had defined the literal sense as covering the whole meaning of the sacred writer, while the mystical sense was the signification which God, the first author of Scripture, had put into sacred history.[4] William lays more stress on the three mystical senses, allegory, tropology and anagogy, than Thomas or Albert

---

[1] M. Burbach, *Early Dominican and Franciscan Legislation regarding St. Thomas*, Mediaeval Studies, Toronto, 4 [1942], 149.

[2] I compared William's quotations of Theophilus in MS. Merton 156, fol. 6rb, 6vb, 7ra, 17vb with St. Thomas's in the *Catena aurea, op. cit.*, fol. 213v, 214, 214v, 138v. They give the same excerpts on the same texts.

[3] MS. Merton 156, fol. 18ra, *Catena aurea*, fol. 138v. There is the same quotation from St. Basil on Luc. i 49: *et sanctum nomen eius.*

[4] *Summa theologica*, I q. i, a. 10; *Quodlibet* vii a, 14-16.

had done. He is reacting against the vagueness and imprecision of the traditional formula, but he cannot bring himself to accept the only doctrine that clears up the muddle. He gets as far as using the Thomist expression, "the literal sense is what the author intended"; he does not like to say that the mystical sense goes beyond the human author's intention. Instead he equates it with the author's 'second intention', which he explains in a lengthy account of the distinction between the literal sense understood in this way and the mystical sense.

Sensus scripture quatuor. Multiplicitas enim sensuum consistit in quaternario numero. Est enim sensus historicus, allegoricus, ⟨moralis⟩, anagogicus. Primus docet quid sit actum, secundus quid sit credendum, tertius quid agendum, quartus quid sperandum, unde:

> Littera gesta docet, quid credas allegoria,
> moralis quid agas, quid speres anagogica.

Et sic communiter dicitur, sed iudicio meo nimis diminute et obscure, et ideo est advertendum quod sensus litteralis seu hystorialis est qui primo intenditur ab auctore et hic duplex est, unus proprius, ille scilicet qui surgit ex prima vocis significatione, verbi gratia, *In principio creavit Deus celum et terram.*[1] Prima huius vocis significatio est creatio vel productio celi et terre ab ipso Deo in principio mundi vel temporis. . . . Est etiam alius sensus litteralis, scilicet figurativus, qui consurgit ex secunda vocis significatione ab auctore intenta vel ab auctoris intentione elicita, verbi gratia, Gen. 49, ubi dicitur: *Beniamin lupus rapax*[2] et Iudicum capitulo 9: *Inierunt consilium ligna silvarum ut ungerent super se regem.*[3] Planum est quod sensus quos iste enuntiationes faciunt per se ex sua prima significatione false sunt. Nam planum est quod Beniamin fuit frater uterinus Ioseph, non est ergo lupus etc. Similiter patet de aliis, et tamen utraque littera sensualiter est vera sive verus sermo. . . . Quid autem fuerit de prima intentione ipsius Iacob verba illa proferentis, *Beniamin lupus rapax*, vel etiam Spiritus sancti eadem inspirantis difficile est dicere. . . .[4] Ex quibus patet quod sensus litteralis frequenter in scriptura exprimit alia quam res gestas et ideo forte non est idem dicere secundum acceptionem auctorum et quoad significata vocabulorum sensus litteralis et sensus historicus, quia sensus historicus solum respicit res gestas. . . . Sensus autem litteralis est plus, quia non solum res gestas, sed etiam alia exprimit,

---

[1]) Gen. i 1.

[2]) Gen. xlix 27.

[3]) Iud. ix 8.

[4]) William here compares the interpretations of the passage given by Jerome, Isidore and Augustine.

ut dictum est. Loquendo tamen de sensu isto qui precise dividitur contra sensum misticum, prout etiam nunc loquimur, secundum communem modum loquendi, indifferenter litteralis, historicus seu hystorialis, qui nichil aliud est quam rerum gestarum vel figuratarum explicatio, que vel ex prima littere significatione vel ex prima loquentis intentione consurgit. Omnis autem sensus qui secundo intenditur ab auctore misticus est. . . . Est autem triplex sensus misticus. . . . (fol. 14ra-b.)

William II, therefore, is the author of the postill, and the sole author. It is a product of the early fourteenth century. The references to Thomas Docking and to Brother Thomas of Aquino do not stand alone. They could not possibly have been interpolated into a commentary written in the mid-thirteenth century. The use of 'correctores', quoted as such, the borrowing from Bonaventure, the near-Thomism of the doctrine on the four senses of Scripture, the lack of manuscripts or notices of them before the second half of the fourteenth century, all this points to an original composition by William II. A. G. Little was mistaken in ascribing it to William I; but what a natural mistake! It must be rare in the history of bibliography to find that two men of the same name, of the same Order, separated by some sixty years, should have been associated in the same work. The share of William I is limited to a transcript of Clement of Lanthony, a transcript of a table of canons and an explanatory note which occupies little more than a column in a folio volume. His authorship of even this modest piece is problematic, resting on an interpretation of Eccleston in the light of the manuscript evidence. It seems certain, however, that he popularized Clement at least among the Oxford Minorites, and his apparatus must have given William II the idea for a work which became classic in England.

Now that the authorship of the postill has been established, one hopes that it will be used for the study of theology and of learning in Oxford in the early fourteenth century. Here is a solid, popular book to swell the evidence for a neglected time.

12

JOHN BACONTHORPE'S POSTILL ON ST. MATTHEW

I

BACONTHORPE AND HIS POSTILL

THE Carmelite Order was just coming on to the academic map when Baconthorpe joined it and was sent to study at Oxford and Paris. Making due allowance for different circumstances, one can see some of the characteristics which the Dominicans had shown at a similar stage of development some hundred years earlier. There was an enthusiasm for Biblical studies based on the old religious obligation to *lectio divina*.[1] This coincided with a general revival of Biblical studies. Postills on Scripture become rare at the end of the thirteenth century and beginning of the fourteenth. Then they multiply quite suddenly. It is enough to mention the names of Augustine of Ancona, O.E.S.A., Dominic Grima, Peter de la Palu, Nicholas Trevet, Thomas Waleys, Robert Holcot, O.P., and Nicholas of Lyre, Peter of Aurioli, Henry of Carreto, O.F.M. We need not ascribe the revival to any single cause, but John XXII most certainly gave it every encouragement. Dominic Grima, Henry of Carreto and the Carmelite Guy Terré, one of Baconthorpe's masters, all dedicated Biblical works to John XXII.[2] He gave a hundred golden florins to the friar who presented him with the *magnum opus* of Nicholas of Lyre.[3] John did his best to promote learning both in universities and in individual scholars.[4] An Avignon correspondent of the Oxford University Chancellor, Master John de Lutterel, writing sometime between October 1317 and October 1322,

---

[1] See the notices of Carmelite masters by the Carmelite chronicler, John Trisse (d. 1363), ed. B. Xiberta, *De scriptoribus scholasticis saeculi XIV ex ordine Carmelitanorum* (Louvain, 1931), pp. 12, 25, 26, 31, 32, 33, 35.

[2] On Dominic Grima see *Histoire littéraire de la France* 36 (1927), 258, on Henry of Carreto, B. Smalley, "Some Latin Commentaries on the Sapiential Books in the late 13th and early 14th centuries," *Archives d'histoire doctrinale et littéraire du Moyen Age*, 18 (1951), 122; on Guy Terré, below, p. 106.

[3] *Histoire littéraire, op. cit.*, 358.

[4] See *Histoire littéraire, op. cit.*, 34 (1914), 521-27.

advises him to come to the Curia to seek advancement. The pope has recently transferred his affection altogether from lawyers to theologians and especially to masters in the sacred page. A theologian worthy of the name is sure of his liberality. Lutterel took the advice, came to Avignon and did very well for himself.[1]

Baconthorpe contributed to the revival. Only his postill on St. Matthew has survived intact out of an impressive series of postills, but this is an ample and highly personal specimen of exegesis.

The Carmelites were bound to John XXII by a special tie of gratitude. He protected them and raised them to the same level as the Orders of Preachers and Minors.[2] A faithful supporter of the pope could hardly keep clear of the great conflicts of his reign. John XXII engaged in three major academic controversies which intermingled with politics. He determined against the Franciscan view of evangelical poverty. The Franciscans had built up their Order on the assumption that Christ and his apostles had owned no property either severally or in common. A system had been devised whereby the friars had the use but not the legal ownership of their endowments. By annulling this system and declaring that Christ and the apostles had owned such possessions as they had in use, John was striking both at the ideal and at the institution. He also condemned the *Defensor pacis* written by Marsilio of Padua in defence of the emperor Louis of Bavaria in his quarrel with the papacy. The two conflicts merged, since the irreconcilables among the Franciscans took refuge with Louis. Lastly John put forward a personal view on the beatific vision; he held that the souls of the faithful departed when released from purgatory did not enjoy the full vision of God until after the Resurrection and Last Judgment. This modified the previously received view that the perfect vision of God was immediate on release from purgatory and ascent to

---

[1] *Snappe's Formulary*, ed. H. E. Salter (Oxford, 1924), 303-305: ... dominus noster summus pontifex magnam et specialem affectionem, quam pre hiis temporibus pretextu sapientie civilis erga iuristas conceperat, modo de novo ad theologos et maxime ad magistros in sacra pagina transtulit integre et perfecte; adeo quod quiscumque magister expertus re et nomine in theologia, dignus habere nomen magisterie dignitatis, hic ad sedem apostolicam veniens, a curia non recedit. ... Pro constanti scio quod cum huc venissetis ... quod plus in brevi reportaretis comodi et honoris, quam unquam de omnibus scolasticis actibus habuistis.

The whole letter is interesting. I have to thank Mr. W. A. Pantin for pointing it out to me.

[2] B. Xiberta, *De scriptoribus scholasticis saec. XIV ex ordine Carmelitanorum* (Louvain, 1931), 131.

heaven. John's opinion aroused so much criticism that he retracted on his deathbed. Though not directly related to politics, this third controversy caused ill feeling and served as another handle against the pope for his many enemies. All three raised important problems concerning the relations between Church and State and papal supremacy over the Church.

Here we have the background to Baconthorpe on St. Matthew. He entered the lists as a champion of the papacy and hence of John XXII in his struggles. The postill has considerable historical interest in showing the close connexion between Oxford and Avignon in the early fourteenth century. It also throws light on Oxford teaching in a little-known period. My study will hardly do justice to the rich material that the postill contains. I shall present it mainly as a "period piece", leaving out the theology and dwelling on the method and on Baconthorpe's political theory.

The spade-work for a study of Baconthorpe in any capacity has all been done by Father B. Xiberta. He has worked out the details of Baconthorpe's life and writings, has described his Sentence-commentaries and Quodlibets and discussed his place in fourteenth-century theology.[1] He has edited the *quaestio* on the Immaculate Conception from the postill on St. Matthew,[2] made some extracts from other places and fixed its relationship to the various Sentence-commentaries. This paper can start where he left off with many acknowledgments to him for laying so solid a foundation.

The essential facts as established by Xiberta are as follows:[3] John Baconthorpe, whose name is spelt in many different ways, was born in Norfolk towards the end of the thirteenth century, joined the Carmelite Order in his youth, studied at Oxford, where he had Robert Walsingham, O. Carm., as his master about 1312, and went on to Paris. Here he had Guy Terré as master. He probably read the Bible and *Sentences* at Paris before Whitsuntide, 1318, and was regent before Whitsuntide, 1324. He held a quodlibet at Paris in 1330. He was provincial of his Order in England between 1327 and 1333. Later he taught at Cambridge and probably also at Oxford, since he disputed with Bradwardine of Merton.

---

[1] *Ibid.*, 167-227; B. Xiberta, "De Iohanne Baconthorpe O. Carm.," *Analecta Ordinis Carmelitanorum*, 6 (1927), 3-128, 516-25.

[2] *Ibid.*, 521-25.

[3] Xiberta, *De scriptoribus, op. cit.*, 167-76.

We shall see that the postill shows some indications of an Oxford origin. There seems to be no place in his life for a degree in canon law, as stated by Bale. He was too young to be a qualified canonist when he joined the Order and as a religious he was restricted to theology. The mistake probably arose from the fact that he called one of his commentaries on Book IV of the *Sentences* "Quaestiones canonicae", and that he quotes the canon law very frequently. Baconthorpe may have been present as "Iohannes anglicus Carmelita" at the recantation of John of Pouilly at Paris, 1321, and he may have been summoned to Avignon with two other members of his Order to defend the pope against attacks on papal authority during his provincialate. He died after 1345 and before 1352, probably in 1348, at the Carmel of London or of Blakeney, where he had first joined the Order. The "doctor resolutus" is described by the Carmelite chronicler, John Trisse, who joined the Order in Baconthorpe's lifetime in 1338, as "minimus in persona sed maximus sapientia et doctrina".[1]

The list of the postills given by Bale covers most of the Old and New Testament.[2] We should probably withdraw the Psalter, since the incipit, "*Beatus qui custodit verba* . . . Apoc. xxii, Crisostomus in homelia super Matheum . . .", is that of a Psalter-commentary by Thomas Waleys, O.P.[3] The postills on St. Paul survive in a *quaestio* from Baconthorpe on Romans printed at the end of his commentary on Book III of the *Sentences*.[4] Xiberta found quotations from Baconthorpe on Romans, Galatians and Hebrews in his theological works and in the postills of Michael of Bologna, a Carmelite exegete of the later fourteenth century. The Paris Carmel had those on Romans, Corinthians I and II and Hebrews.[5] We shall see that he quotes his postill on the Fourth Gospel.[6] Bale gives incipits of two

---

[1] Xiberta, "De Iohanne," 26.

[2] Xiberta, *De scriptoribus*, 185-7. My statements about Baconthorpe's life and writings come from *De scriptoribus* unless any other source is mentioned. John Bale has notices of Baconthorpe in his *Index*, ed. Poole and Bateson (Oxford, 1902), 178-80, his *Illustrium Scriptorum Maioris Britanniae Summarium* (Ipswich, 1548), fol. 137ʳ⁻ᵛ, and in his manuscript note-books, MSS. Oxford, Bodl. 73 (*Summary Catalogue*, no. 27635), fol. 39ᵛ, 207ᵛ, London, British Museum, Harl. 1819, fol. 7, 10, 153. Xiberta has used them all. See also F. Stegmüller, *Repertorium biblicum Medii Aevi* (Madrid, 1951), no. 4167-4219.

[3] B. Smalley, "Thomas Waleys, O.P.," *Archivum Fratrum Praedicatorum* 24 (1954), 66-71.

[4] Ed. Milan, 1511, vol. II, fol. 122ᵛ-3ᵛ.

[5] Xiberta, 186.

[6] Below, p. 296

poſtills on St. Matthew,[1] but one of these is a ghoſt: the firſt is the incipit of Baconthorpe's "Proteſtatio fidei" at the beginning of his comment on the text, the second that of his comment on the prologue *Matheus qui et Levi*.[2] Bale may have seen two manuscripts which put them in different orders. Our one surviving copy begins with the comment on the prologue; the "proteſtatio fidei" would come more logically before than after it and probably did so in some copies. All the other poſtills liſted seem to have disappeared for good. The moſt promising line of research would be to ſtudy the unprinted commentaries of Michael of Bologna on Matthew and Luke.[3] If it turned out by collation that he quoted Baconthorpe on St. Matthew either by name or anonymously, then there would be a chance of disinterring some of Baconthorpe on St. Luke.

The surviving copy of the poſtill on St. Matthew is in MS. Cambridge, Trinity College B.15.12 (348), carefully described in the catalogue of M. R. James.[4] It will be unnecessary here to do more than summarize and supplement the catalogue. The firſt item in the volume has not so far been identified. It is the poſtill on St. John's gospel by St. Bonaventure (fol. 1ra-98va), a very widespread and popular work.[5] Baconthorpe on St. Matthew occupies fol. 99ra-191ra. There is a ſubjeĉt index to his poſtill on fol. 191va-194ra, arranged in alphabetical order, but keeping to the chapters of St. Matthew; thus each chapter is supposed to treat of one ſubjeĉt only. The whole volume was written by Thomas Yarmouth, O. Carm., in 1448. The explicit (fol. 191ra) reads:

Explicit poſtilla bona super Matheum edita a fratre Iohanne Bacunsthorpe doĉtore in sacra theologia ordinis beate Marie genetricis Dei de monte Carmeli, in qua oſtenditur quod Chriſtus eſt verus messias per prophetias et eius opera. Ipsi sit gloria in secula seculorum. Amen. Scripta per manum fratris Thome Zernemouth, anno Domini m°cccc°xl°viii°, ordinis eiusdem.

There was an explicit in much the same terms at the end of the poſtill on St. John (fol. 98va), but it has been erased. A photograph taken under

---

[1]) *Summarium, op. cit.,* fol. 137ᵛ.

[2]) Stegmüller, *op. cit.,* no. 590.

[3]) Stegmüller, *op. cit.,* no. 5607-8.

[4]) *Catalogue of the MSS. in Trinity College, Cambridge,* i (Cambridge, 1900), 475-6.

[5]) *S. Bonaventurae Opera omnia* vi (Quaracchi, 1893), 246-530.

ultra-violet light just shows the words after "Explicit", which has been left untouched, "postilla bona super evangelium Iohannis" and the name Thomas Yarmouth with the date 1448 at the end. Though a few other letters and words can be read in the six lines of the erasure it is not possible to make out the attribution. However, we can be sure that the postill on St. John was not ascribed to Baconthorpe, whether it had the correct attribution to Bonaventure or not. The incipit has also been erased after the words "Incipit postilla notabilis super Iohannem" and a seventeenth-century hand has written "Bacunsthorpii" over the erasure (fol. 1ra). Another seventeenth-century inscription in what looks like the same hand on the flyleaf is an extract from a notice of Baconthorpe by Bale. The writer may have been the John Thornton who owned the book in 1614 according to a note on the end flyleaf. A fifteenth-century hand has written "Bacunsthorpii postille" on the first flyleaf. John Thornton or another owner may have erased the incipit and explicit of the postill on St. John because he thought that Baconthorpe either was or ought to have been the author of both postills. The book belonged to Thomas Whalley, Vice-Master of Trinity in 1637, who gave it to his college.[1] James describes the script as a "good and rather unusual upright hand". The scribe, Thomas Yarmouth, must have had a good exemplar; there are not many mistakes. The marginal notes (mainly "Nota" with a line down the side) show that the book was studied. The incipits and explicit of the postill on St. Matthew are:

Incipit postilla magistri Iohannis Bacunsthorp ordinis beate Marie genetricis Dei de monte Carmeli super Matheum. Prologus. *Matheus etc.* Hic prologus dividitur in iv partes. In prima parte describitur evangeliste status . . . (fol. 99ra).

In hac postilla per concordiam prophetiarum et miraculorum Christi . . . (fol. 99va).

There follows a list of 27 "conditiones messie", to prove that Christ fulfilled the Old Testament prophecies.

Protestatio fidei. Dicit apostolus ad Hebr. xi sine fide impossibile est placere Deo . . . (fol. 100ra).

---

[1] The mediaeval ownership of the manuscript has not been traced. The pressmark "e. 19" on the flyleaf suggested to James the library of the Friars Minor at Hereford, but this has been rejected by N. R. Ker, *Medieval Libraries of Great Britain* (London, 1941), 54.

Modus procedendi in hoc opere erit secundum doctrinam Augustini ... (fol. 100ra).

Modus litteram introducendi. *Liber generationis etc.* Quia hoc evangelium incipit in Christo ... ideo ego Carmelita, beate Marie servus, licet indignus, primo incipio hanc postillam ... (fol. 100rb).

Litterales questiuncule ad naturam evangelii cognoscendum. Incipit evangelium. In primis notandum quod philosophus in primo libro philosophie ... (fol. 102vb).

Liber generationis. Hec genealogia dividitur in tres partes ... (fol. 103rb).

... de eius materia habes § ego baptizo in aqua (fol. 191ra).

There can be no question of the correctness of the ascription to Baconthorpe. Apart from the Carmelite scribe, Thomas Yarmouth, and the fact that the author calls himself "ego Carmelita", there are references to Baconthorpe's own surviving works and some passages reappear in his *Quaestiones canonicae*.[1]

Another copy existed in the Carmel of Ferrara. Here the list of 27 "conditiones messie" were placed at the end instead of the beginning of the postill.[2] This has disappeared. The postill is said to have been edited by Marasca, Madrid, 1754, but I have not seen the edition.[3]

II

DATE, PLACE AND SOURCES

Baconthorpe twice mentions the constitution *Benedictus Deus* of Benedict XII, promulgated on January 29, 1336. As the references come into his comments on Matthew v. 8 (fol. 126va) and Matthew viii. 11 (fol. 139ra), he may have seen it before he finished the postill. Although John XXII had died in 1334, the conflicts of his reign were still fresh in

---

[1] See below, p. 299.

[2] On this and other traces of manuscripts since lost see Xiberta, "De Iohanne Baconthorpe O. Carm.," *Analecta Ordinis Carmelitanorum* 6 (1927), 67.

[3] Stegmüller, no. 4200. Xiberta does not seem to have known of it.

Baconthorpe's mind and he often refers to them. This suggests either the year 1336 or soon afterwards. 1336 would be moderately late in his teaching career. This is borne out by allusions to his earlier works. He refers to his commentary on Book III of the *Sentences*, which Xiberta has dated in its complete form to his regency at Paris, about 1325,[1] and to his third Quodlibet, given at Paris in 1330.[2] Baconthorpe also sends us to commentaries on the Gospel of St. John[3] and on the *Ethics*,[4] both of which are recorded but lost.

The sources indicate that he was working in England rather than in Paris. He uses a commentary which became a classic in England in the fourteenth century but was hardly known on the Continent except in late extracts, William of Nottingham on Clement of Lanthony.[5] Nottingham gave his postill on the gospel-harmony of Clement as a lecture course when he was regent in the Franciscan school at Oxford about 1312. Baconthorpe refers to it as *postilla*, conveying the impression that he thought of it as a standard work, a modern supplement to the *Glossa ordinaria*:

Et ostendit illi omnia regna mundi (Matt. iv. 8): Qualiter potuit diabolus hoc ostendere? Respondet postilla quod hoc potuit facere ostendendo sibi figuras

---

[1] On Matt. xxii. 1: In hoc precepto secunde tabule comprehenditur dilectio sui ipsius et proximi. Quantum ad primum est duplex intellectus. Unus est falsus, (scilicet) quod quia unumquodque diligitur secundum quod est conveniens diligenti et magis convenit diligere bonum suum quam alienum, homo debet se diligere super omnia. Hoc reprobatur in dilectione naturali, libri iii lecture mee, dist. xxviii (fol. 172vb).

See Baconthorpe's commentary on III *Sent.*, dist. xxviii (ed. Milan, 1511), vol. II, fol. 94ra-95rb.

[2] On Matt. xviii. 1: (marginal heading: De modo cognoscendi angelorum) Secundus modus cognoscendi, quo scilicet superiores cognoscunt inferiores angelos ac etiam quecumque alia creata, habet difficultatem. . . . Sed qua ratione hoc est possibile in habitu vel specie, eadem ratione et in essentia angeli. De hoc diffuse quodlibet ii meo, q. vi (fol. 161rb).

The "ii" in the manuscript is a mistake for iii, and the "vi" for v, since the question is treated in the Quodlibet III, q. 5: Utrum angelus intelligendo se intelligat alia a se (ed. Venice, 1527, fol. 51ra). The same quotations from Aquinas and Henry of Ghent appear in both the postill and the Quodlibet III.

[3] On Matt. iii. 16: et ideo quod fuerunt baptizati baptismo Christi et aque ponitur super Iohannem, cap. iv, post principium (fol. 120ra).

[4] On Matt. vii. 13, Baconthorpe is recommending the "happy mean" in judgment: Ergo si vultis esse virtuosi iudices et premium virtutis accipere, *intrate per angustam portam*, id est, nonobstante difficultate, iuste iudicate, quia licet pauci per hanc viam vadunt, hec tamen est via que ducet ad vitam, sicut et spatiosa ducet ad mortem. Maior et minor diffuse tractantur II Ethicorum (fol. 136vb).

[5] For a discussion of the authorship and list of manuscripts of the full work and of its abbreviations, see *Mediaeval and Renaissance Studies*, vol. III, pp. 200-38.

omnium in instrumento artificialiter depicto sicut mappa mundi. Chrysostomus respondet melius ... (fol. 121ra).

The question, the first reply and the second reply, ascribed to Chrysostom, are all to be found in Nottingham (MS. Bodl. Laud. misc. 165, fol. 91va). Baconthorpe has borrowed long passages with only a few omissions, but without naming his source, on the mission of St. John the Baptist and on the whole story of the temptation in the wilderness (fol. 118vb-121vb, MS. Laud. misc. 165, fol. 81va-82ra, 86ra, 90ra, 91vb). This accounts for his quotation from Clement of Lanthony (fol. 120rb), who is quoted by Nottingham (MS. Laud. misc. 165, fol. 90ra). After Matthew iv. 11, Baconthorpe seems to have put Nottingham aside and I have found no further evidence of borrowing. The reason was probably that he thought it too complicated to use a postill on a conflated text of the gospels, especially so vast and elaborate as Nottingham's.

He also had an English handbook to canon law, the *Summa summarum* of William of Pagula, composed about 1320-31.[1] Baconthorpe quotes him as "ille qui fecit Summam summarum" (fol. 120ra) in a reference to Pagula's views on the baptism of the apostles, found in Book III, chapter 52 of his *Summa* (MS. Bodl. 293, fol. 146vb). Elsewhere he quotes the title: "Hoc habes in Summa summarum" (fol. 120va) on the question of fasting, referring to Book III, chapter 56 (MS. Bodl. 293, fol. 149ra). On dispensations from fasting he gives a joint reference to the *Summa summarum* and the *Summa confessorum* of John of Freiburg:

In Summa summarum et Summa confessorum habes multos casus expressos necessitatis excusantes ... (fol. 120vb-121ra).

Collation shows that he drew his material directly from the *Summa summarum*, Book III, chapter 56 (MS. Bodl. 293, fol. 149ra-va), though taking an occasional look at the *Summa confessorum* for the appropriate section (ed. Lyons, 1518, fol. 35r, v). We shall see that he uses the *Summa summarum* without acknowledgment in other places. His acquaintance with the

---

[1] L. E. Boyle, "The 'Oculus Sacerdotum' and Other Works of William of Pagula," *Transactions of the Royal Historical Society*, 5th series, vol. 5 (1955), p. 105. I am grateful to Fr. Boyle for helping me to find the quotations.

298

canons and canoniſts, overpowering at firſt sight, derives partly from this handy compilation.

He tells one ſtory that goes back to his Paris period to illuſtrate the dangers of sorcery apropos of the magi. An abbot employed a magician to find him treasure, but was discovered and died wretchedly in the bishop's prison; his corpse was thrown out to be execrated by the people. The magician was taken to judgment in a cart with the cat he had used for his sorcery. Baconthorpe places the incident at Paris in the year 1326:

Item finaliter teruntur et infeliciter moriuntur, ut anno Domini m°cccxxvi° patuit Parisius. Inquiri enim fecit quidam abbas de quodam thesauro per quendam nigromanticum et capti fuerunt. Abbas vero miserabiliter eſt mortuus in carcere episcopi et proieƈtus coram toto populo in curia palatii ad inspiciendum et maledicendum. Magus vero cum catto (MS. taƈto) suo in quo sortilegium suum fecerat in curru quodam duƈtus eſt ad iudicium malediƈtum et tunc potuit dicere: Contritio et infelicitas in viis eorum[1] (fol. 113ᵛᵇ).

The continuators of Gerard de Frachet and Guillaume de Nangis tell the same tale with many more details, identifying the abbot and mentioning other ecclesiaſtics concerned. They put it under the year 1323.[2] Baconthorpe may have misremembered the year or the "vi" in the manuscript may be a miſtake for "iii". He does not copy from the chronicles, for his account, though summary, gives additional details, the caſting out of the abbot's body into the courtyard and the fate of the cat.[3] His manner of telling the ſtory suggeſts that he was addressing an English audience which would not previously have heard it. There is every reason, therefore, to assign the poſtill to his teaching at Oxford or Cambridge in the academic

[1]) Ps. xiii. 3.
[2]) Recueil des hiſtoriens, vol. XXI (1854), pp. 60-1; Société de l'hiſtoire de la France, vol. II (1843), p. 47.
[3]) The use of a magically processed cat to discover loſt treasure reſts on a long-lived superſtition. Mr. Emden points out to me that John Stokesly, afterwards bishop of London, when bursar of Magdalen paid aſtrologers to hunt for college treasure loſt in the previous year, 1502/3. At the visitation of the college in 1506/7 he was accused of baptizing a cat at Collyweſton, his native place. See W. D. Macray, A Regiſter of the Members of St. Mary Magdalen College, Oxford, N.S. vol. I (London, 1894), pp. 32-3, 46-7. As he purged himself from the two charges together, of praƈtising witchcraft to find treasure and of baptizing a cat, it seems that they were conneƈted (ibid., pp. 58-9). The Paris cat was anointed with holy oil.

year 1336/7 or soon afterwards. That he intended it for a lecture course
appears from his prologue:

Deo igitur duce, intendo in postillatione evangeliorum ut melius et universalius singuli in lectionibus ordinariis eruditionem inveniant . . . (fol. 100ra-b).

The *terminus ante quem* would be given by the composition of Baconthorpe's *Quaestiones canonicae* on Book IV of the *Sentences*, which Xiberta
has dated about 1340. He puts the postill before these *Quaestiones* because
its teaching on the Immaculate Conception stands half-way between that
of the commentary on Books II and III of the *Sentences*, finished about
1325, and that of the *Quaestiones canonicae* on Book IV; Baconthorpe at
first opposed the "pia sententia" of the Immaculate Conception, but
gradually came round to it.[1] This order would be borne out by the fact that
Baconthorpe refers to his commentary on Book III of the *Sentences*, as we
have seen, but does not mention the *Quaestiones canonicae*.[2] On the contrary,
he seems to have incorporated a number of passages from the postill into
his *Quaestiones canonicae*. Comparison shows that the passages in the
Quaestiones look like excerpts. Two of them represent *quaestiones* on the
doctrine of the beatific vision propounded by John XXII. We shall discuss
Baconthorpe's views on the problem later. Here it will be enough to show
how he has shortened a passage from the postill. The first *quaestio* which
is identical in the two works discusses the texts from St. Bernard on which
John XXII relied for his opinion on the beatific vision, concluding that
the pope's deduction from the texts was insufficiently founded: "ergo
anime sanctorum sunt in regno celorum." The postill then discusses St.

---

[1] G. P. B. Couto, "Doctrina Ioannis Baconthorpe," *Carmelus* 2 (1955), 54-84.

[2] Xiberta says that another *quaestio* from the postill is in the commentary on Book III of the
Sentences at dist. 20 (p. 186, n. 1). The two *quaestiones* at the end of III, 20, which might possibly also
occur in the postill are: "Utrum per sacram scripturam et per computationem iudeorum possit probari
quod adventus messie in carnem et ad passionem etc. sit factus in preterito et non expectandus in futuro
(vol. II, fol. 69ra)" and "Utrum per auctoritates iudeorum possit probari quod messias cuius passio erat
promissa venerit in preterito (*ibid.*, fol. 71va)." Neither bear any relation to any part of the postill.
Xiberta may have been misled by the list of topics to be discussed in the postill which follows the commentary on St. Jerome's prologue. The first item reads: "In hac postilla per concordantiam prophetarum
et miraculorum Christi probatur quod Christus est messias in lege promissus, quod negant iudei (fol.
99va)." This certainly sounds as though it might be identical with the discussion in the Sentence-
commentary. In fact the matter as well as the wording differs.

Augustine's teaching on the subject, again deciding against the pope: "et sic habetur propositum et quod iusti, id est anime iustorum, sunt in regno celorum et quod plene perfruuntur Dei visione et presentia." It goes straight on:

> Ex hac sententia Augustini videtur fuisse sumpta condempnatio erroris grecorum xxvii in concilio Lugdunum (fol. 117vb).

The section in the *Quaestiones canonicae* omits the discussion of Augustinian teaching and passes to the condemnation of the Council of Lyons:

> Hec sententia potest haberi ex condempnatione erroris grecorum in concilio Lugdunum (vol. II, fol. 198vb).

Then another identical passage begins. The omission and its smoothing over in the continuation points to an excerpt from the postill rather than to an enlargement in the postill of the *Quaestiones canonicae*.

Xiberta has noticed, however, that the postill itself may be drawing on some earlier writing by Baconthorpe on the beatific vision. Although he refers to the death of John XXII (fol. 117vb) and quotes from the constitution *Benedictus Deus* of 1336, by which Benedict XII had closed the controversy, in another *quaestio*, reproduced in the *Quaestiones canonicae*, he writes as though the matter were still open to discussion:

> De ista visione moderno tempore orta est disputatio in clero, quia licet sanctissimus pater dominus summus pontifex, ut dicitur, dixerit in quodam sermone quod sibi videbatur per dicta doctorum aliquorum et sanctorum quod anima beata non videbit divinam essentiam ante diem iudicii, palam protestando se nichil velle diffinire circa hoc absque consilio fratrum suorum, tamen, ut scriptum est michi de curia, sunt aliqui dicentes quod probabiliter possunt teneri articuli qui sequuntur.

He lists and discusses the articles, saying:

> Secundo, pono modum secundum quem aliqualiter dictum domini pape posset salvari (fol. 124^{va-b}).

The whole tone of the argument suggests that Baconthorpe was writing soon after hearing the news that John XXII had expressed his startling

view on the beatific vision in the winter, 1331/2, and before he heard of
John's retractation and death, December 3-4, 1334.[1] Since references to the
Benedictus Deus come both before and after the passage referring to John
XXII as still alive, we cannot suppose that news of the latest developments
reached Baconthorpe after he wrote this passage. It is more likely that he
revised an earlier draft of his postill.

Xiberta also pointed out that *quaestiones* 11 and 12 from dist. xxv of
the *Quaestiones canonicae* had already appeared in the postill. They have
been taken from the comment on Matthew iv. 22-3 (fol. 122va-124ra). Both
deal with the controversy on the poverty of Christ and with John XXII's
constitutions on the subject. The discussion in the postill again is fuller
than in the *Quaestiones canonicae*; the *quaestiones* 11 and 12 appear to be
extracts.

A block of *quaestiones* on the power of the keys on Matthew xvi. 17-19
(fol. 156vb-157va) are also found in the *Quaestiones canonicae* on *Sent.* IV,
dist. xvii, q. 1 (vol. II, fol. 108va-110va). The introductory phrases differ
in the postill and the *Quaestiones* and each has intersections of its own;
there is also a difference of order; the *quaestio* on whether the pope can
revoke an ordinance of a preceding pope, which comes at the end of the
whole discussion in the postill (fol. 157va), in the *Quaestiones* comes before
instead of after the *quaestio* on whether there are one or two keys (vol. II,
fol. 109ra-b). Otherwise the identity is complete apart from very slight
variations of wording. Again the *quaestiones* on the Eucharist on Matthew
xxvi. 26-29 (fol. 182ra-183va) reappear in the *Quaestiones canonicae* on *Sent.* IV,
dist. viii, q. 3 and q. 5 (vol. II, fol. 77va-79vb), with similar slight variations
in wording, length and order. Only one *quaestio*, "utrum Christus seipsum
sumpserit", in the postill (fol. 182va), does not appear in the *Quaestiones*.
Naturally the corresponding sections in the *Quaestiones* raise and discuss
more problems than the postill.

One *quaestio* in the section on baptism in the *Quaestiones* has been taken
from the postill: whether Mary and the Baptist received Christian baptism.
In the postill it ends with the reference to Baconthorpe's own work on the
Fourth Gospel, already quoted, in the *Quaestiones* with the words: "Creditur pie quod saltem fuerunt baptizati (*Sent.* IV, dist. v, q. 1, vol. II,

---

[1] See the summary in G. Mollat, *Les papes d'Avignon* (new ed., Paris, 1949), 54-6, 71.

fol. 77ra)." I have not found any other identical passages. It is significant that all belong to the *Quaestiones canonicae*, none to the earlier part of the *Sentence*-commentary.

Xiberta places the *Quaestiones canonicae* "probably at Oxford", because Baconthorpe claims to have caused Bradwardine, notorious for his views on freewill and predestination, to reformulate his thesis (*Sent.* IV, dist. 1, q. 4, vol. II, fol. 37vb). Baconthorpe touches on the same problem in his postill, though the argument follows a different line from that in the *Quaestiones*; he calls it the most difficult in the whole of theology:

Hoc probatur in difficillima materia totius theologie, verbi gratia cum arguitur: Deus prescivit tunc dampnandum, ergo necessario dampnabitur... (fol. 107rb).

Hence it seems that he was teaching in Bradwardine's Oxford, where predestination and necessity was the question of the hour.[1]

We can take it as probable, therefore, that the postill was prepared as a lecture course at Oxford between 1336 and about 1340, incorporating earlier material, and that Baconthorpe drew on it for his *Quaestiones canonicae*.

The exegetical sources are what we would expect in an up-to-date commentary of the period. Baconthorpe quotes the *Compendium litteralis sensus totius Biblie* of Peter Aurioli, published in 1319:

... omnes quatuor evangeliste singula capitula sua concordant cum auctoritatibus legis, ut patet in compendio Aurioli (fol. 110va).

He also takes some of the twenty-two *conditiones* for the gospel fulfilment of the Old Testament prophecies from the section on St. Matthew in the *Compendium*.[2] He makes constant use of the *Postilla litteralis* of Nicholas of Lyre. The actual name "Nicholaus de Lira", sometimes "Lyra", appears many times, beginning on the genealogy of Christ (fol. 103rb) and ending

---

[1] It may also be significant that he picks on Pelagianism as one of the principal heresies manifestly refuted in Scripture (fol. 125vb). And see below, p. 309.

[2] On the date and editions of the *Compendium*, which has been published many times, see P. Glorieux, *Répertoire des maîtres en théologie de Paris au XIIIe siècle* (Paris, 1933-4), no. 351 h.

on Matthew xxviii. 1 (fol. 189rb). The quotations are verbal.[1] Baconthorpe quotes him by name when comparing his views with those of earlier commentators, generally those found in the *Glossa ordinaria*. On Matthew xxiii. 15, *filium gehennae duplo*, Lyre is quoted as "quidam doctor" (fol. 174ra). On Matthew xvi. 1, *rogaverunt eum ut signum de caelo ostenderet eis*, Baconthorpe quotes first the explanation given in the *Glossa ordinaria*, which he calls "theological" (secundam glosam theologicam); then he goes on:

> Aliter philosophice secundum postillatores. Aliqui (MS. alique) enim scribe et pharisei iam omisso studio legis et prophetarum studebant in mathematicis et maxime in astrologia (fol. 156)^{ra}.

This second explanation comes verbally from Lyre. Many other passages have been lifted verbally or in substance from the same source. Whenever, in fact, one finds an arresting example of literal exegesis, it proves to be borrowed from the *Postilla litteralis* on St. Matthew. We know that Lyre composed his gospel-commentary before he embarked on his work of postillating the whole Bible. It must have existed in a first edition before 1322. It was then incorporated in the *Postilla* which Lyre began in 1322 and finished in 1329.[2] Baconthorpe knows not only the *Postilla* on St. Matthew but also that on Isaias. He quotes verbally from Lyre on Isaias vii. 14, *ecce virgo concipiet*; he is giving a string of proofs to confute the Jews:

> Quantum ad secundum, Nicholaus de Lira, qui fuit multum instructus in hebreo, arguit contra eos et dicit *almut* in hebreo significat absconsionem . . . idem est tenendum de tertia (fol. 109ra).

The passage comes from Lyre on the Isaias text and has no equivalent in Lyre on St. Matthew. He had reached the book of Isaias by 1327 and was working on Daniel in 1328. Baconthorpe was quoting him by name and

---

[1] I have collated Baconthorpe with Lyre in the edition published with the *Glossa ordinaria* and the additions of Paul of Burgos, Lyons, 1588-90. The editors claim to have used the autograph copy of the *Postilla litteralis* from Verneuil, the house where Lyre made his profession; see H. Labrosse, "Oeuvres de Nicholas de Lyre," *Etudes franciscaines* 19 (1909), 157. The references will be found in vol. VI, *ad loc.*

[2] The dates of Lyre's works, with a summary of the evidence for them, will be found in the *Histoire littéraire*, vol. XXXVI (1927), pp. 355-400.

with respect in his lifetime, since Lyre died in 1349, and quoting him, moreover, within about ten years of the completion of the *Postilla litteralis*. It is another witness to Lyre's brilliant reputation. Baconthorpe in his choice of sources indicates, too, the advance in Biblical studies in the early fourteenth century and its slowing down in the second half. He uses the same two writers, Lyre and Aurioli, as Wyclif in his postill on the Bible, composed some forty years later.[1]

Since Baconthorpe studied at Paris under Guy Terré, it seemed possible that he would use his master's *Summa de haeresibus* and gospel commentary. Terré composed a gospel harmony, based mainly on St. Augustine's *De concordia evangeliorum*, and provided it with a postill, on a more modest scale than Nottingham's postill on Clement. Baconthorpe shows no knowledge of the *Summa*, although he often deals with heresy, or of the postill. Probably they were written too late for him to use; Terré produced them while bishop of Elne, 1332-42.[2] Another possibility was his use of the marginal glosses in the Latin Bible, now MS. Oxford Laud. lat. 87, which he left to the London Carmel on his death. They proved to have no connexion with his postill. A reference to *postilla quedam* in the discussion of baptism remains irritatingly obscure:

Sed numquid mater Christi et Iohannes baptista fuerunt baptizati in aqua? Dicit postilla quedam quod non, quia non acceperunt Spiritum sanctum solum credendo sicut apostoli et alii catechumini, qui tamen essent in aqua baptizandi, ne contemptus religionis in eis appareret (fol. 119vb-120ra).

Baconthorpe himself disagrees with this view. He could not have found it in Hugh of St. Cher, whom surprisingly he does not seem to use, in St. Thomas, St. Albert, Nicholas Gorran or Augustine of Ancona on St. Matthew, or in any of his standard books. Presumably it comes from some lost record of Oxford or Paris teaching.

His theological reference book is the *Summa theologica* of St. Thomas,

---

[1] B. Smalley, "John Wyclif's Postilla super totam Bibliam," *Bodleian Library Record* 4 (1953), 190, 197.

[2] B. Xiberta, *Guidonis Terreni "Quaestio de magisterio infallibili Romani pontificis"* in Opuscula et textus, ed. M. Grabmann and Fr. Pelster (Munich, 1926), pp. 5-6. I used the 1528 edition of the *Summa de haeresibus* and the Cologne, 1631, edition of the *Quatuor unum*.

quoted frequently and exactly.[1] From time to time he refers to the Quod-libets of Henry of Ghent.[2] In his *quaestiones* on the keys of St. Peter he quotes Richard of Middleton,[3] Duns Scot,[4] and Peter of Tarentaise,[5] as well as St. Thomas on the *Sentences*.[6] It is noticeable that he confines him-self to theologians of the late thirteenth or very early fourteenth century. He does not quote contemporaries by name and seldom even anonymously. In this respect the postill contrasts strikingly with Baconthorpe's own theological works, where Xiberta has found so many names of con-temporaries. It also contrasts with his practice in the postill of quoting contemporary or nearly contemporary exegetes. In this, however, Bacon-thorpe seems to be following an established custom: the lecturer on Scrip-ture might be as "modern" as he liked in his choice of exegetical sources; he was conservative and traditional in his choice of theologians. Thus Henry of Ghent on the Hexaemeron quotes William of Auxerre, Philip the Chancellor, and even Simon of Tournai.[7] A postill on Scripture was not the place for theological speculation. The theological faculties provided ample opportunity to indulge in this elsewhere.

---

[1] III, q. xxxi, a. 5, ad 3 (fol. 108va); Suppl. q. lxxxiii, a. 2, ad 1 (fol. 108vb); III, q. xxv, a. 2 (fol. 111vb); II, ii, q. xxiv, a. 9 and q. xxvii, a. 7 (fol. 131vb); II, ii, q. cxi, a. 4 (fol. 133vb); III, q. lix, a. 4 (fol. 160vb, 187va); III, q. lxxviii, a. 3 (fol. 182rb); III, q. lxxxi, a. 1 (fol. 182vb). This is by no means a complete list.

[2] Henry's Quodlibet X, q. 6 (ed. Venice, 1613), fol. 149^{va-b}, is quoted twice (fol. 111^{va-b}). Baconthorpe also ascribes to him a saying which is not to be found in his *Summa* or *Quodlibets* and may perhaps derive from a sermon:

> Propter hoc dicit magister Henricus de Gandavo quod christiani non debent predicare saracenis, quia iam fecerunt statuta quod predicatores christianos interficere seu submergere (licet) (fol. 135vb).

[3] On IV *Sent.*, dist. xix, q. 1 (ed. Brescia, 1591), vol. IV, p. 312 (fol. 152va), and on IV *Sent.*, dist. xviii, q. 3, vol. II, p. 271 (fol. 157rb).

[4] On IV *Sent.*, dist. xix, q. 1, a. 2. Baconthorpe is referring to the view of Peter Lombard that only one key is conferred in ordination, and says: Propter istam rationem negat magistrum Ricardus, dist. xix, q. 1, et Scotus tenet idem, lib. IV, dist. xviii, a. 2 (fol. 152va). As he only says in general terms that Duns Scot disagreed with the Lombard on this point, it is impossible to know which of the Sentence-commentaries of Duns Scot is meant. See C. Balič, *Les commentaires de Jean Duns Scot sur les quatre livres des Sentences* (Louvain, 1927).

[5] On IV *Sent.*, dist. xviii, q. 1 (fol. 157rb), I checked the quotation from MS. Oxford, Bodl. Laud. misc. 605, fol. 67vb.

[6] On IV *Sent.*, dist. xviii, q. 1, ad. 3.

[7] B. Smalley, "A Commentary on the Hexaemeron by Henry of Ghent," *Recherches de théologie ancienne et médiévale*, 20 (1953), 63, 86, 89, 97-9.

306

Baconthorpe's other sources are unremarkable in a postill of the period and need no special comment.

III

PURPOSE, METHOD AND CONTENT

Baconthorpe sets out his purpose and method so clearly that we must begin with his own words. My account of the content of his postill will take the form of a comment on this introductory passage. Few teachers at any period of history can have had as fixed an idea of what they meant to avoid and what they meant to instil into their pupils as had this fourteenth-century Carmelite. Baconthorpe felt that some of his colleagues were frivolous and irrelevant, this at a time when the faith was in danger, when heretics were attacking the Church and when papal supremacy was being questioned. So he aimed at creating stalwart champions of the Church and the papacy. We shall see that he showed discrimination, both in his defence of the papacy and in the means he employed. He did not adopt the extreme position of some controversialists nor did he ban all pagan learning as an aid to exegesis. But wise moderation is often the most effective weapon in controversy.

Baconthorpe shall now speak for himself. He begins from the teaching of St. Augustine in the *De doctrina christiana* on spoiling the Egyptians: it is right for the Christian scholar to use pagan learning as an aid to preaching the gospel. Here he makes a distinction, not found in his source: it is *not* right to moralize pagan fables. His remarks on this point are so interesting that we shall study them in detail. Having justified his objection to fables, he outlines his positive programme. He will set forth briefly and pile up compendiously certain matters relating to philosophy (i.e. pagan philosophy) which contain truth, matters concerning theology and morals, and material from canon law, in order that each student may find better and more general information in his lecture course:

Modus procedendi in hoc opere erit secundum doctrinam Augustini, iio De doctrina christiana, cap. xvo, ubi docet quod si philosophi ac humanorum statutorum doctores aliqua vera dixerunt, in usum predicandi evangelium assumi

debent.[1] Non tamen sunt fabule poetarum admittende, immo nec moraliter expo-
nende in predicatione. In Decr. ii (*sic*) dist. lxxxvi, cap. *Cum multa,*[2] refert
Gregorius quod auditis studiis Desiderii episcopi tanta letitia cordi suo fuit innata
quod sibi negare que petivit non potuit, sed cum postmodum audivit quod grammaticam exposuit glosam, id est recitabat in ecclesia fabulas Iovis et eas moraliter
exponebat in predicatione sua,[3] hoc tam moleste suscepit et vehementius fuit
aspernatus ut ea bona que prius dicta fuerant in gemitum et tristitiam verterentur;
et addit rationem, quia in uno ore cum laudibus Iovis Christi laudes non capiunt.
Alia ratio est quia fabula per se significat falsum, sicut parabola per se exemplum
est veritatis significativum; sed falsum ubique est destruendum, non introducen-
dum; et ideo Philosophus tam in scientia speculativa quam morali primo destruxit
opiniones fabul(os)as et falsas et post veras construxit rationibus et exemplis, ut
patet primo Phisicorum, primo Metaphisice, primo Ethicorum; et hoc ostendit
figura. Quemadmodum enim populus Israel de Egipto exiens, egiptiorum orna-
menta de auro et argento et eorum vestes ad usum meliorem, et non auctoritate
propria, sed precepto Dei, vendicaverunt. . . .[4] Deo igitur duce, intendo in
postillatione evangeliorum, ut melius et universalius singuli in lectionibus ordinariis eruditionem inveniant, quedam philosophica spectabilia veritatis continentia
et moralia et iura canonica pariter cum theologicis breviter ponere et compendiose
cumulare (fol. 100ra-b).

We shall start from the negative part of his programme, his objection
to moralized fables. He supports it by the famous letter of St. Gregory I
to Bishop Desiderius, reproving Desiderius for teaching grammar: the
praises of Jove and of Christ should not issue from the same mouth.
Baconthorpe quotes the letter from Gratian's *Decretum*; it has the authority
of canon law. He brings the reproof up to date by giving it a very personal
interpretation. Gregory writes that Desiderius is reported "grammaticam
quibusdam exponere", which Baconthorpe renders as: "grammaticam
exposuit glosam". Then by a process of free association he interprets the

---

[1]) *De doctrina Christiana*, II, xl (60-61). This is a summary, not a verbal quotation.

[2]) Gratian, *Decretum* I, dist. lxxxvi, cap. 5, from St. Gregory's *Registrum*, lib. ix, ep. 48 (54).

[3]) The words, very freely rendered by Baconthorpe, are: Sed post hac pervenit ad nos . . .
fraternitatem tuam grammaticam quibusdam exponere. Quam rem ita moleste suscepimus, ac sumus
vehementius aspernati, ut ea, que prius dicta fuerant, in gemitum et tristitiam verteremus, quia in uno
se ore cum Iovis laudibus Christi laudes non capiunt.
Nothing in the *Glossa ordinaria* on this passage of the *Decretum* could have suggested Baconthorpe's
interpretation.

[4]) Baconthorpe here quotes from the passage in the *De doctrina christiana* referred to above, on
spoiling the Egyptians.

glossing of a grammatical text, together with the praising of Jove and of Christ simultaneously, to mean that Desiderius recited fables of Jove in church and moralized them in his preaching. He justifies himself further on the ground that "fable" by definition means "falsehood", as distinguished from "parable", which means "*exemplum* significative of truth". The term *exemplum* naturally includes the moral anecdotes used in contemporary sermons, as well as the gospel parables. But, he argues, a falsehood should be exploded, not introduced into teaching. We can learn from Aristotle's method of procedure in the *Physics*, *Metaphysics* and *Ethics*. The Philosopher always begins by exploding fables and false opinions; then he builds up true ones, by means of reasons and *exempla*. Baconthorpe returns to the attack in his comment on Matthew xiii. 18, discussing Christ's use of parables. He refers back to his introduction and quotes St. Gregory's letter all over again, giving it another gloss, which shows rather more clearly how he came to read "moralized fables" for "the praises of Jove" in his original. Christ is invoked when the preacher is inspired by the Holy Spirit to explain the mystical sense of parables; Jove's poet is invoked when he moralizes fables drawn from pagan poetry:

Nota quod per fabulas non est predicandum. Fabula enim, ut iam habitum est, in recto dicit falsum. Falsum enim non assumendum est in testimonium predicationis veritatis ... Quinimmo nec moraliter in predicatione debent exponi fabule poetarum; et ponitur ratio dist. lxxxvi, cap. *Cum multa*. In significationibus misticis parabolarum per Spiritum sanctum expositis laudatur Christus et similiter in figmentis poetarum moraliter expositis laudatur Iovis poeta et sic de aliis (fol. 151vb).

Baconthorpe holds to his principle with only one lapse: he quotes and moralizes the story of the conversion of Ulysses' companions into beasts, introducing it with the words "ut fertur in gentilium libris" (fol. 114ra). Otherwise he refrains from using poetic fables.[1]

---

[1] Baconthorpe tells only two other stories in his postill, apart from the personal reminiscence of the Paris magician already quoted: (1) Socrates makes a mirror for King Philip in which he sees two dragons at the top of a mountain (fol. 112va). From the Pseudo-Aristotelian *De causis et proprietatibus elementorum*; see the commentary of St. Albert, *Opera*, ed. Borgnet, ix (Paris, 1891), 643. (2) A certain man when asked why no one envied him answered that the only way to avoid envy was to be poor and inconspicuous (fol. 153rb). Baconthorpe must have taken this story from Walter Burley's *De vitis et moribus philosophorum*, ed. H. Knust (Tübingen, 1887), cap. 22, p. 88. He ascribes it to "Valerius

This was a very topical protest. The moral interpretation of myths went back to ancient times,[1] but only became a recognized part of sermon technique in the early fourteenth century. St. Gregory could hardly have forbidden it in a letter written in 601. Preachers of the later Middle Ages used to satisfy the general craving for "novelty" by telling stories from pagan sources, which they would moralize as they moralized the Bible, to illustrate some point of Christian doctrine. The worst offenders in Baconthorpe's eyes must have been wholesale producers, who would be retailed by individuals. An anonymous Franciscan moralized the *Metamorphoses* in French before 1329;[2] Peter Bersuire did the same in Latin 1337-1340.[3] Abundant material had been accumulating in manuals for preachers and Scripture commentaries intended for the use of preachers. Baconthorpe might have seen the Old Testament commentaries of Thomas Waleys, O.P., which originated as lectures given about 1320-1330 and circulated widely.[4] Moralized fables crowd thickly on his pages. More likely still, it was no random shot, but was aimed directly at another Oxford Dominican, Robert Holcot, who resigned his chair to his successor soon after 1333.[5] Holcot's great commentary on Wisdom, one of the most widely read of later mediaeval books, and equally crammed with fables, originated in Oxford lecture courses. Baconthorpe's colleagues and students would still be admiring or criticizing them when he was preparing his postill. The expert historian of mediaeval *exempla*, Fr. J.-Th. Welter, considers that Holcot's *Moralitates*, a collection of moralized fables from ancient sources, following on his commentary on Wisdom, mark a final stage in development:

Il faut arriver aux *Moralitates* pour vraiment voir la moralisation recevoir son plus ample développement. C'est dans ce petit recueil, en effet, comprenant une

---

Maximus, lib. iv", which is incorrect; the story does not come from Valerius. But Burley tells it about Simonides, after quoting several other stories of him from Valerius. Baconthorpe might well suppose that Valerius was the source for all of them.

[1] J. Seznec, *The Survival of the Pagan Gods* (translated from the French, New York, 1953), 84-94.

[2] J.-Th. Welter, *L'exemplum dans la littérature religieuse et didactique du Moyen Age* (Paris, Toulouse, 1927), p. 347, n. 35.

[3] *Ibid.*, 345-9. Bersuire began his work on Ovid at Avignon, corrected and revised it at Paris, 1340, and published two later redactions, 1340-1350.

[4] B. Smalley, "Thomas Waleys O.P.," *Archivum Fratrum Praedicatorum* 24 (1954), 50-107.

[5] J. C. Wey, "The 'Sermo finalis' of Robert Holcot," *Mediaeval Studies* 11 (1949), 219.

cinquantaine de récits se suivant au hasard et s'appliquant à des sujets moraux, que Robert Holcot nous a laissé de vrais *exempla* moralisés, dont il a trouvé les modèles du genre soit dans des traités et les recueils d'*exempla*, où le type de l'*exemplum* moralisé se trouvait à l'état isolé, soit dans les *Declamationes Senecae reductae ad moralitates* de son compatriote, Nicolas Trivet.[1]

Baconthorpe was protesting against a technique which reached its perfection just exactly when he was teaching. The ineffectiveness of his protest appears from the whole history of the later mediaeval sermon.[2] It is none the less significant in that it anticipates Wyclif's criticism of contemporary preachers.[3]

Baconthorpe notes a further difference between the preaching of Christ and that of contemporaries. Christ used parables, not fables, and he did not construct his sermons according to the elaborate rules recommended in the *Artes praedicandi*.[4] He did not proceed by division of themes, but by "real conclusions", which we might perhaps paraphrase as "plain statements". Baconthorpe does not expressly condemn the modern method of sermon construction, but shows how it differed from that of the Sermon on the Mount. He says on *Beati pacifici* (Matt. v. 9):

> Est ibi intelligendum quod Christus habuit formam predicandi non per thematum divisiones, sed per reales conclusiones; et secundum hoc hic sermo, qui durat usque ad viii capitulum, dividitur in quatuor conclusiones seu quatuor membra (fol. 124rb).

His disapproval of moralized fables in preaching extended to the study of classical poetry in general. He was consistent in his attitude. How consistent we shall discover if we digress for a moment to look at his short commentary on the *De civitate Dei*. Nicholas Trevet and Thomas Waleys indulged in a one-sided type of commentary on this work of St. Augustine.

---

[1] *Op. cit.*, p. 363. See also B. Smalley, "Robert Holcot O.P.", *Archivum Fratrum Praedicatorum* 26 (1956), 5-97.

[2] Welter, *op. cit.*, 409-52. The recently published sermons of Thomas Brinton have many moralized fables; *The Sermons of Thomas Brinton, Bishop of Rochester (1373-1389)*, ed. Sister Mary Aquinas Devlin (Camden 3rd Series, vol. 85-6, London, 1954), I, 41, 56, 220, II, 489.

[3] On expressions of disapproval of fables in preaching see Welter, *op. cit.*, p. 449, n. 62.

[4] See Th.-M. Charland, *Les "Artes Praedicandi". Contribution à l'histoire de la rhétorique au Moyen Age* (Paris, Ottawa, 1938).

They ignored the anti-pagan polemic in order to concentrate on the classical history and literature. The allusions interested them much more than the argument.[1] Our Carmelite's commentary is so unlike the Dominicans' as to suggest a deliberate contrast. Waleys wrote his at Bologna or Avignon about 1330-1333; Trevet wrote early enough for Waleys to use him; Baconthorpe's is dated after November 10, 1324, by a reference to the bull *Quia quorundam*. He may well have seen Trevet's commentary, even if Waleys' was too late for him. Baconthorpe's commentary exists in an autograph in MS. Paris, Bibliothèque nationale lat. 9540, fol. 76^r-216^v, following his commentary on St. Augustine's *De Trinitate*. He refers to the three bulls on evangelical poverty of John XXII (fol. 87^r). A closer study might date the commentary more exactly. He makes yet another attack on the use of moralized fables, with the same reference to St. Gregory's letter in the *Decretum* (fol. 76^v). He avoids quoting the poets. His introduction sounds like a reproach to the classicists. He summarizes St. Augustine's aim as the defence of the faith in the first ten books, the building up of the faith in the last twelve. In the first ten books Augustine uses arguments drawn from their own poets and historians to refute the idolators; in the following twelve he brings forward the Law and the Prophets. Baconthorpe intends to recast an obscure text in the form of "certain conclusions" and to put the meaning more clearly; he will "follow the letter and its sense in everything".

Intentio Augustini (in) libri(s) x[2] De civitate Dei est defendere fidem Christi contra cultores falsorum deorum per argumenta sumpta a suis poesibus et gestis. Effectus eius in xii sequentibus est introducere bibliam ad astruendum fidem christianam per argumenta sumpta a lege et prophetis. Hec patent in prologo et librorum processu. Modus meus procedendi est reducere confusionem littere in certas conclusiones et littere obscuritatem in claram formam intelligendi, litteram et sensum eiusdem per omnia sequendo (fol. 76^r).

His commentary is mainly restricted to a short summary of the argument. An example in relevance, he must have felt. The controversy on evangelical poverty was perhaps not immediately envisaged by his author, but the

---

[1] B. Smalley, "Thomas Waleys O.P.", *op. cit.*, 86-98.

[2] The top margin and first line of the text have been damaged, so that the first words are difficult to read.

defence of John XXII made an allowable exception to his rule of following the sense of the letter.

Sophistry was Baconthorpe's second bugbear. He cannot have thought it as dangerous as fables, since he does not attack it in the preface to his postill. We may notice his dislike of it here because later he shows that he saw it as the main vice of speculative theologians, just as story-telling was the main vice of practical theologians and preachers; he says early in his commentary on St. Matthew:

Theologi enim speculativi hodie non querunt nisi speciem veritatis, id est apparentiam sophisticam. Iterum theologi practici et predicatores nichil hodie videntur querere nisi per fabulas poetarum aures mulcere et prurire; et tales magistros sibi hodie omnes querunt (fol. 111ra).

Sophistry was another form of irrelevance. He denounces it roundly in the prologue to his *Quaestiones canonicae*. Xiberta has described his attack on sophistry as the words of a man brought up in "the golden age of scholasticism", who sees it being corrupted. He regarded two major trends of his day, destructive logic and early humanism, as dangerous alike in learning and teaching.

We turn now to the positive part of his programme. He is certainly in the Thomist tradition in seeing no basic opposition between Christian theology and pagan philosophy. The philosophers, though not the poets, impress him as respectable and helpful. He fulfils his promise to cite "quedam philosophica spectabilia veritatis continentia". Aristotle and his commentators are used in three ways. Where they agree with Christian teaching they are quoted in support of Baconthorpe's point, together with texts from the Fathers or from Scripture. This is his usual practice. Where they differ, he will either argue on parallel lines, one according to theology, the other according to philosophy, or he will harmonize them in a rather arbitrary way. His comment on Matthew vi. 28, *Considerate lilia agri* will illustrate the parallel line of argument, which is frequently and systematically used. The lilies of the field raise the problem why God has not provided a care-free existence for man as he has provided for birds and plants. The theologian replies that God did provide such an existence for man in the state of innocence before the fall. The philosopher, who does not accept the doctrine of the fall and of original sin, has a different answer.

Plants and animals have only one end, which nature provides for, whereas man, being rational, has other needs; hence God has given him his hands and brain. The theologian can agree in part with this argument, since God did not wholly destroy man's nature after the fall. Man kept his hands and brain, but henceforward he had to endure care as a punishment for sin. Baconthorpe ends the discussion by touching on the topical question of the necessary and contingent. Care is necessary, afflicting man more than other animals, but (as the text teaches) he should not be unduly careful of material needs, and here we have contingency.

Sed quare non providet Deus homini sine omni solicitudine sicut avibus et vegetabilibus? Secundum theologiam est respondendum quod in statu innocentie fuit provisum homini de victu et vestitu sine omni solicitudine. Secundum philosophiam sic est respondendum, quod quia natura et sensus sunt determinata ad unum, ideo natura(lia) et animalia carent arte providendi sibi victum et vestitum. Quia tamen natura non deficit in necessariis, ideo sine solicitudine provisum est eis a natura. Homo vero rationalis, cum non sit determinatus ad unum, sed variis modis habet tam de se quam de aliis per solertiam et per alias partes prudentie providere, ut patet vi Ethicorum,[1] ideo Deus creavit in homine animam rationalem, ut probat Philosophus xvi De animalibus,[2] per quam possit sibi et aliis providere variis modis prout recta ratio suaderet, et cum hoc dedit homini manus per quas universa operaretur secundum rationis dictamen. Et hec ratio tangitur iii De anima, ubi Philosophus tractans de perfectione hominis qua excedit omnia entia dicit quod in homine est intellectus in quo est omnia fieri modo intelligibili et quod homo habet manum que est organum organorum, quia per manus potest homo se iuvare in omnibus qui(bus) se iuvant animalia per diversa organa.[3]

Ad propositum, quia igitur post lapsum hominis Deus naturam eius non penitus extinxit, intellectus et manus sibi reservavit in subsidium, sed in penam peccati solicitudinem quandam sibi adiunxit; et sic sequitur conclusio de mixtione de necessario et de contingenti, quod hominem ultra alia animalia sollicitare necesse foret, sed cum moderamine rationis prout contingentia rerum suaderet (fol. 134ra).

Baconthorpe's explanation of the promise to the disciples, Matthew xix. 27-30, forces an agreement between the gospel and the *Ethics* which shows more goodwill than conviction. The perfect happiness promised

---

[1] *Ethic. Nichom.* vi.
[2] *De part. anim.* iv, 10, 687a, 2 - b, 21.
[3] *De anima*, iii, 8, 432a.

to the Christian in heaven corresponds to Aristotle's definition; it is not mentioned that Aristotle was arguing in terms of this life:

> *Ecce nos relinquimus omnia etc.* Respondet Christus quod felicitas plena, ubi notandum quod antiqui philosophi alii felicitatem posuerunt in honoribus, alii in divitiis. Aristoteles eam posuit in operationibus optimis, ut patet i Ethicorum et x,[1] ubi hoc pulchre probatur, et concordat Aristoteles quod aliqualiter consistit in debitis honoribus ... ac divitiis secundum rectam rationem bene usitatis. ... Principaliter tamen consistit in operatione perfectissima. ... Sic respondet Christus in proposito: Vos qui secuti estis me habebitis extremum honorem, sedentes mecum pro tribunali ... Habebitis multiplicatas divitias pro paucis. ... Habebitisque operationem perfectissimam, Dei claram visionem, perfectam dilectionem comprehendente(m), que est felicitas plena. Ergo etc. (fol. 165vb-166ra).

We leave serious discussion and slide into homiletics when Baconthorpe proves that Christ always chose the "mean" recommended in the *Ethics*. He does so by moralizing all passages in the gospel containing the words "in medio": Christ was born among animals in the stable, was crucified between two thieves, and so on. He also praised the mean in his teaching, as when he said: *Pax vobis* (John xx. 21); a man should be neither reserved nor rowdy:

> *Pax vobis*, in quo docet teneri medium circa conversationem, cuius extrema sunt singularitas et tumultuositas, ut nec homo se separet a communi nec tumultuantibus secularibus se implicet (fol. 163ra).

The theology promised in the introduction accounts for the elaborate structure of the postill. Baconthorpe uses it to refute Jews, schismatics and heretics. He begins in the normal way by commenting on the prologue to St. Matthew;[2] then he lists the twenty-seven points on which he is going to prove against the Jews that Christ is the promised Messias by showing how the prophecies agree with the gospel miracles; then he makes a protestation of faith, submitting his postill to the pope for emendation and correction; then he sets out his programme, transcribed above; then he seems ready to begin his commentary on the text, and we have the opening words, *Liber generationis*, under a rubric "Modus litteram introducendi".

---

[1]) *Ethic. Nichom.* i, 4-7; x, 1-8.
[2]) Stegmüller, *op. cit.*, no. 590.

Instead of beginning to comment, he announces that he is going to consider the question of the immaculate conception. The gospel opens with Christ's birth from Mary: "Therefore I, Carmelite and servant of blessed Mary, though unworthy, begin this postill by treating of the sanctification of her generation or conception."[1] He was unwilling, it seems, to comment on the gospel without having first stated his position on this much-discussed question. This occupies him for several leaves of the manuscript. Then he goes back to solve a few general questions of a traditional kind on the nature of the gospels, why there are four and so on, with a warning against apocrypha. Then we start from *Liber generationis* again, followed by a scholastic division of the genealogy ending with the hopeful words: "Nunc ad evangelii realitatem accedamus." In the next six leaves (fol. 104va–110rb) Baconthorpe proves to the Jews that Christ is the promised Messias, disposing of the first two points in which the prophecies are fulfilled. The remaining twenty-five are noticed when they arise, but the more general part of the argument is over. It is on quite traditional lines, though not copied directly from Lyre. The postillator does not forget to mention the schismatic Greeks on the procession of the Holy Spirit when passing Matthew i. 18; he gives their arguments and answers them:

> Hic ponitur articulus fidei incarnationis . . . Spiritus sanctus ab utroque procedit . . . De isto articulo non fluctuet quiscumque fidelis, eo quod greci christiani hunc articulum non admittunt. Est ratio eorum . . . (fol. 109vb).

The postill on the first chapter, therefore, contains many theological *quaestiones* and much apologetic. The following are expounded on a rather more modest scale. Baconthorpe has dealt with the Jews and can concentrate on heretics, with occasional references to the Greeks. He also gives straightforward doctrinal teaching. His net for catching heretics on theological points has been cast wide. He mentions the condemnation of the opinions of John of Paris on the Eucharist, which was comparatively recent, 1305-6.[2] John's views are stated, with the Church's "determination" to the contrary:

---

[1] Printed by Xiberta; see above, p. 101.
[2] P. Glorieux, *Répertoire, op. cit.*, no. 60.

Hic ponitur contra responsionem illorum qui posuerunt panem remanere in altari, inter quos fuit noviter Iohannes de Parisius, qui dixit quod potuit sustineri quod hec est vera: hoc est corpus meum, licet maneret ibi substantia panis. . . . Sed contrarium determinatur ab ecclesia (fol. 182ᵛᵇ).[1]

He even remembers Abailard's opinion on the atonement. The crucifixion raises three difficulties. The first is whether the devil held man in bondage justly before the redemption. Baconthorpe mentions the error of Peter Abailard, who held that the devil had no right over man. Bernard acted against him at the Council of Rheims (a mistake for Sens) and Peter was condemned, and again condemned by Pope Innocent II after his appeal. Baconthorpe gives Innocent's letter to the archbishops of Rheims and Sens as his authority; but the letter does not specify the condemned views.[2] Baconthorpe must have found them in St. Bernard's *Capitula* against Abailard in a collection of Bernard's letters:[3]

Hec sunt tres difficultates. Prima est an diabolus per iustitiam tenuit hominem vinctum. . . . Error Petri Ballardi (*sic*) fuit iste, quod diabolus non habuit ius tenendi hominem. Bernardus in concilio Remensi egit contra ipsum et fuit Petrus condempnatus. Appellavit et per Innocentium II fuit condempnatus. Hec in epistola quam Innocentius II misit archiepiscopis Remensi et Senonensi (fol. 188ʳᵃ).

Baconthorpe had a certain antiquarian curiosity, as Xiberta has noticed. He collected books and he collected heresies. Abailard's case may have interested him especially because the pope played a part in condemning him. Baconthorpe liked to put the Holy See at the centre of his picture. We shall see how he deals with heresies on the subject of papal supremacy when we describe his use of the canonists.

The latter play a much larger part in the argument than either philosophers or theologians. Quotations from canon law books far outnumber any others. This is no mere trimming; it represents an attitude. We have the awful spectacle of the gospel as it might have appeared to a mediaeval canonist, reading it in a strictly professional capacity. On the text *Nolite*

---

[1]) This *quaestio* is reproduced in the *Quaestiones canonicae, op. cit.*, fol. 78ᵛᵃ.

[2]) The text of the letter of 1141 is given by Otto of Freising, *Gesta Friderici imperatoris* i, 50 (ed. G. Waitz, Hanover and Leipzig, 1912), 71-3.

[3]) *Capitula haeresum Petri Abaelardi*, cap. iv: nec diabolus unquam ius aliquod habuit super hominem (Pat. lat. vol. 182, col. 1050). See J. G. Sikes, *Peter Abailard* (Cambridge, 1932), 206, 219-235.

iudicare (Matt. vii. 1) Baconthorpe explains in a rather perfunctory way that judges must show moderation. Then, having opened his manual at the section *De iudiciis*, he copies out a passage on the various kinds of jurisdiction, secular and spiritual, criminal and civil (fol. 135va), from the *Summa summarum* (MS. Bodl. 293, fol. 65rb). When Christ is accused by the Pharisees of eating with publicans and sinners (Matt. ix. 11), Baconthorpe says briskly:

Hic primo notabis casus in quibus non licet communicare cum publicanis et excommunicatis, et sunt quinque, scilicet in osculo . . . (fol. 141rb).

He then shortens the *Summa summarum* on the prohibitions and valid exceptions to them in communicating with excommunicates (MS. Bodl. 293, fol. 230vb-231ra). The Christian who wishes to follow his Master's example, it is implied, will have to tread warily. The mission of the disciples (Matt. x. 1) is expressed in legal terms:

Hic probatur Christus esse messias per auctoritatem committendi iurisdictionem suam, et commissariis certam formam vite tradendi (fol. 143rb).

On the trial (Matt. xxvii. 1-31), Baconthorpe lists the legal injuries committed against Christ by his judges in their procedure. For instance, Christ was the Jews' own prelate, according to the promise in the Law; and they had already made a notorious conspiracy against Him to exclude anyone who confessed Him as Christ from the synagogue. But subjects notoriously conspiring against their prelate are not to be admitted as his accusers:

Et cum accusaretur a principibus sacerdotum et senioribus, nichil respondit. Hic ponitur tertia iniuria in parte accusantium. Accusabant enim Christum iudei tanquam proprium prelatum, quia promissus fuit eis in lege tanquam pastor eorum vice Dei, secundum illud: Prophetam dc gente tua et de fratribus tuis suscitabo tibi; ipsum tanquam me audietis.[1] Et contra eum iam notorie conspiraverunt, ut si quis eum confiteretur christum extra synagogam fieret, ut dicitur in Iohanne.[2] Sed subditi notorie conspiratores non sunt admittendi ad accusationem prelati (fol. 187^{va-b}).

---

[1] A loose quotation of Deut. xviii. 15.
[2] Ioan. ix. 22.

The exposure of each flaw in procedure is supported by the appropriate canon.

Baconthorpe has a propagandist purpose in his use of the decretalists. He wants to defend the papacy against its enemies, anticlericals, schismatics, heretics or even critics. John XXII had instructed the faculties of theology as well as those of canon law to lecture on his four constitutions against the Franciscan errors on the poverty of Christ.[1] Baconthorpe was obeying. His systematic quotations from the canons provided a suitable framework. True, an extreme anticlerical was not to be persuaded by arguments from the *Decretals*, which he would hardly accept, but only by proofs from reason and Scripture.[2] Baconthorpe assumes that his students will fall outside this category and that they only need warnings and information. We shall see how he uses the canons when we consider his political theory.

Meanwhile we must note the main gaps in the postill. We seem to have lost sight of the "literal and spiritual exposition" which constituted the main body of a normal postill of the period. Both are there, but in a subsidiary capacity. Baconthorpe has promised us *moralia* in his preface, as well as philosophy, theology and canon law. He acquits himself by moralizing his text in the traditional way, chapter by chapter. We find the inevitable attacks on the clergy:

> Est verum de multis ecclesiasticis quod sunt male naturati et male et sine ratione educati. Ab initio in ecclesia sunt defectuosi et vitiosi (fol. 138vb).

The slaughter of the innocents in its moral sense refers to the corruption of youth by bad masters and sages, "qui sunt in civitatibus, villis, universitatibus et collegiis, tam religiosorum quam secularium" (fol. 112rb). This at least points to no lack of educational facilities. Baconthorpe also chooses the parable of talents in its moral sense for teaching on the contemplative life (fol. 179rb-180ra). But the key is pitched lower. Much of the material is conventional. Baconthorpe did not put his heart into the invention of *moralitates*.

---

[1] *Hist. lit.* xxxiv, 460.

[2] Thus Francis of Meyronnes, arguing, as it has been plausibly suggested, against the thesis of Dante's *De monarchia*, never quotes from the canon law, although his other writings prove that he knew it well; see P. de Lapparent, "L'œuvre politique de François de Meyronnes: ses rapports avec celle de Dante", *Archives d'histoire doctrinale et littéraire du Moyen Age*, 15 (1942), 5-151.

The literal exposition is equally derivative. He makes no mention in his programme of those studies which go to make Biblical scholarship in the strict sense. That he had little use for them appears from his cheerful acceptance of the legend of the triple marriage of St. Anne. He notes that she is said to have had three husbands and three daughters called Mary, and he quotes the verse: "Anna solet dici tres concepisse Marias" (fol. 153rb). The legend was anathema to mediaeval purists.[1] Baconthorpe probably felt that Nicholas of Lyre gave guidance enough on the historical sense of the gospel (though he did not find the St. Anne legend in Lyre). He shows some interest and independence in comparing Lyre with Jerome on the exegesis of the genealogy of Christ and will even prefer the more modern scholar, though cautiously:

Nec debet aliquis moveri si ego recedo in hoc a dictis Ieronomi, quia dicta sanctorum non sunt tante auctoritatis quam liceat sentire contrarium in hiis que non sunt per sacram scripturam determinata.

However, he supplies an argument against Lyre and for Jerome as an alternative, to be on the safe side:

Sed quia dictum Ieronomi non est faciliter respuendum et ideo contra Nicholaum potest sic argui . . . (fol. 103vb).

Our postillator was fully occupied in driving his three horses, philosophy, theology and canon law. It would be asking too much to expect him to harness a fourth. Biblical scholarship might well have upset his team.

IV

POLITICAL THEORY

The text Matthew xxii. 30, *erunt sicut angeli Dei in celo*, gives Baconthorpe his chance to set out his theory in general terms. It suggests the

---

[1] For discussions of the Maries in the gospels and refutation of the St. Anne legend see the bibliography in B. Smalley, *The Study of the Bible in the Middle Ages* (2nd ed., Oxford, 1952), p. 363, n. 1, and R. W. Southern, "St. Anselm and Gilbert Crispin, Abbot of Westminster", *Mediaeval and Renaissance Studies*, 3 (1954), 104-12.

nine orders of angels of the celestial hierarchy. He quotes Pseudo-Dionysius and St. Gregory on the hierarchy and then assigns to its nine orders the various classes of good Christians who will join its ranks after the Resurrection and the Last Judgment. It is a neat way of expressing his values. The apostles and all ardent lovers of God join the seraphim. Those who possessed fullness of knowledge, especially the evangelists, join the cherubim. To the thrones, the seat of God's judicial power, go all who judge well and piously of themselves, among them good popes *par excellence*, who occupy the judgment seat in this world:

> Tertius ordo vocatur throni, ad quem pertinet iudiciaria potestas, quia in eis Deus sessurus (MS. cessurus) ad judicandum. Ad hunc ordinem assumuntur omnes bene et pie de seipsis iudicantes, sed per excellentiam boni romani pontifices, qui thronum iudicii tenent in hoc mundo (fol. 172ra).

Baconthorpe has allotted good popes to the first hierarchy. He goes on to the second, assigning martyrs to the dominions, confessors to the virtues, those who have overcome the flesh, especially virgins, to the powers. We must pass to the third and lowest hierarchy before we find good emperors and kings such as Constantine, St. Louis and Edward the Confessor. They belong to the principalities. Their good officials and ministers, dispatched to enforce and proclaim justice, join the archangels, signified by St. Michael. The rank and file of the faithful, who have not been assigned to any of the eight higher orders, belong to the lowest order, the angels. The doctors of the Church seem to have been forgotten, unless they come among the cherubim with the evangelists. Baconthorpe has clearly subordinated the secular to spiritual power. He also sets a high price on law and justice.

Naturally, therefore, he praises the Donation of Constantine, as he found it described in the *Decretum*. Needless to say, he did not question that his source described an actual historical event. Baconthorpe knits it ingeniously into his exegesis. He first refers to it when he is proving against the Jews that Christ was the promised Messias. Christ proved Himself to be a true descendant of David, as is stated in the gospel genealogy. At the time of His advent the Jews were captive. Yet later Christ gathered to Himself not only a multitude of peoples of diverse kingdoms, but also an empire. The Donation fulfils the prophecies of His kingship. Constantine submitted to the Christian faith and granted to the pope his crown, empire and all royal dignity in Rome, Italy and the West. He led the pope through the city of Rome holding his bridle and showed him many other honours. Baconthorpe sends us to the *Decretum* for a fine account of the temporal dignity of the Church; he saw it as the true successor to the Roman empire:

Cum enim iudei sub imperio fuerant captivati in eius adventu, postea Christus congregavit sibi non solum multitudinem gentium diversorum regnorum, sed etiam imperium. Imperator enim romanus, Constantinus magnus, se christiane fidei subiecit et coronam, imperium et omnem regiam dignitatem in urbe romana et Italia et etiam in partibus occidentalibus pape concessit, et eius frenum per civitatem romanam tenendo duxit, et multos alios honores exhibuit, prout habetur dist. xcvi, cap. *Constantinus*.[1] Vide ibi pulcherrime de dignitate temporali ecclesie (fol. 105ra).

The parables of the grain of mustard seed and the leaven (Matt. xiii. 31-33) also refer to the Donation. Christ had prophesied the spread of heresy in the two previous parables. Here He prophesied the rise of the Church through the temporal power. By means of the Donation, the Church, formerly poor and small like a mustard seed, grew into a great branching tree on whose boughs the pope and ecclesiastics, like birds of the air, might nest. The heresies foretold in the earlier parables could now be suppressed. Endowment, with the emperor's help and protection, enabled the Church to wipe out those heresies which had been dividing Christendom. The faith was now strengthened and declared by the Creed. The same parable foretells the Church's universal jurisdiction. Baconthorpe makes a list of the claims put forward by Innocent III against the empire: to depose an emperor who fails in his duty of protection of the Church, to transfer the empire and to examine, cancel or confirm imperial elections. These rights derive from the Donation. It was made by public and private consent; it bound Constantine's successors; the papal right over the empire remained and remains. Baconthorpe has in mind John XXII's refusal to recognize Louis of Bavaria as emperor. He does not mention it, but it explains his warmth on this aspect of the Donation.

---

[1] Gratian, *Decretum* I, dist. xcvi, cap. 14 (palea).

The parable of the leaven described how the Church would prevail over heresies by means of the spiritual power. The leavening signified the union of all predestinate to life eternal in the warmth of the faith. Such a union came about under Constantine, since he decreed that St. Peter and his successors should have primacy over the four patriarchal sees and over all God's churches in the world. Baconthorpe is careful to add that Constantine decreed the supremacy *de facto*; it already obtained *de iure*. Peter's universal authority will be discussed later on chapter xvi.

Baconthorpe is expressing his own deep conviction and also hurling defiance at those who thought that the Donation had "poured poison into the Church". He believed that the riches and power of the Church were right and necessary as a means to overcoming heresy.

Hec est tertia parabola in qua describitur status ecclesie sequens post heresis seminationem. Post enim seminationem heresum exaltavit Deus ecclesiam suam per potentiam temporalem. Ab initio enim fuit ecclesia sicut granum sinapis, id est minima in potestate temporali, Mathei viii: Vulpes foveas habent et volucres celi nidos; filius autem hominis non habet etc.[1] Tempore vero Constantini, ut patet dist. lxxxix, vi (*sic*), cap. *Constantinus*, fuit ditata et facta magna arbor. Tradidit enim Constantinus beato Silvestro pape palatium imperii sui lateranense et coronam et (s)ceptrum et suis successoribus coronam quam in capite portabat . . .;[2] et tunc ecclesia, prius arbor, tunc facta est expansa et ramosa, in cuius ramis, id est provinciis et civitatibus, volucres celi, id est papa et viri ecclesiastici, habitare possent; et sic patet expositio huius parabole, ut ecclesia Christi potestatem temporalem haberet hereticorum perversitates cohercere. Hac enim ditatione facta et ipso Constantino assistente et ecclesiam defendente, tunc primo sunt diverse hereses per quas (s)cissa erat christianitas penitus extirpate et fides ecclesie fidei simbolo roborata et declarata, ut habetur dist. xv, cap. *Canones*.[3]

Ex hac donatione ad quam ex consensu publico et communi[4] facta et obli-

---

[1] Matt. viii. 20.

[2] Baconthorpe quotes at greater length than in the passage above from the *Decretum* I, dist. xcvi, cap. 14.

[3] *Decretum* I, dist. xv, cap. 1: Canones generalium conciliorum a temporibus Constantini ceperunt. In precedentibus namque annis persecutione fervente docendarum plebium minime dabatur facultas. Inde Christianitas in diversas hereses scissa est, quia non erat licentia conveniendi in unum, nisi tempore supradicti imperatoris. Ipse enim dedit facultatem Christianis libere congregari.

[4] Baconthorpe is referring to the preamble to the Donation given in the text of the *Constantinus*, *op. cit.*: Utile iudicavimus una cum omnibus satrapis nostris, et universo senatu optimatibusque meis etiam et cuncto populo Romano.

gatione super hoc suis successoribus per dictum imperatorem imposita[1] remansit
et remanet ecclesie ius imperatorem deponere si ecclesiam noluerit defendere, immo
et imperium transferre et alteri tribuere, ut factum fuit tempore Karoli magni,
ut habetur tit., de electis, libro primo, cap. *Venerabilem* in glosa.[2] . . . Habet ulterius
ecclesia iurisdictionem examinandi electionem et personam imperatoris electam, et
si defectus fuerit in electione seu persona totum irritare, et si bona sit electio
electum inungere, consecrare, coronare et ad imperium promovere, ut habetur
cap. *Venerabilem*. Patet igitur qualiter non solum ecclesia est arbor ramosa in
divitiis, sed etiam in universali iurisdictione, ut non solum populum, sed et ipsum
imperatorem habet cohercere et si heresis vel alia causa exigat corrigere et deponere; et in hac multiplicata iurisdictione iam nidificat ecclesia, et sic patet
dupliciter hec parabola.

Item *simile est regnum celorum fermento*: quarta parabola, in qua describitur
exaltatio ecclesie contra hereses et hoc per potentiam spiritualem. Sicut enim
mulier quedam abscondit fermentum in tribus satis farine donec totum est fermentatum, sic ecclesia, primo quasi absconsa, stetit sub humilitate in tribus satis
farine, id est fide, spe, caritate, donec omnes ad vitam eternam predestinatos
haberet fermentatos, id est in calore fidei sibi unitos; et illa unio facta fuit tempore
Constantini. Ipse enim de facto decrevit, licet de iure sic erat, quod beatus Petrus
eiusque successores principatum teneret super quatuor sedes patriarchales,
Alexandrinam, Antiochenam, Ierosolitanam, Constantinopolitanam, et super
omnes in universo orbe Dei ecclesias.[3] De hac universali auctoritate Petri dicetur
infra, cap. xvi (fol. 152rb-vb).

Baconthorpe seizes his opportunities to attack the *Defensor pacis*. He
shows no sign of having read it and does not mention it by name, but he
knows the five propositions condemned by John XXII in the bull *Licet
iuxta doctrinam* of October 23, 1327.[4] Surprisingly he refers to the condemnation as "the constitution *Certum processum*". Can he mean the lost
letter of 1327 addressed by John XXII to the University of Paris? We
know that it had a list of condemned propositions corresponding to that
of the *Licet iuxta doctrinam*.[5] In any case, Baconthorpe's account of the
propositions and of the pope's arguments against them agrees verbally

---

[1] "imposita" has been written over an erasure. The sentence is not quite grammatical as it
stands. Perhaps it should read: . . . "facta est obligatio".

[2] A quotation from the *Decretals* I, tit. vi, cap. 34, and the *Glossa ordinaria* ad loc.

[3] Quoted from the *Donation* as given in the *Decretum*, *op. cit.*

[4] Text in O. Rinaldi, *Annales ecclesiastici* v (Lucca, 1750), s.a. 1327, 347-354. See G. de Lagarde,
La naissance de l'esprit laïque au déclin du Moyen Age ii (Paris, 1934), 322-5.

[5] *Ibid.*, p. 326, n. 52.

with the text of the surviving bull. His *Certum processum*, whatever else it was, muſt have been a copy of the *Licet iuxta doctrinam* with a difference only in preamble and in non-essentials.

On the text *Sic omnis arbor bona fructus bonos facit etc.* (Matt. vii. 17) he gives a liſt of heresies ending with those of Marsilio of Padua and John of Jandun as condemned by the pope. His account of their five heresies is an almost verbal copy of the papal bull. Even the order corresponds. He does not discuss them in this context, but goes on to describe the inquisitorial procedure in cases of heresy (fol. 137ra). On the promise to Peter, Matthew xvi. 18, he mentions the second proposition, that St. Peter was no more head of the Church than any other apoſtle, and summarizes the proofs brought againſt it by John XXII:

> *Et ego dico tibi.* Hic tertio fit generalis commissio, ubi notandum eſt primo quod una heresis noviter fuit orta que dicebat quod beatus Petrus apoſtolus non fuit plus caput ecclesie quam quilibet aliorum apoſtolorum, et fuit Marcili de Padua et Iohannis de Ianduno, et hanc condempnat dominus Iohannes XXII in conſtitutione que incipit *Certum processum*; et probat Petrum esse verum caput et vicarium singularem Chriſti . . . (fol. 156vb).

John is defended againſt the suspicion of political bias. He did not decide againſt the partisans of the Bavarian usurper (the Emperor Louis) merely because they had spoken against himself. The proof is that the Church had condemned their heresy long ago. Baconthorpe quotes examples from the *Decretum* where to impugn the primacy of Rome is said to be heresy:

> Nec eſt suspicandum quod Iohannes hic favorabiliter diffinierit, eo quod contra ipsum fautores Bavari usurpantis imperium hoc dixerant, quia ab antiquo hec heresis eſt condempnata ab ecclesia, diſt. xxii, *Omnes*, ubi dicitur quod dicendus eſt hereticus et proculdubio in heresim labitur, qui ecclesiam (MS. ecclesie) videlicet romanam cunctis ecclesiis non pretulisse cognoscitur[1] (fol. 156vb-157ra).

The fundamental discussion comes on the giving of tribute, Matthew xvii. 23-26, as might be expected: the firſt condemned proposition was

---

[1] Gratian, *Decretum* I, diſt. xxii, cap. 1, *Omnes sive patriarchae*: Qui autem Romanae ecclesiae privilegium ab ipso summo omnium ecclesiarum capite traditum auferre conatur, hic proculdubio in heresim labitur. . . . Fidem quippe violat qui adversum illam agit, quae eſt mater fidei et illi contumax invenitur, qui eam cunctis ecclesiis pretulisse cognoscitur.

that Christ paid tribute to Caesar of necessity and that consequently the
temporalities of the Church were subject to the emperor. Baconthorpe
supports the papal refutation with arguments of his own and considers
the whole question of the relations between Church and State. From the
point of view of political theory this is the most interesting part of the
postill. He first explains his text as meaning that Christ, as son of God
and descendant of King David, had no compulsion to pay tribute. He did
so to avoid scandal, because the collectors were gentiles, ignorant of the
Law and the Prophets, who did not realize that He was the King's son.
Christ ordered tribute to be paid on Peter's behalf as well as on His own,
because He had already made Peter chief over all the other apostles;
Baconthorpe refers back to his questions on the keys in the preceding
chapter. He then sets out the condemned proposition on the giving of
tribute, with the pope's refutation. To each papal argument he adds a
quotation from canon law. He makes a special point of John XXII's
distinction between taxes on persons and on property. John argued that
even if Christ paid tribute for his *person*, it would not follow that Church
property should be subject to civil authority. He backed his statement by
a general reference to civil law: "Hec patent falsa etiam per iura imperialia
manifeste." Baconthorpe finds chapter and verse in the canons. Then he
leaves the bull and sets out to prove from the canons and from sacred
history that the Church should be exempt as regards both persons and
property. First, Church property from the beginning was of divine institution; men were taught to offer firstfruits and tithes. Secular jurisdiction, on
the contrary, arose in consequence of sin. The same holds good of secular
property. At first all things were common; appropriation resulted from
ambition. Hence ecclesiastical property should be exempt, whereas secular
is deservedly subject to pay taxes to the prince. But this raises a difficulty.
If secular jurisdiction originated in sin, then how can secular rulers have
a just title to their possessions? Baconthorpe replies by expounding the
canon law teaching on the origin of property; he quotes the *lecturae* of
Hostiensis and Innocent IV. In the state of innocence all things were
common. After the fall, God permitted appropriation. Hence by divine
permission even Gentiles and infidels have a just title. In that case we
have to consider the further problem: if secular jurisdiction is just and of
divine institution, then why should the Church interfere in it, excommuni-

cating princes who attack other princes and so forth? Baconthorpe seems to shift his ground a little. We should expect him to adduce the Donation, which he has already praised so fervently. He chooses instead a wider and safer argument. Intervention in secular matters is *ratione peccati*. He quotes Innocent III's letter *via* the *Decretals*, explaining that the pope intervenes on moral grounds and does not wish to disturb or lessen secular kingdoms.

A fourth difficulty has to be considered. Assuming that the part of the Church which is outside the Promised Land has to interfere in temporal jurisdiction only in cases relating to salvation of souls (*in casibus salutis*), did this exclude Christ as the son of David and consequently the pope as His vicar from interfering in the jurisdiction of the Promised Land? He answers that they had a right to interfere there, because Christ was temporal sovereign and had no obligation to pay tribute, though He did not exercise his right to refuse.

The discussion begins from Peter's reply to the question whether tribute is paid by sons or by strangers, with Christ's teaching on tribute: *Reges terrae a quibus accipiunt tributum vel censum? a filiis suis, an ab alienis? Et ille dixit ab alienis. Dixit illi Jesus: Ergo liberi sunt filii.* Christ explains to Peter why He is not bound to pay; He is the son of the eternal King and descended from King David:

Sed tu, Petre, scis quod ego sum filius regis eterni. Iam enim audisti in monte paternam vocem dicentem: *Hic est filius meus dilectus etc.*,[1] supra in hoc capitulo. Fuit etiam filius ex tempore ex progenie David, ad Rom. i;[2] ergo patet quod a me non debent petere. *Ut autem non scandalizemus eos, vade ad mare etc.* Hic ponitur responsio plus quam satisfactoria. Hic notandum quod scandalum aliquando oritur ex ignorantia et tale vitandum est ubi salvari potest veritas iustitie vite et doctrine, sed isti colligentes tributum ignorabant Christum esse filium regis tam temporalis quam eterni, et non erat contra veritatem vite aut iustitie aut doctrine eis tributum solvere, quia ignorabant Christum esse filium regis, et probabiliter, quia gentiles erant, quibus adhuc non fuerat Christus predicatus, nec legem aut prophetas noverant. Ideo voluit Christus eis tributum dari ad scandalum vitandum; et hoc est quod sequitur in littera: *ut autem non scandalizemus eos, vade ad mare et mitte hamum etc.* Sed quare precepit Christus tributum dari pro Petro sicut pro se? Respondetur quod iam Petrum constituerat

[1] Matt. xvii. 5.
[2] Rom. i. 3.

capitaneum super omnes alios apoſtolos, saltem promisso, quod poſtea implevit
faĉto. De hoc supra, cap. xvi, § *tibi dabo claves* et ita per totum.

Ex hac solutione didragmatis orta fuit nova heresis hiis diebus per magiſtros
Marcillum de Padua et Iohannem de Gendino dicentes (MS. dicentium) quod
quando Chriſtus solvit tributum Cesari hoc non fuit condescensione et liberalitate
sue pietatis sed necessitate coaĉtus. Et ex hoc nitebatur (*sic*) concludere quod
omnia temporalia ecclesie subsunt imperatori et ea poteſt accipere velut sua.
Videntur enim supponere quod ex hoc quod Chriſtus tributum solvit, et ex debito,
ut dicunt, quod res temporales Chriſti imperatori subessent, et per consequens
res ecclesie temporales et sic velut suas posse accipere.[1] Utrumque condempnat
dominus Iohannes in conſtitutione *Certum processum*. Primum condempnat quia
direĉte eſt contra textum evangelii, qui dicit hic quod primo oſtendit Chriſtus se
non teneri et poſt subdit: *ut non scandalizemus eos etc.*[2] Idem habetur xxviii, q. 1,
cap. *Iam nunc*, § *Multa*, ubi sic dicitur: Multa sunt facienda non iubente lege, sed
libera caritate. Unde ipse Dominus, cum prius se tributum non debere solvere
demonſtrasset, solvit tamen ne scandalizaret eos quibus ad eternam vitam consulebat.[3] Vide multa ibi.

Secundum condempnat, quia si didragma non solvit ex debito, sed liber
erat de solvendo, ut diĉtum eſt, ergo per solutionem didragmatis non poteſt argui
quod res eius et ecclesie sue sunt subieĉte imperatori cui datur didragma.[4] Ad
idem xi, q. 1, cap. *Si tributum*, et cap. *Magnum*, et in glosis.[5] Item posito quod
solvisset ex debito, non sequitur quod res ipse essent subieĉte imperatori, quia
illa solutio fiebat pro persona, scilicet pro se et Petro, ubi hic dicitur: sed non
sequitur si persona sit tributaria quod propter hoc res tributarie, nec e contra
quod persona poteſt esse tributaria et bona libera;[6] et e contra habes lib. v, tit.
de verborum significatione, cap. *Cum* (*sic*) *quibusdam* et ibi in glosa.[7] Ut enim ibi
patet in quibusdam locis dantur pedagia pro transitu per terram principis et hoc
fit pro persona, non pro rebus; et e contra in quibusdam locis ubi nichil datur pro
persona, pro rebus dantur salinaria, id eſt tributum pro sale duĉto per terram
principis ac etiam pro aliis portatis dantur portaria. In quibusdam tamen locis

---

[1]) Quoted from the bull of John XXII, Rinaldi, v, 347.

[2]) *Ibid.*

[3]) Gratian, *Decretum* II, causa xxviii, q. 1, cap. 8. "Multa ... consulebat" is a rough quotation
of two sentences.

[4]) Rinaldi, *op. cit.*

[5]) Gratian, *Decretum* II, causa xi, q. 1, cap. 27 and 28.

[6]) Rinaldi, *op. cit.*

[7]) *Decretals* V, tit. xl, cap. 26, *Super quibusdam*. The *Glossa ordinaria ad loc.* explains the various
kinds of tolls and cuſtoms duties. Baconthorpe has added the diſtinĉtion between payments on persons
and payments on things to his source. The only mention of it that he could have found comes later on
in the passage in the *Decretum*, "in omni causa, quae ratione personarum vel rerum ad ecclesiaſticum
forum pertinet ...".

328

dantur guidagia que solvuntur pro salvo conductu per terram principis, et quando-
que et pro persona et pro rebus.

Ad plenius sciendum quod modo Christus et viri ecclesiastici non debent
esse astricti iure quod ab initio fuit ad dandum huiusmodi onera per principes
imposita neque pro persona neque pro rebus, notandum quod ab initio ecclesie
status etiam quoad temporalia fuit a Deo institutus. Dicitur enim in historiis
quod cum Abel et Caym optulerunt munera creditur quod Adam in spiritu docuit
filios ut Deo offerrent decimas et primitias.¹ Post diluvium vero optulit Abraham
decimas Melchisedech et hoc fuit ordinatio divina, ut patet ad Hebr. vii,² quia
Melchisedech gessit personam filii Dei Christi, qui est sacerdos in eternum.
Tempore vero Moysi statuit Deus decimas dari tribui Leviticis (*sic*) et primitias
summo sacerdoti, ut habetur Lev. xviii,³ et lib. iii, tit. de decimis, cap. i.⁴ Cum
igitur persone ecclesie et possessiones earum sunt a Deo institute et pro Dei
servitio faciendo, ut dictum est, patet quod tam persone quam res debent esse
libere. E contra iurisdictio secularis fuit propter iniquitatem hominum introducta.
Ab initio enim erant omnia communia. Post diluvium vero filii Laban primo
diviserunt insulas gentium⁵ et post Nemeroth incepit venari homines et eos amore
dominandi sibi subdere, ut habetur Gen. x et in historiis;⁶ et sic propter meum
et tuum et propter iniquitatem inter mortales cepit divisio, ut habetur xii, q. i,
cap. *Dilectissimis*.⁷ Ex hac concluditur quod ecclesia debet esse libera iure antiquo
quoad personas et quoad sua temporalia et adhuc rationabiliter debet esse libera
in huiusmodi, quia iurisdictio a Deo instituta non debet esse subiecta iurisdictioni
propter iniquitatem hominum introducte. Ergo res civiles merito sunt principi
tributarie.

Sed tunc remanet difficultas. Cum iurisdictio secularis sit per iniquitatem
introducta, quomodo principes seculares iuste possident? Respondetur per glosam
super cap. *Dilectissimis*, quod quia ius gentium, ut habetur in Decreto, dist. i, est
sedium occupatio, edificatio, munitio, bella, captivitates et servitutes habens, et
quia hoc ius, quo gentes post diluvium rerum utuntur, est contrarium iuri (MS.
iure) naturali, ideo dicitur hoc ius per iniquitatem introductum (MS. introducti).⁸

¹) Peter Comestor, *Historia scholastica in Gen.*, cap. 26, PL 198, col. 1077.
²) Hebr. vii. 1-17.
³) Actually Deut. xviii. 3.
⁴) *Decretals*, III, tit. xxx, cap. i.
⁵) Gen. x. 5.
⁶) *Ibid.*, 8-9; *Historia scholastica, op. cit.*, cap. 37, col. 1088.
⁷) Gratian, *Decretum* II, causa xii, q. i, cap. 2: Communis enim usus omnium, que sunt in hoc
mundo, omnibus hominibus esse debent. Sed per iniquitatem alius hoc dixit esse suum, et alius istud,
et inter mortales facta fuit divisio.
⁸) Gratian, *Decretum* II, causa xii, q. i, cap. 2. The *Glossa ordinaria ad loc.* refers to I, i, 9: here
"ius gentium" is defined as "sedium occupatio" etc. The *Gloss. ord.* on "per iniquitatem" in the chapter
Dilectissimis has: id est per consuetudinem iurium gentium equitati naturali. . . .

Tamen non est modo iniquitas, sed ius, cuius rationem assignant Hostiensis in lectura et Innocentius, tit. de voto, cap. *Quod super hiis.* Dicunt enim quod licet ab initio omnia erant communia, tamen Deus ex causa sibi nota postmodum concessit terram occupanti et scienter tolleravit per antiquos patres dominia specialia teneri, ut patet Gen. x et Gen. xii de Abraham et Loth; et talia dominia adquiri et teneri tolleravit, non solum apud fideles, sed apud infideles, et rationabiliter, quia non solum pro fidelibus, sed pro natura humana creata sunt omnia et ideo dicitur Mathei v: Deus solem suum oriri facit super bonos et malos, quia Deus sic pro natura humana terram et dominia specialiter concessit occupanti. Ideo gentes et infideles licite et sine peccato huiusmodi dominia possident.[1]

Sed ex hiis sequitur alia difficultas, quia si iurisdictio secularis a Deo sit et iusta, qualiter ecclesia potest de eorum temporali iurisdictione intromittere, principes excommunicando, si alios invadant et in similibus? Respondit papa lib. ii, tit. de iudiciis, cap. *Novit ille,* quod ipse non vult se intromittere, iurisdictionem regum turbare aut minuere, sed si peccaverint eos corrigere, secundum quod Dominus ordinavit in evangelio, quod si in fratrem peccaret et se emendare nollet, tunc dicas ecclesie. Ad hoc vide pulchra in textu et glosis;[2] et hoc fecit ecclesia cum (MS. iam) de facto propter defectum imperatoris transtulit imperium ad teutonicos, ut patet tit. de electionibus, cap. *Venerabilem.*[3]

Hic oritur quarta difficultas. Supposito enim quod ecclesia nostra que est extra terram promissionis non habeat se intromittere de iurisdictione temporali nisi in casibus salutis, numquid libere Christus ut filius David se habuit intromittere et per consequens papa de iurisdictione terre promissionis? Dicitur quod sic per illud Luce i, ubi dicitur: *Dabit illi Dominus Deus sedem David, patris eius; et regnabit etc.*[4]......[5] Ex hoc evidenter probat Christus Petro quod non debet solvere tributum, quia per legem Cesaris fuerunt excepti filii regum et maxime in terra ubi erant regnaturi, sed secundum rei veritatem, ut dictum est, Christus fuit filius David sessurus super solium eius in terra promissionis[6] infra quam erat Capharnaum, ergo in Capharnaum nullo modo veritate considerata debet peti ab eo tributum. Christus tamen illo iure noluit (MS. voluit) uti, secundum illud Luce

---

[1] *Decretals* III, tit. xxxiv, cap. 8. Baconthorpe has summarized the commentaries of Innocent IV and Hostiensis, who are almost identical on this passage; *Innocentii IV in V libros Decretalium commentaria* (Venice, 1578), fol. 176[vb]; *Henrici de Segusio Cardinalis Hostiensis in V libros Decretalium commentaria* (Venice, 1581), fol. 128[ra].

[2] *Decretals,* II, tit. i, cap. 13; *Gloss. ord. ad loc.*: ... nec tamen propterea in hoc derogare vult in aliquo iurisdictione illius, nec intendit iudicare de feudo, sed decernere de peccato illius, cuius censura ad ipsum spectat.

[3] *Decretals* I, tit. vi, cap. 34.

[4] Luc. i. 32.

[5] Further proof texts follow.

[6] A reference to Isa. ix. 7, quoted above.

xii: *Homo, quis me conſtituit iudicem super vos?*[1] De hiis parte 3a, q. 59, art. quarto[2] (fol. 159ᵛᵇ-160ᵛᵃ).

The origin of property in Chriſtian as diſtinct from pagan times is discussed on the queſtion of tithes (Matt. xxiii. 23). Baconthorpe argues that the early Chriſtians held their goods in common and that the apoſtles and then the bishops dispensed them to the laity. It was the Church which granted laymen the right to hold property in private, reserving tithes from it for herself. Conſtantine confirmed this arrangement at the time of the Donation:

> Item ab initio chriſtianitatis omnia bona chriſtianorum erant communia et per manus apoſtolorum, et episcoporum poſt eos, dispensanda. Quod autem laicis concessum fuit habere proprium fuit ex ordinatione ecclesie. . . . Cum autem processu temporis ecclesia dotata fuit a Conſtantino . . . etiam tunc idem imperator totius mundi approbavit decimas per omnes leges predictas ſtatutas. Cum ergo chriſtiani ab ecclesia receperunt (*sic*) proprium et ecclesia sibi tunc decimas reservavit ac etiam imperator totius mundi et omnes sui sequaces et reges et principes universi hucusque in hodiernum diem approbaverunt, patet quod et per legem canonicam et civilem et non solum per divinam tenentur ad decimas. Chriſtus enim eas confirmavit, Mt. xxiii, *oportet illas non omittere.*[3] Ex quibus arguo sic: ab initio chriſtianitatis tota possessio chriſtianorum fuit una communis, cuius diſtributio ad ecclesiam pertinebat, Act. v.[4] Hoc totum quod proprium habent misericorditer ab ecclesia receperunt, ecclesia sibi reservante ius receptionis decimarum. Sed qui totum acceperunt ab ecclesia tenentur (MS. sed) ei reddere decimam partem, quam sibi, Chriſto ordinante, reservavit et leges canonicae et imperiales confirmaverunt (fol. 174ᵛᵇ-175ʳᵃ).

Baconthorpe uses the same argument in his additions to his *Quaeſtiones canonicae*. Here he goes so far as to say that it would be beſt for the earlier syſtem to ſtand, the Church dispensing property to the laity and secular princes defending it on the Church's behalf; he draws the consequence that it would be beſt for the Church to depose some and inſtitute others:

> Esset igitur optimum, quod omnia bona chriſtianorum essent communia et

---

[1] Luc. xii. 14.
[2] *Summa theologica*, III, q. lix, a. 4.
[3] Matt. xxiii. 23, a loose quotation.
[4] Act. iv. 32-35.

per ecclesiam omnibus communiter diſtribuenda ..., et per principes tanquam
per defensores ecclesie essent defensata ... et quod alii deponerentur per ecclesiam et alii conſtituerentur ...[1]

We now have enough material to sum up Baconthorpe's position on
the relations between secular and temporal powers. He takes his ideas exclusively from the canoniſts. There is no reason to suppose that he had even
thumbed any of the controversial literature conneᵉted with Boniface VIII
or with John XXII. His theory of the origin of the State and of property
derives from the patriſtic and early mediaeval teaching, transmitted in the
Decretum and the *Decretals*. These human inſtitutions, unnecessary in the
ſtate of innocence, were tolerated by God as a remedy for the disorder
caused by men's passions after the fall. St. Thomas, holding that man was
a political animal, put some kind of government back into the ſtate of
innocence. He taught that private property was not againſt nature, but
something added to nature and making for the more effeᵉtive use of
nature's provisions.[2] Baconthorpe completely ignores the newer and more
optimiſtic view of the State proposed by St. Thomas. It was not altogether
incompatible with an extreme view of the supremǎcy of the spiritual
power, as we know from the *De regimine chriſtiano* of James of Viterbo;
but it would have involved a reshaping of Baconthorpe's argument. The
canoniſts' doᵉtrine fitted into his scheme more easily. Perhaps, too, he was
following an Oxford tradition. Duns Scot did not fully accept the view
that man is a political animal and thought that only paternal authority
was founded in nature rather than in convention.[3] Both Fitz Ralph and
Wyclif would revert to the patriſtic teaching that secular authority was
brought about by sin, though they drew different conclusions from their
premiss.

Yet Baconthorpe took his canoniſts with a pinch of salt. He might
have held with Innocent IV that Chriſt as supreme Lord of the world committed both spiritual and temporal power to Peter and his successors.
According to Innocent, Conſtantine could not confer even temporal

---

[1]) From Baconthorpe's autograph notes in MS. London, British Museum Royal 11. B. xii, fol.
114ᵛ, printed by Xiberta, p. 226.

[2]) O. Lottin, *Le droit naturel chez Saint Thomas d'Aquin et ses prédécesseurs* (2nd ed., Bruges, 1931).

[3]) G. de Lagarde, *op. cit.*, iii, 330-335.

authority on the pope. On the contrary, he received back his own authority to hold legitimately, having previously reigned as a tyrant.[1] Building on such claims, the papal propagandists, Giles of Rome and Frances of Meyronnes, argued that the pope had supreme temporal as well as supreme spiritual jurisdiction and that secular princes held their power as a delegation. Baconthorpe never actually claims that the pope has supreme temporal power. He says that the pope had universal spiritual jurisdiction before the Donation, which Constantine recognized *de facto*, not *de iure*. He says that Church property, being divinely instituted, ought to be exempt from secular control. He says that Christian laymen originally derived their property rights from the Church at a time when the early Christians were holding all their goods in common, with the bishops acting as stewards. He thinks that it would be best if this were still done and if secular princes acted as a police force directly amenable to the Church. "Optimum esset": the subjunctive is revealing. He does not suggest that it *is* so. Nor does he present the secular power as being purely derivative from the spiritual. Though inferior to the spiritual and a consequence of sin, it is lawful in itself. The pope intervenes in secular jurisdiction by virtue of his spiritual authority, *ratione peccati*. His temporal power derives in some way from the Donation, though Baconthorpe is not at all clear as to what the Donation covered. To argue that the pope as Christ's successor is temporal Lord of Palestine, as Baconthorpe does, might seem an academic point at a time when the Turks had conquered it. He excludes the western states from the Donation when he argues that the Church has only spiritual authority over them: "supposito quod ecclesia nostra que est extra terram promissionis non habeat se intromittere de iurisdictione nisi in casibus salutis." In fact, he limits himself to the claims actually made by the popes *ex cathedra*, as distinct from the higher claims made by some canonists and propagandists. Innocent IV, it has been pointed out, showed more caution in his pronouncements as pope than as commentator on the *Decretals*.[2] Given the practical control exercised by the English kings over the Church in their dominions, the most ardent supporter of

[1] R. W. and A. J. Carlyle, *A History of Mediaeval Political Theory in the West*, v (London, Edinburgh, 1938), 306-7, 318-24.

[2] *Ibid.*, 318-19.

the papacy might well hesitate to slight their authority from a chair in Oxford. Baconthorpe did well to be so prudent.

A casual reference to St. Thomas Becket throws more light on his attitude. The flight into Egypt raises the question: how far should a prelate resist attacks on the Church, and when is he justified in fleeing? Baconthorpe considers the special case where the temporalities of the Church are manifestly injured; should a prelate resist unto death? He discusses the case from the point of canon law and decides that the prelate ought to resist. Then he suggests a "theological" answer. It is not merely a question of injury to Church property but of salvation of souls, since the aggressors endanger their souls by committing sacrilege and set a bad example. John the Baptist resisted Herod unto death, not for the sake of the faith, but for protesting against his bad conduct (in marrying his brother's wife). Here we have clearer proof that Thomas of Canterbury was a true martyr. Some have objected that he was not, since he died for the sake of the temporal jurisdiction of the Church:

Sed numquid prelatus debet se opponere ad mortem pro manifestis iniuriis ecclesie quoad res temporales? Videtur quod sic. . . . Possit tamen per hec verba dici theologice quod contra iniuriatores in bonis ecclesie debet se opponere ad mortem iniurias eorum et peccata corripiendo et compescendo, quia opera sacrilegia eorum vergunt in detrimentum sue salutis eterne et in perniciosum exemplum, sicut Iohannes Baptista qui ingessit se ad mortem contra Herodem, non pro fide, sed contra malos mores eius; et sic clarius potest salvari quod Thomas Cantuariensis fuit verus martyr, contra quod aliqui obicierunt quod moriebatur pro temporali iurisdictione ecclesie (fol. 115rb).

The parallel between the Baptist and Thomas Becket is not immediately clear. It becomes so if we read a sermon on his feast day preached probably by Archbishop Stratford to the monks of Christ Church during the "constitutional crisis" of 1341.[1] The preacher wishes to defend Becket against those who deny that the cause of his martyrdom was sufficient. There were many such. St. Thomas's cause is criticized frequently, he says; many are wont to detract from it in speaking, in writing and in public preaching. Like Baconthorpe, he wants to find an argument that will

[1] W. D. Macray, "Sermons for the Festival of St. Thomas Becket, etc., probably preached by Archbishop Stratford," *English Historical Review*, 8 (1893), 85-91.

appeal to them. According to a life of Becket which he had read at Oseney Abbey, one of Becket's murderers gave as his reason that the archbishop had hindered a proposed marriage between Henry II's brother William and the Countess of Warenne, widow of a son of King Stephen, on the grounds that it would be incestuous.[1] If what the Oseney *Life* says is true, he argues, it is very much to the point. Becket resembled John the Baptist in that he died for having resisted an unlawful union. Baconthorpe must surely have had this episode in Becket's life in mind. He takes the same line as the sermon. In spite of his proofs from the canons, he feels that defence of ecclesiastical privilege as a cause for martyrdom may not carry conviction in all circles. A rebuke to royal morals raises it to a higher level. Becket suffered in his spiritual capacity, resisting sacrilege and incest. His intervention was *ratione peccati*. We can trace a thread in Baconthorpe's reasoning. He sees the weakness of an extreme presentation of his case and is always ready to fall back on a second line of defence.

The two great controversies of John XXII's reign, on the poverty of Christ and on the beatific vision, raised the question of papal authority within the Church. Was the pope's action limited either by the decrees of his predecessors or by any kind of control from his subordinates? We have seen that Baconthorpe had reservations on the temporal power of the papacy. On the subject of limits to the pope's spiritual authority he had none. He goes into both controversies, on the poverty of Christ and on the beatific vision, in great detail, but he always keeps the major problem in the forefront. His discussion of the poverty of Christ (on Matt. iv. 20, *relictis retibus*) takes the form of a commentary on the three bulls of John XXII, condemning the view that Christ and the apostles held no property even in common. Baconthorpe quotes from and explains the teaching of *Ad conditorem canonum*, *Cum inter nonnullos* and *Quia quorundam* (fol. 122va-124ra).[2] He ends by stressing the right of the pope to define contrary to the teaching of a predecessor. Nicholas III in his bull *Exiit qui seminat* (1279) had accepted the Franciscan claim that evangelical

---

[1] See William Fitz Stephen, *Vita S. Thomae*, Materials for the History of Archbishop Becket, ed. Robertson (Rolls Series), iii 142; Stephen of Rouen, *Draco Normannicus*, Chronicles of the Reigns of Stephen, Henry II, and Richard I, ed. Howlett (Rolls Series), ii 676.

[2] Ed. C. Eubel, *Bullarium franciscanum*, vol. v (Quaracchi, 1898), no. 486, 518, 554, pp. 233, 236, 271.

poverty meant a complete renunciation of ownership of property and had forbidden that his bull should be glossed.[1] John's opponents questioned his power to reverse this decision. Baconthorpe left his students in no doubt whatsoever that all who denied this power in a reigning pope to reverse previous decisions were heretics and liable to excommunication. The piece is worth quoting for the passion which informs the argument:

Caveant igitur universi de periculo heresis, quia xxiv, q. 1, sic dicitur: *Hec est fides*. . . .[2] Hic habes quod standum est diffinitioni romani pontificis et qui contradixerit est hereticus. Sed dominus Iohannes XXII primo in constitutione sua *Cum inter nonnullos* diffinivit Christum et apostolos habere aliquid in communi et contrarium esse hereticum; et consequenter in constitutione sua *Quia quorundam* diffinit hoc non derogare perfectione vite Christi et evangelice, ut iam deductum est; nullus ergo qui heresim vult cavere debet dicere quod Christus et apostoli nichil habuerunt in communi, ut vitam perfectionis exercentes, nec presumat quisquam se fundare super hoc quod alii romani pontifices hoc diffinierunt, quia contrarium iam est probatum. . . . Cum igitur dominus Iohannes de concilio fratrum primo diffinierit Christum aliquid in communi in constitutione *Cum inter nonnullos*, et quod hoc stat cum perfectione vite Christi et evangelice iam declaravit, et in fine eiusdem declarationis iterum diffinit, contrarium asserentes aut docentes per se vel per alios in heresim dampnatam insidere, ut patet in constitutione *Quia quorundam*, nullus contraire presumat (fol. 124ra).

Baconthorpe introduces his discussion of the keys as necessary because papal power to revoke a predecessor's decision has been questioned:

Et tibi dabo claves. De clavibus ecclesie tempore Iohannis XXII fuit ortus error magnus, ut patet in constitutione sua *Quia quorundam*. Dicebant enim quidam filii mendacii (MS. mundani)[3] quod papa sequens non potuit per clavem potestatis revocare quod predecessor suus firmaverat in fide (et) moribus, et sic falsificaretur quod hic dicitur *quodcumque ligaveris* etc. Propter quod est necessarium scire de clavibus que sequuntur (fol. 157ra).

The whole discussion on the keys centres on the need to establish this point.

The beatific vision controversy was even fresher and more actual

[1] *Ibid.*, vol. iii, 404.

[2] Gratian, *Decretum* II, causa xxiv, q. 1, cap. 14.

[3] A reference to the opening words of the Bull: Quia quorundam mentes sic pater mendacii dicitur excaecasse. . . .

than that on the poverty of Christ, since it had come at the very end of
John XXII's life. Baconthorpe discusses it thoroughly twice, on the
preaching of John the Baptist, Matthew iii. 2 and on the beatitudes,
Matthew v. 8. He goes over well-worn ground. The most interesting
part for us is where he insists that John XXII never deviated from the
faith. John put forward his views as a private interpretation, without
wishing to define officially, and revoked them at his death. "A certain
theologian" acted imprudently in criticizing him. This is clearly a reference
to the Dominican, Thomas Waleys, summoned before the Inquisition for
a sermon attacking the supporters of John's view on the beatific vision,
preached at Avignon, January 3, 1333. Waleys appealed against the in-
quisitors and was transferred to the papal prison. He was probably still
there when Baconthorpe was preparing his postill.[1] Baconthorpe seems to
have felt that Waleys deserved his fate. But, he goes on to say, even if the
pope should err in a matter of faith, a council summoned to consider the
matter cannot judge him; it can only reverently say that the first see of the
Church is accountable to none; the pope must judge his own cause. The
authority is the *Decretum* on the case of Pope Marcellinus:

Et discant theologi qualiter secundum sacros canones debeant se habere in
reprehensione pape. Nullus enim mortalium eius culpam redarguere presumit nisi
a fide deprehenditur devius et non vult corrigi, ut habetur d. xl, cap. *Si papa*[2] in
textu et in glosa. Sed dominus papa non est deprehensus devius a fide predicando
quod alique auctoritates sanctorum sonant quod anime non recipiantur in regno
celorum nec Deum videbunt ante diem iudicii, maxime cum protestabatur se nichil
velle sententialiter diffinire absque concilio fratrum suorum, et ante mortem sub
bulla confessus est quod anime sanctorum sunt in celis cum Christo et beatis
angelis et vident Deum facie ad faciem, secundum quod congruit ex modis eorum;
et ideo minus prudenter reprehendit eum quidam theologus. Quinimmo si sit
deprehensus devius a fide etiam idolis sacrificando quod maxima est heresis etiam
super hoc congregato concilio nullus debet eum iudicare, sed omnes cum reverentia
dicere: prima sedes non iudicatur a quocumque; tuo ore iudica causam tuam.
Hec habentur de Marcellino papa, qui et idolis optulit, d. xxii (*sic*), cap. *Nunc
autem*[3] (fol. 117vb).

---

[1]) Th. Kaeppeli, *Le procès contre Thomas Waleys*, O.P. (Rome, 1936). Waleys was probably released by Clement VI in 1342 or later; B. Smalley, *Thomas Waleys O.P.*, *op. cit.*, 52-57.

[2]) Gratian, *Decretum* I, dist. xl, cap. 6.

[3]) *Ibid.*, I, dist. xxi, cap. 7.

The second discussion seems to date from the period before John XXII died, when his views were still being canvassed.[1] The relevant point here is that Baconthorpe, while not following the pope in his interpretation of the texts, still tries to do his best for him. He sets forth the scheme of procedure to be adopted: first he will adduce the authorities proving that the souls released from purgatory enjoy the full beatific vision; secondly he will show how the pope's thesis can be favourably interpreted:

> Secundo, pono modum secundum quem aliquanter dictum domini pape posset salvari (fol. 124ᵛᵇ).

Thirdly he will explain the texts from St. Bernard on which much of the discussion turned. He ends with what must be an addition to his original *quaestio*, Benedict XII's definition in the *Benedictus Deus* (fol. 126ᵛᵃ).

The question so disturbed Baconthorpe that it drew from him his only reference to his Order. Devotion to the pope swallowed up lesser loyalties. After his *quaestio* on the Immaculate Conception, where he calls himself a Carmelite, he never mentions Carmel or the vexed question of its origins. But the text Matthew vii. 11 reminds him of the feast of the Patriarchs Abraham, Isaac and Jacob. The Church of Jerusalem and the Carmelite Order celebrated it.[2] He points out that the gospel in this passage justifies the feast and that it is further legitimized by Benedict XII's decision in the *Benedictus Deus*, since the Patriarchs are enjoying the beatific vision in heaven. Hence the feast can be defended. He feels that the pope has thrown his mantle over a cherished practice:

> *Multi ab oriente et occidente venient, et recumbent cum Abraham et Isaac et Iacob in regno celorum.* . . . Ex hac littera roboratur factum quorundam religiosorum qui festum celebrant patriarcharum, Abraham, Isaac et Iacob, non habendo respecta ad statum eorum pro tempore veteris legis, quia hoc esset hereticum, sed pro quanto creduntur esse in regno celorum. Hoc roborat constitutio novella Benedicti XII, que incipit *Benedictus Deus in donis*, ubi condempnando errorem qui dixit

---

[1] See above, p. 300.

[2] *Acta sanctorum*, Oct., vol. iv (Brussels, 1780), pp. 691-3. The feast was kept in the Greek and Oriental, as well as in some Latin churches and in the Carmelite Order; see also S. J. I. van Dijk, "The Breviary of Saint Clare", *Franciscan Studies*, 8 (1948), 36.

animas sanctorum veteris testamenti, qui de hoc mundo decesserunt ante Christi passionem, et aliorum fidelium defunctorum baptizatorum et plene purgatorum ante resumptionem suorum corporum in celo celorum regni et paradisi celestis cum Christo et sanctorum angelorum consortio congregantur. Sed Christus hic inter omnes sanctos patres Abraham, Isaac et Iacob specialiter pre omnibus regno Dei dignos nominat. Licitum est ergo iuxta antiquum usum ecclesie Ierosolomitane et institutionem antiquorum pontificum eiusdem eorum festum celebrare, quia ab antiquo licuit cuilibet episcopo festum sanctorum instituere . . .[1] (fol. 139ra).

V

SIGNIFICANCE

It will be helpful to compare our postill with four others of the early fourteenth century. Its individuality will stand out all the more sharply. Michael of Massa, O.E.S.A., left a gospel-commentary correctly described in the title as "plena documentis plurimorum philosophorum et poetarum ac gestis romanorum secundum Valerium Maximum".[2] It is a compilation of moralized tales drawn from classical writers, threaded together on the gospel text. We have seen that Baconthorpe regarded this kind of exercise with horror. Nicholas of Lyre kept close to the gospel story (his *moralitates* on Scripture came after and were supplementary to his work on the "letter"[3]). He could not use his knowledge of Hebrew and rabbinics to the same extent on the New as on the Old Testament; but he took an interest in the historical setting, in Roman and Jewish customs and institutions; he tried to find out what happened. We have seen that Baconthorpe, while quoting Lyre, regarded this kind of study with indifference. The English Franciscan, William of Nottingham, also interested himself in New Testament history and chronology, taking pains to work out the relationship between the events told by each evangelist. His interest was as sincere, but more naïve and less scholarly than Lyre's. A simple piety

---

[1]) Baconthorpe quotes the *Decretals*, II, tit. xix, cap. 5, *Conquestus est*, and the *Decretum*, III, *De consecratione*, cap. 1, *Pronuntiandum*, on the keeping of feasts as approved by the bishops in their dioceses.

[2]) B. Smalley, "Thomas Waleys O.P.", *op. cit.*, 77, 105.

[3]) See above, p. 303, n. 2.

inspired him which is admirably rendered by the crude, lively little pictures of English workmanship in the late-fourteenth-century copy in MS. Bodl. Laud. misc. 165.[1] Nottingham makes an unspoken protest against the use of "fables": ancient poets and historians are conspicuously absent from his pages. This must have endeared him to Baconthorpe and may explain why Nottingham is quoted in the early part of our postill. But Nottingham has also banned theological controversy. One would expect a Franciscan to discuss evangelical poverty. True, Nottingham worked before 1317 and therefore before the acute stage of the controversy under John XXII. The question was actual when he wrote, nevertheless. We know that he felt strongly in favour of the complete poverty of Christ, since he subscribed as English provincial to the two encyclicals drawn up at the General Chapter of the Order in 1321.[2] Yet none of the texts which were usually quoted in the controversy tempt him into argument.[3] This cannot be accidental. Either Nottingham or a colleague went through his postill after the publication of *Quia quorundam*, cutting out all references to the question; or else he felt from the first that bickering, like fables, clashed with the content of the gospels. Baconthorpe, who had no such scruples, must have found him very tame.

We come closest to Baconthorpe's purpose in the contemporary postill of his master, Guy Terré.[4] Here we find the same hard hitting against enemies of the papacy: the anti-pope, Nicholas V, the Spirituals and Marsilio of Padua and John of Jandun.[5] We find the same staunch defence of the faith. Theological controversy abounds. Xiberta has edited the *Quaestio de magisterio infallibili Romani pontificis* from Terré's postill.[6] It is a fundamental discussion of the problem of authority, defending the magistracy of the Church as the guarantor and interpreter of Scripture. Terré, however, while resembling Baconthorpe in some ways, differs from

---

[1] B. Smalley, "Which William of Nottingham?", XI above

[2] D. L. Douie, *The Nature and the Effect of the Heresy of the Fraticelli* (Manchester, 1932), 155.

[3] For instance, all Nottingham vouchsafes on the beatitudes is that to occupy oneself with spiritual work, such as study, prayer and preaching, is better than to labour with one's hands (MS. Laud. misc. 165, fol. 155[ra]).

[4] *Quatuor unum* (ed. Cologne, 1631); it is dedicated to John XXII.

[5] pp. 67, 222, 275-81, 563.

[6] See above, p. 304, n. 2.

him in the direction of his interests. He is more conscious of his Order and of its hermit background and more interested in religion.[1] Above all, he quotes mainly from the Fathers and mediaeval theologians, hardly ever from the canonists.

Baconthorpe therefore was original in his approach. He had a plan and he carried it out to the letter. After making a clean sweep of irrelevance in the shape of "fables", he "piled up" on his text three types of carefully differentiated material, philosophy, theology and canon law, with the emphasis on the last. To "pile up" authorities on one's text was the mediaeval technique *par excellence*. Philosophers had long joined the theologians as a source for the exegete. Many of Baconthorpe's predecessors had quoted the *Decretum* and *Decretals*; but they had done so occasionally in order to make some particular point. No earlier commentator on Scripture seems to have chosen the canonists as his main authorities. On the contrary, the masters of the sacred page used to denounce them as unscrupulous careerists. To desert theology for canon law was presented as treachery to one's calling. Theology prepared men for cure of souls. Defections robbed the Church of properly qualified pastors. Baconthorpe felt that the deserters after all supplied the best ammunition in her defence. By his use of them the fierce little man put a punch into exegesis which it had lacked since the days of the Investiture Contest. Earlier efforts to make postillating topical had generally taken the form of moralization. The technique of moralizing the text had enabled commentators to attack heretics or negligent prelates on the basis of any passage which lent itself to a "trope". But the spiritual exposition was now discredited as a method of proof. St. Thomas had taught that it could be used for edification but not in argument. Opponents of papal claims against the State had brought their heaviest guns to bear on proofs based on the spiritual exposition of texts; they rejected altogether such arguments as the comparison of the Church to the sun and the State to the lesser light, the moon. The popes tacitly accepted the ruling. The type of argument used by Boniface VIII

---

[1] The fast in the wilderness recalls monks and anchorites, the calling of the disciples the year of novitiate; the text Matt. iv. 22 raises the question whether a son may enter religion if his father needs his support; the Carmelite Order is used as an illustration in a *quaestio* on Luc. x, 1; see *Quatuor unum*, pp. 66, 72, 103, 290.

in his *Unam sanctam* drawn from the traditional moralizations was dropped.[1] Commentators on Scripture had to find a new method if they were to take a "high Church" line in their lectures. Baconthorpe met the crisis. His classroom rang with controversy of the most actual kind. He related his text to current problems without having recourse to the outmoded, round-about method of moralization. He made his attack on the enemy direct and up to date by quoting the canons right down to the latest papal pronouncements.

How did the gospel fare when submitted to this treatment? A student of mediaeval postills soon gets used to comments which have little connexion with the text. Scripture formed the taking-off ground for doctrine or homiletics. Some of Baconthorpe's colleagues were accentuat-ing this tendency by quoting fables and classical writers in general, which caused them to lose sight of the text altogether. Baconthorpe disapproved, but did he do any better by substituting canonists? Let us be honest: he departs from his text and he murders it first. The gentleness of the gospel, felt poignantly by Nottingham, perishes in contact with our Carmelite's harsh legalism. He sees heaven and earth in terms of his "de iudiciis" as a system of jurisdictions. He meets a human situation by consulting his *Summa summarum*.

Here he was in tune with the development of the Avignon Papacy. Although John XXII befriended theologians, his attitude was that of a lawyer. A modern historian, sympathetic to the fourteenth-century popes and their problems, has written acutely:

Les Papes d'Avignon sont des juristes; presque tous avaient fait de l'enseigne-ment du droit ou de l'administration leur profession. C'est parmi les canonistes

---

[1] Boniface VIII made great use of the spiritual exposition in the argument of his bull *Unam sanctam*. John XXII omits it in his *Licet iuxta doctrinam* (see above, p. 125). It is interesting that Boniface in his bull granting a *studium generale* to Avignon, where he praises learning, describes theology in early mediaeval terms as consisting of spiritual exposition of Scripture: "Sic quoque ad sacrarum accedit altitudinem scripturarum et elicitur vivificans spiritus de littere visceribus occidentis (*Registrum*, no. 5256, July 1, 1303, vol. iii, col. 782-4)". John XXII quotes these words in his encyclical of 1316 to prelates, ordering them to make provision for all masters and scholars of Paris, but he gives a clever little twist to the traditional expression to bring it into line with later developments. As he puts it, the expression need not refer to the spiritual exposition, but to any type of exegesis: "Per has etiam ascenditur ad altitudinem scripturarum, et vivificans sensus ex ipsis elicitur multa ibidem obscuritate conclusus" (Denifle and Chatelain, *Chartularium Universitatis Parisiensis*, vol. ii (Paris, 1891), no. 729, p. 184).

342

qu'ils choisissent la plupart des cardinaux qui les entourent et qu'ils consultent. Ils ont tendance à organiser l'Eglise comme une immense machine administrative, à concevoir la vie chrétienne comme faite plus de rapports juridiques que de relations réelles et affectives entre Dieu et les hommes.

He points out that the university of Avignon had no theological faculty.[1] Perhaps by his interest in *sacra pagina* John XXII was trying to redress the balance. Baconthorpe produced a mixture of canon law and theology which reflects the papal ambivalence. He expounded St. Matthew, transferring the legal outlook of the Curia to the pages of his postill. He shows that a conscious attempt at revival is apt to be superficial.

Many of his contemporaries, good catholics, felt a nostalgia for the primitive Church, a natural reaction to the pervading legalism. They contrasted the poverty and detachment of the apostles with the wealth and worldliness of the fourteenth-century clergy and they mourned at the change. Baconthorpe took the opposite view. Without excusing the sins of the clergy, he presented ecclesiastical power and riches as a fulfilment, not a negation of the gospel. They were necessary to the Church's mission. How else could the popes hold Christendom together and police it against heretics and rebels? He must have shocked the sentimental. Perhaps he meant to.

The historian need not take sides against Baconthorpe. He should rather enjoy the picture of someone approving of something. Our Carmelite gives us this rare opportunity. He has a feeling for history and for historical development; it is a consequence of his liking for canon law. One cannot handle the *Corpus iuris canonici* without being aware of a vast process of institutional growth. Baconthorpe was unusual in his time in seeing that growth need not mark a decline from primitive standards. He approved of the transformation of a tiny community in Palestine into a world-wide ecclesiastical system. He approved of wealth and endowment as a means to expansion. He approved of the papal *plenitudo potestatis* and its exercise as a means to preservation. He admired the Church as an institution. Most men carped at its failings without suggesting any workable alternative. Baconthorpe was more logical than the grumblers. He saw no half-way house between the *Defensor pacis* and the *Licet iuxta*

[1] Y. Renouard, *La Papauté à Avignon* (Paris, 1954), 121.

doctrinam. The catholic must choose between the lay-controlled Church of the heretics and the Church as it actually was, endowed and centralized under the Avignon Papacy. He devoted himself to apologizing for the second. A little uncritical praise is refreshing after so much uncritical blame.

Note:

p. 305, n. 7: This commentary has now been edited in full by R. Macken, *La "Lectura Ordinaria super Sacram Scripturam" attribuée à Henri de Ghent* (Analecta Mediaevalia Namurcensia, xxvi, 1972).

p. 336, n. 1: Waleys was released soon before the death of John XXII; see M. Dykmans, 'A propos de Jean XXII et Benoît XII/ la libération de Thomas Waleys', *Archivium historiae pontificiae*, vii (1969) 115–130.

On Baconthorpe see now Walter Ullmann, 'John Baconthorpe as Canonist', *Scholarship and Politics in the Middle Ages. Collected Studies* (Variorum Reprints, London, 1978) n. x, 223–246.

13

Jean de Hesdin O. Hosp. S. Ioh.

Jean de Hesdin is better known as the *Gallus calumpniator* who disputed with Petrarch on the subject of the Avignon papacy than as a biblical commentator. P. de Nolhac and other modern scholars have looked at his *lecturae* only as evidence for confirming his identity : his scholastic works show the same fondness for varied literary allusions as does the letter to Petrarch. But Hesdin may well intrigue us as a biblical commentator too. He was quite a freak. No other brother of the Order of St John of Jerusalem won fame as a master of theology at Paris ; the Order did not even remember him [1]. Alone in his Order, he was almost alone as a lecturer on Scripture. The third quarter of the fourteenth century marked a pause in the production of biblical commentaries [2]. The friars, so busy in the first half of the century, stopped publishing their lectures, with few exceptions. The revival, when it came in the last quarter, was led by secular masters, by Wyclif at Oxford and Gerson at Paris. Hesdin bridges the gap between mendicant and secular activities. He was a religious by profession, though not a friar. He took part in high politics, though in a humble capacity, as the average friar doctor did not. The question arises : do his lectures, given at Paris and Avignon in the late ' fifties and ' sixties of the fourteenth century, represent an intermediate stage in their content as well as in the circumstances of their date and authorship ? Do they fall into the pattern of exegesis current in the first part of the century, or do they look forward to Gersonian piety ? A second line of enquiry runs parallel to the first. Hesdin interested himself in classical scholarship. Can one see anything new in this or does he stand wholly for the older tradition in contrast to Petrarchan humanism ? I shall try to answer these questions.

* * *

1. G. Bosio does not mention him in *Dell' istoria della sacra religione e illustrissima militia di S. Giovanni Gierosolitano* (Rome 1594-1602). The records of the Chapters General of the Order are incomplete for the fourteenth century. Miss A. Williams, who kindly gave me this information from her B. Litt. thesis on the Chapters General of the Knights Hospitallers, tells me that she has found no reference to Hesdin or to university studies in the Order in the surviving records.

2. This emerges from F. STEGMÜLLER, *Repertorium biblicum medii aevi* (Madrid 1950-1961) in progress.

The clearest evidence for Hesdin's career comes from three notices in the *Chartularium*. A document of mid-November, 1364, lists him among the regent masters in theology who assembled to correct errors imputed to Denis Foullechat O. F. M. Hesdin's place in the list, immediately after the chancellor of Notre Dame, suggests that he already held the office of dean of his faculty. He has the title of dean in the roll of petitioners for papal provisions sent from the regents of the theological faculty to the Curia, dated June 14, 1365. A short *curriculum vitae* goes with it :

> Primo fratri Johanni de Hesdinio, O. S. Johan. Jherusol. decano ad presens theologice facultatis Parisius, qui per xxv annos fuit quasi continue actu regens, excepto tempore quo in Avinione cum domino cardinali Boloniensi peregit lecturam supra Job, quam Parisius inceperat, et postea Parisius fecit lecturam supra epistolam Pauli ad Titum, cum pluribus sermonibus et aliis operibus, que per copiam habentur Parisius [3].

He attended with other masters of theology, again heading the list, when a new provost of Paris swore to preserve university privileges, June 23-Oct. 10, 1367. Another man had replaced him as dean by the autumn 1378/9 [4].

The Hospitallers had a house at Paris [5]. Pope Innocent VI gave them permission in a letter dated Feb. 21, 1356 to send brothers to study and qualify in canon law at Paris and elsewhere, on the grounds that the Order lacked learned men and yet had many brothers who wished to study in the faculty of canon law. A Hospitaller is mentioned as doctor of decretals in 1385 [6]. The Order had been founded for the sake of action rather than of study and contemplation ; the house at Paris does not seem to have served as a *studium* before this time. Canon law had practical use, in that the Order must have needed lawyers for its business as a large propertyholder. Still, Hesdin's regency, said to have lasted almost continuously for twenty-five years by 1365, may perhaps be seen against the background of some attempt to raise the

---

3. *Chartularium Universitatis Parisiensis*, ed. H. DENIFLE and E. CHATELAIN, vol. III, p. 122, n° 1299 ; p. 127, n° 1305. For the system of collective petitions from university faculties for papal provisions see E. F. JACOB, *Petitions for Benefices from English Universities during the Great Schism*, in *Transactions of the Royal Historical Society*, 4th series, 27 (1945) p. 41-60.

4. *Chart. Univ. Paris.*, vol. III, p. 163, n° 1336 ; p. 247, n° 1429.

5. It was listed as liable for taxation with those of other religious Orders in 1252 ; *ibid.*, vol. I, p. 232, n° 203. See also A. LE ROUX DE LINCY and L. M. TISSERAND, *Paris et ses historiens aux XIVᵉ et XVᵉ siècles*, Paris 1867, p. 186.

6. *Chart. Univ. Paris.*, vol. III, p. 40, n° 1230 ; p. 396, n° 1518. Benedict XII had already granted permission to religious Orders to allow their members to study canon law.

tone of the Order. Innocent VI had planned to reform it in 1354 [7]. It is also rather surprising to find a religious holding the office of dean of the theological faculty ; this, we are told, 'was always held by the senior secular doctor ' [8]. Perhaps his membership of an Order which did not normally compete with the seculars inclined his colleagues to make an exception in his favour.

We know nothing of his life before his regency. It has been suggested that he came of the same Artois family as Simon de Hesdin, his contemporary, who translated Valerius Maximus into French [9] ; but there is no evidence apart from the fact that both took their surname from the same place. I have not found any references to Jean de Hesdin in the papal registers for this period which have been published. His own writings must fill in the outline drawn in the *Chartularium*.

His commentary on Job, finished on the vigil of All Saints, 1357, begins with a dedicatory letter to Gui de Boulogne, cardinal bishop of Porto, and ends with verses addressed to the same person. Hesdin writes as client to patron, calling himself 'vester humilis et devotus orator '. He praises the cardinal's nobility of birth and character and his *liberalitas*. The patron is asked to examine the commentary and correct what is wrong, so that glory may accrue to the corrector rather than to the author. Indeed, the length is such that a conscientious examiner would have deserved respect, if not glory. But Hesdin hoped for something more. He begs his patron to support the hesitant and hearten the timid, as well as to correct the erring. The verses at the end ask him to stretch a helping hand to the tired sailor coming ashore, with a hint : Job's patience was rewarded at last [10].

His patron's career will throw light on Hesdin's. Gui de Boulogne, an uncle of King John II, entered the sacred college in 1342. He went on a mission to Hungary as papal legate in 1349, travelling via Padua and Venice. He then visited Rome in connexion with the Jubilee in the spring of 1350, held a council at Padua on his way back, and reached Avignon again on June 7, 1350. The Pope created him cardinal

7. G. MOLLAT, *Les Papes d'Avignon*, 9th ed., Paris 1949, 102-103.

8. *Rashdall's Medieval Universities*, ed. F. M. POWICKE and A. B. EMDEN, vol. I, Oxford 1936, p. 326, n. 1.

9. E. COCCHIA, *Varietà letterarie*, Naples 1931, p. 35-36. Cocchia gives a full bibliography on Hesdin as the correspondent of Petrarch in his introduction to his edition of their letters, *ibid*. See also the review by V. ROSSI, in *Giornale storico d. Lett. ital.* 76 (1920) 347-351, of the original paper reprinted in *Varietà* etc.

10. On the dates see STEGMÜLLER, *op. cit.*, nº 4551-6. I have printed the two dedicatory letters in the appendix, p. 321-325.

bishop of Porto late in the same year [11]. It has been supposed, and is very likely, that Hesdin had accompanied him on his mission as a *familiaris*. Hesdin, in writing to Petrarch, gives personal impressions of Milan and Rome and perhaps also of Venice. The miserable state of Rome and the Romans' poverty struck him forcibly [12]. It is known that his patron annoyed the Roman innkeepers by shortening his stay there. All this agrees with the dates given in the *Chartularium*. Hesdin must have been regent from about 1340. He could have begun his *lectura* on Job at Paris before 1349. He would have interrupted it in order to serve the cardinal at Avignon and go with him on his mission, 1349-50. He would have finished it at the papal *studium* after their return. His letter to Petrarch refers to his happy experience of life at Avignon [13].

The *lectura* on Titus was begun at Paris in 1362. The lecturer mentions 1363 as the 'present year' when about a quarter of the way through [14]. He finished on the feast of the Exaltation of the Holy Cross (Sept. 14) in 1364. There are references back to the *lectura* on Job. Hesdin dedicated his second *lectura* to a new patron, Philippe d'Alençon, archbishop of Rouen. The cardinal of Boulogne (as he was commonly called) may have disappointed him. The French government looked askance at the cardinal's intrigues with the king of Navarre and the duke of Lancaster in 1354-5. His candidature for the papacy on the death of Innocent VI in 1362 had failed [15]. On the other hand, Hesdin made a bad choice this time, if he looked for favour at the royal court. Philippe d'Alençon, archbishop of Rouen since 1359, embroiled himself at once in a conflict of jurisdictions, although he was of the blood royal and a nephew of Philip VI. The trouble ended only with his translation to the archbishopric of Auch, with the title of patriarch of Jerusalem, in 1375 [16]. Hesdin now had a more definite post ; he writes to the archbishop of Rouen as 'vester humilis capellanus et devotus orator '. The tone of the letter suggests a respectful

11. *Dict. d'Hist. et de Géogr. ecclés.* 10 (1938) 101-106. On the mission to Hungary see E. G. LÉONARD, *Les Angevins de Naples*, Paris 1954, p. 361.

12. COCCHIA, *op. cit.*, 41, 50, 52. Hesdin says of Rome : ' ...miseriam cuius certe non potuissem credere ne vidissem ' ; of Milan : ' Nonne in Mediolano vidi abhominabile idolum super altare Dei ? ' ; of Venice : ' Et iterum, illa nobilis civitas Venetorum, quam et supér alias sic extollit (i. e. Petrarch), quid habet aliunde non advectum ? '

13. *Ibid.*, on the Church at Avignon : ' Vidi enim eam ibi in omnibus quietam et tranquillam '. He defends the city as a fit dwelling for the Curia.

14. See below, p. 291.

15. R. DELACHENAL, *Histoire de Charles V*, vol. I, Paris 1909, p. 87-89; G. MOLLAT, *op. cit.*, p. 109.

16. *Dict. d'Hist. et de Géogr. ecclés.* 2 (1914) 96-97.

mentor rather than a dependent. The third and last *lectura*, on St Mark, has no dedication. He finished it on July 10, 1367. It contains references back to his work on both Job and Titus. The *Chartularium* tells us that he was still at Paris.

Lastly he wrote his letter to Petrarch. Its background is Franco-Italian polemic on the subject of the Avignon papacy. Petrarch had written to Pope Urban V, begging him to remove to Rome. King Charles V tried to dissuade him by sending an embassy to Avignon. It failed in its object, having arrived only a few days before the Pope set off on his journey, on Apr. 30, 1367. One of the royal ambassadors was Ancel Choquart, a doctor of canon law, professor at Paris and member of the King's council. He made a speech at the Curia, pressing the royal point of view [17]. Petrarch wrote to Urban again : the Pope should not listen to French objections, but should persevere. By this time a lot of mud had been flung on both sides. Petrarch had criticised the French character and the Avignon climate ; Choquart defended the ancient Gauls and their history. The French champion died late in 1368 or early in the next year. Hesdin took up the cudgels on his behalf. He refers in his letter to Choquart's speech at the Curia and to Petrarch's counter-attack, saying that the former would have given a good account of himself, had he lived [18]. Since Choquart spoke officially for the French royal government, it seems probable that Hesdin had a brief to replace his dead colleague as propagandist. Arguments from ancient history and classical quotations played a big part in the controversy : Hesdin, whose lectures were stuffed with literary allusions, must have seemed the right man to choose.

His letter to Petrarch dates itself by the reference to Choquart's death, winter 1368-9, at one end, and by the Pope's return to Avignon at the other, September, 1370. The autumn or winter of 1369 seems the most likely moment between these limiting dates. Hesdin knew of the Perugian rebellion as well as of the earlier anti-papal riots at Viterbo and Rome. The Perugians had been in open rebellion since August, 1368, but the papal bull which publicised their disobedience to the Holy See is dated July 7, 1369 [19]. He writes as though the return

---

17. DELACHENAL, *op. cit.*, III, p. 515-526.

18. COCCHIA, 52 : ' Unde et dominus Anselmus, a domino Rege missus, haec et multa alia, quae D. N. Papam revocare poterant ab incepto, luculenter ostendens, male fuit per istum — salva reverentia — redargutus. Quod, si forte vixisset, vivis rationibus ostendisset '.

19. P. BALAN, *La ribellione di Perugia nel 1368* (pubblicato nel periodico *Studi e documenti di storia e diritto*, Rome 1880) 5-6, 35. Hesdin describes all these commotions as common knowledge : COCCHIA, 48 : ' Et quis est, qui non vidit aut audivit Viterbiorum aggressionem furiosam, Romanorum commotionem iniuriosam, rebellionem Perusinorum et obstinationem animosam, et generaliter tyrannorum contradictionem odiosam ? '

journey to Avignon was under discussion, and not yet settled[20]. Urban V announced his decision to return early in October, 1369 ; the Romans pleaded with him to stay. It must have been clear by the spring of 1370 that Urban would stand by his decision[21]. Hesdin, writing at this juncture, would have used different terms ; he would have rejoiced at the prospect of the Pope's arrival on French soil again. Petrarch did not get the letter until late in 1371, when a friend brought it from Avignon. He commented on the time and trouble wasted by his correspondent and on his slowness in answering a letter written four years ago[22]. But the delay may have been in delivery rather than in composition. A date towards the end of 1369 would fit in with Petrarch's comments.

Hesdin may have met the poet as an honoured guest of cardinal Gui de Boulogne when they were returning from Hungary in 1350. He refers to Petrarch with respect as a great man, whose attacks on France were unworthy of him[23]. Petrarch, for his part, would hardly have noticed a member of the cardinal's large household[24]. He chose to give the impression that he did not know Hesdin, and does not mention his name, but he had some information about 'the anonymous Frenchman' nevertheless. His correspondent, he tells us, was a scholastic theologian, living somewhere in France, and a religious, *fraterculus*, wearing a white habit[25]. Petrarch accused him of currying

---

20. COCCHIA, 49 : ' Et iterum, si adventus ad Italiam ita D. Papam felicitat, et spiritus, quo ductus est in desertum, ipsum moneat ad regressum, nonne eius regressus, *si contingat*, ipsum faciet infelicem ? Absit. Omnia enim sibi licent. Licuit sibi ire ; *licet etiam et redire...* Spiritus enim bonus duxit eum, ut credo ; nec dicam ipsum malum, sed multo meliorem, *si reducat* '.

21. G. MOLLAT, *op. cit.*, 256-257.

22. *Contra cuiusdam anonymi Galli calumnias ad Ugutionem de Thienis apologia*, ed. COCCHIA, *op. cit.*, 62-63 : ' ...epistolam, immo librum dicam, verius homeliam ingentem pariter et ineptam, multo — ut res indicat — sudore confectam et magni iactura temporis, attulisti, dum e longinquo veniens, ...adisses... Epistola enim mea... ante hoc — ni fallor — quadrennium, missa erat. Quid igitur rei est, ut vel tot annis orator iste tacuerit, vel nunc tandem caput extulerit, nisi quod parum iustitiae suae tunc fidebat, sicut obstare suae iracundiae nunc non potest ? '

23. ' O verbum improprium, vere admirabile et ineptum, et non a tali viro saltem sic improvide proferendum ' (*ibid.*, 43) ; ' Consideret iste praedicator egregius, quantum — Deo adiuvante — ipsius praedicatio, sive exhortatio, multis possit proficere, et quod habet in foribus quos facundiae suae lenitate mulceat et profunditate scientiae dirigat exhortando... ' (*ibid.*, 50).

24. On Petrarch's relations with Gui de Bologne see P. DE NOLHAC, *Pétrarque et l'humanisme*, 2nd ed., II, Paris 1907, 310.

25. COCCHIA, 62, 64, 70, 80, 112 : ' ...scholastici nesciocuius epistolam... prolocutor iste, non scribentis epistolam sed sermocantis in morem... candidamque — ut aiunt — togam sui habitus nigris atque deformibus maculis inquinet...

favour with the great in order to get a bishopric, though he was not rich enough to succeed ; he thought of nothing else [26]. It sounds as though Petrarch had heard gossip about Hesdin's disappointed hopes, which is likely enough in view of the dedications to a cardinal and an archbishop.

The date of Hesdin's death is unknown. Petrarch supposed him to be alive when writing early in 1372. We have seen that he was dead or at least retired from the office of dean by 1378/9.

* * *

Stegmüller lists twelve copies of the *lectura* on Job, of which one consists of excerpts and one is incomplete, plus one recorded but now lost, nine copies of the *lectura* on St Mark, plus one recorded but lost, nineteen of the *lectura* on Titus, plus two recorded but lost [27]. The other items listed are noted as non-existent or spurious. There seem to be no significant variants ; in each case the *copies* derive from the same original *lectura*. A full study of the manuscripts and their provenance would be long and expensive, and would be more suitable as part of an enquiry into Hesdin's influence on his successors than to this preliminary survey. A glance at the list suggests that the *lectura* on Job circulated most widely in Germany and Eastern Europe ; only two copies are in Paris now, and one at Toulouse. The *lecturae* on St Mark and Titus are combined in one volume in copies now at Assisi, Avranches and Toulouse. The *lectura* on Titus survives in the largest number of copies and had the widest distribution in France, Germany, Italy and Spain. The reason for its popularity will be discussed later.

It would be a waste of time to search for a good text of a late scholastic *lectura*. Hesdin's commentaries, divided into *lectiones*, bear marks of their origin in the master's own hastily prepared notes. The style is careless and conversational. It is doubtful whether the exemplar as it left his hands would have been free from mistakes. I have therefore used those copies which are most readily accessible to me and have restricted myself to sampling two or three of each *lectura*. I shall

---

Fraterculus hic flammatus ulciscitur... Sin fortassis eum videris, quem credo illo adulationum atque mendaciorum in regno esse... '

26. *Ibid.*, 70, 76-77 : ' Turpibus blanditiis bonum opus, episcopium, aucupatur, ad quod obtinendum sciat se aliis, quam verborum, retibus indigere... Unum ei posset opitulari. Posset — ut ego mentitus videar — episcopus fieri ...an ipse magis exoculatus, qui fulgore panni captus exigui nihil videt aut cogitat praeter episcopatum, quem mendacio fidens stulta et cupida mente preoccupat ? '

27. Stegmüller, *op. cit.*, n⁰ 4551, 4553, 4556. The ' lost ' copy in MS *Balliol College 324* is a ghost from *Cat. MSS Angl. et Hibern. : cat. MSS Coll. Oxon.* (Oxford 1697) 8. It is the MS now numbered MS *Balliol College 181*.

describe those which I have seen, adding details where the catalogues leave something to be desired :

JOB.

London, Brit. Mus. Arundel 64, fol. 1ra-178vb [28]. Late 14th or early 15th cent. English (?) hand, on parchment, blue and red initials, 13 ½ × 10 in. The ink on fol. 1r is so faded as to be almost illegible ; it is faint throughout. Many marginal headings and names of authors quoted. ' Genealogia Iob secundum magistrum in historiis scholasticis ' follows the text, fol. 178vb. A table, incomplete, *Abissus... Superbia*, fol. 178vb-188vb.
Given by Lord Howard of Norfolk.

Paris, Bibl. Maz. 200, fol. 17ra-357rb. Paris hand about 1370 [29], a rather untidy scholar's book, not a show copy. Preceded by a table, *Abissus... Ypocrite*, fol. 1ra-16ra, rest of leaf blank. ' Genealogia Iob ' (as above), fol. 357rb, followed by six lines of verse headed : *Brevis conclusio ad dominum cardinalem bononiensem*. Leaves numbered only at beginning and end.
Provenance unknown.

ST. MARK AND TITUS.

Avranches, Bibl. publ. 33, Tit. fol. 1ra-75vb, followed by table, fol. 76ra-79va ; Mc. fol. 80ra-139vb, incomplete, ending on Mc. x, 48 ; the last leaf discoloured by damp and the rest lost. Two quires missing after foll. 36 and 49 respectively .This enormous and handsome, though now mutilated copy was written in 1391 for Pierre Leroy, abbot of Mont-Saint-Michel [30].

Oxford, Balliol College 181 (= B) ; fol. 1r, blank, fol. 1v : ' Iohannes de Isdinio super Marcum et epistolam ad Titum', Mc. fol. 2ra-79va ; table, fol. 79va-81va ; fol. 82r-85v blank ; Tit. fol. 86ra-169vb.Tables to Tit. fol. 170ra-173vb. 16 × 11 ½ in.
According to a verse on fol. 169vb (see Coxe [31]) it was finished on St. Lambert's day, 1444. Written on paper. The watermark, fol. 174, closely resembles one dated Evreux, 1441 [32]. The hands, like the illuminated capitals, look Dutch ; this is borne out by the mention of St. Lambert's day. The first hand writes in a lightish ink ; the second, from fol. 103v, uses darker ink and is more Germanic. A few marginal headings fol. 2-79v, many more, giving names of authors quoted, fol. 86-169v.
Given by William Gray, a great benefactor to Balliol, bishop of Ely 1454-78 [33].

ST. MARK ONLY.

Paris, Bibl. Nat. lat. 17287, fol. 1-116v ; table, exactly like that in B, fol. 116v-120v. 15th cent., from the Paris Carmel.

---

28. I include the dedicatory letters to Job and Mark respectively in the commentaries.

29. A. MOLINIER, *Cat. des manuscrits de la Bibl. Maz.*, I, Paris 1885, 73.

30. *Cat. gén. des manuscrits des dép.* etc., IV, Paris 1872, 445.

31. H. O. COXE, *Cat. cod. MSS in coll. Oxon., Balliol*, Oxford 1860.

32. C. M. BRIQUET, *Les filigranes* etc., IV, Paris 1907, 755, n° 15054.

33. For Gray's career and classical learning, see A. B. EMDEN, *A Biographical Register of the University of Oxford to A. D. 1500*, II, Oxford 1958, 809-814.

TITUS ONLY.

> *Paris, Bibl. Maz. 271*, fol. 1ra-112va [34]; table like that in MSS *Avranches 33*
> and *B*. Late 14th cent. Another scholar's book with little decoration.
> From the *Grands Augustins* of Paris.

I have also used microfilms of MSS *Toulouse 42*, *Iob*, and *54*, *Titus* (= *T*),
from the Franciscans and the Austin Friars of Toulouse, both late-14th
century. The copy of Hesdin on Titus, lacking the dedicatory letter, is rather
more decorated than MS *42*; and has the names of the authors quoted
written in the margin, as in *B* [35].

* * *

Scholastic lectures on Scripture tend to be more personal in tone
than lectures on the *Sentences*. They often give an impression of the
master's attitude to current problems both within and without the
university. We shall begin, therefore, by studying the *Gallus calumpniator* from this point of view and then go on to study his technique
and sources as a commentator.

How far was he awake or *engagé* in relation to contemporary politics ? These were stormy enough to draw out the most detached
scholar, unless, which is also possible, they were too dangerous to be
mentioned. I have not found any allusions to them in the *lectura* on
Job, which perhaps reflects the tact needed in lecturing to the international audience of the Curia. The *lectura* on Titus offers several
pointers to Hesdin's thoughts. That on Mark shows a return to his
earlier reserve.

The most definite statement comes into a discussion of justice on
the word *iustum* (*Tit.* i, 8). He quotes St Augustine's saying
that kingdoms without justice are no better than robber gangs, and
adds that in the present year, 1363, this is clear in fact : the kingdom
of France is full of robberies now, since justice fails [36]. The remark
may be taken as a trite reference to the aftermath of the Anglo-French
wars and especially to the armed companies ; but it may have been
more pointed than that. The terms of the treaty of Brétigny, 1360,
had left the sovereignty, and hence the right to hear appeals, in

---

34. A. MOLINIER, *op. cit.*, 98.

35. Fully described in the *Cat. gén. des manuscrits des dép.* etc., VII, Paris 1885,
19-20, 24-25. I have to thank Mlle J. Vielliard of the Institut de recherches et
d'histoire des textes for her kindness in procuring microfilms of these two large
MSS for me.

36. *B*, fol. 109ra : ' ...revera sine iustitia regna non sunt nisi latrocinia, ut
dicit Augustinus ivo de civitate Dei, et istud de facto patet in regno Francie modo,
quia sumus anno 1363, quia iustitia deficiente regnum est nunc latrociniis
plenum '. See *De civ. Dei*, IV, 4.

abeyance in large areas of France, pending renunciations on both sides. The renunciations were delayed. 'The practical result of the *Cest assavoir* clause as affecting the administration of justice in the English possessions in France was the abolition of appeals either to Edward III or to King John ' [37]. ' Justice failed ' in the technical sense of the term.

His attitude to current academic developments gives a clue to his whole mentality. He disapproves of ' English doctrine ', that is Ockhamism. This ' now flourishes at Paris ; sound learning has come to an end '. He says so apropos of a tag from Seneca : ' You are taught to dispute rather than to live ' [38]. Hesdin never specifies what he means by ' sound learning ' (*bona scientia*) as opposed to *doctrina anglicana* : we shall soon see that he meant Thomism. The sequel to Ockhamism in the schools was anti-intellectualism and fideism. Moralists would contrast devotion and learning as though they were mutually exclusive, in order to praise the former and blame the latter. Hesdin, as a Thomist, could have no place in the anti-intellectual chorus, though it must have taken courage to stand outside. And stand out he did. This appears in a fascinating passage where he defends Abelard and Gilbert de la Porrée against their accusers. He saw these twelfth-century masters as the founders of scholastic theology and rejoiced that St Bernard failed to win his case against Gilbert at the council of Rheims (Hesdin says Tours by mistake). The passage reads as a manifesto in favour of ' sound learning '. Both the content and the sources are surprising. Hesdin is commenting on *doctrina sana* (*Tit.* i, 9). He gives four reasons why some men oppose the teacher of sound doctrine. The first reason is ignorance. He cites in example the council of Sens. Abelard's apologist, Berengar (of Poitiers) says that the prelates who attended the council opposed Abelard from ignorance rather than for any other cause ; they did not understand what his words really meant. The same thing happened at ' the council of Tours ' (Rheims), where St Bernard imputed heresies to Gilbert de la Porrée, contained in his exposition of Boethius on the Trinity, as St Bernard and others assembled there thought. But Gilbert answered in such a way as to silence them, and left the council unharmed. Hesdin purports to be quoting from ' the archdea-

37. P. CHAPLAIS, *The Opinions of the Doctors of Bologna on the Sovereignty of Aquitaine (1369) : a Source of the Songe du Verger*, in *Camden Miscellany*, vol. XIX (Camden 3rd series, vol. LXXX), p. 52-53.

38. *B*, fol. 129vb : ' Docemini magis disputare quam vivere, quod maxime fit temporibus istis, sicut patet de doctrina anglicana, que modo viget Parisius, et bona scientia cessavit '. From SENECA, *Ep. moral.*, 108, 23 : ' qui nos docent disputare non vivere '.

con of Chartres in his chronicle '. He rounds off the story by citing the text Osee iv, 4-6 : ...*My people have been silent because they have no knowledge.* The second reason for opposition to sound doctrine is envy. St Jerome tells us that he had detractors, and so had Peter Abelard, who says at the beginning of his letterbook that Anselm, dean of Laon, opposed him out of envy, because many scholars followed him and his teaching. Hence it is well said in Ecclesiasticus : *In nowise speak against the truth* :

> Est etiam sciendum quod aliqui sanam doctrinam predicanti aut docenti contradicunt per ignorantiam, invidiam, malitiam, arrogantiam. Primo per ignorantiam, sicut narrat Berengarius in apologia pro Petro Abelardi (*sic*) quod in concilio senonensi prelati plures qui erant ibi dictis magistri Petri contradicebant magis ex ignorantia quam ex alia causa, quia ignorabant quid verba illius pretenderent [39] ; et ita narratur de hoc quod factum fuit contra Gilbertum Porretanum in concilio turonensi, ubi sanctus Bernardus hereses Gilberto imposuit, quas ipse dixerat super expositione libri de Trinitate Boetii, ut sancto Bernardo et pluribus aliis ad hoc congregatis videbatur. Finaliter tamen Gilbertus in respondendo sic se habuit quod eis silentium imposuit et illesus a concilio recessit, ut tractat archidiaconus carnotensis in cronica sua, et de hoc bene dicitur, Osee iv° : Sicut hii qui contradicunt sacerdoti. Sequitur : populus, quia non habuit scientiam [40].
>
> Secundo, contradicunt aliqui alteri per invidiam, et ita, ut dicit Ieronimus in prologo super librum Regum et in prologo super Paralipomenon quod multi dente canino contradicebant dictis suis per invidiam. Etiam Zeusippus contradicebat Demosteni, quia ipse plures scholares habebat [41], et ita fuit de Abelardo Petro (*sic*) quia, ut ipse dicit in principio epistolarum suarum, Anselmus decanus laudunensis contradicebat sibi ex invidia, quia plures scholares sequebantur eum et doctrinam suam [42], et ideo contra eos bene dicitur Ecclesiastici iv° : Non contradicas verbo veritatis [43] (*B*, fol. 111vb ; *T*, fol. 55va).

Hesdin's defence of Abelard is all the more meaningful in that he thought that Abelard had fallen into error on at least one point. He mentions it on the subject of grace (*Tit.* i, 4) [44]. Evidently this did not quench his sympathy for the great rebel.

---

39. PL 178, 1857-1860. Berengar in his *Apologia* accuses Bernard of malice and the other prelates of drink. Hesdin has softened the accusations. On the Council of Sens see A. Borst, *Abälard und Bernhard*, in *Historische Zeitschrift* 186, iii (1958) 497-526.

40. *Os.* iv, 4-6.

41. From the prologue *Si LXX interpretum*, and the prologue *Frater Ambrosius*, prefixed to the Vulgate.

42. *Historia calamitatum*, iii-iv (ed. J. Monfrin, Paris 1959, 66-70). The title has no manuscript authority. Abelard's account of his misfortunes is in the form of a letter which comes first in the collection ; see J. T. Muckle in the preface to his edition in *Mediaeval Studies* 12 (1950) 163-166.

43. iv, 30.

44. *B*, fol. 97vb : ' Male erraverunt aliqui circa istam gratiam, ut Petrus

The references to Abelard may well spring from the interest which his correspondence with Heloise aroused in the late thirteenth and fourteenth centuries [45]. Readers of the so-called *Historia calamitatum* may have turned to his pupil Berengar's *Apologia* to find out more about him. Hesdin's foggy memory of the trial of Gilbert de la Porrée at Rheims in 1148 is less easily explained. He must be referring to John of Salisbury's *Historia pontificalis*. John, who was bishop, not archdeacon, of Chartres (1176-80), says that Gilbert, having agreed to correct errors in his book, ' absolutus est ab adversariorum impetitione et nota ' [46]. This statement in conjunction with John's account of Gilbert's behaviour at the trial may lie behind Hesdin's words :

> ...in respondendo sic se habuit quod eis silentium imposuit et illesus a concilio recessit.

The *Historia pontificalis* was little known in the middle ages. The only existing copy survives as a sequel to the chronicle of Sigebert of Gembloux in a manuscript from Fleury. Guillaume de Nangis, the monk chronicler of St Denis (1285-1300) seems to have used it [47]. The presence of a copy at St Denis would explain how a Paris master of the fourteenth century came to have some idea of its contents. The three primary sources for the council of Rheims are the *Historia pontificalis*, Otto of Freising's *Gesta Frederici* and the version given by Geoffrey of Auxerre. The third, written in favour of St Bernard and against Gilbert, gained the most currency in later compilations [48]. It is interesting to find that the account most favourable to Gilbert turns up in a Paris classroom about 1363.

A later quarrel rumbles like a retreating storm through his pages, seculars versus mendicants. Hesdin tells a personal story which seems to reflect discredit on the friars. He blames superiors who send ignorant and uneducated men out preaching, and prelates who allow them to do so. A religious (probably a friar) once told him that he knew two

---

Abelardus, qui negabat gratiam co-operantem, ut recitat Berengarius in apologia pro eodem magistro Petro '.

45. J. T. MUCKLE, *op. cit.*

46. *Hist. pontif.* XI, ed. M. CHIBNALL (*Nelson's Medieval Texts*), London etc. 1956, 25.

47. *Ibid.*, XLVII-XLIX.

48. For a full discussion of the sources for the trial see M. E. WILLIAMS, *The Teaching of Gilbert Porreta on the Trinity as found in his Commentaries on Boethius* (*Analecta Gregoriana* 56) Rome 1951. There is no mention of the council of Rheims in the *Vieille chronique* of Chartres, ed. E. DE LEPINOIS, *Cart. de N.-D. de Chartres*, I, Chartres 1862, 1-57, nor in the *Breviarium historiale* of Landolfo Colonna, canon of Chartres. Mlle M.-Th. d'Alverny very kindly checked this for me from MSS at the Bibliothèque nationale. By process of elimination, therefore, Hesdin's mysterious archdeacon must be John of Salisbury.

sermons in French ; they sufficed to keep his poor body and soul together. Much harm could come of this sort of thing. Laymen would take such preachers for clerks, going to them as confessors and advisers on many matters which they were incompetent to deal with. They often gave preaching a bad name, although they might say something of value [49]. A *quaestio* proves, however, that Hesdin was no enemy of the mendicant Orders. The text *Sunt enim multi seductores* (*Tit.* i, 10) sends him to the command to the apostles : ...*gratis accepistis, gratis date* (*Mt.* x, 8). It seems from this authority that preachers may not receive even food in return for their work, which would be against the mendicants. Hence it is asked whether it is permissable for any preacher to live upon pure alms. Many have held the contrary. Hesdin instances Guillaume de Saint Amour and also Master Jean de Pouilli. Again he makes odd mistakes, ascribing to the former ' a big book beginning *Angeli pacis flebunt* ' (*Isa.* XXXIII, 7), which I have not been able to identify, and to the latter another ' big book ' beginning *Sapientiam sanctorum etc.* In fact, the second book, *Sapientiam antiquorum* (*sanctorum* must be a slip), is the famous compilation made by Guillaume de Saint Amour against the friars ; it has been dated before October, 1266 [50]. The affair of Jean de Pouilli belongs to the years 1312-21 [51]. Hesdin has confused two quite distinct stages of the controversy. He then promises for brevity's sake to pick out three or four of the many authorities and reasons brought forward by the two masters. These are so familiar that there is no point in transcribing them. The gist of the charges, with Hesdin's replies to them, can be found in the *Summa theologica* II^a II^ae, q. 187, art. 4-5, though he does not mention St Thomas. His conclusion is Thomist. Where such preaching is clearly useful and there is no evil intent, men should not take scandal if preachers depend on alms for the necessities of life. This is what the Apostle meant in the text quoted :

> Ex ista auctoritate videtur quod predicatores etiam nec victum possent accipere pro labore, quod esset contra ordines mendicantium. Et ideo ad evidentiam istius queritur utrum alicui predicanti de puris elemosinis vivere

---

49. Lect. XII, *B*, fol. 96ra : ' Et ideo homines ignari et illitterati nunquam deberent mitti ad predicandum, sicut semel unus religiosus dixit michi quod ipse sciebat duos sermones in gallico, et erant satis pro sustentatione miserie vite sue. Quampropter graviter peccant qui tales mittunt, et prelati qui tales predicare sinunt, quia multa mala possent provenire ex isto, quia laici credunt eos esse clericos et respiciunt ad eos in confessione (et) in consilio et in multis de quibus tales nescirent bene consulere ad salutem, et sepius predicatio infamatur per tales, licet dicant plura bona '.

50. P. GLORIEUX, *Répertoire des maîtres en théologie de Paris au XIIIe siècle*, Paris 1933, n° 160 (1).

51. J. KOCH, *Der Prozess gegen den Magister Johannes de Polliaco und seine Vorgeschichte*, in *Rech. Théol. anc. méd.* 5 (1933) 420-422.

liceat, quia multi tenuerunt quod non, ut Guillelmus de Sancto Amore, qui contra mendicantes predicatores librum magnum composuit, qui incipit *Angeli pacis flebunt*, et est Ysaie xxxii (*sic*), et etiam magister Iohannes de Polliaco, qui etiam composuit contra eos librum magnum, qui incipit *Sapientiam sanctorum* etc. Et licet multas rationes et auctoritates adducant pro se, causa brevitatis sufficiant tres vel quatuor... Et posset dici breviter quod ex quo apparet manifesta utilitas in predicatione talium, et non apparet aliqua mala intentio eorum, non debent scandalizari homines in eis, si ex elemosinis necessaria ad vivendum accipiunt (*B*, fol. 114^{ra-va}).

The interesting point for us lies not in Hesdin's inaccuracy in his cursory survey of the question, but in his moderate championship of the mendicants' case against the seculars. As a member of a wealthy Order and as spokesman of the seculars in his capacity as dean of the theological faculty, he might well have argued differently. The friars' opponents had been condemned ; but jealousy was ready to flare up again. Hesdin could have insinuated dislike of the friars into his discussion of the problem had he really wanted to. Instead, he follows St Thomas.

We find a few strictures on the sins of his fellow men. Hesdin notes on *Tit.* ii, 3 that old women especially tend to dabble in fortune-telling and divination by calling upon demons ; he has seen and heard of many cases [52]. The prevalence of sorcery would form a recurrent theme in Jean Gerson's sermons at the turn of the century [53]. Hesdin, like most moralists, took a gloomy view of the contemporary Church : she was going to ruin for lack of reformers who would correct evils [54]. Describing the virtues required in prelates on *Tit.* i, 5, he complains that no one today will follow the example of Thomas of Canterbury in braving death for ecclesiastical freedom, although there is need for it [55]. This sounds like a High Church pronouncement and suggests that Hesdin may have acted the Herbert of Bosham to his patron's Becket ; the archbishop of Rouen did in fact oppose his king on the subject of clerical privilege [56]. The discussion of Church-State relation-

---

52. *B*, fol. 129ra : ' ...et quia ut plurimum anus et vetule intromittunt se de sortilegiis et divinationibus, que fiunt per invocationes demonum, quia demon se ingerit ad decipiendum maxime eos qui sunt debiles in fide et creduli, cuiusmodi sunt anus tales, ut dictum est ; et multa exempla de hoc vidimus et audivimus '.

53. L. MOURIN, *Jean Gerson prédicateur français*, Bruges 1952, 75, 256, 274.

54. *B*, fol. 98va : ' Et ideo cotidie deperit ecclesia, quia non est qui corripiat, noxia evellendo '.

55. *B*, fol. 100va ; *T*, fol. 32va : ' ...quia revera si aliquis modo pro libertate ecclesie se opponeret, ut deceret, inveniret quos (eum) occideret, sed post Thomam cantuariensem non est inventus talis, cum tamen constantia sit necessaria in prelatis, ut exemplis antiquorum confirmati pro libertate ecclesie mori sint parati '.

56. Above, p. 348.

ship on *argue cum imperio* (*Tit.* II, 15) shows, on the contrary, that it was rather a rhetorical phrase, thrown out in passing. When Hesdin got down to business, he took a moderate line on *regnum et sacerdotium.*

The discussion turns on the question : what meanings are commonly given to *imperium* and which are intended here ? What sort of *imperium* had Titus ? Hesdin distinguishes four kinds : immortal or eternal (God's rule over his creatures), temporal or earthly, spiritual or ecclesiastical, moral or ethical (man's rule over his appetites). The first and last need not concern us. Hesdin says on temporal or earthly *imperium* that kings and emperors, of whom Julius Caesar was the first, may be equated as having the same power. Good rulers should be honoured, loved, feared and obeyed, though it is meritorious not to obey laws which go against God's will. Earthly rule suffers from many defects, being subject to change, decline, loss and overthrow. Hesdin has stated, in spite of these very obvious reservations, that the emperor, and hence kings, hold their rule from God alone. He does not question it. The Pope is not set above them in the secular sphere. Turning to ecclesiastical or spiritual rule, he insists that this is of divine institution, even though kings and emperors have enriched the Church and have endowed her with many possessions. The admission that the Church owes her riches to endowment is significant : Hesdin does not mention the claim made by some papal propagandists that St Peter received temporal as well as spiritual power from Christ. Hesdin restricts spiritual or ecclesiastical rule to the power to bind and loose and to punish, absolve and correct in spiritual matters. He suggests that it might be better for temporal and spiritual power to be undivided. Nevertheless, he admits that temporal power is greater than spiritual in its own sphere, while ecclesiastical is worthier and more honourable in itself. The Apostle refers to the latter, that is the power of ecclesiastical censure, when writing to Titus, whom he had ordained as archbishop, and who therefore had the power to impose ecclesiastical sanctions. All this is Thomist doctrine. It follows that moderate tradition which had reasserted itself after the storms of the early fourteenth century.

> Et de isto quod dicit *cum imperio* possent fieri alique questiones litterales, quas movent etiam doctores. Prima est quot modis accipitur *imperium* communiter secundum scripturas, secunda de quo *imperio* intelligitur litteraliter, tertia quale *imperium* habebat ille Tytus, quarta si *imperium* de quo intelligitur habuerunt soli prelati evangelici.
>
> Quantum ad primum, dico quod quadruplex *imperium* invenitur, videlicet immortale sive eternum, temporale sive terrenum, spirituale sive ecclesiasticum, et morale sive ethicum...
>
> Secundum *imperium* est terrenum et temporale, secundum quod reges regnant et imperant, quia reges et imperatores idem sunt, nisi quia imperator reputatur summus, quia a nullo homine dicitur *imperium* tenere nisi a Deo ;

reges autem ei subsunt. Et istud fuit institutum primo de Iulio Cesare, quia ante ipsum nullus in mundo imperator fuerat vocatus, nec aliquod regnum *imperium* proprie. Sed quando ipse triumphavit de Pompeio, tota terra siluit in conspectu eius, et videns quod omnia regna mundi ei subiciebantur, ipse rediens Romam vocavit primo se imperatorem et regnum romanorum imperium... Et istud *imperium*, etsi in mundo florere videtur, quia si bene regunt sunt digni honorandi, amandi, timendi et obediendi eis... patitur tamen multos deffectus, quia est variabile, defectibile, amissibile, subitabile (*sic*).

Tertium *imperium* est ecclesiasticum et spirituale, quia a Deo institutum est primo, etsi imperatores et reges terreni ecclesiam ditaverunt et dotaverunt multis possessionibus et divitiis, nichilominus a Deo prelatis ecclesie fuit data potestas ligandi atque solvendi spiritualiter, immo etiam et punire contradicentes, absolvere insontes, corrigere delinquentes, immo rebellantes contra fidem catholicam tradere Sathane... In antiqua lege legimus reges sacerdotes fuisse et in matrimonio (*sic*, ministerio ?) sibi invicem miscebantur, et licet regnum et sacerdotium debeant esse indivisa, *imperium* terrenum in terrenis et temporalibus maius est, in spiritualibus tamen ecclesiasticum *imperium* dignius et honorabilius... et de isto plane hic in littera.

Ex dictis ergo patet quod Apostolus, quando Tyto dicebat *argue cum omni imperio*, quod intendebat de *imperio* et potestate quam habet prelatus super subditos, quos per censuram ecclesiasticam potest corrigere, arguere et punire...

Quantum ad secundam questionem, patet per ea que dicta sunt quod Apostolus solum intendebat de *imperio* ecclesiastico, et patet ad tertiam quod Tytus erat ordinatus archiepiscopus a Paulo apostolo, et ideo habebat potestatem ligandi et solvendi, corrigendi et monendi per censuram et potestatem ecclesiasticam, et sic poterat arguere *cum omni imperio*, scilicet ecclesiastico (*B*, fol. 149rb-vb ; *T*, fol. 141va-142vb).

Perhaps we may see an oblique reference to the plight of France in a passage where Hesdin quotes from the *Politics* on the dangers which beset a state. He copies down a saying of Aristotle that a servile or subject state hardly deserves to be called a state at all. Significantly, the context in the *Politics* is the need for soldiers for defence against foreign invaders. He goes on to explain how a state becomes servile. This happens in one of two ways. Strife arises because the rich oppress the common people, whom Aristotle counts as free. All share in freedom, and should share, who dispute concerning the political form of the state. Such dissension brings ruin : *every kingdom divided against itself shall be made desolate.* The second reason why a state may be called servile is that it lives under a tyranny, since no love is lost between a tyrant and citizens. He adds some trite quotations on the evils of tyranny. The starting point is *Tit.* I, 5 : *per civitates.*

Quod civitas debet gubernari libertate dicit plane Philosophus, IV Pol. : *Nichil minus impossibilium quam dignum esse vocare civitatem servam natura. Per se enim sufficiens est civitas. Quod vero natura servum est non per se sufficiens* [57], et quia servitus in civitate fit duobus modis, videlicet quando

---

57. Hesdin quotes, in this case almost verbally, from the translation of

regitur in oligarchia (MS oligantia), id est quando divites dominantur in civitate super pauperes, quos Philosophus vocat liberos, IV Pol., cap. 4 [58], quia tunc divites gravant plebem communem, et fit dissensio in civitate, ut plane tractat Philosophus in III Pol., unde cap. XII dicit quod *omnes* (MS omnis) *libertate participant* et participare debe(n)t semper qui *altercantur de politia* [59], et quia divisio in civitate est causa ruine eius, ideo civitas serva isto modo durare non potest, iuxta illud Mat. XII : *omne regnum* etc. [60] Alio modo dicitur civitas serva quando vivit sub tyrannide, quia nunquam est amor inter tyrannum et cives, ut dicit Philosophus... (*B*, fol. 99[vb]).

Hesdin's audience may have filled in the topical allusions for themselves, thinking of English victories and civil war in France, and of complaints against royal misgovernment. Later, in his *lectura* on St Mark, he applies the prophecy in XIII, 8 to popular risings in various countries or districts in his own time [61]. They were a feature of the late fourteenth century.

But on the whole we glean a small harvest. Hesdin is aware of troubles around him. He does not care to talk of them. The only English invasion of France that he mentions is Ockham's ! He shares in a current reticence. It is difficult for the historian to find any data on French opinion during this critical period. The character stands out more strongly than the opinions. Their very absence has meaning. Hesdin sounds like a discreet, conventional, temperate man, not given to extreme views or to hot language. This accords with his letter to Petrarch : its moderation has made a favourable impression on the poet's most fervent admirers. Petrarch had better scholarship, but worse manners than the Frenchman.

* * *

Hesdin uses the traditional method in his lectures, dividing them into three parts, exegetical, theological, homiletical. There is no room

---

William of Moerbeke ; see *S. Thomae Aquinatis in libros Pol. Arist. expositio*, ed. R. M. SPIAZZI, Turin 1951, 196. This comes from IV, 4, 1291a, 8-10.

58. A reference to IV, 4, 1290b, 1-3.

59. Really III, 9, 1280a-4-7 : ' ...libertate enim participant omnes : propter quas altercantur utique de politia '.

Aristotle is explaining that all citizens enjoy freedom ; hence the dispute : ' wealth and freedom are the grounds on which the oligarchical and democratical parties respectively claim power in the state '. Hesdin seems to be making the point that those who take part in political disputes ought to be free ; perhaps he means to exclude serfs. Neither St. Albert nor St. Thomas says anything of the kind on this passage.

60. *Mt.* XII, 25.

61. *B*, fol. 61[rb] : ' Et ponuntur hic effectus diversi, quorum quidam sunt ex plebis malitia, cum dicitur : *exurget gens contra gentem*. Ita legimus de multis in biblia, et modo videmus de facto in diversis patriis '.

for a study of his theology in this paper. Lecturers on Scripture normally confined themselves to teaching established doctrine : they could discuss controversial matters better in *Sentence* commentaries and in disputations. Hesdin's theological *quaestiones* look unadventurous and non-polemical. He expresses the difference between *quaestiones* in biblical commentaries and *quaestiones disputatae* when he says that he is enquiring ' non disputative, sed magis inquisitive circa fidem divisionem ' (*B*, fol. 91ʳᵃ). The homiletic sections rely on devices familiar in fourteenth-century preaching.

One or two formulae strike me as new, though they only make explicit what had been taken for granted. Hesdin has his own way of introducing a digression. A departure from the text was as old as the commentary on Scripture itself and was essential for teaching purposes. Procedure hardened. Hesdin warns us when he means to go right off the point. He makes his digressions *causa solationis nostre* or *causa eruditionis nostre* or even *causa iocunditatis et eruditionis*. Here is his program for expounding *mendaces* (*Tit.* I, 12) :

> ...et ideo causa solationis et eruditionis videamus de ipso mendacio, primo poetice, secundo autem quomodo philosophice et theologice simul quantum ad mala que mendacium facit, et tertio de mendacio, utrum semper sit peccatum mortale et quomodo (*B*, fol. 115ʳᵃ).

The digressions are homiletic in character as a rule. Where they treat of theology we find *quaestiones* regarded by Hesdin as not strictly relevant to his text. A hypothetical question on the blasphemy of the Jews in killing Christ begins :

> Propter dicta in textu quidam ponunt hic casum, et causa solationis et eruditionis volo illum breviter tangere. Casus est iste. Ponamus quod Iudei non occidissent Christum... et tamen illi estimarent quod ipsum occidere tenerentur secundum legem suam (*B*, fol. 74ʳᵇ).

Again :

> Sed queri potest causa solationis quid anima Christi fecit (*sic*) in triduo quo corpus Christi iacuit in sepulchro (*B*, fol. 75ᵛᵇ).

All this amounts to an admission that extraneous matter must be brought into the lecture to amuse the students. Mere exposition will not do. Hervé de Nédellec had defended *curiosae quaestiones* if they were debated *causa recreationis* [62]. He did not say that such recreation was suited to a biblical commentary.

I shall give a summary account of Hesdin's sources. His main authorities on Job were St Gregory, St Thomas and Nicholas of Lyre.

---

62. In a quodlibet of 1308, quoted by J. Leclercq, *L'idéal du théologien au moyen âge*, in *Revue des Sciences religieuses* 21 (1947) 133.

Some extracts from his commentary on Iob III will show how he treats them (appendix, p. 319). Hesdin adds no fresh interpretation, but he does decide between three divergent views and give his reasons. St Gregory thought that the words in which Job cursed his birthday should be interpreted not literally, but mystically. Such a curse would have been inconsistent with his patience and was anyway ' absurd ' : a day that has passed cannot ' perish '. St Thomas, more alive to the human element in Scripture, thought that Job was expressing poetically the horror which the sensitive part of his nature felt at suffering. His friends did not realise this, and so they supposed him to be blaspheming [63]. Lyre objected to St Thomas's explanation, though he agreed that the episode belonged to the literal sense. He argued that Job's friends, as learned men, would not have mistaken his meaning. They held, with Job, that human life was ruled by divine providence, but differed on the question of rewards and punishments in a future life. If this life were all, as they thought, then Job might well have cursed his birthday ; they urged him to repent of the sins for which God was punishing him [64]. Hesdin defended St Thomas against Lyre. He argued that the discussion between Job and his friends had not yet reached this point. Lyre was anticipating. Neither side could have known as yet what the other was going to put forward. Job's friends, as St Thomas said, took his curses, which really expressed his natural grief, rather than his mental processes, as being spoken deliberately in mental disturbance.

Hesdin generally undertook the defence of St Thomas where the later commentator differed from him. This typifies Hesdin's respect for St Thomas. He quotes the *Summa theologica* repeatedly in all three of his *lecturae*, and sometimes uses it without saying so : his discussion of the duty of obedience owed by slaves to their masters and religious to their superiors (on *Tit.* II, 9 ; *B*, fol. 139^{va-b}) depends on II^a II^{ae}, q. 104, art. 5-6 ; Hesdin has slightly rearranged and abridged his original. The *Summa* is the latest theological work to be mentioned by name.

He uses St Thomas's *Catena aurea* as one of his main sources on St Mark, sometimes referring to the authors quoted in it, sometimes quoting it as ' Thomas ', sometimes quoting it without acknowledgement. Here, too, he relies on Nicholas of Lyre, often without naming his source. He speaks appreciatively of Bede's commentary [65],

63. *Opera* XIII, Antwerp 1612, fol. 4vb-5va.

64. *Post. lit. in Bibl. (Glos. ord. cum post. N. de Lyra et addit. P. de Burgo etc.* III) Lyons 1559, 45-47.

65. *B*, fol. 66vb, on *Mc.* XIV, 22 : ' Beda in commento suo quasi iocunde incipiens istam litteram exponere pulchre incipit, sic dicens : Finitis veteris pasche solempniis... Melchisedech '. See PL 92, 272.

and admires Hugh of Saint-Cher as a postillator [66]. He refrains from quoting the marvels in 'the Gospel of Nicodemus' as apocryphal [67]. Such sobriety was commoner in the thirteenth than in the fourteenth century, when masters had less scholarly restraint.

Lyre's postill on Titus is very thin. Hesdin does not seem to have used it. He fell back on St Jerome, on Peter Lombard and even on Gilbert de la Porrée, though he finds one of Gilbert's explanations 'crude' [68]. It is surprising that, given the vast quantity of medieval commentaries on the Pauline Epistles, he should have relied on the two twelfth-century masters. Perhaps some unnamed source has escaped me; but his habit is to quote his main authorities at least

---

66. *B*, fol. 8[ra] : ' Hugo cardinalis facit hic pulchram digressionem, in suis postillis, dicens quod in isto deserto aliqui pelluntur de spiritu phitonico... '

Fol. 36[vb] : ' Hugo graiopolitanus episcopus, qui post fuit cardinalis et postillavit magnam partem biblie : similis fraus... '

Verbal quotations from *Post. in Mc.* I, 4 ; VII, 11 (*Post. in Bibl.*, Paris 1530-45, VI, *ad loc.*).

67. *B*, fol. 75[ra], on *Mc.* xv, 38 : ' ...multa et mira in evangelio Nicodemi de hoc dicuntur, sed quia apocryphum reputatur, ideo hic dimittuntur '.

The *Acta Pilati*, sometimes called the *Gospel of Nicodemus*, does not contain marvels concerning the tearing of the temple veil ; see M. R. JAMES, *The Apocryphal New Testament*, new ed., Oxford 1955, 104-105. John Lathbury, Hesdin's contemporary, quotes it for the same subject, however ; see B. SMALLEY, *English Friars and Antiquity in the Early Fourteenth Century*, Oxford 1960, 225.

68. *B*, fol. 88[ra] ; *T*, fol. 4[va-b], on *Tit.* I, 1 : ' *Servus Dei*... Unde Petrus Lombardus in expositione ordinaria epistolarum Pauli dicit quod hoc fuit ratio humilitatis, quia ipse creaverat istum Tytum et genuerat in fide, immo archiepiscopum ordinavit, et posset ex hoc tanquam spiritualis pater sic supra Tytum maius dominium reclamare, quia dominus debet servum erudire et monere...

Sic ergo patet quod licet apostolus istis rationibus posset dominium supra Tytum reclamare, causa humilitatis se servum (dicebat ?) et humilis apparebat, et sic poterit intentio Petri Lombardi magistri rationibus sustentari et vallari.

Unde Gilbertus porretanus in expositione quam ipse ordinavit super epistolis Pauli ponit aliam rationem, dicens quia nomen Domini nostri Iesu Christi in primitiva ecclesia erat Iudeis scandalum, gentibus vero ad stultitiam... et quia ipse institutus ab ecclesia apostolus et doctor gentium, et romani erant tunc quasi omnes gentiles, ut inter gentes et in gentibus nomen Iesu Christi predicaretur et annuntiaretur publice... ideo ipse scribens romanis se servum Iesu Christi nominavit, et quia Tytus fuerat iudeus, semper credens vivum Deum et in fide christiana a Paulo instructus, ideo tanquam sufficientem in fide Iesu Christi confirmato suffecit ut ei scribens premitteret sic : *Paulus servus Dei*. Et quantum michi apparet, satis est ista expositio grossa '.

The quotation from Peter Lombard, though not verbal, corresponds fairly well ; see PL 192, 383. I cannot trace the quotation from Gilbert de la Porrée. There is nothing like it in the copy of his commentary on St Paul in MS *London, Brit. Mus. Royal 2.F.I* (late 12th cent.). The copy on MS *Oxford, Magdalen College lat. 118* (also late 12th cent.) has lost the leaf containing the commentary on Titus I. On Gilbert's commentary see M. SIMON, *La glose de l'épître aux Romains de Gilbert de la Porrée*, in *Revue d'Histoire ecclésiastique* 52 (1957) 51-80.

occasionally. The reason may be that his lecture on Titus was of a more discursive kind than the other two ; it resembles Robert Holcot on Wisdom in this respect. Hence the exegetical sources tend to be far outnumbered by others.

It need hardly be said that Hesdin had aids to study in the form of Peter Comestor's *Historia scholastica*, which he constantly uses, and of biblical dictionaries such as Brito's *Vocabularium* and the *Catholicon*. The latest school manual in his repertoire to be mentioned seems to be the *Manipulus florum*, a collection of excerpts alphabetically arranged, ascribed to Thomas of Ireland [69]. He attempted a bit of personal research on ' Jewish fables ' (*Tit.* I, 14). Wanting to know more about them, he found something in the *Speculum historiale* (of Vincent of Beauvais) ; he also had a book by the converted Jew, Petrus Alphonsi, which was the source of the *Speculum* [70] :

> Et quia plus non ponit nec exponit (Apostolus) que sint illa fabulosa ficta vel posita a sapientibus iudeorum, et ideo quesivi et inveni in Speculo historiali, lib. xxvi°, cap. cxviii°, aliqua de ista materia ; etiam habui quendam librum de disputatione cuiusdam iudei conversi contra unum iudeum in iudaizatione, ubi originaliter fabule iudeorum, que sunt posite in Speculo historiali, continentur, et intitulatur liber Petri Alfonsi, qui illum librum composuit, qui fuerat iudeus (*B*, fol. 118[va] ; *T*, fol. 70[ra]).

A sermon by ' Pope Urban ' on the Eucharist represents either a rare work or a slip of the pen [71]. If it were the former, Hesdin might have been quoting from an otherwise unrecorded sermon by the reigning Pope, Urban V, which Hesdin would have received from a correspondent at Avignon. Urban V was elected in September, 1362 ; Hesdin's quotation comes towards the end of his *lectura* on Titus, finished

---

69. *B*, fol. 163[va], on *Tit.* III, 5, he quotes excerpts from St Bernard on *misericordia Dei*, saying ' in Manipulus florum ponuntur '. They are in fact given in *Manipulus florum*, MS *Oxford, Lincoln College lat. 98*, fol. 143[v]. Thomas of Ireland is said to have been a doctor of the Sorbonne, c. 1306-1312 ; see F. M. POWICKE, *The Medieval Books of Merton College*, Oxford 1931, 129 ; P. GLORIEUX. *Répert. des Maîtres en théol.* etc., Paris 1933-34, n° 322 (x).

70. *Dialogus* (PL 157, 555-672) ; *Spec. maius* IV, Venice 1591, fol. 360ra-363va, actually xxv, 118-138 of the *Spec. hist.* Hesdin also quotes HELINAND OF FROIDMONT'S *Responsio Apollinis* (*B*, fol. 116ra) via VINCENT OF BEAUVAIS (PL 212, 725).

71. *B*, fol. 163[vb], on *Tit.* III, 5 *per lavacrum regenerationis* : ' De effusione lavacri sanguinis, qua anima mundatur, bene habetur a Salvatore nostro, qui fuit princeps et primus martirum, qui sanguinem suum fudit in pretium simul et lavacrum, ut redempti a miserabili servitute a peccatis omnibus mundaremur, ut dicit Urbanus papa in sermone de eucharistia '.

It was not a mistake for Innocent III, judging by his printed sermons, nor for Clement VI. Father Th. Kaeppeli kindly verified this for me from the sermon on the Eucharist of Clement VI in MS *Rome, Vat. Borgh. 41*, fol. 47[v]-52 ; see G. MOLLAT, *op. cit.*, 93, for a bibliography on his literary work.

in September, 1364, according to the explicit. The *Vitae* of this beatified Pope do not mention his preaching, but it seems probable that he gave occasional addresses. Hesdin may have had notice of them, directly or through his patron [72]. On the other hand, it may be a careless mistake on his part.

He takes a mild interest in textual variants, noting that the text used by St Jerome in his commentary on Titus differed in some places from that in current copies of the Vulgate. The latter has *argue* where St Jerome' commentary has *increpa* (II, 15). He wondered why St Jerome had used a different text in his commentary from that of his own translation. A prelate had asked Hesdin the reason. He answered that St Jerome did not always comment on his own translation. But he takes his illustrations of this from the books of the Old Testament only :

> Et sciendum quod textus Ieronimi habet *increpa* hic in commento [73], et si queratur, et non immerito, quare in ista epistola Ieronimus discrepat a textu quem ipse transtulit, quia iste transtulit textum qui communiter habetur, quia ibi continetur *argue*, et etiam ibi in multis locis invenitur quod dissonat a textu quem transtulit, et istud ab uno prelato fuit quesitum a me. Potest dici quod Ieronimus in omnibus libris quos commentavit vel super quibus scripsit translationem suam non est secutus, sed translationem Symachi, qui transtulit secundum LXX interpretes, et proprius ipse transtulit quam Theodotion nec quam vulgata editio, et causa forte fuit quod quando scripsit super multis libris biblie adhuc ipse non transtulerat totam bibliam immediate de hebreo in latinum, sicut post(ea) fecit. Et quia LXX interpretes transtulerunt bibliam de hebreo in grecum, alii interpretes de greco in latinum, Ieronimus quasi ultimus et corrector aliorum transtulit immediate de hebreo in latinum (*B*, fol. 149rb).

Similarly St Jerome has *non incentrices* where the Vulgate has *non criminatrices* (II, 3). Hesdin expounds both, the former 'in honour of St Jerome ', a traditional way of dealing with textual variants [74].

> Beatus Ieronimus hic in commento suo ponit *non incentrices* [75] et istud exponit. Biblie tamen quas ego vidi habent *criminatrices* ; et ideo primo pro honore Ieronomi breviter exponimus textum suum, scilicet *non incentrices* (*B*, fol. 128vb).

---

72. Urban on his deathbed submitted to the judgment of the Church all that he had said ' ...conferendo, predicando aut disputando... ' ; see BALUZE, *Vitae paparum Avenionensium*, ed. G. MOLLAT, I, Paris 1914, 382. Richard de Bury, bishop of Durham, boasts in his *Philobiblon* that his agents sent him news of the latest sermons or *quaestiones* from the Curia (ed. A. ALTAMURA, Naples 1954, 102), cap. VII : ' Si in fonte fidei christiane, curia sacrosancta romana, sermo devotus insonuit, ...hoc statim nostris recens infundebatur auditibus... ' Other prelates may have had their own channels of information.

73. PL 26, 589.

74. B. SMALLEY, *The Study of the Bible in the Middle Ages*, 2nd ed., Oxford 1952, 219-221.

75. PL 26, 580.

Although he implies that he has looked at a number of Bibles in this last passage, there is no reason to suppose that he ever handled a *correctorium* or knew that such things existed. He shows no sign of having dabbled in Greek or Hebrew. We miss the curiosity of the friar scholars who preceded him at Paris and Oxford. He did not even exploit the fruits of other men's labour.

* * *

We shall now study Hesdin's attitude to pagan philosophy and secular literature, concentrating on his lecture on Titus : this was his *tour de force* from the point of view of quotations. The lectures on Job and Mark show less, though still not little, use of secular authors. The reason was that he saw the Epistle to Titus as a compendium of wisdom addressed especially to prelates, as he explains in his dedication to the archbishop of Rouen (see appendix). He understood it as a biblical parallel to the *Mirror for Princes*, a *genre* much in favour in the later middle ages [76]. The didactic treatise on the right conduct of rulers and on Christian education in general served as a setting for pearls of ancient wisdom. Hesdin used his lecture on Titus in the same way. The opening to his prologue could be transferred to a *De instructione principum* just as it stands. Hesdin brings forward traditional quotations and *exempla* to prove that rulers ought to receive a liberal education. He begins with *Prov.* XXIX, 17, *Erudi filium*, and Cyprian, *De habitu virginum, Eruditio sive disciplina est custos sive retinaculum* [77]; both were favourites with didactic writers. He goes on to praise the custom of the ancients according to his models :

> Et istud potest patere per antiquos, qui instruebantur a iuventute in liberalibus artibus, sic quod reges et presides erant litterati viri, ad gubernandum populum eruditi, sicut Aristoteles dicit 11º Rhetoric., cap. 49º, quod apud Tebas... [78], unde et Boetius 1º de consol., et recitat Tullium, qui dicit quod beatas fore respublicas, si principes sapientie intenderent [79]. Et licet, quantum ad (hoc), multa exempla possent adduci secundum quod antiqui et nobilissimi principes filios instruebant et erudiri commendabant, sub brevibus pertranseo, sicut Alexander Nequam in libro de natura rerum ponit multa exempla [80] (*B*, fol. 86ᵛᵃ).

---

76. See W. BERGES, *Die Fürstenspiegel des hohen und späten Mittelalters*, Leipzig 1938.

77. CSEL 3, 1, 187. Hesdin quotes the opening lines.

78. Actually 11, 23, 10. Thebes began to prosper as soon as her leading men became philosophers.

79. *De consol. Philos.* 1, pros. 4, where the saying is properly ascribed to Plato, not Cicero.

80. *De nat. rer.* 11, 21 (*Rolls Series*, p. 141-142).

John of Salisbury's *Policraticus* and John of Wales' *Communi-loquium* both figure in his pages [81]. He also used the longest treatise on education ever written in the middle ages, the *Rudimentum doctrinae* of Gilbert of Tournai [82]. All three books suited his purpose. The *lectura* contains much advice on the teaching of young men and boys, on marriage, and on the respective duties of rulers and subjects. Hesdin's interest centred on human beings. Natural science and marvels, popular with contemporary homilists, had less appeal for him. He succeeded in finding an eager public for his biblical *Mirror*, as is proved by the greater number of surviving copies. The vogue of Hesdin on Titus resembles in a small way that of Holcot on Wisdom. Both catered for the taste for a mixture of scriptural, profane and intermediate types of didactic material on a wide range of topics.

Hesdin like Holcot admired ancient sages. He thought it very hard that they should have merited damnation, when so many of them were worthy men and philosophers. He does not seem to doubt that they were damned, however, saying on *Tit.* III, 3 : *Eramus enim aliquando et nos... errantes* :

> Alii qui ante adventum Christi in lege sua vivebant, licet explicite Christum non crediderint, tamen virtuose vivebant secundum mores. Valde durum michi videtur quod dampnabiliter errarent, ut fuerunt multi valentes viri et philosophi multi, quos nimis longum esset narrare, ut post mortem dampnerentur, videlicet pena sensus, quia nulli fideli dubium quin omnes erant filii ire natura, ut dicit Apostolus ad *Eph.* IIº [83], et obligati ad penam dampni. Errabant tamen, quia fidem veram non habebant [84] (*B*, fol. 156ᵛᵇ ; *T*, fol. 156ʳᵇ).

---

81. *B*, fol. 86ʳᵇ, 86ᵛᵃ, 96ᵛᵇ, 102ʳᵇ and *passim* ; he refers to John of Wales as ' Auctor in communiloquio '. On John of Wales see W. A. PANTIN, *The English Church in the Fourteenth Century*, Cambridge 1955, 177-178 ; B. SMALLEY, *English Friars and Antiquity in the Early Fourteenth Century*, Oxford 1960, 51-55 and *passim*.

82. *B*, fol. 87ᵛᵃ : ' De duobus primis pulchre loquitur Gilbertus tornacensis, libro qui intitulatur rudimentum doctrine, parte prima, ubi facit digressionem magnam ad laudem beati Pauli : Videtur michi Pauli anima, id est conscientia, spiritualis paradisus et locus amenissimus omnium virtutum florida venustate... Et post ipse, inducendo per singulos illustres viros, qui fuerunt a principio mundi nominati in biblia... ' (St Paul is given pride of place) ; fol. 93ᵛᵃ : ' Gilbertus tornacensis, liber de eruditione doctrina, parte prima... ' (Gilbert quotes Hugh of St Victor's *De arrha animae* to the effect that the ancients lacked true philosophy).

I have no MS of this rather rare work to hand, but E. BONIFACIO gives a detailed analysis of its contents in the preface to his edition of Gilbert's *De modo addiscendi* (Turin 1953). Hesdin must have been quoting the chapter *De speciali beati Pauli supereminentia* (actually v, 3 ; see BONIFACIO, 24) and the chapter *Quod philosophi erraverunt* (1, 2, BONIFACIO, 22).

83. *Eph.* II, 3.

84. See Peter Lombard on the same text, PL 192, 393 : '...etsi philosophi essent quidam vestrum, vera tamen sapientia carebant'.

Hesdin was therefore less optimistic than St Thomas had been on the salvation of good pagans living before the coming of Christ. He may have been influenced by Gregory of Rimini, who took a much narrower view, holding that they could not plead even their involuntary ignorance [85]. But doubts on the score of their salvation did not prevent Hesdin from quoting them as often as he liked. It is allowable to do so, he says, provided that theologians do not reverse the roles of other sciences in relation to Holy Scripture and make her a handmaiden, whom all sciences should serve, as do those who introduce and dispute questions proper to logic and philosophy in their study of theology [86]. He even cites Seneca on Cato's death among his examples of how the ancients practised the virtue of patience [87]. As a Christian he ought to have blamed suicide, and did blame it in his *lectura* on St Mark. Significantly, he supports himself here on Aristotle's disapproval of a man's killing himself in desperation, though Aristotle is less definite on the subject than he makes out [88].

Again, he seems to condemn the study of secular history more sweepingly than his practice warrants. He says on the text *genealogias... devita, sunt enim inutiles et vanae* (*Tit.* III, 9) :

> Nec mirum si doctores catholici circa talia vacantes deridebant, ut videlicet eos qui in historiis et genealogiis diversarum nationum tempus consumunt, studium perdunt nec profectum inducunt, ut scilicet historiographi, chronographi et tales huiusmodi [89].

Hesdin also quotes Gilbert of Tournai, who said that the ancients lacked true philosophy, not being Christians ; see above, n. 82.

85. L. Capéran, *Le problème du salut des infidèles*, 2nd ed., Toulouse 1934, 191-195, 204-205.

86. *B*, fol. 114va : ' ...ut dicit Petrus Lombardus super illo passu, habemus argumentum quod licet ex dictis paganorum aliquas auctoritates assumere que faciunt ad bonas mores et ad confirmationem alicuius veritatis... dum tamen theologi sacram scripturam, cui omnes scientie debent servire, ancillam non faciunt, sicut faciunt illi qui questiones proprie logicas aut philosophicas in theologicis locutionibus suis proponunt et disputant '.

See Peter Lombard on *Tit.* I, 12 (PL 192, 388) ; it is not a verbal quotation.

87. *B*, fol. 127[va] : ' Unde ibi commendat paupertatem in Fabricio, exilium in Rutilio, tormenta in Regulo, venenum in Socrate, mortem in Catone... '

88. *B*, fol. 71[vb], in a *quaestio* ' utrum se Christus tradiderit ad mortem ' : ' Dico hic quod aliquis potest esse causa mortis sue dupliciter... Culpabiliter, sicut aliquis est causa mortis sue ex desperatione, sicut cum aliquis ex desperatione se suspendit aut occidit, et istud Philosophus, IX° Ethic. vituperat et prohibet '. From *Ethic. Nicom.* IX, 4, 1166b, 13. Hesdin has touched up his original, which contains a simple statement of fact : Aristotle says that men hated for their wickedness even shrink from life and destroy themselves.

89. Peter Lombard glosses *genealogias* : ' id est originum enumerationes ' (PL 192, 393).

He may have had in mind the invention of mock origins for towns and peoples, which tended increasingly to glorify their imaginary pagan ancestry [90]. Anyway, he did not scruple for his own part to refer to *Gesta romanorum*, *Gesta francorum* and chronicles for stories of Charlemagne, Roland or Philip Augustus [91]. He appealed to the glories of ancient Gaul when he defended France in his letter to Petrarch.

The poets come off better than philosophers and historians, probably because no *locus* called for stricture. Hesdin, in common with scholastics and humanists alike, thought that ‘ the poets, who were such great clerks ’, intended their fables to be taken in a moral sense. The metamorphoses which they described referred to man's animal passions and should not be understood literally. He is commenting on *Tit.* I, 12 : *Cretenses... malae bestiae* :

> Quapropter non est sciendum quod poete, qui tam magni clerici fuerunt, quando loquuntur de mutatione hominum aut mulierum in bestias, quod ipsi dicerent hic quasi ad litteram hoc fuisset verum, sed ideo dicebant hoc ad insinuandum hoc sub suis enigmatibus ad metaphoram mores et acta et conditiones eorum (*B*, fol. 116[ra]).

Hesdin found the poets useful to quote by way of illustration : Ovid's *Ex Ponto* struck him as apt when he was commenting on the sufferings of Job [92].

The two dedicatory letters (see appendix) will show how he piled up his *auctoritates*. His repertoire was not unlimited ; otherwise he would not have made the same letter do duty twice, with few changes. P. de Nolhac has printed a list of Hesdin's sources as quoted in the letter to Petrarch ; this gives a fair idea of his classical culture [93]. It was medieval culture. Hesdin does not seem to have joined in the hunt for new texts, which was a mark of the early humanists. The only trait in Hesdin that reminds one of the latter is his fondness for Cicero. Medieval moralists generally preferred Seneca, but Cicero seems to be catching up on him, judging by the number of quotations in the

---

90. A. BORST, *Der Turmbau von Babel*, II, II, Stuttgart 1959, 825-869.

91. For instance, on the next leaf, after his attack on those who waste their time on history, he writes, *B*, fol. 168[vb] : ‘ Debet qui mittitur in arduis habere fidelitatem, non sicut Ganeno (*sic*, for Ganelon), qui proditorie, quando missus fuit ad Marsilium a Karolo rege Francie, Rolandum et alios francos in manus sarracenorum tradidit, ut in gestis francorum ; et econtra patet de fidelitate Fabricii, quem miserunt romani ad Pirrum regem ’.

92. MS *Maz. 200* (unfoliated) on *Iob* XIX : ‘ Et quia, ut dicit Ovidius in De Ponto : Parcendum est animo miserabile vulnus habenti. Ideo Iob, qui miserabile vulnus patiebatur bene erat miserendum ’. *Ex Ponto* I, 5, 23. He has just quoted II, 6, 20 and II, 9, 39.

93. *Op. cit.* II, 308.

lectura on Titus. But Hesdin's was the medieval, not the humanist Cicero. He quotes *De senectute* sixteen times, *De officiis* seven, *De tusculanis quaestionibus* and *De paradoxis* six each, *De amicitia* five, and *De natura deorum* twice [94]. This adds up to an impressive picture of the philosopher and moralist beloved of the middle ages. The humanists' Cicero was more complete and personal. Petrarch rediscovered the orator and politician with his ambitions and frailties, unsuspected by Hesdin.

We find fewer commentaries on classical texts than in works of the English classicists earlier in the century [95], though Hesdin knew such standard books as Albert on the *Ethics*. He may perhaps have used Nicholas Trevet's commentary on the *Tragedies* of Seneca. These had become popular in learned circles before Hesdin's day [96]. He knew and quoted them. Commenting on the word 'earthquakes' (*Mc.* XIII, 8), he mentions the myth that the isle of Delos floated on the sea until Jove fastened it as a resting place for Leto to give birth to Apollo and Diana. He attaches the story to lines 15-16 of *Hercules furens* :

> Quibusque natis mobilis tellus stetit
> Quem profuga terra mater errante edidit.

Seneca just alludes to the legend, which needed no explanation to a Roman audience. Hesdin makes him explain it, as though thinking of a commentary together with the text :

> Seneca in prima tragedia, cap. 1º, dicit quod Delos (MS Dolos) insula fuit facta firma a Iove, quia Lachona, que erat pregnans ex Iove, defugerat Iunonem. Ibi peperit Apollinem et Dianam, unde loquens Appolini dicit: Iam tuus (*sic*) mobilis tellus stetit. Et sic patet de causa motus terre (*B*, fol. 61rb).

Trevet tells the tale of Jove and Leto in his commentary. Hesdin, though he does not quote verbally, may well have remembered the gist of what Trevet wrote :

> Sextum exemplum est de Latona, quam cum impregnasset Iupiter, Iuno ei orbem interdixit. Unde vix accepta est in insula Delo, que tunc mobilis natabat tanquam separata a residuo orbe, que postea peperit gemellos

---

94. I make this rough calculation on the basis of marginal notes giving the names of authors quoted in *B*. *De senectute* was a medieval favourite, but Hesdin had a special reason to quote it so often ; he was discussing ' old age ', and a number of quotations are bunched together here.

95. B. SMALLEY, *English Friars and Antiquity in the Early Fourteenth Century*, Oxford 1960, *passim*.

96. See *ibid.*, 59-61, for bibliography on the *Tragedies* and Trevet's commentary.

Phebum et Dianam, in quarum (sic) nativitate insula, que prius mobilis natabat, fixa immobilis facta est... *mobilis tellus*, scilicet insula Delos, que mobilis natabat, *stetit*, scilicet immobilis in eorum nativitate facta (MS *Oxford, Bodl. 292*, fol. 1ᵛᵇ) [97].

Medieval Latin poets, too, figure in Hesdin's anthology : Bernard Sylvestris, *De universitate mundi*, Walter of Châtillon, *Alexandreis*, Matthew of Vendôme, *Ars versificatoria*, Alan of Lille, *Anticlaudianus* [98], and the Latin comedies, *Alda, Pamphilus* and *Geta* [99]. He was fond of a verse, which he ascribes to Facetus, as a conclusion :

> Qui voluerit plus istud moralizare faciat, quia sicut magister, id est Facetus, dicit in fine poetrie sue induco sic :
>> Illidi metuens scopulis onerata phaselus
>> Ad portum properans, longius horret iter (*B*, fol. 78ᵛᵇ).

---

97. On Trevet's commentary see the bibliography in A. B. EMDEN, *A Biographical Register of the University of Oxford to A. D. 1500*, III, Oxford 1959, p. 1902-1903. Miss R. J. Dean kindly guided me to the MS.

98. *B*, fol. 78ʳᵇ : ' Et ita nominat hominem Bernardus Silvestris, libro de Noym, lib. 11º, metro penultimo, ubi tractat de formatione hominis et eius prerogativa : Sunt alia inferiora... et artis opus. Et prosa sequente dicit : In minori mundo... supereminet'. From *De mundi universitate* (ed. C. S. BARACH and J. WROBEL), Innsbruck 1876, 60, 64.

Fol. 102ʳᵇ : ' Unde Galterus in Alexandride : « Non te emolliat intus (MS intellectus) », scilicet quantum ad voluptatem, « Prodiga luxuries ne fortia pectora frangat » '.

Fol. 75ᵛᵃ : ' ...in Alexandride dicitur : Nobilitas sola est animi que moribus ornat '. See *Alexandreis* (ed. F. A. W. MUELDENER), Leipzig 1863, 11, 9, from lib. 1, lin. 165-166 ; lin. 104.

Fol. 103ʳᵃ : ' de qua dicit Matheus vindocinensis, tractatu de amore : Protervo cubitus in vetitum mores deflectit '. I cannot find this line in the printed poems of Matthew of Vendôme.

Fol. 135ᵛᵃ : ' Vindocinensis, tractatu de descriptione temporum, dicit : Ver roseum tenero lascivit flore, laborat ‖ Picturare Ream floridiore coma '. From the description of the four seasons, *Ars versif.* (ed. E. FARAL, *Les Arts poétiques du XIIᵉ et du XIIIᵉ siècles*), Paris 1924, in B. E. H. E. 146.

Fol. 103ᵛᵃ : ' Unde Anticlaudianus : Ad (sic, for O !) fastus vitanda lues, fugienda Carribdis. Culpa gravis morbus communis publica pestis '. *Anticlaudianus* (ed. R. BOSSUAT), Paris 1956, 116, from lib. IV, lin. 307-308. Hesdin also quotes from the prose part of the *Liber de planctu naturae*, *B*, fol. 159ᵛᵃ : ' Unde Alanus in libro de planctu nature pulchre dicit : Invidia (quid) monstruosius monstrum ? Quid dampnosius dampnum ? Que culpabilior culpa ? Que penalior pena ' ; fol. 160ʳᵃ : ' Si quis in torrente divitiarum natat, cum Cresso (sic) opes spargit... ' See PL 210, 468-469.

99. *B*, fol. 132ʳᵇ : ' Commedia de Alda : Sicut non possunt sine munere numina flecti ‖ Sic sine muneribus nulla puella potest '.

B, fol. 140ʳᵇ : ' in Pamphilo : Concipit ingentes animos fiducia forme ' (for ' immanis egestas ').

Ibid. : 'in libro de Geta et Birrea : Hoc placet ipsa viro ‖ Plus placet ipsa sibi'. See G. COHEN, *La « Comédie » latine en France au XIIᵉ siècle* I, Paris 1931, 139, 44 ; II, 211.

He puts this at the end of a moralisation of the miracles worked by the apostles in his lecture on Mark, and ends the whole *lectura* with the same lines (fol. 79rb). They do not occur in the printed edition of *Liber Faceti docens mores hominum*, but not all the verse ascribed to this twelfth-century writer has been published [100]. Hesdin saw the poets of what we now call 'the twelfth-century renaissance' as prolonging the classical tradition and to be quoted on a level with the ancients. Perhaps, as a good Frenchman, he felt proud of them.

The only contemporary writer to be quoted by name is 'the Prior of Saint-Éloi', that is the classical scholar and friend of Petrarch, Pierre Bersuire. It is almost certain that the two men knew each other. Bersuire came to Paris after his stay at Avignon and lived in the city or its neighbourhood from about 1342 until his death in 1362. He was inscribed as a student at the university [101]. Hesdin was regent from about 1340 onwards, except for the time he spent at Avignon and on his visit to Italy. They would have had ample opportunity to meet.

Hesdin quotes Bersuire's moralisation of the *Metamorphoses*, though not always verbally, sometimes expanding his original :

> Verum aliter prior sancti Eligii luxuriam sub specie Veneris depinxit, et ponitur in libro suo, quem vocat moralisationes figurarum deorum. Est enim ad modum puelle pulcherrime nude... (*B*, fol. 102ra). Sciendum quod prior sancti Eligii in libro suo, quem intitulavit de moralisatione deorum, exponit statum superbi prelati sub figura Saturni... (fol. 103vb). Moraliter istud exponendo secundum priorem sancti Eligii et secundum Fulgentium Mars representat speciem alicuius principis et prelati iracundi (fol. 104ra). Dicit prior sancti Eligii quod hoc est quia ebrietas generat luxuriam et vinolentiam etc., et ardor venereorum viget in mulieribus ardentius (fol. 105ra). Isti fuerunt rudes homines et agrestes et incuriales, qui propter suam ruditatem dicuntur in ranas mutati esse... Ita exponit prior sancti Eligii (fol. 116rb) [102].

Perhaps Bersuire infected Hesdin with his own passion for moralised mythography. Hesdin certainly shared it. But Bersuire was more

---

100. On *Facetus* see H. WALTHER, *Initia carminum ac versuum Medii Aevi poster. lat.* I, Göttingen 1959, 184-185, n° 3690, 3692.

101. On Bersuire's life and writings see F. GHISALBERTI, *L'« Ovidius moralizatus » di Pierre Bersuire*, Rome 1933 ; J. ENGELS, *Études sur l'« Ovide moralisé »*, Groningen 1945 ; B. SMALLEY, *English Friars*, 261-264.

102. Dr J. Engels kindly sent me his reprint of the Paris edition of 1509, *Petrus Berchorius, Reductorium morale, Liber XV, cap. 1. De formis figurisque deorum*, Utrecht 1960. It is useful to have this rare book so easily to hand. I quote the chapter number of the original and the page number of the Utrecht reprint.

Venus, cap. V, p. 15 ; *Saturnus*, cap. I, p. 5 ; *Mars*, cap. III, p. 11 ; *Bacchus* : Muliebrem habet faciem..., cap. XIII, p. 27.

The moralisation of the fable of 'Lathona' comes in a later part of Bersuire's book ; I have checked it from the copy in MS *Oxford, Bodl. 571*, fol. 42^{va-b} ; it is an almost verbal quotation.

than a moralist. He consulted Petrarch on the pictorial images of the pagan deities and tried to describe them as accurately as possible. Hesdin resembled him in that he, too, could delight in imagining a pagan scene. The text *Iuvenes similiter hortare ut sobrii sint* (*Tit.* II, 6) serves as a signal for a youth personifying Spring, crowned with flowers, to take the stage. Hesdin discourses at length on the properties of youth, and then, lest he should leave it too soon, he summons a second personification : the goddess Flora and her train of nymphs and satyrs troop on, *causa solationis*. He claims to have found this particular form of solace in a book which pleased him mightily by Alberic of London. The latter was a twelfth-century compiler, known today as Mythographus tertius, who was often confused with Alexander Nequam. Hesdin gives the incipit of the book correctly. It is interesting that he got the author's name right : the English friars and Bersuire himself ascribe it to Alexander [103]. Neither of the two personifications of Spring appear in it, however. Hesdin must have had an expanded version or he was misremembering. We shall see that his mythographers tend to be as mythical as their subject matter. This was a common trait of fourteenth-century moralists ; he was soberer than many of them. Whatever their intermediate source, his dryades, naiades and silvani look classical enough. He goes on to ask an unusual question : 'what may they be ? ' For answer he quotes Bernard Sylvestris to the effect that they were harmless, happy spirits, living in an early age of the world, and now extinct. That was Bernard's opinion. Hesdin refuses to commit himself as to its truth, and will not discuss the subject any further [104].

Bersuire made contact with early humanism through his friendship with Petrarch. Hesdin looked back to the classical tradition of Chartres. Both Petrarch and Bersuire had a poetic approach to antiquity, which contrasted with the mythographers' dry, prosaic manner. But this passage, where Hesdin shows real feeling for the beauty of ancient myths, stands alone in his *lectura*. Elsewhere the moralist predominates in him. Nothing illustrates his strictly contemporary tastes more clearly than his projection back into the ancient world of his own preaching technique. He makes Virgil's commentator, Servius, say that the ancients made virtues into gods because, when the poets, who were learned clerks, told the people about the properties of virtues or vices, the people carved idols or statues to represent these properties ; and so these images served the people as books, just as ' now we

---

103. E. RATHBONE, *Master Alberic of London, ' Mythographus Tertius Vaticanus '*, in *Mediaeval and Renaissance Studies* I (1941) 35-38 ; B. SMALLEY, *English Friars*, 171, 211, 262-263.

104. See Appendix, p. 387

have pictures in our churches, which are commonly called books for the peasantry '. The same idea is found in a sermon by Robert Holcot : he makes Servius tell of a heathen picture book of virtues [105]. It must have been a moralists' commonplace. How unclassical ! Hesdin goes on to quote a moralised description of the god Apollo, who represents Truth, because he was the mouthpiece of Jove. Hesdin found it in John Ridevall's *Fulgentius metaforalis*, a moralisation of the *Mythologiae* of the mythographer, Fulgentius. He ascribes it incorrectly to ' Brother Robert Holcot ', a common and understandable mistake on his part ; the names of writers having the same interests were often interchanged. The text is *veritatis* (*Tit.* I, I) :

> Causa solationis et nostre eruditionis videamus primo duo. Primo inquiramus de veritate in communi, secundo specialiter. Primo inquiramus quid antiqui de veritate sentiebant, secundo quid moderni. Est ergo sciendum quod Servius, qui fuit commentator Virgilii, super Georgicam dicit quod antiqui faciebant virtutes deos et (MS in) quod quando poete, qui clerici et litterati erant, de aliqua virtute aut vitio populo proprietates dicebant, illi statim idolum aut statuam construebant et fabricabant, in quo significatio proprietatis illius virtutis aut vitii significabatur, et sic tales imagines populo rudi erant pro libris, (sicut) nunc in ecclesiis fiunt picture, que dicuntur communiter libri rusticorum [106]... Erat descriptio Apollonis quasi iuvenis pulcherrimus, arcum tenens et sagittas [107], ...Si ergo causa solationis et nostre eruditionis ista velimus moraliter explanare, sicut frater Robertus Holcot exposuit et Fulgentius, etiam pro parte poterimus de veritate aliquas proprietates declarare (*B*, fol. 92va).

On the same verse, *secundum pietatem*, he quotes without acknowledgment but almost verbally an item from Holcot's very popular *Moralitates*, representing Piety as a man having a split heart. Holcot introduced it by a tale which he claimed to have taken from a letter of Pliny to Valerius Maximus, a pure invention. Hesdin quotes this tale with its ascription to Pliny without any comment [108].

---

105. Quoted in B. SMALLEY, *English Friars*, 171 : ' In cuius signum Servius super primum librum Eneidarum refert quod apud gentiles, qui picturas virtutum habebant in libris, isto modo gratia depingebatur '.

It was an old idea that the ancient gods represented virtues, but a comparatively new one that the poets, like medieval preachers, taught the illiterate people, using statues or pictures as books.

106. It would be interesting from the point of view of the history of education to discover when pictures first came to be called ' libri *rusticorum* ', instead of ' libri *laicorum* ', as in the twelfth century and earlier. See for instance JOHN BELETH, *De divinis officiis*, cap. LXXXV (PL 202, 89), and texts collected by L. GOUGAUD, *Mutus praedicator*, in *Revue bénéd.* 42 (1930) 168-171. The difference points to the rise of a litterate laity.

107. H. LIEBESCHÜTZ, *Fulgentius metaforalis : ein Beitrag zur Geschichte der antiken Mythologie im Mittelalter*, Leipzig 1926, 116.

108. *B*, fol. 93va : ' Restat aliquod dicendum de ipsa pietate, et si velimus

Holcot's ' ancient picture ' of Piety represents a type of *exemplum* which seems to have originated in England. Preachers and moralists were not content to use genuinely ancient fables and figures of deities ; they invented sham antique stories and figures in order to moralise them as well. The Oxford Franciscan, John Ridevall, included a quite unclassical ' picture ' of Idolatry in his *Fulgentius metaforalis* among his gods and goddesses. Both Ridevall and Holcot used this same technique in their biblical commentaries, and Holcot did much to popularise it in his *Moralitates*. It spread to the Continent and found imitators [109]. Hesdin had read at least two *exempla* collections of this kind. His quotations from them lead us into a maze of bibliographical problems. He quotes (1) a book which he ascribes to the Prior of Saint-Éloi, Pierre Bersuire ; this is unknown to Bersuire's bibliographers ; it drew on Holcot's *Moralitates*, as did other compilations of the kind ; Hesdin may have found the ' picture ' of Piety in it (2) a book which he ascribes to Holcot : ' Frater Robertus Holcot in moralitatibus idolorum quas composuit '. At first sight it looks as though he were quoting Ridevall's *Fulgentius metaforalis*, attributing it incorrectly to Holcot, as we have seen him do when describing and moralising the god Apollo. But no ! These ' pictures ' are not to be found in the writings of either Ridevall or Holcot. We thus have a pseudo-Holcot and a pseudo-Bersuire to add to pseudo-Alberic of London.

Holcot's shoulders were broad enough to carry any amount of *spuria*. The items wrongly ascribed to him are Holcot-inspired, if not genuine Holcot. They compensate for unacknowledged borrowings or thefts from his *Moralitates*. Poor Bersuire might have turned in his grave. In the first place, he was scrupulous in specifying his debt to Petrarch and to Ridevall, whose *Fulgentius metaforalis* he used for a revision of his *Ovidius moralizatus*. It is unlikely, therefore, that he would have plagiarised Holcot's *Moralitates*, as the author of the compilation ascribed to him by Hesdin certainly did. In the second place, Bersuire moralised only genuinely classical fables and figures of deities in his *Ovidius moralizatus*. He never demeaned himself to the point of manufacturing shams, and he tried to get his information right. His famous name and the vogue of his *Ovidius moralizatus* could easily have led to the circulation of Pseudo-Berchoriana. True,Hesdin

sicut in aliis virtutibus superius positis alludere causa iocunditatis et eruditionis, quid antiqui de pietate sentiebant videamus... '

From *Moral.* X in the Bâle edition of 1586, 718-719. The *Moralitates* are printed at the end of Holcot's commentary on Wisdom. For bibliography and discussion see B. SMALLEY, *English Friars*, 145-147, 165-183.

109. *Ibid.* 109-121, 145-147, 165-183.

should have been able to distinguish the authentic from the false Bersuire, seeing that he began his *lectura* on Titus in the very year of Bersuire's death, 1362, and had probably known him. But we cannot trust Hesdin, whose bibliography was not impeccable. He dabbled, though shyly, in the manufacture of sham antique 'pictures' himself. A book which suited his purpose, going under the respectable name of Bersuire, may not have disposed him to ask questions on the score of its authorship.

His quotations from Pseudo-Alberic, Pseudo-Bersuire and Pseudo-Holcot may be read in the appendix, together with his own 'pictures'. Hesdin's essays in this curious genre show some enterprise. He tried to find a 'picture' of Justice, feeling sure that the ancients must have personified what they regarded as the virtue *par excellence*. Yet he searched in vain through Fulgentius, Rabanus, Remigius, Robert Holcot and the Prior of Saint-Éloi ; the last two had both taken pains to collect *imagines*. Fulgentius came nearest, since he suggested, in describing the judgment of Paris, that Paris might stand for Justice. Hesdin found what he wanted in Aulus Gellius. He quotes a description of Justice from *Noctes Atticae*, adding on his own account a crown, a chair and a sceptre. He also noted that a Greek commentator on the *Ethics* (translated by Robert Grosseteste) gave Justice a golden face. The traditional weighing scale made her 'picture' complete. His second effort was a 'picture' of Old Age. This image appeared as bowed down (by years). Hope, in the form of a damsel, was offering a staff by way of support. The image had two crows underfoot and looked backward with a sad expression on its face. Young men mocked it on one side ; on the other, grave men of ripe age crowned it with various crowns. Most painters of 'pictures' ascribed them to some author, whether real or invented. Hesdin, on the contrary, admitted that he had not taken his from any book, but had put it together as best he could. Here, in the flourishing sham antique market, is a piece labelled *copy*. Touching honesty ! Did Hesdin suppose that the other wares were genuine antiques ? It almost seems so.

Hesdin deplored the invasion of *anglicana doctrina*, but he acted as a fifth columnist for *anglicana figmenta*. His imitations were clumsy. Holcot would mix grave and gay as deftly as the fourteenth-century sculptor, who puts an impish smile on the lips of the Holy Child. Hesdin's abrupt transitions *causa nostre solationis* to 'pictures' from exegesis sound awkward, as though he were saying to his class : ' I've been boring you. Now for some light relief '. He discarded 'pictures' in his last *lectura*. He may have felt that a gospel commentary was not the place for them, or he may have heard criticism from his colleagues.

* * *

It remains to mention a sermon on the Feast of the Conception of the Blessed Virgin in MS *Saint-Omer 316*, foll. 132-138. Hauréau knew of it, but the catalogue, though correctly noting it as listed among the contents of the volume on the end flyleaf, reports it as missing [110]. It forms part of a miscellany which belonged to the abbey of Saint-Bertin, early fifteenth-century. Some of the pieces are also found in another Saint-Bertin manuscript, *Saint-Omer 273*, late fourteenth- or early fifteenth-century. Both volumes have Trevet's *Declamationes Senecae moralizatae*, the Pseudo-Aristotelian *Enigmata*, and an *exempla* collection beginning *Refert Fulgentius, De ornatu Urbis* [111]. This collection draws on Holcot's *Moralitates* and on Ridevall's *Fulgentius metaforalis*. The first item in it, ascribed to ' Fulgentius, *De ornatu Urbis* ', recalls a work quoted by John Lathbury under the title ' Fulgentius, *De ornatu civitatis* '. This Pseudo-Fulgentius contained *exempla* on statues and buildings of ancient Rome, as circumstantial as they were apocryphal [112]. It is interesting to find Hesdin's sermon in company with this pseudo-classical material. The author of the *lectura* on Titus is not out of place there.

The sermon is written in an unprofessional hand, much abbreviated, and the text is very corrupt :

> Incipit sermo conceptionis beate Marie per magistrum Iohannem de Hisden Ord. Hosp. sancti Iohannis Ierusalem.

> *Tota puchra es amica mea et macula non est in te*, Cant. IV. Quantum michi apparet, in generali invenitur triplex macula in sacra scriptura, qua homines maculantur...

> ...et applica ad propositum, si placet etc.

It is really a draft for a sermon. Hesdin intended it for a clerical audience, since he touches on nice theological points. He may have preached it either at Paris or at Avignon. It is interesting because he gives his opinion on the much discussed question of the Immaculate Conception of Our Lady. After distinguishing three kinds of *macula* (i) *ignorantie* (ii) *omissionis* (iii) *traductionis*, and showing that the Virgin

---

110. *Cat. gén. des manuscrits des bibl. publ. de la France*, III, Paris 1861, 157-158.

111. *Ibid.* 137-138 ; other items in MS *316* are WILLIAM OF AUVERGNE'S, *De penitentia* and what seems to be part of his *De collatione et singularitate beneficiorum*, anonymous and headed ' De prelatis ecclesie ', fol. 82-108, not mentioned in the catalogue ; see GLORIEUX, *op. cit.*, n° 141 (m) and (r).

112. B. SMALLEY, *English Friars*, 353-355. For a list of MSS (which omits *Saint-Omer 273* and *316*) and analysis of the *Refert Fulgentius* collection see LIEBESCHÜTZ, *Fulgentius metaforalis*, 47-53 ; 115-116. John Lathbury's quotations do not appear in *Refert Fulgentius*, though they might well have come from the same original, *De ornatu Urbis* or *Civitatis*, whatever that was.

was exempt from the first two kinds, he considers the third. Here he says with his usual caution that this is too deep a matter to be rashly determined. It is for the Pope to declare and determine doubtful matters of faith. Hesdin's phrasing shows his affection for the Papacy. However, in the absence of definition, he would wish piously to believe in the doctrine, which seems reasonable as well as holy. Though a number of saints and doctors have disputed it, others have pronounced in its favour. He lists the theologians commonly held (whether rightly or wrongly) to have favoured the doctrine : Anselm, Richard of St Victor, Alexander Nequam, Robert Grosseteste, bishop of Lincoln, and Ildefonse, bishop of Toledo :

> Vero et quamvis determinate istud ab homine mortali sciri non possit sine speciali revelatione Dei, quia nemo novit spiritum Dei nec consiliarius eius fuit [113] ...et ideo asserere hoc vel illud pertinaciter temerarium esset donec ab ecclesia sit determinatum et declaratum, quia ad bonum summum pontificem pertinet declarare que dubia sunt in fide nostra... Tamen, quia semper Virgini gloriose est tantus honor deferendus quantus potest sine preiudicio deferri..., ideo, omissis disputationibus que a multis in secundo Sententiarum solent fieri [114], videlicet quid sit originale, quomodo contra hoc (? illegible word), quot modis possit purgari, in quo sit, et multis talibus, breviter ad illud membrum (sic, illam materiam ?) pro predicatione et eius laude, dico tria breviter, sicut dicit Augustinus, sermone de assumptione eius, quia aliter de ea non sentio, aliter dicere nec presumo :
> primum est quod Deus ab originali macula conservare potuit ; secundum est quod hoc etiam fieri decuit ; tertium est quod credo pia fide quod ita fuit...
> Ex quo manifeste concluditur quod rationabile et sanctum est pia fide credere quod ita de facta fuit. Et si plures doctorum et sanctorum ad oppositum opinati fuerunt, etiam multi sancti et doctores (MS doctorum) partem istam tenuerunt, scilicet Anselmus in libro quem apposuit de ista materia et Richardus de sancto Victore, *Igitur huius diei*, Alexander Nequam, exponens *tota pulchra es*..., magister Robertus, qui fuit episcopus Lincolniensis, qui fuit doctor eximius et egregius in theologia ; Hildefonsus toletanus episcopus, sermone de nativitate eius... [115]

---

113. From *Rom.* XI, 34.

114. *II Sent.*, dist. XXX-XXXIII.

115. S. L. FORTE gives a useful bibliography and account of the sources commonly adduced in discussions of the question in the fourteenth century, *Thomas Hopeman O. P. An unknown biblical commentator*, in *Archivum Fratrum Praedicatorum* 25 (1955) 329-334. Hopeman's main sources include three mentioned by Hesdin : Eadmer's treatise, here ascribed to St Anselm, 'the sermon of the Pseudo-Peter Comestor, quoted under the name of Richard of St Victor, and the commentary on the Canticle of Alexander Nequam '. On Grosseteste see F. M. MILDNER, *The Oxford Theologians of the Thirteenth Century and the Immaculate Conception*, in *Marianum* 2 (1940) 296-299 : ' On reading the work of theologians of the thirteenth and fourteenth centuries who wrote in favour of the Immaculate Conception we invariably find Grosseteste named as a theologian in its favour, but unfortunately we never find indicated any work

> Ex quo concludo corollarie quod sanctum et pium est hanc solempnitatem celebrare, non habendo respectum ad aspectus morales seu mariales, sed ad sanctitatem et ad puritatem tante Virginis, que sine omni macula Dei mandatis (*sic*) est imago bonitatis illius (fol. 133-134).

Hesdin has avoided hurting anyone's feelings. He ends his discussion by implying that all, irrespective of precise shades of opinion, can join in celebrating the feast in the Virgin's honour. The rest of his sermon consists of praise of her beauty and of exhortations to virtue. His use of pagan authors is restrained. There are a few quotations from Aristotle and only one from Ovid [116].

* * *

The extent of his influence on later commentators must remain problematic until more work has been done on fifteenth-century exegesis. Jean Gerson did not use Hesdin on St Mark in his lectures on the same gospel [117]. Gerson may even have had Hesdin in mind when he criticised those who piled up snippets of authorities for the sake of display [118]. All the same, the number of surviving copies, especially of the *lectura* on Titus, shows that Hesdin was in some demand in the late fourteenth and early fifteenth centuries. Further study might disclose whether his *lecturae* passed into the school tradition or whether they were read privately.

The questions posed at the beginning of this paper can now be answered. Hesdin was a conservative. He prolonged an older tradition or group of traditions. He did not revive biblical scholarship, though his use of Lyre shows that he appreciated the need for it. He looked to St Thomas in theology. Holcot and Bersuire influenced his technique as a moralist. The homiletic content of his lectures is innocent of *devotio moderna*. He stood for tradition in his moral and religious teaching, just as he stood for medieval classical culture as opposed to

---

wherein he expressed his opinion on the subject '. On Pseudo-Augustine, *Sermo de Assumptione* (PL 39, 2196), and Ildefonse of Toledo see *Clavis Patrum Latinorum*, in *Sacris erudiri* 3 (1951) n⁰ 1251.

116. Fol. 137ᵛ : 'Item Ovidius in arte amandi, lib. 111⁰ : Forma bonum facit (*sic*)... ipsa suo'. *Ars amatoria* 11, 113-114.

117. See P. GLORIEUX, *L'enseignement universitaire de Gerson*, and *Les « Lectiones duae super Marcum » de Gerson*, in *Rech. Théol. anc. méd.* 23 (1956) 88-113 ; 27 (1960) 344-356. I have compared Gerson with Hesdin on the same texts and found no dependence of the one on the other.

118. GERSON, *Opera* IV, Antwerp 1706, 204 : ' Non tamen estimo curiositatem in allegationes huiusmodi consectandam, sed quousque prosunt studiosis et edificant charitatem : alioquin cumulus ille truncatarum auctoritatum male congestus, et informis congeries allegationum sue origini non convenientium quid proficit, quid nisi fortasse ostentationem operatur ? '

early humanism. He had a keen interest in antiquity and he read widely, but where we find a spark of something more poetic he owes it to Bernard Silvestris. Perhaps the most interesting pieces in his repertoire come from the twelfth century. He remembered Abelard and Gilbert de la Porrée as fighters for freedom of debate in the schools; he admired those twelfth-century Latin poets whom the humanists would dismiss as mere versifyers.

A clear character emerges from the *lecturae*, the sermon and the letter to Petrarch. Hesdin disliked controversy and observed moderation in all things. The secular masters of theology accepted him as one of themselves, to the extent of making him dean of their faculty, in spite of his religious habit, yet he did not combat the friars in his teaching. His reverence for St Thomas did not lead him to make any sustained attack on the modernists. He showed self control in defending his country against Petrarch. The Pope's desertion of Avignon, and Italian slights to France and Frenchmen must have stirred this quiet man to the depths of his being to make him fire shots in the French cause. Petrarch may have been right in suspecting that he did it in order to win a bishopric ; but even ambition, which he doubtless had, would hardly have sufficed to push Hesdin into conflict unless some other powerful emotion had lent him strength.

The missed preferment brings us to his noble patrons. They disappointed him, in that he died without a mitre ; but hope unfulfilled belongs to the history of patronage. His patrons, Gui de Boulogne and Philippe d'Alençon, were princes of the Church, not secular nobles, but influential in French politics. Hesdin's relations with them seem to anticipate those between Wyclif and the duke of Lancaster and between Gerson and the duke of Burgundy. University doctors were becoming more reliant on outside help than their predecessors in the thirteenth century had been, and less independent in consequence.

Appendix

On Iob III.

[*MSS Paris, Maz. 200*, unfoliated ; *London, B. M. Arundel 64*, fol. 10^{ra-vb}]

Post hec etc. Postquam descripta est superius Iob flagellatio, et est quasi prosa, hic incipit eius cum amicis disputatio, et secundum quod dicit Ieronimus, ut supra dictum est, ab hinc usque ad medietatem capituli ultimi totus fuit conscriptus versibus exametris ex dactilo et spondeo

382

currentibus [119], et quasi incipit prosecutio libri, et in prima sui divisione dividitur in duas partes, nam primo ponitur ipsius Iob lamentatio querulosa, secundo amicorum obiectio calumpniosa in principio quarti capituli. Et antequam subdividatur capitulum oportet memorare certa dicta sanctorum et doctorum aliquantulum.

Circa quod est advertendum quod beatus Gregorius, iv° Moralium, dicit simpliciter quod verba ipsius Iob, quibus maledicit principium vite sue et continuationem, non pertinent ad litteralem intellectum, et arguit quod verba ipsius Iob in isto capitulo viderentur verba hominis impatientis prima facie, immo desperantis, sed Iob non cecidit a vera patientia, ut patet ex precedentibus, tum ex verbis eius benedicendo Deum, tum ex suasione ad uxorem, etiam quia in ultimo capitulo libri dicitur quod Dominus, loquens ad Eliphat Themanitem, dicit : *Iratus est furor meus* ... [120] Secundo arguit quod, si verba ipsius Iob accipiantur ad litteram, continent impossibilia et irrationabilia, impossibilia scilicet dicendo : *Pereat dies* etc., quia dies illic pretereunt nec redire poterat idem in numero, ut habetur ex primo de generatione : Quod semel est corruptum idem in numero redire non potest [121]. Etiam irrationabilia, dicendo : *Dies vertatur in tenebris*, et alia huiusmodi, que continentur in isto capitulo. Propter quod et consimilia, cum Iob fuisset sapiens, non est credendum quod ipse intelligeret illa ad litteram, immo dicendum, ut ipse dicit, quod ipse enigmatice seu parabolice loquebatur, et ideo mistice ipse exponit totum capitulum istud [122].

Sanctus Thomas de Aquino nichilominus exponit capitulum ad litteram ad cuius intellectum est sciendum... nec erant irrationabilia, ut patebit infra. Magister Nicholas de Lira, quantumcumque istud gratiose et subtiliter dictum (sit), movet dubium... ut patebit in processu [123].

Quantum michi apparet, licet bene arguat contra Thomam, positio tamen sua non est ad propositum, quia quod ipse dicit hic ex suppositione erroris eorum non videtur probabile, quia adhuc verbum non dixerant, ex quibus posset scire opinionem eorum, etiam quia verba hec non sonant recte, et homo non potest arguere ex datis contra aliquem, nisi sibi prius appareat de intentione eius, et ideo, sustinendo opinionem sancti Thome, dicendum quod ipse loquebatur exprimendo passionem naturalis sensitive partis, non ei consentiens per rationem, sed magis ei dissentiens, secundum quod dixit infra : *Si occiderit me, etiam in ipso sperabo* [124]. Sed amici Iob crediderunt eum loqui ex deliberatione et mente turbata, et ideo contra eum arguunt, et ipse postea respondit ad dicta eorum, quibus volebant ostendere quod ipse non debebat ita loqui, cum hoc sustineret ex aliqua culpa commissa, sicut

119. From the prologue *Cogor per singulos*, prefixed to the Vulgate.
120. XLII, 7.
121. Actually ARISTOTLE, *De gen. et corrupt.* II, 11, 338b, 19.
122. Hesdin summarises St GREGORY, *Moral. in Iob* (PL 75, 634-635), adding the argument from Aristotle. He adopts the account from LYRE, *op. cit., ad loc.* (III, 44-45).
123. Hesdin quotes the argument of St Thomas (*op. cit., ad loc.*) via Nicholas of Lyre, *ad loc.* He goes on to quote *in extenso* Lyre's objection to St Thomas.
124. *Iob* XIII, 15.

et aliis afflictis contingit, et sic non arguunt ex equivoco, ut patet, nec potest dici blasphemus, cum hoc non diceret ex deliberatione rationis, sicut ditum est.

DEDICATORY LETTERS.

[*MSS Paris, Maz. 200*, fol. 1^{ra-b} ; *T*, fol. 1^{ra-b}].

Reverendo in Christo patri et domino Guidoni de Bononia, Dei providentia episcopo portuensi ac sacrosancte romane ecclesie cardinali, frater Iohannes de Hysdinio sancte domus hospitalis sancti Iohannis Ierosolitani ordine professus, vester humilis et devotus orator, presentem vitam ducere felicem et gloriam consequi sempiternam.

Quia, ut dicit Cassiodorus epistolarum seu variarum lib. iii°, ep. 6ª, sicut indigna posteritas laudes antiqui generis abnegat, ita preclara egregie de patribus dicta confirmat iuxta illud : Preconia veterum presens donat vena virtutum [125]. Laudabilis enim vena suam servat originem et fideliter posteris tradidit, que in se gloriosa transmissione promeruit [126]. Unde et Philosophus ad propositum ii° Rhetorice dicit, cap. 22° : Ad laudandum aliquem sumenda est nobilitas progenitorum ; bonum enim et honestum prepossedisse honorem in suis parentibus [127]. Et eandem sententiam recitat Seneca, viª tragedia de Andromaca, que filium suum exhortandum, quem de illustri et nobili Hectore susceperat, ad probitatem sequi sui generis invitabat [128], nam ut dicit Aristoteles iii° Poetice, cap. 19° : Meliores est verisimile eos esse qui ex melioribus, quia ingenuitas est virtus generis [129], et secundum veritatem nobiles genere debent habere quasi innatam prudentiam clariorem, clementiam dulciorem, audaciam fortiorem, iustitiam veriorem, ut sicut dicit Philosophus, ubi supra : Ingenuitas apud quoscumque sit honorabilis [130]. Et quia, nobilissime et excellentissime pater et domine, revera possum vobis dicere sicut in epistola Bernardi ad magistrum Galterum de Calvomonte : Genus clarum, corpus aptum, forma evidens, ingenium velox, eruditionis utilitas et morum honestas in te resplendeant, et gloriosa dicta sunt. Si tibi usurpas, est qui querat et iudicet [131]. Ita quod, teste veritate et fama proclamante, que omnino veritate non caret, ut dicitur vii° Ethic. [132], in vobis antiqui generis regia nobilitas regum, ducum

---

125. PL 69, 579.

126. *Var.* iii, 6 (PL 69, 583).

127. Neither in the *Rhetorica* nor in PSEUDO-ARISTOTLE, *Rhetorica ad Alexandrum*.

128. *Troades*, lin. 461-474.

129. Actually *Polit.* iii, 13, 1283a, 35-37.

130. *Ibid.* 33-35.

131. *Ep.* civ (PL 182, 239). For *evidens*, read ' elegans ', for *dicta*, ' quidem '. After *sunt* add ' sed ei a quo sunt '.

132. I cannot find this text either in the *Ethic. Nicom.* or in St Albert's commentary. It may perhaps be a deduction from *Rhet.* i, 5, 1361a, 25-27, where

comitumque nobilis generis non degeneret aut pereat, sed clarius fulgeat, melius vigeat et iocundius floreat vita morum, et ut cogar verius dicere, in tantum quod vena laudabilis illustris generis sic gloriosa transmissione servet originem, quod dictis et vita in vobis nobilitas generis appareat in moribus, liberalitas imminens prefulgeat, moribus humilitas ceteris resplendeat communibus et claritas operis refloreat virtutibus et dicatur verissime de vobis quod dicatur 1º Reg. xº : *Vir Dei est in hac civitate nobilis* [133], et in sancta ecclesia romana, que omnium ecclesiarum mater est et magistra, que est civitas de qua dicitur Hebr. xiº quod *expectabant sancti*, supple *fundamenta, habentes civitatem, cuius artifex et conditor* est *Deus fide* [134]. Et revera illa de qua ille contemplator maximus in Apoc. xxiº dicit quod vidit *civitatem sanctam, Ierusalem, descentem de celo, ornatam quasi sponsam viro suo* [135]. In qua vos, alme pater, tanquam vir *nobilis in portis* eius sedens *cum senatoribus terre*, ut dicit Prov. ultimo [136], presidetis.

Hinc est quod ego inter doctores Iohannes minimus et indignus, in spe tante nobilitatis, refulgentia bonitatis, clementia claritatis, intelligentia et humilitatis benevolentia, lecturam sive postillam supra librum Iob, quem nomine vestro incepi, vestra gratia, ut scio, que multum contulit paupertati ingenii mei taliter, ut scio, minus sufficienter complevi, vestre dignitati ausus sim fiducius presentare, cum revera spes vestre humilitatis gratiose ad supportandum, vestre nobilitatis generose ad excusandum, vestre subtilitatis ingeniose ad corrigendum, vestre bonitatis virtuose ad conducendum penurie et timiditati intellectus et cordis mei audaciam inchoandi potentiamque complendi contulerunt auxilium pariter et iuvamen, maxime quia, ut melius novit alta profunditas vestra, expositio historie libri Iob tanti sit oneris (MSS honoris) et ponderis quod Philippus, commentator libri Iob, vir antiquissimus, doctrina et scientia plenus et in divino eloquio excellens et famosus, ad Nectarum episcopum sic dicat : Aggredior, pater, in opus arduum... [137] De eodem libro ita dixit Ieronimus : Obliquus... Et idem in epistola ad Paulinum dicit : Iob exemplar... [138] Et beatus Gregorius in prologo huius libri post multas protestationes, immo excusationes, concludit : In obscuro hoc... [139] Si igitur tanti viri, tam profundi sermonis tantoque spiritu imbuti, ad expositionem libri sancti Iob, quem magis etiam mistice quam litteraliter exposuerunt, formidabiliter accesserunt, quanto ergo, nobilissime ac reverendissime pater, ego vir tenuis scientie, rudis ingenii, inculti eloquii, librum hunc ad honorem vestrum velut lapillum in acervo preconiarum vestrarum conieci, sciens quod, sicut non habet

---

Aristotle lists good fame among the parts of happiness ; he attaches some importance to it.

133. Actually *I Reg.* IX, 6.

134. Hesdin is adapting *Hebr.* XI, 9-11, glossing *fundamenta* as applying to *sancti.*

135. From *Apoc.* XXI, 2.

136. From *Prov.* XXXI, 23.

137. PHILIPPUS PRESBYTER (STEGMÜLLER, nº 6970).

138. Quotations from St Jerome's prologues prefixed to the Vulgate.

139. PL 75, 512.

unde placeat ex venustate, sic, ut spero, ex devotione scribentis non poterit displicere, quia etiam liber iste diverse loquitur, aliquando poetice, aliquando astrologice, aliquando philosophice, aliquando mathematice, aliquando allegorice, mistice, anagogice, ut melius, pater, novistis, ut vir nobilis genere et moribus, sustineatis trepidantem, confortetis formidantem, corrigatis delinquentem et reducatis oberrantem, et scriptorem vestrum confortetis pariter et iuvetis, quia istius minimi operis omnia vestro relinquitur examini, ut vobis maior et iustior corrigendi quam michi scribendi gloria debeatur.

[*Maz. 200*, fol. 357ʳᵇ; *T*, fol. 264ʳᵃ].

Brevis conclusio ad dominum cardinalem bononiensem.

> Alme pater scitis, est circa verbera lusum.
> Iam patientia Iob premia digna tulit.
> Quod potui feci. Defectus corrige, supple.
> Non michi scribenti gloria, sed tibi sit.
> Ergo laboranti, vir prestantissime, naute
> Ad tua nunc tendenti littora tende manum.

[*B*, fol. 86ʳᵃ⁻ᵇ].

Illustrissimo et venerandissimo in Christo, patri domino Philippo de Alenconio, divina providentia rothomagensi archiepiscopo dignissimo, frater Iohannes de Hisdinio, sancte domus hospitalis sancti Iohannis Ierosolitani ordine professus, vester humilis capellanus et devotus orator, vitam ducere felicem et vestrorum regnum assequi finaliter beatorum.

Quia, sicut dicit Philosophus primo Rhetorice, cap. 22⁰, ad laudandum aliquem sumenda est dignitas primogenitorum bonorum ; bonum et honestum est prepossedisse honorem in suis parentibus. Ratio huius potest esse quia, sicut dicit Cassiodorus lib. III⁰ Variorum cap. sive epist. 6⁰, laudabilis vena suam servat originem et fideliter posteris tradidit que in se gloriosa transmissione promeruit [140], quia, ut dicitur primo Rhetorice, cap. 22⁰, verisimile est ex bonis bonum, et sic nutritum talem esse [141], unde talis nobilitas inter partes felicitatis numeratur, primo Rhetorice, cap. 11⁰ [142]. Quapropter, ut recitat Trogus Pompeius, lib. xiv⁰, bene novit Apius senator romanus, cum romani vellent facere pacem cum Pirro rege grecorum, sed in honestam nobilitatem antiquorum, ut Hectoris, Enee et ceteros nobiles et strenuos a quibus descenderant ad memoriam reducebant. Unde conclusit in duobus versibus Ennii poete sic :

> Nobilitas patrum quondam revocetur ad usum.

---

140. Above, n. 126 and n. 127.
141. Probably a reference to *Pol.* III, 13, 1283a, 35-37, rather than to *Rhetorica*.
142. A general reference to *Rhet.* I, 5, 1360b, 30-33.

Et Tullius hic recitat libro De senectute, parte IIᵃ [143], quia secundum veritatem in nobilibus et excellentibus viris debet esse quasi innata prudentie verioris magnitudo, constantie firmioris fortitudo, clementie dulcioris aptitudo, iustitie melioris rectitudo, et propter hoc, lib. IIᵒ Rhetorice, cap. 33ᵒ, bene dicit Philosophus : Nobilitatis igitur mos est magis amatorem honoris esse eum qui habet ipsum [144]. Omnes cum assit, scilicet nobilitas, ad hoc accumulare consueverunt. Nobilitas enim honorabilitas progenitorum est. Et Boetius, De consolatione, lib. IIIᵒ prosa 6ᵃ, dicit : Si quid est in nobilitate bonum, id arbitror esse, ut imposita nobilibus necessitudo (MS multitudo) videatur, ne a maioribus, id est progenitoribus, virtute degenerent [145]. Et quia, illustrissime ac reverendissime pater, inter nobiles mundi [146] antiquorum potentissimorum ac nobilissimorum regum Francie et Castelle aliorumque totius christianitatis excellentissimorum gloriosorumque progenitorum nobiliter refulgetis, et in ecclesia Dei nobilissima rothomagensi presidetis, sic quod vere dicatur de vobis illud primi Regum Xᵒ : *Est vir nobilis in civitate hac* [147], vero illud Proverb. ultimo : *Nobilis in portis vir eius* [148], non solum nobilitate parentum, sed vera nobilitate virtutum, que secundum sanctos et doctores consistit in intellectus cognitione, virtutum operatione, appetitus refrenatione, morum ordinatione, ita quod in vestra felici et nobili iuventute resplendeat et refulgeat, vigeat et floreat vita morum. Quia quando in nobili genere viget corporis habilitas et iuventutis virtuosa maturitas, tunc talis ad cumulum laudis attingere perhibetur, ut a Philosopho Xᵒ Ethic., cap. 9ᵒ, satis haberi patet textus inspicienti [149], ut sic, a nobilitate ista progrediens de virtute in virtutem, ad nobilitatem supremam veniatis feliciter gloriosus, ut ad exemplum Iulii Hostilii, de quo narrat Valerius Maximus, lib. IIIᵒ, cap. 5ᵒ, quod nobilitas, quam accepit in cunabulis in adolescentia, fuit occupata sic quod validior etas imperium romanum rexit, et senectus in altissimo maiestatis fastigio fulsit [150], ut vobis, alme pater, dicatur quod dicit Apuleius, De deo Socratis : Gene-

---

143. IUSTINI *Epitom. Hist. Philip.* XVIII, 2 (*C. S. L. Parav.* 43, 121). *De senect.*, cap. VI, par. 16. Cicero mentions Appius and Pyrrhus and quotes from Ennius, but not this particular line.

144. *Rhet.* II, 15. This time Hesdin is quoting verbally from the translation of WILLIAM OF MOERBEKE, MS *Oxford, Balliol College 250*, fol. 21ᵛᵇ-22ʳᵃ. See *Aristoteles latinus* I (ed. G. LACOMBE etc.), Rome 1939, 406.

145. *De consol. Philos.* III, pros. 6, with Hesdin's gloss on *a maiorum virtute*.

146. Blank in MS.

147. Actually *I Reg.* IX, 6.

148. *Prov.* XXXI, 23.

149. Perhaps a general reference to the discussion of character training and the advantage of gentle birth in *Ethic. Nicom.* X, 9.

150. VALERIUS MAXIMUS, *De fact. et dict. mem.*, actually III, 4. As well as writing *Iulius* for 'Tullus' (which may be a copyist's mistake), Hesdin has slightly altered the story to suit the case. Tullus Hostilius is cited in the original as an example of a peasant boy, whose youth was occupied in tending flocks and who rose from humble origins to greatness. Hesdin makes him a young noble. Was he hinting that his patron might eventually become Pope ?

rosus es ? In hominibus (MS omnibus) considerandis noli illa estimare aliena [151].

Hinc est, prestantissime pater, quod ego, inter doctores theologie minimus et indignus, in tante excellentie et dignitatis fastigio, clementie et humilitatis suffragio, sanctimonie et bonitatis preconia, benevolentie et paternitatis patrimonio confisus, minimum opus, immo rusticitate persone invalidum et indignum, quod super epistola Pauli ad Tytum taliter qualiter ordinavi et complevi, ausus fui vestro nomini dedicare. Et quia consideravi quod in illa brevi epistola doctrina ab Apostolo necessaria et utilis ad omnium prelatorum quantum ad vitam, doctrinam et instructionem clericorum cuiuscumque gradus aut status ordinationem, dominorum temporalium quantum ad se et subditos gubernationem, subditorum et servorum obedientiam et subiectionem, statum sexuum et etatum conditionem et meliorationem, hereticorum et infidelium detestationem et repulsionem, dignum opere duxi circa ea aliqualiter insudare, et vestre alme paternitati humiliter presentare. Et quia, ut dixit Petrus Comestor in prologo Historie scholastice, stilo rudi opus est lima [152], vestre nobili et profunde discretioni limam submisi, ut corrigatis delinquentem, supporteris negligentem, reducatis oberrantem, conforteris formidantem, et si in hoc minimo opere sit aliquid laudabile prestantissime vestre paternitati non immerito tribuatur.

PSEUDO-ALBERIC.

[*B*, fol. 135$^{rb\text{-}vb}$; *T*, fol. 109rb-110rb].

On *Tit.* ii, 6 : *Iuvenes similiter hortare ut sobrii sint.*

Et ideo propter istas conditiones voluerunt antiqui comparare ver iuventuti, quia ver dat tempori formositatem, cordi iocunditatem, voluntati amicabilitatem et menti hilaritatem... Et quia iuventus veri apte aptari potest per hoc patet, quia sciendum (est) quod antiqui sculpebant imaginem veris, ut dicit Albericus londonensis in libro suo de moralizatione Ovidii et poetarum, qui incipit *Erat vir in Egipto ditissimus* etc. [153], et est in veritate liber delectabilis et utilis, ubi innuit quod ver depingebatur (ut) iuvenis pubescens decorus, floribus ornatus et etiam coronatus, avibus circumdatus, delectatus cantibus, et ingenio dispositus... Verum, ne transeam de iuventute nimis cito, adhuc causa solationis est notandum quod Albericus predictus, ubi supra, dicit quod iuventutem aliqui depinxerunt sub nomine dee Flore, de qua poete fingunt ut erat uxor Zephiri, venti orientalis, et sic est

---

151. Hesdin may well have taken this quotation from *Policraticus* vi, 28 (ed. C. C. I. WEBB, Oxford 1909, II, 84-85). JOHN OF SALISBURY quotes *De deo Socratis* xxi-xxiv. Hesdin excerpts and inverts : ' Similiter igitur et in hominibus contemplandis noli illa aliena estimare... Generosus es ? parentes laudas '.

152. PL 198, 1053.

153. G. BODE, *Scriptores rerum mythicarum* II, Celle 1834, 152.

dea florum. Fingebant eam [154] inter deas gratior fuisse in vultu et corpore, in veste variata diverso colore. In circuitu eius saltabant et ludebant nimphe, driades et nereides cum satiris et silvanis... Sed quid sunt nimphe driades ? Sciendum (est) quod secundum Ovidium et poetas driades dicuntur nimphe silvarum et nemorum, quia inhabitant in locis floridis et delectabilibus, et etiam ibi habitant silvam satiri, et ibi saltant et ludunt in locis umbrosis. Nereides sunt nimphe fontium, que colunt fontes, et ideo in circuitu dee Floride (*sic*) ludere dicuntur, quia in locis floridis manent, ut dictum est. Sed quid sint secundum veritatem ? Dico quod Bernardus Silvestris, libro suo quem fecit de formatione hominis, qui intitulatur liber Noym, lib. ii°, prosa 4°, ponit opinionem suam, ubi tractat de spiritibus diversis, generatis in diversis elementis et materia. Tamen ad propositum ipse dicit sic [155] : Ubi terra delectabilior, nunc herboso cacumine iugoque montium picturato nunc fluminis hilarescit, nunc silvarum viriditate vestitur, illic silvani, panes, nimphe camporum [156] et nerei, id est nereides, innocua conversatione etatis evolvunt tempora longioris. Elementali quadam puritate compositi sero tamen abeunt in tempora dissolvendi.

Ex isto habetur quod sunt spiritus innocui, coram hominibus delectabiliter viventes, per longa tempora viventes. Finaliter mortis exactum patiuntur. Et ista fuit opinio sua. Utrum vera sit an falsa, nichil ad me pro nunc.

Pseudo-Bersuire and Pseudo-Holcot.

[*B*, fol. 90vb-91rb ; *T*, fol. 10ra ; on *Tit.* I, I : *secundum fidem electorum Dei*].

Ergo quantum ad primum videamus de fidei descriptione vel diffinitione, et primo secundum quod describunt antiqui idolatre... Circa quod est sciendum quod antiqui fidem descripserunt mirabiliter secundum figuras, quibus ipsi dei vitia aut virtutes figurabant. Nam antiqui de aliquibus, que non apprehendebant ad sensum, fidem habebant. Et ideo, ut dicit Fulgentius, lib. ii° in Mithol., antiqui fidem depingebant vultu obscuram et quasi velatam, circa spatulas et pectus nudam, lauro coronatam, sceptrum in manibus tenentem, sub pedibus duas vulpes habentem, et in modo constantem (? MS constantiam). Quam picturam exponens prior sancti Eligii Parisiensis, allegans fratrem Guillelmum (*sic*) Holcot, qui figuras Fulgentii moralizavit [157], dicit quod fides est obscura vultu, quia de articulis et credibilibus claram notitiam non habet, sed tantum credentiam... [158]

---

154. MS ' Pingebat inter deas '. Something may have dropped out.

155. BERNARD SILVESTRIS, *op. cit.* 50. I have emended Hesdin's quotation where it is obviously corrupt.

156. ' nimphe camporum ' omitted in the original.

157. Hesdin probably confused Holcot with Ridevall, ascribing to him Ridevall's *Fulgentius metaforalis* ; but this ' picture ' of *Fides* is not in *Fulgen-*

[B, fol. 102ra, on *Tit.* I, 6 : *in accusatione luxurie]*.

Circa primum causa solationis est primo inquirendum quomodo antiqui et poete senserunt de luxuria... Quantum ad primum est sciendum quod frater Robertus Holcot, qui moralizavit figuras deorum, sub imagine Veneris luxuriam descripsit. Depingebatur antiquitus Venus nudata corpore, mir-r(h)a delibuta, visu pulchra sive facie, foliis ficus coronata, sub pedibus concha marina. ... [159]

[B, fol. 103rb, on *Tit.* II, 2 : *pudici]*.

Frater Robertus Holcot in moralisatione sua de figura (*sic*) deorum narrat quod Rabanus, libro de natura rerum, dicit quod Socrates depinxit superbiam ad modum hominis crudelis, coronati tribus coronis, et sub pedibus duo leones. In prima corona erat versus scriptus : Effluo, descendo, quo quis privatur habendo... [160]

[B, fol. 115^{ra-b}, on *Tit.* I, 12 : *mendaces]*.

Et ideo causa solationis et eruditionis videamus de ipso mendacio primo poetice... Quantum ad primum est sciendum quod frater Robertus Holcot in moralitatibus idolorum quas composuit mendacii imaginem descripsit prout sibi ipsemet. Prior sancti Eligii, non, ut dixit, quod antiqui hoc finxissent tanquam imaginem aliquid divinum habentem, et causa adorationis, sed magis sculpserunt ut vitium detestationis et confusionis. Erat enim imago ad modum mulieris, habitu meretricis, variis distincta coloribus, oculis orbata, vultu deformis et morbo languida [161].

[B, fol. 125rb, on *Tit.* II, 6 : *sine crimine]*.

Ad propositum tamen occurrit michi exemplum quod ponit prior sancti Eligii in moralitatibus suis, et est Alexandri magni et invenitur in gestis grecorum, ut ipse dicit [162]...

---

tius metaforalis ; nor have I found it elsewhere in the works of Ridevall and Holcot. Ridevall's 'picture' of *Fides*, expanded by Holcot, is quite different ; see my *English Friars* 175.

158. A moralisation of each separate attribute of *Fides* follows.

159. Not in Ridevall or Holcot.

160. The ascription to Rabanus Maurus is spurious. This 'picture' of *Superbia* is taken from Holcot's *Moralitates*, n⁰ XXXIII (Bâle, ed. 1586, 737) : 'Fertur in libro deorum quod Socrates... '

161. I do not know the source of this 'picture' of *Mendacium*.

162. A variant of the story in Holcot's *Moralitates* I (Bâle 1586, 700) : 'Theodosius in vita Alexandri... '

390

[B, fol. 126ᵛᵃ ; T, fol. 88ʳᵃ, on Tit. II, 2 : in dilectione].

Sed quomodo Deus nos invicem diligit satis possumus habere ex descriptione imaginis amicitie, quam ponit prior sancti Eligii, quam dicit se habere a Rabano, libro de natura rerum. Depingebatur sive sculpebatur specie iuvenis, coronati (MSS coronatus) corona in qua erant quatuor lapides pretiosi induti (MSS indutus) tunica viridi, in cuius fimbriis erat scriptum... [163]

[B, fol. 159ʳᵃ, on Tit. III, 3 : in malitia].

Prior sancti Eligii in suis moralisationibus dicit quod invenit quendam expositorem Tullii in illo passu quo ponebat quod Varro depinxerat quendam imaginem malitie ad similitudinem dee terribilis, iuxta quam ponebantur tres imagines... [164]

HESDIN'S OWN 'PICTURES'.

[B, fol. 108ᵛᵇ-109ʳᵃ ; T, fol. 49ᵛᵃ ; on Tit. I, 8 : iustum].

... ut consuevimus in ista lectura sacra, tractando de vitiis et virtutibus, tria sunt facienda : primo videre causa consolationis quomodo antiqui iustitie imaginem depinxerunt, reducendo ad mores causa nostre instructionis...

Circa primum est sciendum quod, sicut narrat Fulgentius, libro Mithol. in principio post prologum, quidam vocatus Dyophanitus... [165] Remigius in commentario super Martianum de nuptiis Philologie et Mercurii dicit quod Aristenes (*sic*) philosophus fuit primus qui vitiis et virtutibus sub imaginibus deorum aut aliorum antiquorum sive astrorum imagines composuit et formavit [166]. Et quia iustitia tantam excellentiam inter alias virtutes anti-

163. A variant of Holcot's *Moralitas* XXVI (Bâle ed., 731) : ' Narrat Fulgenius in quodam libro de gestis romanorum... '
164. A variant of Holcot's *Moralitas* XXXI (Bâle ed., 734) : ' Tullius in libro de academicis questionibus, questione quarta, commendat Varronem, eo quod ipse tradidit iura deorum. Ubi in expositione inveni quod Varro depinxit peccatum ad similitudinem dee... '
Thus four ' pictures ' or stories, *Superbia*, the Alexander story, *Amicitia* and *Malitia* come from Holcot's *Moralitates*. They have been slightly altered and ascribed to different sources from those alleged by Holcot, but equally fictitious.
165. FULGENTIUS, *Mythologiae* I, I (ed. R. HELM, Leipzig 1898, 15-16). Hesdin quotes Fulgentius' account of the origin of idolatry.
166. I cannot find this passage in Remigius on the *Nuptiae*. If ' Aristenes ' is a corruption of ' Aristoxenus ', then the *locus* should be II, 213 ; see MARTIANUS CAPELLA, *De nuptiis* etc. (ed. A. DICK, Leipzig 1925, 78). Aristoxenus is paired with Orpheus. REMIGIUS in his commentary says that both were astro-

quitus obtinuit, ut nunquam aliquis ex istis quorum scripta vidi et studui, videlicet Fulgentius, Rabanus, Remigius, Robertus Holcot et prior sancti Eligii, qui circa istas imagines componendas multum insudaverunt, sub aliqua figura deorum et astrorum iustitiam descripserunt, nisi quod Fulgentius sub imagine Paridis, filii Priami, iustitiam describere videtur in II° Mithol. [167], verumptamen in legendo Agellium, libro noct. attic. lib. XVI°, cap. 4°, iustitie imaginem descriptam ab antiquis, ut ipse dicit, in hunc modum adinveni. Depingebant imaginem in specie virginis incorrupte, aspectu vehementem, gratiosam et formidabilem, luminibus oculorum acrem, non humilis necque atrocis, sed reverende cuiusdam dignitatis videbatur [168], capite coronatam, in cathedra sedentem et sceptrum in manu tenentem. Unde Eustathius commentator super primo Philosophi v° Ethic., quod iustitia est communis virtus, dicit quod propter hoc ipsi philosophi dixerunt eam habere vultum aureum, stateram vero in una manu habentem equivalentem (MS equilante) [169].

Quid ista significent declaremus. Primo depingitur ut virgo, quia certe iustitia debet esse et est immaculata et incorrupta... [170]

[*B*, fol. 123rb-124rb ; *T*, fol. 80^{va-b}, on *Tit.* II, 2 : *senes*].

... antiqui... etiam senectutis imaginem depinxerunt. Erat autem imago curva, et spes, in specie domicelle, dabat sibi unum baculum pro sustentatione corporis. Habebat autem sub pedibus duos corvos. Vultu tristi et averso retro se respiciebat. Ex uno latere erant iuvenes et adolescentes

---

logers, which might have suggested the *astrorum imagines*, but nothing more. I used the copy of Remigius' commentary in MS *London, Brit. Mus. Royal 5.A.XXXIII*, fol. 69.

167. FULGENTIUS, *op. cit.* II, 1, 36 : ' Fabula de iudicio Paridis '. Only the title of the chapter could have suggested that Paris was a figure of justice ; the mythographer does not say so.

168. AULUS GELLIUS, *Noct. attic.* actually XIV, 4 : ' Facit quippe imaginem iustitiae fierique solitam esse dicit a pictoribus rhetoribusque antiquioribus ad hunc ferme modum : forme atque filo virginali, aspectu vehementi et formidabili, luminibus oculorum acribus, neque humilis neque atrocis, sed reverendae cuiusdam trititiae dignitate. Ex imaginis autem istius significatione intelligi voluit iudicem, qui iustitie antistes est, oportere esse gravem... ' Hesdin has taken some of the traits of *Iustitia* from Aulus Gellius, but has added the crown, the chair and the sceptre.

169. From GROSSETESTE's translation of Greek commentators on *Ethic. Nicom.* V, 1, MS *Oxford, Balliol College 116*, fol. 83vb-84ra : ' hoc Euripidis sapientis Melamppe dicit enim in ipsa iustitia aureum vultum '. Hesdin has added the scale, which is not mentioned here. The collection of ' pictures ' *Prudentia pingebatur* (of uncertain date, except that it quotes Holcot's *Moralitates* ; Holcot died in 1349) has the same reference to Eustatius : MS *Paris, Bibl. nat. lat. 590*, fol. 179 : ' Iustitia et eius imago sic describuntur habere vultum virgineum aureum vel vitreum, ut vult commentator Eustatius '.

170. Hesdin goes on to moralise the attributes of *Iustitia*, ending : ' ...et istud sufficiat de moralizatione imaginis iustitie '.

illam imaginem deridentes, ex alio latere graves et maturi homines, qui eam coronabant diversis coronis... Et sciant auditores quod ista, que ibi recitavi, non eodem modo nec sub eisdem verbis scribuntur in libris, sed eodem sensu et sicut potui ad habendum clariorem intellectum in brevibus collegi [171].

Note:

p. 347: Fr. Jean was a Hospitaller by January 1353 at latest; he probably entered the Order at least several years before that time, however, for by 1353 he was senior enough to be Preceptor of the Order's house at Mont-de-Soissons near Soissons. By 1363 he was better off, being both Prior of Corbeil, an important community of the Order, and Preceptor of Val-du-Provins, positions he still held in 1365/6.' See A. Luttrell, 'Jean and Simon de Hesdin: Hospitallers, Theologians, Classicists', *Recherches de Théologie ancienne et médievale* xxxi (1964) 137–8.

p. 357: The *Angeli pacis flebunt* is the *De periculis novissimorum temporum* of William of St. Amour. On the mendicant-secular controversy referred to by Jean de Hesdin see M.-M. Dufeuil, *Guillaume de Saint-Amour et la polémique universitaire Parisienne 1250–1259* (Paris, 1972).

---

171. I do not know where Hesdin collected these items for his 'picture' of *Senectus*.

Jean de Hesdin a Source of the « Somnium viridarii »

The *Somnium viridarii* is a treatise on public law with special reference to the relation between ecclesiastical and secular government [1]. The anonymous author sets it in the conventional framework of a dream : he organises his material after the prologue as a debate between a clerk and a knight. The treatise is dedicated to King Charles V of France. We know from an explicit that the author finished it on May 16, 1376, « qua etiam die illustrissimus princeps rex Francie, duobus annis revolutis, inter agentes in rebus domus sue et in consiliarium me, quamvis indignum, motu proprio duxit eligendum » [2]. It seems, therefore, that he belonged to the royal household in some capacity and that the king had promoted him to be one of his counsellors. We also know that the *Somnium* is a compilation drawn from diverse sources ; some have been identified, but by no means all. Agreement ends here. Many candidates for authorship have been put forward : it has been the lot of writers of the age to have attributed to them the authorship of the *Somnium viridarii*, as G. W. Coopland expresses it [3]. G. de Lagarde has suggested as an alternative that more than one royal servant may have helped to draw up this vast dossier at the king's bidding ; it was done by 'back-room boys'. Since lesser burocrats remain anonymous as a rule, it would be wrong, he thinks, to look for a distinguished scholar such as Nicole Oresme [4]. This note will be concerned only with the dedication of the *Somnium* and its setting in the prologue. There is no need to discuss the body of the work or the equally disputed question of the relationship between the *Somnium* and the French version, the *Songe du verger*, prepared a few years later.

The sources so far discovered for the prologue are (1) the *Somnium* of John of Legnano, 1372 [5]. Legnano was a professor of Bologna, *utriusque iuris peritus*, high in favour with Popes Innocent VI and Gregory XI. He uses his dream as a framework, soon forgotten, for a debate between two

1. Ed. M. GOLDAST, *Monarchia S. Romani Imperii*, Hanover 1612, vol. I, p. 58-229. For bibliography see R. BOSSUAT, *Manuel bibliographique de la littérature française du moyen âge*, Melun 1951, 544-545 ; *Supplément 1949-53*, Paris 1955, 113 ; *Supplément 1954-60*, Paris 1961, 108 ; P. CHAPLAIS, *The Opinions of the Doctors of Bologna on the Sovereignty of Aquitaine (1369) : a Source of the « Songe du Verger »* (Camden Miscellany, 19), London 1952, p. 51-78 ; M. LIÈVRE, *Note sur les sources du « Somnium Viridarii »*, in *Romania* 81 (1960) 483-491.

2. See the discussion in R. BOSSUAT, *Nicole Oresme et le « Songe du Verger »*, in *Le Moyen Age* 53 (1947) 92-93.

3. G. W. COOPLAND, *Nicole Oresme and the Astrologers, a Study of his « Livre de Divinacions »*, Liverpool 1952, 3.

4. G. DE LAGARDE, *Le « Songe du verger » et les origines du Gallicanisme*, in *Revue des Sciences relig.* 14 (1934) 1-33, 219-237.

5. For what follows see G. W. COOPLAND, *An Unpublished Work of John of Legnano, the « Somnium » of 1372*, in *Nuovi Studi medievali*, vol. 2, fasc. 1 (1925-26), p. 65-88, especially p. 84-87.

queens, representing canon and civil law respectively, accompanied by many other actors in the drama. The author (or authors) of the *Somnium viridarii* adapted both the dream setting and some of its details to his own program. He sometimes borrows verbally : 'At several points of the introduction there is quite skilful use of the exact words of the earlier *Somnians* and the purpose of the writer is evident'. (2) Chapter 1 of Marsilio of Padua's *Defensor pacis*, used cautiously ; the extreme anti-clerical sting has been removed [6]. A third source may now be added. The compiler has borrowed from a letter by the Paris theologian, Jean de Hesdin, dedicating his *lectura* on Job to his patron, Cardinal Gui de Boulogne. Hesdin must have written the letter in the autumn of 1357, since he finished his *lectura* on Oct. 31st, the vigil of All Saints, in that year. He probably died before the *Somnium viridarii* was put together [7]. Its compiler borrows from him in that part of the prologue which dedicates the book to Charles V. The fact that Hesdin's letter itself contains many quotations may arouse suspicion that they were both drawing on a common source, perhaps a letter-book giving model addresses to a noble patron. But this cannot be so. The compiler of the *Somnium viridarii* betrays himself in a tell-tale passage. Hesdin refers to Philip, a commentator on Job, who protested that his task was very difficult. Such a reference was to the point in the dedication of a commentary on Job, but quite off it in the dedication of the *Somnium* ; nevertheless, the compiler has included the reference to Philip among his excerpts.

He uses the same scissors-and-paste method in borrowing from Hesdin as he does elsewhere. He cuts out two passages, inverts the order, and sandwiches other material between them. I have numbered the passages in Hesdin to show how their order has been changed. He also abridges and modifies. Some of the slighter differences may be due to his use of a manuscript with a divergent text, or to mistakes in Goldast's edition of the *Somnium viridarii*. This is not satisfactory, but must do duty here in default of any other. I have copied his text as it is, only making some corrections in punctuation. The identifications of Hesdin's own borrowings from earlier writers will be found with the text of his letter, printed in the paper referred to at the top of the column.

Somnium viridarii (ed. GOLDAST I, 59-60).

Cum igitur tibi Karolo regi Francorum Deus dederit talentum ingenii, veram fidem et fortunam bonorum exteriorum, et veraciter tibi possint applicari verba Bernardi ad magistrum Galterum de Claromonte (*sic*) : *Genus*

HESDIN (in *Rech. Théol. anc. méd.* 28, 1961, 321-322).

(2) Et quia, nobilissime et excellentissime pater et domine, re vera possum vobis dicere
sicut in epistola Bernardi ad magistrum Galterum de Calvomonte : *Genus clarum... iudicet.* Ita quod, teste

6. G. DE LAGARDE, *op. cit.*, p. 16-19.
7. B. SMALLEY, *Jean de Hesdin O. Hosp. S. Ioh.*, in *Rech. Théol. anc. méd.* 28 (1961) 283-330. We hear nothing more of Hesdin after the winter of 1369, except that Petrarch, who could easily have been misinformed, assumed that he was alive early in 1372.

clarum... iudicet, testante veritate et fama proclamante, quae omnino veritate non caret, et (*sic*) ut dicitur VII Ethimologiarum (*sic*), in te antiqui generis regia nobilitas non degenerat, neque perit, sed clarius fulget, melius viget, et.iocundius floret vita morum. Et melius dicamus : in tantum quod vena laudabilis illustris (generis ?) sic gloriosa in transmissione servet originem, quod dictis et factis in te nobilitas generis apparet in moribus, liberalitas muneris praefulget in omnibus, humilitas caeterisque respondet communibus, et claritas operis refloret virtutibus.

Porro inter innumerabilia dona, quae tibi contulit altissimus... (Here follows a passage praising the king's victories over his enemies, and explaining the purpose and form of the *Somnium viridarii*)...

Verum, princeps Christianissime, quia, ut dicit Cassiodorus epistolarum variarum libro tertio epistola 6 : *Sicut indigna posteritas... promeruit*. Nam, ut dicit Aristoteles tertio Politicorum, cap. 19 : *Meliores est verisimile... virtus generis*. Et secundum veritatem nobiles, maxime reges, debent habere quasi ignatam (*sic*) prudentiam clariorem, clementiam dulciorem, audaciam fortiorem, iustitiam veriorem.

Hinc est quod ego humilis servitor vester in spe tantae nobilitatis, refulgentia bonitatis, clementia caritatis, intelligentia et humilitatis benivolentia, sertum ex variis floribus dicti Viridarii duxi componendum, una cum somno meo minus sufficienter concepto, vestrae regiae celsitudini fiducius praesentandum, cum re vera spes vestrae humilitatis gratiosae ad supplendum, nobilitatis generosae ad excusandum, vestrae subtilitatis ingeniosae ad corrigendum, vestrae bonitatis virtuosae ad conducendum penuriae et timiditati cordis et intellectus mei, audaciam inchoandi, potentiam complendi contulerunt auxilium pariter et iuvamen, maxime quia,

veritate et fama proclamante, que omnino veritate non caret, ut dicitur VII Ethicorum, in vobis antiqui generis regia nobilitas regum, ducum comitumque nobilis generis non degeneret aut pereat, sed clarius fulgeat, melius vigeat et iocundius floreat vita morum, et ut cogar verius dicere, in tantum quod vena laudabilis illustris generis gloriosa transmissione servet originem, quod dictis et vita in vobis nobilitas generis appareat in moribus, liberalitas imminens (*sic*) prefulgeat moribus (*sic* in omnibus ?), humilitas ceteris resplendeat communibus et claritas operis refloreat virtutibus.

(1) Quia, ut dicit Cassiodorus epistolarum seu variarum libro tertio epistola 6 : *Sicut indigna posteritas... promeruit*. Unde et Philosophus ad propositum... et eandem sententiam recitat Seneca... Nam, ut dicit Aristoteles tertio Poetice (*sic*) cap. 19 : *Meliores est verisimile... virtus generis*, et secundum veritatem nobiles genere debent habere quasi innatam prudentiam clariorem, clementiam dulciorem, audaciam fortiorem, iustitiam veriorem...

(3) Hinc est quod ego inter doctores Iohannes minimus et indignus in spe tante nobilitatis, refulgentia bonitatis, clementia claritatis, intelligentia et humilitatis benivolentia, lecturam sive postillam supra librum Iob, quem nomine vestro incepi,... (et) minus sufficienter complevi, vestre dignitati ausus sim fiducius presentare, cum re vera spes vestre humilitatis gratiose ad supportandum, vestre nobilitatis generose ad excusandum, vestre subtilitatis ingeniose ad corrigendum, vestre bonitatis virtuose ad conducendum penurie et timiditati intellectus et cordis mei audaciam inchoandi potentiamque complendi contulerunt auxilium pariter et iuvamen, maxime quia, ut melius

ut melius novit alta profunditas vestra, hoc opus tanti est ponderis, ut veraciter possim dicere cum illo Philippo expositore super Iob, sic dicente :	novit alta profunditas vestra, expositio historie libri Iob tanti sit oneris et ponderis quod Philippus, commentator libri Iob, vir antiquissimus, doctrina et scientia plenus et in divino eloquio excellens et famosus, ad Nectarum episcopum sic dicat : *Aggredior, pater, in opus arduum et difficile...*
Aggredior, pater, in opus arduum et difficile. Cum sim igitur, princeps metuendissime. vir tenuis studii, rudis ingenii, inculti eloquii,	... quanto ergo, nobilissime ac reverendissime pater, ego vir tenuis scientie, rudis ingenii, inculti eloquii, librum hunc ad honorem vestrum... conieci... ut melius, pater, novistis, ut vir nobilis genere et moribus,
me suscitetis trepidantem, corrigatis delinquentem, et scriptorem vestrum confortetis pariter et iuvetis, quia istius minimi tractatus, quem *somnium viridarii* volo nuncupari, omnia vestro relinquentur examini, ut maior vobis et iustior corrigendi quam michi scribendi gloria debeatur.	sustineatis trepidantem, confortetis formidantem, corrigatis delinquentem et reducatis oberrantem, et scriptorem vestrum confortetis pariter et iuvetis, quia istius minimi operis omnia vestro relinquuntur examini, ut vobis maior et iustior corrigendi quam michi scribendi gloria debeatur.

What light, if any, does the quotation from Hesdin throw on the authorship of the *Somnium viridarii* ? In the first place, its mosaic-like character comes out even more strongly than before. In the second place, the appearance of a theologian, who taught for some thirty years in his faculty at Paris, does not tally with G. de Lagarde's picture of the compilation :

> Elle est un des premiers aspects de la méfiance mutuelle que ne cessèrent de se témoigner jusqu'au milieu du XVIIᵉ siècle les maîtres de la faculté de théologie de Paris et les conseillers gallicans de la Cour et du parlement [8].

Supporters of the candidature of Nicole Oresme could seize on the fact that he and Hesdin had been colleagues in their faculty : Oresme held the post of Master of the College of Navarre 1356-1361. Further, the college library had a copy of Hesdin on Job, whereas there is no record of it in the library of Charles V [9] : all known copies of the letter are prefixed to the *lectura*. However, it might be argued on the other side that the servants of Charles V probably had the run of Paris libraries. They need not have distrusted Hesdin for ideological reasons. His teaching on the relations between Church and State, as we know it from his *lecturae*, was moderate : he held that each power should be supreme in its own sphere, which agreed

8. *Op. cit.*, p. 11.
9. F. STEGMÜLLER, *Repertorium biblicum Medii Aevi*, vol. III, Madrid 1951, p. 346 ; L. DELISLE, *Recherches sur la bibliothèque de Charles V*, Paris 1907.

with the tendency of the *Somnium viridarii*. I have found no trace of borrowing from Hesdin either in the body of the *Somnium* or in the *Songe*, but his views must have been known to be 'safe' in royal circles. The king would have remembered him, too, as a champion of France and of the papal residence at Avignon against Petrarch. There was nothing to dissuade the compiler of the *Somnium*, however gallican he may have been, from turning to Hesdin when he wanted a model for an elegant, learned, and flattering dedication. The question of authorship has advanced no further. The compiler (or compilers) has only emerged as even more eclectic than had been thought.

From the point of view of a student of Hesdin, the quotation has some interest. It shows that he won fame as a letter writer.

15

THE BIBLE AND ETERNITY : JOHN WYCLIF'S DILEMMA

'Although with one foot he stands in the Scholastic age, the other is seeking a resting place elsewhere.' So says Wyclif's editor in an introduction to *De benedicta incarnatione*, 1886.[1] We need not imagine the reformer in this undignified posture. Wyclif bestrode the narrow world of Oxford like a colossus just because his other foot rested on the Augustinian tradition, represented by Grosseteste and never forgotten. My thesis here will be that in his attitude to time and eternity Wyclif went back past Augustine to Plotinus. He did so not consciously, since he knew Plotinus only indirectly, but because a like situation induced a like reaction. The combination of scepticism and fideism led to a quest for certainty, for a total explanation, which should appeal to reason and should silence all doubters. The mediaevalist who reads Père Festugière on Hermes Trismegistos will have a curious feeling of having been there before. The author in fact makes the comparison himself. The abuse of rational argument leads to a distrust of reason; the worried turn to revelation as an alternative. It happened at the end of the fifth century B.C. after the ravages of Greek sophistry, and at the end of the Middle Ages after the excesses of scholasticism. Père Festugière is describing the rise of mystery cults and of 'salvation mongery' in general in the centuries before and after the Christian era. He has in mind both the fourteenth-century mystics, Catholic or heretic, and the anti-intellectualist bias of fourteenth-century moralists.[2] We can exclude the former. The schoolmen, 'loving their arguments as mothers love their children', as the saying went, had no professional concern with mysticism. Wyclif seems to have been unaware of those devout 'sitters in solitude' who dot the English landscape for us historians. One can answer distrust of reason by finding a better way of reasoning. Plotinus chose this other road. 'We must accept the fact that Plotinus *was* a schoolman', Professor E. R. Dodds has warned us. He built up a metaphysical system from the material that he had to hand. If his system called for mystical union with the divine as its natural sequel, 'the technique of attainment is not for him physiological or magical, but intellectual.'[3] Wyclif, too, wanted to restore belief in revelation by showing that it could be proved by reason. If we chose to look forward instead of backward, we could see him as an early leader in the 'Holy War', waged against the neo-Pyrrhonists, 'to overcome doubt so that man could be secure in his religious and scientific knowledge'.[4]

The contrast between time and eternity must play a central role in any system of dispersion from and return to the *one*. The one for Plotinus was

> a point where all lines meet without ever spreading outside it; this point remains in its sameness in itself; it experiences no change; it is always in the present and has neither past nor future; it is what it is and

[1] Edward Harris (Wyclif Society), p. xxv.
[2] A.-J. Festugière, *La révélation d'Hermes Trismégiste*, i, 1950, p. 64.
[3] E. R. Dodds, 'Tradition and Personal Achievement in the Philosophy of Plotinus', *Journal of Roman Studies*, l, 1960, pp. 1–7.
[4] R. H. Popkin, *The History of Scepticism from Erasmus to Descartes*, Assen, 1960, p. 112. This is a parallel which should not be pressed too far; I do not mean that the neo-Pyrrhonists derived from the fourteenth-century sceptics.

is always this. Hence eternity is not the substrate of intelligible beings, but in some way shines forth from them, thanks to this sameness which it manifests, not with what will later be, but with what it is. It is what it is and will not be otherwise.[5]

Plotinus agreed with Plato in seeing time as 'imitating eternity, just as this universe is the image of the intelligible world.' But time implied deficiency, appetite for the future, and hence absence of plenitude. The philosopher must free himself from tense if he wished to rise from the temporal and visible to the intelligible, the eternally present. In that sense time was the enemy.

St. Augustine had to break with the neo-Platonists on two essential points. His system could not be wholly intellectual, since he admitted faith. As a Christian he could not dismiss the fact of time: belief in the teaching of Scripture bound him to those Christian theorems, 'God's transcendence, time's reality, and the existence of the particular event in time.'[6] History rejoices in tense; the Christian must rejoice in history in so far as he understands it as the history of salvation. Recent studies have shown that Augustine did not take kindly to a positive view of time. He persisted in preaching its punitive character. His exegesis of the Old Testament especially suffered from his lack of historical sense. Jewish history became prophecy rather than story in his treatment of it.[7] Nevertheless, he came to believe that it mattered that things had happened and would happen. God's eternal Word had been written in time and of time, just as the Word had been made flesh. Pagan philosophers could allegorize their myths so as to reduce them to a timeless present. The Christian Church had her Scriptures as a bridge between time and eternity. Only through the first could the Christian get guidance to reaching the blessedness of the second.

What Plotinus and Augustine had in common was the experience of conversion. We can only guess at Plotinus's by inference. Perhaps it was rather a vocation. At least he taught the need for conversion of the mind, heart and will as a condition for return to divine unity.[8] We know more of St. Augustine's conversions, including the decisive one; or rather we know what he thought of them in later years and what his historians now think of his thoughts on his conversion. Wyclif was a convert too. We have enough evidence to compare his conversion with that of Plotinus, who was little more than a name to him, and with that of St. Augustine, who was more real to him probably than any living person whom he ever met. But a sense of kinship, such as he felt for Augustine, amounts to less than true likeness. Wyclif resembles Plotinus more closely than he does Augustine.

The background of a comparison must be the Oxford schools and their problems when Wyclif started on his Arts course about 1350. There was one marked contrast between fourteenth-century schoolmen and fourth-century

[5] *En.*, iii, 7, 3. I have used the French translation by E. Bréhier, iii, 1956, p. 130.

[6] J. Guitton, *Le temps et l'éternité chez Plotin et Saint Augustin*, 3rd ed., 1959, p. 17; see also E. Lampey, *Das Zeitproblem nach der Bekenntnislehre Augustinus*, 1960.

[7] M. Pontet, *L'exégèse de Saint Augustin pré-* *dicateur*, 1944, pp. 161–66, 305–83; H.-I. Marrou, *L'ambivalence du temps de l'histoire chez Saint Augustin*, 1950; G. Straus, 'Schriftgebrauch, Schriftauslegung und Schriftbeweis bei Augustin', *Beiträge zur Geschichte der biblischen Hermeneutik*, i, 1959, pp. 53–73.

[8] J. Guitton, *op. cit.*, pp. 127–45.

philosophers: the schoolmen as such had as little concern with poetry as they had with mysticism. Did they ever muse on the *topos* of time in the gentle melancholy induced by October on the banks of the Cherwell? We shall never know. Wyclif in exile waxed lyrical on the beauties of Oxford; what homesick don would not do so? Some may have regarded it as a conventional theme to be used in preaching. The true ethos of the schools apropos poetry may be illustrated by a passage in the argument between Wyclif and Dr. John Kenningham O. Carm. about 1372–74. They discuss the question whether the antiquity of a document adds to its authority. Kenningham contests Wyclif's opinion that it does. He cites the example of ancient poets, such as 'Orpheus and others who wrote fables of the gods'. They lived, he says, long before the philosophers Plato, Aristotle, Pythagoras and others. 'But now the *philosophers'* writings are held in great authority, when those of the ancient poets *quasi nullius sunt momenti*.'[9] So much for the poets and their poetry. The dilemma arose from logical and metaphysical and hence from theological and moral doubts.

It might seem at first sight that the fourteenth-century crisis must have been less acute than that of late antiquity: the Church offered certainty to her faithful, based firmly on the teaching of the Bible and the Fathers. Fideism could surely counter scepticism if one had something solid to believe. It was all the more frightening when this apparent security came to look like an illusion. The inhabitants of an ancestral home discovered that the foundations had cracked while death-watch beetle powdered the roof. The problem as Wyclif saw it was summarized in a passage of one of his favourite books, *De doctrina christiana*; he quotes it twice at least in his *De veritate sacre Scripture*. St. Augustine was explaining why we must have faith in the authority of Scripture, and why the effect of doubt will be loss of charity:

> Faith will waver if the authority of holy Scripture should fail. If faith wavers, then charity weakens. If a man falls away from the faith, then he needs must fall away from charity also. He cannot love that which he does not believe . . .[10]

Just what had happened in Wyclif's time. The rot had set in with terminism, the casting of doubt on the reality of universals, and the use of God's *potentia absoluta* to dissolve the whole divine order. Now the sceptics had turned upon their own last refuge against anarchy, faith in the Scriptures. Who could question, as he looked around him, that charity had weakened in consequence? The Church (for reasons which do not concern us) was coming under fire increasingly. Men were more critical and the intellectuals were naturally more vocal than others. St. Augustine's analysis fitted like a glove.

[9] *Fasciculi Zizaniorum Magistri Johannis Wyclif*, ed. W. W. Shirley (Rolls Series), 1858, pp. 4–5 (referred to henceforward as *F.Z.*). On its compilation see J. Crompton, '*Fasciculi Zizaniorum II*', *Journal of Ecclesiastical History*, xii, 1961, pp. 155–66.

[10] *De doctrina christiana*, i, 37 (41), ed. J. Vogels (Florilegium patristicum fasc. xxiv, Bonn, 1930, p. 19): '. . . titubabit autem fides, si divinarum scripturarum vacillat auctoritas. Porro fide titubante caritas etiam ipsa languescit. Nam si a fide quisque ceciderit, a caritate etiam necesse est ut cadat. Non enim potest diligere quod esse non credit.' Quoted in *De veritate sacre Scripture*, ed. R. Buddensieg, (Wyclif Society) i, pp. 157, 389 (referred to henceforward as *De veritate*).

The scepticism hated by Wyclif has been described often enough to excuse me from going into detail. Modern historians differ on the significance rather than on the facts of this fourteenth-century phenomenon. Dr. Gordon Leff has gone back on his earlier view that it represented a conscious attack on Catholic doctrine, but persists in holding that, if we look at the effect instead of at the intention, it did sap the foundations of belief. Aquinas had contrived a carefully distinguished balance between faith and reason. Then faith had to take over more and more ground as criticism disposed of one metaphysical proof after another, making God's very existence and the working of divine Providence open to doubt.[11] Father Trapp takes it less seriously. Questioning of dogma, he thinks, indicated an outburst of activity in the classroom: masters experimented with a new teaching method; they sharpened their pupils' critical faculty by showing them how to pick holes in statements which hitherto they had accepted without testing. It was not heresy to deny articles of belief on grounds of logic, since no one dreamed of disbelieving them in consequence. He admits that a lunatic fringe may have trespassed over the borders of orthodoxy, but sees the trespassers as unrepresentative.[12] Dr. Robson, considering Wyclif's reaction to the new method, finds it 'easy to exaggerate' its importance, adding that one 'should not dismiss it as of no serious significance'.[13] Wyclif had grown up with it. He did not object to 'the sophists', as he calls them, as a lunatic fringe, but as a vanguard of the devil's army. Why, rightly or wrongly, did he see them in this way?

The early-fourteenth-century critics, of whom Robert Holcot is the best example, had questioned or denied reason's power to prove that God existed or that man's soul was immortal, but had cast doubt aside when they lectured on Scripture. Holcot, it seems, neither dared nor wished to pick holes in that sacred text which as a fideist he had to save at all cost. The next generation, as was bound to happen, rushed forward where their elders had held back in fear. Wyclif found the sophists in full cry against the unlogical, imprecise language of the Bible and the liturgy. They found heresies in the Lord's Prayer and in the Hail Mary. The following illustration is relevant, since it concerns the problem of time apropos tense in customary usage. It comes from *De benedicta incarnatione*, one of Wyclif's earliest theological works. 'The sophists cry out against the Church's prayers in which she asks the Lord to be freed from harm by (the merits of) the Incarnation, the Nativity, the Passion and Resurrection etc. "Vain," they say, "is the offered prayer, when all the aforesaid events neither *are* nor *can be*." ' They lodged their objection to the petitions on the ground that a past event, such as Christ's resurrection from the dead, could not be invoked in the present tense, as though it had not happened, but were still in process of happening.[14] A second illustration of such criticism, directed against the text of the gospel, comes from *Opus evangelicum*, Wyclif's last work. The sophists enrage him still. Here they object

[11] G. Leff, *Gregory of Rimini: Tradition and Innovation in Fourteenth Century Thought*, 1961, pp. 20–21. For a good introduction to the subject see now L. Baudry, 'Les rapports de la raison et de la foi selon Guillaume d'Occam', *Archives d'histoire doctrinale et littéraire du Moyen Age*, xxix, 1963, pp. 33–92.

[12] D. Trapp, 'Augustinian Theology of the Fourteenth Century', *Augustiniana*, vi, 1956, pp. 147–231.

[13] J. A. Robson, *Wyclif and the Oxford Schools*, 1961, p. 143.

[14] *Op. cit.* (see note 1), pp. 110–11.

to Jesus's own saying: *If any man come to me, and hate not his father and mother and wife and children and brethren and sisters, yea and his own life also, he cannot be my disciple* (Luke xiv, 26). The sophists argued that Adam and Eve had no father or mother; further, many persons living in the time of grace (i.e. celibate clergy and religious) had neither wife nor children, just as many at all times had no brothers or sisters. It followed that none of them could be Christ's disciple.[15] Wyclif, as we shall see, thought that his theory of time provided a short and easy way to deal with these attacks on Christian texts.

Was he to shrug off sophistry as a silly waste of effort? Or was it really detestable, both in itself, and as causing faith to waver and charity to cool? A modern reader may sympathize with the sophists, regarding them as 'advanced' in outlook. He should remember that, unlike their successors, the neo-Pyrrhonists, they lacked the courage of their convictions, if they had any. None of them dared to apply the new method in a written commentary on Scripture. Their criticisms, transmitted by Wyclif, must have been mainly oral. If we can believe him, they mocked or insulted when their arguments failed. Perhaps he mistook a symptom for a cause when he diagnosed the sickness of his time. But most of us have done so at some period of our lives. Sophistry was no mere academic wrangle: clever young men could be dangerous. The rise of a literate upper-class laity meant that theological debates would leak out. We know what traces the discussions on necessity and contingency, on freewill and predestination, have left on English poetry; Bradwardine's name had become a household word. Langland complains that gentry now dine in private instead of in hall; comfortably secluded, they exchange half-baked arguments on theological matters:

Carpen as they clerkes were. of Cryste and of his miȝtes.[16]

The sophists' criticism of Scripture might impinge on private dinner-party conversation quite soon. Wyclif thought they were leading the laity astray already.[17] He would appeal to secular lords, magnates and knights, to help him reform the Church as soon as he had a positive programme to offer them.

His horror of sophistry becomes more understandable when we realize that he had joined in it as a student. This brings us to his conversion. A sketch of his character, however impressionistic, must come first. Wyclif lacked that feeling of sexual guilt which makes a conversion interesting. His worst enemies never accused him of loose living at any stage of his career, but rather paid tribute to his austerity. Nor does he show any sign of the puritan's revulsion from sins of the flesh. Pride and greed in the clergy struck him as worse faults than concubinage, though he did not approve of it. His treatise on the Ten Commandments offers mere commonplaces on the precept against adultery. It interested him less than the others. Casuistry on the subject of sexual relations he thought unfitting and time-wasting.[18] This shows incidentally

15 Ed. J. Loserth, (Wyclif Society) ii, pp. 183–84.

16 *Piers Plowman*, B. text, passus x, line 92.

17 *De veritate*, i, pp. 385–86.

18 *De mandatis divinis*, ed. F. D. Matthew (Wyclif Society), pp. 437–53; *De veritate*, iii, p. 32. For Wyclif's biography and the chron-

ology of his works see A. B. Emden, *A Biographical Register of the University of Oxford to A.D. 1500*, iii, 1959, pp. 2103–6. Broadly speaking, the metaphysical works belong to the period before about 1369, when he was a B.D. (bachelor of divinity); then come his early theological works, composed before he

how little the routine of parish work and the problems of the confessional bothered him. He was far from puritanical in his attitude to church music.[19] He put his own energy into academic activities in his early life, and some later on into his essays in politics. He had grave defects of character in being self-opinionated and in hating to be contradicted, when he would lose both his temper and his manners. His colleagues put up with him in spite of his crustiness because they admired his mind. The factor of personal ambition in his career is difficult to estimate; all of us, I think, would allow it something. He certainly degenerated under the strain. He grew ruder and bitterer. His last book, the *Opus evangelicum*, sounds like a cracked old gramophone record. His habit of quoting his own works with shocking complacency had increased with the years. But one trait redeems him. If Wyclif was hard on others, he was also hard on himself. He admits in his treatise on the Commandments, an early, non-polemical book, that his preoccupation with worldly business distracts him at prayer. Worldlings cannot say the Lord's Prayer without sin because they lack the right disposition: 'At least, I'm sorry to say, I'm afraid that this happens to me.' He knows by experience that worldly thoughts and feelings cause distraction.[20] *De veritate sacre Scripture*, written about 1378, when he had already plunged into politics, contains his answer to criticism of his motives. If perverse vanity, ambition or spite move him, then he regrets it and will beware of them. His enemies accuse him of hypocrisy owing to his austere way of life. On the contrary, he has failed to practise the apostolic poverty which he preaches. He pleads guilty on the score of spite: 'I know that all too often I mix perverse vindictiveness with my good intentions, if I have them. As to the imputation that hypocrisy, spite and envy underlie my pretence of holiness, I'm afraid, I'm sorry to say, that it happens too often. I deserve to have even more mud thrown at me than has been.' He prays to God on the subject of his spiritual sins, and only denies any open crime.[21] He sometimes associates himself with those worldly university clerks whom he denounces.[22] The willingness to admit his faults decreased with age; but here we shall be watching him at a stage nearer to his conversion.

Our evidence comes entirely from what he tells us himself: he was converted to realism from terminism. First, an early philosophical work shows that he had not as yet reached a fully realist position. Secondly, pointers to his evolution towards realism occur in his later philosophical works. I quote Dr. Robson:

> There are a number of hints in the *Summa de ente* that he had once been less than a full-blooded realist, that he had, for example, regarded the

incepted as D.D. (doctor of divinity) in 1372 or 1373; of these I shall refer to his *De Trinitate* and his *De benedicta incarnatione*. *De mandatis divinis* and *De statu innocentie* are non-controversial theological works and probably belong to 1373 or 1374. From this date onwards his writings become polemical in character. I shall refer, apart from a few passing remarks, to *De veritate*, 1378, and *Opus evan-*gelicum, which he was still working on at the time of his death, 31 December 1384.

[19] *De mandatis*, p. 251; *Opus evangelicum*, ii, p. 262. Wyclif's views on church music and the liturgy would repay study.

[20] *De mandatis*, pp. 97, 261.

[21] *De veritate*, i, pp. 296–97, 360, 365–66.

[22] *De officio regis*, ed. A. W. Pollard and C. Sayle (Wyclif Society), p. 34.

singular as prior to the universal. And on one occasion, at least, he suggests that as a young man he had not been a realist at all: "and so, when I was younger, I used ignorantly to confuse universals."[23]

Thirdly, not hints, but frank admissions punctuate his theological works. Before he became a realist, Wyclif impugned the truth of Scripture and criticized the Fathers. He says in his early *De benedicta incarnatione*: 'When I understood as a child, I used to think that St. Ambrose was very ignorant of logic.'[24] Worse follows. 'It is imputed to me,' he writes in *De veritate sacre Scripture*, 'that I once said that Scripture was very false.' Instead of denying or palliating the charge, he can only say that he does not think so now: 'I profess that if ever I should have said that holy Scripture was very false, this greatly displeases me now, and I humbly revoke and retract it as most ill-sounding, heretical and blasphemous.'[25] He next passed through a stage when he tried to refute the sophists' attacks on Scripture, but with the wrong arguments. He had not yet worked out his metaphysical system. Further, he admits to having shown off by turning their own weapons against them:

I confess to vainglory; for I often fell away from the teaching of Scripture both in arguing and in responding, because I wanted at one and the same time to win fame among the people and to expose the sophists' arrogance.

When I was younger, I rejected the mystical expressions of Scripture partly owing to my pride and partly to destroy the sophists' vainglory; for they rejoice if they can make out a seeming case against their brother.

When I spoke as a child, I tied myself up in my anxiety to understand and defend the Scriptures according to their way of speech. . . . At last God of his grace opened their sense to me to understand the equivocation of Scripture.[26]

Two passages in *De dominio divino*, written in 1375–76, a few years before *De veritate sacre Scripture*, tell how he realized that his theory of ideas linked up with his view of Scripture. He thought or came to think that it was part of God's eternal plan to bring him to this realization with the help of Augustine

[23] Robson, pp. 139, 145, 188.
[24] p. 103: 'Et quando sapiebam ut parvulus, putabam istum sanctum multum ignarum logice.' See 1 Cor. xiii, 1.
[25] ii, p. 5: 'Sed quia impositum est michi, quod ego quondam dixi scripturam esse falsissimam . . . primo tamen profiteor, quod, si umquam dixero scripturam sacram esse falsissimam, hoc multum displicet michi modo, et illud humiliter revoco et retracto tamquam pessime sonans, hereticum et blasfemum.'
[26] *Ibid.*, i, p. 23: 'Unde de ista vana gloria confiteor, sepe tam arguendo quam respondendo prolapsus sum a doctrina scripture, cupiens simul apparentiam fame in populo et denudationem arrogantie sophistarum.'

Ibid., p. 100: 'Quando autem fui minor, abieci locutiones misticas partim propter meam superbiam et partim ad destruendum inanem gloriam sophistarum. Ipsi enim gaudent, si possunt habere apparens inconveniens contra fratrem suum.'

Ibid., p. 114: 'Unde quando loquebar ut parvulus, fui anxie intricatus ad intelligendum ac defendendum istas scripturas de virtute sermonis, . . . et demum Dominus ex gratia sua apperuit michi sensum ad intelligendum equivocationem predictam scripture.'

In *De statu innocentie* Wyclif had suggested that his earlier views on contingency had not been strong enough; *De stat. in.*, ed. with *De mandatis*, p. 158.

406

and others. God enlightened him to reach it *perfunctorie*, which I take to mean 'suddenly' or 'unexpectedly':

> For I cannot demonstrate and understand the creature except by demonstrating and understanding God. I took a long time to understand this theory of ideas from Scripture. When I had discovered it unexpectedly, having been enlightened by God, I gave joyful thanks to him, with his servant Augustine and others, whom God eternally ordains to help me to this as his ministers.

Later on he exclaims:

> Blessed be God, who has freed us from the superficial snares of words in order to direct our mind's eye to penetrate to their meaning.[27]

Wyclif, therefore, in his own mind connected his realist metaphysics with Scripture. They supplied him with his key. He believed that God had led him to study St. Augustine 'and others', i.e. Robert Grosseteste, in order that they might put it into his hand. It must have been one of those flashes which come to many a scholar when least expected: something clicks; he sees the connecting link. Wyclif had a common experience, and took it for divine guidance: it taught him how to confute the sophists and his earlier self together with them.

That is his account of his conversion. It brought him neither the holiness of the saint nor the detachment of the sage. He had no need to be converted from an evil life, which he had never lived. Nor was it a sudden illumination. He came round to realism as a result of deep thought and study. As a young student of Arts he accepted the prevalent terminism and applied it to Scripture. Then his study of philosophy brought him to realism. He had formed himself as a philosopher by the time he took his bachelor's degree in divinity. Henceforward, having seen in a flash how to co-ordinate his ideas on a crucial point, he applied his realism to theological questions and to exegesis. Can we speak of a conversion at all? We can and must. Conversion may be gradual; even St. Augustine's had been prepared for. A convert may be no nicer afterwards. Wyclif's own statements forbid us to classify it as purely intellectual. Platonists of all shades incline to take up a religious, 'holier than thou' attitude, whereas Aristotelians just treat their opponents as stupid. Wyclif thought that God loved the Platonists (though he admired Aristotle) and that any other approach would dishonour the divinity:

> 'It was by the eternal ordinance of the Holy Spirit that the faithful doctors of the Church, gathered together to treat of the dispute between Abbot Joachim and Peter Lombard, were instructed on the truth of universals.'

[27] Ed. R. L. Poole (Wyclif Society), p. 63: 'Non enim possum demonstrare vel intelligere creaturam, nisi demonstrando et intelligendo Deum. Et diu fui antequam ex scripturis intellexi istam sententiam de ydeis; quam cum illustratus a Deo perfunctorie repperissem, cum gaudio gratias egi Deo, cum suo famulo Augustino et aliis quos Deus eternaliter ordinat ad hoc ministerialiter me iuvare.'

Ibid., p. 65: 'Sed benedictus Deus qui nos liberavit ab inviscationibus superficialibus verborum ad penetrative dirigendum mentis intuitum ad signata.'

A knowledge of universals is the pre-eminent step on the ladder of wisdom, by which we search out hidden truth; and this, I believe, is the reason why God does not permit the school of universals utterly to fail.[28]

The falling off of the old school of logic concerning universals and the right metaphysic was the cause of all heresies and errors on the subject of Christ's humanity. Wyclif's *De universalibus* offered the moderns an answer to all their problems. Errors on the subject of the Trinity had the same source.[29] He never wavered in his conviction. An old Yorkshirewoman once explained to me why her son had ruined the village band by refusing to play in it on Sundays: 'Well ye see, 'e's converted an' pig'eaded and all that.' Wyclif came from Yorkshire. He was converted and pigheaded. 'And all that' involves his theories on time and eternity.

A metaphor must serve as an island whence we can survey the deep waters. It occurs in his inaugural lecture, delivered when he incepted in divinity in 1372–73. The inceptor had to give his *principium* in the form of a sermon in praise of Scripture. Wyclif argued, as he had in his earlier *De benedicta incarnatione*, that a knowledge of the true philosophy and especially a true view of time were essential to a right understanding of Scripture. The inceptor had also to find suitable comparisons for Holy Writ as a means to praising it. The exercise had been gone through so often that only the most fertile brain could invent a new one. Wyclif compared the Scriptures *inter alia* to a mirror of eternal truths:

Ipse enim sunt speculum in quo veritates eterne relucent.[30]

It sounds conventional enough, but I have failed to trace it. The mirror image was used for Scripture. St. Augustine calls the Bible a mirror reflecting 'the true face of its readers'.[31] The *distinctiones* listed under *speculum* in Pitra's *Spicilegium solesmense* are numerous, but include no mirror of eternal truths.[32] Wyclif's metaphor, as far as I know, belonged neither to the Augustinian nor to Latin school tradition.

Whether original or not, it throws light on his mental processes. One should bear it in mind when reading certain passages of his *De Trinitate*, another early theological work. They show us the other side of his anti-terminism. He was anti-fideist. The fideist holds that God has revealed certain truths which a Christian must believe even or because he cannot understand them by the use of reason. It follows from this position that the truths must have been revealed at a given time. Eternally present to God, they are only temporally present to men. They remained out of man's reach before God revealed them, because they were inaccessible to human reason. Apart from cases of special illumination, these truths have been revealed in the Bible. Apprehension of the Blessed Trinity was one of such truths, the schoolmen

[28] Robson, pp. 153–54.
[29] *De ben. incarn.*, pp. 12, 81–82, 144–45; *Tractatus de Trinitate*, ed. Allen duPont Breck, Colorado, 1962, p. 71.
[30] The *principium* is still unpublished; I have edited it in a paper which is now in press for a forthcoming volume of the Oxford Historical Society, n.s., xvi, p. 295.
[31] *In Ps. ciii enarratio*, ed. Migne, *P.L.*, xxxvii, col. 1338.
[32] iii, 1855, pp. 162–64.

almost unanimously held. Pagan philosophers had failed to grasp it. The Third Person, corresponding to charity, as the Father stood for omnipotence and the Son for wisdom, was least knowable to their intelligence, unaided by revelation. This is an extreme and traditional example of the limits set to reason. Naturally enough, the terminists by their scepticism narrowed the limits and left more to faith. Yet Wyclif shrank from admitting even this old, generally received limit to the power of reason. He wanted to think that the Trinity was after all capable of rational demonstration: therefore the philosophers could have grasped it in some way. First he argues that we have no factual evidence to show that they did not do so. We could not be sure unless we had all the writings of all the ancient philosophers who ever lived, and could find it in none of them; such evidence as we have suggests rather the opposite.[33] Later he grants that the philosophers lacked a clear knowledge of the Third Person, but holds that they knew him 'confusedly'.[34] He goes on to discuss the whole problem of reason and faith, standing as we might expect at the opposite pole to the fideists. A man who exalts the power of human reason to grasp divine truths, such as the apprehension of the Trinity, will have difficulty in finding a small corner for faith. Wyclif has already argued that the reasons persuading us to believe in the Trinity are more plausible and evident to the right kind of philosopher than any reasons to the contrary.[35] Now he turns to authority, since we also have authority for what we believe. The Bible is our authority: why should we believe it? How do we know what parts are true and canonical? A wayward man might say, when offered proof from the Saviour's words as found in any of the gospels, that he would believe it only if it really was said by Christ. We must therefore fall back on the Church's authority as determining both the canon of Scripture and the faith. If we could not trust the Church to determine in so important a matter, what could we believe? All arguments from authority would go by the board. St. Augustine said that he would not believe in the gospel unless he first believed in the Church, and that if one part of Scripture were false, then all the rest would be suspect. Wyclif at this early stage of his career had not yet begun to attack papal authority, but even now he could not bring himself to recognize the Church to be the sole guarantor of revelation. He adds after quoting Augustine:

> It is impossible for the Church to determine anything concerning the faith unless there is an underlying reason why it should thus be determined; and so it *is* thus in the order of nature before it is thus determined; and so if we subtracted all the Church's authority it should thus have been said on grounds of reason.

[33] *Ed. cit.* (above, n. 29), p. 26: 'Sed dico . . . quod negativa talis non potest probari ab eis nisi indirecte ut puta si noverunt omnes philosophos qui umquam fuerunt, et omnia scripta et habitus eorum et in nullo eorum fuerit notitia trinitatis in lumine naturali. Sed modo diu esset expectare probacionem antecedentis. Ideo dico quod multi philosophi probaverunt trinitatem :am ante incarnationem quam post. . . .'

[34] *Ibid.*, p. 111: 'De philosophis conceditur quod cognoverunt possibile esse distincte gignens et genitum, ignorando distincte spiritum sanctum. Verumtamen eo ipso cognoverunt confuse spiritum sanctum . . .'
[35] *Ibid.*, p. 95: '. . . secure possumus asserere contra protervientes, vel fideles vel infideles, quod ratio suadens trinitatem est coloracior et evidencior cuilibet recte philosophanti quam aliqua ratio fienda ad oppositum.'

Then he puts it even more clearly:

> I consider that the Church ordains nothing unless there is an under-lying reason on account of which there is rational cause that it *is* so before it be ordained by man. I consider that in whatsoever way we speak of the uncreated Trinity by means of our signs, unchanging truth is signified, which is not subject to our ordinance.[36]

Note how 'our', i.e. man's, 'ordinance' has slipped into the place formerly occupied in the argument by the Church's determination. Note also Wyclif's persistent use of the present tense. Eternity has no tense but the present. Scripture must be believed because it mirrors eternal truths, accessible, so it seems, to man's reason, if rightly directed. The metaphor certainly mirrors Wyclif's mind.

His readers will have many questions to ask him. How do we know the size of the mirror? Does not authority have to determine its frame by declaring which books are canonical? At some point in time certain books were accepted and others rejected from the canon. Wyclif does not see our problems, because he starts from eternal truths, and then finds them reflected in his mirror. There is no difficulty in finding them, if one first, as a metaphysician, knows what to look for. Why should the size of the mirror matter? Wyclif would have accused the objector of terminism for putting such a question. Scripture for him was not properly speaking its outward signs, words written in ink on quires of parchment, a human artefact which could be taken apart at will; it was rather God's eternal Word, 'the Book of Life, in which all is written.' He amplifies this passage from *De beata incarnatione*[37] in *De veritate sacre Scripture*. Here he distinguishes five grades of meaning in Scripture in descending order of merit. In the highest sense of all it is the Book of Life; in the next it is the truths inscribed in the Book of Life according to their intelligible being; in the next it means the truths to be believed *in genere*, which are inscribed there according to their existence or effect; next it means the truth to be believed

---

[36] The text as printed has some obvious mistakes; I have suggested a few emenda-tions; *ibid.*, pp. 159–60: 'Patet ex hoc quod non crederetur aliquid esse dictum Christi vel scripture sacre ex sentencia spiritus sancti revelatum nisi ex informacione et fide adhi-bita ecclesie, ergo prius naturaliter et plus oportet credere ecclesie quam auctoritati ⟨et⟩ de canone Biblie tamquam loco ab auctoritate ⟨;⟩ ut allegata protervo qua-cumque auctoritate scripture ut sentencia Salvatoris in quocumque evangelio ⟨,⟩ pro-terv⟨i⟩us diceret quod illa sentencia esset vera si esset dictum Christi. . . . Ideo presup-posita auctoritate et doctrina ecclesie iam ut superius dictum est quicquid homo credat, oportet primo omnium hoc credere fide et evidentia topica. Sed quomodo, queso, esset probabilitas in aliquo dicto ecclesie si tam matura et exquisita determinacio ecclesie in precipua materia fidei non daret fidem? . . .

Et periret omnis locus ab auctoritate ut in assimili arguit beatus Augustinus . . . dicens quod non crederet evangelio nisi crederet ecclesie, et si una pars scripture esset falsa totum residuum scripture esset suspectum. Dicetur ergo quod impossibile est ecclesiam determinare quicquam concernens fidem nisi subsit racio quare sic est determinandum: ideo prius naturaliter sic est quam sic est determinatum et ideo subducta omni auctori-tate ecclesie sic esset rationabiliter dicendum.'

p. 162: 'Secundo considero quod ecclesia nihil ordinat nisi subsit racio propter quam causa racionalis est sic esse antequam sic ab homine ordinetur. Tercio considero quod quomodocumque loquimur cum signis nostris in materia de trinitate increata semper est veritas immobilis significata que non subicitur ordinacioni nostre.'

[37] p. 73.

as this is inscribed in the book of natural man, as in his soul; in the fifth and lowest sense it is the mere signs of Scripture, such as manuscripts or other artefacts, which remind us of the prior truth.[38] As Robson puts it, Wyclif has equated the Bible with an emanation of the Supreme Being, transposed into writing.[39]

His aim in doing so was to put it high above the reach of doubters and critics. Each word of Scripture was eternally true. Another problem posed itself in consequence, which he could not ignore. How should he link the eternal idea to a record of change, and how fit biblical history and prophecy into the eternal present? The problem had arisen before in various forms. The most relevant to our understanding of Wyclif concerns 'the immutability of faith'. Theologians of the twelfth and thirteenth centuries had disputed as to whether the object of faith was the thing believed, the fact of Christ's Birth or Passion, or on the contrary the proposition stating it: Christ *was born* or Christ *suffered*. The tense of the proposition caused difficulty. Today it must be stated in the past tense, whereas the patriarchs and prophets of the Old Testament believed that these events would take place in the future. Is the object of faith the same or different according to the tense of the verb in the proposition? Some theologians, wishing to save 'the immutability of faith', held that the object of the faith was the thing believed; they avoided in this way the difficulty about tense. Others preferred the second opinion in spite of its difficulties. Subtle arguments developed. It could be held, for instance, that the object of faith remained constant, but that the subject, the believer, accepted it as past or future according to his own particular place in time. St. Thomas showed his common sense in dismissing the problem as false. To the question whether the object of faith is a concept or a judgment, he answers that it can only be a judgment, since we have to do with mere human knowledge. A human being must judge, he cannot know, when he assents to an article of faith. We must therefore admit variations in judgment as regards tense according to the time at which the judgment is made. Man needs to use tense, because he is temporal; it cannot be otherwise.[40]

Here was a down-to-earth solution; but Wyclif could never have agreed to it. He put forward instead his own theory of time, which complemented his view of Scripture as a mirror of eternal truth. He prescribes his theory of time in his inaugural lecture. He calls it the highest of his 'three nests for Christ's chickens' in his debate with Kenningham: by it 'we uphold Scripture as true according to its speech (*de vi sermonis*) against the pompous arguments of the sophists.'[41] He would hardly know how to save the truth of Scripture against their attacks without it, he admits in *De veritate sacre Scripture*.[42] He was repeating it to the end in *Opus evangelicum*.[43]

[38] pp. 107–13. This passage of *De veritate* is too long to quote.

[39] Robson, *op. cit.*, pp. 146, 163.

[40] M.-D. Chenu, 'Commentaire historique de la IIa IIae q. i, a. 2', *Mélanges thomistes* (Bibl. thom. iii), 1923, pp. 123–40; *La théologie au douzième siècle*, 1957, pp. 91–107.

[41] *F.Z.*, pp. 453–54.

[42] i, p. 172: 'Unde sine isto scuto fidei, quo credimus creaturas mutabiliter succedere et Deum immutabilem ratione eternitatis omni preterito vel futuro assistere, non video, quomodo salvaretur scripture metaphisica de Dei notitia intuitiva vel philosophia de successivis edocta.'

[43] i, p. 118: '. . . et necesse est loquentem libere in ista materia bene cognoscere ista duo, primo quod omne quod eveniet de

Robson has summarized Wyclif's theory of time as found in his *De tempore*, a fruit of his teaching in the Arts course. It forms a companion piece to *De universalibus*: 'The first treatise asserts that being is universal; the second that it is eternal.' There are two time schemes, the one extra-temporal, *duratio*, the other 'particular or successive time as apprehended by men', *tempus*. What has eternal being in God's eternal present is individuated by its occurrence in time, which God created with the world. Everything, therefore, has its being stored up as it were in the external exemplar, which knows neither past nor future; it enters into time in due course according to God's ordinance. His theory had the advantage for Wyclif of abolishing contingency even in the future: 'Everything happens of necessity.'[44] It justified his doctrine of predestination and its consequence, worked out later, that the true Church comprised the elect, chosen eternally, whether patriarchs and prophets or saints and apostles, and their successors up to Doomsday, as opposed to the *presciti*, those foreknown to damnation.

Wyclif applied his theory to the text of Scripture in order to dispose of all problems relating to tense. Had he known that the verb in Hebrew was tenseless, it would have helped his argument and would have strengthened his belief that Scripture was on his side; but he did not know. A comforting formula, 'the amplification or extension of time' served instead. He brought it to bear on those apparently imprecise statements in which Scripture abounds. The prophet Amos said to the high priest Amasias: *I am a herdsman plucking wild figs* (Amos vii, 14). Amos was amplifying the present tense, so as to cover the past; he was not *plucking wild figs* at the moment of speaking to Amasias. Amos also said: *I am not a prophet.* This could not have meant that he was not a prophet either then or ever; he was. He meant only, according to Wyclif, that he was not inspired at that moment to prophesy.[45] The same formula of amplification of time could save Scripture from the sophists. It enabled Wyclif to answer their objection, which I have already quoted, that no one who lacked a wife or relatives could be Christ's disciple, since he could not hate and leave what he never had in response to Christ's call; Adam and Eve had no earthly parents. Wyclif replies to the objection about Adam and Eve that Christ's words apply to the time of grace only, and that Adam and Eve did 'hate' their mother, the earth; they were ashamed after the Fall of their own power of fleshly generation. He deals with the objection about hating one's wife or relatives by arguing that we are called upon to hate our own flesh and blood; hence it can apply to ourselves as well as to our wives or relatives, and hence to a bachelor or widower. His third answer relies on his theory of time:

It is clear that if we extend time as the faithful do [the faithful being Wyclif and his disciples], granting that all things are present to God, then every man has brothers and sisters.[46]

necessitate eveniet et secundo extendendo tempus de presenti sic quod omne quod fuit vel erit est pro tempore suo . . .'

[44] Robson, pp. 156–217. This paper could not have been attempted without Dr. Robson's invaluable account of Wyclif's philosophy as guidance.

[45] *F.Z.*, pp. 458–62. Wyclif discusses the same question on the text of Amos in his *Postilla*; I have transcribed the passage and compared it with the corresponding part of his discussion with Kenningham in my forthcoming paper, see above, n. 30.

[46] *Op. evang.*, ii, p. 184: 'Et quantum ad

He means that all men are children of Adam and Eve; as such they have had brothers and sisters at some time in the past, which is the present to God. The sophists' objections to the petitions in the liturgy fall neatly into the trap. They argue, as we have seen, that we pray in vain when we evoke a past event such as the Nativity, as though it were present, since it is not now and can never be again. Wyclif answers:

> But it is agreed that each one of these things, although past to us and future to the fathers of the Old Testament, really *is* in its time; hence it is the cause of our praying God to have mercy upon us.[47]

What has happened or will happen in its time is nonetheless ever present to God.

He disposed of the sophists to his own satisfaction; but the victory led to his undoing. Wyclif's attempt to save the Church from herself by his theory of time soon aroused misgivings. The first heresy imputed to him was:

Quod si aliquid fuerit vel erit, ipsum est.[48]

The Carmelite doctor, John Kenningham, deduced a number of heretical consequences from his colleague's theory. We may omit technical details. Kenningham accused Wyclif in general of being both 'high falutin'' and absurd. If each particle of Scripture be true *de vi vocis*, as Wyclif argues, then a lie reported there would have to be true. Wyclif withdrew, ungraciously, from this position: he no longer insisted on *de vi vocis*, but said that he really meant *de vi sermonis*. A lie reported in Scripture would not be true, but it would have to be true that the persons reported to have lied would have done so; the report that they lied would have to be true.[49] Kenningham objected to Wyclif's theory of future contingents also, on the score that the future tense does not denote the same thing as the past; it is not fixed and certain as the past is. He realized that Wyclif had flattened out time, and that this had the effect of defacing sacred history. The New Testament, Kenningham agreed, was eternally true *from* its starting point in time; he could not agree that it was eternally true *before*. Wyclif's *extensio temporis* led to *confusio temporis*.[50] His proposition *omne quod fuit erit* amounted to a return to the 'great year' of Plato and his disciples, the cyclical view of time held by pagan philosophers and condemned by St. Augustine.[51] Wyclif supposed that he had covered himself

etrtium obiectum, patet quod extendendo tempus ut faciunt fideles, concedentes quod apud Deum omnia sunt presentia, omnis homo habet fratres et sorores.'

[47] *De ben. incarn.*, p. 110: 'Sed constat quod unumquodque illorum, cum sit nobis preteritum, et futurum suo tempore pro patribus veteris testamenti, vere est pro suo tempore et per consequens causa misericordiam impetrandi.'

[48] *F.Z.*, p. 2.

[49] *Ibid.*, pp. 20, 456–58, 466–67.

[50] *Ibid.*, p. 20: 'Si igitur auctoritates praemissae probarent quod omnia quae fuerunt sunt: a pari ex ista cum similibus sequeretur

quod omnia quae erunt fuerunt, conformaliter loquendo utrobique, et sic esset nedum extensio sed confusio verborum.'

p. 47: 'Ulterius in eadem materia dicit Doctor quod novum Testamentum est aeternum, etiam a parte ante . . . : quod sit aeternum a parte post, testatur auctoritas . . . , sed de aeternitate eius a parte ante, non memini me vidisse rationem vel auctoritatem quae hoc affirmat.'

[51] *Ibid.*, p. 56: '. . . et est quasi in eodem error philosophorum ponentium magnum annum Platonis, et reditum omnium rerum in statum pristinum, (et) est reprobatum, sicut patet ibidem, per Augustinum.'

by arguing that the Creation was unique and that each moment of time was unique. But this admission did not keep his theory quite safely within the bounds of orthodoxy.

Kenningham's insight into its consequences helped me to solve a problem which had puzzled me in reading Wyclif. The reformer's philosophy and hence his theology had struck me as being anti-historical: what thinker possessed of the least inkling of historical sense would frown so severely on the distinction between past and present? And yet he shows a developed and searching sense of history in his criticisms of the contemporary Church. He was unusual in this. Anyone could point to the contrast between primitive Christianity as described in the New Testament and the wealth and corruption of fourteenth-century prelates. Wyclif had only to collect and repeat common-places, when he attacked the clergy. But he went further. He excelled at tracing changes of doctrine and custom since apostolic times, with especial reference to the changes marked in canon law. A modern historian reading his account of the process will warm to him and will hail him as a younger brother; his most astringent biographer softens a little.[52] True, Wyclif saw what some would call 'development' as decline; but he tried to find out how and why it happened. His thought ran to cycles all the same. We must see his researches into ecclesiastical history within that framework. It explains his seeming inconsistency.

His early *De statu innocentie* gives a clue to his historical thinking. Genuine emotion pervades his otherwise scholastic treatment of the state of man before the Fall. Wyclif feels homesick for that lost garden, where man would have drunk fruit-juice and would have busied himself with care of the animals,[53] a true Englishman's paradise. Man in the state of innocence is a norm for the theologian, just as a healthy man is a norm for the doctor when he treats the sick. Christ restored the state of innocence on earth, living in poverty and in the open air.[54] He left no body of written law to his disciples, because to live without written law keeps man closer to the state of innocence, where there was none. Wyclif had no use for *civilitas*, by which he meant 'government'. It was absent from the state of innocence, is due to man's sin, and will not obtain in heaven. Hence *civilitas* smacks of imperfection and does not suit the function of clergy.[55] Wyclif's logic and metaphysics fit into the picture: they agree better with the state of innocence than do those of his opponents.[56] There was no sophistry in the garden of Eden! Now the time had come to

[52] K. B. McFarlane, *John Wycliffe and the Beginnings of English Non-conformity*, 1952, p. 95.

[53] *De stat. innocent.*, pp. 493, 522.

[54] *Ibid.*, p. 475; *De potestate pape*, ed. J. Loserth (Wyclif Society), p. 173; *Speculum ecclesie militantis*, ed. A. W. Pollard (Wyclif Society), p. 42; *Op. evang.*, i, p. 6.

[55] *De potestate pape*, p. 85. Wyclif defines *civilitas* (*ibid.*, pp. 83–84): '... maius bonum foret tam clero quam laicis, quod laici occuparent totam civilitatem secularis dominii ... Nam nulli dubium quin secularia iudicia, contentiones, pugne et alia laboriosa manua-

lia sunt laicis plus pertinentia.' 'Government' here is taken in its most sordid and oppressive sense. On contemporary use of the word *civilitas* see L. Minio-Paluello, 'Tre note alla Monarchia', *Medioevo e Rinascimento: Studi in onore di Bruno Nardi*, 1955, pp. 513–21.

[56] *De veritate*, i, p. 48: 'Conceditur ergo cum scriptura sacra habet omne genus logice, quod logica scripture est ... tenenda, cum sit logica celestis a primo magistro edocta, ut discatur logica statui (*ed.* logice status) innocentie simillima et per consequens subtilissima, utilissima et certissima.' Wyclif had come to think that his logic was that of Scripture.

414

restore the clergy to the state of innocence, as it had been restored by Christ on earth once before. Men degenerated after the Fall and before Christ's coming; then they degenerated again (apart of course from the few elect, who lived in all ages); things could hardly be worse than they were in Wyclif's day.[57] His prescription was to restore the clergy to the state of innocence again by stripping them of their worldly goods, by force if necessary. And it would be necessary. Let the secular government apply the laity to the clergy as a doctor applies a leech to his patient, medicinally, to suck out the evil humours.[58] Wyclif differed from contemporary moralists in two ways: he advocated the use of force in reforming the clergy; he saw his reform as a second return, whereas others contented themselves with setting up the practice of the primitive Church as their ideal standard. The ideal for Wyclif was rather that man should return for the second time to that blessed state in which God had intended him to live. The merits of his reform programme need not concern us: how force could effect a return to the state of innocence was a question that he did not raise. His plan embraced a part of society only, the clergy, not the laity, who would be left with their own possessions, plus the goods of the dispossessed clergy. Perhaps he hoped that a reformed clergy would set about reforming the laity by preaching and example more effectively than 'Caesarian prelates'. The important point here is that both his interpretation of history and his remedy for present ills depended on his view of time as cyclical.

We have enough evidence now to compare him with Plotinus and Augustine respectively. The comparison suggests a metaphor. Plotinus murdered Father Time and dissolved the body in acid, so that no trace remained. Augustine subdued Time and fettered him, while still keeping him alive. Wyclif, a murderer like Plotinus, but less expert, killed Time, but did not get rid of the corpse. Wyclif's Time is dead time, dead but unburied. He therefore resembled Plotinus more than he did Augustine, just as his type of conversion was more Plotinian than Augustinian. To make the comparison at all is to risk an estimate of Wyclif as a thinker. It exposes him as too rigid and backward-looking to rank very highly. On the other hand it brings out the fact that he had the power and courage of his metaphysical convictions.

The strength he drew from them gives him more affinity with St. Augustine. Plotinus lived as a private person, surrounded by his group of disciples. It would have been alien to his ideas to enter into public life or to try to change the world: why change what was subject to time in any case? He taught that the way to rejoin eternity lay through individual effort. Augustine and Wyclif both felt obliged to act on the world according to their beliefs. Membership of the Church involved action, if not in secular, at least in religious and ecclesiastical matters. Wyclif plunged into politics. The mental processes and motives of his political action are still unclear; but one thing we do know: all the conclusions which he used as weapons derive from his academic work as M.A., as B.D. and as a newly incepted D.D. The student who follows his political career will realize too that it affected his scholarship disastrously. He had to distort both facts and texts in order to fit them into

[57] Ibid., i, pp. 68–69; Op. evang., ii, pp. 191–193.   [58] De officio regis, pp. 214, 280.

his theories. To choose the most arbitrary interpreter of Biblical texts of the Middle Ages would be rather like awarding a prize for the ugliest statue of Queen Victoria. Yet I would back Wyclif to win. He ended his life as a mere bore, inventing fresh insults in default of new ideas. The government left him to die in peace and isolated at Lutterworth. He had ceased to be dangerous, though some of his disciples were.[59] *Tempus* and *temporalia* had their revenge on the champion of Scripture as a mirror of eternal truths.

[59] K. B. McFarlane, *op. cit.*, pp. 116–21.

See now my 'Wyclif's *Postilla* on the Old Testament and his *Principium'*, *Oxford Studies presented to Daniel Callus* (Oxford Historical Society, New Series, xvi, 1964) 253–296; G.A. Benrath, *Wyclifs Bibelkommentar* (Arbeiten zur Kirchengeschichte, xxxvi, 1966).

BIBLIOGRAPHY
of BERYL SMALLEY
exclusive of items reprinted here
and of reviews

1931

With G. Lacombe, 'Studies on the Commentaries of Cardinal Stephen Langton', *Archives d'histoire doctrinale et littéraire du Moyen Âge* v. 1-220.
With G. Lacombe, 'The Lombard's Commentary on Isaias and Other Fragments', *The New Scholasticism* v. 123-162.
'Stephen Langton and the Four Senses of Scripture', *Speculum* vi. 60-76.

1933

'*Exempla* in the Commentaries of Stephen Langton', *Bulletin of the John Rylands Library* xvii. 121-129.

1935

'Master Ivo of Chartres', *English Historical Review* 1, 680-686.
'Gilbertus Universalis Bishop of London (1128–1134) and the Problem of the "Glossa Ordinaria" ', *Recherches de théologie ancienne et médiévale* [RTAM]vii. 235-262.

1936

'Gilbertus Universalis Bishop of London (1128–1134) and the Problem of the "Glossa Ordinaria" 'II, *RTAM* viii. 24-64.

1937

'La Glossa Ordinaria', *RTAM* ix. 365-400.

1938

'Andrew of St. Victor, Abbot of Wigmore: A Twelfth Century Hebraist', *RTAM* x. 358-373.
'A Collection of Paris Lectures of the Later Twelfth Century in MS Pembroke College Cambridge 7', *Cambridge Historical Review* vi. 103-113.

'The School of Andrew of St. Victor', *RTAM* xi. 145-167.
Hebrew Scholarship among Christians in xiiith Century England, as Illustrated by some Hebrew—Latin Psalters, (Society for Old Testament Study, Lectio 6, Shapiro, Valentine & Co., London).

1941

The Study of the Bible in the Middle Ages (Oxford).

1943

With H. Kantorowicz, 'An English Theologian's View of Roman Law: Pepo, Irnerius, Ralph Niger', *Mediaeval and Renaissance Studies* i. 237-252.

1945

With S. Kuttner, 'The "Glossa ordinaria" to the Gregorian Decretals', *English Historical Review* lx. 97-105.

1946

'Two Biblical Commentaries of Simon of Hinton', *RTAM* xiii. 57-85.
'A Commentary on Isaias by Guerric of St. Quentin O.P.', *Studi e Testi* cxxii. 383-387.

1948

'Some More Exegetical Works of Simon of Hinton', *RTAM* xv. 97-106.
'Robert Bacon and the Early Dominican School at Oxford', *Transactions of the Royal Historical Society* 4th series, xxx. 1-19.
'The *Quaestiones* of Simon of Hinton', *Studies in Medieval History Presented to Frederick Maurice Powicke*, ed. R.W. Hunt, W.A. Pantin, R.W. Southern (Oxford). 209-222.

1949

'William of Middleton and Guibert of Nogent', *RTAM* xvi. 281-291.
'Some Thirteenth Century Commentaries on the Sapiential Books', *Dominican Studies* ii. 318-355.

'Some Thirteenth Century Commentaries on the Sapiential Books' II,
III, *Dominican Studies* iii. 41-47; 236-274.
'Some Commentaries on the Sapiential Books of the late thirteenth and
early fourteenth centuries', *Archives d'histoire doctrinale et littéraire
du Moyen Age* xviii. 103-128.

1951

'A Commentary by Herbert of Bosham on the Hebraica', *RTAM* xviii.
29-65.

1952

The Study of the Bible in the Middle Ages, 2nd ed. revised and enlarged
(Oxford).

1953

'A Commentary on the Hexaemeron by Henry of Ghent', *RTAM* xx.
60-101.
'John Wyclif's *Postilla super totam Bibliam*', *Bodleian Library Record*
iv. 186-204.

1954

'Thomas Walcys O.P.', *Archivum Fratrum Praedicatorum* xxiv. 50-107.

1955

'Gerard of Bologna and Henry of Ghent', *RTAM* xxii. 125-129.
'The Biblical Scholar', *Robert Grosseteste Scholar and Bishop*, ed. D.A.
Callus (Oxford) 70-97.

1956

'Robert Holcot O.P.', *Archivum Fratrum Praedicatorum* xxvi. 5-97.

1957

'John Ridevall's Commentary on *De civitate Dei*', *Medium Aevum* xxv.
140-153.

'Capetian France', *France: Government and Society an historical survey*, ed. J.M. Wallace-Hadrill, J. McManners (London) 61-82.

1959

'Flaccianus, *De visionibus Sibyllae*', *Mélanges offerts à Étienne Gilson* (Toronto, Paris) 547-562.

1960

English Friars and Antiquity in the Early Fourteenth Century (Oxford).

1962

'Problems of exegesis in the Fourteenth Century', *Miscellanea Medievalia, Veröffentlichungen des Thomas-Instituts an der Universität Köln* ed. P. Wilpert, i, *Antike und Orient im Mittelalter* (Berlin) 266-277.

1963

'Moralists and Philosophers in the Thirteenth and Fourteenth Centuries', ibid. 2, *Die Metaphysik im Mittelalter, ihr Ursprung und ihre Bedeutung*, 59-67.
'The Bible in the Middle Ages', *The Church's Use of the Bible Past and Present*, ed. D.E. Nineham (London) 57-71.
'L'exégèse biblique dans la littérature latine', *Settimane di Studio del Centro Italiano di Studi sull'Alto Medioevo* x, *La Bibbia nel Alto Medioevo* (Spoleto) 631-656.

1964

'Wyclif's *Postilla* on the Old Testament and his *Principium*', *Oxford Studies presented to Daniel Callus* (Oxford Historical Society, New Series xvi) 253-296.

1968

'L'exégèse biblique du xiie siècle', *Entretiens sur la renaissance du xiie siècle* (Décades du Centre culturel international de Cerisy-la-Salle, New Series, ix) 273-283.

'Church and State, 1307–77: Theory and Fact', *Europe in the Late Middle Ages*, ed. J.R. Hale, J.R.L. Highfield, B. Smalley (London) 15-43.
Introduction to *Trends in Medieval Political Thought*, ed. B. Smalley (Oxford) vii-xii.

1969

'The Bible in the Medieval Schools', *The Cambridge History of the Bible*, ed. G.W.H. Lampe ii (Cambridge) 197-220.

1971

'Sallust in the Middle Ages', *Classical Influence on European Culture A.D. 500–1500*, ed. R.R. Bolgar (Cambridge) 165-175.
' "Privilegium fori": un dialogue entre la Théologie et le Droit canon au xiie siècle', *Atti del secondo congresso internazionale della Società Italiana di Studio del Diritto* ii (Florence) 749-755.

1973

The Becket Conflict and the Schools. A Study of Intellectuals in Politics in the Twelfth Century (Oxford).

1974

Historians of the Middle Ages (London).

1978

'Some Gospel Commentaries of the Early Twelfth Century', *RTAM* xlv. 147-180.

1979

'Peter Comestor on the Gospels', *RTAM* xlvi. 84-129.

1980

'An Early Paris Lecture Course on St. Luke', *"Sapientiae Doctrina" Mélanges de théologie et de littérature médiévales offerts à Dom Hildebrand Bascour O.S.B.* RTAM, Numéro spécial i (Leuven) 299-311.

'L'uso della Scrittura nei "Sermones" di Sant'Antonio', *Rivista Antoniana di storia dottrina arte* xxi. 3-16.

In Press

'The Gospels in the Paris Schools in the Late Twelfth and Early Thirteenth Centuries: Peter the Chanter, Hugh of St. Cher, Alexander of Hales, John of La Rochelle', I and II, *Franciscan Studies* xxxviii and xxxix.

PAGINATION OF ORIGINAL ARTICLES

I	93	1	IV	93	42	V	69	83	VIII	13	123
	94	2		94	43		70	84		14	124
	95	3		95	44		71	85		15	125
	96	4		96	45		72	86		16	126
	97	5		97	46		73	87		17	127
	98	6		98	47		74	88		18	128
	99	7		99	48		75	89		19	129
	100	8					76	90		20	130
			V	35	49		77	91		21	131
II	655	9		36	50		78	92		22	132
	656	10		37	51		79	93		23	133
	657	11		38	52		80	94		24	134
	658	12		39	53		81	95		25	135
	659	13		40	54		82	96		26	136
	660	14		41	55					27	137
	661	15		42	56	VI	113	97		28	138
				43	57		114	98		29	139
III	15	17		44	58		115	99		30	140
	16	18		45	59		116	100		31	141
	17	19		46	60		117	101		32	142
	18	20		47	61		118	102		33	143
	19	21		48	62		119	103		34	144
	20	22		49	63		120	104		35	145
	plates			50	64		121	105		36	146
	21	23		51	65		122	106		37	147
	22	24		52	66		123	107		38	148
				53	67		124	108		39	149
IV	78	27		54	68		125	109		40	150
	79	28		55	69		126	110		41	151
	80	29		56	70		127	111		42	152
	81	30		57	71		128	112		43	153
	82	31		58	72		129	113		44	154
	83	32		59	73		130	114		45	155
	84	33		60	74		131	115		46	156
	85	34		61	75					47	157
	86	35		62	76	VII	179	117		48	158
	87	36		63	77		180	118		49	159
	88	37		64	78		181	119		50	160
	89	38		65	79		182	120		51	161
	90	39		66	80					52	162
	91	40		67	81	VIII	11	121		53	163
	92	41		68	82		12	122		54	164

424

VIII	55	165
	56	166
	57	167
	58	168
	59	169
	60	170
	61	171
	62	172
	63	173
	64	174
	65	175
	66	176
	67	177
	68	178
	69	179
	70	180
	71	181
IX	307	183
	308	184
	309	185
	310	186
	311	187
	312	188
	313	189
	314	190
	315	191
	316	192
	317	193
	318	194
	319	195
	320	196
	321	197
	322	198
	323	199
	324	200
	325	201
	326	202
	327	203
X	277	205
	278	206
	279	207
	280	208
	281	209
	282	210

X	283	211
	284	212
	285	213
	286	214
	287	215
	288	216
	289	217
	290	218
	291	219
	292	220
	293	221
	294	222
	295	223
	296	224
	297	225
	298	226
	299	227
	300	228
	301	229
	302	230
	303	231
	304	232
	305	233
	306	234
	307	235
	308	236
	309	237
	310	238
	311	239
	312	240
	313	241
	314	242
	315	243
	316	244
	317	245
	318	246
	319	247
	320	248
XI	200	249
	201	250
	202	251
	203	252
	204	253
	205	254
	206	255

XI	207	256
	208	257
	209	258
	210	259
	211	260
	212	261
	213	262
	214	263
	215	264
	216	265
	217	266
	218	267
	219	268
	220	269
	221	270
	222	271
	223	272
	224	273
	225	274
	226	275
	227	276
	228	277
	229	278
	230	279
	231	280
	232	281
	233	282
	234	283
	235	284
	236	285
	237	286
	238	287
XII	91	289
	92	290
	93	291
	94	292
	95	293
	96	294
	97	295
	98	296
	99	297
	100	298
	101	299
	102	300
	103	301

XII	104	302
	105	303
	106	304
	107	305
	108	306
	109	307
	110	308
	111	309
	112	310
	113	311
	114	312
	115	313
	116	314
	117	315
	118	316
	119	317
	120	318
	121	319
	122	320
	123	321
	124	322
	125	323
	126	324
	127	325
	128	326
	129	327
	130	328
	131	329
	132	330
	133	331
	134	332
	135	333
	136	334
	137	335
	138	336
	139	337
	140	338
	141	339
	142	340
	143	341
	144	342
	145	343
XIII	283	345
	284	346
	285	347

INDEX